DANNY YATOM
Former Director of the Mossad

THE LABYRINTH OF POWER

Senior Editors & Producers: Contento
Translator: Eran Levy
Editor: Michael Kadichevski
Book Design: Liliya Lev Ari
Cover Design: Oksana Kravtsova
Production Manager: Eran Aviad

Copyright © 2016 by Danny Yatom and Contento

All rights reserved. No part of this book may be translated, reproduced, stored in a retrieval system or transmitted, in any form or by any means, electronic, photocopying, recording or otherwise, without prior permission in writing from the author and publisher.

ISBN: 978-965-550-494-1

International sole distributor: Contento
22 Isserles Street, 6701457 Tel Aviv, Israel
www.ContentoNow.com
Netanel@contento-publishing.com

Danny Yatom
Former Director of the Mossad

The Labyrinth of Power

Table of Contents

Introduction and acknowledgements 7

Chapter 1: Assassination Gone Wrong 11

Chapter 2: Hot Potato 31

Chapter 3: Inappropriate Considerations 41

Chapter 4: Gil: The False Magician 57

Chapter 5: Leaks and Evasions 77

Chapter 6: "Thank You – and Farewell" 97

Chapter 7: "Roots" 107

Chapter 8: The Unit 119

Chapter 9: A Physician and a Murderer 133

Chapter 10: A Leader, a Friend and a Mentor 155

Chapter 11: Pathways to Peace 187

Chapter 12: "The Deposit" 231

Chapter 13: "Not a Single Inch" 247

Chapter 14: Assad: "I am Serious" 277

Chapter 15: Peres: Vision but Also Naiveté 291

Chapter 16: "Look Me in the Eye" 311

Chapter 17: "How to Enter the Room" 321

Chapter 18: Gains vs. Price 351

Chapter 19: Shepherdstown: Barak Insists 367

CHAPTER 20: Albright and Clinton Run Out of Patience 395

CHAPTER 21: "I Swam in the Sea of Galilee" 411

CHAPTER 22: "The Best Friend I Ever Had" 439

CHAPTER 23: Oslo: "Danny, I Never Thought Anything Would Come of It" 485

CHAPTER 24: "Dr. Tibi, Please Leave the Room" 515

CHAPTER 25: "Netanyahu Might Win" 543

CHAPTER 26: Full Power, on Both Tracks 551

CHAPTER 27: "I'm Willing To Go Much Further Than Rabin" 569

CHAPTER 28: After 18 Years, The IDF Exits Lebanon 581

CHAPTER 29: "Dear Friends, We Are Not Making Progress" 595

CHAPTER 30: The Suitcase Packers 623

CHAPTER 31: "I Do Not Want To See Anyone" 651

CHAPTER 32: "Arafat Cannot Make a Decision" 667

CHAPTER 33: To Practice What You Preach 691

CHAPTER 34: A Look to the Future 705

EPILOGUE 717

APPENDIX I 720

APPENDIX II 721

INDEX 724

Introduction and Acknowledgments

During my many years of service in the IDF, the Mossad, the Prime Minister's Bureau and the Knesset (the Israeli parliament), I amassed many experiences in matters related to the State of Israel's national security.

I participated in the peace process with Jordan, Syria, Lebanon and the Palestinians from 1993 to 2001.

I chose to write a book that will offer readers in Israel and abroad a unique glimpse into the world of the country's leadership and national-level decision makers.

I am of the opinion that it is highly important for ordinary people to be exposed to decision-making processes in the Prime Minister and governmental levels on matters that are crucial to the State of Israel, and to each and every one of us.

The book contains a detailed description of the foremost process that Israel has gone through in the political-military area, namely the peace process.

From the following pages, one can learn about the dynamics that characterized decision makers behind closed doors, about the many uncertainties and decisions that had to be made at different crossroads during negotiations.

The book follows developments in Israeli society that led to the murder of Prime Minister and Defense Minister Yitzchak Rabin, a traumatic murder that sent the State of Israel into a whirlpool and left us with immense pain and bloody scars that will never heal.

The various chapters cover a wide range of events, affairs and processes, but due to its limited breadth I did not include all the national experiences that have happened in recent years.

Additionally, you will find descriptions pertaining to my family and the home I grew up in. I saw much importance in including these descriptions, aimed to clarify the foundations of my worldview and behavioral patterns as they are expressed in my life and in this book.

My late parents, Pnina and Simha Yatom, may they rest in peace, greatly influenced my personality and instilled in me the core values that accompany me to this very day. They were not rich people, but they refrained from spending on themselves so that I and my brothers Ehud and Moshik and my sister Etti could be given the best education, and never feel a lack of anything.

They raised us with an eye for excellence, to love our fellow man, our people and our country, and to love the heritage of Israel. It is no coincidence that the four of us served the State of Israel for many years. I served in the IDF, the Mossad, the Prime Minister's Bureau and the Knesset, Ehud in the IDF, the Shin Bet (Israel Security Agency) and the Knesset, Etti in the defense establishment, and Moshik in the IDF.

To my parents I owe tremendous thanks for the way they raised me, and the wonderful love they showered upon me.

I owe a great debt to the late Yitzhak Rabin. I was lucky to have been chosen by him as his military secretary, first during his time as Defense Minister, and later when he served as Prime Minister and Defense Minister. I learned much from Yitzchak, and working alongside him was a uniquely powerful experience. Yitzchak deeply affected my way of thought and perceptions on military matters, peace and the way to run a country.

Ehud Barak, whom I have followed for over forty years, has been my guide and a true friend. From Ehud I have also learned very much. Ehud set a personal example for me in his courage in battles and operations behind enemy lines, and in his logical and far-reaching way of thinking. I thank Ehud for all of these.

I thank Professor Moshe Arens for choosing me to serve as his military secretary in his term as Minister of Defense. Moshe gave me a rare chance to take part in decision-making on the national level, and from him I learned what is intellectual openness and organized, systematic work.

To Shimon Peres I owe special thanks. Shimon appointed me as Director of the Mossad and has set a personal example for me in his vision and special talent to solve complicated issues in an uncommon and creative way.

Finally – special thanks go out to my dear family. To my wife Tova and my children Omer, Nir, Tal, Roey and Itai, who encouraged me throughout my journey, were my comfort at difficult times, supported me fully and were sympathetic towards the choices I made at different crossroads in my life and in the many roles I have filled. They showered me with tremendous love, encouraged me to write this book and supported me throughout its writing.

Danny Yatom
October, 2015

Chapter 1

Assassination Gone Wrong

The tall brunette whispered some words into the ear of the tourist resting near the hotel pool. The man, bearded and in his forties, was careful to maintain a frozen expression, although the woman's presence there meant a nightmarish scenario was coming true. He put down the English version of The Catcher in the Rye that he had busied himself reading until she arrived, and followed her to a secluded corner in the garden.

The meaning of her appearance at the hotel was clear to him even before another word was exchanged. Her presence at this place was strictly forbidden, unless some horrible mishap had occurred - which meant that the operation to assassinate Khaled Mashal, head of the political bureau of Hamas on Jordanian soil had gone wrong.

Shortly afterwards, I was asked to leave an operational discussion I was holding in my office at the Mossad headquarters in central Israel. H., head of the Mossad Operational Department, was standing outside the room. "There's trouble," he told me, "Several operatives have been captured, apparently by Jordanian police, and the others have contacted me and requested authorization to evacuate to the embassy." H. gloomily advised that I authorize an evacuation.

At that moment I knew with certainty that the operation had failed and had already decided to travel to Jordan immediately in an attempt to minimize damages.

Paradoxically, the operation had been put into motion a few months earlier, just as I had returned from a vacation with my family in Jordan on July 30, 1997. During a holiday in Eilat with my wife Tova and three of our sons, King Hussein had invited us to go on a trip to Jordan. The king's royal helicopter awaited us in Aqaba and flew us to Petra for a tour, after which we were invited to a cruise on one of the royal yachts along the Jordanian coastline, finally ending the day with dinner at the Royal Palace in Aqaba. The king, who had not been present during our visit, sent one of his men to escort us throughout that pleasant day. My family and I enjoyed our excursion very much, although later my son would write in the family album, next to photos of that day: "Trip to Jordan, Summer of 1997, I have a feeling there won't be another visit like this soon."

On our way home, while we were at the airport in Eilat, I received an update that there had been a terrorist attack in the Mahane Yehuda market in Jerusalem. My wife and children went home and I immediately returned to Mossad headquarters. That same evening I participated in a situation briefing at Prime Minister Netanyahu's office. Among those present were Defense Minister Yitzhak Mordechai, IDF Chief of Staff Amnon Lipkin-Shahak and Head of the Shin Bet Ami Ayalon. At that time, Hamas had already assumed responsibility for the bombing in which sixteen people were killed and 200 were injured, and Netanyahu instructed all present to return to him with Hamas targets that could be attacked.

Several weeks later, on September 4, Hamas committed another terrorist attack in Jerusalem, this time on Ben Yehuda Street. The bombing killed four people and 200 were injured. Due to these two bombings there was an air of urgency on the side of the Prime

Minister and the Security Cabinet to receive Hamas targets which could be attacked. The IDF and Shin Bet had no recommended targets, claiming there were no valuable targets to attack, and I alone had come to the Prime Minister with a list of targets in different countries. Here is the place to present my position regarding the roles of the operational and political echelons in operational activities. The role of the operational echelon is to fight terrorism and hostile nations' attempts to obtain unconventional weaponry, recommend operations – almost always dangerous ones – which could go bad, present the possible benefits and risks, and not sit idly or explain that there are no targets, no objectives, and really nothing to be done. The political echelon's role is to supervise the operational echelon and consider the general and broad military and political ramifications before each operation is authorized.

The list of targets I presented was based, among other things, on the person's importance within the organization, the importance of removing him, the difficulty involved in reaching him and the results of his assassination. This list included eight names, and only the last ones were in Jordan. Mashal was fifth on the list and after him came Mousa Abu Marzouk, who had filled Mashal's role before him. Abu Marzouk's placement stemmed from his transfer to Jordan a short period earlier by the Americans, and there was concern that attacking him could create a problem with the United States. The targets in Jordan were at the bottom of the list because ever since the signing of the peace treaty with Jordan, operations on Jordanian soil were deemed extremely sensitive, militarily and politically.

Regarding Mashal, the summary of the Mossad's professional echelons was that his assassination, in itself, would not achieve the required objective, as it would only cause a temporary shock, and he would soon be replaced by someone else in Hamas leadership.

Members of Hamas who appeared at the top of the list presented to Prime Minister Netanyahu were central members in different countries. The material gathered about them showed that these people were recruiting and managing terrorist activities on a daily basis, and that attacking any one of them would hinder the organization's activity in the countries in which they were working. The Jordanian members were heads of the Hamas political bureau that had set the terrorist policy, funded terrorist acts and ordered others to commit terrorist attacks. Due to the sensitivity of the Jordanian field of operations and the high rank of Mashal and his counterparts, they were placed at the bottom of the list in terms of priority, and for this reason I recommended to Netanyahu an operation against a Hamas target in a different country.

The Prime Minister gave me the green light to proceed in preparations for the operation I had recommended, and operatives from the relevant unit in Mossad were dispatched to the location and began gathering intelligence.

However, a short time later on Friday evening, I received a call from the Military Secretary to the Prime Minister, Major General Ze'ev Livne, who informed me of a change in the mission. I was very surprised and asked him how there could be a change in the mission without my being consulted. Livne replied that after a meeting with the head of the Shin Bet, Ami Ayalon and Defense Minister Yitzhak Mordechai, it was decided that one of the heads of Hamas' global apparatus – possibly Mashal – would be targeted on Jordanian soil.

I was stunned. I could not understand how the Mossad was being given a mission that I, as head of the organization, had not been involved in its decision. I tried to speak to the Prime Minister but he was unavailable. I tried to glean further details, and all I could discover was that the head of Shin Bet and the Defense Minister had been informed of the original mission assigned to the Mossad.

They subsequently turned to the Prime Minister and convinced him that the original target - that I had suggested and had been authorized by the Prime Minister - was not significant enough and that it was not worthwhile to waste the Mossad's special abilities on him. The two of them recommended targeting the heads of Hamas in Jordan.

Eventually, when I spoke with the Prime Minister I expressed my firm objection to the way the decision had been made. I argued that I had to check the feasibility of action on Jordanian soil. Finally I came to accept that Mashal or one of the other members of Hamas leadership would be the target of attack.

The issue of action on Jordanian soil was raised in my first conversation on this matter with the Prime Minister and resurfaced many more times until the date of implementation.

I was concerned about the plan being situated in Jordan, but I took broader considerations into account, weighing the importance of peace with Jordan against Hamas terrorist attacks. These attacks had already hindered the peace process with Jordan during the Peres administration, and the current attacks could hurt the peace treaty with Jordan, as intelligence reports indicated that all attacks were being directed by Hamas headquarters in Amman.

Our repeated requests to the King of Jordan to take action to halt Hamas activities on Jordanian soil had been entirely fruitless. At the time of the previous administration, after terrorist attacks in Hadera and Afula, Prime Minister Rabin had already decisively demanded of the king to take action against Hamas, which had been responsible for the attacks, and terminate its activities in Jordan, but nothing happened. The Jordanians explained they preferred to keep Hamas headquarters close so they could keep an eye on its endeavors. The Jordanians also claimed that Hamas was only occupied with publicity in Jordan, rather than operational activity. However, we had proven to them that Hamas in Jordan was supplying financial and logistical support, outlining strategies, guiding and providing arms for terrorist activities in the Palestinian Territories. Hence, a large-scale terrorist attack originating from Jordan could potentially ruin relations between Israel and Jordan as well as the continued peace process with the Palestinians. Hamas terrorism had caused tension between us and the Palestinian Authority, which we had also expected would prevent terrorist attacks. The Palestinians' lack of preventive action had led to Israeli activity in Palestinian territory – which greatly strained our relations with the Palestinian Authority and impeded the possibility for a functional peace process.

It should be noted that when King Abdullah rose to power after his father's death, he realized the destructive effect of having Hamas' global headquarters located in his capital. Abdullah adopted a different approach to his father and was quick to abolish Hamas headquarters from Jordan along with Khaled Mashal, Mousa Abu Marzouk, Ibrahim Gosha, Mohammed Nazal and other senior officials, who since then became welcome guests in Damascus, hosted by Syrian president Assad.

On a personal level, I was faced with a twofold uncertainty; on the one hand, I was the king's friend, from as early as when I had served as Military Secretary to Prime Minister Rabin, and this was significant on many levels. On the other hand, I was head of the Mossad, and was responsible along with others for Israel's national security, and one of the Mossad's main objectives is to preventi terrorism. Due to my role, I knew in detail the terrorist activities of Hamas' headquarters in Jordan, headed by Mashal, and thus despite the problematic nature of an operation on Jordanian soil I did not disagree with the idea.

Simultaneously, it was assessed that even if an operational mishap would occur, it would not be irreparable, in light of the importance of the relations between Israel and Jordan and the king's personality; this was an assessment that eventually turned out to be accurate.

Assassinating Mashal was also in line with my notion that the Mossad's primary purpose is to prevent terrorism and prevent hostile nations from obtaining unconventional weapons. This is in addition to the Mossad's other roles, such as to gather military, strategic and political intelligence, form connections with nations with which we do not have diplomatic relations, bring Jews from nations in which they were in duress (such as Yemen, Syria and Ethiopia) to Israel, and covert cooperation with intelligence organizations in allied nations.

Khaled Mashal replaced Mousa Abu Marzouk after the latter was arrested in the United States. His official title was Head of the Political Bureau of Hamas, but in a terrorist organization such as Hamas there is no separation between the political and military ranks, as the primary activity of the Political Bureau was dictating terrorist strategies, ordering terrorist attacks and providing financial and logistical support for their execution.

Based on the information we possessed, it was asserted that Mashal and his people in Jordan were considerably more extreme in their terrorist policies than the Hamas command posts in the Palestinian Territories. We discovered that the Jordanian headquarters had refused requests from command posts in the Territories to reduce the scale of terrorism in fear of the IDF's responses.

All of these facts were part of the decision-making process regarding the operation's target, and once the Prime Minister gave me the order to terminate Mashal, the Mossad began to look into the target and examine the operational possibilities.

A suitable method of action was chosen so as not to create tension between Jordan and us.

After the operational plan was finalized, I came with H., head of the Operations Directorate, and with Mishka Ben David, head of the Intelligence Department within the Directorate, to a meeting at Netanyahu's office. Besides us, the Military Secretary and the stenographer were present at the meeting. I presented the plans to Netanyahu, stressing that due to the sensitivity of action on Jordanian soil, it would be an operation conducted under strict orders in regards to the terms of completion. This meant that the operation would only be set into motion if conditions were such that they would ensure a clean and seamless completion, and if this would not be the case, the operation would be immediately terminated, even seconds before it was to be carried out.

During the course of these discussions, I reported the state of preparations for the operation to the Committee of the Chiefs on Intelligence Services ('Varash'), which included head of Shin Bet Ami Ayalon and head of the Directorate of Military Intelligence Moshe "Bogie" Ya'alon. None of those present said a word in regards to the operation's target and location, and certainly none raised any objection, which of course did not prevent them in days to come from stating they had no idea of its existence.

When the operation was presented to the Prime Minister, he asked his secretaries to call the Minister of Defense into the room. Yitzhak Mordechai came in and after Netanyahu asked him to join the meeting, he said he was in a hurry and could not stay. Netanyahu asked Mordechai to meet me and learn what was happening, and we agreed to meet the following day at noon. At the end of the meeting with Netanyahu, it appeared that Netanyahu wanted to assassinate the chiefs of Hamas in Jordan by rank, one after another. Netanyahu's instruction was that after Mashal was targeted we would examine the responses of Jordan, Hamas and others as a whole, and then decide if we would continue to target other members of Hamas leadership.

On the following day, Friday, August 1, at noontime, I arrived at the Defense Minister's office along with Mishka Ben David. While we were waiting for the appointment, the door opened and the head of Military Intelligence, Bogie Ya'alon, left Mordechai's room. I took Bogie aside and updated him on how preparations for the operation were progressing.

Immediately afterwards, Mishka and I entered Yitzhak Mordechai's office and found his military secretary there with him. I directed the Military Secretary' attention to the fact that he was about to be exposed to matters which I had not been exposed to when I had been Military Secretary to the Defense Minister, and that he must keep them top secret. The Military Secretary was present during the entire meeting and busied himself recording it in writing. We sat with Mordechai for an hour or so and presented him with all the intelligence regarding the chiefs of Hamas in Jordan. In this meeting too, just as in the meeting with Ayalon and Ya'alon, there was no objection to the target of choice and the place of operation, and no attempt was made to halt preparations or cancel the operation. Mordechai later claimed that he was not informed of the operation and there was no documentation of that meeting, but on that Friday afternoon he bade me and Mishka good luck as we departed.

My instructions to the field operatives were clear and unequivocal. The strict terms that had been determined as conditional for the operation's implementation were complete certainty of the man's identification and suitable surrounding conditions, which would allow for execution with minimal risk of the operatives being captured. The operatives were presented with detailed and precise scenarios of what they were and were not allowed to do, according to the circumstances. They were to ensure an area that was free of the presence of others in Mashal's surroundings - from companions, acquaintances and family members, to bodyguards, lookouts and Jordanian police. I made it clear to them that this was by no means a case of completion at all costs and that if conditions did not fit the plan, it would always be possible to come back at another time and complete the mission.

This was stated repeatedly, but I am sad to say that this is not what actually happened - and nearly everything that could go wrong, did.

The Mossad's best field operatives were sent on the mission, operatives belonging to the Operations Branch. These were the cream of the crop of Israeli intelligence services - highly experienced operatives, most of whom had taken part in similar or even more complex, complicated and dangerous operations. These operatives had served in special forces units in the IDF and had later undergone extensive training at some of the highest professional levels worldwide in the Mossad. When preparations were complete, a group of operatives departed to Jordan to execute the mission.

On the morning of September 25, 1997, which was supposed to be the group's last day in Jordan, the squad informed the group that Mashal was on his way to his office and that he and his driver are alone in the car. The implementation group began preparing when the first mishap took place – the squad had failed to notice that Mashal's two young children were also in the car.

The operatives assumed their positions as planned and awaited Mashal's arrival. When he arrived and began walking towards the building's entrance, the operatives approached him and one of them raised his hand in an attempt to hit Mashal.

Mashal's driver noticed the hand in motion towards Mashal's back and began to shout. Mashal turned around, realized something was happening - although he did not know exactly what - and began to flee the scene.

Mashal turned right and ran and the operatives hastily moved towards the vehicle. When they reached the corner of the alley in which the car was parked, a messenger from Hamas headquarters named Mohammed Abu-Sief arrived there. He was carrying documents that were to be delivered to Mashal's office, and he heard the driver shouting and noticed the people who were gathering around Mashal. Abu-Sief also saw Mashal fleeing in the other direction and the two operatives quickly approaching him. He did not understand what was happening, but realized that the two were connected to what was happening with Mashal. He tried to block the operatives by extending his leg in an attempt to trip them. The operatives bypassed him, entered the vehicle and taking a rash decision, decided not to proceed towards their hotel as planned, but to make a few more turns and lie low. They were worried that Abu-Sief would call the police and that they might be arrested if they arrived at the hotel with that car. After two turns, they felt safe enough and got out of the car. The driver had kept driving in search of a parking spot in a different area, and to get rid of the car. This was an error in judgment on the two operatives' part, since even if the messenger had written down the car's license number, they still would have had enough time to distance themselves from the area before the police cars would have received the information. There had been no need to leave the car a mere 200 meters from the scene.

What the two didn't know was that Abu-Sief, who the media reported had been promoted to Mashal's bodyguard and was a veteran of the war in Afghanistan, had been chasing them the whole time. The two decided to separate and walk on two separate sides of the street. It was then that Abu-Sief spotted one of them, grabbed him by the shirt and began shouting to bystanders that the man had done something to Mashal. The operative pushed him away and then the second operative rushed to his associate's aid, and threw the messenger into a nearby ditch, cracking his head. The second operative bent over to Abu-Sief and began strangling him in an attempt to knock him unconscious. The whole event lasted mere seconds, but this was enough time for hundreds of people to gather round, as is characteristic of street life in large and busy Arab cities.

The sight of two foreigners thrashing an Arab created a lynch-mob atmosphere around them, and the two operatives, who had released Abu-Sief by then, were now surrounded by hundreds of people. Suddenly, a police officer who was in the area emerged from the masses. He distanced the crowd from the two men, hailed a taxi, and placed the two men inside it along with the wounded man who was bleeding and unconscious, and this party was led to the nearest police station.

The operatives estimated that any violent action they take on the way to the police station would lead to a chase in Amman, and after neutralizing Abu-Sief they thought that the police would release them within minutes and believe them when they would say that he was the one who had attacked them.

Either way, they found themselves at the police station. At this point, the policeman thought he was bringing them there as part of his civic duty. He was certain that the two had been attacked by Abu-Sief and tried to convince them to file a complaint against the unconscious messenger.

Unfortunately for them, Abu-Sief started to regain consciousness, and when he recovered he stated that he thought the two men had tried to hurt Mashal. Due to the conflicting versions, and because of Mashal's name suddenly being brought up, the policemen decided to keep Abu-Sief and the two operatives for further investigation.

A short while later, H. took me out of my office, told me what had happened and requested authorization to evacuate some of the operatives to the embassy.

As we were worried that the border with Jordan might be closed and an escape via the airport or a land border crossing would be impossible, the operation's commander recommended that he and his men be evacuated to the Israeli embassy.

I accepted the squad commander's suggestion to prevent any further complications, believing his presence at the field gave him knowledge of all the details, and authorized his request to evacuate to the embassy along with additional operatives. Escaping to the embassy was, as always, the very last option and was meant to be used only when all other means had failed. Nevertheless, I chose to authorize the request because I believed that an evacuation to the embassy would prevent further complications that might occur if the operatives would attempt to escape and I did not want King Hussein to get the feeling that I had more people hidden elsewhere.

Mishka, who was handling communications with Israel, was commanded to transfer the operatives to the embassy. He contacted the embassy and began transferring the operatives to a rendezvous point from where they were taken to the embassy. Afterwards he went back to his hotel.

During those moments, it was clear to me that the operation was over and that I had to present the full picture to the Jordanians. I had received the report on the operation's progress with a feeling of immense failure and immediately called the Prime Minister.

Netanyahu received the call in his car as he was on his way to a celebratory new year's toast at Mossad headquarters. I reported the mishap to him and we agreed that I would continue updating him when he reached his destination. When he arrived, we had an initial consultation and he authorized my suggestion that I would fly to Jordan immediately, meet King Hussein and attempt to straighten things out with him before the affair spiraled out of hand.

The situation was completely surreal. All Mossad employees who were in Israel were waiting for the Prime Minister in a hall at Mossad headquarters. The passageways, stairs and lower floor were full of people awaiting the Prime Minister's festive greeting, and no one was aware of the great drama that was taking place behind the scenes. Netanyahu and I stood on one of the inner balconies, which we used as an elevated vantage point from where we could view all those present. Despite the immense pressure we were under, we had to assume a festive expression and greet everyone, while my thoughts wandered far away, going through all the king's possible reactions. My greatest fear was that the identity of the operatives would be revealed in their interrogation at the police station. For this reason, I suggested to Netanyahu that we tell the king the whole truth, to avoid unnecessary complications due to contradictory accounts that might be given in the course of police investigations. Netanyahu agreed with my approach.

What I was most concerned with at that moment was not the relations with Jordan and the king, but the question of how I would manage the safe extraction of all my people from there and bring them back to Israel as quickly as possible. Relations with Jordan, I told myself, could be handled later. I knew that I had to take that unpleasant mission upon myself, to face the king and tell him what had happened. The responsibility for the operation's execution had been mine and so was the responsibility to resolve the mishap.

Netanyahu called King Hussein from my office and told him that I was being sent to him for an important meeting. The king immediately agreed, even though he did not have the faintest idea what this was all about at this stage. On my way out, Netanyahu told me, "Offer the king the means to save Mashal's life."

A short while later, I landed in Jordan on a private jet and was taken to the king's palace.

King Hussein greeted me very warmly, as usual. My counterpart was also present – Samih Batihi, head of the Jordanian General Intelligence services, and General Ali Shukri, the head of the king's bureau.

"Your Majesty the King, thank you for having me," I said, and immediately added, "I have come to you due to an emergency."

I told the king and the others present that a few hours earlier we had attempted to assassinate Khaled Mashal in Amman. I told them that during the course of the operation the Mossad operatives were captured and they were being held by Jordanian police, and that more operatives were in the embassy. I said I had come to this meeting in an attempt to end the affair quietly. I added that the operation had taken place following terrorist attacks carried out by Hamas and that Israel had no intention of acting against Jordanian interests. I offered to try and save Mashal's life.

"I have told you everything," I told the King. "I am hiding nothing from you, everyone is to trying to solve this problem as quietly and quickly as possible. I apologize for what happened, but as I have said, the goal is not to hurt you and the Jordanian people but to hurt the terrorists who are acting against us. I cannot return to Israel without my people and I ask that you allow me to return with all of them."

A silence fell upon the room.

The king adopted a severe expression. He took a deep breath and immediately turned to his men and asked them to find out Mashal's state. In a short while, it was reported that Mashal had fallen ill and was taken to the hospital. The king ordered he immediately be transferred to the Royal Hospital and accepted my suggestion to give the Jordanians the means to save Mashal's life. He thanked me, departed from me warmly, told me, "The rest you can conclude with my men," and left the room.

I was later criticized by people in Israel for presenting the full picture to the king. However, to me it was clear that I had to tell him everything, and that only the truth would bring our people back home safely and prevent relations between Israel and Jordan from being disrupted. I believed that the king's trust could only be regained when he felt that nothing was being hidden from him. It should be noted that this way of conduct was known and authorized by Netanyahu.

I stayed at the palace with Ali Shukri and awaited reports of Mashal's state. It was clear to me that Mashal's fate would determine further proceedings; his death would further complicate the situation and his recovery would make restitution possible. Thus, I found myself praying for the same person twice in the same day, once for his death and once for his life.

José Saramago, the Portuguese author and Nobel Prize laureate, once said that the magic of literature is its ability to kill people and bring them back to life. In the long hours during which I sat in the Jordanian palace, wishing for the recovery of the man whom hours earlier I had sent people to kill, I thought of how often reality can surpass any literary fantasy.

A few hours later, at the embassy, I met the operatives who had arrived there. The atmosphere was gloomy and I found myself consoling them. I went over to each one of them and shook his hand. They could not look me in the eye and seemed completely withered. It must be understood that these were the very best of the Mossad's people who had failed their mission and were burdened by their sense of failure. They seemed to be struggling with difficult emotions. At that stage, none of them was concerned with not being able to leave Jordan. It was only after the media had reported the occurrences that Hussein forbade them from leaving. At this stage, they were more worried about their sense of failure and their arrested associates.

I told them that above all else, I was committed to getting them and the operatives held by Jordanian police out of there, and bringing them home as quickly as possible.

It was then that I first heard their version of the events.

Having been instructed to leave Jordan the next day by regular flight, Mishka and the woman who accompanied him stayed in their hotel rooms, and there they encountered their third surprise of the day. In the evening, they turned on the television and set the broadcast frequency to Israel Channel One. To their shock and anguish, while they were in a hotel in Jordan unprotected and with their identity revealed, news anchor Haim Yavin appeared on the screen and announced to the entire world that according to reports in foreign media, a group of Mossad operatives had attempted to assassinate Khaled Mashal, and that some of the operatives had been captured and were being held by the Jordanians.

This news report was particularly aggravating, because the operatives' wives did not know where they were, and hearing such a report on the news, could not know which of their husbands had been arrested and which had not. Mishka's companion refused to leave by regular flight, out of fear that she might be arrested by the border police since the matter had been revealed by the media and her identity was known to Jordanian intelligence. Therefore I asked her and Mishka to meet me at the embassy and come home with me.

At the end of that long and suspenseful day, King Hussein authorized that I return Mishka and his companion back to Israel. A few operatives stayed at the embassy, while those held by the police were transferred to Jordanian General Intelligence. The king refused my request to fly back to Israel with the remaining team members from the embassy.

We drove to the airport late at night and boarded the plane that had brought me there earlier that day. The flight was very short and passed in complete silence. Each of us fell deep into our own thoughts. I felt great anguish, because I had learned from my initial inquiry with the operatives at the embassy that everything that should not have gone wrong, had done just that.

We landed in Israel at four in the morning and immediately drove to Mossad headquarters, which was lit and bustling with activity as though it was the middle of the day. I went to my office with the difficult feeling that I had left people on Jordanian soil. Our operatives had gone on a mission in the name of the organization I was leading. I knew that for the following days I would be entirely occupied with the task of getting them home.

A large crew, headed by the Prime Minister, awaited me at the Mossad headquarters to discuss further management of the affair. Netanyahu seemed bothered and worried although his attitude towards me was businesslike and regular. I told myself that in these moments, one must act calmly and level-headedly, and the settling of scores can be left for future times.

Within the Mossad itself there was a sense of unease. The dire restlessness was noticeable, composed of a mix of concern and disappointment. This was especially apparent among the field officers, who on the one hand felt immense pain and great concern for those left behind, and on the other felt sorrow mixed with anger for the damage caused, nationally and internationally. This event hurt their pride, and they found it difficult to understand how something like this could happen to the best of our people - who are usually very successful in completing their missions, most of them even more complicated and dangerous than the Mashal operation, and thankfully, only very few mishaps had ever happened to these operatives. One such famous mishap occurred in Lillehammer, Norway, in the 1970s. In that affair, operatives assassinated an innocent Moroccan waiter named Ahmed Bouchiki as a result of a misidentification. The original intent was to terminate Ali Hassan Salameh, of the terrorist organization Black September, who was one of the leaders of the terrorist attack in which eleven Israeli athletes were murdered in the Munich Olympics. Salameh was killed later in Beirut, however the six Mossad operatives from the

Lillehammer affair not only failed their mission, but were caught by Norwegian authorities, tried and imprisoned.

In other departments of the Mossad there was criticism of the operatives, along with concern for their fate. The hallways were full of people, including Mossad retirees who came and gathered with everyone in joint frustration. On a personal level, I had neither internal criticism for myself nor the operational concept and the way it had been planned.

Chapter 2

Hot Potato

As far as I was concerned, my primary task as Director of the Mossad was to get the people back home, and afterwards to mend relations with Jordan. I'm happy to say that I managed to convince the Prime Minister and others of the importance of saving the operatives who had remained on Jordanian soil.

All Mossad operations carry a potential risk to the operatives. The operatives commit illegal acts, from surveillance to tresspassing on private property and finally to charges of espionage and attempts to injure or kill terrorists. At any given moment, the operatives might be caught and be accused of breaking the laws of the country in which they are operating.

The operatives embark on their missions after being trained and prepared to overcome obstacles and extricate themselves from difficult situations. Whatever happens, an operative knows he will not be abandoned and that someone is watching out for him. The State of Israel will back them, in public or clandestine means. Things will be taken care of and the bottom line is that there is a safety net and the State will tend for him. Nevertheless, like any soldier leaving for battle, a Mossad operative who embarks on a mission also knows he is assuming a risk.

I had insisted that every operative involved in an operation would be safe - that if, God forbid, something would go wrong, we would attend to him and do everything to extricate him. The operative embarks on his mission for his country's sake, and his country will take care of him. While this might sound obvious in the Israeli military ethos, it should be noted that in the Mossad, due to the covert nature of its work, there were times – such as during the Lillehammer affair – when operatives knew that if something goes during an operation and they are captured, their fate would be in their own hands; the State would deny any connection to them and any aid they would receive would take place behind the scenes. According to this approach, the needs of the State come before those of the individual – and if the State's interests would be compromised by acknowledging and accepting responsibility, then the State would be preferred over the individual operative.

After I had finished reporting the events that had transpired, a larger system was put into action. The Prime Minister held many meetings and assessments with the heads of other services, with ministers and with anyone who could help with their connections and experience. One day after the operation, on Friday, it was decided to bring Efraim Halevy, formerly of the Mossad and then the Israeli ambassador to the European Union in Brussels, back to Israel. Halevy was brought due to his special relationship and close ties to King Hussein.

Halevy arrived and from that moment his behavior seemed strange and reticent, although those who knew him told me it was characteristic of him and that he did not even trust himself. Halevy had many telephone conversations with Jordan and elsewhere, and always took care not to do so in my presence. It seemed odd to me that he excluded me, as I was the Director of the Mossad and bore all of the responsibility, while he was supposed to be acting according to my instructions. Halevy would retire to the side to hold his telephone conversations, and would return with an impassive and lukewarm demeanor, saying "I've spoken" and nothing else.

When I asked "Who did you speak with?" he would answer, "Never mind," or "I spoke to who I needed to." Sometimes he would return and mumble, "The situation is very difficult," "very complicated," or "very problematic." To me it felt very strange and unpleasant. I called Efraim, slammed the door behind him and informed him that I do not condone his methods, and demanded that he report to me on any step or action he wishes to pursue. After this difficult and harsh conversation the situation improved, and Efraim began to share his activities with me. All that stood before my eyes at the time was to release the operatives and get them back home in peace, and I told myself that what was important at that moment was that anyone who could do something to help actually do so.

In all of our meetings, Efraim painted a strictly bleak picture, and argued that to appease the king we must make a very generous gesture towards him. Thus Halevy came up with the idea to offer the king the release of Sheikh Ahmed Yassin, leader of Hamas in Gaza, from Israeli imprisonment. This suggestion was based on the premise that Israel had attempted to hurt a chief official of Hamas and so the solution should pertain to Hamas. I supported the suggestion since I would have supported almost any reasonable idea that would get the operatives back home safe and sound. I didn't think releasing Yassin would worsen the state of terrorism, since even in confinement he was giving instructions, maintaining ties to his people in the Gaza strip, and was considered an important spiritual leader. Since I am familiar with the methods and decision-making processes in Hamas, I do not believe that the terrorist attacks that occurred before he was released and those that came afterwards are related to Yassin's presence in prison, in Gaza or outside, since during his imprisonment Hamas continued to commit horrible acts of terrorism. Furthermore, Hamas headquarters – initially located in Amman and afterwards in Damascus and Qatar – was the one who dictated the organization's terrorist policy, and was always more extreme and militant than the headquarters in the Palestinian territories. Further support of this notion can be found in the fact that when Hamas won the Palestinian elections, its local leaders tried to display a form of moderation, mostly towards other Palestinian organizations. However, the global Hamas headquarters, headed by Khaled Mashal, did all in its power to stoke the flames. Mashal accused Fatah and its chiefs of treason and cooperation with Israel, which led the Fatah chiefs to accuse him of inciting rebellion and an attempt to invoke civil war ('Phitnah') against the Palestinian Authority. Similarly, after the Israeli soldier Gilad Shalit was abducted in the Hamas attack against the IDF's Kerem Shalom outpost, Mashal's fingerprints and extremism were noticeable. While the stance of the Palestinian government, headed by Ismail Haniyeh, was in favor of finding a quick solution to release the soldier, Mashal made certain from his offices in Damascus to thwart almost any effort and set obstacles in the way of Shalit's release. Apparently, Mashal was also behind the attack on Kerem Shalom.

In fact, the issue of Yassin's release from prison had been discussed many times in the past, as early as during Rabin's term as prime minister, with concerns looming in the background that Yassin might die in prison from old age and sickness and Israel would be held responsible for his death.

King Hussein, who at the time was feeling very vulnerable, made it clear that if the situation were to escalate, then all the current complications would become much more complicated, and threatened to take drastic measures. He threatened to forcefully enter the embassy and capture the operatives who took shelter within it, and even considered suspending the recently-signed peace treaty with Israel, including a severe crisis in diplomatic relations, closing of embassies and ending all political, military and economic cooperation. The king further added that if Mashal were to die, he would have no choice but to consider executing the two operatives in his custody in order to appease the masses and the heads of Hamas in Jordan. At the same time, King Hussein reported the developments and his plans to the American President, Bill Clinton.

Our estimate was that the king would not follow through on his threats, and that it was a way to pressure us, but in my opinion, his remarks reveal just how deeply Jordan was entangled with Hamas on its soil, without even realizing the full extent of it.

Meetings, discussions and assessments were constantly held throughout the entire day. Many people were involved in the process and tried to contribute based on their experience. These included a former head of the Mossad, ministers and experts, with me and the Prime Minister participating in almost every discussion and brainstorming session meant to come up with a way to prevent any further escalation and find a solution for what had already happened.

Eventually Netanyahu decided, with my full concession, to give the Jordanians everything they asked for. Immediately afterwards, the Jordanians began treating Mashal and breathing new life into him. It was with a sigh of relief that I received updates of his initial recovery, which to me signaled the beginning of the recovery of our relations with Jordan.

At midnight of September 27, a helicopter landed in the center of Amman, and in it were Prime Minister Benjamin Netanyahu, Ministers Ariel Sharon and Yitzhak Mordechai, and their aides. The delegation arrived at the king's palace in order to try and set things straight, but the resentful king refused to meet them, and instead sent his associates to the meeting.

The king was never particularly fond of Netanyahu and always treated him with a cold and alienated attitude. In one of my past visits to Jordan, I asked Samih Battikhi, Director of Jordan's General

Intelligence, why Hussein refused to meet Netanyahu and in effect almost shunned him. Battikhi told me that in one of his meetings with the king at the royal palace, Netanyahu sat before the king with his legs crossed and the sole of his shoe facing the king's direction, and so it was that every time the king looked at Netanyahu he met the sole of his shoe. In Arab culture, there is almost no greater insult and humiliation, and the king was angered by this behavior. Battikhi also told me that the king did not like the affable, almost 'chummy' demeanor Netanyahu allowed himself to assume in his presence. When I returned to Israel I told Netanyahu about the king's offense from the sole of his shoe, but Netanyahu responded in an offhanded shrug. Clearly Netanyahu did not mean to offend the king, but he was also unaware of his sensitive nature.

Thus it was no wonder that when the Israeli delegation led by Netanyahu landed in Amman, at the height of the Mashal crisis, the king chose not to meet them, and sent his brother Prince Hassan in his place, along with Samih Battikhi and Chief of the King's Bureau Ali Shukri. The main issue that was discussed in this meeting was the release of Sheikh Ahmed Yassin.

The next day, on the morning of Sunday, four days after the operation had begun, Efraim Halevy arrived at the Jordanian Royal Palace and managed to convince the king to release the operatives who were in the embassy. A special helicopter was quickly dispatched from Israel, and they came back home with Halevy.

At this point, hasty negotiations with the Jordanian Royal Family began regarding the release of the two operatives in custody in exchange for Yassin's release. These negotiations, which lasted eight days, were placed under the responsibility of the Minister of National Infrastructures, Ariel Sharon, who was asked to employ all of his powers and talents to help bring a quick solution to the problem, due to the Jordanian leadership's trust and appreciation of him. The Jordanians asked that twenty Jordanian citizens who were imprisoned in Israel be released along with Yassin, and Sharon made the agreement with them. However, on the night when the agreement was to be put into motion, the Jordanians changed their mind and asked that more prisoners be included. As this was the third time the Jordanians had tried to change the agreement, Sharon lost his temper when he heard of the new demand and told the king, "If you keep this up, you'll keep our people, and we'll shut off your water supply and kill Mashal."

This outburst was effective; the Jordanians realized they had reached the limit, and the agreement was closed. Twelve days after the operation began, a helicopter landed in Jordan with Yassin in it, while another helicopter with the two operatives left for Israel.

After twelve days of being held by Jordanian authorities, it was clear that the two operatives were very happy to be home. The joy of their return was especially significant for them because during their days in custody they had no clue as to their fates, while being constantly interrogated by the Jordanians.

After they returned, I met with them at the Mossad headquarters. They voiced their deep regret for the operation's failure and thanked me for my efforts to return them. During the whole of their arrest, I was in touch with their families who were very worried.

To me, being a commander means being under the immense pressure of responsibility for people's lives and fates. My most difficult moments as a commander were always when people under my command were killed. I believe that this is the most difficult emotion that a commander must deal with. It is a feeling of utter failure for the loss of a life I had failed to prevent. My concern for the lives of the operatives and desire to bring them back home are what followed me throughout those days, and I was very much relieved to see them back.

This relief was mixed with the feeling of failure, yet as they returned I was able to look into their mothers' eyes and tell them that I had completed the mission I set out to achieve twelve days earlier; to bring our operatives back home in peace, and that the State of Israel had fulfilled its obligation to these operatives, sent on a mission in a foreign land.

While these nerve-wrecking efforts to return the operatives were taking place, as well as afterwards, I was forced to handle a second front. Mossad operations, usually operating far from the light of day in the cover of false identities and absolute secrecy, had suddenly found itself in the unfamiliar territory of the spotlight.

The Mossad, due to the nature of its activities as a covert organization, is always a broad and fertile ground for mythical fairy-tales and never-ending curiosity which can almost never be satisfied.

For this reason, any publication regarding the Mossad is the subject of public fascination and considered 'media gold'. The Mossad's operational activities are numerous, almost daily, and they take place in different countries, some of them hostile. Most of these activities carry some potential to become extremely complicated and transform into a crisis. Fortunately, the vast majority of these activities had succeeded over the years, and subsequently remained unknown. It is only when an event fails that some of the shroud of secrecy is compromised, giving the signal to the media to start an ongoing carnival of "revelation", "sensational discoveries", and "knowledgeable commentary", all of which bear no semblance to reality.

It had become the 'flavor of the month' in that time to present Mossad workers as clumsy, and publications to that effect fueled this notion. One example can be found in the publications that gleefully presented the Mossad operatives as a couple of losers who were defeated by "a burly bodyguard, who was a veteran of the battles in Afghanistan", while Mohammed Abu-Sief's testimony was ignored – that same "bodyguard", who was merely a delivery boy for Hamas headquarters. A German newspaper published an interview with Abu-Sief, who spoke of how the moment he made contact with the two operatives they beat him to near-death and knocked him unconscious in seconds, and testified that they were very skillful and well-versed in Krav Maga.

I believe that the media circus was further encouraged by the fact that Netanyahu was a controversial prime minister, that the media was harshly critical of his conduct, and here they were awarded a chance to rebuke him for another failure handed on a silver platter.

As far as the media was concerned, it was a celebration of continuous besmirching, unlimited in time and with almost no rules being applied, and as far as I was concerned it was the start of a new battle, this time for my own name and the prestige of the body I had headed.

The irony was that Khaled Mashal, the terrorist who was given his life back, returned to his previous role with the glory of martyrdom, while I had to fight a battle for the Mossad's reputation and name.

The Prime Minister's office, which is in charge of the Mossad, was flooded by endless petitions and questions from the media. One day after another, a torrent of questions landed upon the Prime Minister's spokespeople in regards to the questions of who knew and who didn't, who authorized and who gave the orders. Netanyahu asked me to brief some leading military journalists on these matters.

When I met with the journalists, I told them about my meetings with the *Varash* forum (Committee of the Chiefs on Intelligence Services), the Head of Shin Bet and Head of Intelligence, the Defense Minister, and the reports and updates these people had received from me before the operation commenced. I even described how aerial photographs and maps of Amman were laid out in Defense Minister Mordechai's office during the meeting on August 1, to which I was accompanied by Mishka Ben David, Chief Intelligence Officer for the Operations Branch.

Immediately after this conference, journalists contacted all the relevant people to cross-check the information, and all three of them - Yitzhak Mordechai, Bogie Ya'alon and Ami Ayalon, in coordination or not - vehemently denied that they were informed of the decision to take action in Jordan and assassinate a Hamas official in Amman. A media circus began from that moment onwards, and with each passing day it was fed with more and more different types of information, until it received a life of its own. The media jumped on this hot potato with a passion, and it only cooled off many months later, after the public inquiry had finished.

Chapter 3

Inappropriate Considerations

After the affair exploded in the media, the Prime Minister was under constantly increasing pressure to investigate the happenings, with some recommending the establishment of a national commission of inquiry.

Netanyahu accepted these demands and decided to form the commission. Immediately upon its appointment, members of the Mossad and I discovered two things; once it was named "The Committee on the Operational Failure in Jordan", it became clear to me that Netanyahu who appointed it, had given it the type of mandate that would prevent it from placing any of the blame on him – as the commission would not examine decision-making on his level, only operational issues. Secondly, it was clear from its members that there was no chance it would understand the intricacies of the Mossad's work; its operational methods, cases and reactions, the fact that the gathering of intelligence must be completed in real time because the target is in constant movement, and also that the planning can only be completed at the place of operation, because of constant changes to surrounding conditions.

The decision to form the commission was wrong in my opinion, because the subject was an operation that had not been accomplished. This was similar to many other operations done by the IDF or the Shin Bet that had sometimes also ended in great disaster and loss of human life – such as the Naval Commando disaster, when a squad was ambushed in Ansaria, Lebanon – and not once was a governmental commission of inquiry appointed to examine such operational occurrences. It was always customary that operational mishaps were handled by internal investigation teams, with the goal of discovering all the malfunctions, amending the shortcomings and settling the score with those responsible if necessary.

I shared my opinion with Netanyahu, but in those days I was speaking from a position of weakness, since I was perceived as one who had a personal interest in thwarting the appointment of such a commission. While I did not want to appear as one who has something to be concerned about, I believed that this type of commission of inquiry might hurt the Mossad since there was a good chance that details would be leaked from it. I was also concerned that the commission would take inappropriate and inadequately professional considerations into account, and I regret to state that from almost the very first moment of its activity all of my concerns turned out to be justified.

However, despite my reservations, once Netanyahu decided to form the commission, I cooperated with it completely, and merely asked that one of its members be a former senior Mossad official, one who was very familiar with the agency's work. Netanyahu accepted my request and appointed Nahum Admoni, former director of the Mossad, as a member of the commission. However, a short time earlier, Admoni was interviewed in the press and made some statements that were construed as supporting the Mossad. All the malcontents immediately raised an outcry, claiming that it was unreasonable that a biased person who supports the Director of the Mossad beforehand, be member of the commission. Admoni was forced to leave and in his place Netanyahu appointed Rafi Peled, CEO of the Israel Electric Company at the time and a past member of the Shin Bet and Commissioner of Police. Joseph Ciechanover, chairman of the board of directors at El Al, was appointed as chairman of the commission, and another member of the commission was Dan Tulkowsky, former Commander of the Israeli Air Force.

The commission members had no familiarity with the Mossad and its workings, since there are key differences between the nature of the Mossad's work and that of the IDF, the Shin Bet and the Israeli police. The Mossad always operates in hostile environments beyond Israeli borders and always unlawfully in the local country. Most of the IDF's activity is in the Gaza Strip, the West Bank, within national borders or outside of them with immediate evacuation possibilities, and the Shin Bet and police generally work in areas where Israel has authority and responsibility. The chairman of the commission, Mr. Ciechanover, was a senior civilian executive, who knew nothing about issues related to covert activities in general and the Mossad in particular. The former commander of the Air Force, who understood aerial issues, was also a member of the commission, as well as the former Police Commissioner whose expertise was in policing and crime. Thus it was clear that they could not understand us, as we, the people of the Mossad, work against the laws of the target country, and must make every effort to avoid being caught by police and security forces. One who is used to having the power and the law on his side, one who enters a battle backed by tanks, airplanes and missiles, could never understand the Mossad operative. This operative usually works alone, always clandestinely, covertly, always has to hide, has no means of defending himself with the use of force while he is in the target country, and acts unlawfully. His superb professional abilities, equanimity, discretion, adherence to a pre-made escape plan and acting according to the debriefing in case something goes wrong – these are the only things that will extricate him from trouble.

Mossad operatives work covertly, their only armor being the covert nature of their activity. When they are undiscovered they are safe, and if something goes wrong and their unlawful activity is discovered – regardless of whether they are in a hostile or friendly nation – this immediately creates a diplomatic crisis for Israel.

The Mossad has developed for itself a modus operandi for such situations, a combat doctrine that was never required from the Shin Bet, the police, or the military. Therefore, I felt that the make-up of the commission would limit its ability to accurately evaluate the occurrences.

Some people in the Mossad were also worried about Rafi Peled, who was forced to resign from his role as Commissioner of Police after it was revealed that he bathed in a luxury hotel Jacuzzi-bathtub with senior police officials. The concern was that someone who was forced to retire under these circumstances, would find it mentally difficult to allow lower ranks in general, and seniors in particular, to go unscathed from such a mishap. Indeed, Rafi Peled did not "disappoint" and fulfilled all our concerns.

Despite all of these objections, it was clear to me that I and anyone else in the Mossad who would be required to do so would cooperate fully and unabashedly with the commission. Immediately after it was appointed, I gave written and oral instructions to all relevant members of the Mossad to appear before the commission as they would be asked to do, and to present it with any material that would be requested. Anyone who wanted legal aid was entitled to receive it. I had employed the help of attorneys Robbie (Reuven) Bachar and Zvika Bar Natan, while at the same time continued to work in two different and highly demanding areas, neither of which could hinder the other. On the one hand, I was to continue and direct activities of the Mossad, whose operatives had not for one moment stopped participating in bold operations to thwart terrorism and the efforts of hostile countries to obtain weapons of mass destruction, while simultaneously gathering materials and preparing for my appearance before the commission.

This state of affairs created some very embarrassing situations, since my routine workdays forced me to meet many people who were involved in the operation in Jordan, and to have discussions with them concerning the Mossad's ongoing regular activities, while at the same time I was forbidden from discussing the matter itself with any of them, so as not to be suspected of obstruction of justice.

The commission began its work under a constant background buzz of leaks, mudslinging, "exposés", and interferences, and very turbulent public opinion. From living room conversations to daily newspaper headlines, none remained indifferent and everyone had their own firm opinions on what had happened.

These publications and the atmosphere led to bleak spirits and severe unease at the Mossad. There was a feeling that the Mossad had become the national punching bag at that time, and that some were after my head.

I was regularly requested to answer the question of why I refused to resign, and was forced to explain over and over again that until the commission finished its work there was no reason for me to do so. I explained that although I was responsible for what had happened, there is still a big difference between responsible and guilty, and I believed with all of my heart that I was not guilty.

I thought that I, as the one who was most informed about what had happened, could amend the shortcomings that were revealed after gaining a more in-depth understanding of the affair – better than any new Director of the Mossad who would be appointed. Since its founding and until the Mashal affair, the Mossad had suffered more than one failure, none of which led to the Director of the Mossad being impeached.

These calls for me to resign were joined by the Jordanians, who – aside from the diplomatic damage caused by the affair - were personally offended by the fact that I of all people, someone who was close to the royal family, was involved in it.

In those days, an interview with King Hussein was published in the prestigious Saudi paper *Al-Hayat*, which is based in London. The king chose his words with care, he did not mention Israel and the Mossad, but he said that he felt as one who "decided to open his house for a complete stranger, and host him with the honors fit for a king. Yet when the host turned his back for a moment, he discovered that the guest was exploiting his hospitality to rape the lady of the manor, or his daughter…" The king added that he felt as though someone had "spat in my face."

The Jordanians conditioned reconciliation upon my resignation, but I refused to do so and awaited the results of the commission to decide on my next steps. I had hoped that Netanyahu would also refuse to agree to this.

Those were difficult, nerve-racking days, and the publications in the media could have caused rifts within the Mossad.

An extreme example of this occurred when one evening I had gone to Kfar Saba to pick up my young son from the movie theater. While I was walking from the car to the entrance to the movie theater, I randomly encountered a journalist from *Ha'aretz* who asked me offhandedly, "So, Yatom, what's gonna happen?" I replied, "I think everything will be okay." To me it was but a meaningless question that received a meaningless answer. The next morning I opened the *Ha'aretz* newspaper and was horrified to read the main headline, which exclaimed – "Yatom blames his subordinates for everything." This was of course plain nonsense, but from the phrase "everything will be okay", the journalist had inferred that I was going to be okay, and hence certainly there was someone else who would not be okay, and thus a headline was born.

This headline invoked unrest at the Mossad and a difficult notion that I was abandoning my men. "If he's declaring that he's calm and unworried even before the commission's findings are published, the blame will eventually land on those who had carried out the operation," said some people at the Mossad, and claimed that if that was the case, it meant I didn't care about anyone except myself.

These types of events forced me to meet with the operatives, calm them and promise them that I had no intention of turning them into scapegoats, and that my intention was only to present the facts as they are to the commission.

Immediately upon the start of the commission's work, it became clear to me that information was leaking from it like a sieve. On one occasion, I was appalled to hear journalist Amnon Abromavich proclaim on the television news that he was receiving leaked materials from the commission on a daily basis, and telling tales of things that had never happened and could gravely hurt the Mossad. I was forced to phone the television broadcast, request to go on the air and deny his statements on live television.

This conduct angered others and myself, especially considering the fact that I had a very well-established suspicion as to the source of the leak.

At a certain stage, I made contact with the commission, through my lawyers, with claims against Rafi Peled's conduct. One of the things he had done and which I considered the 'last straw' was that some weeks after his testimony at the commission, the Head of the Branch's Intelligence Department, Mishka Ben David who had taken part in the operation, was called to appear before the commission again. When he came to where the commission had gathered, he found out that he had not been asked to appear before the commission plenum, but for a personal meeting called by Rafi Peled.

Peled told him that the commission had finished its work and that he was currently writing the chapter related to intelligence of the final report, and hence there was no need to reassemble the whole commission just to fill in the small details he needed.

"I only have some clarification questions to ask," Peled said to Mishka, who at that stage still thought everything was in order. Yet once the "clarification questions" began, Mishka realized that Peled was in fact giving him the opportunity to clear his own name in exchange for incriminating others.

Mishka was asked questions, such as: Did you evaluate that there were intelligence gaps during preparations for the operation and were told by your superiors, "We don't have time to fill this gap and it is unimportant to us?" When Peled said "your superiors," he could only have meant two people: me and H., the head of the Operations Wing.

At that moment, Mishka told Peled that the situation made him uneasy and it seemed wrong for him that the two of them were sitting in private without their conversation being recorded.

Mishka asked to end the meeting and told Peled that he was to inform the rest of the members of the commission about it and about what he asked during it. Mishka did not report the event to me or anyone else at the Mossad, as we were all under strict instructions to avoid any form of obstruction of justice. The first time I heard of the event was after the commission's initial summary, when the commission sent letters which detailed its claims to those who might suffer harm from its conclusions – and once these letters were sent, their recipients received the opportunity to review all the materials collected by the commission. Here is the place to stress that the chairman of the commission, Ciechanover, had made it clear to me and others that the commission did not intend to issue warning letters, but only letters which he defined as "detailing the commission's claims," which would be sent to those who might be harmed by the conclusions. The reason for this, according to him, was that the commission did not intend to suggest personal recommendations. Since I was one of those who received letters from the commission, I reviewed all the materials and within them found the report Mishka had written about his meeting with Peled. From this report I learned that Peled, a member of the commission, had acted in a gravely inappropriate way, attempting to get a witness to talk outside of the commission's formal work process.

I'm afraid to say that Mishka's case was not the only troublesome detail we – my lawyers and I - had discovered in the materials we were given. We found several instances in the commission's protocols in which Peled quoted to some witness or another inaccurate or even falsified statements allegedly made by others, in order to provoke the witness and undermine his self-confidence. These were methods Peled was very familiar with from his work at the police - but they are unacceptable in the work of a commission of inquiry.

Due to these actions, Peled received a slap on the wrist from Attorney General Elyakim Rubinstein, who stressed that Peled would not be replaced. At the same time, the leaks did not stop and it drove me mad. Due to this I contacted Ciechanover and asked that everyone who was involved in the affair and had testified before the commission – from commission members to typists to secretaries – take a polygraph examination. I asked that one question be asked, "Did you leak details from the commission?"

Ciechanover said this was a good idea and asked to check with the rest of the members of the commission. The next day he came back to me with an incredible and insulting answer: "We, the members of the commission, are certain we did not leak any information," he said to me, and added, "but I authorize that you check whoever you want from the Mossad." I explained to Mr. Ciechanover that I did not need his authorization to check Mossad employees and realized the torrent of leaks would not cease.

I'm certain that if such an examination were held, the source of the leak would have been found and unnecessary damage to the Mossad and to Israeli national security could have been avoided. The things that were published, whether true or not, received worldwide publication and hurt national security as well as the morale of Mossad operatives.

So the commission continued its work with my unease regarding its activity and its leaks mostly continuing to increase, and though I was supposed to see it as an authoritative body, I could no longer feel that way.

Throughout the inquiry of the Ciechanover Commission, my people and I felt that Ciechanover and Tulkowsky were asking relevant questions, while Peled's treatment of us was very much diffident and often even prejudicial.

This was expressed even in his tone of voice and accusatory questions.

He asked questions such as: "Did you know how the Jordanian intelligence and security forces are organized if a mishap occurs? Where do they place road blocks? Who do they check?" These were legitimate questions and Peled received answers to the extent that we had sufficient information regarding the conduct of Jordanian police and intelligence bodies. However, he was unwilling to accept our answer that we could not know in advance where each and every roadblock would be placed due to constant changes.

Indeed, in retrospect, even after the mishap occurred, no roadblocks were set up nor was there any attempt to check traffic at border checkpoints, including at the border with Israel. Hence a basic requirement for this operation was that all conditions were right for its commencement. The fact that the operatives were struck with a form of all-encompassing determination and carried out their mission - despite the fact that conditions, by all accounts, did not allow for it - is an operational flaw rather than an architectural flaw. It's always possible to keep collecting a near-infinite amount of intelligence and still not reach a state in which one can say with surety that 'we know everything.' When Mishka said to H., the Chief of the Directorate, that we needed more information regarding a certain operation, H. would respond that you can gather indefinitely but eventually it's time to act. Military officers are used to working plans and operations that include aerial photographs and maps, but a regular intelligence operative is used to a different type of collection work, in which things happen and change within seconds. The final intelligence is always collected by operatives when they are already at the locale.

Throughout my testimony before the commission, I felt that I was asked questions that stemmed from ignorance and a misunderstanding of the unique situation which Mossad operatives face in this type of operation. When the commission had finished its work, others shared the same emotion with me.

The commission members dwelled considerably over the way the operation was planned when in fact its main flaw was in the execution.

Due to my claim that the execution was flawed, I was accused of trying to blame my subordinates for the failure, which is absurd. It should be understood that the chain of command in the Mossad is similar to the military chain of command: a department director is subordinate to the Director of the Mossad, just as the Director of Military Intelligence, Regional Commander and Branch Commander are subordinate to the IDF Chief of Staff. The one who is at the head of the pyramid is responsible, as a commander, for anything that happens, but cannot be responsible for the shortcomings of anyone down the chain of command. Commanders and soldiers alike, in all ranks, carry the duty and responsibility of making sure that what they take upon themselves is executed to the best of their abilities.

About three weeks after the Ciechanover Commission began, the Subcommittee for Covert Services, which is a subcommittee of the Knesset's Committee for Security and Foreign Relations, also decided to investigate the Mashal affair.

The chairman of the commission was MK Uzi Landau and the rest of its members were MKs Ehud Barak, Ori Or, Gideon Ezra, Benny Begin and Yossi Sarid. In those days, the same people found themselves, once again, rushing between Morasha Junction and the Knesset in Jerusalem.

The parliamentary committee, which included a former chief of staff (Barak), a major general in reserve service (Or), a former Shin Bet deputy-director (Ezra) and Knesset members devoid of personal interests and past grudges with the Mossad, turned out to be a more astute and far more professional organization than the Ciechanover Commission.

In light of the works of the commissions, security authorities – from the Defense Minister to the Director of the Shin Bet and the Director of Military Intelligence - began making firm claims that they had not been informed of the operation and thus could not have agreed to its implementation. I claimed that they had undoubtedly known, but I was in a position of weakness and the burden of proof fell upon me to prove that I was right and the three of them were wrong.

The three of them claimed that the matter was presented to them as a mere idea. I claimed that the matter of principle – the fact that it was an operation on Jordanian soil and the target to be assassinated would be from among the chiefs of Hamas, including Mashal – was known to them well in advance, when preparations for the operation could have been stopped and its commencement canceled. Not only did none of the three do so, but it was Itzchak Mordechai and Ami Ayalon's initiative that the Mossad act in Jordan rather than in the country that I had recommended, and in which the operation had been planned in the first place.

I do not know what caused all three of these senior officials to be struck with such a severe case of amnesia in regards to the information they held before the operation about the possibility that one of the Hamas chiefs in Jordan would be assassinated. I am but left to assume that as always, no one wants to have the failure stick to them, and that success will always have many authors while failure will remain orphaned.

One of the things I learned from my days in different commissions of inquiry was that you are only trusted if you have written proof, and luckily I had. I understood that I might be right but without proof it would be useless. I had to face Itzchak Mordechai, Ami Ayalon and Bogi Ya'alon – who were plainly saying 'You are not telling the truth, we were not informed of the operation ahead of time' – and say the opposite. Luckily I had the documents to support my version. I had the testimony of Mishka Ben David, who was with me at Itzchak Mordechai's office; Major General (Res.) Ze'ev Livne, Netanyahu's military secretary during the operation was called back from the United States where he was serving as military attaché. I demanded that he be present before the commission because of what he had documented in his notebook regarding the meeting between Netanyahu, Mordechai and Ayalon in which the latter two recommended to send the Mossad to assassinate one of the chiefs of Hamas. Lastly there was the testimony of Prime Minister Netanyahu, who also said he had updated Mordechai. Eventually my version was accepted. The subcommittee fully adopted my version as the truth, and in effect completely rejected the versions voiced by Itzchak Mordechai, Ami Ayalon and Bogi Ya'alon.

In those days, a new accusation was brought up against the Mossad, according to which Hamas had offered Israel a ceasefire several days before the operation to assassinate Mashal. The claim was that the message was delayed in the Mossad, did not reach the Prime Minister and the assassination went ahead. If the Prime Minister would have received this message on time, perhaps the assassination and subsequent failure could have been avoided.

What had actually happened was that two days before the operation, when its date of execution was not yet known and was reevaluated in the field every day by the squad that was already in Jordan, D. – who was in charge of open diplomatic relations between the Mossad and Jordan – arrived at the royal palace. For D. it was but one of many regular visits. He met with the king and they discussed various issues. Among other things, the king talked about the peace process and was critical of Netanyahu and his actions. At the end of the conversation, as a side note, the king told him that he had received information from Hamas that one of its senior officials, apparently Mousa Abu Marzouk, had an idea that was still undeveloped about the possibility of a *'hudna'* (ceasefire) with Israel. The king stressed to D. that he was still unsure about the seriousness and reliability of this information, and mentioned that he had to conduct further checks, and asked that we make no use of it at that moment.

D. returned to Israel, informed me of this conversation and added that Hamas might just be running the idea up the flagpole. D. stated his impression that the king himself was unsure of whether this matter was serious or not.

For five to ten years, as early as Rabin's time, the State of Israel had received numerous suggestions from Hamas, regarding a *hudna*. In return for the promised ceasefire, Hamas was willing to suffice with some "modest" demands. These demands included: the full evacuation of all settlements in the West Bank; the withdrawal of all IDF forces from the Palestinian Territories and their return to the June 4, 1967 border; the release of all terrorists imprisoned in Israel, and Israel's agreement to the Palestinian refugees' right of return.

These different *hudna* proposals reached Israel constantly and in varied ways: through Arab members of Knesset, European emissaries, collaborators and the Civil Administration in the West Bank and Gaza. The subject, as mentioned above, had already been discussed during Rabin's term as Prime Minister, and continued to surface during the tenures of Peres and Netanyahu as well. On all these occasions, the prime ministers were given evaluations by all the directors of intelligence apparatuses (IDF, Mossad and Shin Bet) that they were not serious. The explanation was that Hamas was under pressure and had asked for a ceasefire in order to regroup and regain strength. The experts explained that this custom stems from Islamic history and tradition, and is meant to strengthen the warring parties whenever they find themselves in a position of weakness. In these cases, a ceasefire - *hudna* - is suggested, with the party who requested it, in this case Hamas, free to end it at any time it desires to do so. The professional authorities recommended that these petitions be disregarded, especially considering that the "price" demanded from Israel for the *hudna* was completely inconceivable.

Be that as it may, immediately after D. gave me the king's message, I ordered the head of my bureau to prepare a report on the matter and send it to the Prime Minister's bureau. Due to a mistake, the material was not sent, but I knew nothing of it. Regardless of the Head of the Bureau's report, I had meant to bring up the matter when I met with the Prime Minister at the start of our weekly update meeting, which was scheduled for the next day. However, this meeting was postponed at the last moment as Netanyahu had just returned from an excursion abroad and was tired. Thus it occurred that I thought D.'s report had already been transferred to the Prime Minister, and in any case I knew that the next day I would meet with Netanyahu when he would arrive to the Mossad headquarters for the annual New Year's toast. When Netanyahu arrived the next day, it was already too late – the operation had already been carried out, and had failed. Either way, I should note that I had not thought that the message had been important enough to justify canceling the operation, and I had meant to say this to Netanyahu in our canceled meeting.

The claim that was made against me was that if this message would have been brought to the Prime Minister's attention, perhaps the attempted assassination of Mashal would have been prevented. However, in the committees that examined the Mashal affair, the issue of the Hamas's *hudna* offer was reviewed, and the directors of Military Intelligence and the Shin Bet said that if they had known of this proposition they would have treated it similarly to former ones. Netanyahu himself, who only heard of this message in retrospect, never claimed that it would have changed his decision. Despite all that, I am still occasionally surprised to see that to this very day – years after the affair – some people occasionally enjoy brushing the dust off the old tale of this "delayed message" and make hackneyed use of it to strengthen their criticism of the operation and its decision makers.

This way or that, the assortment of tales, leaks and publications did not cease. The commissions of inquiry finished the witness examination stage and proceeded to review the materials and reach their decision, while I had to continue working and be very focused on managing one of the most important intelligence agencies, in a country where hardly a day goes by without security concerns.

Chapter 4

Gil: The False Magician

While the commissions of inquiry were laboring over the testimonies and conclusions, and the atmosphere at the Mossad was tense and stressful, I made immense efforts to convey a sense of business-as-usual. Since terrorism and hostile nations' attempts to arm themselves with Weapons of Mass Destruction (WMDs) do not work according to the schedules of Israeli commissions of inquiry, Mossad operations continued to take place, intelligence was still being gathered and at the same time, large-scale staff work on different matters was being conducted at the Mossad.

It was amidst all this activity that A., who was in charge of the Agent Handling Division, arrived at my office one day. He presented an operation for my authorization, whose essence was a meeting between a veteran agent and his Mossad case officer, namely Yehuda Gil.

Usually when people use the term 'Mossad agent,' they are making one of the most rooted terminological mistakes in trade craft: a Mossad agent is not a Mossad operative. An agent is one who is recruited into the ranks of the Mossad by a Mossad worker who becomes his case officer. An agent is a person who provides information that he knows he is forbidden to provide according to the laws of his nation, and receives material benefits in exchange for this information. At times, the recruited agent is witting – aware of the fact he is working for a certain intelligence agency - and sometimes the agent is unwitting.

A. told me that Yehuda Gil was a veteran Mossad worker who recruited the agent some twenty-three years ago. Since that day, the agent had vehemently refused to meet anybody else, so the Mossad continued to employ Gil's services in this matter, despite the fact he had already retired.

A. told me that Gil's meetings with the agent happened once in a while, in meetings which the Mossad refers to as Scheduled Update and Report. According to A., the agent was one of the most important assets in his nation, an army general with broad and unique access to decision-makers in his nation. From the conversation, it appeared that the agent had previously delivered highly valuable information about the nation's military, its alertness level, and changes in its deployment.

"However," A. said to me, "There is some controversy regarding the agent and his case officer, and there have previously been some doubts and questions raised regarding the credibility of the information provided by the agent."

A. proceeded to tell me that previous information provided by the agent had failed to correspond with subsequent happenings. As the years passed, said A., a heated argument had developed between analysts and intelligence professionals in the IDF and in the Mossad, with the military officers treating the information as highly valuable while Mossad officers occasionally raised doubts regarding the trustworthiness of these reports. Nevertheless, Mossad officers continued to treat these reports as significant reports that must be considered during the preparation of the overall intelligence assessment. Despite these doubts, both Military Intelligence and Mossad personnel were careful not to say that the agent was deceiving us or that his reports were worthless.

A. went on to say that throughout the years, attempts had been made to replace Gil with another case officer. On one occasion, a second Mossad operative was dispatched to accompany Gil in one of his meetings with the agent, in order for him to be presented to the agent as Gil's replacement. However, Gil met with the agent, and upon his return from the meeting informed the substitute that the agent unabashedly refused to switch case officers and refused even to meet the substitute.

A. stressed that the agent's reports were always taken into very serious consideration.

I asked A., "So then, what are your suspicions, and what do you recommend we do?" A. responded, "Nothing, I'm just giving you the background."

I found it difficult to suffice with this answer and told A. that if there were uncertainties, they should be checked. A. updated me that during the time of my predecessor, Shabtai Shavit, suspicions had already surfaced and Gil was asked to record his conversation with the agent using a hidden recorder during one of their meetings. Gil returned from the meeting without the requested recording, claiming that the recording device malfunctioned, but with a meticulous and comprehensive written report which described every small detail of the meeting.

From start to finish, officers in the Mossad wanted to end Gil's contact with his source, and in Shavit's time, it was even terminated once. However, the Mossad soon received impassioned letters from Military Intelligence, arguing that it was unheard of to terminate contact with such a strategic source in one of Israel's greatest enemy nations. There was a lot of pressure from Military Intelligence, in particular from the Director of the Research Department, to immediately renew contact between Gil and the agent.

While there were some disagreements within Military Intelligence, the prevailing approach there was that he was an invaluable source.

His reports received such high esteem at Military Intelligence that in the early eighties, when Menachem Begin served as prime minister, the IDF covertly recruited a limited amount of reserve forces based on Gil's information.

At the time, the Syrian army was attacking the Christians in Lebanon and Syrian artillery was bombing Ashrafia. Israel responded with an IAF flyover above Beirut. At a certain stage, the Syrians began sending forces into the Beqaa Valley, into places where they had not been before. The Syrians' intentions were unclear and there was some concern that the Syrians were preparing for a broader military move. Gil was sent to retrieve information from his source and came back with a report stating that the Syrian military movements were a preliminary step to an offensive against Israel, through the Beqaa Valley and Beticha Valley towards the Galilee. Eventually it turned out that Syria had no such intentions, but that reserve recruitment cost the state a fortune, and could have deteriorated into a military clash.

This source's reports had reached the Prime Minister, the Defense Minister and the Chief of Staff. Having been Military Secretary of a prime minister and defense minister in the past, I knew what affect this type of report had and how dangerous it was if it was inaccurate.

In the course of that conversation, I gleaned much information from A. regarding Yehuda Gil. I was told he was one of the pillars of the case officers and one of the notable intelligence-gathering officers in the Mossad. Gil was perceived as highly accomplished, especially in light of his relations with the high-ranking agent.

I realized we were dealing with a colorful, charismatic person, with an almost hypnotic presence; bright, with a phenomenal ability to improvise and alternate between identities; known as "the man with a thousand faces." He was fluent in a great many languages – including English, Arabic, French and Italian – and could use his incredible personal charm to convince anyone of almost anything. Mossad folklore told that he could "make even a telephone pole talk." He was considered a field operator turned trade craft legend in regards to operating human intelligence sources, HUMINT in professional terms. His ability to adopt a European persona which completely blurred the fact of his Israeli identity was absolutely perfect. He put a lot of effort in creating the cover of his borrowed identity, from his outward appearance to the contents of the character, and had an excellent ability to convince whomever necessary that he was not Yehuda Gil. His hair would change colors and his well-kept mustache would disappear and reappear – as the role dictated.

Part of his personality was expressed by a never-ending need to be at the center of attention and to always feel that he was needed. Ego was the heart of his personality and his driving force. He managed to cause his entire environment to treat him accordingly: everyone found him charming on account of his appearance; his ability to rally everyone around him, from opponents to allies; and his professional reputation.

He was considered a one of a kind intelligence-gathering officer and none could ignore his colorful reports and the narrative abilities he displayed when telling them. The information he would bring from his sources and the reports of his conduct with them impressed each and every one.

In his role as senior trainer for intelligence-gathering officers in the Mossad, Gil raised a generation of case officers, and was admired by his trainees. His colorful, dominant character was very unusual, and when combined with the myths of his operational abilities abroad and his phenomenal talent as an actor – it put a spell on the new recruits. He would hypnotize his students with his tales and turned them into faithful fans of his thrilling character.

His lectures were thrilling and unusual. One time, he went into the classroom and immediately gave his students an amazing performance of a heart attack, which the students were certain was real. These are things that a trainer in such a course is not supposed to do. It is not his responsibility to teach the students the art of impersonation – he can give examples of what can be done, but not how to do it.

A. finished talking and I began scratching my head in discomfort, asking myself: What do we do now? One things was clear to me – I could not ignore this matter now, after what I had been told.

I authorized Gil's planned departure to meet with the agent, once again requesting he be equipped with a recording device.

Determining Yehuda Gil's credibility required organized and highly sensitive work within the Mossad, since after dozens of years working for the organization and due to his charismatic character, he had plenty of friends who might warn him of the suspicions against him.

After the meeting was authorized, Gil went to meet with the agent, once again with a recording device at my request. Gil returned to Israel from the meeting with a long and detailed report about what he had been told by the general. The report was in line with all previous reports regarding Syrian military preparations, but once again, we heard the claim that the recording device had malfunctioned.

I asked that the device be taken for examination at the Mossad's technical department, and the device was returned with a diagnosis of working perfectly, audibly recording even the street noises and traffic.

This event raised my level of suspicion.

A while later, during a series of new appointments in the Mossad, I appointed M. to be director of the Agent Operations Division.

After interviewing all the candidates and looking into others, I decided, in opposition to some dissenting voices within the Mossad, that M. was the most suited person for the job. M. would later proceed to reach higher ranking positions within the Mossad.

From the first meetings I held with M., immediately after he had assumed his new position, we discussed the main issues that the Division was to handle, and the matter of Yehuda Gil was notable among them. Despite the marked discomfort involved, M. made it clear that his position was similar to mine – that Gil's credibility must be tested.

M. believed Gil was savvy enough to guess that he had been tested before when he had been asked to retrieve tapes of his meetings with the agent. M. added that he felt that Gil had given a sigh of relief during Shavit's time when he had been asked to stop the meetings, which were later renewed at the request of IDF Military Intelligence.

R., M.'s second in command, also felt uncomfortable with Gil's reports, although both were aware of the grave implications of their words. The notion that an intelligence-gathering officer might also be a liar had a far-reaching and grave influence on the organization's morale and its prestige. If intelligence agencies and governments in Israel had made decisions based on his false reports for twenty-three years, it could lead to serious national and international harm to the Mossad and the State of Israel.

M., who was aware of the moral and professional meaning of a decision to test Gil, said outright that if the examination revealed that Gil had been honest, he would resign from duty, as this meant he had doubted the credibility of an intelligence officer, which is against every code of conduct the Mossad follows.

A while later, M. came back to me and presented me with another meeting between Gil and the agent. We would later discover that Gil, who was a man of the world with a hedonistic approach and who understood a thing or two about the good life, had a special weakness for the City of Light. Hence he scheduled his meetings there, with an emphasis on a certain bohemian quarter and its famous cafés, previously inhabited by philosophers, intellectuals, authors and artists.

In one of our discussions and under M.'s recommendation, I decided to try and crack the mystery of the material's credibility. We also wanted to examine the uncharacteristic conduct, in which one intelligence officer operated an agent for twenty-three years without interruption, and understand how and why an agent would "dig his heels in" and refuse to meet another case officer. We also aimed to examine how it could be that every technical means we entrusted Gil with in order to bring back testimony from his meetings, mysteriously stopped working immediately upon his arrival at the rendezvous point.

As far as I was concerned, and as far as M. and his deputy R. were concerned, it was a difficult decision to make: to follow a case officer, a Mossad veteran operative, and gather information regarding his conduct.

It was no coincidence that such an unprecedented and far-reaching decision had not been made for years. It must be understood that in the organizational culture of the intelligence community, it is an accepted belief that if something appears to be wrong, then the agent must be examined, not his case officer. The thought that one of our "own people" was deliberately doing something that could hurt the organization was unimaginable. A great deal of the Mossad's activity is carried out by individuals, in interactions between a case officer and agent.

The basis for accepting the case officer's reports from his meetings with the agent is complete trust between the organization and the intelligence officer, that the latter is actually carrying forth his mission: that he is in fact meeting with the agent, hearing what he is hearing, and recording it in as accurate a written report as possible. This trust is one of the significant foundations of the Mossad's operations.

Nevertheless, assumed identities, disguises, subterfuge and deceit are often part of the routine work of a Mossad operative in his field activities. There is always the concern that boundaries become blurred as the years pass, due to force of habit. People become accustomed to living under assumed identities and presenting cover stories riddled with lies and fabrications that do not bear even a coincidental similarity to reality. On the other hand, when reporting to their superiors, these same people must re-assume their true identity and stick to the absolute truth. This gives rise to concern due to the nature of the sharp transition between fabrication and truth. Therefore, it must be made certain that despite their living in such a dichotomous world - with frequent and extreme transitions between identities and between reality and fantasy and the need to assume and abandon shapes, often in short time intervals - they retain the ability to distinguish between fabrication as a tool of the trade and the need to deliver truthful reports. This further requires that they remain transparent in their dealings with superiors at the Mossad and legal authorities, including obeying any neighborhood traffic policeman and minor tax official. Doubtless, these people require a special personality to help them successfully switch between both worlds without developing minor schizophrenia or forgetting how to distinguish right from wrong and what is allowed and forbidden.

One of the occasions that convinced me that things had gone too far and led me to demand of M. to act decisively and creatively in order to solve this riddle, was when Gil delivered a report that said President Assad had tired of the foot-dragging in diplomatic negotiations with Israel and was planning a military offensive. The report suggested that Assad believed he was being deceived by Israel and that Israel would refuse any compromise, and surely there was no chance for it with Netanyahu's government. Therefore, Assad had decided to take quick action in the north, apparently at Mt. Hermon - a ground-based assault at the end of a Syrian military drill in the Golan Heights. Meaning, the Syrians did not intend to initiate all-out war, but only to conquer a limited-scale territory in the Hermon area. Gil reported of a new Syrian deployment in the Golan Heights and the Beqaa Valley. The only obstacle to launching the attack, said Gil, would be if strong rain began to fall in the Golan Heights. In such a case, the offensive would be delayed until springtime. This information caused havoc in the defense establishment, and a high-level alert was declared in the north, which significantly raised tensions on the Syrian side as well. Fortunately, the affair ended in nothing, but the rising tension levels in the north could just as well have led to a declaration of war.

After this event, it was clear how critical this matter was, and how it could spiral into a terrible ending.

The decision to track these meetings to extract further information than was given by Yehuda Gil was an unprecedented decision, the likes of which had never been taken in the Mossad until then. However, my suspicions were so severe that I saw no other way to act.

In order to delve a bit deeper into the nature of Gil, I invited him to a personal meeting with me. I presented it as an acquaintance meeting, nothing of which could have raised his concern, and Gil behaved like a reliable person who could be trusted, and told me different things about himself. Among other things, I learned from him that after he retired from the Mossad he looked for a new position of influence and attempted to run in the local elections in the regional council of the settlement in which he lived, Gedera. Afterwards, he took part in political activism in the Moledet movement, where he was allied with Rehavam Ze'evi (nicknamed

Gandhi), and was latter appointed the party's General Secretary. He also became part of the Hevra Kadisha (the Jewish religious burial service) in Gedera, while at the same time served as chairman of the Be'er Association, responsible for delivering water from the settlement's wells to the older neighborhoods in the town.

It was clear to me that these various humdrum occupations could not give this life-lusting man even an eighth of the exhilaration he was used to at the Mossad, and I had no doubt that his continued employment as a retiree was very valuable for him. This arrangement was very comfortable for Gil and suited his lifestyle. He was still in the center of affairs, receiving a generous paycheck for his services and his expenses in Europe, in addition to the sums of money he was given to pass on to his source, and like many others, he did not find his trips abroad to be a suffrage.

At this stage I met with E., head of one of the operational divisions of the Mossad, and asked him to prepare a squad of operatives to watch Gil's next meeting with the agent.

Gil departed for the meetings as usual, and the squad left after him. Several days later, they returned to Israel and reported they saw that Gil had indeed met with someone. The followers attempted to get nearer and hear what the two were talking about, but failed to do so. Their main finding was that it was obvious by lip and body movements that Gil did most of the talking, while his partner sat opposite attentive, occasionally nodding or making short, fleeting statements. All this did not stop Gil, as usual, from preparing a long and detailed written report of all the things that the agent allegedly told him. Gil also reported that the meeting lasted for seven hours, while the surveillance squad saw it last for a mere forty minutes.

These details gave some basis to our suspicions, or at least the initial suspicion that part of Gil's reports included statements which were never made by the agent. This was all in contrast to our initial suspicion that Gil was merely "spicing up" his reports.

The Prime Minister was regularly updated of my suspicions towards Gil and my intentions to act upon them. After being updated about the latest findings, we decided to consult Attorney General Elyakim Rubinstein and Chief Prosecutor Edna Arbel. Following these consultations, it was decided to involve Shin Bet investigators in the affair, and ask for authorization to search Gil's house.

On November 24, 1997, it was decided to arrest Gil and hold him in custody for investigation. At my request, a gag order was issued in order to avoid harming the investigation itself, as well as prevent a needless scandal.

We knew that it must come as a surprise. We invited Gil to meet with M. at his office at Mossad headquarters, with Shin Bet investigators sitting in an adjacent room. M. asked me to give Gil one last chance to confess before being handed over to the police and the prosecution. I agreed, since as a commanding officer I understood his feelings. M. explained that he felt he had to give an operative who had misconducted himself a chance to say "I failed," otherwise he would not be able to look his other subordinates in the eyes.

Gil arrived at M.'s office with his usual attitude of business as usual. M., who unlike Gil knew what was about to happen, was very tense and agitated to confront the man who had been his mentor, the one who had trained him in his first days in the Mossad, a man whom he adored and held in such high esteem.

However M. was careful to maintain a calm outward countenance and told Gil, "Yehuda, we have reason to believe that in operating the agent, you crossed some uncrossable lines in our organization, and your actions were in contrast to basic principles of honesty and credibility."

Gil kept his poker face and answered with stoic serenity, "I have no idea what you're talking about."

M. said once again, "Yehuda, look, I'm asking you, think one more time before you answer me. I'm speaking on the basis of firm evidence. I care about you very much and don't want you to leave this room into a series of unpleasant events. In the other room there are people who, if you don't lay out the entire truth right here, will have to deal with you in other methods."

Once again, in utter indifference, Gil answered, "I don't know what you're talking about."

At that same moment, the Shin Bet investigators entered the room, headed by "Sheriff", and took him to a nearby room.

Two hours later, Gil had signed a confession. We found it hard to believe that such a man would break after a mere two hours, but the Shin Bet investigators were highly professional and knew how to make him surrender, and lead him to confess immediately at the onset of the investigation, that the contents of his meetings with the agent were born in his vivid imagination.

When the investigation ended, it turned out that Gil had indeed attempted to recruit that officer twenty-three years earlier, but his efforts had failed. The officer refused to take part in covert work for any espionage service. Gil was afraid that his failure to recruit the officer would harm the aura of almightiness he had gained, his reputation and promotion. Therefore he had decided to hide the affair and from then until the day he was arrested, for twenty-three years, he had fabricated and fooled the Mossad and other intelligence services with false reports of the hostile nation's military, all of which he had invented.

Throughout this entire time, he had continued to meet with the officer, for whom it was apparently not much more than a vacation in Europe to meet an old and generous acquaintance who would reimburse his expenses.

Gil, who would regularly teach new recruits at the Mossad a course titled "Lying as an Art Form", which focused on methods of lying and deceit as an instrument to achieve goals, had apparently decided to go all the way with the material he taught.

In order to create a guise of credibility for his reports and ensure they would be accepted as authentic, he would use background material he had received from Military Intelligence personnel who would brief him before he departed on a round of meetings. Military Intelligence would guide him as to what questions to ask, and he would very sophisticatedly use his excellent descriptive abilities and mirror these questions with answers that were in line with the background materials he had received, and thus would appear to verify the evaluations he had received from Military Intelligence. This was also what he had done in regards to the planned Syrian surprise attack in the Golan Heights, and regarding Syria's intention to declare war in the early 1980s – he had heard of all these matters from Military Intelligence researchers who had prepared him for his meeting.

Another matter that added an air of credibility to his false reports was his use of information regarding the Syrian military doctrine, which he had studied carefully. The search in his home revealed a library rich with military journals, books and research papers about Syria, the Arab armies and Soviet doctrines, which the Syrians adopted. Being an immensely curious person who read extensively and invested most of his energy in studying these matters, he managed to extract a vast amount of knowledge from these materials and gained an excellent grasp of the matter. He would structure his reports based on his broad and deep education, and the background materials he received from Military Intelligence. The information he gave managed to convince most of the research officers, as it was in accordance with what the agent would reasonably report. None could have imagined that what was coming from the agent, who we viewed as a strategic asset, was nothing but a collection of fibs hatched by his case officer. The basic perception of the organizational system in the Mossad and Military Intelligence could not imagine that Gil would lie, but only that something was not quite right with the agent - and that if there was a liar involved, it must have been the agent.

Furthermore, Gil's reports, which matched some of the existing evaluations, were of service in a way to all involved, since they were in line with the perception Military Intelligence had developed with regards to certain matters.

At a later stage, when concerns began to surface that the source of the problematic nature of the material was Gil's credibility issues and not those of the agent, it was decided to enforce certain restrictions and limit Gil's ability to receive information, so as not to enable him to use it in his reports. Yet in his characteristic sophistication, Gil managed to charm those briefing him, and due to the vast knowledge he had amassed, he managed to ask the right questions and receive exactly the right answers that would later be of service to his reports.

Thus it was that for twenty-three years, he had fed the system false reports, which had managed to fool many intelligence professionals.

True, there were some people in the Mossad and in Military Intelligence who had doubted the credibility of the reports at some points. The Mossad constantly checked itself regarding the authenticity of material. His information was crosschecked against other information, but no one imagined that Gil was taking existing data and recycling it. Since the examination was only with regards to the reasonableness of the content, it was always possible to find other information that was similar to Gil's content, and so in retrospect, all these examinations were worthless.

It was interesting to understand the motives for such an unusual act. Apparently, this was not a matter of greed. True, throughout the years, Gil was given incredible sums of money to transfer to the agent in exchange for his services, and the money of course was never transferred to the agent but remained in Gil's possession. Gil himself told his investigators about the money he possessed and led them to a hiding spot in his house, where they found several dozen thousand dollars, which he claimed was the total amount he had received over the years to transfer to "the agent." However, according to certain assessments in the Mossad, $150,000 was still missing from all the sums he was given to transfer to different people.

Gil had apparently become his own victim. His extroverted and charismatic personality and his uncontrollable urge to be at the center of attention and receive positive feedback from his environment, had turned him into a slave of his own ego. This was quite a lot of ego indeed - one that had degraded a man to servitude and inability to admit his failings.

The work of an intelligence officer is very individual and competitive, and ego plays a central role in it. Gil's problematic personality caused him to lose his boundaries, an occurrence that is fortunately rare in Mossad officers, and that was what made Gil's actions so anomalous and unusual.

It's amazing to think that such an affair could go on for twenty-three years. For that entire time, even when suspicions about Gil arose, the necessary steps to reveal the truth were not taken. This despite the fact that the writing was written in great big letters on the wall, and even though the directors of the Mossad who preceded me were aware of the matter.

At some point, the story of Gil's arrest was leaked to the media. Claims then began to appear that I was the one who had manufactured the affair and then leaked the story, in order to divert public attention from the Mashal affair, which was still being featured prominently in the headlines at the time. However, it was very much in my interests, as well as in the interests of the Mossad and the state's national security, to ensure that the story not be leaked, in order to make the most of the investigation and limit the damage to national security – hence that claim is absurd. That is the reason I demanded a full media blackout be enforced with regards to the investigation and that a gag order be issued.

These things were done, but I'm afraid they did not prevent the malicious leak. Furthermore, I had reached the decision to begin inspecting Yehuda Gil's behavior far before the Mashal affair even happened, and real steps had already been taken to begin to get to the bottom of this matter.

An operational mishap is something that is taken into consideration, and it can happen at any time, but the discovery of an extreme unreliability, which is analogous to actual treason, in one of our own ranks, was utterly unacceptable. Besides the professional, security and reputational damage, there was also a feeling of personal grievance, and betrayal of the most crucial and essential element, which is a foundation of the Mossad's work: trust in the commanding officers and the operatives to provide full information and tell the whole truth in every situation, even in embarrassing and uncomfortable circumstances. Every Mossad member who embarks on an operation knows that even if the operation fails – the subsequent inquiry must always be truthful.

People at the Mossad were so shocked, that in a meeting I had with Mossad retirees, one of them turned to me and asked why Gil's treatment had to be taken outside of Mossad boundaries. The man argued that the media reports had caused us immense damage, and that everything should have been taken care of within the Mossad.

This man failed to understand how severe Gil's actions were, to what extent his behavior had transgressed every moral code and necessitated involvement of legal authorities in order to allow for his criminal prosecution and to give him his just desserts - processes that could not take place within the boundaries of the Mossad. The internal commission I appointed in the Mossad examined all the operational and managerial aspects in order to gain future insights, but no internal commission had the power to punish Gil for such grave offenses as damaging national security, fraud, deception, breach of trust and theft of money.

The Mossad, which could not bring Gil to justice and punish him, could at least check itself and learn its lesson to prevent this sort of matter from recurring in the future.

Indeed, following the affair, which was known as the False Information Affair, some changes were made:

It was revealed from Gil's actions that he viewed the price of lying as lower than the price of failure. He thought that if he would lie, the price the Mossad and the State would pay would be lower than the price of his personal failure in attempting to recruit the agent. Hence, it was clear that a way must be found to further instill the principle of abrogation of lies, and to ensure that the Mossad would only employ people who report the truth in its service. In the past, there was a tendency to recruit all sorts of "special fellows" to the Mossad, brought by other "fellows" who knew them, people who were highly talented in recruiting and operating agents, but basic qualities of honesty and reliability were not given first priority. One of the internal commission's conclusions was that there was no longer a place for recruiting these types of people, and the basis would have to be honest and reliable people.

One thing was clear: the internal controls had failed in this case, otherwise such a mishap could not have developed – that for twenty-three years, Gil could feed the system false materials without anyone finding out.

It was also decided to enhance the way sources are evaluated by crosschecking information between different teams that would check the source's credibility. If such a procedure had been in place, a case like Gil's would not have happened, because one of two things would have been discovered: either that the source was unreliable, or that his case officer was fabricating the material.

I determined that anyone who would be found unreliable, or to be giving false reports, would immediately be expelled from the Mossad, even if this person was a talented professional in other aspects. I ordered that Gil's case be analyzed and studied as part of different training courses, to show how never to behave, and to instill the principle that the price of lying is higher than that of failure.

Nevertheless, it is important to remember that the False Information Affair is not a characteristic case, and the vast majority of Mossad people are excellent, reliable, talented and professional, with actual and not imaginary accomplishments.

In one of the days before the trial, M. went to visit Gil in prison. Gil appeared very down in spirits in the moldy cell that stank of Lysol and bore no resemblance to the luxury hotels to which he was accustomed. M. still hoped to hear some words of apology or regret from him, and asked him again, "Why did you do it?" However, Gil, who apparently had difficulty accepting his new situation, mumbled incoherently. As usual, he was attempting to use his verbal skills to cover up for a lack of any real substance in his statements.

Gil was put on trial in the Tel Aviv District Court and charged with providing false information with the intent to harm national security, theft and fraud, and sentenced to five years of imprisonment. He attempted to appeal against his conviction to the Supreme Court, but his appeal was denied.

The next time the two of them met was when M. came to testify in court. M., who was embarrassed because of Gil's presence – apparently more so than Gil was embarrassed for himself – tried not to meet his glance, but at the end of his testimony, when he walked past Gil, he heard him call to him, "M., what's wrong, you don't even say hello anymore?"

The man of a thousand faces still found it difficult to accept that the game was over and that the rules had changed.

Gil was born in Libya and his original surname was 'Ganach.' In Libyan Arabic, the word means 'bird's wing.' After the False Information Affair was revealed, one of his friends said of him, "Gil tried to fly his whole life. He was a master of improvisation and maneuvers, one for whom most of the rules simply do not apply from his perspective. This time he fell."

If Yehuda Gil would not have been caught, and would have continued with his shenanigans, the damage done to national security could have been tenfold.

Chapter 5

Leaks and Evasions

The work of the inquiry commissions, which began five months earlier, was about to be finished. However, the leaked information from the Ciechanover commission continued to cause me much duress and to have absolutely no trust in the commission. This was entirely contrary to the way the Subcommittee for Covert Services (which oversees and monitors the activities of Military Intelligence, the Mossad and the Shin Bet) was conducting itself, and from which no information leaked.

At an earlier stage, during one of the commission's gatherings, Ciechanover voluntarily told me, in the presence of two other members of the commission, "Our commission will not recommend that any personal decisions be made, despite having the authority to do so, and hence we will not issue warnings to you."

At one stage, the commission sent me a document that included claims regarding the nature of the operation, its implementation and the preparations towards it. These claims came with an explicit notice that this was not to be considered a warning letter, but a letter meant to enable me to respond to the commission's claims in regards to me.

In response to the Ciechanover commission's claims, my lawyers and I prepared an entire booklet of answers that presented my side of the matter. However due to censorship issues, I was unable to reveal its contents at the time, and still cannot do so now.

In the background, there was still a constant buzz about me, mainly the issue of my resignation, but I restated my position that we must wait until the commissions finish their work. PM Netanyahu also held a similar stance, at least outwardly, and stated that he awaits the results of the commissions in order to decide on his next steps. However, after every work meeting I had with him, his office would anonymously leak to the press that he was looking for my replacement. This was not the type of support I was expecting. When I confronted him, Netanyahu answered that he does not know who is behind these leaks and that he would take action to stop them, but they did not cease.

On February 13, 1998, the Prime Minister received the conclusive report of the Subcommittee for Covert Services, and three days later, he also received the Ciechanover commission's report. The report by the Ciechanover commission was around 300 pages long, most of them confidential, and approximately only fifteen pages were ever made public.

Naturally, I did not suffice with the non-confidential abstract that was made public, and asked to receive a copy of the commission's full report, but my request was refused. In order to know exactly what was attributed to me, to what level of severity and which changes I was asked to make in the Mossad, I thought it would be right that I read the entire report. I was told it was being sent only to Netanyahu and that I was to receive it from him. I contacted the Prime Minister's bureau but there was no trace of the report, and instead was answered with an embarrassing evasion. I saw this as improper and petty behavior as well as bad governance. Only after media pressure was I asked, on February 17, one day after the conclusions were published, to visit the Prime Minister's bureau in Jerusalem in order to sit there and read the full report, with its hundreds of confidential pages.

The report detailed the faults that had occurred based on the opinions of the commission members. Several faults were attributed to me.

The Subcommittee for Covert Services determined that the Prime Minister was the one who authorized the operation, and that he consulted the Defense Minister on the matter, who had raised no objection. The committee further determined that several weeks before the operation took place, it was brought to the attention of the Director of the Shin Bet, Ami Ayalon, and Head of Military Intelligence, Moshe "Bogie" Ya'alon, members of the Committee of the Heads of Services (*Varash*) and they also had no objections. This was the case despite the fact that all of these people – Defense Minister Yitzhak Mordechai, "Bogie" Ya'alon and Ami Ayalon – claimed they did not know about the operation beforehand. The committee further determined that the considerations made when the operation was decided upon were reasonable and justified; this was similar to other successful operations in the past. The committee found that the failure was due to planning and execution, but noted that the failure itself was also due to far deeper reasons stemming from shortcomings that had existed for years. The reason for this was that for many years the Israeli government had not created a comprehensive policy for combating terrorist organizations, one that was based on thorough consideration and a logical, consistent and long-term approach. The introduction of the Special Anti-Terrorism Office in March 1996 had also failed to change this problematic state of affairs. In lieu of a complete anti-terrorism doctrine, the element of responding to terrorist attacks – as had happened in the Mashal affair – became prominent and counter-productive.

The parliamentary committee further noted that after the operation failed, the media was flooded with leaks containing details of the operation, which were very harmful to confidential systems and to national security. It was stressed that the source of these leaks was in the bureaus of high-ranking officials, and noted that this phenomenon was ugly and dangerous, and that special effort must be made to eliminate it. The committee noted that the shortcomings it found in the ways of combating terrorism, in the political and operational echelons, had been going on for many years but had not been identified and handled. This led all members of the committee, except for MK Sarid, to the opinion that no personal decisions should be made about any of those involved in the failure of the operation. Furthermore, it was their recommendation that I stay in my position in light of my knowledge and due to their belief that I could amend the shortcomings better than anyone else could.

MK Sarid was the only one who held the minority position that my role should be terminated. Nevertheless, and despite his conclusion, Sarid was careful to state that I was the most reliable witness of those who appeared before the committee, and that everything I said in my testimony, from start to finish, turned out to be accurate. Hence, the others – Defense Minister Yitzhak Mordechai, Head of Military Intelligence "Bogie" Ya'alon, and Director of Shin Bet Ami Ayalon, who claimed they had not been updated about the operation before its commencement - had not been entirely accurate in their claims, to understate the matter.

The Ciechanover commission also decided not to make any personal recommendations, but nonetheless, in a manner that was entirely unsurprising and opposed to the commission's previous commitments, their report included Rafi Peled's minority position that I must resign from my position as Director of the Mossad. Ciechanover and Tolkowsky, who had decided in advance that they would not submit personal recommendations, left the decision at the Prime Minister's discretion.

I was significantly strengthened by the Intelligence Subcommittee's recommendations that I remain in my position, and even from the Ciechanover commission, in which two of three members chose to leave the decision to the Prime Minister. H., who was the head of the division that had carried out the operation, decided to resign as he viewed the conclusions as a blemish on the operational echelon. H. had acted despite being appointed my second in command only a short time earlier, and set to replace Aliza Magen who was appointed Deputy Director of the Mossad in the days of my predecessor, Shabtai Shavit. Magen was supposed to conclude her service and leave for advanced studies according to our agreement.

From the very beginning, I did not deny that the chief superior responsibility in the Mossad was mine, but I made the distinction between being responsible and being at fault. The person who is responsible is not necessarily always the one at fault. It is my opinion that the operation was prepared in accordance with strict professional standards, and had gone through all the necessary stages of inquiry and authorizations, but had ultimately failed in execution, not planning, due to grave errors made by the operational team. The basic terms to carry out the mission had not been met and it was wrong to execute it. Nonetheless, an attempt to attack Mashal was made. Furthermore, at the stage when the operatives could still have escaped without being caught and the operation revealed – the operatives made another mistake: they left the vehicle too early, in complete contradiction to the plan. Thus, they enabled those who had been chasing them to catch them after the altercation developed. Hence, the prepared escape plan was never even tested, due to the operatives' misguided judgment.

The matter of superior responsibility is very important to me, and I am well familiar with the phenomenon in which more often only the lower ranks are accounted for their actions, instead of the higher ones. However, the unique conditions that were known and clear to the operatives – and which were a non-negotiable condition to implementing the operation – had not been met. Hence, the attempt to assassinate Mashal, in the manner and time in which it took place, should never have happened. I was and remain convinced that the strength of the method we chose for this operation was that if a decision was made not to execute in the last moment, according to the circumstances on site – nothing would have happened and no damage would have been done because there was no incriminating sign that anything of this sort was about to take place. The late Zvi Malhin, a legend among Mossad operatives, who had participated in the operation to capture Adolf Eichmann, said of the Mashal affair, "Sometimes the bravest thing to do in the midst of an operation is not to act, but I'm afraid we're not familiar with this concept."

Since this was my opinion with regards to the reasons for the operation's failure which comprised not even the smallest part of my superior responsibility, I reached the conclusion that I was responsible but not at fault because of some misdoing or something I had failed to do. My responsibility was superior-vicarious, since I was the one who sent the operatives on their mission, but it was not personal.

In regards to the target and location of the operation, both commissions of inquiry found that Jordan could not be given immunity when it comes to actions that are necessary for defense of the State. The commissions also found that Khaled Mashal and his counterparts were not immune in light of their deep involvement in the terrorist campaign against the citizens of Israel.

Accusations that I had "fixated mindset" remind me of something that Meir Shalev wrote after the Ciechanover commission's report was published - that if arriving at an Arab capital and injecting a substance into the leader of a terrorist organization's ear is a fixated mindset, we can consider ourselves lucky that people in the Mossad are not creative.

I felt better after the commissions concluded their work, and saw it as approval to continue my service. Not only had I stood the test of bringing the operatives back, but I had also stood the test of the commissions' critical review and received authorization to stay in my position.

Although I was very relieved to read the commissions' reports, I awaited Netanyahu's decision. He had announced earlier that he would decide on his steps after reading the conclusive reports written by the commissions. Yet Netanyahu, whose role as Prime Minister had apparently taken up most of his time, was slow to read the report. Some days after it was submitted, he claimed to have read thirty pages of it, and ten days later he was still on page 200. I wondered if Netanyahu was hoping that by the time he finished reading, someone else would do his work for him.

In the meantime, as far as I was concerned, the submittal of the reports and conclusions of the commissions of inquiry ended five nerve-racking months, filled with stress and frustration, and intensive round-the-clock work. I wanted to see it as the end of an era and the beginning of a new one, and decided to take a short one-day rest. I wanted one day to relax with my family after the Mashal storm. I thought it would be the ultimate vacation for me, before returning to the demanding and weighty position of Director of the Mossad. It was an opportunity to spend one whole day at home, in the company of my family, after a long period away except for brief intervals for some few brief hours.

I did not have any special plans for this rare vacation day, which was set to take place on Thursday, February 19. "Just some rest, quiet, and mostly one day to do nothing," I told myself before falling asleep on Wednesday night.

A strange and unexpected knock on my door at six in the morning of the next day took me out of a pleasurable sleep and forced me to leave my bed half-asleep to see what was going on.

As I went downstairs towards the entrance to the house, I was certain it was the newspaper boy who wanted to become acquainted with the household's residents or the delivery boy from the grocery store who had the wrong house. However, I was amazed to find my neighbor, A., head of an operation division in the Mossad, standing at the door.

A. appeared agitated as he told me, "We had a blunder in Switzerland last night."

I looked at him with a shocked expression, wondering if this was due to not being fully awake yet, or if I had been struck by a sudden forgetfulness. One thing was clear; I had no idea what he was talking about.

"Which operation are you talking about?" I asked, and A. responded, "It's an operation that your deputy Aliza authorized to carry out, the day you were not at the Mossad and went to read the Ciechanover commission report in Jerusalem."

A single knock on my door had now reduced my coveted vacation day to ruins, and my plans to have some peace and quiet that day, and in the days that followed, disappeared without a trace.

A. told me that the operation was meant to gather intelligence regarding a Hezbollah operative in Bern, Switzerland, who had been in contact with Lebanon. The operation included a squad of operatives who had been discovered in action. The local police had been called, some of the squad members had been captured, and the fate of the others was still unclear.

A. finished talking and I thought to myself - never a dull moment.

A squad that revealed information to the local police which led to arrests – truly it was a while since this last happened, and I was starting to miss it. Only two days earlier I had finished reading the report of one commission of inquiry, and already another calamity was knocking on my door.

I immediately left for Mossad headquarters to begin another session of round-the-clock work. The atmosphere at the Mossad in those days was unbearably difficult. Everybody felt that we were being chased by bad luck, a very difficult feeling that something was wrong at the organization that usually worked flawlessly.

I immediately phoned the Prime Minister and told him what was going on. In the background, I heard two words: "Oy vey…" Just like me, Netanyahu also thought this was the last thing we needed, especially two days after the Ciechanover commission and the Subcommittee for Covert Services had filed their reports.

I could hear Netanyahu was very upset. "How could this happen?" he said in that conversation, which sounded more like a scolding and expressed extreme dissatisfaction.

I cannot say I was offended by his response. I had known for a long time that what Rabin was able to provide for his subordinates, in terms of support, cooperation and shared responsibility, Netanyahu would never learn.

I felt I was alone, and not in a good way.

Many problems and unclear issues bothered me about this operation, one of the main ones being: how could such an operation be planned and executed without me knowing and authorizing it, in absolute contrast to the Mossad's rules of conduct?

My investigation revealed that from the moment the operation was authorized, on that day when I was in Jerusalem, two days had passed in which neither Magen, my deputy, nor A. the division director, bothered to update me. I made many attempts to understand what had happened there; why I was not informed; why they did not wait for me to return from Jerusalem - which might be a bit of a distance from central Israel but still is not abroad; and why the operation had been launched without me knowing of it. All I encountered in response was eye rolling, staring at the floor and the shifting of responsibility from one to the other.

I felt that those responsible had chosen not to inform me of the operation due to their concern that I would not authorize it. Indeed, in retrospect, now that I am familiar with the details of the operation, I can say that it was highly doubtful that I would have authorized it. Surely I would have asked to make a deeper examination into its necessity, the escape routes, potential responses in the event of a mishap and the chances of success.

Furthermore, the operation took place a short time after conclusions were reached from the Mashal calamity, and as a result, in all operations that began between the Mashal operation and the Swiss operation, additional emphases were made compared to what had been done earlier. The emphasis was on getting out of problematic situations and overcoming mishaps.

During that period, I drove the operatives mad before every operation, demanding exact and very detailed plans for possible responses and escapes.

Now we were facing the same mess, as if no lesson had been learned, once again forced to inform the authorities of a foreign nation that we had acted on its soil unlawfully, and again I found myself dealing with the concerning matter of bringing the operatives back home and trying to minimize damages.

I immediately turned to M., who was our representative in Europe. M. was dispatched by the department in charge of the Mossad's foreign relations with various covert and other organizations abroad. Her responsibilities included the Mossad's contact with covert services in European countries, including Switzerland. I asked her to inform General Rigley, head of the Swiss intelligence services, of what had occurred. I asked that she tell him everything about the Hezbollah operative and the operation's objective. I also asked her to stress to him that there was no intention to harm anyone or to act against Swiss interests.

M. informed Rigley of what had happened and asked him to minimize damages and release the detained operatives, in order to avoid further unpleasantness and escalation. She promised full cooperation and offered to end the affair quietly and without making a scandal of it, as had happened many times before in the course of relations between foreign espionage agencies. I also spoke with Rigley on the phone a few times, and he promised he would do everything in his power to end the affair quietly, but also noted that his was only a recommendation in this case, and he was not the final decision-maker.

A few hours later, a report came in that some of the operatives who were captured had managed to extricate themselves from Swiss police and were in the midst of escaping Swiss borders. Another optimistic report was that contact had been made with the first operative who had disappeared and that they were already beyond the border. Therefore, as of early noontime, only one operative was still detained and we had to act urgently to release him.

I later discovered additional details, from which I learned that carrying out the mission had involved occupying a building for several hours. The operatives' presence there had created noises.

The mishap began when the building's caretaker, who had difficulty sleeping that night, heard the noises late at night. She went to check on their source and discovered that the place the noise was coming from was blocked.

The caretaker went back to her apartment and called the police. The squad members were unaware of her actions, but could have assumed she would do this when she had tried to reach the place where they were located.

Squad commander Y. was forced to make a dramatic decision: one option was to leave immediately, prevent the squad from being captured, but leave traces that would clearly point to the nature of the mission on the scene. A second option was to attempt to partially complete the mission, in a way that would allow the squad members to return later and finish the work. Y. found himself facing the possibility of the police arriving within ten minutes, but if the police had not been called, the mission could be accomplished. He took into account that the entrance to the building was blocked by two operatives tasked with stalling the police if they arrive and alerting those inside of their arrival.

There was disagreement among the operatives on the scene, with two arguing to leave immediately, but Y. decided to at least attempt to complete one more stage of the mission in order to prevent the operation from being revealed. A few minutes later, when the work was done, he sent the two operatives who were with him outside and decided to stay inside to finish the last part himself. At that moment, the police arrived. The two operatives outside did not manage to succeed in their task and decided to flee. The policemen met another pair of operatives leaving the building in their direction. The two made an evasive maneuver, and fled from the police at the first opportunity. Y. was caught carrying all the instruments used to complete the mission.

The squad commander's judgment was a classic case of making a decision that could lead to triumphant or miserable consequences. If the police had been delayed for two more minutes or if the blocking team had been more successful – the squad commander would have received all the acclaim for his courage and devotion to a mission that had been successful despite all the risks. However, in practice, the results were miserable. The squad commander was wrong to stay on the scene, because his decision led both to his capture and to the nature of the mission and identity of the target being revealed, resulting in a much greater calamity.

In this case too, similar to the failed operation to assassinate Mashal, the operational squad was professional and experienced, with innumerable successful operations in its track record compared to a single botched one. The operational squad that undertook this task had been frequently involved in dangerous and complex operations throughout the world.

Europe, which in the seventies and eighties served as the main base of operations for Palestinian terrorism, had turned into a problematic region for terrorist organizations to operate in, after some twenty years of intense work done by operational units. The bulk of the work done by operational Mossad units had been gathering intelligence on terrorist elements and thwarting their activities. This gathering and thwarting had ended the activity of terrorist organizations in Europe, either due to our actions against them or joint actions with other nations. This broad and intensive labor of eliminating Palestinian terrorism in Europe could not have been done without a very large number of operations similar to the one in Switzerland. All in all, we were dealing with a success rate of nearly one hundred percent, and anyone who thinks a higher rate could have been reached should probably not be involved in covert operations.

From past experience I already knew that in this kind of operation, you only know how it starts, and never how it will end. Hence I once again called for the attorney, R., who was still recovering from his work on the Mashal affair, and asked him to begin to ready himself for a new affair. We brainstormed in the Mossad's headquarters, mapped all our connections in Switzerland and began utilizing all of them. At one point, I thought to go there myself and meet General Rigley in an attempt to reach a faster solution, but after discussing the matter with him it was decided that this would only complicate matters further and should be avoided.

We located a Jewish lawyer in Switzerland named Ralph Zloczower, who was also a reserve officer in the Swiss military, and asked him to represent the captured operative.

At the same time reports were coming in from M., and it turned out that while we were trying to prevent the matter from escalating via the Swiss security services, the matter had already reached the desk of the Swiss Minister of Justice, and that we were to prepare for the possibility that the matter would be leaked and made public. We further discovered that the Swiss were planning to charge Y. with illegal trespassing and declare the escapees wanted for investigation. Yet even that was not all: we also learned that all the instruments that had been used had been discovered by Swiss authorities.

Since I understood this was about to turn into a diplomatic incident between the two nations, I involved the Ministry of Foreign Affairs, the late President Ezer Weizman, who was in good relations with the Swiss president; Israel's attorney-general, Elyakim Rubinstein; state attorney Edna Arbel; and the Israeli ambassador to Switzerland, Yitzchak Meir.

I also used all my connections with world leaders who I thought could assist. I contacted Schmidbauer, Germany's Minister for Intelligence Affairs in Chancellor Kohl's regime, and he agreed to my request to go to Switzerland and attempt to help solve the crisis.

The deeper I delved into the Swiss affair; the more horrified I became when I realized more and more things the Swiss could discover in the course of their investigation. From that moment on, I started focusing on preventing the operative's investigation from dealing with additional issues.

We did all we could to formulate a suggestion in which the detained operative be released and be allowed to return to Israel while awaiting trial, on condition that he returns for his legal proceedings. We told the Swiss that we were willing to deposit bail that would ensure his return.

Once the situation began stabilizing and we managed, through extensive efforts, to define and limit the scope of the investigation to one specific area, diplomatic efforts began aimed at releasing the man on bail.

While these negotiations were taking place, we did all we could to prevent the matter from becoming public in Israel and in Switzerland. However, pressure on the Israeli censorship authorities became greater due to various leaks. At one stage, in an attempt to prevent the matter from becoming public, I met with the Editor's Committee at the Sokolov Journalism Center in Tel Aviv - after consulting Netanyahu. I told them all that I could in a background briefing that was to be neither quoted nor published. This was all so they would understand the severity of the harm that could be caused if the media outlets published the affair. I stressed to them time and again that they should not publish anything about the matter and warned them that such publication could endanger the operative in Switzerland, as the Swiss conditioned his release on bail on the matter not being made public.

I was naive enough to believe them and thought I could rely on their promises to avoid any publication, but the following morning, one of the newspapers came out with a main headline about the affair, and published all the details of the story in a leading report.

As was expected, madness ensued: the Swiss immediately stated that under the circumstances the matter would be much more difficult to handle, and as a result of the publication, questions had been raised in the Swiss parliament, members of which complained that the matter had been hidden from them.

In those hectic days of urgently dealing with the Swiss affair, I reached the conclusion that I had to resign. A streak of two failures by the organization I was in charge of left me no other choice.

I decided my superior responsibility had to be expressed in light of the string of affairs, despite not being aware of the Swiss operation's existence and despite not authorizing it.

I believed that I had to act according to what is known as superior-vicarious responsibility. It was an entirely personal decision, and the only people I shared this notion with were my wife Tova, my five sons, and my brother Ehud. There were different opinions among my family members with regards to my decision to resign, but they all supported me.

It was clear to me that if I were not to resign; I would find it very difficult to continue directing Mossad operations, due to the feeling that I had to reach personal conclusions due to my superior responsibility. If I had not done so, my authority as supreme commander would be diminished and it would send a problematic message to my subordinates. I knew that if I would not do so, I would always be haunted by frustration and discomfort with myself.

I wanted the resignation to be done in a dignified manner and in line with basic codes of decent conduct. I did not want the matter to reach the press, and for PM Netanyahu to learn of it from the media. Hence, taking into account the atmosphere at the Mossad in those days, I decided to write my resignation letter by hand and did not type it.

I wrote to Netanyahu that in my role as Director of the Mossad I bear full responsibility for the Mossad's activities, for better and worse. I added, "In light of the failure of the operation in Jordan and the calamity surrounding the operation in Switzerland, I hereby submit my resignation. I do not accept the findings in the Ciechanover commission's report regarding shortcomings in my conduct. These findings were made despite the clear evidence I presented to the commission that is utterly opposed to these findings. Nevertheless, I do not intend to ignore the report. Therefore, in light of its findings and the mishap in Switzerland, and as bearer of the ultimate responsibility for the Mossad's activities, I have decided to submit my resignation. You of all people know that besides these calamities, the Mossad has carried out courageous operations that succeeded and contributed much to national security. However, as is the nature of the Mossad's covert activities, they are not known to the public, and all for the better."

On February 24, I met with Prime Minister Netanyahu, informed him of my decision and handed him the letter of resignation.

Netanyahu accepted my decision, and by his response it was clear that he viewed this as an inevitable step that he had been expecting.

It reminded me of the way that after the botched US invasion to the Bay of Pigs in Cuba in the 1960s, US President Kennedy invited Allen Dulles, then head of the CIA, and told him, "In a parliamentary government, I would resign. In this government, the president can't and doesn't and so you... must go."

I did not expect Benjamin Netanyahu to act any differently.

He made no attempt to dissuade me and immediately issued a press release stating, "The Prime Minister regretfully accepted the Director of the Mossad's decision. The Prime Minister expressed his great appreciation for Danny Yatom's immense contribution to the State of Israel's security. The Prime Minister said that Danny Yatom had always been characterized throughout the years by his deep dedication to the security of Israel, his spirit of devotion, personal sacrifice and honesty."

Now that I had announced my resignation, I also wished to set things straight with Jordan. It caused me great grief that the king had taken personal offense from my involvement in the Mashal affair, and that along with General Batikhi, who was in charge of intelligence services, expressed the personal injury he had suffered to Netanyahu and Mossad representatives time and again. This was very difficult for me, especially in light of the very special relationship I had formed with the king, and how close we had grown over the years. Eventually, I turned from one of the king's close associates to a persona non-gratis in Jordan, by which the king was personally offended.

All throughout the time that had passed since the attempted assassination of Mashal, the Jordanians were sending messages to the effect that they would find it better if I were to leave my position. Naturally, the burden of causing tension between the nations was not easy on me. Hence, immediately after my resignation, I called my friend Eitan Haber, and with his help wrote a letter to the king, informing him that I had had no intention to hurt him or the Kingdom of Jordan, and all I had done was attempt to fight terrorism and its initiators. I expressed my apologies in case the king had taken personal offense and told him that I hoped that the personal relationship between us would return to its previous state. A short while after sending the letter I met with the head of the king's bureau, General Ali Shukri, who told me on behalf of the king that the king had forgiven me and would be happy to meet with me. Unfortunately, this meeting never took place due to the king's passing.

Chapter 6

"Thank You – and Farewell"

I had intended to do many things as Director of the Mossad. Some, but unfortunately not all, I managed to fulfill.

When I started my position, I had a large assortment of plans to upgrade the operative systems, with an emphasis on strengthening the Mossad's ability to complete its operations. I had placed two items at the top of my agenda: international counter-terrorism and preventing hostile nations from acquiring WMDs; mainly Iraq and Iran.

With regards to international counter-terrorism, the emphasis was on fundamentalist Islamic organizations, mainly Hamas, Hezbollah, and the Palestinian Islamic Jihad (PIJ).

Both of these missions are difficult and complex, since we are dealing with hostile nations and organizations regarding whom it is very hard to penetrate and collect information. Terrorist organizations work in a very secretive, compartmentalized manner. They are driven by religious and ideological zeal aimed to spread the Islamic revolution, as envisioned by the Ayatollahs, throughout the entire world. One of their methods is to attack democratic nations and moderate Islamic elements.

The typical course of action is to form militant terrorist organizations, consisting of local citizens, such as Lebanese members of Hezbollah and members of the Muslim Brotherhood in Egypt. The goal of these organizations is to combat withdrawal from Islam. The Muslim Brotherhood murdered President Sadat after he signed the peace treaty with Israel, and Hezbollah presented itself as an authentic Lebanese organization aimed at freeing the conquered lands of Lebanon from Israel.

Al-Qaeda was still unfamiliar in those days, and we were not aware of its international activities, but there was a lot of intel about the connections and cooperation between organizations such as the Islamic Jihad and Hamas.

From this intel, we discovered that Iran was behind worldwide Islamic terrorism and provided religious and ideological support, training, guidance and intelligence, and financial and logistical aid.

The challenge of collecting intel on nations such as Iran, Saddam Hussein's Iraq, Syria and Libya, lies in the vast distances involved, and the totalitarian regimes in these nations. Due to these factors, the circle of confidants involved in classified matters such as unconventional weapons is very small, and a deliberate effort is made to hide the information and prevent it from leaking to other nations.

In such countries, it is very difficult to convince internal elements to cooperate because they are driven by ideological zeal and due to fear of the punishment that would be dealt to one who was caught as a collaberator.

The way to obtain information despite these difficulties is through difficult, complex and complicated espionage operations, carried out far away from Israeli soil in great peril and courage.

My emphases were on strengthening the operational units and giving preference to recruiting field operatives with regards to resources and priorities.

I placed a special emphasis on the task of locating hostages and MIAs in order to bring them back home. For years, the Mossad had carried out complex and dangerous operations, some far away from Israeli soil, and no resources were spared in order to complete this important mission. However, I am afraid to say that all of our efforts did not produce the results we had wished for, and to this very day, Ron Arad, Zecharia Baumel, Tzvi Feldman and Yehuda Katz have yet to be found. Since then, IDF soldier Guy Hever has joined this list, after more than seventeen years of ongoing efforts failed to discover what happened to him.

All this was done in addition to the Mossad's other roles, such as collecting strategic diplomatic and military intelligence, forming connections with nations with which we did not have diplomatic relations, bringing Jewish people from countries in turmoil to Israel and cooperating with intelligence organizations in friendly nations.

Another thing I dealt with immediately after assuming my position in the Mossad, and fortunately also managed to complete, was to prepare a multi-year work plan. When I started my position, I knew, due to my previous role as Military Secretary of the Prime Minister, that the Mossad does not have this type of work plan. I believed that a single-year plan does not allow this type of organization to properly handle its responsibilities and purposes.

Processes related to shifting resources according to various priorities, building new operational capacities, recruiting and training new personnel and other matters – are all processes that should be dealt with over a multi-year perspective.

When I talked about a broad long-term strategic view and how the Mossad would look in ten years, I met a lot of raised brows within the Mossad. Some tried to convince me that intelligence issues constantly change from one day to the next, and hence it would be difficult to make even a single-year plan.

I, who was 'raised' in the army, and among other roles served as Head of the Planning Division for four years and introduced multi-year work plans in the military, including for the Directorate of Military Intelligence, was convinced such a plan was possible and moreover – necessary. Thus, under my management, the Mossad took upon itself to prepare this plan. For this task I recruited the help of a very special woman: the late Col. Tehila Sadeh, may she rest in peace, who in her last role in the IDF served as Secretary of the General Staff, and had served under my command for many years as Head of the Planning Division, in the process gaining immense, unique experience in dealing with long-term strategic work plans.

With her one-of-a-kind personality, her persistence and unique skills, Tehila, along with others, managed to navigate the headquarters' activities, and a year after I assumed my position she presented a multi-year plan at the Forum of Heads of Divisions and their deputies in the Mossad.

Coincidentally, the Ciechanover commission and the Subcommittee for Covert Services were investigating the Mashal affair while the multi-year plan was being prepared. Thus, while others in the Mossad and myself were busy handling the Mashal affair, many discussions regarding the plan and its commencement were held at the Mossad.

These were parts of the things I dealt with. Along with them were many others which I had planned to deal with, but unfortunately did not have the time to do so.

Once word of my resignation spread in the Mossad, I received many written and spoken requests from Mossad employees to stay. Many spoke of my departure sadly and recounted how well they felt under my command and how challenging it was to work with me. Among these were several men and women, including tough and courageous operatives, who shed a tear in personal meetings with me. All of these meetings touched me, but did not change my decision.

These reactions were in line with my feeling when I had arrived at the Mossad – that I had been accepted with open arms. Shabtai Shavit, the previous Director of the Mossad, gave me a professional and highly organized onboarding, allowed me to meet anyone I asked to, presented the whole of the Mossad's activities before me and did not spare any of his time, energy and experience to tell me everything I needed to know.

There were sporadic, marginal and minor objections to my appointment, since I had not come from within the ranks of the Mossad. The decision to bring in someone from outside of the organization was due to the fact that there was no dominant candidate from within the Mossad who could replace Shabtai. In any case, it was not unprecedented – before me were Directors of the Mossad and former Generals Meir Amit, Tzvi Zamir and Yitzchak (Haka) Hoffi, and this trend continued in Meir Dagan's appointment in 2003.

One of the heads of Division who believed he was fit to fill the position as Director of the Mossad, informed me upon my arrival that he did not intend to continue working with me and indeed he proceeded to resign. Some heads of division needed to be replaced and I had to handle this matter and receive the Prime Minister's authorization to appoint the new heads of division. Naturally, these changes also caused a stir, some water-cooler conversations and an active lobby. After I felt that I was more familiar with the structure of the Directorate and its people, I decided on a series of new appointments, which were also received critically by those who were not appointed. However, excluding one or two of them, the critics also continued to serve the Mossad.

Routine daily work eventually resumed in a short period of time. As in similar roles I had previously fulfilled, the Mossad does not grant you even one day of grace. Immediately upon assuming the position, one must study and become knowledgeable in thousands of details, while at the same time managing day-to-day activities and handling problems that arise.

In daily proceedings I felt there was full cooperation from all directorates and subordinates. Yet along the way, some took care – out of their own interests – to whisper in my ear that some of the matters presented to me were false and some of the reports were inaccurate. I was not affected by this, despite later finding out – in the Mashal, Swiss and Yehuda Gil affairs – that indeed the truth was not always the deciding factor in some of these reports. However, I believed then and still believe that, with the exclusion of some marginal occurrences, the Mossad is a professional and reliable organization.

My appointment as Director of the Mossad, in May 1996, was for me in many ways the crowning achievement of my thirty-three year long career in the security services. The position stirred great interest in me from day one.

I was appointed by Shimon Peres, who had been appointed Prime Minister after the murder of PM Yitzhak Rabin. Peres appointed me after deciding that I was the most suitable person to serve as Director of the Mossad. He was free of any previous commitment to me, and free of any unwritten will and testament, after I made it unequivocally clear to him that PM Rabin had never promised to appoint me to the position.

A short while after the appointment, while I was in the middle of the onboarding process with my predecessor Shabtai Shavit, Peres lost the elections and was replaced as prime minister by Benjamin Netanyahu. However, even though the appointment had been finalized only one week before Netanyahu started his position, and despite not being appointed by him, I did not sense that he treated me as one whose appointment was imposed on him.

My acquaintance with Netanyahu started many years ago, when we were young officers in the IDF's General Staff Reconnaissance Unit. Yet despite the many years I served in Special Forces, being deputy commander of the unit and participating in dozens of operations behind enemy lines, I had never participated in a Mossad operation before.

I thought it was essential for me to participate in a few of the Mossad's operations, because I placed high significance on setting a personal example. Furthermore, I learned from conversations I had with operatives that this was something that raised their morale and motivated them.

Since I had not come from the Mossad, I thought it was essential to become familiar with its operational activities, not only by knowing and authorizing operations but also through personal experience. I was aware of the risk I was taking upon myself in case something went wrong, and therefore decided to take part in operations that I thought were relatively less risky. Since all of these activities are covert and secretive, and since my appointment as Director of the Mossad had been publicized, I had to act accordingly. I was the first Mossad director whose name was made public in the media immediately upon appointment, rather than after his retirement, as was customary until then.

Prime Minister Rabin was the one who had decided to reveal the identity of the heads of the secret services, such as the Mossad and the Shin Bet, due to his conclusion that retaining the secrecy of these identities would not pass the test of the Israeli Supreme Court. The media involved the Supreme Court in the matter, and the State Attorney also supported abolishing the secrecy surrounding the chiefs of these services, as is customary in most Western democracies.

This decision raised difficulties for me and forced me to be extra-careful in my travels abroad.

In light of all these experiences and the expressions of empathy towards me, I sent a farewell letter to all the staff and operatives of the Mossad, in which I wrote: "I say to you today: thank you, and farewell. I regret having to leave before my time. This is not the way I wanted it, yet under the circumstances, there is no other option but for me but to resign. I will not hide my pain at having to depart from you. I decided to resign as Director of the Mossad following the failure of the operation in Jordan and the mishap in Switzerland. I hope and believe that I am expressing my overall responsibility for all happenings at the Mossad, for better or worse. Thus I was taught by my educators, commanders and leaders. Thus I too attempted to teach.

"The pain in my heart is great, because I resign from an organization that is the apple of the State of Israel's eye, whose staff and operatives are a unique occurrence among the organizations responsible for national security. However, excellent people and a magnificent organization cannot always guarantee success. In the Mossad there are troubling signs of an estrangement from these core values that throughout the years have led all security services, and mainly ourselves, to incredible achievements. I found that in the Mossad's activities there are issues that need to be improved and amended, some requiring comprehensive, laborious and continuous work. You know how many achievements the Mossad has accumulated throughout the years, as well as lately - achievements to which few can compare. You are the ones who know to what peaks we have climbed. Much thought, planning skills and execution abilities were devoted to dozens and hundreds of operations, lately as well. In all but a bare few of these, we were triumphant. We performed our duties as was required of us, clandestinely, far away, in tense situations and with a high level of professionalism. Yet these great achievements are only ours to know. They expand our hearts but must be kept silent. Failures, on the other hand, are public knowledge. Thus a distorted picture of our true abilities is formed, and is further distorted by malicious, false and unfounded leaks of information, at least some of which came from within us and were meant to sabotage me personally. I find this regrettable.

"I do not accept the findings of the inspection committee, but could not ignore their moral aspect. I was heavily burdened by King Hussein's decision to cut off contact with us, thereby harming crucial interests. The pain this matter causes me is great, also because I was part of the small group who took part in the initial efforts of the peace treaty with Jordan, and am very proud to have done so.

"After the blunder in Jordan, I spared no effort, together with others, to bring our operatives back home, and indeed, our efforts were fruitful. Since the blunder in Switzerland, I am working tirelessly to bring back home the operative who is still there. We will not rest and will continue working until he returns home as soon as possible. The comradery of warriors is not a fairy tale.

"The time to lay down our arms has yet to come. The way before us is still long and much still needs to be done. Many are still after our lives, and the Mossad was and always will be the long arm of the State of Israel. The people of Israel are relying on you.

"Through yourselves I would like to thank your family members: the husbands and wives, mothers and fathers, daughters and sons, who come to your aid in difficult times and help you fulfill your important tasks. A thousand thanks to them, from me.

"I seek to strengthen your hands, to ask you to keep following the path of commitment and security, to thank you for your immense contribution to the nation and its security, and to wish you all the best and good luck. For the comradery and the job well done, for your part in fortifying national security, and for who you are – thank you, from the bottom of my heart."

When I left the Mossad, Y. was still detained in Switzerland. However, to my great joy, the intensive efforts I had been making for many longs weeks were fruitful – and a week after my resignation, he was released on bail of $1.8 million and an obligation by the Israeli government that he would appear for his trial. Y. returned to Israel after sixty-four days of detainment, until the start of his trial, two and a half years later, in the federal court in Lausanne. At the end of the trial, he was sentenced to one year of probation and was forbidden from entering Switzerland for five years.

After Y. returned to Israel, the media in Israel immediately published a glorified account by my successor Efraim Halevy, to the effect that in one single week he had managed to bring the operative back home. Only one journalist bothered to note that it was impossible that such an affair had been wrapped up in one week, and that the release of Y. was the result of prolonged and intensive work that preceded Halevy's arrival at the Mossad.

I finished my service at the Mossad two years after it began. I regret to say that I did not manage to fulfill many of the plans I had. I did not leave the Mossad with a feeling of failure, but only one of missed opportunities – a uniquely nasty feeling.

As far as I was concerned, the Mossad chapter of my life was done but unfinished.

Chapter 7

"Roots"

My resignation from the Mossad signaled the end of thirty-five years of service in national security, including thirty-three years in the IDF.

As I examine my own personal journey in the national security system, I can start by looking at the boy I was at eighteen, when I climbed on to a bus in the central bus station at Netanya, the city where I was born, on my way to the recruiting office.

Yet in many other ways, the roots of this journey are planted many years earlier, in small steps taken by big men, the majority of whom I had never had the chance to meet, and all of whom were of my family.

One part of this journey took its first steps already in the plains of Russia, when my grandfather Shimon Segal emigrated from there to Israel and settled in Tiberias, where he met the woman who would eventually become my grandmother – Yehudit Paikov. Yehudit was born in Tiberias, a third-generation daughter of a family who had arrived from Russia with the Bilu pioneers during the First Aliyah. Yehudit was the daughter of Henya of the Friedman family and Rabbi Abraham Paikov. My great-grandfather Abraham was the Chief Rabbi of Tiberias, son of a religious family who was a descendant of the Baal Shem Tov. He was born in Tiberias to parents of the Karlin Hassidic sect, who had immigrated to Israel from Russia at a young age after a series of pogroms.

Rabbi Abraham Paikov and his wife Henya were well-known and prominent figures in the Galilean landscape.

Abraham's personality and lifestyle portrayed a combination of his zealousness towards holy work along with hard and highly demanding physical labor as the owner of a dairy farm. He was a God-fearing hassid who took strict care to rise each morning at dawn, cover himself with the *talit* and lay *tefillin* (phylacteries) before embarking on the day's labor, as the laborious work in the cowshed that began at dawn did not allow for him to participate in prayer with a regular *minyan*. Yet while this saddened him deeply, he did not change his habits and forsake his commitment to the herd of cows he was nurturing.

He devoted most of his time to his work in the farm, and after finishing the daily milking, would make his way each morning on the back of his mule, to market the fresh jugs of milk.

Henya of the Friedman family was born in Minsk, Belarus ('White Russia'), to an impoverished hassidic family of bread bakers. When the persecutions of Jewish people increased and Jewish children began to be kidnapped to serve in the Russian military, her parents decided to flee with their family to Palestine and settled in Tiberias. Henya was kind and modest. The bulk of her time was devoted to helping others, and she was very popular among both the Jewish and Arab residents of Tiberias. Abraham and Henya had four daughters: Shoshana, Rachel, Yehudit my future grandmother, and Nehama.

My great-grandfather Abraham had commercial ties in all of northern Palestine, as well as with traders from Syria. Many times, he took the train to Damascus to trade with them, with Grandma Henya joining him to shop in her favorite market in the heart of Damascus. They both spoke perfect Arabic, and when they were with their acquaintances from the ranks of the traders of Damascus, they felt completely at home in the Syrian capital.

Grandpa Abraham was very much involved in the Karlin sect, but at the same time maintained close ties and a great empathy towards the farmer pioneers. Among the Karlin Hassids some frowned upon his hearty attitude towards the pioneers, and the fact that he integrated the ones they called "youngsters with handkerchiefs on their heads" in the prayers at the Hassidic *beit midrash*. On account of this, Grandpa Abraham decided to leave this *beit midrash* and pray in the *beit midrash* run by Bouyan Hassids in Tiberias.

His home attracted these young pioneers and one time, on a Saturday night, as he was singing the songs of Sabbath, they knocked on his door and told him that the music coming from his home reminded them of their families and filled them with yearning. Thus these young people, as well as the watchmen of the settlements Migdal, Mitzpe and Kinneret, became regular guests at the home of Abraham and Henya Paikov.

In the Ottoman period, the Paikov family suffered, as did many agricultural families, from repeated lootings of property and produce at the hands of the Turkish troops. One day, one of the pioneers asked for permission to leave a sack of ropes in Grandpa Abraham's courtyard, until he returned from his duties. Grandpa Abraham agreed to store the sack in his courtyard, but later that day, when the Turkish troops came for another round of looting, they saw the sack, opened it and found weapons in it. Grandpa Abraham was sentenced on the spot to death by hanging on the charge of possessing illegal firearms.

All Tiberias was ablaze from this matter, and its people begged the Turks for my grandfather's soul. They gathered money to release him and bribed all persons necessary. The Turks finally agreed to release Grandpa Abraham, not before they tied him to a galloping horse that dragged him all the way to Tebha, at the north side of the Lake of Galilee.

The German Templars of Tebha untied Grandpa Abraham from the horse, and began treating his ailing and bloodied body. In the meantime, the members of the Paikov family were certain that Abraham had passed away in his journey of suffering with the horse, and were sitting *Shiva* for him. However, after several long weeks under the devoted care of the Templars, Grandpa Abraham regained his strength and returned home. The family's amazement was immense and its joy boundless. At some stage later, Abraham and Henya Paikov decided to move to the settlement Hadera, and later to Rishon LeZion, but they missed the Galilee greatly and eventually returned to Tiberias.

My grandmother, Yehudit of the Paikov household, one of the four daughters of Abraham and Henya, was also born in Tiberias, where she met Shimon Segal, who had immigrated to Israel from Russia several years earlier.

Shimon and Yehudit married, and during the Arab persecutions at the time (*Ha'meoraot*), my grandfather was hit by a bullet in his abdomen, fired by one of his Arab friends with whom he had lived side by side peacefully before the events started. My grandfather came very close to death from his grave injury, and after a long recovery decided, along with my grandmother Yehudit, to join some of Tiberias's long-standing families who had decided to leave their homes, and found the settlement of Pardes Hana.

In Pardes Hana, Yehudit and Shimon bore their seven children: the eldest was my mother Pnina, born in 1925, and her six siblings were Ya'akov, Rivka, Sarah, Yoseph, Miriam and Abraham.

My mother grew up in Pardes Hana and excelled in her schoolwork and sports. Excellence was a significant aspect of her worldview and was central in the encouragement and education she gave to my brothers and me.

As she belonged to a religious-oriented family, my mother was sent to study in the "Beit Ya'akov" religious high school in Jerusalem. However, due to financial troubles, she was forced to end her studies there and return home to help provide for the family. My mother came to Netanya, where her aunt Rachel, my grandmother's sister, had lived, and began working as a diamond polisher. The diamond industry was still in its infancy, but in the years that followed and for many years to come, Netanya became a central hub in the diamond processing and trade industry in Israel. My father Simha also worked as a polisher in the local diamond trade, and that was how my parents met in 1943.

My father was born in 1918 and came to Israel with his parents Moshe and Pesia Yussim in 1936, from the town of Belz, Bessarabia, on the Russian-Romanian border, which at the time was ruled by the Romanians. Yussim, his surname, apparently originated from the custom of giving surnames that described one's profession or situation. Apparently one of my family members had been an orphan (in Hebrew – *Yatom*), and in Yiddish their name was Yussim. Later this name would be adapted to the Hebrew: *Yatom*.

My grandfather Moshe's first wife died of illness at a young age, leaving behind two children: Dov and Dina. After her death, Moshe married his niece Pesia, who was twenty-five years younger than him. She was exotically beautiful with dark skin, and rasping blue eyes, which could leave no man indifferent. Moshe and Pesia were married in Russia and gave birth to Simha, Shlomo and Sarah.

The roots of service in the armed forces, which became a cornerstone in the life of my family for generations to come, could perhaps be found in my grandfather Moshe Yussim. He served in the Russian military, and was the only Jew to be chief of the personal guard in the court of the Russian Tsar. Grandpa Moshe was a well-disciplined soldier in the Tsar's army, but was also a devoted Zionist. At a certain stage, he decided to immigrate with his whole family to Israel, but knew that if he would ask to be released from the Russian military, he would be denied and he and his family persecuted. Hence he decided to arrange a "discharge" for himself from the military on medical grounds. With his own two hands he pulled all the teeth out of his mouth and was immediately discharged.

Moshe and Pesia immigrated to Israel with their children Dina, Simha, Shlomo and Sarah. Their eldest son Dov, who was active in *Hashomer Ha'tsair*, had immigrated to Israel some years earlier and lived in the Kibbutz Ma'abarot.

My grandfather Moshe and grandmother Pesia also came to Ma'abarot, following their son, but disliked life at the Kibbutz and soon moved with their children to the adjacent city of Netanya, where they opened a fish store.

My father Simha, the youngest son of Moshe and Pesia Yatom, justified his namesake (*Simha* in Hebrew means happiness): a hearty, optimistic and joyful man, who was always adored by others and insisted on seeing the upside of any situation. His living he made from road paving and working in the orchards of Hefer Valley. In 1937 he was recruited to the *Hagana* and later served as a guard in the "Hebrew Settlement Police", which was the only legal armed force in Israel under British rule, and in effect acted as the executive branch of the Hagana organization. In his role as guard my father was tasked with security missions, and at night he aided in covertly smuggling, along with his associates, illegal Jewish immigrants who came in the dead of night to the shores of Israel and were quickly scattered throughout the residing settlements. In 1942 my father was sent by the Hagana to serve in the British-founded 'coast police.'

In February 17, 1944, about one year after they met, my parents married in the home of Rabbi Werner in Netanya, with their wedding ball held that evening in Café Rimon in the city. They built their home in the *Ein Hatchelet* neighborhood in north Netanya, where my grandfather and grandmother Moshe and Pesia had rented a plot of land for ninety-nine years, which over time became a private asset. After my parents' marriage, my grandfather and grandmother built their home in Ein Hatchelet with two living quarters: one for themselves and one for my parents. During my youthful years, I lived with my brother Ehud and sister Eti in one single room, and only when I reached seventh grade were separate rooms built for me and Ehud.

In this house in Ein Hatchelet, my brothers, sister and I were born, and there my parents lived until the day they died. I was the eldest of their children born about a year after their marriage, on March 15, 1945 in Beilinson Hospital in Petach Tikva. My birth certificate bears the stamp of the Palestine government over the land of Israel.

When I was born, the country was still under British rule. I do not remember much from those days, though I do have a vague childhood memory of British troops patrolling the neighborhood.

Ein Hatchelet was a neighborhood composed of supplementary estates, littered with low housing. The estates were relatively large and as either a secondary or central source of income, small farms were built on these estates. One of our neighbors had a cowshed and made his living selling cows to be slaughtered, and dairy milk, and the other had chicken coops. My parents had a small chicken coop producing eggs for home consumption, with one of the chickens occasionally being sacrificed for the sake of family dinner. The garden was full of fruit trees – lemon, orange, grapefruit, fig – and green meadows, which never sufficed for the home's consumption, serving only as a supplement.

However, the official king of our courtyard was Pompidou.

Pompidou, who I named after the then President of France, was a rooster of unmistakable presence and charisma. He ruled the garden assertively and with a kind of violence, with his crest held high.

Pompidou came to us as a chick, grew up to be the only rooster in the coop and formed a forceful, dominant personality. He terrorized every stranger who wandered into the yard, and would banish any uninvited visitors with his cooing and yelling. When he occasionally managed to escape into the street, wild shouts were immediately heard, and we would witness Pompidou running amok through the street, his red crest waving, and before him one of the neighborhood children fleeing for dear life. Before the daily excursion, we would tie a rope round his neck and walk him through the neighborhood like any other pet.

Ein Hatchelet was the ideal neighborhood to pass my youth. Next to us was 'Neve Shalom', the old Yemenite immigrants' neighborhood, and a neighborhood populated with European and North-African immigrants who came to Israel in the early 1950s. Therefore it was that in our vicinity, was a population of older immigrants who had come to Israel at the turn of the century, as well as newer immigrants.

Ein Hatchelet was shrouded in the green colors that encompassed the houses and gardens. It had streets without asphalt and a very great deal of sand. The sea was at the tip of our fingers and we walked there barefoot, in almost every free moment we had. Our relations with our neighbors were very close; the doors were always open and people came to visit each other, always ready to lend a helping hand.

The great waves of immigration that came to Israel from North Africa in the 1950s led to the construction of one of the famous immigrants' camps a mere few hundred meters from my home – the Ein Hatchelet Immigrant Camp, where Kiryat Sanz is located today.

We, the immigrants of the previous generation, would visit them and aid them in any way we could. Any unneeded item in our house – blankets, ovens, kitchenware and furniture – was given to the new immigrants out of a deep feeling of solidarity and desire to help.

The atmosphere at home was embedded with patriotism. Every second sentence would start with "Ben-Gurion said…" The notion that this was our country and we had no other place to go was an essential part of our upbringing. From early childhood, we had absorbed Father's stories of his life as a guard and the tales of the struggle to found the nation. It was but natural for all of us, both boys and girl, to serve in frontline units in national security. We grew up in the atmosphere of old Israel, where everyone was devoted to the same idea and worked to accomplish something beyond their personal needs. We were brought up to help others and saw our parents giving anonymously.

Another thing my mother embedded in us from a very young age was striving towards excellence and accomplishment, along with the feeling of togetherness and our mutual commitment to each other. The message was; we are always together in the face of the entire world.

In those years, my father was head of the Netanya *Shekem* branch, and in 1948, during the War of Independence, he was recruited to the IDF and served in the Seventy-first Regiment of the Seventh Brigade, which fought in the Galilee front against the Arab Liberation Army headed by Fawzi al-Qawuqji. My father was a squad commander and participated in the conquest of the Arab village Miyar and the city of Nazareth. During the war, my brother Ehud was born, and it was only two days after his birth that my father was located and given the message of his second son's birth. In the years that followed, my Sister Eti and young brother Moshe (Moshik) were born.

After my grandfather Moshe turned ill, my father was asked to assist with work in the family fish store. Over time, my father became the owner of the store, which enriched the family menu in proteins. My mother knew how to prepare all forms of fish, and when one of us refused to eat fish occasionally, she took care to remind us, "All the brains in your head are from fish."

My father's store was the only fish store in Netanya in those days, and was very popular. It provided for us well and in the days to come would turn my father into the chairman of the trader's union in Netanya.

The store was in a central location in town next to the Berkowitz's shoe store. Yehuda, Berkowitz's son, who later became the actor Yehuda Barkan, would occasionally come to help at his parents' shop, as would I. Each Saturday, I rode my bike from Ein Hatchelet for a distance of four kilometers, under my father's orders to check if the water in the fishpond at the store was running and the fish were safe and sound in it.

My father continued to work at the shop until he reached an age where the required physical exertion prevented him from carrying on, and he turned to managing the neighborhood post office until he retired. As one of the founders of Netanya and on account of his lifelong work for the city and the benefit of its traders, he was awarded a token as a 'Notable Citizen of Netanya' as well as 'Notable Member of the Histradut' (Israel's central trade union).

I made my first steps in the education system in the worker's city kindergarten in Ein Hatchelet, at the teacher Ahuva Madenlater's kindergarten.

From there I proceeded to Be'eri School. I was a good student, an excellent athlete and had an interest in painting. In June 1959,

I won a school painting contest, and was subsequently sent by the City of Netanya to a summer camp for art loving students in Jerusalem. In that camp I met children from all over Israel, most of whom came from richer families than mine. It was there that I first met Moshik Teomim, who would later become a famous advertising professional, and Dudu Goldenberg, who would later be known as Dudu Topaz.

From a young age I was active in youth movements. I started in *Hashomer Ha'tsair* and the Boy Scouts, but most of my activity was in *Ha'noar Ha'oved*, alongside my studies in Tchernichovsky High School in Netanya, where I studied Science and Physics.

Since I was the eldest and a fairly good student, when it was my time to enlist for the military, my mother wanted me to join the academic reserves and study medicine. I also wanted to fulfill my lifelong dream of being a doctor, but was much more inclined to complete a regular military service, even resigning from a *Nahal* group I was a part of at the time, which was headed for the Kibbutz Ma'ayan Baruch in northern Israel. At the end of my last year of high school, I joined the group for a two week stay at the Kibbutz, to become acquainted with it before our enlistment. Two weeks of working in the Kibbutz's groves were enough for me to understand that a military service of '*Nahal* tomato-picking,' as it was called at the time, was not for me, and I decided to apply for the Paratroopers.

Chapter 8

The Unit

Come my enlistment day, on August 8, 1963, my mother packed a small bag for me, I bid my parents farewell and left our house, walking towards the nearest bus station to take the local bus that passed through Netanya's neighborhoods. I rode it to the central bus station in Netanya and there I boarded a bus to the recruiter's office in Petach Tikva. There was none of the carnival we have grown to expect nowadays, with parents, friends, video cameras and cellular phones. In those days everything was much more concise, focused and to-the-point.

When I reached the induction center, I immediately turned to the Paratroopers Brigade shack and volunteered to serve in the unit.

When I left the shack, I met on one of the Induction Center's paths, my neighborhood friend Shaul Levy.

"You're the one I'm looking for," he said to me.

I knew Shaul belonged to the Paratroopers, for as a curious young man who would gaze with appreciation mixed with adoration at the older fellows who had enlisted for combat units, I would see him coming home for weekend vacations with the Paratroopers' uniform.

I told Shaul I had already volunteered for the Paratroopers, but he said, "I have something even better for you - the Paratroopers

Commando Unit." I had no idea what he was talking about, but it sounded interesting and I told him that could work for me.

Hence, I was in effect recruited to the *Sayeret Matkal* commando unit ('the Unit'), whose existence and role I was not even aware of but moments earlier. Few had heard of this unit back then, and they were mostly those who came from a *Kibbutz*. The unit recruited its members on a recommendation basis.

Immediately after Shaul Levy decided I was a good fit, I was admitted to a preliminary interview in a tent in which three officers were seated: Lt. Col. Abraham Arnan, the unit's founder and commander, and on either side of him were two young Second-Lieutenants, the most noticeable feature of whom – besides their red berets – was their dark complexion. These were Abraham Muchtar and Amnon Brochiel, also known as 'Bruchi.' I was asked what I know of the unit, and my answer was 'Nothing.' I was asked why I wanted to join the unit, and I answered that Shaul had told me it was 'commando' and that had sounded interesting to me. I told them about my background, my Finals grades and my activity in the youth movement.

After passing all the interviews, I joined a group of young recruits who had also been through the preliminary interviews for the Unit, and we waited for the next stage. Then Abraham Arnan came and told me, "I'm sorry, but we can't let you join the Unit." I asked him why, and he answered, "Look at the skin-tone of everyone here, and then look at yours, and you'll understand." I was redheaded with light skin and everyone had dark skin.

At the time, the prevalent belief in the Unit was that those with dark skin and a Middle-Eastern look would find it easier to blend in with the Arab population in the Unit's operations. I was not really disappointed as I had no great expectations from something that I knew nothing of, and I thought that joining the Paratroopers would also be excellent.

However, a few hours later, I was once again tracked down by the Unit's representatives in the Induction Center, and informed that I had after all been accepted. When I looked at the others who had been accepted that day, I saw they were also not particularly dark-skinned, but I truly was especially fair and completely redheaded. Bruchi and Muchtar were then newly appointed platoon commanders, and the recruits were meant to staff the platoons under their command.

After a short period of initial training, we proceeded to complete the regular Paratroopers' basic training boot camp. After basic training the Company Commander Giora Hayke called me for a talk and said to me, "Why do you need to go to *Sayeret Matkal*, stay with us in the Paratroopers!" but I refused, although at this stage it was still unclear to me what it was all about and where I was actually headed. The shroud of secrecy that engulfed the Unit was heavy, and the only thing that was clear to me was that it would be an interesting service, and that the Unit was involved in operations outside Israeli borders.

In the August '63 recruitment, some thirty new soldiers joined the Unit, not all of whom managed to stay on board until the end. Every platoon has around fourteen soldiers. Asi Dayan was one of the new recruits in my platoon, but he was ejected during boot camp and stayed in the Paratroopers. Another soldier in the platoon was a darkish fellow named Meir Huberman, who used to draw commando knives and throw them from afar, straight into any random tree log or electricity pole (these were made of wood at the time). I was very impressed by this, and I thought to myself that I had reached a unit of real 'killers,' and that perhaps I had no chance to survive in a place like this. Meir Huberman was dropped from the Unit during boot camp and stayed in the Paratroopers, but over time, he became Meir Dagan and would later be appointed Director of the Mossad.

Although at the beginning I had failed to realize exactly where I was, with time I understood that I had come to an amazing place, in which my service would be an amazing, life-changing experience, deeply affecting my life in the future and contributing to the formation of my personality as an adult.

It was a very demanding service, one that posed great mental and physical challenges. Training involved immense physical hardships, via hikes and navigating through dozens of kilometers, with heavy weights on our backs, by day and night and in any weather. On numerous occasions, what was actually being tested was willpower rather than physical strength, since when you are very tired and your legs can barely carry you anymore, the only thing that propels you forward is your willpower and determination to complete the mission.

A few years after I enlisted to the Unit my brother Ehud also joined, but we never spoke explicitly of our service there while at home. Mother never asked but it was clear she knew what was happening. Whenever we came home, she would launder our uniforms, and one look at the stains and mud that they were covered with could have told her what we were up to more than a thousand words. She asked no unnecessary questions, and would only gaze at the filthy uniforms and say, "It doesn't matter where you've been, and I don't want to know what you did. The important thing is that you came back in peace and that God will continue to protect you."

After the operation to release the captives from the Sabena aircraft she saw my picture in the paper, standing on the wing of the plane dressed in white overalls next to Ehud Barak, with our eyes covered by a black line to protect our identity. When I came back home a few days later, she asked me if it really was me, I answered yes and asked her to tell no one. I knew she could be relied upon to keep a secret.

During my service in the Unit, I took part in many operations behind enemy lines, such as the raid on the airport in Beirut. There were of course dozens of other covert operations that cannot be spoken of until this very day.

All of these experiences defined my personality and turned me into an adult who feels the burden of responsibility on his shoulders – since as early as age twenty, when I was but a second lieutenant and platoon commander, I had commanded operations outside of Israeli borders. In these moments and places, you are a great distance from Israel, responsible for the soldiers and officers under your command. In these operations, you are alone in the locale, and no one is there to help you, evacuate you or advise you. The first operation I commanded was in Lebanon, after I had already gained a breadth of experience as a combatant but not as a commander. The instruction I was given by my commanding officers before embarking on the mission was: "You are the commander-in-chief in the field; we are back at the command center and can only advise, the decision is ultimately yours."

I served in the Unit from 1963 to 1972, years that were rife with retaliatory action and many operations outside of Israeli borders. When I finished my role as platoon commander, and the soldiers under my command were released from service, I decided it was also time for me to leave after five years of service, and turn to higher education. As I was studying Mathematics, Physics and Computer Science at the Hebrew University in Jerusalem, I formed the training squadron of *Sayeret Matkal* and was its first commander. When I finished my Bachelor's degree, I came back to the Unit as deputy-commander under Ehud Barak. In 1972, I finished my service in *Sayeret Matkal* and switched to the Armored Corps.

Some six months before I was discharged from service and turned to academic studies, when I was still a young officer in the Unit, on one of the weekends when I was home for vacation, I was walking through Herzl Street, Netanya's main street. When I passed by Café Papa, one of the town's more established venues, I heard a call, "Danny, how are you?" I turned my head and saw Ranny Langer, my classmate from elementary school, sitting at the café with two pretty girls.

Ranny introduced me to them, and it turned out that one of them, Tova Raich, had recently been discharged from military service. I sat next to them and started talking with Tova, who I was fond of immediately. We sat by that table until the next morning, having a conversation that goes on to this very today. Tova and I were married in 1971, some three years after that chance encounter. We have five sons - Omer, Nir, Tal, Roey and Itay - and six grandchildren - Lior, Adi, Tamir, Tamar, Dolev and Maya.

As I stated, I began studying in 1968 at the Hebrew University of Jerusalem for my Bachelor's degree in Mathematics, Physics and Computer Science. I 'inherited' books from my companion from the Unit, Ehud Barak. He had recently finished his studies in the same place. Along with those books, I was also 'granted' more books by his classmate Liora Rubin (who would later become Meridor). Ehud left us and went back to the army, leaving Liora with a mission, "Liora, from now on you are in charge of Danny," he said, and declared that she was responsible for my success.

After the first academic year, Abraham Arnan convinced me to have the rest of my studies funded by the military, and return to service once I finished them. At first, I was reluctant to agree, as I felt I had reached the height of my experience in the army after five years, and I did not see myself further partaking in a military career. I was very keen to study, but after half a year of academia, I began to miss the Unit and decided to accept Arnan's offer. I was not discharged from the army but rather was put on unpaid leave. The IDF funded my studies while at the same time I formed the training squadron of the Unit, the squadron responsible for training the different units before they became operational.

Each Friday, I would come to the Unit, sit with the platoon commanders and authorize training plans for the coming week. Thus, throughout my three years at the university, I remained active as the commander of the training squadron, and when necessary I embarked on raids and operations with the Unit.

My service in the Unit led me to sign long-term contracts with the military and remain in service for many years, which was entirely opposed to my initial plans to finish my service and begin studying Medicine or one of the exact sciences.

Service in the Unit, which was so fascinating and unique, changed the course of my life, and led me to spend some ten years (including the University period), from age eighteen to twenty-seven, in the Unit.

I felt that I was part of a group of amazing people, of extremely high quality, who had been meticulously chosen, and there was a feeling of great satisfaction in being a part of them. The course of training and operations was extremely physically and mentally difficult, but at the same time was very special. The training was so unique and entirely different from other units.

There was a direct connection between the taxing training and their goal. As a young soldier, I had already participated in operations and offensive raids deep behind enemy lines. There was a sense that what we learned in training came in handy a relatively short time later during operations. Soldiers in field units usually do not gain much operational experience in cross-border activity, barring an ambush or other event, and combat experience is mostly gained during wars and counter-terrorism activity in Gaza, the West Bank and Lebanon. In the Unit, operations are a routine - our day-to-day consisted of a long line of complex, complicated and dangerous missions behind enemy lines.

When I was appointed platoon commander, I recruited soldiers from the August '65 enlistment. Among my platoon members were: Moshe Siboni, the late Rafi Barlev, who died while serving as a tank company commander in the Yom Kippur War, the late Baruch Zuckerman (Zur), who died as a reserve soldier of the Unit in the Yom Kippur War, Shlomo Gelber, Danny Snir (Shukragi), Reuven Cohen, Hanan Gilutz, Itzik Gonen and Mordechai Rahamim. They were in addition to other soldiers who had not managed to complete the difficult and taxing course. A special bond is formed between these elite soldiers, who undergo unique moments together, some of which stretch their human capabilities to their very limits. To this very day, we remain in touch and take care to meet.

Service in the Unit is a test for each of its members. It is a test of willpower, personality and physical fitness. The training is very difficult and requires a complex and demanding struggle with a very high achievement bar which must be reached. For example, we learned to memorize navigation across an axis, and to navigate dozens of kilometers without opening a map in order not to be revealed.

Many times, we were required to complete difficult personal missions by ourselves. Working in small squads causes each physical difficulty to be accompanied by mental difficulty as well. In the final kilometers of the journeys, the only thing leading you forward is willpower, because other powers have long been depleted.

These training sessions taught me more than anything else to know my abilities and myself. I discovered I could do things which I had no idea I was capable of. I understood that nothing withstands the will, and that this is not merely a cliché; and I gained values of comradery and mutual commitment.

We learned the meaning of commitment to the mission, persistence and determination. Members of the Unit gain a lot of self-confidence on a personal, operational and military level. It is no coincidence that two prime ministers came from this unit (Ehud Barak and Benjamin Netanyahu), two Commanders in Chief (Ehud Barak and Bogie Ya'alon), one Director of the Shin Bet (Avi Dichter) and two Directors of the Mossad (Shabtai Shavit and myself).

In 1971, after finishing my studies in Jerusalem, I returned to the Unit and was appointed deputy unit commander under Ehud Barak, then the commander of the Unit. After finishing my position in the Unit, I was offered some very attractive positions, such as commanding the Golani special forces unit, but I chose to continue my service in the Armored Corps.

When I turned to the Armored Corps, I underwent a very long process of career change. I studied the roles of the Armored Corps in the school for Armored Corps, as any recruit might. This started with driving and cannoning lessons, participation in Armored Corps workshops where we learned to dissemble and reassemble tanks along with mechanics, electricians and technicians, on to being a regular participant in Tank Commander training, a full course in Armored Corps Officer Training and Company Commander Training. This preparation took an entire year, and I partook in it despite already being a Major after fulfilling the role of deputy-commander of *Sayeret Matkal*, because I believed it was essential to go through this course if I wanted to become familiar with the intricacies of work as a member of the Armored Corps. Hence, I insisted, despite my experience and rank, to command a company.

Two weeks before the Yom Kippur War I was appointed Deputy Commander of Battalion 195, whose commander was Uzi Levtzur. The battalion was part of Brigade 401 whose commander was

Dan Shomron, who later would be appointed Chief of Staff. Our battalion was meant to replace Amnon Reshef's battalion in the Suez Canal, but due to rising tensions the IDF Upper Command postponed the replacement. When the war broke out, Reshef's Brigade was still in the position we were meant to man, while we were still training at the edge of Sinai in Bir Gafgafa.

On the eve of Thursday, October 4, 1973, I went home to visit my wife, who was pregnant, as well as my oldest son. Yet on Friday, October 5, I was already called back to the battalion due to the alert that was announced over concerns that a war was about to begin. Later on we were informed that there was information that the Syrians and Egyptians would launch an offensive at 5:00 PM on Saturday, October 6, but that international efforts were being made to prevent the outbreak of hostilities. Eventually the war did start on Saturday, and it caught us completely by surprise. A few minutes before 2:00 PM on Yom Kippur, October 6, which was on Saturday, I was sitting with Uzi Levzur in the Battalion Commander's office and we were occupied with preparing the battalion for the possibility of war. Most of the soldiers were in their quarters and the tanks were scattered under camouflage nets. The tanks were armed and outfitted, but there had been no order to go to battle. While we were sitting in that office a bombardment by Egyptian planes began, and the first sentence I said, completely innocently, was "Guys, don't worry, if there are Egyptian planes around, the Israeli Air Force will take care of them."

Uzi and I immediately went out of the office and activated the battalion siren, which signaled the tank staff to leave their quarters and get into the tanks. In this commotion Egyptian planes appeared, flying low, and bombed us while we were running towards the tanks. Nine soldiers were killed in this bombardment. It was clear to Uzi and me that we no longer needed to wait for the official announcement that war had broken out, and that it had begun.

We immediately began moving towards the area of Hagidi Strait, and from the very first day, we did battle until we crossed to the other side of the canal. We went as far as Adabiya, the Egyptian military port on the other side of the Red Sea, south of the Canal, where we were ordered to lead the entire brigade and in effect the whole of the IDF's forces until the 101st kilometer, where the ceasefire was declared. We secured the ceasefire talks between the IDF and the Egyptian army, and there, when the battles died down and the War of Attrition began, I replaced Uzi Levtzur and became Battalion Commander.

As Battalion Commander I led the battalion out of Egypt to the Tassa junction.

After this role of Battalion Commander, I was appointed G3 of Division 252 in Sinai, a regular Armed Corps division, and later received command over a reserves Brigade. I was a young lieutenant colonel at the age of thirty-one, when Mussa Peled, who was commander of the Armored Corps, suggested I leave to the United States for a continued education program with my family. I was very pleased at the suggestion, it gave me a chance to rest a little, to be with my family and be exposed to a different culture. At the time, I had three young sons: four-year-old Omer, two-year-old Nir, and one-year-old Tal. We went to Fort Hood in Texas and I was the first Israeli officer the Americans had accepted to this place.

It was the biggest military base in the United States, and it served as the permanent headquarters of two armored divisions: the Second Armored Division, whose commander was General Patton, son of the legendary General Patton of the Second World War, and the First Cavalry Division. This base was also host to the only attack helicopter Brigade the Americans had at the time, and there was also a corps headquarters at the place. I was assigned to a small base nearby called West Fort Hood, where the American army planned and executed the first field experiments of new military systems before they became operational. Those at the base were exposed to the most advanced, state-of-the-art systems of the American army.

It had taken the Americans a long time until they had agreed to allow an Israeli officer on the premises, and I was honored to be the first one allowed to do so. We stayed in the United States for a year and three months, and it was a fascinating time that contributed much to my family and me. I saw other patterns of thought, other emotions, and for the first time realized that perhaps Israel was not the center of the world after all, that there are stronger nations than us and people who were just as qualified and talented.

I was not just an educational emissary, but I was actually assigned to project teams that were involved in planning and executing different field-tests. I functioned similarly to any local officer there.

When we came back to Israel, I was appointed G3 of the Armored Corps. Afterwards I commanded a regular Armored Brigade No. 14, under division commanders Yossi Peled and Ehud Barak, who was once again my officer in command. Afterwards I was appointed Head of Armored Corps and in 1982 was given the rank of brigadier general and appointed head of the IDF's R&D (Research and Development).

I served in this position for six months, and then was appointed Military Secretary to Moshe Arens, the Minister of Defense. Arens took the position following the decision made by the Kahan Commission, which had investigated the massacre committed by the Christian militias in the Palestinian population of the refugee camps Sabra and Shatila in Lebanon, and Israel's responsibility for the affair. One of the Kahan Commission's decisions was to end Arial Sharon's term as Minister of Defense.

Around one year after Arens was appointed Minister of Defense, the elections were held and Yitzhak Rabin replaced him. In 1985, I asked to leave the Minister of Defense's Bureau, and was appointed commander of a regular Armored Corps division – the Steel Division in Ma'ale Efraim, above the Jordan Valley.

In 1986 I left for MBA studies in Tel Aviv University, and during my studies in 1987, I was approached by Chief of Staff Dan Shomron and offered to be appointed head of the Planning Division. At the age of forty-two, I was given the rank of major general, along with a role that carried much responsibility over the IDF's working plans, both yearly and multi-yearly. This included resource appropriation, budget and manpower, the plan to build the fighting force, including structuring and organization of the IDF, forming new units and dissembling existing ones, developing arms and equipment, responsibility over the organization and allocation within the army and responsibility for all diplomatic and strategic matters that the IDF was involved in. It was a fascinating four-year period that gave me important thinking and implementation tools. Chief of Staff Dan Shomron's deputy was Gen. Ehud Barak, and thus I once again found myself working alongside him.

In the First Gulf War in 1991, I was responsible for coordinating with the US armed forces, including the introduction of the satellite system that provided real-time alerts when Iraqi missiles were fired at Israel, bringing the Patriot missiles and coordinating operational and intelligence matters between the IDF and the US armed forces.

At that time, I was sent to Germany to meet Chancellor Kohl, along with Dr. Hanan Alon from the Defense Ministry, in order to convince the Chancellor to award Israel close to one billion German Marks meant for the construction of two new Dolphin submarines. After an exhausting night of negotiations, Chancellor Kohl agreed to give Israel 880 million German Marks to construct the two submarines.

In 1991, when I was deep out at sea on a military missile boat during a Navy drill, I received a message from the deputy Chief of Staff Ehud Barak. The message said, "Congratulations. You have been appointed Commander of Central Command." The Navy Commander was Micha Ram and he immediately invited me to celebrate the navy way: they opened a bottle of whiskey and congratulated me for the appointment.

I replaced Gen. Yitzchak Mordechai who was appointed Commander of Northern Command, at the height of the First Intifada. I was replaced as Head of the Planning Department by Gen. Amram Mitzna.

After close to two demanding years in Central Command, I received an offer from Yitzhak Rabin, who was then elected as Prime Minister and Defense Minister – to serve as his Military Secretary. The Prime Minister's military secretary is usually a brigadier general, but Rabin, who also took the role of Defense Minister, thought it would be appropriate for his military secretary to be a general. I told Rabin I would be happy to fill the position, but would only be available in a few months, once I had completed two years as Commander of Central Command.

In April 1993, I started my role as the Military Secretary to PM Rabin, a position I continued to staff after Rabin was murdered. For six months, I continued as the military secretary of Shimon Peres, who replaced Rabin as Prime Minister and Defense Minister.

In 1996, after almost thirty-three years of military service, I laid down my uniform and was discharged from the IDF in a modest ceremony in the Prime Minister's office. A few days later, I was already Director of the Mossad.

Chapter 9

A Physician and a Murderer

The Commission of Inquiry on the Mashal affair was not the first commission of my career in the defense establishment. It was preceded by another commission of inquiry, the seeds of which were sown in the ringing of a telephone, which shattered the morning silence in my home, on Friday, February 25, 1994.

Over the years, I have developed a sense for the sound of ringing telephones, especially those that appear at unusual hours such as a quarter to six in the morning. Yet despite my experience that there is a low probability of hearing good news from a phone call at such an hour, I still did not imagine the size of the catastrophe that would proceed to unravel over the next few hours.

On the other side of the line was Col. Amnon Sofrin, intelligence officer from IDF Central Command, who was the officer on duty at Central Command headquarters that morning, with an initial report regarding gunshots being heard in the Cave of the Patriarchs.

The questions of who had fired, who was fired upon, whether there were any wounded and how many – could not yet be answered, and the first possibility that went through my mind was that it was a terrorist attack by Arabs against Jews. However, despite the temporary vagueness of detail, one thing was already clear as crystal to me: shots fired at a charged and historical place such as the Cave of the Patriarchs was an omen with highly volatile potential and very severe implications.

A short while later, I was picked up from my house and reached Hebron by helicopter. When I reached the cave the event was already over, and all the killed and wounded had been evicted from the Hall of Isaac, where on that morning a prayer of 500 Muslim men was held. I entered the prayer hall and before me was a horrific scene. Although the victims were no longer there, it was obvious that a massacre had occurred in the place. The hall was full of blood, littered with dozens of empty gun shells and remnants of medical equipment.

At this stage, the exact number of wounded and killed was not known yet, but the identity of the perpetrator of this massacre was becoming clearer. As it turned out, contrary to my assumption in the first moments, it was a Jewish person who attacked Arabs, and the name of the terrorist was Dr. Baruch Goldstein, a captain in reserve service, physician and resident of Kiryat Arba.

According to details gathered later on, it was revealed that Goldstein was born in the United States thirty-eight years ago, was married and had four children. He immigrated to Israel in 1982, about a year after finishing medical school, was enlisted for regular service along with other physician immigrants and served for three years as a military doctor in Lebanon, Jerusalem and Hebron. Goldstein was described as a responsible, disciplined officer who conducted himself efficiently and performed his role to the best of his ability.

After being discharged from the military, he worked as a family doctor in Kiryat Arba in the Leumit HMO as well as in a nonprofit organization that operated a medical center. He also continued to serve as a reserves doctor at the rank of Captain in one of the regional defense units of the Judea Brigade, and was part of the staff that operated an emergency care vehicle in the area of Mt. Hebron, serving both the military and civilian sectors. Due to the many terrorist attacks in the region, he had become an expert in treating trauma victims, and was considered a devoted and appreciated physician, for which he had even won an award from the Leumit HMO.

Goldstein possessed ultra nationalist opinions. In the United States, he had already been active in Meir Kahane's league, and continued this activity after immigrating to Israel. He was a candidate for the *Kach* political party in the parliamentary elections, and was even elected on its behalf to the council of Kiryat Arba but resigned in 1993 to make room for Baruch Marzel. His views were highly extreme in both the religious and the political-ideological aspects.

In his media appearances, at different times he was interviewed, Goldstein stated his view that peaceful co-existence with the Arabs was impossible. He criticized Israeli society that he saw as tired of fighting, and the IDF for mistreating the Jewish settlers by prohibiting them from taking retaliatory action against Arab attacks. He believed that the Arabs would drive us out of Israel if we would not drive them out first, and as far as he was concerned, they were successors to the Nazis. Goldstein had been investigated by the police several times on account of breaching the peace on political grounds. He obstructed a soldier in the course of his duty, ripped to shreds a decree prohibiting the entrance of non-Muslims to the Cave of the Patriarchs during a Muslim holiday, and turned over a cabinet of Quran books in the Hall of Isaac, the Muslim hall of prayer in the Cave of the Patriarchs. Furthermore, he once refused to treat a wounded terrorist in Lebanon; organized retaliatory attacks in Arab villages in the Hebron district, and in November

1990 – following the murder of Rabbi Kahane – issued a pamphlet that stated, "Many acts of vengeance shall blessedly come."

Yet despite his sympathy for the extremist views of the *Kach* movement, he was not a part of the violent core of its activists. Furthermore, his type of statements were also common with others in Kiryat Arba. Goldstein's prominence in his environment was actually as a physician and a public activist, and he was perceived as a quiet and friendly individual, naïve, decent, idealistic, kind and serious. This relaxed persona, which concealed his hidden intentions, was retrospectively helpful for him in the way the Cave's security treated him on that fateful day. His extremist views, religious fanaticism, feelings of persecution in light of the terrorist attacks and his frustration with the conduct and rule of law and state combined into a passion to commit such an extreme and severe act and to commit the horrific massacre of dozens of praying Muslims.

After a tour of the perimeter and a short investigation I conducted, certain details of the horror committed by Goldstein began to become clear.

Officers and soldiers who had witnessed the happenings stated that a short while before 5:30, they heard gunshots from inside the Cave of the Patriarchs, in which there was only a single officer. They ran inside but could not manage to enter the Hall of Isaac on account of a flood of people fleeing in panic. When the first soldiers finally managed to enter the hall they found the shooter dead, and on the floor was a horrific scene of dozens of people groaning with pain, the dead and wounded stacked one on top of another in terrible chaos.

The Cave of the Patriarchs and its surroundings were controlled by the IDF. At the time, security of the perimeter was handled by a regular Armored Corps company under the command of First-Lieutenant Yitzchak Hamudout. At 01:00am that same day, there was a shift change in the place's security force, and twelve soldiers under the command of Rotem Revivi started their shift. Two soldiers were stationed near the main entrance, their task being to secure the entrance and check those entering. Two additional soldiers patrolled between the various standpoints in the Cave. At 04:30, the eastern gate was opened and two soldiers were stationed at its entrance. From that hour, the inner security staff included six people: two in the main entrance, two in the eastern, and Second-Lieutenant Revivi and Corporal Melnick who were patrolling. According to the orders of the Commander of the Judea and Samara Division, Maj. Gen. Shaul Mofaz, at 05:00 am a reinforcement of three Border Guard troopers was to join the force securing the Cave of the Patriarchs. Two of these were meant to stand at the main entrance to the Hall of Isaac, and one in the Hall of Abraham. Additionally, according to my instruction one policeman of the Israeli Police was meant to reinforce the shift starting from five in the morning.

Nevertheless, the Border Guard troopers were late to rise that morning, and only reached the Cave at 05:35 am, some five minutes after the shooting had begun. The policeman had also not arrived to his shift. From the soldiers' testimony, we discovered that the policeman's absence from the morning shift was a routine affair. Additionally, one of the soldiers who was supposed to patrol inside the Cave had just gone outside, and so it was that instead of ten people who were supposed to secure the Cave's interior, only five were there in those fateful minutes.

At 05:20 am, Goldstein arrived at the cave dressed in his IDF uniform with Captain's rank, and carrying a Glilon rifle, a pistol and a handbag that was later discovered to contain seven loaded magazines. Second-Lieutenant Revivi spoke to Goldstein, who was known to be a frequent visitor of the Cave, and asked him if he was on reserve duty. Goldstein said yes and turned to the Hall of Jacob, where he used to pray by himself. The fact that he was armed did not raise suspicion and was not unusual or forbidden. Since the murder in *Beit Haddasa* in 1980, settlers were allowed to enter the Cave of the Patriarchs armed. In 1982 this permit was revoked and was reinstated in 1986.

Apparently, Goldstein proceeded through the Hall of Jacob into the Hall of Isaac, where the Muslim worshippers were located, without being noticed by the soldiers. Goldstein, who would frequently come to pray at the Cave of the Patriarchs, was very familiar with the prayer procedures in place and exploited them to his advantage.

Prayers at the Cave of the Patriarchs were held according to the arrangements that existed since the Six-Day War and were authorized by then Defense Minister Moshe Dayan. As the years went by the political echelon was not required to change the status-quo in the Cave, despite the Intifada and the rise of fundamentalist Islam in Hebron. These arrangements enabled both Jewish and Muslim prayer in the Cave of the Patriarchs, partially at the same hours, in different rooms and halls.

According to these arrangements, during Jewish holidays and events, when there was a large amount of worshippers, prayer could also be held outside of normal hours, and sometimes in the halls that were used for Muslim prayers on regular days.

On that morning, the Jewish worshippers began to arrive at the Cave starting from four in the morning. It was a group of prayers known as *Minyan Vatikin*, who would pray at the stroke of dawn in the Hall of Abraham. According to the arrangement, at this hour the site contained both Jews and Muslims, who began to gather at the Cave to pray at an especially holy day for Muslims – Friday, the fifteenth day of Ramadan. Due to the holiness of the occasion, some 800 worshipers had gathered at the Cave by 05:30 am; 500 men who prayed in the Hall of Isaac and 300 women who prayed in the Hall of Jawaliya.

The worshippers in the Hall of Isaac stood in tightly packed lines, facing southwards. When the Imam began to read the *Sajada* passage, the worshippers kneeled down as was ordained by the customs of prayer, and at that moment the hall was filled with bursts of automatic gunfire. The fact that the worshippers were in the process of kneeling, with their back to Goldstein and in close rows, caused his shooting to be particularly deadly.

After 90 seconds and 108 shots fired, with the floor of the hall already littered with twenty-nine dead and 125 wounded, Goldstein ceased his shooting to switch magazines. One of the worshippers took advantage of the momentary lapse in gunfire, pounced on him and removed the weapon, which was burning hot, from his hands. At this stage, several of the worshippers attacked him, swung at him, and killed him with a fire extinguisher and iron poles used to support the partitions between the Hall of Isaac and the Hall of Abraham.

Since violent clashes between Jews and Arabs are a daily affair in Hebron, and at its center stands a holy site to both religions, I immediately ordered a curfew be instated in the city to prevent friction between the hostile populations, and to enable the security forces to better control the situation.

I demanded the forces in the area act with maximal constraint in regards to using firearms. My instruction was to fire only under clear and present danger to life, and to minimize the use of the 'suspect arrest protocol' (shouting a warning of "Stop or I'll fire!", firing a warning shot into the air if the suspect does not halt, another warning call and finally – if the suspect has not halted –

firing towards his legs). All this was to avoid additional deaths and to enable the burial ceremonies to be held under curfew.

Word of the massacre spread throughout Hebron immediately, and people began to gather, mostly around the 'El-Ahly' hospital where the wounded and dead Palestinians were taken. At the same time, reports began to come in of Israeli cars being stoned, roads being blocked and riots by Arabs in Hebron. Throughout that day, clashes formed between Arab protestors and Israeli security forces, in which nine more Palestinians died and dozens were wounded.

As was expected, the horrific massacre became one of the most difficult moments of the Jewish-Arab conflict, and threatened to become a significant stumbling block in the peace process with the Palestinians.

As a result of all these occurrences, their volatile potential and the severe implications of the act on the political-diplomatic-security levels, the government decided to form the "National Commission of Inquiry regarding the Massacre in the Cave of the Patriarchs in Hebron."

Prime Minister and Defense Minister Yitzchak Rabin were not in favor of forming the commission, which he saw as a major mistake. He said, "We know what happened in Hebron, and we'll change the arrangements there. The commission's proceedings will hinder the Peace Process. The Investigation will concern many in the Army and all will want attorneys, but the members of government think otherwise, and therefore I suggest that we decide to form a commission of inquiry."

The commission appointed five members. It was headed by the then President of the Supreme Court, Justice Meir Shamgar. Its other members were Justice Eliezer Goldberg, Justice Abd El-Rachman Zoabi, Prof. Menachem Ya'ari and former Chief of Staff Lt. Gen. (Res.) Moshe Levi. Thus, I found myself for the first time, and unfortunately not the last, a central witness before a national commission of inquiry.

In fact, I had only recently been reappointed Commander of Central Command at the time of the massacre due to a coincidence, since I had finished my position ten months earlier, having been appointed the Military Secretary of Prime Minister and Defense Minister Yitzchak Rabin.

I returned to the position of Commander of Central Command due to particularly tragic circumstances, and it began like other significant affairs in my life with the telephone's ringing disturbing the peace of my family's home at an unlikely hour of morning or night.

The operational telephone in my home rang several weeks earlier, late at night on January 13, 1994. It was a rainy night, stormy and dark. When that telephone rang, I could also feel that it did not bear good news, but nothing could have prepared me for the dreadful news that awaited me from the other side of the line. On the other side was the reporting officer in the Operations Wing, who informed me of a gruesome helicopter accident in which a beloved friend and decorated officer had lost his life – the Commander of Central Command, Nehemya Tamari.

Just ten months earlier, after my appointment as Military Secretary to Prime Minister Rabin, Tamari replaced me as Commander of Central Command, and in one minute of gloomy night his short cadency ended, and with it, his long and eventful life in the IDF.

When I had heard that Nehemya would replace me in Central Command I had been very pleased, because I knew I was passing my command onto sure and faithful hands, in a very problematic and charged position.

Nehemya was very familiar with Central Command since in his previous position he was in charge of a command-wide drill in which the Command and all its systems were tested, including myself as its commander. Running this drill, Tamari witnessed the Central Command, with all its wings and the units that reported to it, which gave him a very broad picture of the command.

Nehemya was the younger brother of Dubik and Shay Tamari. The Tamari brothers served for many years in the army, in combat and command roles in the Paratroopers and the Armored Corps. Dubik and Shay were both discharged at the rank of brigadier general after many years of service, and young Nehemya followed in their footsteps and enlisted to the Paratroopers, and would later command *Sayeret Matkal* as did his eldest brother Dubik.

In other periods of his service, Nehemya commanded over a Paratroopers reserves brigade (belonging to Division 96), the regular *Nahal* brigade and the regular Paratroopers brigade (Brigade 35). Nehemya was one of the only people to command two regular brigades, and was an excellent and highly appreciated officer. However, beyond being a fighter and a commander, he was an impressive man and one whose presence was pleasant. In the IDF, there was a widespread assumption that he would one day be Chief of Staff.

Tragically, the telephone to my house that winter night cut all that in its prime.

Nehemya Tamari was killed in a helicopter accident along with the head of his bureau and the two pilots of the helicopter they were on that night. The helicopter was called several hours earlier to fly Nehemya to an area where an operation was taking place. On its way back when he was about to land in the Command headquarters in Jerusalem, it hit a metal cable that supported a tall communications antenna, crashed into the ground, and all on it were killed.

The terrible accident meant a replacement for Nehemya had to be found urgently. The big round of appointments in the IDF was to happen some four months later, in April of that year. Prime Minister Rabin and Chief of Staff Ehud Barak did not want the IDF's upper command to enter the whirlwind of new appointments too early, which would be the case if a new Commander of Central Command were to be appointed. Furthermore, there were not many officers volunteering to assume this difficult, complex and demanding position. That was why they contacted me and asked that I return to my previous role for the coming months. In fact the two were a few steps ahead of me. When I saw the dilemma regarding staffing the position at Central Command, I reached a decision to suggest myself as a temporary solution until the permanent appointment, as I thought it would be unheard of to have a Command in such a sensitive state to be left without a commander, and so obviously I agreed to their request.

In retrospect, despite the charged and coincidental circumstances that led me back to the role of Commander of Central Command and in such a problematic period, I have never felt bitter over reassuming the position, never asked myself why I needed that headache. When would ask myself I would answer that I was certain I should have agreed to the mission given to me by the Prime Minister and the Chief of Staff, and the question of whether I regret my choice was irrelevant. I had ended my previous cadency in this difficult, complex and problematic role as the head of Central Command unblemished and having achieved great success in the war on terror.

Since I returned to the Command only ten months after leaving, I still knew the people and the matters that needed to be handled, and I quickly assumed my position without the need for an onboarding process.

However, being familiar with the areas of responsibility and complex problems it includes could not prepare me for the horror that unfolded before my eyes on the morning of February 25, 1994, in the Hall of Isaac in the Cave of the Patriarchs in Hebron.

The role of Commander of Central Command requires one to carefully and very discretely conduct one's self between the need, pressures and the demands of settlers to take a tougher stance against the Palestinian population, and the duty to protect the security and rights of both Jewish and Arab residents. This must be done while at the same time establishing as much of a sustainable framework as possible for both populations. One needs to distinguish between the uninvolved Palestinian population and the Palestinian terrorists and outlaws from both sides. It was a complex, demanding and difficult mission that required the head of the Command to be constantly involved in daily life at the Command.

In Hebron, Kiryat Arba and other places there are spots where settlers with extremist ideologies, driven by Messianic zeal, live and operate. This requires even greater involvement from the senior ranks in the relationship between Jews and Arabs.

This entire set of considerations was at play when Goldstein's family and friends asked that Dr. Goldstein be buried in the Jewish graveyard in Hebron. I decided to refuse the request since I estimated that a funeral passing through Hebron would spark a new flame between Jews and Arabs and the grave would become a point of constant friction between the two.

I authorized to bury Goldstein in Kiryat Arba, in a Jewish settlement where no Arabs lived at all. This decision raised criticism from right-wing activists, including threats, objections and appeals that went all the way to the Prime Minister and Defense Minister, but my decision was backed.

After the immediate occurrences following the massacre, preparations for the commission of inquiry began. Much like Rabin, many in the IDF were disappointed with the decision to form it. Senior officers complained that while their hands are full of work, they must hire attorneys, prepare records and recreate events. However, once it was decided that the commission would be formed it was clear that everyone would cooperate with it.

There is no doubt that the abundance of commissions of inquiry, or other committees external to the IDF, is an element that can negate the willingness, the will and the independence of commanding officers to initiate action and reach decisions as they are required to do in their positions, and whose results might include failure. The military life and situation is a fertile ground for many uncertain, unexpected and perplexing moments, which require decisions be made within short periods of times based on information which is only revealed at that moment, and which is usually partial and perhaps even not completely accurate. In these situations, a commander who fails to reach a decision could lead to disaster. I am referring to decisions such as when to open fire, when to charge forward, whether to continue negotiating with a terrorist who is holding hostages or to storm in and as a result endanger the rescue squad and hostages, and similar occasions. The fear of a future commission of inquiry could cause officers to include irrelevant considerations into their decision-making process and will not do what is needed out of fear that they will need to stand trial or be investigated regarding the results of their decision.

The solution relies on building a military justice system that is separate from the civilian one. The problem is that many times boundaries are crossed and something that should be handled in a military inquiry or investigation, goes to the civilian tribunals in the form of commissions of inquiry, civilian courts or the Supreme

Court. Of course, it must be ensured that proper behavioral norms are kept and that those who act wrongly and against these norms be brought to justice. However, it needs to be done within the operational frameworks because the reality of military life often puts officers and soldiers in situations that are unique to the military environment.

A great effort must be made to enable the officers at all levels and ranks to regain the feeling that their actions are supported, that they do not have to enter the battlefield with an attorney close at hand, and avoid a situation in which their ability to make decisions and take risks which they see as calculated is compromised.

The way to build a better, more experienced chain of command is to acknowledge the fact that the baby should not be thrown out with the bathwater, as well as to learn the difference between the British and Japanese methods. In Japanese tradition, a mistake leads to Hara-kiri, while the British believe in learning from mistakes and implementing the conclusions – unless it is a case of negligence or acting against orders.

A commission of inquiry always causes a stir with those involved, since everyone tries to establish an alibi even if it is at the expense of those above, below or to alongside him. There is an atmosphere of mudslinging even when others could get hurt, since this is usually the approach recommended by the lawyers which are consulted. However, I am happy to say that in this case this phenomenon did not occur in the upper levels from Brigade Commander and above. The sense of support came from the top, starting with the Defense Minister and Chief of Staff, through the Commander of Central Command, and downwards. Hence there were also very few sparks flying from this commission, which was focused and professional.

This commission focused on two main issues: the security at the Cave of the Patriarchs and an intelligence warning regarding such an event.

On Tuesday, March 8, the Commission began hearing my testimony, which started at eight-thirty in the morning and lasted for four hours, in the Supreme Court in Jerusalem.

At the heat of my testimony was the notion that the massacre could have been prevented. I argued that if the security plan for the Cave of the Patriarchs was followed as written, and if the forces securing the perimeter - which is supposed to include eighteen people - would have arrived on duty, the massacre could have been prevented or at the very least the murderer would have found it more difficult to perpetrate his act. Furthermore, even if the shooting had started – it would have ended completely differently. However, inside the Cave of the Patriarchs, at the time of attack and contrarily to the orders given, there were only four Border Guard troopers and one army officer, while half of the force – including three Border Guard troopers, a soldier and a civilian policeman – were missing.

I believe that platoon or team commanders are responsible to fulfill their duties, and we must by no means shed this responsibility from them.

If it was something systematic, a pattern that spread to all units, the commanding officers would also be at fault. However, if it was an isolated incident and a commission of inquiry investigated and found that it happened due to miserable coincidence on that same morning, and does not reflect on the whole – responsibility should not be placed on the higher ranks of command.

Towards the end of the testimonials in the commission, I was asked to testify again in my role as the Military Secretary to the Prime Minister and Defense Minister. I was asked to weigh in on the testimony of Director of the Shin Bet Ya'akov Perry and the Police Commissioner Rafi Peled, since in their statements they mentioned a period in which I was the Military Secretary. In my first testimony, I said that as Head of the Command I received no warning that a Jewish settler might commit this kind of terrorist attack, and that such a warning was to be given by the Shin Bet. In my second testimony, I added that I had also not heard of such a warning during my role as Military Secretary, who attends the Prime Minister's meetings with the Director of the Shin Bet.

I asked to testify behind closed doors because I was discussing my role as Military Secretary and matters that had arisen in the Prime Minister's bureau. In my testimony, I spoke about two main issues: whether I had early information or any focused kind of warning regarding Jewish terrorism against Arabs, and whether this possibility was even discussed.

I said that both in my role as Commander of Central Command and in my role as Military Secretary, this possibility was never discussed. I told them that the intelligence never came to the level of warnings from Jewish terrorism in general, and no terrorist intentions regarding targets in Hebron were mentioned in particular, and of course there was no mention of the Cave of the Patriarchs or other holy sites besides the Temple Mount.

I said that when I re-assumed the position of Commander of Central Command I knew that the Shin Bet was following violent groups from the ultra-nationalist right, and that if the need would arise, the Shin Bet would act to prevent Jewish terrorism.

During the month that preceded the massacre, when I was once again in command, I met several times with Gideon Ezra, who was head of the Jerusalem and West Bank District in the Shin Bet, as well as many of his intelligence coordinators. In none of these meetings, discussions, face-to-face or telephone conversations with any of these people did I receive any kind of warning or information regarding Jewish terrorism against Arabs.

The situation is appraised according to intelligence, historical developments and close contact between many different officers from the IDF, the Civil Administration, the Shin Bet and the Police - and the local Arab and Jewish populace. The possibility of Jewish terrorism was never mentioned and was unprecedented for twenty-seven years, since the area was occupied by the IDF. Furthermore, crimes committed by Jews against Arabs were mostly expressed in breaches of the peace. Hence, I believed that the massacre in Hebron was an act of madness by a lone individual, which could not have been predicted, and hence was extremely difficult to protect against and prevent.

During my testimony, I was asked why there were no rules of engagement against Israelis. I answered that reality had not set such a requirement, but further stressed that we also do not have rules of engagement when it comes to soldiers and other security service personnel. Nevertheless, if a soldier would endanger the lives of soldiers or civilians who are not a threat to himself, his counterparts are obliged to act, even to open fire in order to prevent a crime from taking place.

Cases of Jewish settlers making illegal use of their firearms were handled on a personal basis, and from the beginning of 1993, firearms were taken from around one hundred Israelis in the West Bank. In 1991, I issued restraining orders to several Israelis in different areas, including the Cave of the Patriarchs.

Another crucial issue that stood in the way of eradicating violence by Israelis against Arabs was the lack of law enforcement against them. In December 1991, the State Attorney, Dorit Beinish, held a discussion about police and military handling offenses committed by Jewish settlers in the West Bank. The discussion was held at my initiative due to the difficulties we had encountered in our dealings with the settlers. One phenomenon kept repeating itself:

the investigation was no investigation at all, when there was room for charges being pressed it was not done, and even when there was a verdict of 'guilty' the punishments given were ridiculous.

Beinish concluded the discussion by turning to the Defense Minister, Police Minister and Justice Minister, and asked to turn their attention to the understaffed and unprepared state of Israeli police in the area. Beinish wrote that this state of affairs would necessitate that manpower be added to the police to allow it to fulfill its role of maintaining law and order and acting against Jewish and Arab lawbreakers. I also thought that there was no resort but to massively reinforce the police. I said that the army was often called to assist the dwindling police forces. I asked for improved deterrence in the form of sentences against lawbreakers.

In November 1993, when I was already Military Secretary, Rabin held a discussion titled 'The Treatment of Jewish Settlers in the West Bank by the Police and Security Forces.' Most discussions were dedicated to finding ways to combat Arab terrorism, but once in a while, when the Jewish rioters had gone too far, we could no longer ignore the need to find ways to end the Jewish people's attacks against their Arab neighbors, and often against the security forces themselves.

Many times just claims were made by ministers and different army officials who were responsible for law and order in practice, that law enforcement against Jews in the West Bank was a sluggish affair.

Many times settlers acted violently, cursed soldiers and physically attacked the security forces. We began using video cameras in outbreaks by Jews or Arabs to have proof in court, and despite gathering testimonies and soldiers filing complaints against unlawful settlers, the police hardly even investigated the matter. It took a very long time for the investigation to produce an indictment (if at all), and in many cases when charges were pressed, the punishments given were ridiculous. As a result, it was difficult to enforce law and order on the settlers because they felt that they were the ones in control. We found ourselves playing a game of cat-and-mouse with the settlers on various hills. In the morning, a report of a caravan on a certain hill would arrive, we would be asked to remove it so as not to open the gateway for others; and every day, there was a new chase, done by soldiers who were supposed to be devoting their time to fighting terrorism and instead bouncing across the hills chasing illegal caravans.

Rabin was furious with this phenomenon and more than once turned angrily to the Attorney General, who would be present at government proceedings, and demanded he overhaul the legal system and police to empower the administration and law enforcement system in the West Bank.

My approach was and is that the conduct of the Police and the courts, in regards to Jewish offenses committed on political or ideological grounds, made life very difficult for the IDF and the Shin Bet in their work in the West Bank.

It was very frustrating. For instance, I had many times tried to issue restraining orders against Rabbi Levinger, forbidding him from leaving Hebron, due to the provocations he caused everywhere. I did not succeed because the Shin Bet did not produce material that could have been the basis for issuing such decrees, as it was concerned about its sources being revealed. Rabbi Levinger is one example of many.

In the period before the massacre, ninety-nine investigations against Jewish transgressions, which were opened as early as 1989, were still open; eleven investigations were closed from reasons such as lack of evidence, lack of public interest or stay of proceedings. There were also nine acquittals. When a guilty verdict was achieved, in twenty-four cases the punishments were fines and conditional prison sentences, one case ended with a fine without a conditional sentence, only six cases ended with actual imprisonment and two cases ended in parole periods without a verdict.

The cases that were investigated came in many forms: riots, window breaking, overturning shops in the market, violence against Arabs, provocations, illegal use of firearms, breaches of the peace, attacks and provocations against soldiers and opening fire on Arabs.

I believe there has been no meaningful change in the way Jewish lawbreakers in the West Bank are treated, and law enforcement against them is problematic to this very day.

The findings of the Shamgar Commission pointed out that the security forces did not predict the massacre at the Cave and in any case did not warn of such a massacre about to happen. In the period before February 25, 1994, the security forces had no concrete forecast regarding a terrorist attack against Arabs in the Cave of the Patriarchs, but there was no fault in that since in any case there is a very low probability to prevent a terrorist attack orchestrated by one person, Arab or Jewish.

The Commission stated that security at the Cave had been increased over the years: an IDF reserves company had been replaced with a regular one, and had been reinforced by a team from the Border Guard. I had also ordered a civilian policeman be stationed at the Cave as an additional reinforcement to the perimeter security force, and there had been an order from the Brigade Commander to add a vehicle patrol outside the Cave during daytime.

In its conclusions the commission determined that Goldstein was the one directly responsible for the massacre and that the missing personnel during the massacre was a miserable coincidence whose roots can be found in improper coordination between the different forces and a low level of discipline in some of them.

The commission determined that clear and understandable rules of engagement must be published, the wording of which would be according to Israeli law with the necessary adjustments for soldiers serving as keepers of the law in the West Bank. The law must be enforced vigorously, decisively and equally against any person who breaks it.

The commission recommended changing prayer arrangements of Jews and Arabs in the Cave of the Patriarchs, in order to avoid a situation in which these two populations would be in contact at the place. It was recommended that either the time or the place be divided differently, so that Jews and Arabs could pray simultaneously, but completely separated from one another.

I suggested accepting only the first alternative, and so it was done. I thought we could not rely on physical separation inside the building, as it would quickly lead to the rules being broken and contact being made. Hence, I recommended only a separation in times, without authorizing Jewish worshippers to enter while Arabs were praying and vice versa.

The commission further recommended that responsibility for security outside the Cave be given to a regular or reserve military unit, while the inner and outer entrances to the Cave be secured by a special unit that will act as 'Cave Guard.' It was recommended that carrying weapons into the Cave by civilians or soldiers be strictly forbidden, except by the special security force. It was further recommended to install means of surveillance and alerting, to enforce the law equally on everyone, while stressing that this responsibility would be on the Police, and to increase Police budgets and manpower in the area.

The Cave was once again opened for prayer only several long months after the massacre, after recommendations and lessons from the horrific massacre had been implemented.

Nevertheless, none of the changes and amendments could atone for the disgrace and the horror of this evil murder of innocent people, while they were kneeling to pray to their maker, with their backs to the murderer, helpless. Unfortunately, as it turned out, this was not the last time in which a single person was able to cause so much harm, pain and sorrow.

Chapter 10

A Leader, a Friend and a Mentor

Close to midnight on the night of November 4, 1995, I entered the operation room in the Trauma Center at the Ichilov Hospital in Tel Aviv. At the center of the room lay the deceased Yitzchak Rabin. His lower body was covered and no signs of injury were apparent on him. His face was peaceful, its normal redness replaced by deep paleness. An unholy silence dwelt upon the room.

I looked at his face and knew that the sight of Rabin's dead body would haunt me until the end of my life, along with the feeling that his death was a personal and national loss, which would forever mark the end of an era in the lives of the dwellers of this country. It was for them that he had fought for all of his life, and in my own life as one who had followed him in dramatic and fateful years.

The State of Israel lost one of the last of its greatest generation, while I lost a leader, a friend and a mentor, whom I had known for a great many years.

My first meeting with Yitzchak Rabin was in 1964, during a *Sayeret Matkal* operation, the unit to which I had been enlisted a short time earlier. In those days I had yet to complete my training as a soldier in the Unit, and my role in the operation was to secure the frontline command room in which the Chief of Staff Yitzchak Rabin and other senior officers were seated. I saw Rabin from afar and of course, we did not exchange a word. An entire hierarchy of ranks and positions was between us, and I could not imagine that one day I would get a chance to work with this battle-worn and highly experienced man, and that it would become one of the defining experiences of my life.

Later on, when I was already a regular combat soldier, I encountered him often when participating in the Unit's operations. Rabin, faithful to his obligation and responsibility for his soldiers, would always come to bid the troops farewell before they embarked on an operation, and welcome them back when they returned.

The first personal meeting between us was brief and happened around one year later in the finishing ceremony of my Officers' Course. I had finished the course with honors and the Chief of Staff Yitzchak Rabin gave me my Platoon Leader's pin. In the future, he would also give me the Chief of Staff's Medal for my role in an operation behind enemy lines.

Further down the road we met many times when I was a team commander in the Unit, leading my soldiers to perform operations. These meetings were of a military and professional character and there was no personal element in them.

A different type of connection began to form through Dalia Rabin, Yitzchak's daughter, who served in the Unit when I did. Dalia and I were and still are good friends, and her wedding ceremony with Abraham Ben Artzi, an officer from the Unit, was my first personal connection with Rabin and his family.

In the Yom Kippur War, I served as Deputy Commander of the Tank Battalion 195, which fought in Sinai. The Battalion Commander was Uzi Levzur, and the Brigade (known as the Iron Footprints Brigade) Commander was Dan Shomron. One time during the war, in the midst of the difficult battles, I heard a call through the communications radio: "Danny, this is Ben Artzi."

Ben Artzi, who had finished his career change to the Armored Corps, recruited a platoon of three tanks and reached an area in which my battalion was fighting by himself. We had many wounded and dead and were in desperate need of any additional tank or crew. Ben Artzi joined us through the radio and was accepted with open arms. From that moment on, his platoon was an inseparable part of the battalion and participated in all stages of the war.

After the ceasefire agreement with the Egyptians was signed, on the 101st kilometer, Uzi Levtzur was appointed G3 of Division 162, and I replaced him as Battalion Commander. Ben Artzi was a company commander in the battalion under my command, and Yuval Rabin, Yitzchak's son, was a platoon leader in the same battalion.

More than once, when I would call their house looking for Company Commander Ben Artzi or Platoon Leader Yuval Rabin, I heard from the other side of the line the familiar voice of then Prime Minister Yitzchak Rabin.

However, the deeper acquaintance between us and our work together began many years later when Rabin was appointed Defense Minister after the formation of the national unity government in 1984. In those days, I had served for a year as the Military Secretary of Moshe Arens, who preceded Rabin as Defense Minister, and Rabin had in effect "inherited" me from Arens. That is why, immediately once news of his appointment to Defense Minister was made public, I called him at his house, and after congratulating him for the appointment I asked him, with the forwardness and honesty that characterized our relationship throughout the years, if he was interested that I remain in my position. The question came from my understanding that it was not obvious for me to stay in a role for which I had been chosen by his predecessor. The immediate and definitive answer I received was, "I want you to stay."

Our work together in the Defense Ministry took place between mid 1984 to mid 1985, and was very intensive. During this year I was with Rabin more than I was with my wife and son, and we formed very close ties that crossed the generational and experience gap, and that helped us develop a shared language and efficient, trustful work relations.

Rabin came to the position of Defense Minister ready and highly experienced. He was a true professional, with a phenomenal memory, reliable, very intelligent, with a quick perception and very wise, a man whose journey through life had made him levelheaded, and whose quiet presence relayed authority and calm on his surroundings.

Once he arrived at the Ministry of Defense, the place was filled with a feeling of having received a person of indisputable professional and military authority.

To his subordinates he was a military, diplomatic and security authority of the highest level, and this was evident from the first Chiefs of Staff who served under his command – Moshe Levi, Dan Shomron and Ehud Barak – and to the last of the officers and soldiers in the frontlines.

In light of the constant clashes in Lebanon and the many casualties, Rabin was an island of stability, and everyone had the feeling that he was someone they could rely on. As early as his first days on the job, he delved into the huge piles of intelligence material, and in a short time became very knowledgeable of the intelligence, the landscape, the units and commanders. Aside from his professionalism and knowledge, Rabin also took care to have endless in-depth discussions on Lebanon and the West Bank. These were very complex matters, with a diverse range of opinions being heard regarding them. He would frequently consult and listen and was never quick to make a decision. He always used to say, "We'll decide when we need to decide, in the meantime we'll collect more information."

He would sum up every discussion, and gave clear and specific instructions, so that each participant knew exactly what he had to do and until when.

Years later, when I served as his Military Secretary during his tenure as Prime Minister and Defense Minister, I was impressed time and again from his authoritativeness and preciseness in his conduct with subordinates, which left no room for misunderstandings or misinterpretations.

Like Arens, Rabin was also cast immediately upon arrival into the fervor of Lebanon, and was forced to devote much time to this sector, in which events, bombings, terrorist attacks and retaliations against the IDF or SLA (South Lebanon Army) followed in quick succession. Rabin, in his own unique way was involved in every step, since his authorization was required for any operation that crossed Israeli borders or was carried out to the north of the Security Zone. His conduct while approving operations highlighted his military experience, his familiarity with the area and his authoritativeness. He drilled down to the smallest details, down to the location of the evacuation squad and of each observation post in the location. His intent was to ensure proper planning, that all the elements which would ensure the success of the operation were taken into account, and that all measures were taken to ensure the safe return home of our troops. The soldiers' well-being was always his topmost concern and was a most crucial issue for him. Therefore, the most difficult moments at his side were when he learned of casualties among our troops.

Delivering news of casualties was part of my job, and sometimes it happened on the phone in the deep of night. After reporting an incident with casualties, I would hear nothing but a long silence from the other side of the line, and then I was asked to find out more about the event. Immediately afterwards he would ask to visit the location of the occurrences as soon as possible.

When I had to inform him of casualties face to face, it was evident that he received the news with great sorrow and pain. He would light a cigarette, shrink into himself, take a few quick short puffs from his cigarette, and immediately start a string of rapid-fire questions: How did this happen, and why and when and how could it be? Again, he would immediately ask to depart to the location, "because I want to see what happened there!"

At the location he would conduct an initial debriefing, during which he wanted to know everything he possibly could: where were the terrorists hiding, where were our forces, who opened fire first, what happened later, when the evacuation squad showed up, how long it took them to arrive and how were the wounded treated.

He always ended meetings with the soldiers and commanders who took part in combat with a handshake, a pat on the back and words of support and encouragement.

Rabin, who knew bloody battles past and had firsthand experience of bereavement and the loss of comrades, well understood the feelings of the soldiers and their commanders. However, he would not hear of superficial investigations. He demanded strict, unabashed examination and that those who were found to be in misconduct receive their just deserts.

I remember him coming back from these investigations many times, slamming his hand against the table in frustration and saying to me, "It could have been different!"

There was much frustration on professional and personal aspects alike, since Rabin had a special weakness and a great love for soldiers and members of the security forces. He loved to visit the field and was prone to do so. It was evident that among the combat troops and during military maneuvers his conduct was the most natural and relaxed. I could see that this is where he truly thrived, and he found these hours much more favorable than discussions at the Ministry of Defense, the government and the Knesset.

Soldiers and officers returned Rabin's love. His attitude toward them was paternal, his speech was soft and he was interested in everything related to them: from the conditions of service to operational preparedness. He was interested in questions such as whether they had enough food, or whether they were cold, and projected an atmosphere of tranquility, peace and security upon them.

The large age gap did not prevent him from conversing with the soldiers as equals and having long conversations with them. Despite his shyness, he easily created a rapport with them, and the young soldiers felt comfortable enough to have long conversations with him during which they presented him with various questions, and he always replied at length and openly.

This attitude towards the troops and concern for their welfare were also expressed in his special and warm treatment for the families of POWs and MIAs, bereaved families and the injured. Rabin would often visit the wounded in hospitals and meet with the families of the fallen and the MIAs. I do not remember even one such family who asked to meet him and was rejected out of hand. He would immediately clear his schedule and accept them. The meetings with the families of POWs and MIAs were naturally often difficult and complex, and the families had many complaints, mainly that not enough was being done to retrieve their sons.

Even though sometimes he could not appease them, and did not always have answers, he was careful to give them the feeling that the IDF and the security services were doing everything to discover what happened to their loved ones and bring them home.

Rabin felt responsible for the life and the fate of every combatant sent to battle, and never ceased to allocate limitless resources to this cause. Some of his efforts were successful: the soldier Hezi Shai, who for years was considered missing in action in Sultan Yacoub, was returned home. The body of the late Zohar Lipschitz was also returned, as were the eight *Nahal* soldiers who were captured in the Lebanon War following the Jibril Agreement in which 5,000 terrorists were released. Rabin went through with the agreement in spite of harsh public criticism against him.

However, four soldiers Rabin spent tremendous efforts bringing home have still not returned: the three missing soldiers from the battle of Sultan Yacoub - Zachary Baumel, Zvi Feldman and Yehuda Katz - and IAF navigator Ron Arad, who was captured in October 1986. Arad abandoned his plane, which was hit during an Israeli air strike near Zur in Lebanon, and fell into the hands of the Amal Movement. The last sign of life from him came in 1988, and according to Israeli claims, Arad was later transferred to the Iranians.

Rabin made every effort to obtain information to promote negotiations for the release of prisoners and missing persons. In July 1989, during his first term as Defense Minister, Sheikh Abdul Karim Obeid was abducted from Lebanon by *Sayeret Matkal*. Sheikh Obeid was a central figure when it comes to Hezbollah's terrorist attacks against Israel. He was commander of the Islamic resistance in southern Lebanon and a member of the Hezbollah's Revolutionary Council of Shiite Clerics. Obeid was involved in the distribution of funds to perpetrators of terrorist attacks against Israel and the transfer of weapons, and took part in planning terrorist acts and harboring perpetrators of terrorist attacks. He was considered a charismatic preacher, who recruited many supporters in the struggle against Israel, and legitimized Hezbollah's terrorism as a religious authority. Rabin ordered the capture of Obeid as a bargaining chip in negotiations for the return of Ron Arad.

In May 1994, during his second term as Defense Minister and Prime Minister, Yitzhak Rabin authorized the abduction of Mustafa Dirani. Dirani was previously head of the security apparatus of Amal. He was deposed by the organization's leader Nabih Berri, who opposed the connections Dirani created with pro-Iranian organizations, one of which was Hezbollah. After the impeachment, Dirani, along with officials who were expelled from the Amal Movement, established an organization called the Believing Resistance. One of Dirani's organization's first actions was the kidnapping of Ron Arad from the hands of the Amal Movement. According to one version, Ron Arad was transferred by Dirani to the Iranians in exchange for monetary compensation. According to another version, Ron Arad was kidnapped while under the responsibility of Dirani from where he was hiding, the village of Bani Sheet in the Baalbek region, by the Iranian Revolutionary Guards. As far as Israel was concerned, Dirani had held Arad for some time, and was responsible for his transfer in some way or another to the Iranians. Rabin said at the time that the purpose of this operation, also carried out by *Sayeret Matkal*, was to exhaust every possibility and every course of action that could provide insight into Ron Arad's condition.

Dealing with issues such as POWs and MIAs, as well as the troops, publicly exposed a human and very soft side of Rabin, who despite his age, experience and duties as Chief of Staff, Ambassador, Member of Knesset, Defense Minister and Prime Minister, was extremely shy and remained so until his last day. People who didn't know him tended to mistakenly think he was distant and arrogant.

Indeed, his shyness made him uncomfortable in the presence of strangers, but with those near and dear to him he was relaxed and loose. Only when he was at home, surrounded by his family and close friends, you could see him let out a free, big laugh.

It was very difficult to penetrate Rabin's intimate circle, which included only intimate friends who had gained his trust. He was suspicious, and his confidence was difficult to win over and easy to lose if one had failed him. However, once he trusted someone, he hid nothing from him.

Rabin came to his first post at the Defense Ministry with a group of people who accompanied him for years that included Eitan Haber, Shimon Sheves and Niva Lanir. This group zealously maintained its position in Rabin's intimate circle, and was impenetrable. Though I was not part of this inner circle in the first place, I was added to it very quickly, and since then our relationship gradually tightened.

I became close with Rabin, largely to the mad, nonstop work and an increasing breadth of shared experiences, which included both harsh and joyful events. Our work together required an almost twenty-four-hours-a-day connection between us, in demanding and pressing situations that appeared day after day and night after night.

The nature of such circumstances led those involved to extreme states, from a strong intimate connection to severe disputes, and sometimes up to crisis and separation. I think I was lucky that Rabin had a favorable view of me and gave me the feeling that he trusted me completely.

In my opinion, Rabin's assessment was that, as was my way, I always used to tell him what I thought, not what I thought he would like to hear. He saw me as a loyal assistant, a man of integrity and without manipulation. He was assured that I was not one to exploit my closeness to the Defense Minister and Prime Minister to promote my personal affairs, and always listened to me attentively and appreciated my knowledge of different subjects, acquired from many years' experience in the field corps of the IDF in a variety of combat and command positions.

Almost a decade after serving as Rabin's Military Secretary when he was Defense Minister, I returned on April 1994 to fill the position of Military Secretary at his side, but this time I was already at the rank of Major General and Rabin was serving his second tenure as Defense Minister and Prime Minister.

My appointment to the position of Military Secretary to the Prime Minister and Defense Minister was unique, because until then, appointed military secretaries held the rank of Brigadier General. Rabin decided that as he was filling the positions of both Prime Minister and Defense Minister, it was important that he have a military secretary at the rank of Major General, who had previously filled positions at this rank. As Prime Minister who was also Defense Minister, Rabin knew he was going to deal with turbulent times, highly demanding and very much preoccupied with security affairs. It was a time when much was happening: the peace process began, the Southern Lebanon front knew no moment of silence, and Hamas and Islamic Jihad did not cease their attempts to undermine the peace process. On top of all that, as Prime Minister and Defense Minister, Rabin was in charge of a very large span of control when it came to defense issues, such as the IDF, Mossad, Shin Bet, Coordinator of Government Activities in the Territories, the Atomic Energy Commission, the Ministry of Defense and the defense industries. Hence, Rabin came to the conclusion, which in my opinion was justified, that he should have someone next to him who could assist him and be of any use in regards to any of these matters. The position of Military Secretary was offered to me by Rabin. Chief of Staff Ehud Barak, who managed to see the big picture of things and also wanted to be involved in political processes related to the military, realized it was important that these issues were properly handled within the Prime Minister's Office.

The fact that I was not a junior officer, but a Commanding General of the Central Command and a Major General in such a turbulent period, and the previous acquaintance and confidence I had received from Rabin in my previous position as his Military Secretary, were the basis for why he approached me specifically.

Rabin decided that in addition to my responsibility for military and security issues, I would coordinate the work done in the Prime Minister's Office on the peace process and relations with the United States, and I would be in contact with all other ministries in regards to these issues.

In the course of my duty, I attended all of Rabin's meetings that dealt with diplomatic and security issues. It was agreed between us from the start, on my recommendation, that aside from exceptional cases, the Prime Minister's meetings would not be held tête-à-tête, but in my presence, and would also be recorded. I discussed this in the wake of past episodes, where the Prime Minister had met with senior officials and high-ranking officers and afterwards disputes had arisen, often quite substantial, in relation to what was said and decided there. I asked Rabin to ensure my presence in these meetings, along with have them being properly recorded, and Rabin agreed.

Most of the procedures were confidential and classified, and much of the material on which the assessment was based was intelligence material provided by the Shin bet, Military Intelligence and the Mossad. These were matters only few people were exposed to, and Rabin, who was familiar with my discretionary practices, felt comfortable with the thought that I would be a part of these discussions.

It was important for me to fill this position, because I understood that I was to expect an interesting role and was going to take part in the dramatic processes involved in decision-making on the highest levels of defense and diplomacy in the State of Israel. I thought that if I could contribute, if only slightly, to the right decisions being made, I would be fulfilling a highly crucial mission.

Furthermore, I was delighted to work with Rabin. I appreciated and was very fond of him and we had become close friends. We felt comfortable with each other and I felt confident knowing that Rabin was serving as Prime Minister and Defense Minister, as I thought that he was the best man for the job, I believed in his way, and I wanted to assist him throughout it.

I felt that the combination of working alongside this very special man, along with the peace process and exposure to other issues being dealt with by the Prime Minister pertaining to diplomacy and security, could serve as an excellent base for a very exciting period in my life, and so it was.

The same qualities that I had known him for from years ago as Minister of Defense were expressed in his capacity as Prime Minister. This time his professionalism and experience were combined with an additional dimension of national responsibility that went beyond security issues, and the solemnity of a man in the seventh decade of his life, with the scars of war behind him and a determination to realize the vision of peace.

I participated in most government meetings and some of his work meetings with ministers, and I once again came to realize how his conduct within the government made him an authority in the eyes of his ministers, who never disputed the fact of him being a source of leadership and knowledge.

As was his custom, Rabin was quick to study in depth the various issues handled in the various ministries and gained a broad knowledge of them.

Faithful to the promises he made during the elections, he turned his attention to intensively promoting peace and a complete overhaul of national priorities. This was done by directing very large portions of the budget to education, welfare and infrastructure within the Green Line, at the expense of reducing the allocation of funds for infrastructure in Judea, Samaria and the Gaza Strip and cutting defense spending.

Rabin saw education as a key to the strength of Israeli society and its future achievements, and allocated the largest budget to education, even larger than the defense budget. Along with Minister of Housing, Binyamin Ben-Eliezer, he charged head-on to tackle the long-neglected road system, and during three years changed nearly the whole country's transportation system, by building a modern infrastructure of roads that shortened the travel time between the outlying areas and central Israel.

Against the backdrop of economic growth, progress in the negotiations for peace with our neighbors and creating new relationships with countries in the region, Rabin won eternal glory. Often in meetings with foreign leaders, I was amazed by the awe and appreciation he was awarded.

The most notable relationship in this context was that which had developed between Rabin and US President Bill Clinton. The two developed an amazing relationship, to the extent that some believed Clinton viewed Rabin as the father figure he never had. It was amazing to see the leader of the free world, the most powerful person in the world, talking to the leader of a small country in the Middle East and listening to him attentively, thirstily drinking in his words.

The situation in which the leader of the world looks up to Rabin with sincere interest and respect might have appeared as though it were taken from another world, but to me it seemed perfectly natural and almost obvious. It was clear that the weight Rabin carried, the course of his life, his political and military wisdom and personality were such that even the most powerful person in the world could not remain indifferent before him.

The two formed a very special bond, expressed even in their body language. Knowing Rabin I could easily tell if he was at ease. As is well known, Rabin was a very introverted man who did not openly express his feelings, but it was clear in his encounters with Clinton that he felt very comfortable. During their meeting, it sometimes seemed as though Rabin was the leader, and the president of the United States his junior. Clinton praised Rabin for his courage and vision, always stating how much he had learned from him, his experience and his leadership.

I think Clinton saw in him what he himself had never been: a hero and military leader who devoted many years of his life to his country's security. Clinton also viewed Rabin as a highly experienced and courageous statesman from whom he should learn. He appreciated Rabin's honesty and directness - Rabin was an unceremonious prime minister and would always put things on the table immediately. Clinton also admired the phenomenal memory of Rabin, who would not carry papers but could give organized, in-depth lectures when required to do so.

Rabin had a tendency to dominate the conversation and talk most of the time. During meetings he tended to immediately 'take command and navigate' the conversation. Sometimes we would pass him a note to the effect that we also ought to hear the other side... and then he would immediately internalize the note, stop talking and let the other side speak properly. Clinton had a great appreciation for Rabin and considered him a completely dependable person, and he knew that any agreement with Rabin would be carried out as planned.

Qualities of reliability and integrity carry much weight in American tradition. As far as they are concerned, if you're caught lying once - you have lost all credibility. Clinton's assessment of

Rabin was mixed with a sense of deep commitment on the United States' behalf to the existence and security of the Jewish people and of Israel, due not only to the political responsibility of the country towards Israel but also from his religious education. Clinton believed in the significance and contribution of the Jewish people to human history.

Rabin learned to appreciate this young man, his integrity, his intellectual ability, his detailed knowledge of the matters discussed in meetings between them, the ability to understand the complex situation in the Middle East and the fact that Clinton had devoted so much of his time and energy to his attempt to resolve the Arab-Israeli conflict.

At a farewell party held in the summer of 2002 for Haim Israeli, who served as assistant of all Defense Ministers from the country's first days until Benjamin Ben-Eliezer tenure, former President Yitzhak Navon spoke. In his speech Navon mentioned his joint work with the Defense Minister and first Prime Minister David Ben-Gurion, and said of him that unlike other leaders, Ben-Gurion was a person whose character intensified the closer you got to him. I felt likewise at Yitzhak Rabin's side, and many others around the world did too.

An impressive demonstration of the worldwide admiration Rabin had at the time was expressed two weeks before his assassination, at a meeting in New York in honor of fifty years to the establishment of the United Nations. The leaders of the world gathered together for the occasion, and before our incredulous eyes a spectacle occurred the likes of which we had never seen before. We witnessed supreme leaders and the rulers of rising nations making a pilgrimage to Rabin's room, seeking his favor, making requests of him that assumed he had tremendous influence on world leaders and especially President Clinton, trying to squeeze in five minutes in

Rabin's tight schedule – requests we were often forced to refuse. This was at the peak of the peace process, and Rabin was considered one of the five leaders of the world. Everyone appreciated and admired him for his vision and courage.

During our stay in New York, Rabin was invited to a meeting with Jiang Zemin, President of China, and as the Chinese president ranked higher than Prime Minister of Israel, Yitzhak Rabin made his way to it. The meeting was set for the weekend, and in order to avoid violating the Sabbath we took a walk to the hotel in which Jiang Zemin was staying.

It was a rainy winter day and Rabin, who forgot his coat, put on mine. I am taller than he was, so the coat did not exactly fit him and its edges lapped the sidewalks of New York. And so we walked, a large and strange group, surrounded by bodyguards, and in its center a grown man with a long coat, sweeping the city. Even New Yorkers, accustomed to strange phenomena, did not remain indifferent. Everyone recognized him, pointed at him, waved and called out to him. Rabin waved back and we had no doubt that if in his place walked a leader of a larger and more important country, he still would probably not have received the same attention from passersby.

At the start of the meeting with the President of China, Rabin gave a start and said, "I am the Prime Minister of a small country and you are the president of a huge country." and then Jiang interrupted Rabin's words with a gesture. We were very much surprised, because the Chinese are generally reserved and patient, and wait perfectly politely until their counterpart finishes talking, but Jiang asked to respond immediately and said, "In one of my previous positions, I was China's Minister of Electronics. At that time I learned about the power of Israeli science and technology, and I have to tell you that the strength of a nation is not measured in its territory and number of residents but in its intellectual and technological strength, and in that sense Israel is a greater power than China."

Rabin turned completely red at hearing this, which was just one example of the power and influence attributed to Israel in those days by other leaders.

Presidents and prime ministers gathered in a long line to see Rabin, whom they considered to be all-powerful within the US government. All were under the impression that Bill Clinton responded to Rabin's every whim, or at the very least worked on his behalf. They incessantly asked Rabin for help with the US government, to speak with Clinton, to arrange a meeting, say a kind word to benefit their interests in the United States, so that America would be responsive to their distress and help them.

Suharto, President of Indonesia, asked Rabin to contact the Portuguese in order to work out his problems with them in regards to East Timor, which is Indonesian territory, but Portugal had claims in relation to its control (eventually East Timor was granted independence).

Tansu Çiller, Prime Minister of Turkey, asked for Rabin's help to get Turkey accepted to the European market, and to soften the United States' approach to it in light of allegations of human rights violations in Turkey. Ciller claimed they were instigated by the powerful Greek lobby in the United States, which was exploiting Turkey's war against the PKK (Kurdistan Workers' Party, led by Abdullah Öcalan).

The Azerbaijani President sought to learn from Rabin's experience regarding how to solve its border dispute with Armenia. He asked him to persuade President Clinton to remove the embargo imposed by the US government, and improve relations between the United States and Azerbaijan, which was being sabotaged by the Armenian lobby in the United States.

The President of Costa Rica spoke of a US company called 'Chiquita,' which exports bananas from Costa Rica. "Chiquita," said the president, "claims the Costa Rican government is discriminating against it, and because this company supports Senator Dole, the Senator is causing difficulties for Costa Rican interests in the Senate. If so," the President turned to Rabin, "can you talk to Senator Dole and change his position towards us?"

Thus an endless convoy of favor-seekers formed, from which we learned that Rabin was widely perceived as a leader who was almost all-powerful.

However, it turned out that this glory and appreciation of Rabin was not shared by all.

As negotiations with the Palestinians progressed, the Israeli right-wing's incitement against Rabin grew stronger. Demonstrations, statements and billboards presenting Rabin as a traitor became a daily affair. Yet even in light of the vocal incitement against him, two extreme events were noteworthy. One was a right-wing demonstration in Jerusalem's Zion Square, attended by the heads of the Likud, in which photos of Rabin depicted him wearing an SS uniform. The other was a demonstration at the Ra'anana junction, with the participation of opposition leader and Likud chairman Benjamin Netanyahu, during which a coffin marking the Oslo Accords' burial was carried at the front of a procession. This was the visible layer of activity against Rabin's legitimacy. The second layer was hidden, and in it extremist rabbis issued a judgment of *Moser ve'Rodef* ('traitor and persecutor') against Rabin.

They accused him of giving away parts of Israel and hence they permitted his life to be taken.

It was in this atmosphere that the Shin Bet became increasingly concerned for Rabin's security, and he was asked to avoid direct contact with the public, wear a flak jacket at public events, and travel in armored vehicles. Rabin did not like these recommendations - he refused to wear a flak jacket, avoided traveling in the armored Cadillac car, which struck him as luxurious and ostentatious, and said he must have direct contact with the citizens. "You worry about my security," he told the Shin Bet.

Rabin preferred not to make public statements on these issues, but during our shared travels I could see that the sight of protesters and banners denouncing him at intersections were very hurtful to him.

Although these sights offended him, they never reduced his motivation to continue and strive for peace. He never worried about his personal safety, and to us, the people around him, it never occurred that he might be hurt. The possibility that a Jewish terrorist would attack him seemed completely delusional. Although much information was open and spread out before us, it did not seem to indicate immediate danger.

Weeks before his assassination, Rabin said he understood the difficulty of Arab leaders to make peace with us: "They might be killed for it and lose their lives. For me, the worst thing that can happen is to lose my seat in the Knesset."

So when I said goodbye to Rabin on Friday, November 3, before the Sabbath, at the end of a long workday at the Ministry of Defense, I could not imagine that this would be the last time I would see him.

The next day, late in the afternoon, I received a report from Col. Shimon Shapiro, my assistant for intelligence affairs, stating that the Shin Bet had issued a warning about a terrorist who was going to attempt to attack in the *Malchei Yisrael* Square during the peace rally to be held there that evening. The possibility that the terrible event that eventually occurred would be perpetrated by a Jewish terrorist was never even discussed. Upon receiving the report, I told

Shapiro to ask the Shin Bet to increase security around Rabin. As Military Secretary, I did not have the authority to instruct the Shin Bet, but I decided to intervene because of that particular warning.

Immediately afterwards I called Rabin, who was already in the car with his wife Leah on their way to the square. I told him about the warning, and he told me he had already heard it from his personal security guard.

It was a perfectly normal conversation, informative, relevant and brief. In fact, this was our last conversation, about an hour before the murder.

Although I accompanied Rabin in many events, I was careful not to join him at this rally. When I was an officer on active duty, I believed this duty included the obligation to never set foot in any event of a political nature.

About an hour later the phone rang, and on the other end was the hysterical voice of Aliza Goren, Rabin's media adviser: "Danny, they shot him! Danny, they shot him!" She screamed into the receiver, words that will echo in my mind for the rest of my life.

I asked her, "They shot who?" And she replied, "They shot Yitzchak!" I asked how he was, and she replied, "I don't know, there's a big mess," and then the call was disconnected.

I felt the blood draining from my face. For a moment, I thought I felt crushed under an immense weight. I was in total shock. Seconds later, I called my son Omer, told him Rabin had been shot and asked him to accompany me, as there was no time to call my driver. I wanted Omer to take care of the car when we reached the place, as it was already clear to me that there would be much commotion there. Within seconds, I was wearing my uniform, and I drove to Tel Aviv as fast as I could with my son next to me. On the way, I was informed that Rabin was being taken to Ichilov Hospital. I turned on the radio and tried to focus on driving, although I was very nervous and upset. While on my way, I telephoned my friend Dr. Yitzhak Shapiro, Deputy Director of Ichilov.

I tried to inquire into Rabin's condition, and found I was the first to tell him of the assassination while he was still at home. Dr. Shapiro at once gathered all the details from the hospital and called me back. "The situation is very bad," he said. Until that point I had hope, because on the radio they had said that Rabin apparently only sustained minor injuries

When I arrived at Ichilov some half hour later, I went down to the surgical floor of the Trauma Department, where I met the Rabin family, some of the ministers including Shimon Peres, Aliza Goren and Eitan Haber, Shimon Sheves, President Ezer Weizman, Chief of Staff Lipkin-Shahak and other staff. As the minutes passed, more and more people gathered.

Shortly after my arrival, Prof. Gabi Barbash, Director of the hospital, came to the room where Leah Rabin sat with her children and grandchildren. A nerve-wracking anticipation stood in the air. Leah looked very sad and worried, her face white as a ghost, and she could not stop crying.

Prof. Barabash came to her and said, "I'm sorry to tell you that we were unable to save the Prime Minister." The first reaction was one of paralyzing shock, followed by uncontrollable crying from everyone.

Eitan Haber, the head of Rabin's bureau and one of his close friends, approached the large crowd standing outside and announced the death of the Prime Minister.

Shimon Peres looked absolutely stunned. His face gray, he called me and asked, "Now what?" I told him he should immediately convene the government.

I called Hollander, the cabinet secretary, and asked him what the procedure for such cases was. He said that a Prime Minister must be elected by the government because the country cannot be left without a Prime Minister even for a brief period of time.

While preparations for the special session of the government were underway, I went with a small group of people in to the operations room for a last farewell from Yitzhak Rabin.

I was struck by the sight of his lifeless body. I realized that this moment would forever separate a period of peace and hope at the national level, and a close friendship on the personal level, from one of terrible loss and crisis.

The killer, who turned out to be a religious Jew, a Yarmulke-wearer, who had killed an Israeli prime minister, made us lose our innocence and our belief that Israeli society is unlike others. We never believed that a murderer would emerge from within us, one who acts out of disagreement with the Prime Minister's opinions and actions. This act, which we believed could only happen in other countries, had made us a nation like all nations. The killer, supposedly driven by an ideological mission, tore a deep rift within us, one that we would try to mend for many years.

After leaving the hospital, I went on auto pilot. I arrived with Aliza Goren and my son Omer at the Ministry of Defense in Tel Aviv, where the irregular cabinet meeting was to be held. The place was full of people, as though this was not a Saturday night. Everyone was encompassed by gloom. Every room was occupied by staff members, some crying, some wandered the corridors shocked. Immediately after the special cabinet meeting, feverish preparations began for the funeral, which was attended by leaders from almost every corner of the world. This show of international solidarity and hurt reminded us all of the place where Israel had been a few days earlier and the vision that Rabin had wished to fulfill but could not.

Among the leaders who took part in the funeral was King Hussein of Jordan, who during the peace process had formed a very special relationship with Rabin and the people around him. After the funeral, I was invited along with Eitan Haber to the king's room at the King David Hotel in Jerusalem. The king received us in tears and told us, "You lost a man close to you who was a leader and I lost the best friend I had."

Rabin's era had ended, but the man and his work continues to accompany me in all my ways. In every one of the roles I filled since then, his image looked back at me every day from the walls of the room where I was sitting. My office at the Mossad, in my room at the Prime Minister's Office alongside Barak, the offices of the Knesset and every one of my civilian roles, my shared photographs with Rabin were put up, telling the story of a different era and ineradicable distant memories.

The two periods I worked with Rabin were the most fascinating in my public and security-related career, in both the professional and personal aspects.

Rabin gave me a sense of being a full partner in the military and diplomatic proceedings, which contributed greatly to my motivation. I felt I was learning a lot from the way he saw things, from his ability to distinguish immediately between trivial and crucial parts of security and political issues.

Many times, I found myself listening with thirst and curiosity to his brilliant analyses, aware of the depth and wisdom revealed in them. These analyses reflected a broad vision and deep knowledge of every subject. Rabin had the power to draw a general picture without losing the important details, he could see the forest, but also distinguish each individual tree.

The clarity with which he presented the issues and the way he gave instructions, prevented misunderstandings and the unproductive meetings that are familiar to anyone who has worked within various governmental institutions. Meetings with him were not idly wasted, and discussions always ended in decisions, with clear tasks given to those involved.

However, Rabin's decisions were never reckless, and were reached after long and thorough deliberation. He never rushed to decide, and his approach was that if you do not have to decide today, you can wait for tomorrow or the day after that as the situation might change. Rabin would deliberate, and sometimes you could clearly tell he was pained with the knowledge that the wrong decision could incur a painful price. However, once he had decided, his decision was very clear and precise, not an ambivalent one that could be interpreted in several different ways as was the case with many others. Instructions were accurate and were given so that anyone who was in the room understood exactly what he was required to do. He was not influenced by the pressures of anyone and even in decisions related to national security you could see how he refused to fold under the pressures of the army and the Chief of Staff.

Working alongside such a man gave me a deep sense of confidence. I felt that the State was led by a sage, responsible and experienced man who knew exactly what he was doing and where he was headed. The feeling we had with him was that we could never be lost.

It was clear that his behavior as a leader who confidently leads the convoy came naturally to him. There was no artificial conduct or forced behavior on his part, which helped his environment immediately recognize who he liked and who he did not, with whom he agreed and with whom he did not. It was enough to track his unenthusiastic gestures and facial expression in order to understand what he thought of the speaker, even when dealing with senior ministers or high-ranking officials.

I had a deep respect for Rabin's ability to translate ideas into action, to make judgments and avoid recklessness. These characteristics, along with providing support and accountability, are in my opinion the fundamental elements of a leader's personality.

The failed rescue attempt of the soldier Nachshon Wachsman is one of the most prominent examples of these qualities of Rabin, which made me greatly respect the man and his leadership.

Wachsman was kidnapped on Sunday, October 9, 1994, by a Hamas cell.

Wachsman's family knew some nerve-wracking days, as did the political and military decision-makers and the people of Israel who were closely following the developments. Two days after the abduction, the Prime Minister's Office received a video tape showing Salah Jadallah (a.k.a. Khaled), a resident of Sheikh Radwan in Gaza, who was wanted by the security forces. While holding Wachsman's ID card and shortened M16 rifle, Jadallah appeared on tape as he detailed the demands to release Sheikh Ahmed Yassin and other Hamas prisoners in exchange for releasing the captured soldier.

On Wednesday of that week, a second tape was published showing Nachshon Wachsman with masked kidnappers. "The guys from Hamas kidnapped me... I ask you to do what you can to get me out of here alive... I hope to get back to you, if Rabin decides to release Hamas prisoners," said Wachsman, facing the camera with downcast eyes and a boyish tone. The tape left a deep impression, and the sight of Wachsman's face begging for his life from among masked men was forever engraved in our collective memory.

Stress, anxiety and helplessness encompassed the entire country that week. The videotape removed the kidnapping from its political and national security context, and turned it into a personal story in most homes in Israel.

The ultimatum set by Hamas for Wachsman's execution was set to expire on Friday at eight o'clock. That day a special prayer was held at the Western Wall for Wachsman's safety, organized by Rabbi Israel Lau, Chief Rabbi of Israel. Hundreds attended the prayer, while thousands of Shabbat candles were lit around the country at the request of Esther Wachsman, Nachshon's mother, who turned to all women in Israel on live television.

As a result of intelligence officials' estimate that the abducted Israeli soldier was being held in Gaza, Rabin declared Arafat responsible for Wachsman's life. He made it clear that he considered him responsible that Wachsman return safely, and stressed that if this was not done, it would have far-reaching consequences that would bring into question the authority of Arafat on the territories under his responsibility. "You have to act against Hamas. It's time to choose between peace with Israel and peace with Hamas," Rabin stressed to Arafat.

US Secretary of State Warren Christopher, who was in the area at the time, told Arafat that the kidnapped soldier also held US citizenship, and if anything would happen to him, the US would have to respond.

Since the initial assumption was that Wachsman was being held in Gaza, Rabin sought to gain time and build a military alternative. He also wanted to make it clear to Arafat that Israel would be prepared to release security prisoners later on, including Hamas members, but refused to tie his gesture with Wachsman's release.

Rabin ordered to prepare for a possible rescue of the soldier in a military operation, if his exact hiding place in Gaza was revealed. "We must do what we would do anywhere else in the world to rescue hostages, and certainly this is true of Gaza," he said.

MK Taleb El-Sana together with Dr. Ahmed Tibi tried to mediate informal negotiations with members of the political bureau of Hamas in Gaza, but things did not materialize into a real offer for an exchange agreement. There was no evidence that the kidnappers were responding to instructions from these levels.

Rabin's approach was to hold no negotiations with the kidnappers, as long as there was another alternative to release the hostage, as this could be a precedent for further abductions.

As a result of this background, criticism began to be voiced against him that when he had served as Minister of Defense in 1984, he had agreed to release 5,000 terrorists in exchange for the release of the *Nahal* soldiers in the Jibril Agreement. Rabin explained that in that case, there was no military alternative to rescue the hostages, and it was feared they would die in captivity.

At the time, Arafat made efforts to locate the kidnapped soldier. Hundreds of Palestinian policemen took part in searches, arrests and interrogations of Hamas members, but they were in vain. "The soldier is in an area under your control, look for him there," said Arafat, who was greeted at first with utter disbelief.

However, Shin Bet officials in Jerusalem, under Deputy Director of the Shin Bet Gideon Ezra, worked tirelessly throughout the week, and on Friday morning managed to obtain accurate information regarding the location of the kidnapped soldier. As it turned out, Wachsman was being held in a villa at the village of Bir Nabala, about a mile from his home in the Ramot neighborhood in Jerusalem.

From that moment on, it was clear to Rabin that there was only one alternative: rescue the kidnapped soldier through military action.

In a unique precedent, Rabin made all the decisions himself without consulting the Cabinet or other ministers. Later, Rabin explained this absolute compartmentalization as stemming from a concern over leaked information.

Pursuant to his authority as Defense Minister and Prime Minister, Rabin approved the military operation to be carried out by *Sayeret Matkal*. General Shaul Mofaz, Commander of the Judea and Samaria Division, was the one who chose the commando unit for the job, as he preferred its proposed course of action over the one presented by the SWAT.

Rabin, who was situated at the Defense Ministry in Tel Aviv, accepted the recommendation of the field commanders, who in addition to Mofaz also included the head of Central Command Ilan Biran and the Chief of Staff Ehud Barak.

He trusted the judgment and assessments of these officers, all of whom were experienced and had rich experience in combat, but he was clearly distressed. Many cigarettes were lit one after the other, and once it was reported that the operation was underway, he became very alert and focused with anticipation.

The television in the room was on, and was reporting on the case in detail. Rabin was restless and spoke of his hope that the operation would go well. He said that even though these were the best combat soldiers, he knew that these types of operations could also fail.

One hour and fifteen minutes before the ultimatum expired, the commandos stormed the villa in which Wachsman was held. A short delay of one of the storming squads led to a chain of events, during which the kidnappers realized very quickly what was happening. Contrary to what had been planned, the house was surrounded and filled with Israeli soldiers. A hail of bullets showered upon the soldiers, nine of whom were wounded and Nachshon Wachsman was shot and killed by his captors. During the firefight, Captain Nir Poraz, Commander of the storming forces, was also killed. Poraz was buried two days later in the military plot in Kiryat Shaul, next to his father, Maoz Poraz, a pilot who was killed in the Yom Kippur War.

Immediately after the operation, the red phone, connected to the field troops headquarters, rang and the secretary said that Barak was on the line. I looked at the intent Rabin as he went to the phone and prayed Ehud was bearing good news. Rabin took the phone and I followed the look on his face closely. I could not hear Ehud's words on the other side of the line, but according to Rabin's expression, I realized something had gone wrong. Rabin listened silently and attentively to Ehud's report, and then sat down in his chair, withdrew into himself, and quietly said, "The operation failed. Nachshon Wachsman was killed and the unit has a casualty and several wounded." Another cigarette was lit.

In a short time, Rabin decided to hold a press conference, and immediately at its start, he took the floor. Looking straight forward and in unequivocal words, he turned to the audience and said, "I am responsible." Without contortions, cover-ups and attempts to place blame or responsibility on his subordinates, he deployed a protective umbrella over the heads of the IDF Chief of Staff and all his subordinates. "I made all the decisions, and I bear responsibility for the consequences," he said.

At that moment, Rabin displayed the full glory of his leadership. The strength of his determination in taking responsibility for both the decision and its execution showed that it had never occurred to him to try to say that the Chief of Staff was the one who recommended it or that the field commander was in charge. He had decided on the policy of an attempted rescue operation, and from that moment on, he had trusted the judgment of the entire chain of command to decide how it would be carried out.

Later on, as I continued my public activity, I found it difficult to find a parallel for this type of behavior, that was so characteristic of Rabin, in other leaders and bearers of responsibility.

Even then, during the days when I worked alongside Rabin, I felt that it was an extraordinary privilege that had crossed my path and I was extremely lucky for it.

More than once, in the course of my other roles in the years that followed, I looked for someone to consult with, to rely on and to hear his opinion, and no such person existed. In these moments, in addition to many others, I missed Rabin very much. Many times, especially in my role as Director of the Mossad, I thought what Rabin would have done in this situation or another.

He had a remarkable ability to give the entire system a sense of stability. Unlike other periods, I do not remember one time when a conflict arose between him and the Chief of Staff, or criticism was published about him in the media, after being timely leaked by senior officers or officials in his office.

Respect for him was all-encompassing, ranging from the defense establishment to ministers and senior government officials, including those who did not always agree with his opinions.

This behavior did not go on to characterize the relationship between Prime Minister Barak and IDF Chief of Staff Shaul Mofaz, between Prime Minister Benjamin Netanyahu and Chief of Staff Amnon Lipkin-Shahak and between Prime Minister Ariel Sharon and Chief of Staff Moshe Ya'alon.

I have no doubt that the special relationship that existed between Rabin and his subordinates was due to his personality, his experience and him being a diplomacy and defense authority who could not be argued with. Very few Israelis have the honor of possessing a resume similar to Rabin's, and no less impressive was the fact that all this took place while he was also a modest person, shy and without aggression.

Those who filled these roles after him only raised more longing for him and emphasized his absence.

Chapter 11

Pathways to Peace

Rabin's murder was a traumatic event in the history of Israel and the Jewish people. I have no doubt that if he had lived, he would have led the country to peace with the Palestinians and Syria, and our current situation would have been decidedly different.

The murderer Yigal Amir, who shot Rabin, killed the peace process and the prospect of Israel being a normal, flourishing and thriving country in the years that followed.

Rabin tackled the peace process headfirst, as he did with every matter that was under his care and responsibility. As was his way, he was determined, full of faith, confident and focused on the goal.

Many years in national security and treading pathways that passed through bloody killing fields led him to become the Prime Minister of Israel for the second time in his life, when he was seventy years old, a seasoned person with broad and diverse life experience.

Rabin felt that one of the duties assigned to his generation, the *Palmach* fighters and the founders of the state and the army, was to give future generations an end to the bloodshed along with a stable Middle East and a better future. As Defense Minister, he felt personally responsible for the safety of every citizen, and was of the opinion that the degree of his knowledge of the problems Israel's security and very existence faced was one that would allow him to weigh all the factors required to take calculated risks, as he defined them.

The man who led the fighting forces of the State of Israel from the role of a soldier to Chief of Staff and Minister of Defense, came to realize that the seeds of peace will never sprout on the battlefield, but rather at the negotiating table. This time, he wanted to be the one who would head the forces leading the process. "It is the only war which is a pleasure to participate in – the war for peace," he said in his speech before the US Congress after signing the peace treaty with Jordan, at the end of another successful journey on the path of peace.

However, in the summer of 1992, the road to formal speeches and pampering receptions was still long and wrought with difficulties.

Rabin entered the Prime Minister's Office in June 1992, some six months after the Madrid Conference in October 1991. The Syrian delegation to the Madrid Conference, headed by Foreign Minister Farouk al Shara, agreed to hold bilateral talks with the Israeli delegation but refused to join the multilateral talks. From December 1991 to April 1992, four rounds of direct negotiations were held between the Israeli delegation headed by Yossi Ben-Aharon and the Syrian delegation headed by Muaffaq Allaf. The rounds, which were held in Washington and supported by the US, were mainly characterized by mutual bickering, no progress was made in their duration, and they were discontinued as the elections in Israel neared.

The first round that was held in Rabin's tenure was in August 1992, and it was the sixth round since the Madrid Conference was convened. Rabin appointed Israel's ambassador to the United States, Itamar Rabinovich, as head of the Israeli delegation that participated in eight rounds of talks during his tenure, from August 1992 to

February 1994, when they were rejected by the Syrians following the massacre in the Cave of Machpelah. In any case, these rounds left the impression that discussions were in fact taking place but with no progress to show for them.

Talks with Palestinian, Lebanese, Syrian and Jordanian representatives were accompanied by the issue that Rabin, his predecessors and those who followed him were forced to face. The question was whether to create a list of priorities in terms of whom to speak with first.

During his Knesset election campaign, Rabin presented the striving for peace with our neighbors as one of the main steps in his policy. His strategy in those days was to begin with progress with the Palestinians. Rabin assessed that progress in the Palestinian sphere could lead to an arrangement of autonomy within six months.

This line of thought was the result of his estimation that an agreement with the Palestinians would pave the road towards a quick agreement with the Jordanians, and then the time for negotiations with Syria would come. Rabin sought to isolate the process with Syria at the end of the maneuver, partly because as he saw it, the Syrian issue was less urgent than the Palestinian one. He saw the Lebanese problem as part of the Syrian one, since it was at the time a Syrian sponsored state.

"Operation Accountability" was launched after a long period of escalation on the northern border. The IDF suffered casualties and injuries in clashes with Hezbollah in southern Lebanon, and residents of northern Israel were forced into bomb shelters time and again due to rocket and mortar fire on their communities. Life along the Lebanese border had become dangerous and intolerable.

Even before the operation, many meetings were held between Rabin and US representatives. In all these meetings, Rabin raised the issue of Hezbollah's terrorist activity, and made it clear that this situation could not continue. On July 10, 1993, Rabin met with Dennis Ross. Rabin began by saying, "Since our last meeting, we are seeing an increase in Hezbollah's hostile activities, as well as that of Ahmed Jibril's organization and other organizations who are under Syrian influence. Even the Lebanese army occasionally fires at Israeli soldiers inside the Security Zone. We cannot ignore these developments. We know that all the weapons used by Hezbollah are shipped from Iran to Damascus via airplane and from there by automobile to Hezbollah. Syria is playing a dangerous game. On the one hand holding peace talks with us, and on the other hand helping Hezbollah."

Rabin asked the Americans to clarify the risk of escalation to Syria, stressing that Israel wanted peace, but would defend its vital interests and protect its citizens.

The next day, on July 11, Chief of Staff Barak presented the IDF's recommendation for an operation in Lebanon, aimed to hurt Hezbollah and to stop the rocket fire aimed at northern communities. The program was based on the assumption that if pressure were exerted on the population that lived north of the Security Zone, and many residents would flee to Beirut, these refugees would then pressure the Lebanese government, which would consequently turn to Syria and ask it to take action to restrain Hezbollah.

Rabin concluded the discussion saying, "The escalation that has developed is quantitative as well as qualitative. The main problem is Hezbollah's intention to deprive us of the ability to respond at targets north of the Security Zone, because any such reaction causes rockets to be fired at northern communities."

As mentioned, Rabin viewed moving the population from southern Lebanon towards Beirut as the central element in our ability to cause pressure that would lead to Hezbollah's restraint. The message that Israel planned to deliver in the operation was:

As long as there is no normal life in northern Israel, there will be no normal life in southern Lebanon as well.

When Dennis Ross and his team returned from their meeting with President Assad, they reported that the Syrian president's response to Rabin regarding escalation in Lebanon was the usual one: he said that Syria is not interested in a confrontation with Hezbollah in Lebanon. Hezbollah, he claimed, is a grassroots movement that has generated a popular following in southern Lebanon and aims to expel the Israeli occupation from Lebanon. The only solution to the problem is political, and must be based on the implementation of Security Council Resolution No. 425. A complete solution to the problem could only be achieved through peace between Israel and Syria.

On July 14, the Prime Minister and Chief of Staff presented "Operation Accountability" to the Security Cabinet for approval. In the presentation, the IDF made it clear that it aimed to complete the operation solely using firepower, and there were no plans to send ground troops into the area north of the Security Zone. It was further clarified that the operation could take about ten days, and residents of the north would have to stay in shelters throughout this period.

Age two, with my parents Pnina and Simcha, may they rest in peace

At my sister Eti's bat mitzvah celebration, with my parents, my brother Ehud (left) and Moshik

My parents celebrating at our wedding

With my wife Tova at our wedding ceremony, 1971

With my wife Tova, our sons and my brother Ehud. From right: Omer, Roey, Itay, Tal, Nir and Ehud at my inauguration ceremony as Head of the Planning Directorate, 1987 (Image by IDF Spokesperson)

With our eldest son Omer, laying tefillin (phylacteries) before his bar mitzvah

My wife Tova at our son Omer's wedding ceremony

Omer completes his basic training in the Paratroopers Brigade. Next to him are Nir (left) and Tal. Front: Roey and Itay

With Tova at our eldest son's wedding, 1999

With Tova on my birthday, at Prime Minister Barak's bureau (GPO)

Chief of Staff, Lieutenant General Rafael Eitan (Raful) and Brigadier General Amnon Reshef awarding me my Colonel's rank (IDF Spokesperson)

Tova and Chief of Staff Rafael Eitan (Raful) awarding me my Brigadier General's rank (IDF Spokesperson)

Tova and the Chief of Staff, Lieutenant General Dan Shomron, awarding me my Major General's rank. From the right are Defense Minister Rabin and Major General Avihu Ben-Nun, the outgoing Head of the Planning Directorate (IDF Spokesperson)

As a young soldier in Sayeret Matkal during a navigation expedition in the Galilee

As a Soldier in Sayeret Matkal during naval training, 1964

Having finished the Officers Course with honors, Chief of Staff Rabin awarded me my Platoon Commander's pin. On the right is Commander of Officers School Colonel Meir Pail, 1965

As commander of "Danny's Squad" in Sayeret Matkal

With the soldiers of my Sayeret Matkal squad during a navigation expedition in the Negev

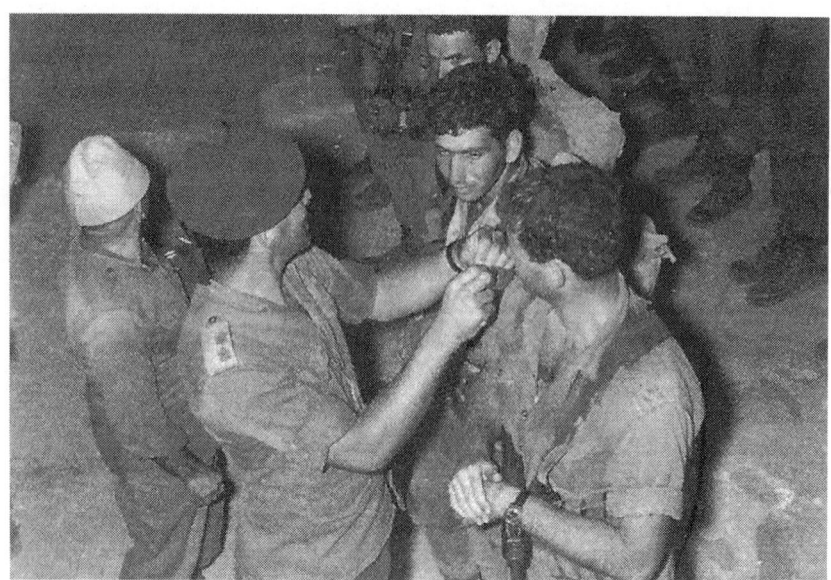

Commander of Sayeret Matkal, Dubik Tamari, awards me my First Lieutenant's rank after an arduous training exercise

As a Squad Commander in Sayeret Matkal near the Suez Canal, at the end of the Six Day War

"Danny's Squad." Standing, from right: Me, Hanan Gilutz, Shlomo Gelber, Danny Snir, Itzik Gonen and Baruch Tsur, may he rest in peace
Kneeling, from right: Moshe Siboni and Rafi Bar-Lev, may he rest in peace

Directly after overtaking the Sabena airplane. I'm in white overalls at the upper end of the ladder.

Sayeret Matkal overtaking the hijacked Sabena Flight 571. On the wing, in white overalls: Ehud Barak (right) and me, May 1972 (Ron Ilan)

With Defense Minister Rabin, who was attending an exercise at the division I was commanding at the time (IDF Spokesperson)

In 1986, at the end of my term as Commander of the Armored 162nd Division, Omer and Tal watching me

With Defense Minister Moshe Arens. I was serving as the Defense Minister's Military Secretary (IDF Spokesperson)

The changing of Defense Ministers, Rabin replaces Arens. I continued to serve as Military Secretary for Defense Minister Rabin (IDF Spokesperson)

With Defense Minister Rabin and Director of the Shin Bet Avraham Shalom during a tour in Lebanon (IDF Spokesperson)

As Commander of Central Command during a visit by Chief of Staff Barak in the Paratrooper's Brigade drill, under the command of Ya'alon (Bogie) who is sitting first on the right. Behind the Chief of Staff is Major General Shmulik Arad, may he rest in peace (IDF Spokesperson)

With Rabin, the Prime Minister and Defense Minister, during a visit to Central Command (IDF Spokesperson)

A restful moment with Prime Minister Rabin and General Director of the Prime Minister's Office Shimon Sheves, during a flight to the United States (GPO)

A visit to a Paratroopers training exercise as Commander of Central Command (IDF Spokesperson)

"Undercover" – from right: Commander of the Judea and Samaria Division Bogie Ya'alon, Assistant to the Director of the Defense Ministry Chaim Israeli, and me – Commander of Central Command (IDF Spokesperson)

As Commander of Central Command with Brigadier General Ya'akov ("Mendy") Or, Commander of the Judea and Samaria Brigade, during a pursuit of terrorists who had perpetrated an attack. Behind me is Bureau Chief Major Eyal Moshkato (IDF Spokesperson)

Chief of Staff Barak's debriefing after a terrorist attack in Hebron. I am Commander of Central Command. Behind and on the right: Brigadier General Ya'alon, Major General Shmulik Arad may he rest in peace, and Brigadier General Gadi Zohar (IDF Spokesperson)

With Sultan Qaboos, the Sultan of Oman

With Egyptian Defense Minister General Tantawi (GPO)

With Rabin before his historic meeting with Indonesian President Suharto

With President of the United States Bill Clinton, center: Eitan Haber, Prime Minister Rabin's Bureau Chief (Government Press Office)

Prime Minister Rabin introduces me to King Hussein

With the Queen of Jordan, Nur, after the signing ceremony of the peace treaty with Jordan

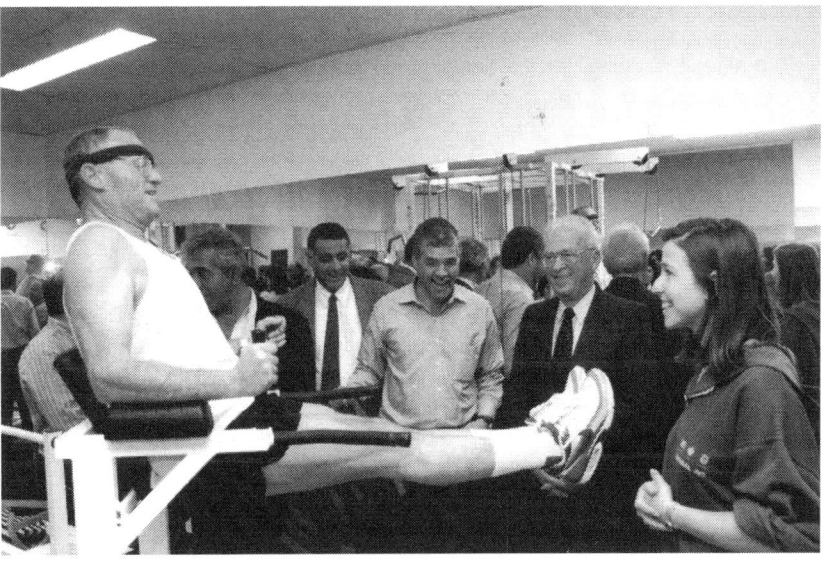

Inauguration of the gym at the Prime Minister's office. Admiring my performance are Prime Minister Rabin, General Director Sheves, Deputy General Director Mizrahi and Rabin's Driver, Yechezkel Sharabi (GPO)

Rabin concluded his presentation by saying, "I see three options. The first is to keep the status quo. This is a bad alternative as it will lead to rocket attacks on northern Israel every time we shoot within the Security Zone and north of it. The second option is to expand the Security Zone. I am against that: we will not solve the problem but merely take upon ourselves more populace under our control. The third option is Operation Accountability, and is the preferred alternative in my eyes. I recommend that we approve the operation in principle."

The Cabinet gave the IDF the 'green light' to continue preparations, and agreed to another cabinet meeting in which the detailed plan for the operation would be approved.

Therefore, on July 23, the Cabinet convened to hear updated reports and additional information about the operational plan. The Cabinet approved the first two stages of the operation, in which targets in the Bekaa Valley, in southern Lebanon and north of the Security Zone would be attacked from the air and ground.

The purpose of the third stage was to initiate the flight of villagers from southern Lebanon northwards. This would be achieved through the use of artillery fire aimed close to the villages and by sending warning messages, according to which the residents were to leave their villages to avoid being harmed.

It was decided that the third stage and any further action required the further approval of the Cabinet and the Israeli government.

"Operation Accountability" began on July 25, 1993, and continued until July 31. The IDF hit many targets. The third stage was also carried out after being approved by the government. About 300,000 Lebanese left their homes and moved towards Beirut.

During the operation, some one thousand sorties of fighter jets and attack helicopters were made, tens of thousands of artillery shells were shot, and approximately fifty terrorists were killed as well as some 120 Lebanese civilians. Hezbollah fired 272 rockets, half of which landed in Lebanese territory. An Israeli soldier was killed during the operation and two civilians were killed in Kiryat Shmona by rocket fire.

Warren Christopher, US Secretary of State, began working towards a ceasefire.

On July 31, Israel announced its conditions for ceasefire. Israel demanded that Hezbollah not fire rockets or other weapons at Israeli territory under any conditions and in any situation, both presently and in the future.

Israel had made it clear that the IDF and the South Lebanese Army would act to protect the Security Zone and against terrorists north of the Security Zone. We also clarified that if rockets were to be fired from the villages situated north of the Security Zone, we would return fire towards the sources of aggression, and we would continue to act against terrorist cells in the Security Zone. The Americans told us that they would try to get the Lebanese to commit to these understandings, as well as a Syrian commitment to make sincere efforts to restrain Hezbollah and prevent future escalation.

With the help of the Americans, a ceasefire was achieved and understandings were reached, the main ones being: the two sides would not fire on civilian targets; Hezbollah would refrain from firing from within the villages; and if rockets were fired from the villages, the IDF would return fire at the sources of fire in the villages.

Christopher and his team arrived in Israel and met with Rabin, who thanked the Secretary of State for his efforts to achieve the ceasefire and understandings. Rabin said that the test would be in the implementation of the understandings, adding that the announcement of the Lebanese government headed by Rafik Hariri, stating that it was ready to deploy the Lebanese army south of the Litani could bring about a dramatic change for the better in the situation in Lebanon. "I am willing that the Lebanese army be deployed on the northern border of the Security Zone. If it manages to stop Hezbollah's attacks for six months, this will open many possibilities for improvement in the situation between Israel and Lebanon," the Prime Minister said.

Rabin would later state that if the Lebanese army would stand the test of six months, he would be willing to withdraw the IDF from Lebanon and allow the deployment of the Lebanese army on the border with Israel.

Rabin's intuitive approach after his election was to hold parallel talks with the relevant parties. Yet on September 1993, after another round of talks, Rabin shared with me his deliberation regarding the progress of negotiations in the peace talks. At the time, Rabin was actually mostly considering peace negotiations with Syria, but stated that this would not impede the process with the Palestinians, and if a breakthrough were to be achieved on the Palestinian track – it would be moved forward.

"If we achieve peace with Syria, we will cancel one remaining strategic threat to Israel," Rabin said, adding, "Until recently Syria has also been at the front of the Palestinian problem, but now the Palestinians have taken responsibility for themselves." Rabin, who chose to hold bilateral negotiations with the Palestinians, Syrians and Jordanians at the same time, refrained from doing so when on the opposite side was a group who represented more than one Arab faction. He claimed that when two or more Arab factions were in the same room, the negotiations would lead to nowhere, because the moderates would always be destined to line up with the extremists. Rabin described the talks held at the same time as three and a half tracks - Jordan, the Palestinians and Syria, and Lebanon, which was seen as half a pathway due to its state as a Syrian satellite.

In effect, Syria remained the most nearby, imminent and immediate threat to Israel in the Middle East. Hence, Rabin believed that this threat should be neutralized by means of a peace agreement with Syria, as without it stability in the region could not be achieved.

Of the two parties that had to be negotiated with to reach a stable Middle East, Syria and the Palestinians, Rabin estimated that the Syrian matter was the less complicated, inasmuch as the dialogue was taking place with an existing country over what was essentially a border dispute. It also seemed to him that in the end it would be easier to convince the Israeli public to make concessions in the Golan Heights, even far-reaching concessions, compared to concessions in the West Bank and Gaza. The Golan Heights had only 5,000 Jewish residents living in it and the West Bank already contained more than 114 settlements, and the sum of the Jewish population there was close to two-hundred thousand people. In addition, the historical relationship between parts of the people of Israel to Judea and Samaria was much stronger than its historical ties to the Golan. Rabin estimated that while it would be difficult to concede simultaneously in the West Bank and Gaza and the Golan Heights, it would be possible to move forward on those two fronts and convince the Israeli public when the time came to make compromises both with Syria and with the Palestinians.

Syria had a clear address for negotiations – President Assad. It was estimated that an agreement with Assad would be something stable that Syria would uphold, just as it had upheld the separation and ceasefire agreement from '74 between Israel and Syria in the Golan Heights.

Rabin estimated significant progress with Syria would lead to acceleration in the Palestinian track, because Arafat feared that if Israel would reach agreements with all parties, he would remain last on the list and his bargaining power would be significantly reduced. Resolving the problem with Lebanon also included solving the Syrian problem, because Lebanon, Syria's puppet state, would not have dared to sign an agreement with Israel without Syria's approval. Rabin wanted very much to reach a peace agreement with Lebanon, which posed a major security problem and was brimming with border incidents, terrorist activities and rocket fire at northern communities by Hezbollah.

Rabin wanted to decipher the motives of Assad, who was careful to remain in splendid isolation at all times from the West and from everything that resembled closeness to Israel, including to take part in a plan intended to promote a peace treaty. "I do not think that Assad is rushing somewhere," said Rabin. "I believe that ninety percent of his own reasons to come to Madrid are related to his relationship with the US and his ambition to strengthen his ties with them, rather than his will to make peace with Israel."

Our assessment was that Syria had a complex array of national interests. The main reason Assad had joined the process was the need to preserve the survival of his regime and leave the rule of the Alawite minority in place. Assad also understood that the world had become unipolar once the United States became the exclusive leading player after the collapse of the Soviet Union. Hence, Assad realized he had to improve his relationship with the United States, and he knew it would not be wise for him to refuse the Madrid Conference initiative. Assad's additional interest was continued Syrian control over Lebanon, which was important to him because as Syria saw it, Lebanon was a place that from which Israel could attack, while he viewed the presence of the Syrian army in Lebanon as something that put pressure on Israel and deterred it from attacking. The importance of Lebanon was based on the economic interests of the families who controlled Syria, and the fact that a million Syrians worked in Lebanon and would send their salary to Syria each month.

Assad was also very interested in recapturing the Golan Heights, and he knew that he could not do so by force. If Assad believed that

Syria could regain the Heights without peace with Israel, he would prefer to do so, because Assad was very apprehensive about peace. He feared anything that might cause Syria to become more open to the West. He envisioned the Ceausescu syndrome - that opening a window to Israel and the West could cause a strong wind to blow into his country, one that might blow away his regime. As far as Assad was concerned, rapid and overly broad exposure of Syrian citizens to the free world could undermine his regime's ability to survive.

Itamar Rabinovich also believed that Assad came to the negotiations because of his relationship with the United States, since unlike the Palestinians he was not under daily existential pressure that peace with Israel could improve. Assad, according to Rabinovich, was looking five years ahead, and he was chiefly occupied with choosing his successor and how he would be remembered in history.

Because of his strong concern for his image and how it was perceived in the region, Assad refused to take any additional steps to contribute to the peace process – namely open diplomacy, expressed by granting media interviews, sending public messages and taking confidence-building measures. Secret diplomacy, which plays a central part in moving such processes forward, especially in the early stages, also worried Assad. According to the Americans, the Syrians opposed it for fear that the existence and contents of secret meetings might leak.

At one point, in an attempt to move things forward and to make Assad feel comfortable, it was suggested that Israel send a message to Syria through the Americans regarding Lebanon: Israel would not undermine Syria's status in Lebanon and would agree not to reach an agreement with the Lebanese prior to an agreement with Syria. In exchange, we asked the Syrians to discontinue Hezbollah's activity in southern Lebanon. This proposal did not receive any form of positive response from Syria.

In those days of the summer of 1993, US Secretary of State Warren Christopher began visiting the area, constantly commuting between Damascus and Jerusalem. During their meetings, Rabin would still complain about Syria's violations of the understandings regarding Lebanon. Rabin mentioned an increase in terrorist attacks against Israel from Lebanese territory, including the killing of Israeli soldiers and civilians in the Security Zone in southern Lebanon and within Israeli borders, and rocket fire on northern communities. It was evident that this explosive situation in Lebanon also affected Rabin's motivation to prioritize the attempt to reach an agreement with Syria.

At the end of 1992 and early 1993, during Rabin's frequent meetings with US representatives who tried to weave the threads of peace with Syria, he made sure to raise the issue of Israeli POWs and missing persons. At the time, this included Ron Arad and the three MIAs from Sultan Yacoub, and Rabin would always state the request to bring the bones of the late Eli Cohen to Israel for burial.

Israel estimated that the Syrians held information on this matter, as Ron Arad had been captured by the Lebanese who acted as Syrian satellite organizations, and the battle in Sultan Yacoub had been against Syrian forces. Assad's unchanging answer to the Americans in this regard was that he had no new information on the subject.

Beyond the humanitarian aspects of the matter, Rabin also stressed to the Americans that Syria's lack of cooperation in such a human and sensitive issue creates discomfort in the Israeli public and does not reflect well on Syria's reliability and willingness to make peace with Israel.

The difference between the Syrians and us was rooted in our different approach to the peace process: We chose peace as a strategic choice, while the Syrians made sure to note that, of all existing options, they prefered the peaceful one.

The Americans, who were familiar with Rabin's approach that Syria was a key strategic country in the process, and that peace with them would solve the Lebanon problem and lead to peace with other countries, used it as bait. They assumed that if peace with Syria was so important and was the key to peace with the entire Arab world, the price for it should accordingly be considerable. However, Rabin explained to the Americans that he was dealing with a more complex equation. Rabin argued that on one hand, the Syrians wanted the results of the peace negotiations with them to be similar to those held with Egypt, namely the return of land they claimed belonged to them, up to the last grain of sand. However, on the other hand, the Syrians were unwilling to do even a small bit of what Egyptian President Anwar Sadat had done in exchange: take part in a secret diplomatic channel along with public diplomacy; make gestures to prove that they strived for peace; visit Jerusalem; send peaceful and confidence-building messages, and stop the activity of Hezbollah, which had direct contact with Syria. "We are facing a strange situation," Rabin said, "On the one hand the Syrians are involved in the peace process and on the other they aid Hezbollah's hostilities against us."

Assad was a tough negotiator who always knew how to walk the line. He did not want to yield the Hezbollah card which he thought could be used to bring Israel to make concessions, to put pressure on it, and demotivate the Israeli public. He viewed public actions, such as education and preparing Syrian public opinion for peace with Israel and messages of reconciliation and peace, as something that could endanger the Alawite sect, a minority within the Sunni majority, to which he belonged.

For Rabin, confidence-building measures and the dividing of any agreed upon withdrawal over a period of time were important steps in any peace process, including the one with Syria. Among other things, he relied on the conduct of events during the implementation of the peace treaty with Egypt. Egyptian President Anwar Sadat's dramatic visit to Jerusalem was in November 1977, and only in April 1982 did Israel's military withdrawal from Sinai end. For two years and two months out of four years and five months between these two dates, Israel continued to control the Sinai while the various elements of normal relations with Egypt were put to the test.

These actions were taken despite the fact that the Egyptians had already taken many steps that had revealed their sincere willingness to make peace. Hence, when it came to Syria, it was even more crucial for Israel to examine whether these elements of normalization would be kept. Assad, unlike Egypt, said time and again that he wanted peace but declined to state which elements of normalization he was referring to.

Rabin said he was willing to commit to a military withdrawal but would not bind himself to full withdrawal, and he requested a ten-year interval between signing the peace agreement until the time full withdrawal would be in place, during which the seriousness and depth of the process would be tested. He later settled for five years.

Rabin asked to outline three stages for the withdrawal. The first phase would include a minor and symbolic withdrawal, which would not include the evacuation of a single Israeli settlement, and in the four years that followed, we could test whether the conditions of normalization were being fulfilled by the Syrians. In the second stage, Israel would withdraw further, and in the third stage - another withdrawal, up to the line determined by the two countries during the negotiations as a border between them.

Rabin devoted much of his attention to security arrangements. He demanded that some of the territory become fully demilitarized, and that in part of the areas the volume of forces deployed be diluted. Warning stations would continue to exist on the Golan Heights, settlements and military bases would be moved, and Israel would receive a security package from the Americans that would include money, airplanes and early-warning systems.

The importance of security arrangements Rabin explained thus: "We and the Syrians have the same number of armored divisions, except the difference is that here most of the divisions are reservists and the Syrians are all regular servicemen. If we're going to lose that which ensures our security, meaning a large part of the Golan Heights, and our situation changes completely, we cannot accept not getting something in return. We are serious in our desire for peace with Syria, but it must be a peace that will ensure security," he said.

Rabin placed great importance on security arrangements, unlike Peres who believed that security arrangements were less important because peace itself was the main component of security, according to his view that peace is what brings security. For Rabin peace did not stand alone, unless it included security arrangements that would prevent surprises and ensure our existence.

The next issue was the depth of the withdrawal, which would determine the location of the final border between Israel and Syria and the components of normalization.

"How can we make peace with Assad when he will not even speak with me personally?" Rabin asked US Secretary of State Warren Christopher during their meetings, pointing out that he had no problem getting on a plane and flying to Damascus if that's what was required to advance the cause of peace.

Christopher told Rabin he agreed with him, "But," he would say, "keep sending your messages through us in the meantime."

Throughout all of the meetings, Rabin stressed time and again that the depth of the withdrawal, setting of the border line, scheduled withdrawal phases, the application of normalization components and security arrangements - are the elements that will be the building blocks of the peace process with Syria.

During those days of the spring of 1993, a channel of dialogue, which would later be known as the Oslo process, began developing behind the scenes. In late April, the names of Yair Hirschfeld and Ron Pundak first began to appear in information submitted to Rabin, as well as mentions of personal contact with the Palestinians, along with Yossi Beilin. It was also mentioned in the regular update meetings held between Rabin and Peres once a week, in private.

Rabin thought this was an interesting attempt, one with a slim chance of success, and preferred to leave this in Peres's court, as he was putting his full weight on promoting the Syrian matter.

In April 1993, Itamar Rabinovich told us that one of the main controversies in discussions between the Israeli and Syrian delegations revolved around the issue of withdrawal and the nature of peace. The Syrians constantly strove to receive a precise definition as to what line we were willing to withdraw to. They mentioned the statement made by Rabin, that "the depth of the withdrawal would be equal to the depth of peace," and restated their position that Israel must withdraw to the border of June 4, 1967 (on the eve of the Six-Day War). Meanwhile, the Israeli delegation first tried to understand the Syrian's concept regarding the nature and depth of peace. Our position was that the depth and breadth of the withdrawal would be determined after we understood how the Syrians viewed the notion of peace and what kind of peace they were referring to. Peace for us meant full normalization, open borders, immediate diplomatic relations, open economic and tourist routes, and everything else that makes peace realizable, present, alive and public.

Rabin and Itamar tried to find a formula to define the withdrawal in a way that would not lead to a misunderstanding, so as not give the wrong impression that Israel was willing to withdraw in full from the Golan Heights.

"Say we're talking about an Israeli withdrawal **in** the Golan Heights, not **from** the Golan Heights, withdrawal from territories occupied in the Six-Day War to secure and recognized borders," Rabin said to Itamar.

At the same time, the US team, which included the Secretary of State Warren Christopher and Dennis Ross, and sometimes just Ross and his team, kept hopping between Israel and Syria. The Americans – who had orchestrated the Madrid Conference and the rounds of talks between the delegations, and had spearheaded the negotiations between Israel and Syria – found it important to repeatedly mention the importance of their role and how vital their presence was.

However, Rabin, who did not wish to undermine the importance of US involvement, was still careful to emphasize to them: "We cannot agree with you on some things, but basically we believe that the efforts of the United States are positive and helpful. I cannot remember any agreement, since the first agreements signed between Israel and the Arabs, which was achieved without the United States' involvement and leadership, and there is no doubt that the Madrid Peace Conference certainly would not have come to be if not for the efforts of the United States. We accept that the United States is a full partner in the process, but needs to remember that it is not an arbitrator, mediator or agent, but a messenger who skips between the parties."

What Rabin was stressing was that he expected the Americans not to surprise us by presenting to the other side new ideas or ones that had not received our approval, and not to bring their own proposals for compromises unless these were coordinated with us beforehand.

Dennis Ross told us, on one of his visits to Jerusalem after his return from Damascus in the summer of 1993, that Assad had repeatedly requested that the US act as an intermediary. He additionally stressed that Assad had mentioned on four occasions Henry Kissinger's actions after the Yom Kippur War, when the latter would travel between Israeli Prime Ministers at the time Golda Meir and Yitzhak Rabin, and himself. Assad asked the Americans to keep commuting between the parties in order to reach an agreement in principle in the first stage, and then a detailed agreement. Ross reported that Assad believed that there should be a breakthrough that same year, and the major issues that he considers essential to achieving an agreement in principle were the essence of peace, security arrangements, the depth of withdrawal and timetables.

The Americans interpreted this to mean that when Assad expressed his agreement with this type of negotiation, it was clear to him that he would have to present ideas to advance the process.

Nevertheless, when it came to our requests from Assad via Ross, to curb Hezbollah's terrorist activities from Lebanon against Israel, Assad responded that no one wanted a confrontation in Lebanon, but the only solution that would bring peace would be a political solution. Assad was also quick to give Ross a scholarly lecture regarding Hezbollah, claiming that it was a national liberation movement fighting against the foreign occupation, namely Israel, and not a terrorist organization. However, Assad was careful not to commit to concrete steps such as stopping Hezbollah.

To Rabin's proposal to establish a secret channel of communication between them and us, Assad chose to respond with a resounding 'no,' and Dennis Ross explained that he thought Assad viewed the American negotiations between Israel and Damascus as the covert channel.

In May 1994, Warren Christopher arrived from Damascus bearing a dramatic innovation: for the first time, he had brought with him the Syrian concept of peace and the components of their 'peace package.'

Despite the importance of his message, Christopher opted to start by rebuking us. The US Secretary of State told Rabin he found it very disruptive and hindering to his work that every time he came to Syria to present the Israeli position, he would discover it was already appearing in the press.

These leaks drove Rabin out of his mind as well. Rabin was a very discreet man and very aware of the damage caused by leaks in such sensitive matters. For this reason, he would communicate the truly significant messages only to leaders such as Mubarak, Clinton, Hussein and Christopher himself in very limited forums. When the meetings with these people included a broader audience, it was only to fulfill a formal obligation, and nothing really important was said.

Following the rebuke, Christopher turned to Rabin, Peres and me, and told us that in this meeting Assad had done something he had never done before: he had read his speech from the paper rather than speaking freely. This signaled the significance Assad had attached to what he had said, his wish to be very accurate and his serious attitude towards Rabin's ideas.

All attendees, including Rabin, Peres and myself, listened with the utmost anticipation and concentration to Christopher due to the importance of what he was saying, and also because it was often very difficult to understand his explanations. His English was complex, he had a tendency to swallow words, and as a lawyer by profession, his language was very legalistic in nature. Christopher used to start at some point, assuming we already understood the background, while we could not understand where this was coming from and how it belonged. However, the most fundamental thing that made it difficult to understand him was that he was not always completely aware of all the details, at least not at the level of the head of the peace talks in the State Department, Dennis Ross, who was part of Christopher's entourage. Ross was knowledgeable in the minutiae of details and the history of negotiations since the days of Madrid, and since he understood our plight, he would gently come to our aid unprompted, and was often quick to answer questions we directed to Christopher before the latter had a chance to answer.

Christopher began to present Damascus' position, as it was told to him by the Syrians.

Assad had agreed that the security arrangements had to ensure the following: a) prevent a surprise attack; b) prevent misunderstandings between the parties, which could lead to a deterioration towards hostilities.

Assad spoke of guarantees between the two sides that would allow them to realize their right to self-defense. He also accepted the idea that after peace would be established there would be a joint Syrian-Israeli committee to oversee the agreement, an emergency phone line between the two sides, as well as joint and international patrols along the border, in which the United States would participate. Assad also accepted the principle of diluted areas where only limited military forces could be deployed.

Assad realized that public diplomacy would be required, during which the Syrian and Israeli public would have to be convinced to accept the components of peace, but said that before this, there needed to be significant progress in the peace process.

Assad demanded a full withdrawal from the Golan Heights, including the uprooting of all Israeli settlements. He asked that the timetable for the withdrawal end six months after signing the agreement, in contrast to Rabin's proposal of five years. Assad demanded that the withdrawal be completed in a single step, as opposed to Rabin's proposal of three stages.

Assad expressed his satisfaction with the approach of Israel regarding the reciprocity of security arrangements, although he thought there was no need for early-warning stations. He wanted peace to be based on friendly relations between the peoples.

Referring to the components of normalization in peaceful relations, Assad said that the two sides would decide on public diplomacy that would take place in parallel to progress in the covert channel. Regarding statements in support of peace, Assad said he had already made many statements on the subject, all of which together weigh more than the statements made by Israel.

Assad promised that after signing the peace agreement, Syria would cease its warfare against the State of Israel and respect the territorial sovereignty of Israel. Additionally, Syria would participate in the multilateral talks, stop the secondary and tertiary boycott against Israel but not the direct boycott. This boycott would be lifted only after Israel would complete its withdrawal from the Golan Heights, up to the border as it was on June 4, 1967.

Christopher continued his report stating that Assad had agreed that after all these steps had been completed, both sides would declare diplomatic relations, and tourists would be permitted to visit each country under its respective rules and laws in order to avoid adverse effects.

Exchange of ambassadors would only take place after the peace treaties would be signed with Syria, Jordan and Lebanon. At that time, the Palestinians had already decided to move forward in the peace process independently and had already signed the Declaration of Principles, and hence Assad refrained from making progress in the talks with the Palestinians a condition.

Christopher continued to state that when he had brought up the issue of operational headquarters of terrorist organizations located in Damascus, and violations of the understandings in Lebanon by Hezbollah, Assad had said that Syria was ready to negotiate an agreement in which neither side would allow fire towards the communities of the other.

Christopher said he could tell that this time Assad could see a real start of negotiations, and noted that it was the first time he had heard the Syrians discuss the essential issues in detail rather than in vague terms.

Christopher had estimated that despite the large gaps between the Israeli and Syrian positions, there were still some flexible areas that could be used to bridge these matters. In regards to the withdrawal stages, Christopher thought that although Assad spoke of one stage and we of three, an agreement could still be reached. Regarding the withdrawal timetable, Christopher estimated that despite the fact that Assad spoke of six months and we spoke of five years, Assad understood that a period of half a year did not make sense, and that he would be willing to compromise on that.

Regarding the components of peace, Christopher found many points of similarity between us and the Syrians, the main difference between the two approaches being the application of these components over time.

Christopher did not mention fully demilitarized zones near the border line, after which there would only be areas of diluted military presence, but noted that Assad had expressed a willingness for restricted areas on the condition that they would continue on the Israeli side of the border as well.

Chapter 12

"The Deposit"

One of the most significant points that appeared in Christopher's message from Assad was of course the matter of the return of the Golan Heights. Throughout his election campaign, Rabin spoke of the need for painful compromises in the West Bank and made it clear that territories would have to be returned. However, when it came to the Golan Heights, he said that the settlements situated there should be strengthened and must not be abandoned. Rabin had hinted there might be compromises in the Golan, but not deep and significant ones. However, he later came to recognize that without a significant Israeli withdrawal **"in** the Golan Heights, not **from** the Golan Heights", as he was careful to point out, peace could not be achieved. His approach was to try to reach an agreement with Syria in which the IDF would remain deployed on the western edge of the Golan Heights – meaning, evacuating most of the Golan but with continued Israeli presence in the western area.

At first, Rabin spoke of some compromises, such as demilitarized zones, but without uprooting Israeli settlements from the peninsula. However, he later reached the conclusion that peace with Syria would require a very deep territorial compromise. I think what made him change his mind was the transition he made from the mindset of the Six Day War Chief of Staff, who remembered the high military significance of the Golan Heights and how important it was to conquer it, to the perspective of a prime minister and statesman. He now reached the conclusion that true peace with Syria was worth even the price of a deep withdrawal in the Golan Heights.

An example of these differences in perspectives, between the narrow military one and the broad political point of view, could also be seen in one of the meetings between Christopher and the then Chief of Staff Ehud Barak, who would later become Prime Minister of Israel and try in his own way to advance the peace process with Syria. In those days, while still in uniform and responsible solely for the military needs, Barak was careful to recommend that the Golan Heights remain under Israeli control.

"As Chief Of Staff, I need the Golan as leeway to block a Syrian surprise attack, and as a grip from which to perform a counterattack in case the situation deteriorates," Barak told Christopher.

Once this conceptual change had gradually seeped into Rabin's consciousness, he began to formulate an approach wherein he was willing to withdraw deep into the Golan Heights, but without leaving it completely, i.e., to keep IDF forces deployed on top of the western heights. Rabin believed that every meter Israel evacuates in the Golan Heights had to become a demilitarized zone, clear of the Syrian Army.

Rabin even considered the possibility of leaving Israeli communities as they were, including their inhabitants, even if the land would be returned to Syrian sovereignty. Rabin wanted to allow Israeli citizens who wished to do so to continue living in the Golan Heights with Israeli citizenship and under Syrian sovereignty. However, later negotiations made it clear that the

Syrians categorically rejected the notion of any Israeli presence, military or civilian, in the Golan Heights.

Since his election campaign, Rabin had only mentioned withdrawal in the West Bank, and not the Golan Heights. Furthermore, it was made clear to him throughout negotiations with Syria that it would be impossible to achieve peace with the Syrians without a very deep withdrawal from large parts, if not the entirety of the Golan Heights. Therefore, Rabin announced that if a peace treaty were to be achieved with Syria, it would need to be approved by means of a referendum.

Rabin attributed great significance to a leader's reliability, and felt a strong moral obligation to turn to the public to request its approval for an act that was contrary to what had been presented during the election campaign.

At the same time, signs began to appear that suggested Assad was also starting to prepare his own people for peace, as could be seen in banners set in the street and various statements. Assad realized that he could not bring about a complete psychological reversal of his people's opinion of Israel without gradually preparing the population beforehand. It should be remembered that for many years, the Syrian regime taught its subjects to hate the State of Israel, which was presented as the ultimate enemy that had to be eradicated. Now public opinion had to be accustomed to the idea that Syria was discussing peace with this monstrous enemy.

Assad told the American delegates that when he takes such steps, he has no intention of going back.

Rabin thought Assad was a leader who stood behind his words, who complies with the obligations he takes upon himself and with whom a lasting agreement could be reached. This feeling was expressed in mutual messages being transferred through the Americans, in which Rabin expressed his belief that Assad was a leader who could be trusted, while Assad said he appreciated Rabin and saw him as a brave man.

Dennis Ross believed Assad's activities among his people stemmed from his notice of Rabin's very serious attitude towards the peace process, which led him to respond seriously as well.

However, every time we started to discuss the details, it became clear that the gaps between Syria and Israel were still very large on two major issues: the depth of the withdrawal and the timetable.

Rabin told the Americans that finalizing peace with Egypt lasted more than four years from the moment the treaty had been signed until the day the withdrawal was complete. In the background, was Sadat's visit to Jerusalem, a visit that broke the wall of the Israeli public's psychological fear of peace with Egypt. Assad responded that the Egyptian model was completely unsuitable for Syria, and in his opinion was unsuitable for Egypt as well, as could be witnessed by the fact that Sadat did not properly prepare the Egyptian public for peace and was subsequently murdered. Assad explained that he had to reach an agreement that he could defend within the Syrian public. When we talked about our need for a gesture from him, so that we could prepare public opinion in Israel, Assad replied that there was also public opinion in Syria.

However, it turned out that nevertheless, there was a certain warming in the atmosphere, and even if it was only semantic, Assad proceeded to declare his willingness to establish normal peaceful relations with Israel during his meeting with Clinton in Geneva in January 1994.

After this declaration, the Americans kept hopping between Damascus and Jerusalem and rounds of talks between the Israeli delegation headed by Ambassador Itamar Rabinovich and the Syrian delegation headed by Ambassador Muaffaq Allaf, in which almost nothing happened.

Rabin wanted to bring a new momentum to the process and began to stress the need for direct meetings. He suggested two possibilities: establishing a secret direct channel between Assad and himself or their representatives, or meetings between military personnel to discuss security arrangements. The idea behind this proposal was that by discussing security issues, we could currently evade the political questions, such as where the border will be drawn and the duration of the withdrawal, issues that served as stumbling blocks to progress whenever they were raised. We had a feeling that a meeting between military personnel would add meaningful new momentum to the process, and estimated that if during the military meetings we could reach a breakthrough - this would affect the progress of the peace process.

Assad refused these proposals for a long time, and asked to continue in the same pattern. However, at some point he agreed to send the Syrian Chief of Staff Gen. Hikmat Shihabi, who in the Syrian hierarchy served not only as chief of staff but also as the second highest ranking government official, to a meeting with his Israeli counterpart Ehud Barak.

Rabin decided that I would join Chief of Staff Ehud Barak in the meeting with his Syrian counterpart, and we both began to prepare for the meeting that was to take place in Washington.

The Blair House is the official guest house of the President of the United States in Washington, and is a quintessential part of the American establishment. Every corner of the house underscores how deeply this establishment respects itself and its guests. The interior design combines the warm and inviting with the official and binding, as is expressed in symbols of government, heavy wooden furniture and portraits of past leaders gloriously hung up on the walls. Formal elegance and dignity are used interchangeably, while constantly reminding its guests of US history and the obligation to it.

The meeting between the Israeli and Syrian chiefs of staff, scheduled to take place in December 1994, was put into motion much earlier, far away from the peaceful scenery that surrounds the Blair House. It happened in the simmering Middle East, in the wood-paneled room of Israeli Prime Minister Yitzhak Rabin in his office in Jerusalem.

During the long period in which Assad insisted on continuing the futile rounds of talks between Syrian and Israeli delegations, Christopher reported, towards the end of 1994, that Assad had "responded positively" to some of Rabin's public statements on the matter of peace with Syria.

This meeting at Rabin's office was also attended by Itamar Rabinovich, the Secretary of State, and Dennis Ross, who stressed that he "must bring something concrete" to his next meeting with Assad.

"This is a self-contained circle, and we are constantly going and coming back to the same place," said Christopher, and continued to appeal to Rabin, "You coined the expression that 'the depth of withdrawal will be equal to the depth of peace.' The Syrians insist on a full withdrawal, and I would like to know if I am able to tell them that in the case of full peace, the withdrawal will also be a full one?"

Rabin told me in detail about the contents of this meeting. He understood that when the Syrians spoke of a full withdrawal, they meant withdrawal to the border as it was on June 4, 1967, which means a retreat to the Jordan River and the east side of the Sea of Galilee, and in effect - a withdrawal from the entire Golan Heights.

Following relentless pressure on Rabin by the Americans in their attempt to understand what his maximal meaning for the term 'withdrawal' was, and the farthest he would go if he were offered a "comprehensive peace agreement" with Syria, which he was striving to reach, Rabin decided to reveal his cards to the Americans.

Rabin began by emphasizing to Christopher, "I'm going to tell you something that I do not authorize you to tell the Syrians. I trust you with this information, which I give to you as a deposit to prove to you that my intentions are serious. I will give you a picture of the limits of the political courtyard in which I am willing to act."

Rabin knew that the territorial card, that is to say the withdrawal, was the most important card in the negotiations, and with regard to the Syrians, he wanted to keep it very close to his chest. At this point, he did not want to give them the idea that he was willing to consider, or even come close to considering, the Syrian demand for withdrawal to the 1967 lines, without receiving proper compensation from them first. So he again said to Christopher that his words were meant for American ears only.

Then everyone in the room heard what was later known as the "deposit" or the "pocket", because Rabin was promised it would remain strictly in Christopher's pocket, and would not be passed on under any circumstances to the Syrians as an Israeli initiative.

Rabin went on to say, "If all of Israel's needs are met in the negotiations, Israel will withdraw to the June 4, 1967 lines."

This announcement by Rabin was extremely dramatic. By making it, Rabin, in effect, became the first prime minister since 1967 to voice an agreement to discuss a withdrawal in the north in general, and particularly the willingness to withdraw from the entire Golan Heights, up to the border of June 4, 1967, the border that had existed on the eve of the Six-Day War.

However, Rabin was careful to attach two very important conditions to this statement. The first condition was to keep power in his hands in determining the needs of Israel. The second condition was to carefully point out to the Americans that this information was for their ears only. One should note the essential distinction that Rabin was careful to make in his words, namely the distinction between "I am willing to withdraw", and, "I would be willing to withdraw only if Israel's needs are met". These needs were to be defined by Israel, and Israel would be the one to determine whether they were fully met. Rabin, who was a very careful and deliberate person, gave the Americans a very meaningful and important statement, but made sure to dress it immediately in a belt and suspenders. Rabin was not expressing consent to withdraw from the Golan Heights, but making an explicit provision that this type of withdrawal would be possible only if the needs of Israel were met in full, and if they were not - there would be no withdrawal. When Rabin spoke of the needs of the State of Israel, he was referring to the security needs, intelligence, water needs, nature of peace and normalization, confidence-building measures and a timetable for the combination of withdrawal and normalization.

This statement was uttered by Rabin after he had given the matter much time, thought, deliberation and consultation, and as always examined it and analyzed it at every angle.

The background for this statement was that Rabin was very determined to try to bring an end to the bloodshed. He quickly learned that for the Syrians, the key to peace with Israel was an Israeli withdrawal from the Golan Heights. Rabin had deliberated much regarding the depth of the withdrawal, and had even entertained the notion that it would be possible to leave IDF forces on the western cliff of the Golan Heights. But having learned from the Americans that Assad viewed the transfer of the entire Golan Heights to Syrian sovereignty as a deal-breaker under any circumstances, Rabin decided to skip past this hurdle.

Those were days in which progress was being made in negotiations with Jordan and intensive negotiations with the Palestinian Authority. On the other hand, Hezbollah terrorism was running rampant in the north, hitting Israeli troops in Lebanese territory and civilians in Israel. In Judea and Samaria, Hamas and Islamic Jihad's terrorism was also running amok. I believe that all of these occurrences taking place in the background made it clear to Rabin that he had to hurry to bring the bloodshed to an end, even at the cost of painful concessions in the Golan Heights, Judea and Samaria and Gaza. Thus, he was willing to take risks which he saw as calculated, rather than dangerous gambles.

This was a gradual process for Rabin, and it is difficult to pinpoint one precise turning point. He pondered the matter for a very long time. He asked experts, studied the consequences of military withdrawal from the Golan Heights, and also considered other alternatives. Rabin was a very cautious person, and anything that did not require reaching a quick decision, was decided very slowly. Rabin was an introvert, so one could not notice any special emotionality about him around reaching this decision. Before establishing his position - he did not express it. Ehud Barak always used to open discussions with the words, "This is my opinion ..." and after he finished presenting his opinion, he would say, "and now I want to hear you." Rabin was the exact opposite: he always opened discussions by presenting the problem, and immediately let other people talk. I was often moved by his patience as he sat there listening to each and every one. Barak, in contrast, was impatient, and used to hasten people to finish talking.

At that time, when I would enter Rabin's room on occasion, I would find him sitting in his chair, thinking, and smoking incessantly in short and quick puffs. It was a sign that he was going through some kind of process that was disturbing and tormenting him.

Even in his definitions we can see steps he went through on the way to the "deposit": first, he said that the depth of withdrawal would be equal to the depth of peace. Then he began to talk about withdrawal from the Golan Heights, including the possibility of a very deep withdrawal in exchange for full peace, but he was not willing to define the boundary to which Israel would withdraw its forces. Rabin always maintained that the position of the border between Israel and Syria would be decided by the leaders of the two countries. In the next stage, he made it clear to the Americans and all foreign leaders with whom he met that there was only one border was recognized by the international community, and that was the international border defined by the powers in 1923, in the agreement between Britain, which ruled Palestine at the time, and France, which controlled Syria. This line was better for Israel than the one from June 4, 1967, because it left the east bank of the Jordan River in Israeli hands, and passed 10 meters east of the northeast bank of the Sea of Galilee, thus leaving the whole of the Sea under Israeli sovereignty. Only in later stages, around July 1994, when Christopher told Rabin that there was no chance that Assad would agree to the international border, did Rabin agree that the term 'full withdrawal from the Golan Heights' could also mean withdrawal to the border as it was on June 4, 1967.

I thought that since the deposit was conditional, it retained all the degrees of freedom and flexibility required to decide whether all of our needs in terms of normalization, timetables, security arrangements, water, etc. had been answered, before we would consent to a withdrawal from the Golan Heights.

The "deposit" was, in fact, a conditional willingness, rather than a conditional obligation, and its purpose was to try to understand, through the Americans, what Assad would be willing to do and where he would agree to concede if Israel agreed to withdraw from the Golan Heights. In any case, it was clear that Rabin gave it to the Americans without any intention of them passing it on to Assad. They could only use it as a form of American examination of such a scenario, and under no circumstances as a statement made by Rabin.

However, sometime later we began to realize the possibility that Christopher, contrary to his promise, had not kept this statement as a deposit entrusted to him, and to him alone. Instead, he had passed a variant of it on to the Syrians by telling them that the US understood that if all the requirements of the State of Israel would be met, Israel would withdraw to the 1967 borders.

We discovered this after we heard about a letter Christopher was about to send to Assad, stating among other things that the Americans believed that Israel would withdraw to 1967 lines if all its needs would be fulfilled. We knew that if Assad were to receive such a letter, he would realize that the Americans would not have reached such an assessment if it were ungrounded and without hearing it from Rabin beforehand.

It is true that at one stage, after the "deposit" was given, and following Christopher's repeated pleading to transfer the contents of the deposit to the Syrians in the form of an "American assessment," Rabin agreed to let the Americans inform the Syrians of an American assessment. This assessment was to the effect that if Israel's demands were satisfied in terms of security arrangements and water, as well as the contents of peace and normalization and timetables, Israel would consider, among others, the possibility that the final border would be that of June 4, 1967. However, as mentioned, that was not what Christopher did.

When Rabin learned about the letter Christopher intended to send, he was very angry, and an angry phone call to Christopher prevented it from being sent. In another telephone call, at a later time, I heard Rabin repeat to Christopher, "I remind you again that I said what I said under very clear conditions. I did not commit to withdraw to the 1967 borders, but presented it as an explicit condition that does not stand by itself, but depends on the fact that all of Israel's needs will be met, and in any case, these things were intended for your ears only."

However, we believed that even though Christopher did not send the letter, he conveyed the message to Assad orally. Looking back, considering that both Hafez Assad, as well as his son and successor as President of Syria, Bashar Assad, still regularly mention the "deposit", I believe that the message was passed on to the Syrians in contrast to what was agreed upon with us. I further believe that the Syrians adopted only half of the statement, decided that Rabin had committed to a full withdrawal from the Golan Heights, and forgot that it had been conditional, and that they were to fulfill Israel's needs as a prerequisite for a possible withdrawal to the 1967 lines. The Syrians decided that the border Rabin had allegedly committed to was the June 4, 1967 border, and since then they demanded in every meeting with us that Israel commit to withdraw to this line at the start of negotiations.

Syria's attitude had been the main cause of dispute between Israel and Syria, and had raised many difficulties and problems during Rabin's tenure and later during Barak's. The Syrians made it clear in every meeting that Israel had to commit to a withdrawal to the 1967 lines first and foremost, and then they would be willing to discuss other issues such as security arrangements, timetables, normalization, and the nature of peace.

In light of all this, Rabin prepared Barak and me for the meetings with the Syrians in Washington. He made sure to emphasize to us that our mandate was to talk only about the security arrangements.

I wanted to understand if Rabin saw a connection between the border and security arrangements, i.e. - if security arrangements would change if the border line moved. My question implied a situation in which the border would pass, hypothetically, through the middle of the Golan Heights, and in this scenario, there would be demilitarized zones devoid of military presence on the Israeli side and on the Syrian side. However, in the event of a full withdrawal from the Golan Heights, the future borders would pass along the Jordan River, and the reciprocal nature of the demilitarized zones on both sides would become problematic. This is because Israeli settlements are located on the Israeli side of the Jordan River, and the army should protect them and act as a buffer between them and the border.

To that Rabin replied, "If we need to draw a line during the talks for illustrative purposes and discuss security arrangements with respect to that line, you will outline two options. One line that passes through the Golan Heights so that the IDF holds the western part of the plateau and controls the Golan Heights cliffs, and a second line drawn on the slopes of the Golan Heights without any precise definition."

This appeared to be a statement of sorts, but all Rabin meant at that moment was that he did not want us to discuss the issue of the border's location, and he did not want the dealing with this issue to prevent the development of a discussion on security arrangements, which was the agenda for the meeting with the Syrians. The solution Rabin found contained the Syrian approach of withdrawal from the Golan Heights as an illustration, while in the same breath we were to discuss a border that passes through the middle of the Golan Heights.

Rabin made sure to keep all these things confidential as he did not want to cause much ado about nothing. Rabin was well aware of his wording and the conditioning of the "deposit", but he was hesitant to make them public because he wished to avoid the possibility of political opposition elements using only the parts of his statement that would serve their interests, while failing to mention the conditions he had set. Even without revealing the "deposit" and its contents, his opponents were frequently attacking him for his statement that "the depth of the withdrawal will be equal to the depth of peace."

Rabin was so secretive about the matter, that when Shimon Peres was appointed Prime Minister after Rabin's assassination, he first found out about it via the overviews he received from Itamar Rabinovich and myself regarding the progress in negotiations with the Syrians.

During the updates on the negotiations with the Syrians that Peres received from the Americans, they tried to sell him the notion that there had been, in fact, an Israeli commitment to withdraw to the June 4, 1967 border, and that was also Syria's understanding. However, I made it clear, time and again, that there had been no talk of an agreement or commitment, but a very clear and unequivocal condition, stating that Israel would not agree to withdraw from the Golan Heights if all its needs were not met.

This confidentiality also accompanied the preparations made by Barak and me to meet with the Syrian Chief of Staff. The meeting with Chief of Staff Shihabi, on November 1994, began a few days earlier as far as we were concerned, in an attempt to reshape the appearances of Shihabi's counterpart - Israeli Chief of Staff Ehud Barak, and mine.

To ensure that the meeting not be revealed, Rabin asked us to leave the country covertly, which required us to use costumes and alter our appearance. The secretive nature of the talks was due to Syrian demand. They threatened that if news of the meetings became known, they would cancel them. However, secrecy was very important to Rabin as well. He wanted to avoid creating a false impression that a treaty between Israel and Syria was about to be signed at a time when a political majority for it was far from certain. If information regarding the meeting was revealed it could thwart any attempt to advance the negotiations between Israel and Syria, due to the discussions and controversies that were expected to develop within the Israeli public. Rabin also wanted to save the Chief of Staff Ehud Barak the need to answer questions from members of the Knesset Foreign Affairs and Defense Committee, and thus prevent giving opposition Knesset members information he did not want them to possess.

We knew that if the Israeli Chief of Staff and Military Secretary to the Prime Minister would be seen together in airports and boarding transatlantic flights, it would raise interest, be leaked and lead to the publication of damaging information that could undermine the intended meeting. In retrospect, we discovered that despite our best efforts to mask our appearances and keep the meetings confidential, their existence was revealed immediately after the meeting on December 21, when the Syrian news agency in Damascus reported a meeting between Syrian and Israeli ambassadors in Washington, in which "military experts" had participated. In late December, the news agency had already confirmed that these "military experts" were Barak, Yatom and Shihabi.

However, a few days before the Syrian leak, on our way from Israel to the meeting in Washington, we were still doing our best to avoid exposure, and we left the country dressed up - wearing wigs and thick-framed glasses.

When I looked into the mirror for the first time after wearing the wig and putting on the glasses, I could hardly recognize myself. The first time that Barak and I saw each other after our revolutionary makeovers, we were seized by huge bursts of laughter. I started to laugh because the person before me was actually Esther, Ehud Barak's mother. Ehud, wearing a wig, looked exactly like his mother! It took us hours to calm down and get used to it. However, that was not the only problem with the wig that had landed on my head. Unfortunately, the material out of which the wig was made caused me to experience serious allergic reactions, and throughout the long journey designed to obscure the final destination, which began in Tel Aviv, continued to Paris and ended in Washington, I suffered from watery eyes, a running nose and a constantly itching scalp.

The flight on board the Concord airplane from Paris to Washington shortened the duration of the journey. We arrived at Washington in the evening, and Itamar Rabinovich, who was in on the secret, picked us up in his car and took us to a hotel in a quiet and humble district of Washington. The journey came to an end, and finally I was relieved I could take off the itchy wig. Each of us turned to his room to prepare for the meeting that was to take place the following day in two stages: an initial meeting with the Syrian ambassador in Washington, Walid Muallem (currently the Foreign Minister of Syria), and then a meeting with the Syrian Chief of Staff Shihabi. Barak and I arranged to meet in the morning in the hotel gym and we bade each other good night.

As agreed, at six in the morning, I stood in the gym wearing my athletic gear and wig. Sometime later, while I was in the middle of training on the treadmill, running and panting, sweat pouring off me and the wig on my head wreaking havoc on my body, I heard Barak's familiar whistle approaching my way from the hallway. I looked at him and my heart missed a beat: he was without his wig!

I told him, "Ehud, are you crazy?! All the way here we suffered and ached for nothing, you will be recognized in a second." Yet Barak, who was supposed to climb the treadmill next to mine, uttered at me, "Forget about it, who around here is going to recognize me?" He lightheartedly passed by the treadmill and proceeded in a cheerful skip towards the hot tub.

Chapter 13

"Not a Single Inch"

Later that morning, Itamar took us to the Blair House, and once we entered, Dennis Ross and Martin Indyk erupted with thundering laughter and could not relax even after many minutes. Only removing the wigs from our scalps succeeded in calming us down.

In the room where the meeting was to be held, all its participants gathered: on the Israeli side - the Israeli ambassador to Washington, Itamar Rabinovich, Chief of Staff Ehud Barak and myself. The Americans were Dennis Ross and Martin Indyk, and from the Syrian side appeared in splendid isolation Rabinowitz's counterpart, the Syrian ambassador to Washington, Walid Muallem.

Barak and I knew we were standing on the brink of an important landmark and felt the weight of responsibility assigned to us. We realized that a meeting of this kind could end with the process getting a running start, or put an end to it right there and then.

We felt great curiosity, mixed with uncertainties regarding the Syrian response. We could not avoid the excitement and curiosity that came with the first face-to-face meeting with a Syrian representative. Until that day, I had seen Syrians only through military binoculars. This new situation of being in their company in the same room, around a formal and ceremonious negotiation table, was one I found very appealing, intriguing, challenging, and exciting.

Muallem began by saying that he was pleased to see in front of him two brilliant generals dressed as diplomats. "I hope this is a good sign, that will make you think as diplomats as well," added Muallem, and I wondered if that was what he would have said if he had seen us a few minutes earlier, still donning wigs.

"If time will allow for it, maybe we'll reach an agreement," said Muallem, adding, "When Assad says Syria sees peace as a preferred strategic alternative, he means it. Assad understands that peace is a positive development for future generations, and together with you, we want to change the situation from war to peace."

In that room, there was a feeling that we were in the midst of a historic moment. We knew that this meeting was essentially a preparatory meeting for the meeting with the Syrian Chief of Staff Shihabi. This was to be the first meeting between the two chiefs of staff in the history of negotiations between Israel and Syria.

I felt that we were approaching the moment of truth, and that the talks with the Syrians were finally getting on a track in which we could seriously examine the extent of the gaps between us, as well as the chance to bridge them. I felt Assad's decision to send his Chief of Staff to meet with us meant that he really intended to reach an agreement. Shihabi had already served as the Syrian army's Chief of Staff for twenty years, and was considered the second most important man in Syrian leadership immediately after Assad.

A mix of hope for peace stood in the room, along with the understanding that it would not be easy.

From his body language and facial expressions, it was clear that Walid Muallem was nervous and excited. He read his words from the writing in Arabic, and they were translated by Assad's personal interpreter, Bouthaina Shaaban.

Muallem said that those who had followed the process since the days of Madrid could see that Syria had come a long way. He said that the peace agreement had to deal with four issues: schedules, line of retreat, security arrangements and normalization.

"Today we will focus on discussions of the security element and maybe from there we can reach a breakthrough in the other elements," said Muallem.

"Security arrangements," continued Muallem, "should prevent incidents between Syrian and Israeli forces that will be deployed along the border that will be determined, and they must ensure the prevention of a surprise attack by one side against the other. The security arrangements should respect the sovereignty of both parties, and therefore, they must be mutual and equal. Demilitarized zones on both sides of the border will be of the same dimensions."

It was clear that Muallem's basis for discussion was an assertion that the Israeli withdrawal line would be the line of June 4, 1967, even if he had not stated so explicitly.

Barak began to reply, opting to play on Muallem's patriotic spirit: "We are very respectful of the Syrians, their soldiers, their commanders and their leadership," said Barak. "Your leadership, professionalism and courage can be seen from the level of platoon commander to President Assad. Your president is highly appreciated in Israel and considered one of the most important leaders in the Middle East. He was a tough opponent in the war, and we take into account that he will be a tough opponent during negotiations as well. We see President Assad as an honest man who honors his word." Barak noted that the border in the Golan Heights is the quietest border of Israel, thanks to the Syrian commitment and leader who gave his word and honored it. He added that in all the intelligence assessments the IDF delivered to Israeli leadership regarding Assad, these things were always mentioned. Muallem, who remembered that Barak was formerly the Head of Military Intelligence, could appreciate these words.

"Danny and I have served in the army for a long time, and we have dedicated a considerable amount of time to thinking how to defeat the Syrians on the battlefield," continued Barak. "Now it seems to us that after so many years of our lives which we have devoted to security and war, the time has come for a peace of the brave between the Syrians and ourselves.

"I do not know if or when we will achieve peace. It depends very much on those sitting around this table. We can have a major impact on the decision-making process in the way we work out the details between us and the recommendations we give to our leaders," Barak said, noting that it would be impossible to imagine stability in the Middle East without peace with Syria.

The meeting, which ended that evening, continued the next morning, with Barak opening the discussion this time by speaking of the important need to reduce the possibility of a surprise attack to zero. Barak explained that Israel needs a 48-hour warning to recruit its reserve forces, noting it has to be accurate and effective, in any season and any weather, around the clock and at any time.

Barak's statement was in reference to things that had previously been told by the Syrians to the Americans, to the effect that in the age of airplanes and satellites, Israel does not need a warning system based on a ground station. Our counter-argument was always that the weather conditions in the Golan Heights make these measures entirely unsatisfactory.

Barak explained that security arrangements were important in order to reduce the incentive to launch a full-scale or partial attack, even if it would not be a surprise attack. According to Barak, stable demilitarized zones would place the forces far away from each other, prevent any possibility of friction, and reduce the chance of conflict starting. "Security arrangements," said Barak, "are designed to ensure that if a crisis occurs it does not lead to attack, and early-warning stations are meant to prevent a surprise attack or military clashes of any kind. Furthermore, we must avoid a situation that will lead to the other side taking counter-steps that could lead to deterioration. This, for example, is what had happened during the proceedings prior to the Six-Day War, when Egypt closed the Straits of Tiran and declared high military alert, which forced Israel to mobilize its army, and the rest is history."

Barak explained that the bulk of our ground forces consisted of reserve troops, whose enlistment paralyzes day-to-day life in the country. He added that we should reach a state of affairs in which situations that raise tensions and force us to recruit reserves, despite the existence of peace, will not occur.

"Such situations," said Barak, "could lead to a crisis without a single bullet being fired. Hence it is important that your forces be deep in Syrian territory and that the security arrangements be sufficient to remove all concerns from our minds."

Another element Barak discussed, in addition to the demilitarized zones, was diluted Syrian and Israeli forces on both sides of the border. Dilution, as was presented by Barak, was to be mutual but not equal. This concept was derived from Israel's narrow geographical layout. Barak explained that if we were to withdraw from the Golan Heights, and the Syrians were to dominate the cliff, we would have then significantly weakened our ability to protect the heart of the country. Therefore, we would require security arrangements to compensate us for the loss of a strategic asset. Israel would be taking great risks and must ensure that it would still able to defend itself in light of these risks.

On the issue of early warning, our position was that we needed early-warning stations in the Golan Heights, and that we would have to continue holding the one on Mt. Hermon. In the interest of reciprocity, we offered in exchange that the Syrians place their own warning station in the Galilee.

Another component in the security arrangements referred to verification, inspection and observers. We demanded to establish teams of observers composed of Syrian, Israeli and US representatives who would engage in supervision and control. In addition, we asked for a US observer force, to be deployed between the two armies, and remote supervision and observation via cameras.

In light of the struggle taking place at that time between Iraq and the international community in regards to the latter's demand to station observers and cameras in Iraqi military camps and other Iraqi facilities, Muallem barged in and said, "What do you think, that we are Iraqis and need to be inspected by cameras?!"

Barak explained that he was suggesting a specification for the security arrangements, from which the sides could choose what they found agreeable. Barak meant that supervisory arrangements would be such that they could immediately identify cases in which either party had violated the security arrangements and taken action that could deteriorate the situation.

Barak estimated that supervision which would enable the international community to monitor the situation would prevent deterioration, since neither side would want to be accused of breaching the peace.

Barak spelled out some "confidence-building measures" that would give a sense of security and ease of mind between the two parties, and relieve the suspicions that existed between the two countries after so many years of ongoing conflict. The steps included: advance notices of military exercises in order to avoid misunderstandings between the parties, "hot" telephone lines between the parties with a direct line between Israeli commanders and Syrian field officers, placing observers between the two sides, and mutual visits of Israeli officers in Syria and Syrian officers in Israel.

Barak also brought up the issue of Lebanon, stressing that Israel had no territorial claims in Lebanon. He added that we viewed the SLA as Lebanese patriots, for whom an appropriate solution should be found in an agreement between Israel and Lebanon, one that would integrate them into the Lebanese population as a whole, and not just that of southern Lebanon. It should also be ensured that no punitive actions be taken against them, because they are patriots who fought to defend themselves in a war-torn country, and never fought against Lebanon.

So as not to embarrass the Syrian sitting in front of him, Barak referred to the matter of terrorism in gentle terms. "Even if you are not behind Lebanese and Hezbollah terrorism, you have a big impact on the Lebanese government and have the ability to influence it to curb this activity."

Regarding the withdrawal timetable, Barak told Muallem honestly and fairly that we asked the Prime Minister for a longer period of time than was presented to the Syrians by the Americans. "It took us a few days to conquer the Golan Heights, but quite a few years to build our line of defense there," said Barak, adding, "We do not expect to be given ten years to withdraw, but maybe half that time."

Muallem listened attentively to Barak's words, and wrote down every word at breakneck speed without saying a thing. However, his expressions betrayed his emotions. When Barak praised Assad, he nodded in agreement and contentment. When Barak spoke about optical surveillance in emergency arms depots, you could tell he was extremely displeased with the idea and was even insulted by it.

Barak stressed that the dialogue between the two sides should be done in an air of mutual respect and sensitivity of each party to the other party's concerns. For example, Barak began to describe a meeting he had with King Hussein, and the way negotiations with him were handled, but Muallem immediately shushed him and said, "Do not compare us to the Jordanians. In general, the Syrians are not like the rest of the Arabs."

"Assad respects and admires Rabin," continued Muallem and noted, "In fact, Assad has a similar disposition to that of Rabin, and he aspires for a peace of the brave; peace that people will be committed to, that the Syrian people will benefit from and will have an interest in keeping."

At this point, Barak dropped a bombshell inside the room, saying that he was not authorized to negotiate the final borderline, and that this issue would be subject to the statesmens' decisions. He immediately continued by telling Muallem that at the same time, he wants to share with him his professional position, which he had presented to Rabin as a military professional. "I told Rabin," Barak said, "that even if there will be peace with Syria, we prefer that the border will pass in the middle of the Golan Heights, and it should be a minimum distance of at least ten kilometers east of the Jordan River and the Sea of Galilee." It is important to note that this statement by Barak had been agreed upon in advance during the preparation sessions with Rabin.

This information had a noticeably grave impact on Syrian Ambassador Walid Muallem. Hearing it, Muallem was overtaken by the demeanor of one who has a bone lodged in his throat, and while pondering whether to swallow it or spit it out, is in the throes of losing his breath.

"Along this borderline," Barak continued calmly, as if there was no drama unfolding on his Syrian counterpart's face, "I would suggest that our forces be deployed even in peacetime."

Barak explained that in his opinion, to reach zero probability of a surprise attack, regions that the IDF would vacate in the Golan

Heights and other areas east of the current ceasefire line, should be demilitarized.

When Barak introduced this concept regarding the border, he did it because we thought it was right to introduce it as a starting point. We did not estimate that when Assad would hear it he would be appalled by the thought that Israel demanded he withdraw his forces deeper than their current location, all in order to protect Israel from a surprise attack. It never occurred to us that Assad would subsequently decide to stop the talks.

We all had a chance to hear Muallem's detailed opinion of Barak's proposal in our next meeting. Muallem arrived at the Blair House on the morning of the next day (November 3, 1994), still under the effect of the previous day's meeting, and especially under the influence of the Israeli Chief of Staff's remarks.

This time Muallem opened the meeting, and immediately at its inception he addressed Barak, stating "The meeting yesterday was very important. I appreciate your commitment to peace and your personal effort in presenting the security arrangements. I appreciate the way you prepared the matter, but I admit that trying to understand the logic of your words gave me little sleep last night. "

Thus Muallem joined a long and distinguished line of Israeli politicians and statesmen from around the world, who during their lives had lost many precious hours of sleep trying to understand what Barak was saying.

Muallem went on to say, "You will find it difficult to find a single more optimistic person than myself regarding the chances of peace between Syria and Israel, but I hope my optimism will not vanish after what you presented yesterday. The Syrian position is very far from what you presented, and after I heard it, I am forced to ask myself, are we actually negotiating the transition from a state of war to a state of peace?"

Muallem meant to imply that the security arrangements, as presented by Barak, gave the Syrians the sense that we were trying to prepare for a state of war rather than a peace treaty between the two countries.

Muallem added, "I appreciate what you said about President Assad, Chief of Staff Shihabi, the Deputy Chief of Staff Ali Aslan and the Syrian army. This indicates you possess a very deep understanding of the subject of our military and leadership. For us, as long as leaders like Assad and Rabin are in rule, there is a good chance for peace. And I once again assure you, that when Syria will reach a peace agreement, we will keep our word and we will be bound by it. We have no doubt that Rabin would do the same, and like us - would be committed to every word, whether it is written or not. "

These remarks by Muallem illustrate the extent to which, later on, Rabin's murder struck a fatal blow to the peace process and how great a regional tragedy it was. He was immensely respected by leaders in the region, and time after time it leads me to think that if Rabin were alive, we would have reached peace agreements with Syria and the Palestinians under his leadership, followed by peace agreements with many more Arab and Muslim nations.

Muallem went on to state that the Syrians believed that an agreement with Israel is not something that needs to be hidden. "When we do reach it, we will defend it, we will promote and respect it, and we will act against any country or group attempting to hinder it."

Immediately after these sayings, Muallem made a series of statements that left no room for misunderstanding regarding the most crucial issue for them: "We cannot give up even a single inch of the land that we held on June 4, 1967," he said. "Therefore, we believe that Israel must withdraw to the June 4, 1967 line, and it is my understanding that our negotiations are based on an Israeli withdrawal to this line."

From this we could understand that when the Syrians came to Washington to negotiate with us on security arrangements, they were under the assumption that the debate over the border's location had already been settled, and that there was an understanding and agreement that the line would be the one of June 4, 1967. Apparently, the Americans had given them the impression that this had been accepted by Israel.

Muallem referred to the statement made by Barak about that line needing to pass six to eight miles east of the Jordan River, and once again stressed, "I can understand this notion from your point of view, but as far as Syria is concerned the line is June 1967."

Regarding the security arrangements, Muallem voiced a familiar and tired Syrian argument, which for us was a rhetorical argument that would be repeated over and over again, stating that when peace would be achieved there would be no need for security arrangements and no reason to fear a surprise attack. Muallem explained that there is no law in the world more powerful than equality, and even God had said so. "We must not create a situation where the security of one party comes at the expense of the other's," continued Muallem. "I accept the goal of preventing a surprise attack, but security arrangements are not necessary because peace will mean that there will be no surprise attack, and I accept the goal of preventing conflicts and incidents on a routine basis."

Regarding respecting the sovereignty of each party Muallem said, "I respect your sovereignty and independence, and I do not want the security arrangements to conflict with the sovereignty of any of the parties." Muallem was implying that after Israel withdraws to the 1967 borders, and no longer controls a single square inch of Syrian soil - then Israel will find that Syria is no longer a threat. In this state of affairs, after Israeli withdrawal from the Golan, a pretext for war will cease to exist and there will be no reason for Syria to wish to attack Israel.

Regarding the timetables, Muallem said he was convinced that as military men, we would be able to fulfill any task within a limited timeframe, and that we could influence the politicians to improve the timetable. "Syria needs a short time frame," he explained, "to keep the momentum of peace. And when Assad says he is committed to normalized peaceful relations with Israel - he means it."

Regarding security arrangements, Muallem clarified that they should be mutual and equal, and that he agrees to the principle of demilitarized zones, provided that they are equal in size on both sides.

All zones would start from the border of June 1967, and from there we would examine which restrictions would be imposed on the parties while maintaining the principle of equality.

Muallem stressed, "An attack on Israel by an Arab coalition, as has occurred in the past, will not happen again. You have peace with Egypt and Jordan, and are in the process of creating an agreement with the PLO. Then, when you have an agreement with Syria and Lebanon, the matter of an Arab coalition will become a thing of history. Hence there is also no need for security arrangements against the possibility of attack by such a coalition. "

With regard to our demand for warning stations, Muallem stressed that when the Syrians speak of "complete withdrawal" they mean that no Israeli soldier, citizen or warning station will remain on the Golan Heights. He added that in a state of peace, they will not need any warning station west of the Jordan River, and we will not need warning stations to its east. Muallem also rejected the possibility that we brought up regarding warning stations under US responsibility, saying, "We cannot agree at this point to an American presence."

He also said that if he is asked by Assad for his opinion on this matter, his recommendation would be to delay the decision until relations between Syria and the US are normalized.

"We refrained from internal discussion of bilateral relations between Syria and the United States," added Muallem, "so as not to fuel the Israeli claims alleging that Syria viewed peace primarily as a means to normalize relations between Syria and the United States. So all the Israelis who claim that our entire goal in these negotiations is to improve our relations with the United States, can rest assured."

It should be noted that despite the content of Muallem's remarks, and the disagreement he voiced with most of Barak's statements from the day before, the atmosphere in the room, while formal and correct, was not at all severe. Muallem proved to be an easygoing person, and after he had managed to break free of the tension in meeting the people whom he saw as symbolizing the highest levels of the Israeli military and defense establishment – his frozen face, tense expression and stiff body language eased into a more relaxed demeanor with the occasional smile. Walid Muallem is a short, rotund man, and according to reports is sociable, pleasant and courteous. As the hours passed by, he relaxed, regained his composure, and you could feel the atmosphere in the room turning into one of productivity.

However, the relaxed atmosphere did not impede Muallem's assertiveness and objection to Barak's statements from the previous day. Muallem rejected Barak's suggestion to deploy American observers, explaining that Syria preferred UN observers. "After all, you are aware of the United States Congress' unsympathetic attitude towards us," said Muallem, referring to accusations in Congress that Syria was sponsoring terrorism and human rights violations.

Muallem, who could not ignore Rabin's preference for US observers, said, "I do not rule out the possibility, but I cannot agree to it at this moment, because we must first normalize relations between the United States and Syria. In any case," he added, "I feel that we will reach an agreement on the issue of international observers."

At this, Barak hurriedly asked, "Am I to understand that we will not reach an agreement on all the other elements?"

"I read much about you," said Muallem. "I know you are very intelligent, and are a strategist who is looking for a way to achieve peace, which is why I'm speaking to you fairly. You and General Yatom are very close to the Prime Minister, and if you value the importance of a peace agreement with Syria, I have no doubt that you can influence your leadership."

Regarding the size of the forces on both sides of the border, Muallem explained that although the Syrian army is much greater in terms of soldiers, the Israeli army is far better equipped. He further added that Syria has longer borders than Israel, and said, "We have problems with several neighbors, and so we need a large army. Reducing the size of the forces will not be part of the peace treaty. This can only be an independent Syrian decision."

Muallem addressed confidence-building measures and agreed that they indeed would reduce the suspicion on both sides, but argued that the time to discuss them would come later.

On the issue of Lebanon, and Israel's demand that Syria work to stop the activities of Hezbollah against Israel, Muallem presented the known Syrian thesis, that an agreement between Israel and Lebanon should be negotiated with the Lebanese. He added, "We will be able to help because we believe that peace between Israel and Syria will also promote peace between Israel and Lebanon."

On the issue of terrorism, Muallem said decidedly, "I assure you that no terrorist activity originates in Syria, and as for Lebanon - we do not encourage nor support any terrorist group, although we define them as freedom fighters."

Barak made it clear to Muallem that there is great concern in Israel that Syria is supporting terrorists in Lebanon. Muallem explained, "We estimate that the Lebanese cannot stop Hezbollah, which is why we are so keen to see progress on the Syrian-Israeli track.

"We will not make peace on one front and war on the other. We will not allow any Arab element to affect the peace between Israel and Syria and proudly defend the agreement."

Throughout his remarks, Muallem stressed the vital importance Syria placed on balance, reciprocity and equality in any arrangements we agree upon.

Barak explained to Muallem that this Syrian demand was problematic for Israel, since as he put it, "You have a large country, and we have a small one."

To illustrate this, Barak used the peace treaty with Egypt as an example: "The entire Sinai Peninsula, which is an Egyptian region of vast proportions that goes deep into Egyptian territory, became demilitarized," said Barak. He continued, "While on our side only a small strip, which includes a few kilometers along the border, is demilitarized. With the Egyptians, we reached an agreement which is mutual, but not equal, due to the fact that Egypt's territory is far greater than that of Israel."

Dennis Ross suggested a solution in which the security arrangements would be mutual and equal in nature. This meant that the aim would be that in any place where the arrangements could not be equal, for example due to geographical and topographical conditions, another agreement would have to be found that would maintain mutuality, but not necessarily equality.

Towards the end of the meeting, Muallem summarized his impression of our approach, saying, "I understand you agree to most principles besides that of equality, unless it is formulated as 'equal in nature.' As for the rest of the components, it is my impression that you are willing to discuss the Syrian positions, the relations between the different components, and the possibility to compensate with certain components for a lack in others.

"The most important thing is that both nations have a common goal, namely: to prevent a surprise attack," said Muallem and turned to Barak, "Do you agree with this definition?"

"I agree completely," said Barak, "Except with the matter of equality. Instead of saying we agree to 'equal in nature.' which could lead to mistakes or a misunderstanding, your reports should include the positions we presented."

Therefore it was in our meetings with Muallem that we discussed matters related to the need to reduce the risk of surprise attack to zero, to eliminate the interest to attack and prevent total war, and to prevent daily incidents. We further discussed preventing the possibility of a national-military crisis, such as deterioration caused by unilateral actions (e.g. recruiting reservists), establishing security arrangements that will ensure definite identification of an attempted attack and determining a timetable for redeployment.

Thus ended the talks in the round of meetings between the Syrian ambassador and us, and we began to prepare for the meeting for which we had actually come: the meeting with the Syrian Chief of Staff Hikmat Shihabi.

The meeting with Shihabi was also meant to take place at the Blair House, with the Syrian side represented by Chief of Staff Shihabi, Ambassador Muallem and interpreter Bouthaina Shaaban. The

Israeli representatives were Ambassador Rabinovich, Chief of Staff Barak, Major General Uri Sagi, then the Head of Military Intelligence, and myself.

Even though in the meetings with Syrian Ambassador Muallem there had also been a ceremonious atmosphere, highlighting the size of the occasion, it was clear that the meeting with the Syrian Chief of Staff would raise the threshold of sensitivity, commitment, vigilance and the feeling that a historical event was taking place in the dialogue between Israel and Syria. It was the first time that Israeli representatives would meet with such a highly-ranked representative within the Syrian hierarchy. In those days, Shihabi had already served as Chief of Staff for twenty years, and during those years, he had gained a very strong political position in Syria, and most importantly - was highly appreciated by Assad. All this put much emphasis on the centrality of this meeting in Syrian eyes. In the advance meeting between Dennis Ross and the Syrian Chief of Staff, the latter said, "The fact that I – the Syrian Army's Chief of Staff and a member of the most senior political leadership in Syria - am here, shows that we attach great significance to this meeting." We knew that if Shihabi recommended the continuation of the talks, it would be so.

At the beginning of the meeting, the atmosphere was frozen. Shihabi appeared like us in civilian clothes, including a suit and tie. It was impossible to ignore the strong air of authority that surrounded him and his frozen demeanor, which betrayed none of his emotions.

The Israeli representatives took their place facing the Syrian representatives round the rectangular table, with Americans sitting at both ends of the table. At the outset of the meeting, Barak, famously a big fan of watches, noticed Shihabi was wearing a particularly expensive watch. In an attempt to ease the tension, Barak asked Shihabi which watch he was wearing. Shihabi responded nonchalantly that he did not know, but it was a "perfectly normal" watch. We estimated the watch was worth several dozens of thousands of dollars, while the average monthly wage in Syria at that time amounted to no more than $120.

During the meeting, I noticed Shihabi was listening attentively and intently to Barak, and did not write down a single note during the long time he was talking. I could not help but be impressed by the fact that when he spoke himself, Shihabi presented the Syrian position fluently, clearly and without drawing assistance from any written material. Even when he addressed the points raised by Barak, he did it with sharp precision using nothing but his memory.

The Syrian attitude towards Shihabi served as clear evidence for the latter's seniority. Walid Muallem was not as independent as he had been before. He was hunched over in his chair, and did not dare say a word in front of Shihabi. It was clear that there was only one speaker on the Syrian side.

On the Israeli side, on the other hand, there was much activity: we all took part in the discussion occasionally, and passed notes to Barak with comments and requests to participate in the discussion.

During the meeting the atmosphere warmed slightly, although the meetings with Shihabi did not receive a social nature over time, and he continued to keep his distance. During the meetings, there was an occasional relaxed moment, and even a smile here and there.

With Muallem, who was, in fact, a diplomat, a man of the foreign service, Itamar Rabinovich could sometimes engage in small talk, but with General Shihabi it was impossible.

Warren Christopher opened the meeting and said, "We have great faith that the right people to advance the peace process are in this room. Barak and Shihabi can bring creative solutions regarding the security issues and are committed to peace. You all have the ability to discuss not only the principles but also the details in a pragmatic way, in order to bridge the existing gaps. "

Barak turned to Shihabi and said, "I have been following you for about twelve years, since I was Head of Military Intelligence, and we greatly appreciate you as a professional and as one who is capable of strategic thinking. Both of us have enjoyed the privilege to serve under leaders of high stature. Through our experience in the battlefield, we have learned to respect the courage, toughness and commitment of the Syrian soldiers and officers who fought for their goals. We have fought for over forty-five years and can continue to fight, but we came here to bring an end to wars."

Immediately after this opening statement, Barak began detailing the elements of the security arrangements that were important to us, and stressed that in peacetime the frontline of our forces should be on the Golan Heights, rather than beneath it. "However," Barak was quick to clarify, "It would not be my decision as a military professional, but of the government, and what the government decides we as the military will completely oblige." Barak explained that early-warning capacity was very important to us in light of the bitter memory of the Yom Kippur War, and was a crucial aspect of Israeli leadership's ability to convince the Israeli public that it was taking all the necessary measures to ensure its safety. Barak said that the Israeli public still sees Syria as a significant threat, and finds it difficult to trust. "Hence," said Barak, "it is necessary to see action that convinces the Israeli public of the purity of Syrian intentions."

Regarding limiting Syria's offensive powers (ORBAT), Barak softened our position as was voiced in the meetings with Muallem. This was due to Rabin's understanding that the Syrians had a problem here, because for them, this was a form of Israeli intervention in an internal Syrian decision. Hence, after the meetings with Muallem, he debriefed us to soften our position, and present the matter not as an Israeli demand, but to say that Israel would be happy if Syria were to decide to reduce the size of its army.

Barak said that we limited our order of battle considerably as a result of a decision to balance between building a modern army, investing in training and effective use of budgets.

At this point, Shihabi took the floor. At the onset, he spared himself the words of praise for Barak and Israeli leadership, which Barak had obliged him, and began by saying, "I believe that the meeting today is a very important step in the peace process since Madrid. The strategic alternative that Syria would prefer is to achieve a whole and true peace in the region. I thank you very much for the kind words you said about me, but..." and here he smiled for the first time, "you need to check the reliability of your sources because they have given me too much credit."

Shihabi then abruptly proceeded to address the security arrangements as were presented by the Israelis. At this point, in contrast to Barak, who tried to create a constructive atmosphere, he began repeating the familiar and trite Syrian mantras, explaining that Syria needs more collateral than the Israelis because Syria is the one who has always been the victim of Israeli aggression.

Syria is the one whose soil is occupied by Israel and Syria is the one that suffered many casualties. "However," said Shihabi, "Although Syria needs more security arrangements than Israel, I believe that security arrangements should serve both sides in a common and compelling manner, and after hearing you, I say that the gap between us is very wide."

Shihabi repeated the familiar sayings, to the effect that our security arrangements gave the impression that they were designed not for peace but for future war. "With your suggestions, we cannot achieve peace," he told Barak.

At that Barak could not hold back and interrupted, "I defined goals, such as preventing a surprise attack, and in order to achieve them, we need adequate and reliable security arrangements.

"However, you're going in the opposite direction: you begin with principles such as that Syria will not agree that Israel retain one square centimeter of the territory conquered in 1967, and from there you derive the principle of security arrangements!"

To this Shihabi answered emphatically, "There are preliminary and basic matters from which the discussion must start, and if we do not agree on them, the discussion is moot."

Shihabi proceeded to elaborate that the Syrians did not accept their emergency depots being monitored by cameras, and did not accept early-warning stations being placed in the Golan Heights since Syria was operating under the principle that no Israeli soldier or citizen would remain on the Golan Heights after Israel's withdrawal from it.

Barak answered Shihabi, saying, "You are treating these discussions as a series of steps, where each time we agree on one step, then we move on and continue to talk about the next step, as one would go about building a brick wall, but this is not the right way."

Shihabi was enthralled with Barak's analogy and replied, "It is like construction: the foundation comes first, then the walls, then the roof."

So Barak then began to explain things and articulate them in the manner characteristic of him, "At least at this stage, it is better to look at the process as a painter painting a picture rather than a builder constructing a building," Barak explained. "In the painter's case, the process is one of creation in which you do not know in advance what will come out in the end. In contrast to a building's blueprint, the painter starts with a series of blots that later combine to make a comprehensive picture.

"The process is circular - that is, discussing a topic, exploring, returning and correcting, and so forth."

Barak tried to find out which solution Shihabi was envisioning to Israel's concerns over a surprise attack.

"On that," reiterated Shihabi, "we can exchange views, we can discuss and review. Only after we agree on the principles that will define the nature of the security arrangements can we agree on everything else, and if we do not agree - then everything falls apart.

"Security arrangements have to start from the principle that the demarcation line is that of June 4, 1967, and there must be mutual and equal security arrangements on both its sides, which will not offend the sovereignty of either party."

Barak wanted to make it clear that we do not see the security arrangements as "equal" but as "equal in nature." That is to mean: we accept the principle of reciprocity and will not suggest anything that we will have and you will not, for example an Israeli warning station on the Golan Heights along with a Syrian warning station in the Galilee.

Yet Shihabi was not impressed, and continued to stick to his approach. "As far as we are concerned, all security arrangements must be equal in their geographical dimensions and character."

To illustrate his point and prove that Syria was also taking risks, Shihabi noted that from the border of June 4, 1967, the distance from Tel Aviv was much greater than the distance from Damascus - which in his opinion would give an advantage to Israel.

At this point, I decided to enter the discussion, as I had reached the conclusion that the exchange was moving us farther away from the practical essence of things.

I suggested that each side present its problems, and the other side say how it suggests these problems could be solved, and thus we could relieve each party's worries and concerns from the other.

The meeting was about to end, and Shihabi concluded it by saying that he demanded security arrangements be equal and mutual, and noted that he agreed with Barak that the goals of the security arrangements were to prevent surprise attacks, incidents and conflicts, and of course prevent total war.

Dennis Ross concluded that there was an agreement on the vitality of security arrangements, and proposed to continue the discussions as I suggested.

Representatives of the two delegations went their separate ways until the next day.

The next day, unlike its predecessor, Shihabi came armed with papers, and was careful to read from them. In his opening remarks, he referred to the statement made in Dennis Ross's summary of the previous day, noting that Ross did not mention that the process should begin with principles, and through them to proceed to the objectives agreed upon. Shihabi's remarks were made in a manner that revealed to us that the Syrians had not liked Ross throughout the entire process. Apparently, they were under the impression that he was pro-Israeli.

Shihabi reiterated that security arrangements were more important to Syria than to Israel, because according to him, Syria was the victim of Israeli aggression. I was very surprised to hear him openly say that Israel has the benefit of known and recognized military superiority over Syria. He also noted that the strategic alliance between Israel and the United States greatly strengthens Israel and decisively contributes to its military superiority.

Shihabi's remarks revealed that this was the approach towards Israel in the Arab world as a whole. Therein lies the attitude towards Israel as an almost demonic nation, which does not need any special security arrangements to protect its vital interests, and whose military might is so great that the ones who should be concerned are actually Syria and other Arab countries.

Therefore, according to Shihabi, security arrangements have to start from the border of June 4, 1967. On Barak's proposal that the borderline pass in the middle of the Golan Heights, Shihabi said that such a border cannot ensure security. He stressed that security arrangements be mutual and equal and not conflict with the national sovereignty of any party. Demilitarized zones on both sides and the presence of a multinational force will meet the need to prevent routine incidents. In the diluted zones, military forces would be equal in size.

Once we'd agree on the principles and security arrangements that result from them, we could also agree on day-to-day policies to ensure adequate handling of mishaps and misunderstandings.

Shihabi mentioned the Ceasefire Commission that had been established in 1949 between Israel and Syria, and that would convene during any event that required it to. "I was a brigade commander myself in the central area of the Golan Heights near the *Benot Ya'aqov* bridge between 1966-67, and I took part in such meetings," he added.

"Achieving a just and full peace will ensure that a surprise attack does not occur," said Shihabi and added, "A solution that fails to ensure the rights and dignity of each party will not last. It is Syria's belief that if we sign an agreement in which you will remain on the Golan Heights, it will not last."

More and more I was overtaken by the recognition that as far as the Syrians were concerned, there was no chance to achieve peace without a full Israeli withdrawal from the Golan Heights.

Syria's starting point was that if there is peace, there is no war, literally. Yet for us, in light of historical experience and the problematic nature of our presence in the region in the eyes of many nations, it was difficult to be satisfied with only a peace treaty, and we were committed to ensuring that we would have the ability to protect ourselves if the peace were to collapse. History shows that many wars have erupted between nations that were bound by a peace treaty.

I was impressed by Shihabi's statements and the way he presented them. He was determined, educated, devoted to his principles and he presented all the points eloquently and clearly, although he repeated some familiar 'mantras' from time to time. It seemed that he was careful to present his position in a logical, organized and relaxed way. It was no longer the type of Arab representative we knew from the past – fierce and unreasoning, answering every question with "just because."

Barak said that the Israeli public must receive guarantees and assurances that the State of Israel would be able to defend itself even after making very deep concessions. "Security arrangements are part of a supportive and encouraging environment for a process that will be in its infancy," said Barak.

He went on to explain that Israel's security is based on the combination of a small core of regular army recruits, a larger reservist force and effective warning. "It is in light of this perception that we are required to give answers," concluded Barak.

Shihabi argued that an early-warning station on Syrian land will perpetuate the signs of occupation, which will result in greater sensitivity on the Syrian side and will appear to be a violation of Syrian sovereignty and dignity. Shihabi also opposed joint patrols within the territory. It was interesting to follow and see how measures suggested by Barak, such as joint patrols, early alerts regarding military drills, a hotline between officers – which we viewed as confidence-building measures – appeared to be violations of sovereignty and dignity in Syrian eyes.

The meeting was almost finished, although it was clear that the parties needed more hours of joint discussions. All the participants went from the meeting to the White House to meet with President Clinton and Vice President Al Gore. Clinton's participation symbolized the importance attributed by the US administration to the process that the Israelis and Syrians were trying to advance.

Shihabi said at the meeting that the talks with the Israeli delegation were being held in a frank and open manner, and although gaps still existed, he made it clear that he intended to recommend the continuation of these talks to Assad.

However, unfortunately, this did not happen. In retrospect, it seems that the issues of dilution and reduction of the military order of battle, which had already been raised in the meetings with Muallem, were far more sensitive matters than we had expected.

During the meeting with Shihabi, he told us emphatically that, "this issue is an internal Syrian matter, and we are not willing to discuss it with you openly or secretly. The size of the Syrian army is not related solely to our relationship with Israel - Syria has other borders to defend." Nevertheless, as I have mentioned, Shihabi said he would recommend to Assad that the talks be continued, and we were confident that Assad would accept the recommendation of such a close confidant.

Yet when Assad read Muallem's transcripts of his meetings with us, and saw that Barak spoke about the need to dilute Syrian forces deep inside Syrian territory and not only at the frontline with Israel during the discussion on security arrangements, he was very angry. Assad said these demands were illegitimate, and that decisions on reducing or diluting the Syrian army's forces are an internal Syrian affair. This angered Assad so much that he decided to halt the talks between the Chiefs of Staff, which were resumed only six months later, when the role of the IDF Chief of Staff was already filled by Amnon Lipkin-Shahak. Assad also urgently summoned Muallem back to Syria, and delayed his return to Washington for many weeks on account of his participation in "discussions" in Damascus.

As a result of this cessation of talks, Warren Christopher and Dennis Ross began a new era of commuting between Israel and Syria, in an attempt to persuade Assad to continue the discussions between military experts on the subject of security arrangements. The Americans were very creative in the negotiations, the most prominent of them being Dennis Ross, who was the moving spirit in driving new ideas forward.

Since Assad refused the Israeli demands, Dennis, along with Rabin, conceived a framework which would be called "purposes and principles of the security arrangements." This framework aimed to serve as a frame of reference in which Assad would feel comfortable and agree to continue the discussions between military experts.

During this commuting between Jerusalem, Washington and Damascus, the framework or document of understanding began to form, which had been dubbed the 'non-paper'. The non-paper is a term borrowed from the legal world, referring to an unsigned draft representing understandings between the parties.

The non-paper is a document recording statements made orally, and it was acceptable to the Syrians, who were looking to avoid an official document to which we would both be sides, as long as an agreement was not yet reached.

The emerging document presented principles designed to ensure that the purposes meant to be achieved by the security arrangements, which had already been agreed upon by Barak and Shihabi, would be met. These included eliminating the risk of a surprise attack, preventing military friction on a daily basis, and eliminating the danger of all-out war in any circumstances, not just in the event of a surprise attack.

Syria continued to insist that security arrangements be "reciprocal, mutual and equal." We had a problem with equality since geographic and topographic conditions within Israel and Syria are different: Syria is a country of 16 million people and holds a regular army, unlike the IDF which is essentially a reserve army; Syria's territory is larger than that of Israel, and especially - the Golan Heights would give Syria a topographical advantage.

We argued that the Golan Heights dominate over the northern part of the State of Israel, topographically and strategically. Therefore, we requested that in the principle of equality, the text that relates to the geographical-topographical aspect would indicate that there is room to consider the dimensions of the territory and topographical conditions. Furthermore, if during negotiations it would become clear that realization of a certain security arrangement is impossible, the matter would be discussed by experts from both sides who would find a satisfactory solution.

Our achievement was that despite the Syrians' insistence on equality, we were creating a mechanism for handling differences of opinion on the matter. In addition, the Syrians' adoption of the document would, in effect, be an admittance on their part that there is still room for disagreement in the matter of geographical equality, and there would be a mechanism for resolving disputes. Hence, the result would be that geographic equality would, on the one hand, be the "principle" as the Syrians wanted, but on the other hand, not be a "literal principle" - since the Syrians had agreed to the Israeli approach that there was a problem, and therefore a mechanism for solving problems was necessary.

This document is a good example of achieving a creative solution in which each side feels it is getting what it wants, and each side views their counterpart as taking a step in their direction.

Behind the scenes, creating this document involved a great deal of transatlantic flights made by Dennis Ross, countless phone calls between him, Damascus and Tel Aviv and vice versa, and discussions and deliberations regarding the precise wording of each letter in the document.

Ross would call me from Damascus, and recount the Syrian comments to me, and with them, I would enter Rabin's room, voice my opinion and await his decision. I would then return to Dennis in Damascus, who would write down Rabin's comments, forward them to Assad or someone on his behalf - and back again. The original document contains my hand-written comments. The document was completed in May 1994 (the original document appears in English, as Appendix A on page 720).

Chapter 14

Assad: "I am Serious"

Following the 'non-paper,' Assad agreed to a three-pronged process: Step one – A meeting between Chiefs of Staff Shihabi and Lipkin-Shahak (who had replaced Barak in office); Step two – Shuttle diplomacy by Dennis Ross; Step three - A meeting between military experts to further discuss security arrangements.

The Chiefs of Staff meeting was meant to resume talks on security arrangements, including all military aspects related to a possible peace agreement. In Israel, a team was established which I was to head, and which included the Head of the Strategic Department in the Planning Directorate, Brig. Gen. Zvi Stauber, the Head of the Operations Division, Gen. Gabi Ashkenazi, the Head of the Research Division, Gen. Jacob Amidror and the Head of the Operations Department in the Operations Division, Col. Dan Harel. The team met frequently and built extensive and thorough foundations that were used as a basis for discussions with the Chief of Staff, and from there on to Rabin, and along with their comments and decisions formed the basis for presenting our views during the meeting between Lipkin-Shahak and Shihabi.

In the briefings Rabin gave Lipkin-Shahak towards his meeting with Shihabi, he did not tell him about the "deposit", even after deep down inside he had already decided on the formula wherein Israel would withdraw to the line of June 4, 1967, if all our needs were met. He still told Lipkin-Shahak that there was no final answer regarding the withdrawal line, but added that "it would be a substantial withdrawal."

In shared briefings he held with Lipkin-Shahak and me, Rabin told us that since we were going to talk about security arrangements, and we had no authority to speak about the border's location, we had to suggest two options to be used as hypothetical scenarios around which the security arrangements would be built; one in which Israel remained on the western cliff of the Golan, and one in which Israel withdrew from the Golan.

While preparing for the meeting with the Syrians, we formulated a request for a large aid package from the United States. The aid package was designed to compensate us for the loss of important territory if and when we withdraw.

Our requests from the Americans included: intelligence and warning measures, long-range combat aircraft and precision air-to-ground and ground-to-ground weaponry. In addition, we asked that the US would refrain from providing offensive weapons (fighter jets and tanks) to Syria during peacetime, and settle for defensive weapons (such as means of communication) that could not endanger us.

Our argument was that we needed advanced offensive weapons, since as a result of the withdrawal, we would lose our defensive capabilities that relied on the Golan Heights and thus worsen our strategic position. The Syrians, on the other hand, would be in control of the Golan Heights and thus significantly improve their situation if they were to decide to attack Israel.

Towards the Lipkin-Shahak–Shihabi meeting, Dennis Ross had been commuting frequently along the Syria-Israel line, as Assad sought to determine the exact participants and location of the meeting and other such procedural issues, which were very significant in the Syrians' eyes. Ross let Assad determine these things because it gave the Syrian president the sense that he was in control of the process. For Rabin, all these things were uninteresting and seemed entirely insignificant.

Dennis told us that he found Assad and Shihabi to be in a much more practical and serious approach towards the dialogue than in the past.

In the final preparatory meeting Lipkin-Shahak and I had with Rabin, before departing for the meeting in the United States, Rabin stressed to us that he was very interested in the continuation of the talks, and hence we had to avoid a breakdown, especially on issues such as demilitarization, dilution and early-warning stations.

The Syrian approach was that all limitations imposed by security arrangements would apply only on the Syrian side of the territory vacated by Israel in the Golan Heights, while on the Israeli side they would be applied in the area between the Jordan River and the city of Safed. I should remind here that the security arrangements included demilitarized zones and diluted zones in which restrictions would be applied on the size of the military force and the types of permitted weaponry.

Israel's position was that the area in which we were willing to apply security arrangements would reach Safed, but that the Syrian area should reach Damascus (more precisely, the Daraa-Damascus highway. Daraa is a small Syrian town located on the border between Jordan and Syria). Our position delineated the relevant area for security arrangements in Syria as deeper than the Israeli one.

The meeting between Lipkin-Shahak and Shihabi was held on June 27, 1995, in Washington, in the Fort McNair military base situated on the river bank. Once again, as was the case in Camp David, the Wye River, and even the Blair House, I could not help but think of how much the beauty of the spot, the breathtaking scenery and the power of nature were so far removed from the weight of the differences trying to be reconciled by representatives of two rival countries from the tempestuous Middle East.

Present on the Israeli side were Chief of Staff Amnon Lipkin-Shahak, Brig. Gen. Zvi Stauber, Ambassador Itamar Rabinovich and myself.

The Syrian delegation included Chief of Staff Hikmat Shihabi and Ambassador Walid Muallem, General Ibrahim Omar, Head of Military Intelligence, General Hassan Khalil, Head of Field Security, and an interpreter. Shihabi seemed more relaxed than he had been in previous encounters we had with Barak, but still had difficulty bringing himself to engage in 'small talk' or even drink coffee with us.

We were very sensitive to the matter of dignity, which we knew the Syrians saw as crucial, and made sure to be very courteous. We tried to appear relaxed, which was quite in contrast to the Sphinx-like expressions of the Syrians, who made sure to sit upright and tense, wearing a sullen countenance resulting from tension or from superior orders. The Syrians even took care to avoid handshakes at the start of the meeting.

In his opening words, Lipkin-Shahak praised Shihabi and Assad in an attempt to dispel the tension. Of these accolades, Shihabi said, "Thank you for the kind words you have said of me, but you are giving me too much credit," and Lipkin-Shahak was quick to reply, "Next time we will bring the file we have on you and see if I'm exaggerating or not."

The Syrians were very formal and distant, and their conduct revealed Shihabi's undisputed seniority. None of the Syrians dared to make a peep, only Shihabi spoke. Muallem dared to speak out only after Shihabi turned to him and said, "Mr. Ambassador, please answer the Israelis' question." Again, as before, there was no exchange of words or notes among themselves. Our side, as usual, was very active, mainly in exchanging of notes and smiles and requests from Lipkin-Shahak to take the floor, which were always granted.

However, as the hours passed, it was clear that progress was being made during this meeting and it was much more productive than the meetings with Barak. This time, in-depth and concrete discussions developed regarding the various matters at hand, gaps and points of agreements between the parties were more precisely defined, and the atmosphere was much more relaxed than in previous sessions. The extent to which this was true could be garnered by Shihabi's remarks to Dennis Ross after the meetings, to the effect that he felt that with Lipkin-Shahak he could "do business." It seemed that there was something in Lipkin-Shahak's conduct that was perceived as far less threatening than Barak's, and his simple, clear explanations were much easier for the Syrians to digest compared to Barak's complex analytical explanations.

Christopher opened the meeting by saying that the Americans had three criteria by which they would evaluate the meeting's success. The first was an open exchange of opinions so that each side would understand the needs of the other; the efforts made by each party to creatively meet the needs of the other party, and the ability to reach points of agreement in the context of security arrangements.

Here the American side adopted the idea that I had raised at the meeting between Shihabi and Barak – that we tend to stray from discussing the main issues, and the most important thing was that each side present its concerns and needs, and the other side try to meet these needs and concerns.

On this matter Shihabi said that if talks were to fail this time as they did before, it would have very significant negative consequences on the peace process. "Our policy is based on our choice of peace as the preferred strategic alternative," said Shihabi. "We aim to reach a full and true peace based on UN resolutions 242 and 338 and the principle of land for peace."

Reading his words from written notes, Shihabi began presenting the Syrian conception of security arrangements, based on the non-paper.

Shihabi said they demanded that demilitarized zones devoid of military presence, except for civilian police, would be present on both sides of the border. In some areas, an international force would oversee the implementation of the security arrangements. The size and mission of the multinational force would be decided by the political levels. Beyond the demilitarized zones would be diluted zones, in which military forces would be present, but they would be limited in size. "The size of the diluted areas, size of the force and types of weaponry, will have to be discussed and agreed on the military level," said Shihabi, adding that in order to assist the international force, US satellites would monitor the security arrangements by photographing the relevant areas on a daily basis, and sending the intelligence to both sides every day.

Shihabi said he was willing to take confidence-building measures, such as advance notice in the case of recruiting reserves. This was a change from the last time when he had said that this was part of the normalization and there was no need to report it. He also agreed to exchange information regarding exercises that were about to take place.

"If both sides have an attitude of peace, it should be enough," said Shihabi. "Peace must ensure stability, dignity and the sovereignty of each one of the countries."

Shihabi noted in this context that an Israeli early-warning station on the Golan Heights would violate Syrian sovereignty and dignity.

Lipkin-Shahak expressed disappointment from Shihabi's statements, saying that the Syrian army's Chief of Staff's suggested components were not enough to dispel Israel's concerns. Demilitarized and diluted zones are important, said Lipkin-Shahak, but they must be on an appropriate scale.

Lipkin-Shahak said that Israel demands to remain on the Golan Heights since defense of northern Israel required the IDF's presence on the Golan Heights. Regarding security arrangements, Lipkin-Shahak said that they must include the following: a demilitarized buffer zone throughout the area evacuated by the IDF, which should be off limits for Syrian military forces, and contain only civilian police forces meant to maintain law and order. On either side of the demilitarized zones there would be diluted strips, in which the forces would be limited in scope and types of permitted weapons. On the Israeli side, this would be up to Safed, and on the Syrian side, up to the Daraa-Damascus highway. Lipkin-Shahak also talked about moving Syrian armored and mechanized divisions, which constitute the bulk of Syrian ground forces, eastwards and northwards.

Warning measures that would satisfy us, added Lipkin-Shahak, would include three early-warning stations on the Golan Heights and verification and inspection mechanisms that would operate on the Israeli side and the Syrian side, in which Israeli, Syrian and US officers would partake.

Israel would be able to conduct inspections in Syrian bases in diluted and demilitarized zones, and the Syrians would be able to conduct similar inspections on our side.

Lipkin-Shahak said Israel wished to discuss the framework for an agreement with Syria on the deployment of the Syrian army in Lebanon, with the intention being to keep it north of the Beirut-Damascus highway. To this Shihabi answered that Lebanon is a sovereign state, and Syrian forces are in Lebanon on its invitation. He also said that they do not encourage the activities of Hezbollah but also do not prevent them. They do not provide weapons to Hezbollah but do not disarm them either. It seemed that Shihabi was being knowingly inaccurate, since Syria has supported Hezbollah in munitions and in other matters, then as now.

Lipkin-Shahak said that Israel has no territorial claims in Lebanon, but only security concerns. He explained that we ask that the Lebanese army disarm Hezbollah and be deployed on the northern border of the security zone in southern Lebanon, for six months, and during this time we would have to be convinced that the Lebanese army can prevent attacks and prevent terrorists from entering the security zone and harming us. If that goes well, Israel undertakes that within three months it will withdraw from Lebanon completely and sign a peace treaty with it. The SLA troops will not be harmed, and will be integrated into Lebanese society and in the military and security apparatus of Lebanon.

Lipkin-Shahak proceeded to speak of the confidence-building measures that needed to be undertaken during the negotiations, and even before agreements would be reached regarding security arrangements. He suggested that Syrian officers begin to accompany the UN officers' patrols of the Golan Heights as part of the disengagement agreement of 1974.

Shihabi rejected the idea, just as he had disliked most of the proposals, and rejected the entire suggestion outright. He expressed his dissatisfaction that no mention was made of the following: The fundamental basis of an Israeli withdrawal to the 1967 borders; that Israel continues to insist on Israeli warning stations on the Golan (and does not accept the satellite compromise); that we think "relevant territories" (areas of demilitarization and dilution) should be deeper in Syria than in Israel; and that Israel broached the issue of the scope and deployment of the Syrian army (Lipkin-Shahak said that the offensive Syrian forces must be distanced). This was – as we had learned in the past – a sensitive matter for the Syrians.

Afterwards began a discussion of various security issues, such as aerial warnings, which was fascinating, thorough and professional. However, it was clear that a cloud hung over the proceedings. The Syrians still insisted that "full peace will provide full security", and deflected any attempt of ours to clarify the necessary security arrangements, with clichés.

When we returned to the hotel after the meeting, we received news from Israel that the political system and public opinion were most turbulent due to the publication of a certain paper, which would later be known as the "Stauber document." General Stauber, a member of the team that I had formed for the excursion, had prepared a document analyzing the non-paper. Stauber's analysis had criticized some of the contents of the 'non-paper.' It seemed that someone from within the establishment received a copy of the document and transferred it to the leader of the opposition at that time, Likud leader Benjamin Netanyahu. Netanyahu took this hot potato, and protected by his parliamentary immunity, read parts of it in the Knesset. Netanyahu wrongly claimed that the document proved that Rabin had already conceded the Golan Heights, and was negotiating with the Syrians on this basis. Netanyahu also claimed, wrongly again, that the document proved that Rabin had retracted previous promises he had made regarding unequal depths of demilitarization, insistence on an early-warning station on Mount Hermon and that Israel would be defended solely by IDF forces. We were shocked to hear these things, just as we were on our way back from an encounter in which we had not stopped for one moment to insist and argue over these exact issues.

Leaking this document was a gravely serious act. The leak was investigated. All the members of the team I had formed, myself included, underwent polygraph examinations and were all found to be telling the truth. We were not the source of the leak. Civilians exposed to the document did not undergo polygraph examinations and the leak has not been found to date.

In any case, Rabin, who was a very discreet, cautious and suspicious person even before the affair, became even more discreet after the document's publication, and made a point of further reducing the number of his confidants, which was small to begin with.

On the second day of talks, Lipkin-Shahak agreed with Shihabi that satellites and aircraft could contribute to the warning mechanisms, but explained that an aerial warning was of limited value. This is because when a military occurrence takes place on the ground, a satellite can only perceive it once it is already at the advanced stage of an event that began long before and this might already be too late.

In regards to Shihabi's claim that Damascus was much closer to the Golan Heights than Tel Aviv, and therefore the Syrians' territorial depth should be smaller than that of the Israelis, Lipkin-Shahak said that the comparison is irrelevant. This is because the Galilee Panhandle is along the border with Syria, and due to Israel's narrow waistline; if the Syrians were to cross the border during an attack in the area of the Galilee Panhandle, their throughway to the Mediterranean would be short and quick. To Shihabi's claim that Israel has a remarkable capability to recruit reserves and operate emergency depots (neither he nor we knew what would be discovered during the Second Lebanon War), Lipkin-Shahak responded by reminding him that in the Yom Kippur War, the Syrians had tried to disrupt these capabilities with missiles, implying that they might do so again.

In regards to "relevant zones "(the area in which security arrangements would apply), Shihabi surprised us by changing the Syrian approach to "equality" of demilitarized and diluted territories and suggested that they stand at a ratio of ten to six. "I took into account your comments regarding the imbalanced topography and geography, and we agree to relevant areas between Quneitra and Safed, with the size on the Syrian side being 1,000 square kilometers and only 600 square kilometers on the Israeli side," said Shihabi.

Lipkin-Shahak told Shihabi that we had another front to deal with at home, and had to work hard to sway Israeli public opinion in favor of peace with Syria. "Not all Israelis are pleased with my presence here today with you," said Lipkin-Shahak to Shihabi, and added, "Yesterday, at the time we met here, there was a demonstration in front of my house by people who are opposed to the process."

The concluding session of the meeting also took place in the White House under President Clinton.

Shihabi said that as opposed to the last time, this time sessions were very serious but the political leadership in Syria would have to decide how they would continue. It seemed that this time Shihabi took care to choose his words more carefully, as opposed to last time when he announced at the end of the talks that he would recommend Assad to continue them, and Assad had rejected the recommendation as mentioned.

After hearing both sides, in a meeting that was in actuality far more ceremonial than substantive, Clinton said he had emerged encouraged, and planned to send Ross to the region and then move on to the next step, which was the continuation of meetings between military experts.

The meeting between Shihabi and Lipkin-Shahak was in fact the end of the first phase of the three that had been agreed with Assad after the non-paper was written. The second stage was Dennis Ross's shuttle diplomacy between Damascus and Jerusalem, and the third phase included planned meetings between military experts from both sides. Yet on one of Ross's visits to Damascus, in July 1995, Assad surprisingly told him that he did not wish to continue meetings with Israeli representatives, since he had come to the conclusion that Syria's position had been compromised as a result of its meetings with Israel, while Israel was only benefiting from them.

Assad expressed his disappointment from the fact that Israel continued to demand early-warning stations in the Golan Heights, after he had received the impression that Israel had given up this demand, as he claimed. It turned out that he had got this wrong impression after hearing from Shihabi that Lipkin-Shahak had agreed to warnings via aircraft and satellites, while Lipkin-Shahak's intention was that he agreed that these means provide additional warning, but not replace early-warning stations.

The Americans tried to suggest a compromise to the effect that the meetings would continue at the ambassador level, with military experts joining them occasionally. Yet Rabin insisted that military experts be the ones discussing security arrangements.

Rabin told Ross that he was not ready to concede essential issues and that he saw warning stations as a matter of essence. "The expert meetings are meant to solve exactly these types of problems," said

Rabin, "Assad is asking for something essential and in exchange is willing to give something procedural. We agreed on meetings of military experts, and what was agreed upon must be honored unconditionally."

In late October, the Syrians suggested to Ross that the Americans prepare a second non-paper related to security arrangements, in which the demilitarized and diluted zones would be discussed, the areas themselves would be agreed upon ("the relevant zones"), and the matter of early warning would be handled.

However, Dennis made it clear to the Syrians that on these issues there had to be direct talks between the Syrians and the Israelis, and without them there would be no additional 'non-papers.' Finally Assad relented and agreed to send the military experts to another meeting.

On October 31, 1995, Dennis Ross and Martin Indyk came straight from the economic conference in Amman to a meeting with Rabin in Jerusalem. Ross reported to Rabin in my presence that in his meeting with Assad in Amman, Assad had said that he accepts the notion that the Americans will work on a new 'non-paper' on the issue of security arrangements. This would include suggestions to resolve the two fundamental issues – early warning and the size of the "relevant zones" (in which the security arrangements would be applied), in preparation for the meeting between military experts. Ross also said that Assad was serious in his intentions, that he was committed to the process and wanted to reach a peace agreement, and that he was willing to make difficult decisions and show flexibility in regards to the details of the security arrangements. However, he stressed that he could not compromise on the principles of Security Council resolutions 242 and 338.

Ross, who had known Assad for many years, said that he had expected to find a crankier and more belligerent Assad in light of the convening of the Amman conference and Israel's presence in it, as well as the progress being made at the time with the Palestinians; but, Ross emphasized, Assad hardly complained - contrary to his habit.

Hence Rabin shared with Ross the timetables he had planned for the near future: Until January 1996, the Americans would prepare the foundation for the new 'non-paper,' and the parties would reach a final agreement on its basis through direct meetings that would begin in January, and then the time for substantial decisions would come. I think Rabin was ready at the time to push the Syrian track forward in full swing, and was willing to reach a peace agreement with Syria within a short period of time. This was after having accepted that it would only be possible if Israel were to agree to withdraw from the Golan Heights to the line of June 4, 1967, and provided all our needs were met.

However, unfortunately, fate had other plans.

Four days later Rabin was murdered, and the peace process – as well as the State of Israel - has never returned to its previous track, until this very day.

Chapter 15

Peres: Vision but Also Naiveté

Shimon Peres assumed the role of Prime Minister and Minister of Defense immediately after Rabin was murdered, and was determined to continue the peace process just like his predecessor.

"I am committed to everything that Rabin pledged to," Peres told Clinton during their meeting in Jerusalem, when the president came to Rabin's funeral to pay his last respects to whom he considered a leader, a symbol, a role model and a friend.

Throughout this meeting, Clinton's behavior, body language and facial expression conveyed the extent to which he was shocked by the murder. His face was elongated, gray and sad, and it was clear that he saw the loss of Rabin as a personal tragedy. Rabin had influenced Clinton quite a bit with his mature and responsible vision, his courage and the way he handled the peace process negotiations. The relationship between Rabin and Clinton contained the combination of the leader of the free world, the most powerful and influential person, and the leader of a small country; the young man and the experienced older man.

Clinton saw Rabin as a brave fighter, a war hero who had become a hero of peace - and this combination captured his heart.

Doubtlessly, this is what led Clinton to tell Peres during that meeting that the United States had benefited more than it had given in its relations with Israel.

At that meeting, Peres suggested that Clinton announce a US plan to end the war in the Middle East before the year 2000, of which a peace agreement between Israel and Syria would be a part.

To this Clinton replied, "I need time to think about it," and added, "It is important to get Assad out of his shell. He is very intelligent and has an amazing memory, but it is enclosed inside a shell and I have to get him out of it. He has a big brain which he preoccupies with small matters."

It was agreed that Clinton would telephone Assad and offer to resume negotiations.

Over the last few months of Rabin's life and the progress being made in the peace process, Peres had been updated by Rabin on all developments and processes. Collaboration between the two was very tight and reached its peak at that time, reflected in long face-to-face meetings held weekly between them. Previous disputes and grudges did not pose a hindrance at that time, and they worked in full harmony and partnership. Rabin viewed Peres as a companion - he was reliable in his eyes and he trusted him. It seemed that both of these older gentlemen were able to overcome past disagreements, and strove together towards a common goal in which they both believed - peace.

As soon as he was appointed as Prime Minister and Minister of Defense, Peres was updated of the details of negotiations with Syria, which he was less familiar with, since Rabin had handled them until then. This was in contrast to the negotiations with the Palestinians, in which Peres was actively involved.

I led a team of security professionals that reviewed for Peres the steps taken and progress made in the negotiations. Chief of Staff Lipkin-Shahak and Ambassador Rabinovich attended briefings in which we discussed this issue. In meetings with military personnel, the subject of the "deposit" was not broached, because it was classified and only few people were aware of it – those in on the secret included Warren Christopher, Dennis Ross, Itamar Rabinovich and myself.

A few days after assuming office, a report appeared in the newspaper to the effect that Peres was surprised to learn that Rabin had agreed to withdraw to the border as it was on June 4, 1967, under certain conditions.

I was very surprised to read this, because I assumed that Peres had been updated on this matter, in light of his good relationship with Rabin and in light of the many update meetings he had held with him and the Americans, and sometimes only with the Americans. I thought he had been aware of the matter of the deposit.

One of Peres's first decisions was to advance the talks with the Syrians, and he appointed Uri Savir as head of the delegation for negotiations with Syria and Ambassador Rabinovich as a member of the delegation.

Due to the atmosphere after Rabin's murder and Peres's willingness to take brave steps, Syria agreed to renew negotiations immediately, and delegations from the two sides met in the Wye Plantation in December.

Our delegation arrived at Wye driven by Peres's approach, that peace would bring security. According to his statements, I was under the impression that Peres did not attach the same importance to security arrangements as Rabin had, and it was not the main thing that interested him. Peres focused mainly on peace and normalization. This was due to differences in nature and attitude between the two men: Rabin had refused to settle for a peace agreement that was dependent entirely on the other side's willingness to fulfill it, and had asked for security arrangements that would ensure Israel's ability to defend itself in case of failure. Rabin was more of a son of this land in a sense - he knew the Middle East well and knew that many years were needed to overcome the mutual suspicions, gaps and psychological fears between the parties. Hence, it was so important for him to build a safety net that ensured that a catastrophe would not occur in the event that the peace agreement faltered.

Peres, on the other hand, viewed peace as something that inherently included security. "Why do we need security arrangements in peacetime?" he asked. In my opinion, this approach encapsulated much vision, but also a considerable degree of naiveté. Peres based his outlook on economic cooperation between Israel and Syria, and international economic aid that would improve the Syrian economy. According to him, the more the Syrians would enjoy the fruits of peace – the deeper the commitment to it would be. Anyway, when we departed for the talks at Wye Plantation, he agreed we leave with a plan to try and reach an agreement with Syria on the subject of security arrangements, although he attributed far less importance to them than Rabin.

When it came to the borderline, Peres' opinion was that the demarcation line of June 4, 1967, was not a viable possibility, since it gave the Syrians control over the Sea of Galilee. Peres, who was willing to go very far in the interest of peace, refused to allow Syrian control over the lake's waterfront. Peres said that June 4, 1967 is not a well-defined line but a concept, a collection of positions taken to mean different things for different people depending on the map they held in their hands. Unlike the international borderline between Israel, Syria and Lebanon, which was set by France and the UK, recognized by the League of Nations in 1923, and marked on the ground by concrete pillars, Peres said that the line of June 4, 1967 had never previously been marked. He added that the line presented by the Syrians was actually their own opinion of the whereabouts of this line. Therefore Peres wanted us to say at the Wye Plantation that Israel would be willing to withdraw its forces according to Security Council resolutions 242 and 338.

Peres also knew that an outright statement that Israel would be willing to withdraw to the line of June 4, 1967, or the international border, could be very damaging for his chances of winning the elections that were set to take place in October 1996 (before being moved earlier to May). "I do not want to lose both the Golan Heights and the elections," he would say. However, if Peres would have been convinced that in exchange for withdrawal he would receive a full, just and secure peace, there would have been a high chance he would have agreed to take such a step. As he put it, "If we're going to reach an agreement before the election, I need the dramatic effect of an end to the conflict." Peres was referring to a drama that would greatly upstage the major concessions required and give the Israeli public a sense of great historical achievement.

Dennis Ross, who met with Peres at the time, said that the US estimated that there was not much difference between the line of June 1967, as the Syrians understood it, and the international border. Israel viewed this border as the preferable option, since it was a recognized border that appeared in maps and kept the entire Sea of Galilee in Israel's hands. It was also preferable because it passed ten meters east of its northeast coastline and on its southern side moved away from the Sea of Galilee eastwards, so that the entire lake remained under Israeli sovereignty. The Syrians on the other hand argued that until June 4, 1967 they had been located right on the waterfront, on the northeast part of the lake. For Syria it was important to return to this exact line due to their attitude towards the land, and because of the precedent in which the Egyptians had regained all of their land, up to the last grain of sand in Taba, in their peace treaty with Israel. Dennis told Peres that he believed Assad had a firm notion that in exchange for the fulfillment of all the requirements and needs of the State of Israel, Rabin had been prepared to withdraw to the border as it was on June 4, 1967.

Assad for his part, could not afford to settle for less, because then the question would arise in Syria, and rightfully so: if Syria was willing to settle for less, why did it wait for so long rather than join Sadat's peace initiative in 1977?

In earlier stages of the negotiations, the Americans offered to examine the possibility of leaving Israeli settlements in the Golan Heights under Syrian rule. Assad had replied: "I do not understand you - a few years ago you asked me to allow all Jews to leave Syria, and now you are asking for Jews to return to live under Syrian rule?"

Dennis said that what mattered to Assad was a public commitment that Israel was willing to make a full withdrawal, and that for him this was the key to obtaining an agreement on the rest of the issues.

The Americans estimated that Assad had high expectations from Peres' arrival at the Prime Minister's office, since he believed that Peres would be more flexible and moderate than Rabin. However, Ross' reports revealed that Rabin's death had undermined Assad's certainty regarding the process. Assad referred to Rabin as an island of stability, and was convinced that Rabin would fulfill any obligation he undertook. Ross also said the murder had severely shaken Assad, who never imagined that such a thing could happen in the Israeli democracy. In that regard, Assad was no different than most Israelis.

Peres sent us to the Wye Plantation to discuss the various issues pertaining to the Israeli-Syrian conflict, except for the border issue. This matter was to be resolved between the senior ranks of both countries. Peres thought he could reach a framework agreement that would discuss principles and solutions to the conflict, stages of withdrawal, timetables, the nature of peaceful relations and normalization, economic cooperation and the issue of water - and how all of this would affect the state of the Middle East.

In Ross' reports in those days came a message from Assad that he was serious in his intentions, he wanted to jump-start the negotiations and move them forward hastily, and that he was willing to discuss all of its components, in contrast to his previous position before the murder – when he was only prepared to discuss security arrangements.

I believed this change in Assad's attitude was due to the shock caused by Rabin's murder, and his feeling that with Peres - whom Assad perceived as a prophet of peace – there would be less insistence on the Israeli side regarding the issues that had previously been fiercely insisted upon.

Participants in the Wye Plantation talks from the Israeli side were Uri Savir, who was appointed as head of the delegation in place of the Israeli ambassador in the United States; Itamar Rabinovich, who also remained a part of the delegation; Head of the Planning Directorate Maj. Gen. Uzi Dayan; Legal Advisor to the Ministry of Foreign Affairs Attorney Yoel Singer; and myself.

The Syrian delegation included Syrian ambassador to the United States Walid Muallem; Syrian Chief of Intelligence Gen. Ibrahim Omar; Head of Syrian Field Security Gen. Hassan Khalil, who was sent to monitor his colleagues within the Syrian delegation; Legal Adviser to the Ministry of Foreign Affairs, Riad Daudi; and the Head of the Foreign Minister's Bureau, Mihail Wa'ava (who later became the Syrian ambassador to the UN).

The Americans were Martin Indyk; Dennis Ross and Mark Paris of the National Security Council; Ross's deputy Aaron Miller; and Toni Verstandig of the State Department.

Talks began in a frozen atmosphere with all of us seated in the same room. In fact, we were "trapped" at this site, which was a collection of wood huts dipped in green. Again there was the deceptive sight of the beautiful American nature, two hours from Washington by car.

Local conditions dictated more than a bit of physical proximity. We were near each other from morning to night in a mix of discussions, breaks and shared meals in which the Syrians and Israelis sat together at round tables - and slowly but surely, the severe formal atmosphere, which the Syrians had been careful to maintain until then, began to crack somewhat. It was clear that Assad was behind this, and we felt a similar influence in the opposite direction later on, when in the meetings in Shepherdstown in Barak's time, the same Syrians refrained from talking to us outside of formal discussions and refused to shake our hands.

During the discussions, Walid Muallem once again stated that the Syrians' starting point was that Israel had to withdraw to the line of June 4, 1967, and we again reiterated that we were not authorized to discuss that, and steered the discussion to the essentials of the arrangements.

Muallem repeatedly insisted, "You know, you have committed to the 1967 line - why do you refrain from saying so?" And we responded that we had committed to nothing.

Muallem, who never dared utter a word during the meetings between Chiefs of Staff Barack and later Lipkin-Shahak and Shihabi, had apparently been granted authority this time, and was obviously enjoying running the show on the Syrian side and subjugating the generals, who did not dare to speak. During one shared evening meal, Gen. Ibrahim Omar was revealed to be a most intelligent man, and he eloquently articulated the Syrian military position over the course of the meal. Muallem very much disliked the informal talks with his generals, and rushed to clarify that only what was said during the official plenary would be binding.

The silence of the Syrian generals seemed problematic to me, because in my opinion, it was very important that there be direct dialogue between the military experts.

Throughout the discussions, Muallem promoted a particular notion – that there is a link between the political elements and the security arrangements. He reiterated his claim that peace would be the best guarantee for security, reminding that the Syrians have been known to fulfill their obligations.

According to him, components such as normalization and diplomatic relations would compensate for some of the required security arrangements. "Do not overstate the importance of security arrangements," Muallem said to us, "After all, if there is a political decision to go to war, no deterrent and no warning could prevent it. Once we accept peace, then we eliminate the possibility of a political decision to go to war. Peace, then, is the best security arrangement."

Muallem, like the Lebanese and the Palestinians, said that the most important thing was to remove the cause of the war, namely our occupation of the Golan Heights. When the occupation would be abolished – there would no longer be a pretext for war.

This approach was a new and revolutionary concept in the Arab worldview. Until 1967, the reason for the war had been that Israel had no right to exist and therefore must be destroyed. The talk of 'occupation' as the sole cause of war was in fact recognition of Israel's right to exist, an understanding that Israel is part of the region and a decision that all that's left to do is solve border disputes. This groundbreaking change in perception actually began with Sadat, who recognized Israel's right to exist, and continued at the Madrid Conference in late 1991. During the conference, delegations from Israel and the Arab states conferred on the basis of UN Security Council resolutions 242 and 338, meaning among other things, recognition of Israel and its need for secure borders.

"Peace with Syria," Muallem said, "is far more substantial than the peace you have with Egypt and Jordan, in that it will precede a complete peace in the Middle East."

Referring to normalization, Muallem said that we must understand that after so many years of hatred, the Syrians would find it very difficult to see an Israeli flag flying over the Israeli Embassy in Damascus. He wished to make it clear to us that for them it would be a much greater sacrifice than we imagined.

The immediate results of the conference were that for the first time, Syrian and Israeli delegations were sitting together for several days, and dealing with a wide range of matters that included not only security arrangements but also the nature and essence of peace and normalization, without touching on borders. For the first time, we discussed issues such as trade, tourism, transport, aircraft landing and ship-docking - matters related to the development of normal relations between the two countries.

For the first time, Assad was showing interest in economic issues, indicating that he had an interest to promote peace, and had begun to understand the economic advantages Syria could reap from peace.

The Syrians always made sure to demand that the withdrawal be fast and abrupt, but that normalization processes be as slow as possible. They feared that rapidly normalizing relations would open the window for a Western wind from Israel and the United

States, to be followed by a storm that would blow the entire door away and remove the Alawite sect from power. Our approach was precisely the opposite - we wanted slow withdrawal and rapid normalization processes, which would strengthen our confidence in the existence of peace and facilitate the withdrawal.

An international economic package was also discussed for the first time, and the Americans agreed to help Syria develop its economy. Christopher told us that Assad thought in very outdated economic terms, and was interested in two things: agriculture and construction.

There was a sense of positive momentum in those meetings, and the Syrians came with a certain openness and willingness to discuss new ideas, despite their refusal to change their positions on the core issues.

Issues related to security arrangements were fleshed out: the Syrians repeatedly insisted that the relevant areas in which restrictions (demilitarization and dilution) would apply, would be between Safed and Quneitra. They additionally stressed their great sensitivity to the defense of Damascus, which is not far from the Golan Heights (and from the location where IDF forces were currently deployed), and after we mentioned how narrow Israel is, they said it was outweighed by the short distance between the Jordan River and Damascus.

In the meeting between Lipkin-Shahak and Shihabi six months earlier, Lipkin-Shahak had said that most of the Syrian army was then concentrated along the border between Syria and Israel, even though the Syrians had said they need a large army because they also have borders with Turkey and Iraq. Therefore Lipkin-Shahak had asked: "How will your troops be deployed in peacetime?" To this, Assad's answer to the Americans, which was further clarified in Wye, was that that is an internal Syrian affair, and a matter Assad himself would decide upon in light of Shihabi's recommendations.

From this we learned that there are only two people in Syria who affect the army's deployment: the Chief of Staff and the president. Furthermore, there was a mechanism within Syria for dealing with this issue, and hence there was a chance that this mechanism could also lead to other decisions. Another thing the Syrians said at the Wye Plantation was that after they would reach a peace agreement, in principle, there would no longer be terrorism originating from Lebanon.

Two rounds of talks were concluded in Wye, which evoked a sense of progress.

After Rabin's murder, the possibility of holding general elections was raised. Peres, who did not want to be perceived as exploiting the terrible murder for his own election, rejected the idea. He finally decided to hold early elections on May 1996, instead of on their specified date - October 1996. He felt that he must gain legitimacy in the elections so that he can lead significant political moves, and do so from the position of one who has been elected by the people, rather than merely appointed due to the murder.

Prior to the start of a third round of talks with Syria, Peres was very optimistic, and said that it was possible that a solution would be reached as early as 1996. However, this round collapsed midway, after Assad refused to condemn the murderous terrorist attacks that Israel suffered at the time.

This round began on February 5, 1996, and within a few days, Israel suffered several severe terrorist attacks. Peres insisted that the Syrians condemn the attacks, and they refused.

Peres told the delegation to return to Israel, and no direct talks with the Syrians were held from then until the meeting between Barak and al-Sharaa.

During March, security tensions in Lebanon rose, and Assad was appealed to restrain Hezbollah.

Assad's view of terrorist attacks in Lebanon was that they served his interest because they hurt Israel. Assad believed that Israeli casualties exert psychological pressure that could lead the Israeli leadership to make concessions.

At the time, Peres was open to the US idea of convening a second Madrid Conference, to give impetus to the peace process and try to resolve the sense of insecurity in Israel due to the incidents in Lebanon and suicide bombings by Hamas and Islamic Jihad.

From the end of 1995, tension between Hezbollah and the IDF in southern Lebanon had been on the rise. Hezbollah had violated the understandings of Operation Accountability. Contrary to what had been agreed upon, Hezbollah terrorists opened fire from within the villages. We responded by firing at the sources of fire in Lebanese villages. Hezbollah claimed that we were violating the understandings by firing into civilian communities, and responded by firing rockets at Israeli communities near the northern border. The situation again became unbearable. Prime Minister and Minister of Defense Shimon Peres ordered the IDF to present him with options for a series of actions that would stop the firing of Katyusha rockets.

On March 21, 1996, a consultation took place in Peres' office, where it was agreed that an operation, similar to Operation Accountability, be prepared. The modus operandi for the operation, which was to be named "Grapes of Wrath", would be based on mobilizing hundreds of thousands of Lebanese living north of the Security Zone towards the capital, Beirut. These would put pressure on the Lebanese government, which would work vis-à-vis Syria to restrain Hezbollah and cease its fire.

In this discussion, I estimated that such an operation could not achieve better results than the understandings following Operation Accountability, but at most would result in the previous accords being honored. I further argued that we should not be content with attacking Hezbollah targets, but should also attack targets that are important to the Lebanese government.

Operation "Grapes of Wrath" was launched on April 11, 1996, and ended on April 27, 1996.

On April 15, four days after the start of the operation, US Ambassador Martin Indyk met with Peres and told him that the United States had begun to work on the memorandum of understanding, but before it would be passed on to the Syrians, he wishes to coordinate it with Peres.

Martin updated Peres that US Secretary of State Warren Christopher, had said in a conversation with Syrian Foreign Minister Farouk al-Sharaa, that Israel had refrained from accusing Syria of causing the escalation, and that Hezbollah was taking advantage of the existing understandings to cause provocations. The new understandings, said Christopher, must be clear and unambiguous. They must ensure that northern Israel will not be attacked and that civilians will not be attacked on either side of the border. The understandings were meant to prevent tension and calm down the situation, but would not constitute a final agreement. Martin further recounted that al-Sharaa had said he would like to examine the wording based on a written text that would be sent to him by the Americans.

Peres told the Ambassador that it is also necessary to establish a group comprised of representatives from Israel, Lebanon, Syria and the United States, who would monitor the implementation of the understandings and handle complaints of violations. I added that the understandings should include a paragraph stating that Israel would act on the basis of its right to self-defense and be allowed to attack terrorist targets, even those that are in the villages, if Israel or IDF targets in the Security Zone are fired at from these villages.

On April 18, 1996, while still in the midst of the operation, Peres held a sitation briefing. He asked how long it would take to bring an end to the firing of Katyusha rockets, and the Commander of Northern Command, Amiram Levine, answered: Three days. I intervened and said that I did not accept this answer, and that the firing of Katyusha rockets would not cease unless Hezbollah was very severely hurt, or if following intense pressure exerted by the Lebanese government and the Syrians, the organization's leadership would decide to hold its fire.

Indeed, Katyusha rockets continued to fall in Israeli territory until a ceasefire was achieved.

On April 18, 1996, IDF artillery returned fire at the source of fire near the United Nations camp in Qana. A stray shell landed inside the camp, hitting Lebanese civilians who sought refuge there. One hundred and two civilians were killed and one hundred were injured. Among the casualties were four UN soldiers.

When news of this reached Peres, he asked to discontinue the operation for fear that Israel would be overwhelmed by a huge wave of criticism and lose its legitimacy for the operation, which was intended to stop the firing of Katyusha rockets on our civilian population. He called for the Chief of Staff Lipkin-Shahak and ordered the operation be put to an immediate halt. Aliza Goren, Avi Gil and I spoke with Peres in an attempt to persuade him that failures were bound to occur, and that we must not stop the operation as it would make our situation worse tenfold. Peres was convinced, canceled his intention to halt the operation and later spoke at a press conference, stating that "we are very sorry but we do not apologize."

Efforts to achieve a ceasefire and better understandings did not cease for a moment. French Foreign Minister de Charrete, and Russian Foreign Minister Primakov came to the region. Christopher and Dennis Ross engaged in shuttle diplomacy between Jerusalem, Beirut and Damascus and met with Peres many times.

In a situation briefing that Peres held three days after the incident in Qana, the event's impact on him was very noticeable. Peres said, "We made a major mistake in Qana and I cannot ignore it. It doubtless tipped the scales in favor of the Syrians, raised the whole world against us and changed the situation completely. Today we have an immense interest to present a humane face and not an enraged one. Those who fail to understand this are ignoring what happened."

Peres met that day with Primakov, who had arrived from meetings in Beirut. The Russian Foreign Minister said that the situation in Lebanon was worrisome, and could lead to a halt in the peace process. Russia was prepared to ensure that quiet be restored, and wished to be involved. He said that Lebanese Prime Minister Hariri, President Hrawi and leader of the Shiites who do not support Hezbollah, Nabih Berri, sought to send a message to Peres. This message stated that if Israel would withdraw from Lebanon on the basis of Resolution 425, Lebanon would take full responsibility for the security in the territory Israel would vacate, and the Lebanese army would be deployed along the border. The Lebanese army was given the opportunity to do so years later, after the Israeli withdrawal from Lebanon, and as we know, they did not even try to take it. Only after the Second Lebanon War, eleven years later, and UN Security Council Resolution 1701, did the Lebanese army head to southern Lebanon and deploy along the border with Israel, with the support of a multinational force that was deployed in southern Lebanon between the border and the Litani River.

Peres welcomed the Russians' willingness to assist, but was quick to clarify to Primakov that his efforts must be coordinated with the United States. Peres added that in our opinion, there was an organized campaign orchestrated by Iran and in which Hezbollah,

Islamic Jihad and Hamas were partners, aimed to harm Israel and Peres himself. The campaign had gained momentum since the announcement of the elections date in Israel.

Throughout all proceedings, Peres stressed that Israel did not wish to remain in the Security Zone, but as long as there were two armies in Lebanon, the Lebanese army and Hezbollah army, and as long as Hezbollah was not disarmed, the Lebanese government would fail to fulfill its intention to provide security along the border.

Meanwhile, the Americans continued their diplomatic activity in an effort to reach an agreement. In Christopher's shuttle diplomacy, he met with Assad, and both reviewed a draft of the memorandum of understanding, word by word. Although Assad said he preferred "more simple ideas", in practice the Syrians did not make significant changes in the document.

In the next meetings between Peres and Christopher, we reviewed the wording of the memorandum of understanding with the Americans. As time passed, meetings became more and more frequent. There were days when we would meet with the Americans several times a day. By the end of the shuttle diplomacy period, the Americans had managed to present a formula that was accepted by Syria, Lebanon and Israel.

The document noted that the two parties responsible for the implementation of the understandings were Israel and Lebanon, but Syria was also mentioned as having been consulted with. For us the mention of Syria was very important. While the Syrians refused to be a party to the agreement, their mention made it clear that they had accepted the agreement and contributed to its achievement.

The memorandum of understanding, which was published on April 26, 1996, and brought about the end of Operation "Grapes of Wrath", was based on the understandings of Operation

Accountability, and its foremost innovation included the establishment of a monitoring group from the US, France, Syria, Lebanon and Israel. Its mission - to monitor implementation of the understanding, and handle the parties' complaints regarding violations of the understanding.

It was also agreed that the United States would organize a consultative group comprising France, the European Union, Russia and other interested parties, in the interest of aiding in Lebanon's rehabilitative needs.

As a result of our demand, and as was known to Syria and Lebanon, the US sent a side letter to Israel stating that Israel would be permitted to fire at the sources of fire even if these were inside Lebanese villages, in the event they were fired on Israeli targets in the Security Zone or in Israel.

Similarly to the understandings of Operation Accountability, the "Grapes of Wrath" understandings were also violated frequently, and the region of southern Lebanon continued to bubble and boil for many years.

During the discussions on a ceasefire, the opposition did not hesitate to release baseless publications to the effect that the operation was part of the election campaign, and was intended to strengthen Peres' image in security matters. In terms of the elections, there was no doubt that the Qana event would be a major weight on Peres' shoulders among his constituents in the Arab sector, and so it was.

In early May, Martin Indyk informed us that the Syrian Ambassador Walid Muallem would like to meet Uri Savir for an informal meeting, and Peres replied that he did not see the necessity for this, twenty days before the elections.

On May 28, the elections were held in Israel, and contrary to all forecasts and surveys, Benjamin Netanyahu was elected Prime Minister. Thus ended the brief period in which Peres served as Prime Minister and Minister of Defense.

Chapter 16

"Look Me in the Eye"

Two months before the elections, I was appointed Director of the Mossad by Peres and I was supposed to take office immediately after the elections. So it came to be that the new Prime Minister Benjamin Netanyahu received me as a new appointment, but one made by his predecessor.

I was appointed to the position at the Mossad after thirty-three years of military service in fascinating and interesting roles, which began as a soldier and platoon commander in *Sayeret Matkal*, and culminated in the rank of Major General and Military Secretary to the Prime Minister.

On my first day without uniform, I started working at the Mossad. I did not have time to engulf myself in contemplation, to meditate, sit on the beach and ponder my personal history over the past thirty-three years, since I dived right into the difficult, fascinating and demanding position of Director of the Mossad.

During the election campaign, I took care, as I had throughout my military career, not to get involved in the political system in any way. I was always careful to make a clear and unequivocal distinction between my official role in the office of the Prime Minister and Minister of Defense and the political activity that naturally stirred in these places. In the past, military secretaries used to accompany the Prime Minister to political conventions, but to me this seemed wrong and inappropriate.

On the day of the elections, I followed them on the television set at my house, and like many others I went to bed late at night that day, with Peres - who was leading in the polls - to be elected as Prime Minister, and woke up with Netanyahu as Prime Minister.

The next day I went to the Prime Minister's office and found an atmosphere of doom and gloom accompanied by deep shock. Hearing the results was difficult for Peres but he kept a dignified face that did well to hide his emotions. The sense of a missed opportunity was common to all, since we were aware of Peres' many plans, and felt they would be put to an abrupt halt. Peres, to his credit, accepted the results with dignity and immediately conducted an orderly transfer of power, which of course included the transfer of all relevant information on the peace processes.

After Netanyahu assumed the role of prime minister, I was sent by him twice, discreetly, to conduct "proximity" talks with the Syrians. These meetings took place in hotels in Washington, where I met with US representatives such as Martin Indyk, who was in charge of the Middle East and Africa desks at the National Security Council, Dennis Ross and Mark Paris of the State Department.

In these meetings, I gave the Americans various formulae, which had been agreed upon in advance with Netanyahu, the goal being to try and renew the negotiations with Syria on their basis. The Americans took note, left the hotel, crossed the road, went to another hotel, where they met Walid Muallem, Syria's ambassador to the United States, and told him what I had said. After receiving his comments, they went back to me, and so on. Ultimately these meetings, in which the Americans hopped back and forth across two sides of the same road, were unfruitful and did not lead to any progress whatsoever.

All throughout his tenure Netanyahu tried to renew direct negotiations with Syria, but to no avail. In the past, when the Syrians had renewed discussions, it was based on their understanding that the Israeli side had consented to the "deposit." They did not request this to be uttered aloud, and would settle for it being conveyed behind the scenes and in the Americans' promises. For them, it was necessary to know that Netanyahu also agreed to the understanding implied by the "deposit", and until they could see proof of that they refused to hold direct talks. In addition, the Syrians had a considerable degree of suspicion towards Netanyahu, who had come to power carried by a strong right-wing election campaign, stressing that there would be no withdrawal from the Golan. In Syrian terms, Netanyahu's rise to power did not herald an optimistic period, and they assumed in advance that not much would be gained from their relationship with Netanyahu - if it would even exist.

In fact, throughout the period in which Netanyahu was in power, there was no direct contact between any Israeli and Syrian representatives. I was told so by Uzi Arad, who was Netanyahu's diplomatic adviser, during the onboarding he gave me as Chief of the Political-Security Staff in Barak's bureau, after the latter had replaced Netanyahu as Prime Minister.

According to Arad, the only contact with Syria during Netanyahu's period was through intermediaries such as Ron Lauder and Miguel Moratinos, the EU representative to the Middle East, and even these small efforts ended in September 1998.

Arad refused my request for a report on the contents of Lauder and Moratinos's meetings with the Syrians, saying he was not authorized to disclose this information, although he promised that Netanyahu would disclose it to Barak. Netanyahu did indeed give Barak an oral briefing on the content of the meetings with the Syrians, but it was completely general and did not reveal much. Having noticed that I had not received all the information I needed on the matter, I asked Dennis Ross for a summary of the American contacts with Syria regarding peace negotiations during Netanyahu's periods. A few months later, I received it.

The truth about the contents of the meetings between Netanyahu's emissaries to the Syrians and the messages conveyed in them was revealed by the testimonies of Ross and others, and from documents that came into our hands.

In the vaults of the Prime Minister's office we found two documents that were used by Lauder. One was written by him on August 25, 1998, and included discussion points Lauder had used with Assad, and the other was from September 29, 1998, and was a list of ten provisions entitled "Peace Agreement between Israel and Syria." From the information that came to us, we learned that under Lauder's initiative, Netanyahu had agreed to withdraw to the border as it was on June 4, 1967.

Patrick Seale, a British journalist and the official biographer of Hafez Assad, and who was considered his close friend and confidant, met with Barak about three months after his election, on August 25, 1999. The meeting was attended by Uri Sagi, whom Barak intended to lead the negotiation team with the Syrians, and myself, and it was in Barak's vacation lodge in Beit Hillel.

Seale came to the meeting after convening with Assad, and disclosed a message to Barak in which Lauder's emissary and its contents were mentioned.

Seale told us that during his meeting with Assad, in which Faruq al-Sharaa also participated, Assad had told him that he had met with Ron Lauder, whom he referred to several times as "Ambassador Lauder."

In that meeting, al-Sharaa said that Lauder had telephoned the Syrian ambassador to the United States Walid Muallem, and informed him that Netanyahu had authorized him to say that Israel would withdraw to the line of June 4, 1967 as part of a peace treaty. According to al-Sharaa, Lauder also added that he was willing to say these things to Assad as well, if the latter would agree to meet him – and on the basis of this statement, Lauder had come to Syria.

Seale told us that Assad said to him, "Lauder met with me and stated Netanyahu's agreement to a full withdrawal to the line of June 4, 1967. However, Lauder said that Netanyahu would not be able to say these things out loud, because they were contrary to his election platform, based on which he was elected. To my astonishment," Assad continued, "I heard from Lauder that Netanyahu believes it is possible to reach an agreement with Syria within fifteen days, and that he wishes to announce a full agreement as early as possible, and surprise the entire world."

Seale went on to quote Assad, who had said, "Lauder went on to talk about other matters, and I realized that a map is required to ensure that we are talking about the same things. I asked Lauder that at our next meeting he bring a map from Netanyahu, on which should appear the outline of the June 4, 1967 line as Israel sees it. It was my understanding that Netanyahu was willing to give us this map, but this did not happen, so the talks were suspended. "

Seale said that Assad had mentioned the willingness he had heard from Rabin, through Warren Christopher, to withdraw to the June 1967 line in exchange for fulfilling all of Israel's requirements, and noted that Peres had reiterated this commitment to Clinton immediately after Rabin was murdered.

Hence in this meeting Assad gave Seale a message to pass on to Barak, to the effect that the basis for resuming negotiations between Israel and Syria was an Israeli commitment to a full withdrawal to the line of June 4, 1967.

After the Lauder documents, which Netanyahu had authorized him to present to Assad, had come into our hands and confirmed everything that Seale had said, Clinton approached Lauder and invited him to a meeting in which he asked him to report on his contacts with the Syrians during Netanyahu's period.

On November 12, 1999, Lauder wrote a letter to Clinton, in which he sought to clarify some matters after having reviewed his notes. In his letter, he stated that he was referring to a period of five meetings during the summer and fall of 1998. Lauder wrote that although great progress was made in the talks they had not been completed, because it was impossible to delineate the security zones between Syria and Israel as long as Syria did not receive an Israeli map on which the line of June 4, 1967 was marked.

Lauder further wrote that in the meetings he had held with the Syrians, an agreement had been reached on some points, "I believe that these points still need to be finalized by defining the security zones on both sides of the border. These points were agreed to by both parties on September 12." The letter continued to list the points on which the parties had agreed, according to Lauder:

> Israel and Syria have decided to establish peace between their countries. The peace will be based on the principles of security, equality, respect for sovereignty, territorial integrity, and the political independence of both. The parties agree to the following provisions:

1. Israel will withdraw from the Syrian land taken in 1967, in accordance with Security Council Resolutions 242 and 338, which established the right of all states to secure and recognized borders in the "land for peace formula", to a commonly agreed border based on the line of June 4, 1967. The withdrawal will be implemented in three stages and it will last 18 months, with normalization implemented during the third stage. A mutual declaration of an end to the state of war will take place during the first phase of the withdrawal.

2. Due to the existing agreements between Syria and Lebanon, the two tracks should be conducted simultaneously, both with regards to solutions as well as with regards to the signing of the peace agreements between Syria and Israel and Lebanon and Israel.

3. In the framework of the peace process, Syria and Lebanon with other parties will discuss paramilitary activities across the borders with Israel with the aim of finding an appropriate solution.

4. The adoption of the paper reached between the parties during previous negotiations on "Aims and Principles of Security Arrangements", includes the establishment of demilitarized zones of limited forces on both sides.

5. In the case of a pressing need for an early-warning ground station, it is agreed that:

    a. EWS can remain on Mt. Hermon for a duration of ten years after total withdrawal: five years followed by a yearly extension for another five years upon agreement by both sides for a total of ten years.

b. It will be an American-French facility under the total auspices and responsibilities of both countries.

6. Peace is to comprise of diplomatic and normalized relations including the opening of embassies and various agreements about peaceful relations, provided that it is done according to laws and regulations.

7. The issue of water is to be addressed by Syria and Israel in accordance to international laws and norms, including the development of new water resources.

8. Syria believes that achievement of a just and comprehensive peace will solve many problems in the region at the forefront of which is the achievement of real and lasting peace between Syria and Israel.

(Lauder's original letter to President Clinton, dated November 12, 1999, appears in its original form as Appendix B on pages 721-723)

Before the Lauder documents came to our hands, I had already held an update meeting with a US team that included Dennis Ross, Martin Indyk, Aaron Miller and Rob Malley of the National Security Council.

During that meeting, I asked Ross if there had been talks between Israel and Syria during Netanyahu's period, and if so - what their contents had been.

Ross replied that Netanyahu had told Assad that he was committed to withdraw to the line of June 4, 1967. Ross noted that Netanyahu's statement was much more substantial than Rabin's, as Netanyahu had undertaken a commitment, while Rabin had spoken in conditional terms - only if all conditions would be fulfilled, would he agree to a full withdrawal.

Ross said he had heard this from two people: Walid Muallem, Syria's ambassador to Washington, told him that one day, Ron Lauder and Daniel Abraham (a Jewish-American businessman and millionaire) came to his office, asking to convey a message from Netanyahu to Assad. Muallem said to them that there was no point passing a message from Netanyahu to Assad unless Netanyahu would commit to withdraw to the line of June 1967. Eight months later, Daniel Abraham came to Muallem once again and said to him: I have received a commitment from Netanyahu to withdraw to the line of June 1967.

Ross proceeded to tell us that the other source for Netanyahu's willingness to withdraw from the Golan was Miguel Moratinos, the European Union's special envoy to the Middle East. Moratinos updated Ross that Netanyahu had told him that he had committed to the Syrians to withdraw to the line of June 1967, and was working to prepare a paper that would ratify this.

At this point, Martin Indyk intervened, adding that Ron Lauder had had nine meetings in Damascus with Assad, and in their final meeting, Assad had demanded a map with Netanyahu's signature on it, upon which the line of June 4, 1967 would be marked – the line to which Israel undertakes to withdraw. Indyk added that Yitzhak Mordechai, who was then the Israeli Minister of Defense, had refused to give this map to the Syrians, because he was dissatisfied with the security arrangements. He also said that on his way to meet with Arafat in the Wye Plantation, Netanyahu had made a detour in his journey, specifically in order to meet with Lauder and give him a message to pass on to Muallem – to the effect that Netanyahu himself had been willing to give Assad the map, and that he had been willing to go to Damascus for this purpose, but Assad had refused the offer.

Therefore, from the documents and various reports we had received, it could be seen that in total contrast to his statements, and according to Lauder and others, Benjamin Netanyahu had been prepared to withdraw from the Golan to the line of June 4, 1967, and had even pledged to do so before the Syrians.

Hence, when Mordechai told Netanyahu on live television that he had, in fact, promised the Syrians to withdraw from the Golan Heights, and Netanyahu denied it, Mordechai fixed his gaze at Netanyahu and said to him, "Look me in the eye!" At that point, both knew exactly what Mordechai was referring to.

Whenever Barak said that three prime ministers had promised to withdraw from the Golan Heights, including Netanyahu, he knew what he was talking about, and when Netanyahu responded that "nothing of the kind ever happened" - he was being inaccurate, to say the least.

Chapter 17

"How to Enter the Room"

Not long after the Syrian demand to receive a map containing the withdrawal line from Netanyahu, new elections were held in Israel, and Ehud Barak was elected the next Prime Minister.

During his election campaign Ehud Barak drew a fairly accurate picture of his approach to security and diplomacy. He said he was committed to peace, and that his administration would leave no stone unturned in its attempt to exhaust the process and make peace with Syria and the Palestinians. Barak also stated that within a year of establishing his administration, the IDF would withdraw from Lebanon as part of an agreement.

During the election campaign, Barak did not hesitate to say that he would be willing to make far-reaching concessions in the Golan Heights, and spoke very highly of Assad. He said that he was a courageous leader whose word could be trusted, and he was confident that when he would reach an agreement with Assad, it would be an agreement that Syria would honor.

While Barak was busy forming his coalition, I met with Ned Walker, US Ambassador to Israel, and he gave me a report on the talks held in mid-June 1999 between Assad and James Baker, Secretary of State under Bush Sr., and Ed Djerejian, ambassador to Syria and Israel. Baker and Djerejian reported that they had found a calm and focused Assad, who said that he had always wanted peace, and was under the impression that Barak wanted the same, and that in Lebanon there was greater support than ever for peace. "But," he added, "Syria does not have the ability to completely control Hezbollah."

Baker stressed to Assad the need for quiet in Lebanon, because otherwise Barak would have to respond in order to prove his ability to protect Israeli interests. Baker stressed that it was important that Syria send public statements in the media, the contents of which would convey positive signs regarding the peace process with Israel.

Assad said Barak's arrival at the Prime Minister's office was a good time to resume negotiations, and noted that he was encouraged by the people with whom Barak chose to surround himself, because he believed in their ability to contribute to the process.

The wind that blew from their meeting with Assad was that an opportunity had been created in which both sides wanted peace, and should be exploited.

Immediately upon entering office as Prime Minister, Barak said that he does not prefer one track of the peace process over the other, and that he wanted to move forward simultaneously and vigorously on both tracks, the Syrian and the Palestinian.

After establishing his government, Barak entered the diplomatic track in earnest, and soon planned his visit to Washington for meetings with Clinton.

Under my recommendation, the visit to the United States was preceded by three visits by Barak to regional leaders: President Mubarak in Egypt, King Abdullah in Jordan, and Chairman Arafat in Erez. The purpose of these meetings was to convey the importance of bilateral negotiations to achieve peace and that the American assistance would stay in the background.

The meeting with King Abdullah was after the latter had returned from Syria. Abdullah updated Barak that Assad was pleased, knew that Barak was committed to the peace process, and that he believed that Barak and Clinton wanted what was good for the Middle East.

Abdullah explained that Assad was conflicted regarding the Lebanese issue, since Lebanon – which was once an asset to Syria and a burden to Israel - had become a burden on Syria as well, since Hezbollah would occasionally act against Syrian interests.

In response to Abdullah's question about lowering the tension in Lebanon, Assad had said that an Israeli withdrawal from Lebanon could be a problem for Syria, as Syria was in Lebanon on the basis of the "Taif Agreement," in which the Lebanese had invited the Syrians to Lebanon to aid them in their defense. As soon as Israel would withdraw from Lebanon, the official reason for Syria's presence in Lebanon would disappear.

Another matter that came following the meeting with Assad was the king's hypothesis that Assad might appoint a person of trust to serve as a mediator shuttling between Assad and Barak, similar to Ron Lauder who had been the middleman between Netanyahu and Assad. Barak replied that if there would be someone who holds proof that he is indeed Assad's emissary, then Barak would have no problem cooperating with him and using his services.

As part of his efforts to promote his approach to the international community, Barak believed in direct diplomacy, rather than using couriers. In this Barak represented a process that is becoming increasingly prevalent in modern diplomacy, wherein many phone calls and direct meetings between leaders take place. Rabin also believed in this method, and when he wanted to clarify something that was fundamental and important to him, he did not hesitate to get on a plane and visit four European capitals in two days.

In his first months in office, Barak conducted a blitz of journeys in order to engrave his approach to end the conflict between Israel and the Arabs in the minds of regional leaders, the United States and Europe.

One of the first of Barak's meetings with world leaders was with Soviet President Boris Yeltsin who, according to rumors that prevailed at the time, was not in good health, and had an affinity and intimate familiarity with heavy drinking. Indeed, the meeting with him could be described as somewhat strange.

Yeltsin went into the meeting with an odd gait, heavy and stiff. He sat straight and stiff, and his whole body language seemed forced.

His body movements were sharp and without human softness, his face was blank and expressionless, and when he spoke he seemed to be giving a speech rather than conversing – his entire appearance gave the impression of a marionette operated by strings. After the meeting, when he stood up to take the closing picture, he was supported by two assistants, and when he began walking toward Barak, it seemed for a moment that he was going to fall flat on his face, even though there was no obstacle, and only the assistants, who quickly stabilized him, prevented his fall.

Throughout all the meetings with world leaders, some of whom had also met with Assad, Barak was repeatedly told that the Syrians believed his statements about his readiness and determination to make peace with Syria and the Palestinians. Additionally, the Syrian demand for full Israeli withdrawal from the Golan Heights in exchange for peace was heard time and again.

The most important visit Barak held, immediately at the start of his term, was with a president who was much more vigorous, healthy and active than Yeltsin - US President Bill Clinton.

Even before the visit to the United States, there was preliminary meeting in Zurich between a US team - which included the Special

Envoy of the Ministry of Foreign Affairs to the Middle East Dennis Ross and his assistant Aaron Miller, Martin Indyk and Rob Malley, both of the National Security Council - and the Israeli representatives Zvi Stauber and myself.

At the meeting, we received an update on what the Americans had heard on the subject of Syria from Arab representatives. King Abdullah told the Americans that Assad had been very pleased to hear the things I had said near Barak's election in an interview with Razi Barkai on the Israeli Galei Tzahal radio station, that the negotiations between Israel and Syria would probably start from the point where they had stopped in the Wye Plantation, during Peres' period.

Abdullah said that Assad wanted an early understanding that a withdrawal to the line of June 4, 1967 was not open for discussion. Abdullah stressed that Assad would be satisfied with an understanding rather than a commitment, even an indirect one, and a US-Israeli-Syrian understanding would satisfy him at that point.

Assad's formula was to publicly continue the talks from the point where they had been stopped, and confidentially have a joint understanding that the withdrawal would be to the line of June 4, 1967. Assad, according to King Abdullah, further added that in this situation, he would be flexible on the subject of security arrangements, and an agreement could be reached within four months.

The Americans also reported that Egyptian intelligence claimed that Israelis had been holding secret talks with Syria in Paris, which of course was a complete fantasy.

Such reports are an example of different messages that had been transferred by different means and understood in different ways, which tend to change and/or be distorted in the process. This is further evidence that the most effective and shortest route is via direct negotiations.

At that meeting, it was agreed that the Americans would pass a message to the Syrians, stating that the Americans feel that the gaps between Israel's positions and Syrian demands are not large, but that the Israelis feel that there are significant gaps when it comes to Syria's fulfillment of Israel's requirements. In view of this, the Americans would offer Syria to open a channel of private talks between Israeli and Syrian representatives, which would not constitute an official renewal of negotiations between the two countries, in order to increase the level of trust between the parties.

Barak sought to renew negotiations on the basis of the Lauder document, which for us was a good document that mentioned the existence of early-warning stations on Mount Hermon. The document also indicated that Netanyahu had pledged to withdraw to the borderline of 1967, which Barak saw as something that could greatly assist him in neutralizing domestic political opposition from the right wing, when the issue of withdrawal from the Golan Heights would come into public debate.

Barack attached great importance to his meeting with Clinton, since this was the first opportunity to fully present his approach regarding security and diplomacy to the US president, and to try to obtain the President's support and backing.

Barak prepared extensively for the trip to Washington. He sat for many secluded hours making notes for himself. I was the only person with whom he shared his feelings and thoughts.

At the same time, many phone calls between him and Clinton were already taking place, a matter that would later become a routine part of their relationship. In these talks Barak had already started purveying his ideas, and from Clinton's reactions it was clear that he was beginning to accept and become sympathetic of them.

Barak wished to convince the President of his intention to act decisively in order to promote diplomatic processes, and that this was possibly a propitious time to design the relations with Syria and the Palestinians, to upgrade relations with the United States and to lead future changes in the Middle East and beyond.

In the US government it is customary that prior to meeting with the President, many long meetings are held with the President's aides and the Secretary of State and her aides, and only after these preparations comes the climactic moment - a personal meeting with the President. Barak, as was his way, disassembled the rules of protocol, and reassembled and bent them according to his needs and preferences. He insisted on the need for many face-to-face private meetings with the President, and even managed to change the order of the sessions, so that he immediately met directly with the President in a round of long and personal meetings. In these meetings Barak sought to receive the US President's full support for Israel's position, as he believed that recruiting the United States to our side would improve the chances of Israel's position having greater influence in the negotiation processes with our neighbors.

Barak insisted on presenting his views to Clinton without presenting them first to senior US officials, including the US Secretary of State, as was customary, and this greatly annoyed the latter. However, Barak, with his extraordinary force of conviction, persuaded Clinton that this was the right way. Barak did not want only to speak, but also to listen to Clinton's advice, and create a dialogue between them through which he would finalize the details of his plan on the Palestinian and Syrian tracks.

His success in bending the US government's rules of protocol stirred criticism and anger towards Barak among US officials. These people were offended when Barak had skipped them on his way to the President. They do not like people meddling in their work and wanted to work as they were accustomed to for hundreds of years. They did not like that the head of this tiny Middle Eastern state was changing their time-honored traditions.

In his meeting with Clinton, Barak raised three issues: Presenting his new approach for the Palestinian track, i.e., that before the third and final stage of Israeli withdrawal, as had been agreed in the Oslo Accords, the parties should reach a framework agreement for the permanent settlement, which would outline the principle components that would form the basis for solving problems in the permanent settlement - refugees (right of return), Jerusalem, borders, settlements, security arrangements and the nature of the Palestinian state to be established.

Regarding the Syrian track, Barak presented his determined intention to make every effort to achieve peace with Syria, noting his willingness to make far-reaching and painful concessions on the Golan. Barak was careful to not use terms like complete withdrawal. He made it clear that although we do not retract Rabin's "deposit" and are not canceling it, he was not ready to ratify it, that is to say, was not ready to adopt Rabin's formula.

The third thing Barak discussed with Clinton was US-Israeli relations and the need to upgrade the relations.

The two of them agreed to establish a senior Israeli-US consultative group, which would convene twice a year and discuss strategic and various other issues, in order to form coordinated and common goals. They spoke of the need to ensure that the United States did not surprise Israel with regard to negotiations with the Arabs, that the Arabs would not suddenly hear an American position that had not been heard by the Israelis beforehand. It was agreed that the United States would continue to ensure Israel's qualitative advantage in the region, so that Israel could always defend itself by itself.

Barak told Clinton that he intended to move forward on both tracks, the Syrian and Palestinian simultaneously, without either undermining the other, but noted that for the first stage, and temporarily, he had chosen to devote the bulk of his efforts and attention to the Syrian track.

Barak estimated, correctly in my view, that the problems with Syria were less complicated and easier to solve than those between Israel and the Palestinians. President Assad was seen as someone who could make decisions and important resolutions, as opposed to Arafat who was constantly caught zigzagging, maneuvering and having trouble deciding. In addition, Barak understood that an agreement with Syria would stop the bloody situation in Lebanon, and had a very great interest to withdraw from Lebanon as part of an agreement with Syria. Barak also thought that one of the byproducts of an agreement with Syria, or even significant progress in the negotiations with it, would also be an acceleration in negotiations with the Palestinians, and that other Arab and Muslim nations would join the peace process.

Barak came to the meeting with President Clinton with his "three paradoxes" theory.

According to this theory, devised by Barak, the first paradox was the "Wye paradox", wherein Benjamin Netanyahu had pledged to transfer thirteen percent of the West Bank and Gaza territories to the Palestinians.

Barak believed that this transfer would increase friction between the Palestinian and Israeli populations, make it difficult for Israel to ensure the security of its citizens, and create a jumble between Palestinian and Israeli territories.

The paradox lies in that the Wye Agreement had been meant to promote peace between Israel and the Palestinians, but in fact the transfer of additional territory to Palestinian responsibility would only increase the friction between the sides, and raise the risk of violent outbreaks, and thus deepen the mistrust and rivalry between the two sides.

The second paradox was the "Lebanon paradox." Barak believed that, unlike in the past, Hezbollah was not a burden only on Israel but had also became a millstone on the neck of the Syrians. This was due to Hezbollah having received a sort of unofficial veto power on the negotiations between Israel and Syria, and had the ability to thwart the peace process by increasing terrorist activities. Barak stated that he could not and would not be willing to negotiate with Syria alongside terrorism in Lebanon.

The third paradox was the "Golan Heights paradox." Barak was convinced that if we would meet directly with the Syrians, we would leave the room with an agreement. However, Assad refused to enter the conference room without Israel announcing in advance that the outcome of the discussions would be an Israeli withdrawal from the Golan Heights to the line of June 4, 1967.

"I have received a mandate to strengthen the security of Israel," Barak said, "and I cannot enter talks while announcing in advance that I have conceded the most important element of our security."

Here Barak connected substance with process, as he believed Israel would be perceived as weak in the eyes of its neighbors and residents if it were to agree to the Syrian demand to withdraw to the line of 1967 before discussions had even started.

During the visit, most of the conversations between Barak and Clinton were intimate, and were attended only by the two of them, but having returned from the talks Barak would dictate their contents to me to ensure that they would not be kept only in his memory.

Clinton felt a deep commitment to the peace process in the Middle East, and invested much time in it. Clinton devoted about seven of the eight years of his tenure in the White House to the Middle East, because he realized that the conflict there had a negative effect on global stability, rather than merely regional stability. Clinton's approach to international affairs was that conflicts in the world should be resolved, including by the use of force, as was done in Kosovo. He had an additional ambition in the Middle Eastern conflict, stemming from his sense of mission, his religious beliefs and special attitude towards Israel, its values and its long-standing history.

During their meetings, Clinton asked Barak, "Assad will ask about Rabin's 'deposit.' What should I say to him?" Barak replied, "I cannot see a situation where the Syrians are on the shore of the Sea of Galilee, and I would also like to present to you the importance of the early-warning station on Mount Hermon. About the 'deposit' – tell Assad I am not canceling it and am not asking to retract it." However, Barak refused Syria's demand and the US request to ratify Rabin's deposit.

From the meeting notes, one can learn the extent of Barak's suspicions that the Syrians were setting a trap for him.

Clinton asked to hear from Barak about the reality he envisioned following the establishment of peace with Syria, and Barak described a situation where full peace would be established and there would be real normalization between the two countries. Furthermore, in this situation, a solution would be found to the issues surrounding Lebanon, terrorism would desist, Hezbollah would be disarmed, Syria would stop supporting terrorism and would abolish all terrorist headquarters from Damascus. Syria would not be on the Sea of Galilee and the Jordan mountains, would not have direct contact with our water sources, and embassies would open in the first phase of the agreement's implementation.

Clinton told Barak that he would give him his full support, and help reduce the risks that Israel would assume as part of peace treaties with Syria and the Palestinians, by maintaining Israel's qualitative edge compared to the Arab nations, as well as via broad and in-depth intelligence cooperation.

It was agreed to establish a fixed encrypted phone line between Clinton and Barak, and that Albright would visit the region to advance the process.

In talks with Clinton's Vice President Al Gore and others, Barak said that he intended to proceed on parallel tracks with Syria and the Palestinians, and promised that he did not intend to use one of the tracks in a way that would disturb or undermine progress on the other.

On the agenda was Albright's visit to the region, a visit that Barak preferred not take place. Barak was concerned that Albright's shuttle diplomacy in the region could lead to a series of leaks that would create an unnecessarily ugly atmosphere between Syria and Israel.

Barak constantly tried to find the best and most effective way to reach Assad, including his meeting with Patrick Seale, a close associate of Assad and his biographer. In his vacation lodge in Beit Hillel he reiterated, "The gap between me and Assad is a few hundred yards. I feel that if Clinton, Assad and I would sit in one room, we would solve all the problems faster than people think. My ability to make concessions depends on me not having to announce them right at the start. There are two possibilities for the process to develop: one is a confidential meeting between representatives whom we trust, and the other is that the Lauder document be the basis for further negotiations."

Seale said that the issue of the waters of the Sea of Galilee was very important to Assad, stressing that Assad had to have access to this water even if it would be limited.

Access to the waters of the Sea of Galilee was very symbolic in Assad's eyes, because the Syrians knew that Syria had controlled the shore of the Sea of Galilee in 1967, and there had been a few fishing villages there. That is why Syria believed that if it did not return to the actual waterline, then it would not have really returned to the borderline of 1967.

When Barak spoke about the components of normalization and security arrangements, it was evident from Seale's expression that he was displeased. Seale said that Assad would not accept the existence of a ground warning station on Mount Hermon.

Throughout the conversation, Barak and Seale exchanged opinions about different formulations that would allow the resumption of talks. Barak said we needed to reach a phrasing behind the scenes that would satisfy Assad and would be different from the public phrasing.

Barak asked Seale to check with Assad about his opinion on the Lauder document, and his thoughts about a meeting between Assad, Clinton and himself in Geneva, to take place on Clinton's invitation. He suggested that initially only Clinton and Assad attend the meeting, and when Clinton felt that the time was ripe, Barak would be invited to join the meeting.

Hinting at the state of Assad's health, Seale noted, "You only have a few months with Assad."

At the same time, Barak, during phone conversations he had with Clinton, continued to try to find the phrasing that would enable Assad to resume talks. Barak felt trapped in this matter, because

Assad demanded that Barak agree in advance to withdraw from the Golan Heights, as a condition for resuming negotiations, a demand that was impossible in Barak's terms. All this transpired while Barak was convinced that once the parties would sit together - problems would be solved quickly.

Barak said of this absurdity that, "If we enter the room – we'll surely find a solution; the problem is how to enter the room."

For long hours I sat with Barak trying to find formulations that would be transferred to the Americans and that could bring the Syrians back to the negotiating table.

Finally, following a telephone conversation between Clinton and Assad, the latter agreed to send his own representative to a meeting in Europe with Barak's representative, in the presence of a US representative.

The Syrians viewed these talks as negotiations, while we saw them as clarification and exploratory talks, intended to build a springboard for negotiations. Barak did not think it was possible to handle such critical negotiations between only two representatives.

Barak wanted to appoint Uri Sagi for the position and I supported this idea.

The relationship between Barak and Sagi had had its ups and downs since the days of their military service. The biggest crisis in their relationship was due to what happened after the 'Tze'elim 2' disaster, and furthermore Sagi was disappointed that Barak had not acted vigorously to appoint him Deputy Chief of Staff. In his book, *Lights in the Fog,* Sagi harshly criticized Barak, which did not improve the murky relationship between them. However, at the moment of truth, Barak transcended above all personal considerations, because he estimated that Sagi was the best man for this type of contact with the Syrians.

When he was Head of Military Intelligence, Sagi had specialized in the Syrian issue and had devoted much time and thought to it. Even at that time Sagi had estimated that Syria was open to negotiations, and was interested in reconciliation with Israel. For Barak, it was important that the meeting with the Syrians be attended by a person who was both highly knowledgeable in the issues between Israel and Syria, and who believed that the negotiations were likely to succeed.

Therefore, to be able to consult with Sagi in real time during the talks in Switzerland, the Prime Minister's Office established a confidential encrypted connection station, and Sagi was accompanied by a contact who carried the required communication equipment.

In the briefings before the meeting with the Syrians, Barak stressed to Sagi that the goal was to bring about a resumption of negotiations without committing to withdraw to the line of 1967.

Barak asked to stress the issue of Israeli presence on Mount Hermon, the timetable of three to five years to execute the agreement, security arrangements, components of normalization, cessation of terrorism from Lebanon and the disarming of Hezbollah, and a resolution of the Israeli-Lebanese dispute. Another issue was finding a regional solution to the water issue: setting up desalination plants along the coastline to provide water to Israel, Jordan and the Palestinians, and cooperation with Turkey on the water issue. This involved transferring water from Turkey to Syria, to compensate the Syrians for their claim that the Sea of Galilee should also serve as a water source for them.

Barak stressed that Syria's demand that Israel withdraw to the 1967 lines and that Syria should reach the Sea of Galilee's coastline was problematic, as it would not allow Israel to maintain the only reliable reservoir of fresh water in Israel. Barak argued that Israel had to maintain sovereignty over a strip of land east of the Sea of Galilee in order to secure complete control of the waters, and made it clear that the issue of withdrawal from the Golan was a very sensitive public and political issue in Israel.

Barak asked to offer the Syrians to set up three discussion groups: one to discuss the issues of water, borders, normalization and timetables, a second group that would focus on security arrangements and third to contemplate the Lebanese issue.

Barak asked Sagi to convey the message to the Syrians that Barak would be the Prime Minister for eight years, and that he and only he would be the person with whom Syria would have to try and achieve peace, whether they liked it or not.

Barak believed that some decisions could only be made in a direct meeting between leaders. Furthermore, in his opinion, far-reaching concessions in the Golan Heights would be better received by the Israeli public if they were part of a package that would also include considerable Syrian compensation to Israel, and only if they would be reached in a trilateral summit attended by Clinton, Assad and Barak.

The messages I gave the Americans on Barak's behalf, before the meetings between the representatives, were that Barak was not reinventing anything, but was also not retracting Rabin's "deposit." This was due to his opinion that we had to first try and build confidence that the conflict could be resolved without creating a binding commitment at this preliminary stage, which Barak would not currently be able to make good on. I further added that we were not ignoring what had happened during Rabin and Netanyahu's periods – namely the Lauder document. Barak took care to mention Netanyahu in the context of negotiations with Syria, in order to make it easier when the time would come to convince the public to agree to the concessions he realized he would have to make.

In addition, I had to make it clear to the Americans that the conflict could not be resolved "within a week" as Clinton believed, and that there needed to be an understanding that the meetings between Israeli and Syrian representatives were not meant to replace peace talks, but were only a preparation for their renewal.

Barak stressed that the psychological, political and public effect would have a major impact and that time had to be spent to solve these problems. He therefore wanted to create drama around a leaders' summit headed by Clinton, a meeting that would end the conflict in a historic peace agreement between Syria and Israel.

Barak knew that Assad wanted a public or secret promise to withdraw to the lines of 1967, and claimed that this was much more than what Assad had received from Rabin, as Rabin's "deposit" was not a promise but a conditional statement. Rabin had not pledged to withdraw to the line of June 4, 1967, but had said that Israel would be willing to withdraw to this line only if its requirements would be fully addressed.

Barak thought it would be wrong to return to the border of 1967, as it is perceived by the Syrians, because it was important for Israel to retain unquestionable sovereignty over the waterways: all the sources of the northern Jordan River mountains up to the Sea of Galilee, and the Sea of Galilee itself. Hence, Barak wanted the borderline between Israel and Syria to pass east of the Jordan River and the Sea of Galilee.

In a telephone conversation with Clinton, Barak said, "You can tell Assad that with me, he is not exposing himself to risks as he did with Lauder, because this time you are in the picture and you remember the 'deposit'." Barak was hinting at the fact that talks with Lauder had taken place without American sponsorship or involvement, and so there had been no "Keeper of the Seals", or historical memory keeper present.

Barak told Clinton that he felt that they were putting a historic move into motion and Clinton replied, "You can do what no one has done before: make peace with Syria."

Barak gave Sagi a briefing prior to the latter's meeting with his Syrian counterpart, Riad Daoudi, who was Legal Adviser to the Syrian Foreign Ministry (who also handled indirect talks between Syria and Israel, via Turkey, with Prime Minister Olmert's Chief of Staff). In the briefing, Barak said that Lauder had been given the impression that Assad had been willing to discuss some flexibility regarding a few hundred yards on this side or that of the 1967 border.

Barak asked Sagi that talks remain confidential, devoid of any official and binding record, and would require the ratification of the leaders.

If the talks would succeed, Barak said, there would three options for moving forward. The first was to move the process from confidential to public negotiations, and then hold a summit that would lead to peace. The second was that the confidential process would continue and lead directly to the summit with Clinton and Assad, in which the key elements to resolve the outstanding issues would be finalized, and would later be translated into a detailed agreement. A third possibility was that following the confidential process, a summit would take place, and based on its principles, open negotiations would continue and lead to peace. The difference between the second and third alternatives was that according to the third only the principles would be finalized at the summit, and no further negotiations would be required.

Lauder's travels to Syria were accompanied by George Nader, a Christian citizen of Lebanon. Nader had lived for many years in the United States, was the editor of the *Middle East Insight* journal, and had been trying to help the peace process for numerous years and in different ways. Nader was a welcome guest in Syria, and as early as Rabin's period, he would come to us with different messages and met with me many times.

Nader had participated in Lauder's talks with Assad, and had carefully taken note of their contents, including of course the Syrian responses.

Therefore, Barak wanted to meet him and learn from him of the Syrians' answers to Netanyahu's offers.

At a meeting with him, which lasted two hours, Nader told us everything he knew about the talks between Bibi and Assad, through Lauder.

Nader said that Assad's meeting with Lauder and himself, as Netanyahu's emissaries, was based as far as Assad was concerned on the assumption that Israel would accept the principle of withdrawal to the 1967 lines - which would be delineated by Israel and Syria together. This was because each party had its own 1967 line, and Assad assumed that the parties could reach an agreed line. Assad, according to Nader, wanted to reach an agreement without the Americans' intervention - and surprise them. In Assad's view, US involvement could ruin everything. He viewed some within the US State Department, led by Dennis Ross, as leaning towards the Israeli side. Assad believed that the Americans' presence in the talks causes leaks, and as evidence noted the fact that the contacts during Rabin and Peres' periods had not yielded anything.

Nader said he had visited twelve times in Syria, nine of them with Ron Lauder.

He said that the meetings were held from the beginning of June 1998 to September 6, 1998 – the meeting in which Assad had asked to receive a map.

Nader stressed that all these conversations had been recorded and had still been kept in the Syrian palace to that day. He also said that already in the first meeting, Assad had demanded a full withdrawal to the 1967 lines, and Lauder had responded by saying that in principle, his answer was affirmative and that the line itself would need to be delineated later on.

Nader said that on a few occasions he met with Uzi Arad, Netanyahu's diplomatic adviser, and from him he received confirmation several times that this referred to a full withdrawal to the line of June 4, 1967. Nader noted that he had not heard Netanyahu say this, but stressed that Lauder had heard it from Netanyahu and had repeated it to him and to the Syrians.

Nader also said that Uzi Arad had called him and Lauder while the two were in Paris, and informed them that the map Assad asked for – with the delineation of the withdrawal line - was ready. "We immediately got on a plane and came to Israel," said Nader, "but we did not receive the map."

The matter of the map came up after Lauder asked the Syrians if they wanted to work with a Syrian or an Israeli map of 1967 - because these showed two different versions of the line. The Syrians asked for an Israeli map.

Nader said that Netanyahu had been willing to give the map, and that twice he and Lauder had been called to come and get it. Nader said that on one occasion, Minister of Defense Yitzhak Mordechai had been willing to give the map, and then he had changed his mind. "On both times, we were told upon our arrival that the map was not ready," said Nader. "Once, Uzi Arad was even waiting for us in the VIP lounge, and when we arrived he said, 'We're sorry, the map is not ready.'"

It is my impression that Netanyahu had intended to give the Syrians a map with the line of June 4, 1967, according to the Israeli position, but the map was not transferred, probably due to opposition by Yitzhak Mordechai and Ariel Sharon.

Nader also told us that in the second half of August, when Netanyahu understood that Mordechai was unwilling to provide the map, the former brought Ariel Sharon into the picture.

"Sharon said he was willing to go to Syria himself to meet with Assad, and in this case would also be willing to give him the map," said Nader and continued, "Netanyahu's answer was 'I'll go with the map to Assad.'" Sharon did not agree to this, and they agreed that if it had been decided to transfer the map, then all three - Netanyahu, Mordechai and Sharon - would bring the map to Assad."

Nader said that he and Lauder had received the impression that Netanyahu did not have Mordechai and Sharon's support to present the map.

Nader went on to say that in one of the meetings, Assad had told them that he would accept Israeli sovereignty over the Sea of Galilee, but stressed that the Syrians would have to be given presence on the coastline.

At that Barak asked Nader if he thought it was possible that Assad would agree that Israel also retain sovereignty in a certain territorial strip of several hundred meters east of the Sea of Galilee. To that Nader replied, "It would be very hard to achieve this."

Nader's report, the Syrians' consent to the Switzerland meeting and preparations for Sagi's journey made us feel that there might be progress with Syria. We were happy that nothing had been leaked, and felt we were building a foundation for the talks to continue, one that could lead to a historic reconciliation process with the Syrians.

Barak had a telephone conversation with Dennis Ross who was already in Bern, waiting to serve as best man between Daoudi and Sagi.

Dennis said to Barak, "The goal is to reach a formula by which Albright will be able to announce the resumption of talks."

Barak updated Ross about Lauder's 'ten provisions' document, as well as our meetings with Nader and the things we had heard from him. Barak told Dennis that following the meetings with Lauder and Nader he was beginning to understand the way Assad had reacted, and his demand that before the meeting between Sagi and Daoudi take place, as a condition for starting any form of talks, he wished to receive a promise, even a secretive one, for a withdrawal to the 1967 lines. "Now I understand," said Barak, "that as Assad sees it I'm backtracking in my positions, compared to Netanyahu who promised him the line of June 4, 1967."

Dennis noted that from his acquaintance with Nader, the latter tended to speak honestly, carefully and precisely. "What he reports is what happened as he understands it," said Dennis, "and it is reported faithfully."

Sagi came to Switzerland, and immediately after his first meetings with Daoudi reported back to Barak, "Daoudi said he wants to reach a quick formula and is open to hear our constraints."

Barak asked Sagi to tell Daoudi on his own behalf (and not on Barak's behalf), that he believed that Barak would like to sign a peace treaty with Syria before signing an agreement with the Palestinians. This was because the problems with the Syrians were simpler, while with the Palestinians everything was much more complicated and difficult, even in the emotional aspect, because of the special bond the Israeli public feels when it comes to the areas of Judea and Samaria.

Talks between Sagi and Daudi lasted two days, and ended without an agreement being reached and without a redeeming formula being obtained.

A few days later Ross visited Israel, after a visit to Syria, and told us that he had met Assad for the first time in two years, and that he had seemed older and on the mental side was not as sharp as he had been previously. Ross reported that Assad had expressed concern that the "deposit" would be taken from him, and had agreed that Ross commute between the parties to construct the formula that would allow the resumption of talks.

Ross said that the Syrians were interested in continuing the Daoudi-Sagi talks, and wanted to come to Washington two days later and start working immediately.

At the meeting Barak and I had with Sagi and Amnon Lipkin-Shahak, Barak instructed Sagi that talks had to be confidential and undocumented. This was in order to enable both parties to examine the areas of flexibility on issues discussed in the previous session, and lead to a formula we would be comfortable with and would be agreed upon between us, the Syrians and the Americans - a formula that would allow the resumption of negotiations.

Barak reiterated to Sagi to maintain our position regarding holding the waterline. This referred to a strip of a few hundred meters east of the Jordan River mountains, and a few hundred meters east of the Sea of Galilee, in the area where the Syrians claimed they had been on the coast of the Sea of Galilee in 1967, that would remain under Israeli sovereignty.

At a meeting with Ross, Barak said that if as part of a signed agreement we would receive sovereignty over the entire land strip east of the Sea of Galilee, we would be willing to consider allowing Syrian citizens to access the Sea of Galilee through this strip. This would allow the Syrians to enter the waters of the lake under Israeli sovereignty, and they would be able to sail, swim and fish in them.

Barak insisted on the meeting including the contents of the talks that had been held in Netanyahu's period, since according to Lauder Syria had agreed to a ground warning station on Mount Hermon for ten years, under US and French control. From what Lauder had said it had been implied that this American-French control could also informally include the presence of Israeli experts, and for internal political reasons it was important for Barak to make use of the fact that Netanyahu had agreed to withdraw to the line of June 4, 1967.

In preparatory meetings with the Syrians, the Americans discovered that the strip of Israeli sovereignty on the northeast of the Sea of Galilee infuriated the Syrians. However, Barak insisted that everything would depend on the question of control over all water resources.

Americans later announced that they felt they had exhausted the dialogue with Daoudi and al Sharaa, and had decided to meet with Assad.

This decision caused us considerable consternation, and left us feeling that another attempt to resume peace talks with Syria had failed.

Clinton sent Assad a letter stating that we had reached the moment of truth. "I have found that the requirements of both parties can be fulfilled. The key issues are the relationship between the control of water sources and the borderline, and the matter of early warning." Clinton wrote. "There is no substitute for direct meetings between the two sides, and I fear that unless we move on to the political level we will vanquish the opportunity. I would not suggest this if I did not think that these matters could be resolved. The deposit Rabin entrusted in me stays with me and has not been taken back. I am also offering Barak to come to a meeting on the political level."

Lord Michael Levy, the British Prime Minister's Envoy to the Middle East, met several times with al-Sharaa and Assad and also reported that the Syrian approach was that they wished for peace, and Assad would be flexible on all issues except that of the border, which had to return to the line of 1967. Assad also said that he did not believe that Barak would withdraw from Lebanon unilaterally.

Barak always said that he would not be able to start negotiations with the Syrians with a confidential or public statement that goes beyond Rabin's "deposit", but stressed that he could defend a position that stated that he would be willing to ratify the "deposit."

Following Clinton's letter to Assad, Assad agreed to resume high-level talks from where they had been stopped. Assad's representative would be Syrian Foreign Minister Farouk al-Sharaa.

The US accepted Barak's request for two sessions to be held: a short one meant to form a framework for negotiations and to set an agenda, and a second meeting, which would be more material and would last as long as necessary until an agreement would be reached. This was a process similar to the one that was used in Camp David with Begin and Sadat, in which both sides sat together in the presence of Americans, until a breakthrough was achieved.

An issue that arose in the talks between Clinton and Barak was that the Palestinians might worry that the progress being made with the Syrians might hurt them, and Clinton promised to speak with Arafat in order to reassure him that the talks with the Syrians would not come at their expense.

Ross told Barak that even though it was the month of Ramadan, the Syrians were willing to come, which indicated the high importance they attached to this matter. The Syrians would of course refrain from eating and drinking during the talks but, as Ross said, "They said they would understand if the Israelis would ask for an hour-long break to eat…"

The lunchtime break was not the only one. Al-Sharaa wanted to have a break between two rounds of talks to reorganize. It was agreed that the parties would not make any press releases, except for the Americans. It was agreed that the opening ceremony at the White House would be brief and would only include a statement by Clinton.

The Syrians did not like the idea that the essentials would not be discussed at the first meeting. Al-Sharaa wanted to talk about everything except the withdrawal, under the assumption that it was agreed and understood that it would be a withdrawal to the line of 1967.

Assad told the Americans that in order to reach a final agreement, he understood there would have to be a summit between the three leaders - Barak, Clinton and himself. At this point, there would not be a handshake between Barak and al-Sharaa. We found Syria's attitude bewildering, but we agreed because we attached greater importance to the meeting itself being held and did not see a reason to insist on shaking hands, an insistence that could delay or cancel the meeting. Furthermore, insisting on something that was mostly symbolic, and later conceding it, would make us look ridiculous.

In negotiations, you have to keep a sense of proportion. This is because on the one hand, it is clear that the parties declare certain positions in public in order to strengthen their opening positions in the negotiations. However, on the other hand, it should be clear to each side that the final positions will not be similar to the opening ones, and that they will have to make concessions during negotiations.

Hence insistence should be focused on important and vital matters, and not ones that are highly likely to change over the course of negotiations. Once you concede a position which you previously declared to be a 'deal-breaker,' it lets the other party understand that the more pressure it exerts the higher its odds to make you cross more and more lines.

Ross told us that Assad wanted a simple agreement, and not a complicated one such as Oslo, which might not work.

Barak updated Ross that if an agreement would be reached with the Syrians, he would need to request it be approved by the government and the Knesset, and then the public would have to approve it in a referendum.

Barak believed that a peace agreement with Syria would lead to peace agreements with additional Arab and Muslim nations. Barak was well aware that the price Israel would need to pay in the Golan Heights would be a very painful one. Therefore on the other side of the scales there would have to be not only peace with Syria but also with other Arab and Muslim nations, particularly in North Africa and the Persian Gulf, an agreement with Lebanon and the complete cessation of terrorism. It would also require massive US aid to strengthen the security of the State of Israel and compensate it for the loss of its control of the Golan Heights.

Barak believed that in the face of such a peace and aid package, the members of the Knesset and the Israeli public would find it easier to accept the heavy price of withdrawal from the Golan and understand that it would be beneficial. The greater the compensation Israel would receive, the easier it would be to accept the calamity of withdrawal from the Golan.

The Americans agreed with this position completely and began to act by proxy in Arab and Muslim countries, in order to promote a much broader process that would lead to peace agreements with other countries. The responses the Americans received from the Saudis, the Persian Gulf countries and the North African countries were that when Israel would achieve an agreement with Syria and Lebanon, they would also join the peace process with Israel.

When the US Secretary of State Albright visited Israel, after a visit to Syria, she told Barak that al-Sharaa had accompanied her to the airport and had told her there that he would have to return from the meeting with Barak with an understanding that the Israeli withdrawal would be to the 1967 lines.

Barak replied to Albright, "I cannot make such a promise to him, because it would ruin the entire negotiations. The Syrians will have to suffice with me not retracting Rabin's 'deposit.' They want the border of 1967 and I want full sovereignty over the Sea of Galilee. I think we can bridge the gap between these two aspirations."

In those days, Barak's approach seemed very prudent to me, despite the Syrian statements that conditioned the peace agreement solely on withdrawal to the line of 1967, and their emphasis that they would not give up one inch of the Golan Heights. At the time, I thought that Syria could be convinced to accept the entire Golan Heights, with the border being determined on the basis of a line, which could be defined by both parties' agreement as "the line of June 4, 1967."

I wish to clarify that our line of June 4, 1967 was not identical to the Syrian one, since this line had never been drawn on a map. Due to many incidents that occurred before the Six-Day War, each side had a different definition for the territory under its control. Between the Israeli and Syrian outposts was an area that each side claimed as its own. For example, to ensure greater control over the Sea of Galilee and demonstrate sovereignty, the Israeli navy made patrols that tried to get as close as possible to the east coast of the Sea of Galilee, on its northern part. In response, the Syrians fired on Israeli ships when they came too close to the eastern bank of the lake, in their eyes. On the other hand, whenever the Syrians tried to enter the Sea of Galilee and display this kind of control, we fired at them to prevent their entry. Examples such as these led to the fact that we claim to have had sovereignty over the entire Sea of Galilee, while they claim to have had direct access to its waters at the time.

Our approach in the days leading to the talks with al-Sharaa was established on the fact that there was no 1967 border clearly delineated on the map. Given this, if Israel would offer Syria a borderline that was very close to the 1967 line as Syria saw it, along with a small piece of land that was indisputably under Israeli sovereignty before the Six-Day War - there was a good chance that the Syrians would agree.

Later, the Syrians made it clear, in no uncertain terms, that there was nothing to discuss, opting to end negotiations as a result of their insistence that the line would be that of June 4, 1967, and no other. After this, I realized that this was a 'red line' the Syrians would not be willing to cross in the future as well. I also realized that if offered adequate arrangements to ensure full Israeli sovereignty over the Sea of Galilee, and security arrangements to meet all the needs of the State of Israel, Israel would have to agree in principle to the line of June 4, 1967. Israel would additionally have to move it as eastwards as possible in the negotiations as part of the discussions on its exact location, which as previously mentioned, had never been defined or delineated.

CHAPTER 18

GAINS VS. PRICE

Barak was harshly criticized for his decision to attend the talks with al-Sharaa. Some claimed that by deciding that the Israeli representative to the talks with the Syrian Foreign Minister would be the Prime Minister himself, Barak had left no latitude for involving higher ranks as negotiations proceed.

It was quite clear that Assad would not join the negotiations between the parties, except in their last stage, and would only arrive after most of the work had already been completed and when it would be necessary to resolve the difficult issues, such as the borderline and Israeli early-warning station on Mount Hermon.

Barak's approach was that in order to maximize the chance to pave a way to the summit, there was no reasonable alternative but to send the most senior person who can decide on issues in which Israel must reach decisions, and to do so already in the stages before the leaders' summit.

Barak believed that if Israeli Foreign Minister David Levy would be sent to handle talks with al-Sharaa, very soon the same disputes would surface, as in fact did eventually happen during al-Sharaa and Barak's discussions. What would happen then? After all, the problems had to be decided by Barak, and the discussions could dissolve, which would waste precious time and possibly lead to a loss of momentum.

If that would be the case, the argument would have been that since Barak had not attended the talks with al-Sharaa, a rare opportunity to advance talks with Syria had been missed, because if the talks between the foreign ministers of Israel and Syria would have reached a dead end, Assad would not have attended the "next level" of the talks.

Moreover, it was clear that Assad was not yet ready to participate in the meetings and discussions with Barak himself, but sent to the talks the most senior person responsible for foreign relations in Syria, who was considered one of the most senior officials in the Syrian regime.

We thought that this was an elusive opportunity, and as soon as it would dissipate it would be difficult to produce a second chance, and hence would be wrong to miss.

We arrived in Washington and after a short meeting between the three leaders - Clinton, Barak and al-Sharaa - they left the White House lawn for a short formal ceremony.

I was very excited by the weight of the occasion, and I had a feeling that this time it was going to succeed and that we were facing a historic breakthrough that would change the face of the Middle East and open a new era that would bring an end to wars.

I was already familiar with some of the Syrian representatives from previous meetings. I met Walid Muallem, Syrian ambassador to Washington, who had taken part in our discussions with the Syrian Chief of Staff, Hikmat Shihabi, and later headed the Syrian delegation in Wye during Prime Minister Peres' administration, and I knew Gen. Ibrahim Omar, whom I had met in the Wye Plantation, while he was head of Syrian Intelligence. Omar came to the talks with Barak after having left the army and while serving as a reserve general and military expert. I also knew Wa'ava, head of al-Sharaa's bureau during the Wye talks, but this time they all seemed decisively tense and gave us only a distant nod, took care not to say a single word to us and avoided handshakes.

In the short meeting between Clinton, Barak and al-Sharaa a few minutes earlier, it was agreed that only Clinton would speak, that his speech would be festive and short, and that the two other leaders would suffice with short greeting words.

Clinton played his part, delivering a very hopeful opening speech, and then came al-Sharaa's turn. To our amazement, on his way to the podium, he was approached by a member of the Syrian delegation and given a pre-written speech. Al-Sharaa read from a blatant and aggressive speech, accusing Israel of the current situation, the incidents leading up to 1967, and of Israel's responsibility for five hundred thousand Syrians fleeing the Golan Heights and becoming refugees. The speech lasted a long time, much longer than planned and was the opposite of what had been agreed upon minutes earlier in Clinton's office.

To Barak's credit, he did not step into the trap set by this provocation and did not continue in the same belligerent line, so as not to muddy the waters. In his speech, Barak addressed al-Sharaa only by saying that Israel rejects these claims and that we have our own truth, but emphasized that the most important thing was to look forward and solve the problems, because there was a very important opportunity here.

When al-Sharaa spoke, one could notice the Americans cringe. They sent al-Sharaa glances that made it clear that they did not believe their ears. They were obviously very angry, and so were we.

The anger was expressed in the statements that followed.

A meeting between Clinton and Barak took place immediately after the event. Others present at the meeting were: myself on Barak's side, and on the US side, Rob Malley – assistant to Bruce Riedel, who was in charge of the Middle East and Africa in the US National Security Council.

Barak began by saying that we were at a historical moment, and it felt like walking on thin ice covering a river flowing beneath it.

The main leverage that could be used on Syria, Barak said, stems from what the United States can contribute to the "larger package" - meaning not only to bridge the gaps between Syria and Israel, but to add Saudi Arabia, North Africa, the Gulf States and Lebanon to the circle of peace, and leverage the Syrians to take action to stop terrorism.

Barak stressed, "I cannot partake in peace negotiations here, while Hezbollah terrorism is directed against us at the same time. It offends me."

Barak added that we need to enhance our military capacity as compensation for giving up territories in the Golan Heights, which would also reduce the resistance in Israel to making concessions in the Golan. He noted the importance of building trust in the process of negotiations between Israel and Syria, and that we would need Clinton's support for our "red lines." These lines were: A) Control of the Sea of Galilee in the sense of sovereignty, including a strip of land all along the east side of the lake; B) An Israeli presence in the warning station on Mount Hermon, even if it will be American-French; C) The immediate beginning of full normalization, in exchange for the first stage of withdrawal.

Withdrawal from the larger part of the Golan, including the evacuation of settlements there, would take place only in the final stages of the timetable. The idea was to "receive" a lot of normalization upfront, and "give" a lot of withdrawal at the end.

As an example, Barak mentioned the fact that in the peace process with Egypt, the two countries opened embassies in each other's lands many years before all the territories and settlements in Sinai were evacuated.

It was clear to us that al-Sharaa would not decide alone but would turn to Assad, who would be willing to consider the Israeli demands, which were opposed to the Syrian ones. But only if he saw the whole package; and only if he understood what he was set to receive from Israel, what benefits he would gain when it would come to the survival of his regime and the continued rule of the Alawite sect over Syria. He needed to be convinced that following the signing of a peace treaty with Israel, the Alawite hegemony would not be lost after his death and his son would rise to power after him. It was also important for him to know what financial aid Syria would receive from the United States, and how peace would affect the strengthening of Syria's position in Lebanon and the Middle East.

Only when Assad would realize that there was a chance for these things to happen, would he be willing to examine Israel's demands in a more sympathetic light.

Clinton asked Barak what he intended to answer when asked by al-Sharaa what the Israeli demands were, as it was clear that if Barak would give a direct answer, the talks might reach a very early dead end.

Barak said he would not answer directly, but would steer the conversation to issues such as when to hold the next meeting, how to build its agenda, where it would be, and which work-groups would need to be formed before the meeting. He said that this was because the right way to deal with all the issues was to see the whole picture and understand that there was a 'give and take' relationship between its various components. "We will neither lie nor manipulate the Syrians," Barak said, adding, "and we expect the Syrians to do the same."

Clinton noted that al-Sharaa realized he had made some mistakes in his speech that morning, and suggested that the Israelis also speak with al-Sharaa about it.

Barak said that an agreement with Syria would change the face of the entire Middle East.

It was clear that Barak considered this agreement an important lever to achieve additional agreements, and was truly concerned that there could be a problem approving the agreement in a referendum in light of possible concessions in the Golan Heights. He constantly contemplated the justifications that could help such an agreement win the votes of the Knesset and the Israeli people.

Before meeting with the Syrians, Barak also had time to meet with Albright, who said that she had told al-Sharaa that his speech was a big mistake. Barak responded that two minutes before this embarrassing incident, al-Sharaa and Barak had promised Clinton to deliver only brief greetings. "If it took him two minutes to break a promise to the President of the United States," Barak said, "what will be the fate of other Syrian promises, ones that are far more meaningful?"

Albright replied that al-Sharaa's explanation for the incident was that he felt that the Syrians had made a great concession by coming to the talks without their basic condition - receiving a promise that Israel would withdraw to the 1967 lines. He felt that in light of this major concession, he had needed to mention Israel's crimes and the Syrian claims in order to balance the picture.

On the morning of September 15, 1999, the first meeting between the Israeli and Syrian delegations was held in the Blair House, the official guest house of the President of the United States, across from the White House. The two delegations sat around a long rectangular table, with the Syrian representatives on one side: Foreign Minister al-Sharaa, Assad's favorite interpreter Bouthaina Shaaban, Wa'ava, head of al-Sharaa's bureau and future Syrian ambassador to the United Nations, General Omar Suleiman, Riad Daoudi the Legal Adviser General to the Syrian Foreign Ministry, and Walid Muallem, Syrian ambassador to the United States. On the other side sat the Israeli delegation, which, in addition to Barak, included Foreign Minister David Levy, Uri Sagi, Attorney General Rubinstein and myself. On both sides of the table were US representatives: Madeleine Albright, Martin Indyk, Dennis Ross and others.

The room had an air of tension mixed with a sense of history, but without ceremony.

Barak opened the meeting by saying that we attached great importance to this event and hoped that it can lead to a peace of the brave. "We will hear you and try to understand your demands," said Barak. "We will present our approach, and we ask that you try to understand it."

"I and all the members of the delegation feel the weight of the responsibility resting upon us. It is time to leave the path of war and build peace. Peace with Syria is the way to full peace and I suggest that we focus our discussion today on how to continue, what issues we have to deal with, which work-groups to form, which issues they will deal with and what kind of agreement we aim to achieve. Do we want to achieve a full and detailed peace document or agree on a core of subject matter and include maps and documents?

"When I came to power," continued Barak, "I announced that I would do everything in my power to resume negotiations with Syria, while continuing negotiations with the Palestinians. I made it clear I would not manipulate between the two tracks, and I say this to you, too, Mr. al-Sharaa: our approach is that each track stands on its own feet, but we will try to make progress on both. "

Al-Sharaa answered, "I want to thank President Clinton for successfully making progress in what seemed impossible a month ago. We came to get results, not to discuss procedures. We hate to read in the media that Syria is being led by the nose by the United States. While it is important for us to have good relations with the United States, we are here to try and make peace with Israel and not to use Israel to get closer to the United States. "

Al-Sharaa's comments were made in response to commentary in Israeli media to the effect that Syria's interest to advance the peace process stemmed from its need to get closer to the United States, and that peace with Israel was a very low priority for them. Against this argument stood many others, myself included, who believed that Syria understood that it could not retrieve the Golan Heights except by peace. The Syrians had several interests, one of which was peace with Israel, along with other interests such as the continuation of the Alawite regime, continued Syrian control over Lebanon and improving relations with the United States.

Al-Sharaa went on to say, "Since Assad was elected President, he has been striving for peace, and has tried to convince the Syrian public that the path of peace is preferable. I know that it was not pleasant to hear what I said this morning, but I did it to draw your attention, and that of the American people, to the fact that Syria does not accept the way the conflict is usually presented in the media - unilaterally in favor of Israel - and I wished to balance the picture.

"To describe the conflict between Israel and Syria as an existential conflict is a mistake, because then the conflict will last forever and neither party will concede anything."

In his last sentence, al-Sharaa implied criticism of the way Israeli officials present the conflict as an existential threat to Israel. Al-Sharaa wanted to emphasize that this is a border dispute and not an existential conflict, which makes it solvable.

"However, you cannot make peace," al-Sharaa proceeded, "and still keep even a single square inch of the Golan Heights. If we do this, the Syrian people will rise up against its leadership. The Golan Heights, to the best of my knowledge, is not a biblical land and your ancestors have no ties to it."

Al-Sharaa was hinting at the position towards the West Bank and the conflict with the Palestinians.

"Peace must be fair in the sense that Syria will get all of its land and will open a wide door to Israel. After peace with Syria," said al-Sharaa, and turned to Barak, "you will be able to visit every capital in the Middle East. Assad was very happy when you were elected, and what he said of you publicly he had not said of any Israeli leader in the past. Peace is Syria's strategic choice and we will be willing to go very far and try very hard to achieve it. "

"We would like to emphasize," added al-Sharaa, "that we do not wish to control Lebanon, but on the other hand, we will not accept it becoming a country that is hostile to us, and we will fight to prevent this."

Here al-Sharaa was hinting that Syria has interests in Lebanon, which they seek to protect without controlling the country.

"Leaks to the press are severely detrimental to the chances to make progress," continued al-Sharaa, "and I want to be fair to you and tell you: we will not advance an inch in negotiations if you do not withdraw completely to the lines of June 4, 1967. On August 1993, Rabin agreed to a withdrawal from the Golan Heights. A month later, the Oslo Accord was signed, which made us very wary. We were certain that Rabin had given the 'deposit' to neutralize Syria in the Palestinian track, so at the time, we asked to receive answers to two questions, through the Americans: Does Rabin mean that all the land that was Syrian before 1967 will return to Syria after a peace agreement is signed? The answer was yes. The second question was: Does Rabin have any claim to any part of the territory that was Syrian territory on the eve of 1967? The answer to that was no.

"We are prepared to reach full peace in return for a full withdrawal. The Americans said that it would stand against Israel's demands on security issues, and we agreed. If you respect Rabin's deposit, then there is nothing further to discuss regarding the border, as it has in fact been agreed upon, and this is the Syrian interpretation of the term continuing the talks from the point they had reached."

From these statements by al-Sharaa, we realized that the Syrians came to the Blair House with their basic assumption being that they had already received the borderline of 1967, and all that remained was to talk about all the other issues.

"It is true that there is no such line, 1967," said al-Sharaa, "and it will be the responsibility of experts from both sides to delineate it. However, when it is agreed upon, we will be flexible in relation to the other components of peace. I apologize if I have spoken for too long, but I wanted things to be clear, since ambiguity could lead to confusion, and we wish to avoid this and to achieve peace."

Now it was Barak's turn to reply. "Your statement this morning bothered me very much, not only because of its contents, but also because a few minutes earlier, something completely different had been agreed upon.

"There are several ways to relate to historical events. Israel has a different view of what transpired but I do not think now is the time to discuss history. The position I can voice at this point is that my government has not taken upon itself any prior commitment. On the other hand, we have not erased the past - not the negotiations with Rabin, not with Peres and even not with Netanyahu. We have other important needs beyond the border issue, and if they are not met it will not be easy to reach an agreement and this situation requires a high degree of responsibility on both sides. "

At a meeting between Albright and Barak that took place later that same day, Albright told Barak that he had left a good impression on al-Sharaa. The Secretary of State mentioned that she was angry at al-Sharaa. "He broke every diplomatic norm and rule of conduct in his speech," she said, adding, "By violating a promise given minutes earlier to Clinton, he insulted the President and me."

When we started talking about establishing work-groups, Barak offered that the borders work-group be postponed, and the work-groups start by discussing security arrangements and normalization. The water and border issues Barak asked to postpone to the days following the other issues, to ensure there was progress on issues that were important to us and represented our needs. What drove this concept was Rabin's formula: If all our needs will be met we will withdraw.

The water and borderline were connected to each other in Barak's perception, since we needed full sovereignty over the Sea of Galilee and the Jordan mountains, which is fed by the Hasbani, Banias and Dan rivers and flows into the Sea of Galilee.

To Albright Barak said, "If we move forward on the border issue it would be very embarrassing for me. I have said before that we can define the border only after we hear what the Syrians are willing to offer in terms of security arrangements and normalization."

At a meeting the next day with the Syrians there was a discussion about the technical nature of the agreement that would ultimately be reached. Al-Sharaa said that it should be a full peace agreement, not an interim agreement or declaration of principles. He said Assad wanted to achieve as comprehensive a peace agreement as possible.

The Americans asked when the Lebanese negotiations would begin, since as part of the package that Barak outlined, it was stated that during the negotiations with Syria, negotiations with Lebanon would also start – which would serve to calm the northern front and help Barak convince the Israeli public of the necessity of peace with Syria and the concessions it required.

To our surprise, al-Sharaa said that the Syrians supported Lebanon joining the negotiations as soon as possible. However, in his next sentence he was quick to dampen the enthusiasm and said, "As soon as we see that our discussions are advancing, the Lebanese will also join."

Albright drew al-Sharaa's attention to the importance of restraining Hezbollah and preventing deterioration in Lebanon, which could undermine the negotiations between Israel and Syria.

Al-Sharaa immediately replied that the Syrians did not control Hezbollah, although they had influence over it, "And with them one needs to act with persuasion rather than force. We tried to exert power over them fifteen years ago to no avail," he stressed.

Al-Sharaa suggested that the discussion topics for the next round of talks include withdrawal from the Golan Heights, mutual security arrangements, the nature of peace - meaning normalization - and a timetable for its implementation. Al-Sharaa added, "These are the four legs that Rabin defined, and as for water – there will be an appendix."

Here you can see the difference between the parties: Barak saw the connection between the water issue and the border issue, and told al-Sharaa that water was part of the core of the agreement and not an appendix. In addition Barak sought to discuss the border issue gradually, after discussions on security and normalization had begun, to make sure that the Syrians intended to fulfill Israel's demands in these areas, while al-Sharaa asked to discuss all these issues at the same time.

Al-Sharaa accepted the challenge of connecting the water and border issues, and proposed to convene the water and border work-groups as early as the following week so they could start working. The Syrian position was that the border work-group should delineate the border of June 4, 1967 on the map, because for them there was only one possible border.

In contrast, Israel's position was that the border group would discuss the determination of the borderline and define its components, but would not delineate it at this point.

Throughout the discussions, when Barak would say that the group should deal with determining the borderline, al-Sharaa would immediately barge in and correct him, "the group will deal with delineating the border."

Barak sought to reject al-Sharaa's suggestion to begin the discussions on borders and water immediately one week later, and asked to postpone the issue to the next round of talks. "Perhaps we should postpone the negotiations on the borderline for a short while so we can see the results of the other groups' work and thus the overall picture," said Barak.

This shows that Barak did not hide from anyone, including the Syrians, that the subjects of water and borders would eventually be the focus of discussion, and his approach was that these matters must be brought to Assad's decision. Since these were such delicate matters, discussing them at the same time as other issues would soon cause the essential disagreements to surface, and would lead to the talks breaking down. However, if this discussion were to be postponed, and there would be progress on other issues such as normalization and security arrangements that would satisfy both sides, then it would be easier for Assad to consider the Israeli position regarding the border.

Assad, according to Barak's plan, would then see how the whole world had joined forces to turn the Golan into a free trade zone, how America had helped him financially and international companies were prepared to invest in the Golan Heights. This entire array, thought Barak, could bring Assad to favorably consider the position that the border not be identical to the line of June 4, 1967 along its entire length, but rather be a "revised" line of 1967.

According to the Syrians, the 1967 lines had passed across the whole of the Jordan River, with Syria and Jordan sitting on the waterfront on the northeast part of the lake, or in the term that had become popular in Israel: "dipping their feet in the Sea of Galilee."

At that stage of the negotiations with Syria, it would have been a grave mistake to tell them that in Israel's view, they would not sit on the waterfront and would not control the Jordan mountains. That sort of thing could stop the process with the Syrians refusing to even consider such a possibility.

In retrospect, it was claimed that at the last moment Barak withdrew his consent to the Syrian demand for withdrawal and refused to sign a peace treaty, after public opinion surveys had indicated that the Israeli public would not support an agreement that would concede Israel's hold on the eastern part of the lake along its full length. These types of statements are false. From the description of the way Barak handled negotiations, it is clear that he was talking about retaining Israeli control east of the Sea of Galilee – as a necessary prerequisite.

Barak was very interested to achieve peace with Syria, and he realized that Assad would find it very difficult to accept our suggestions. Therefore, he constantly strove to give Assad the full picture of the benefits Syria would enjoy as part of a peace agreement with Israel. This was because Barak believed that only then would Assad understand that if he were to refuse the agreement because of amendments in the line of June 4, 1967 as he defined it, he would lose all the benefits and advantages Syria stood to gain in the agreement. Barak did not imagine that such a formula would be rejected out of hand by the Syrians, since he thought they would understand that they have a lot to lose. This was a tremendous change for Syria against the required price of conceding its positions, mainly in regards to the border, but also in other issues such as normalization, timetables and security arrangements.

CHAPTER 19

SHEPHERDSTOWN: BARAK INSISTS

The Israeli delegation returned to Israel from the meetings with the Syrians with the feeling that al-Sharaa, who was not satisfied with the meetings, was convinced that the substantive discussions would take place in the next round, and so upon his return to Syria he would recommend President Assad to continue the talks.

Therefore, we immediately began preparing for the talks' renewal, and work-groups were established, including a group for the talks with the Lebanese in case they join the negotiations. Major General (Ret.) Menachem Enan was appointed the head of this team; General (Ret.) Uri Sagi was appointed head of the team for negotiations with Syria; Rubinstein was head of the legal team, and I as Chief of Staff continued to coordinate the activities of all the teams. In addition, I was appointed as head of the team that dealt with coordination with the Americans, collateral and the aid that the United States will give to Israel to prevent our security being compromised due to future concessions.

The border and water issues did not cease to preoccupy Barak. In one of our many conversations on the matter, he told me that the substantive discussion of these issues would be in the round of talks in which Israel and Syria would sign the agreement.

Barak's conception resulted from his recognition that these issues required dramatic and substantial concessions from both sides: ours in the Golan Heights and the Syrians in the Sea of Galilee. Due to the explosive potential of these charged issues, there was concern that once they would be on the table, it would lead to the talks being stopped, the parties returning home for consultations and leaks would begin regarding the parties' willingness to make concessions, which would lead to the breakdown of negotiations. Due to their sensitivity, Barak thought that these matters should be discussed, agreed upon and immediately afterwards the peace treaty should be signed.

Meanwhile, it was decided that the next round of talks between Israel and Syria would be held in Shepherdstown, and intensive preparatory discussions began.

Barak was busy defining what he wanted to achieve; for him, the main component for the next round of talks was normalization, with the idea being to "get" a lot of normalization early and to "give" the majority of the withdrawal only near the end. Normalization for him was the exchange of ambassadors immediately upon signing the agreement, opening borders and allowing free movement of citizens, ending the boycott on Israel, economic and commercial relations, connecting road networks and more.

The other things which he considered *sine qua non* included: physical control and sovereignty over the water (the Jordan River mountains and the entire Sea of Galilee), Israeli presence at the Mt. Hermon warning station and settlements being evacuated only after normalization begins.

On the water issue, Barak spoke with the Americans about a regional water settlement, according to which there would be an international effort to build desalination plants on the

Mediterranean coast. These plants would produce fresh water for Israel, the Palestinians and Jordan, while Turkey would contribute water to Syria from its abundant sources.

He considered the possibility of meeting with Turkish President Demirel on his way to Washington to suggest the water solution to him personally. However, Dennis Ross did not think this was a good idea, saying, "This may be perceived by Assad as a conspiracy, as if on your way to the talks you are coordinating positions against him."

Barak was convinced, and later sent me to the president of Turkey to discuss the issue. In the meeting Demirel said to me, "No problem at all, we are prepared to provide unlimited water to the Syrians, but we will not give them even a single liter for free."

In his conversations with Dennis Ross, Barak explained the paradox of the new round of talks. "In the coming round, we cannot determine the border, because if we discuss it before fully addressing the other issues, such as normalization and security arrangements, there will be a leak. This will create a situation wherein the price Israel will pay will be clear from the start, even before we find out what Syria is willing to give in exchange," explained Barak. He continued, "Therefore it is possible to extend the discussions beyond ten days and finish everything. A second possibility is that as Prime Minister I cannot be away from the country for too long, so I will have to return to Israel while the teams continue their work, and I shall return later. A third option is to avoid dealing with the issues of water and the border altogether, and instead to begin discussing other matters, and only return to those issues towards the end of negotiations. And then," explained Barak, "after I will be satisfied that Israel is receiving substantial compensation from the Syrians, we can talk about the two sensitive issues – the border and the water, and convince the Israeli public that the price we will have to pay is worth the compensation we receive from Syria."

In preliminary talks with the Americans, Barak tried to promote the notion of turning the Heights into a free trade area, and tried via President Clinton to get the president of the World Bank on board and convince him to get the bank to invest in the project. The intention was to make the Golan Heights under Syrian sovereignty a demilitarized free trade zone – an area in which factories of leading international companies will be established with the help of international investments, which will provide many jobs for the Syrians, and whose products will be exempt from tax across the world.

Dennis Ross updated Barak that al-Sharaa's goal was to leave the next round of talks with the Israelis with a promise that Israel withdraw to the 1967 borders.

Barak reiterated to Ross, that he felt that the discussions on security arrangements and normalization should precede the discussions on the withdrawal. This is an example of Barak's insistence when he believed something to be vital and true. In these cases he makes extraordinary efforts to convince, firstly the Americans - through dozens of phone calls to Clinton - in the hope that the reasoning behind his proposal will convince the Americans and the Syrians will follow. Despite the estimate that the chances of the Syrians being convinced were low - which could cause a long delay in negotiations and possibly their breakdown - he would not change his position, and was unwilling to reach an agreement with the Syrians at any cost. He does not concede what he believes is a vital interest; on the rest of the things he is willing to compromise.

Barak was the first Prime Minister who said exactly and explicitly what he wanted. Unlike Rabin, who said that the depth of the withdrawal would be equal to the depth of the peace, deposited a conditional statement with the Americans and left things vague, Barak made clear to the Americans where the limit of his flexibility lies. Aside from a narrow strip of a few hundred meters along the northeast side of the lake, which would give us physical control and sovereignty over all of its waters and full sovereignty over all of the Jordan River mountains- he expressed his willingness for a full withdrawal from the Golan Heights, the largest Israeli concession. However, Barak also had many demands in regards to security arrangements, normalization, timetables and intelligence warning, and without those requirements being fulfilled, he was not prepared to withdraw from the Golan Heights.

As part of the preparations for the Shepherdstown talks, Barak constantly emphasized to the Americans the importance of resuming negotiations with Lebanon, which among other things would deal with the IDF's withdrawal from Lebanon, the disarmament of Hezbollah and cessation of terrorist attacks from Lebanon. Barak said that this development would encourage the Israeli public to support the process with Syria and help deal with his opponents: "When the Israeli public feels that serious negotiations are being conducted, I will be able to be more flexible," Barak said.

Barak realized that the Israeli public was tired of the IDF's presence in Lebanon, and believed that tying negotiations with Syria with the development of negotiations with Lebanon would convince the Israeli public that concessions in Syria's favor were justified and appropriate.

The dilemma was how to plan the meeting with the Syrians without them being overly disappointed by the border issue, which would cause Assad to refrain from coming altogether, while on the other hand to avoid advancing too much in regards to borders and water, thus killing the process due to leaks.

The preparatory work of the team dealing with relations between Israel and the United States, which I headed, focused on the goal that Israel and the United States will declare themselves strategic allies. This means that the US will give Israel weapons systems and military technologies it was not willing to give us until then, such as Tomahawk missiles that we were very interested in, and acknowledging that an unconventional attack on Israel would be considered as an unconventional attack on the United States. The team I headed also prepared lists of new weapons meant to increase Israel's ability to defend itself as a result of the withdrawal from the Golan Heights. The idea was mainly to receive F-22 aircraft - the futuristic aircraft that was being developed by the Americans at the time. We also prepared a request to receive a large financial aid package and deepen intelligence, operational and diplomatic cooperation. The aim was to ensure Israel's qualitative, military, and diplomatic advantage over its neighbors. Widening the qualitative gap in Israel's favor was supposed to be one of the achievements of the peace process.

After formulating the list of requirements, which was composed through the joint work of the Ministry of Defense, the Ministry of Foreign Affairs, military officials and the Ministry of Finance, we presented our conclusions to the Prime Minister for his approval, and they were later presented to members of the National Security Council in the United States.

The administration was sympathetic towards the Israeli requests and accepted them, and it was necessary to begin an extensive effort to persuade Congress – which is the one that decides on these matters in light of the White House's recommendation. We were told in advance by the Administration that the chance we would be given Tomahawk missiles was slim. The Tomahawk is a long-range cruise missile with a maximum cruising range of 2,500 km. The Americans have several versions of it - with nuclear or conventional heads. We requested the missile without nuclear warheads.

This missile's flight path is set and programmed in advance, and according to this path, it navigates itself to the target area, comparing the preset image in its memory to what is being perceived by its electro-optical eye in flight. Thus the missile "knows" how to hit the exact target that was set. Tehran, the capital of one of our enemies, for example, is 1,500 km away from Israel, so that one of the longer-range Tomahawk missiles could be very useful to us in time of need.

In my many conversations with the Americans, as with Dennis Ross, Sandy Berger and US Ambassador to Israel Martin Indyk, I tried to get them to convince the Syrians to take confidence-building measures. Again and again I gave the example of Sadat, who came to Jerusalem and thus broke the psychological wall and gave tremendous momentum to the peace process.

It was clear that Assad would not repeat such a dramatic step, but we tried to look for other ways that would increase trust between Israel and Syria and will instill in the Israeli public, which over the years became wary of the Syrians, a new and different feeling to help it overcome its concern.

Some confidence-building measures we proposed at the time included stopping terrorism from Lebanon, Israeli MKs visiting Syria, scholars visiting Syria and inviting Syrian officers to visit the Golan Heights. However, all the proposals were rejected by the Syrians. Their attitude was that this was not necessary at the moment, and that all the steps we proposed are part of normal relations and will occur by themselves when there are peaceful relations between the two countries.

Barak felt at the time that the Syrians would ultimately agree to the concept of an Israeli withdrawal from the Golan Heights with some "corrections" around the Sea of Galilee. I argued on the other that the Syrians will not be flexible on the subject of withdrawal, and the position of Military Intelligence was also that the Syrians will not give up their demand for withdrawal to the line of June 4, 1967.

As mentioned above, the 1967 line is not really a "line." It is neither delineated on the ground nor on the map. Each side has "its own" 1967 line, so it is actually more of a concept, within which in our opinion there was room for some flexibility that would allow the Syrians and us to determine the "line" together. The Syrians, who understood this, agreed at a later stage that experts from both sides would work together to delineate the 1967 line on which we would agree, but demanded a clear commitment that Israel will withdraw to the line of June 4, 1967, and once this commitment is received, the experts will start their work.

I thought that since the Syrians claim they had villages on the Sea of Galilee's waterfront before 1967, they will not be flexible on the matter, but I agreed that we should try, so I supported Barak's approach that we must strive to maintain Israeli sovereignty over a land strip along that part of the lake.

In early January we were off to meet with the Syrians. We landed in Washington late at night and drove to Shepherdstown. The misty night and long, dark road on which the convoy moved slowly left much space for the thoughts and concerns that raced through my mind.

Immediately upon arrival, around two in the morning, Barak called a meeting with Uri Sagi, who arrived on the previous day, in order to be updated of the latest details. Sagi reported that in preliminary talks he had with the Americans he received their approval for Barak's intention to postpone the talks on the water and border issues to the final stage, but Syria's position on this matter was yet unknown. Barak told us at that nighttime meeting that he would view this round of talks as a success if progress would be made on security and normalization issues while a substantive discussion on the border issue would be avoided.

The Syrians and the Americans were at the facility when we arrived, as were the journalists who were housed outside of it. For

Barak, it was very important to completely isolate the area from the media, and to ensure as far as possible that there would not be leaks through telephones or encounters. It was clear that such an occurrence could completely devastate this peace effort.

The first day was devoted to internal discussions of the parties at Shepherdstown and meetings between the parties and the Americans.

As in previous meetings, the Syrian officials were once again careful to exhibit callousness and reserve.

The delegations were housed on different floors and dining rooms were adjacent but separate. The Americans and the Israelis ate in the general dining room, and the Syrians were invited to join at any time. On our way to the dining room we saw the Syrians but did not speak with them. They made do with exchanging courtesies by nodding their head when seeing someone whom they knew from previous rounds. It was clear that they did everything they could to avoid meeting our gaze and maintained a cold and distant expression.

The message that the Syrians tried to convey through their behavior was that they would not make any gestures, even the smallest and most symbolic ones such as shaking hands, before seeing progress in the talks. It was clear that they were instructed to behave this way by Syrian leadership.

Later, in the rooms where the different groups' discussions were being held, there were handshakes and hallway chats.

Before the meeting between Barak and Clinton, the senior ranks of the Israeli delegation convened. Among them were Barak, Foreign Minister David Levy, Minister of Tourism Amnon Lipkin-Shahak, Uri Sagi, Elyakim Rubinstein and myself. At this meeting, Barak asked Rubinstein to meet with Dennis Ross and start thinking about the formulation of a draft agreement between Israel and Syria.

In his meeting with Clinton, Barak began by saying, "The fact that I, Lipkin-Shahak and Levy are here indicates the Israeli side's seriousness and its will to move forward. However, we have no illusions, and we know the difficulties in the three major issues: effective warning, normalization first and Israeli sovereignty around the Sea of Galilee."

"All of these issues," continued Barak, "can only be decided by Assad, and al-Sharaa has no authority to make any concessions on them. Therefore, we will never know if we did everything possible to achieve peace unless at the end of the process there will be a meeting with Assad."

Assad wanted to meet with the Israelis for the first time only at the signing ceremony of the peace treaty. However, Barak wanted the end of the negotiation process to be with Assad in order to reach an agreement on the last issues still in dispute, with the peace treaty signed only at the end of this process.

Assad thought that unlike other countries, such as Jordan and Egypt, and the Palestinians - where leaders from both sides met and participated in the process - he need only receive a promise from Israel to withdraw to the border of 1967, and then there would be no more to discuss. From that moment, in Assad's view, it would be possible to finalize all other matters with the negotiation teams, and even if one or two things would not be finalized, he would arrive, finish what needs to be finished and sign the peace treaty.

Barak explained to Clinton that until the meeting with Assad, progress must be made to the extent that both parties can see their benefits and losses from signing a peace agreement or lack thereof. Barak stressed that it was essential that the US and Israel remain in agreement on every stage, that they would be closely coordinated, and that the Israelis and the Americans would maintain transparency, openness and trust between them. "I will not surprise you in any of my positions, and I expect that you do not surprise me," Barak said to Clinton.

"I'm prepared to reach an agreement, but not at any cost," Barak said to Clinton, adding, "I will not accept an agreement in which Israel has no effective presence on Mount Hermon, and in which Israel is required to evacuate large parts of the Golan Heights before the Syrians begin to fulfill their part in normalization. The Israeli side is taking major political and security risks, we are walking on a tightrope and it is important that you not let the Syrians rip it."

Barak was well aware of the complexity of the process he created with his wish to avoid discussing the border issue early on, in order to prevent a situation in which the most significant Syrian demand would be discussed without Israel knowing what the Syrians were willing to give and which concessions they were willing to make. He did not want to move too fast on this subject, for fear that it will substantially reduce every aspect of his leeway in respect to negotiations and the political situation in the country. On the other hand, he did not want to raise anger or further suspicion in the Syrian side by refusing to discuss the border issue substantively – which could also pose a threat to the future of the negotiations.

It was clear that Barak expected Clinton to help him solve this problem.

In his conversation with Clinton, Barak stressed that for him it was extremely vital that the Syrians show flexibility on the water issues, i.e. Israeli control over the Sea of Galilee, which provides a third of Israel's drinking water, a warning station on Mount Hermon with Israeli presence and normalization first.

Barak cited to Clinton an article by Amos Oz, published a few days earlier, in which Oz wrote that he would not accept a peace in which the Syrians arrive at the Sea of Galilee, and the only thing they give in return is a fax containing the peace agreement.

"Do not be surprised if my opening position with the Syrians will be that Israeli communities and factories will remain in the Golan Heights under Syrian rule for another thirty years," Barak said to Clinton. Thus he implied that this should not necessarily be seen as the Israeli position, but merely a starting point, since even at that time there was unofficial Israeli willingness to evacuate the Golan Heights of all its settlers and keep the settlements intact for Syrian use, in contrast to the precedent of Sinai where the settlements were uprooted.

Barak spoke about the psychological and moral aspects of the Israeli public, whose main concern was the issue of security. "Therefore," Barak said, "we must ensure that Israel is strong and equipped with the most advanced means."

Barak proceed to tell Clinton that in order to make it easier for him to make difficult decisions and increase his ability to convince the Israeli public of them, it was very important to him that the whole of the peace agreement would include additional components. Such components could be, for example, an agreement with Lebanon, Saudi Arabia, the Gulf and North African nations joining the peace process, and substantial US aid in money and weapons.

Barak also believed the US should not agree to erase Syria's external debt in the amount of twenty billion dollars before Syria showed willingness to make concessions in negotiations. Additionally, Barak thought that it would be wrong to remove Syria from the list of state sponsors of terrorism, but they can imply that progress will result in their removal from this ignominious list.

The high sensitivity towards benefits Syria could reap before conceding anything at all, and before signing a peace treaty, could be seen even years later, when in June 2008 reports began to surface of intensive meetings between Syrian and Israeli representatives during Ehud Olmert's administration. Terje Larsen, the senior UN official who was appointed by the UN Secretary General to be responsible for the implementation of Security Council Resolution 1559, which called for respect of Lebanon's sovereignty and the disarmament of Hezbollah, strongly criticized the negotiations that took place in Turkey. Larsen said that "Syria is receiving international legitimacy for free. So far Israel is giving Syria a huge gift without getting anything in return, Europe is courting the Syrians due to negotiations with Israel and they, on their part, are no longer expected to give anything in return."

In light of Barak's refusal to ratify the "Rabin deposit" to the Americans, and as he was looking for ways to reassure Assad, Barak offered Clinton to tell Assad that he had Rabin's "deposit", and that Barak had not retracted it. "Tell Assad," said Barak, "that the border will be based on the concept of the line of June 4, 1967, with all the modifications required to fulfill the needs of Israel. Since it is not a line but a concept, there is some flexibility that can be exploited."

"The problem is," continued Barak, "that Syria's public propaganda argues that the border issue has already been decided and that the border is no longer a matter for discussion – this bothers us very much."

This line of Syrian propaganda created many internal problems for Barak. Severe accusations were made against him - in part by Ariel Sharon, leader of the opposition at the time - that negotiations with Syria had already been decided, that Israel had essentially conceded the Golan Heights, and that the negotiations in Shepherdstown merely served as a front for things that had already been finalized.

In response to Barak's statements, Clinton said, "I must tell you that as usual, you have once again considered everything. I agree with you that Lebanon should enter into negotiations. We have started working with countries like Bahrain, Oman, Qatar, Algeria and Tunisia to join them into the peace process. We started to address the issue of free trade and international investments. The problem is how to convince the Syrians that they have nothing to worry about regarding the border issue, even if it is not being discussed in this round. I suggest I tell Assad that I intend to convince you to ratify Rabin's 'deposit,' making it yours as well, in the event that negotiations with Lebanon begin immediately, as well as signs of normalization and confidence-building measures are taken that prove the Syrians have sincere intentions with respect to normalization with Israel. I will also tell Assad that if this is leaked by the Syrians - the whole thing will be canceled. "

"I prefer something else," Barak replied, "I would rather you say that you heard me say that not only have I not retracted the 'deposit,' but that I also do not intend to retract it in the future."

Clinton raised the idea to offer the Syrians that the discussion on the final line of 1967 will start only after negotiations with Lebanon, but Barak expressed concern that this would leak and subsequently the matter would disintegrate.

At a meeting that took place that day between Madeleine Albright and Barak, Albright told him that the Syrians were in a somber mood and that she is concerned that if they do not receive an Israeli commitment to withdraw to the 1967 borders, they will not be able to continue the talks. Albright further said that the Syrians accuse the Israelis of leaking details of the talks.

Albright suggested three options for reassuring the Syrians: one - Barak says he ratifies Rabin's deposit, but it will be stressed to the Syrians that if this matter leaks, the ratification will be canceled. Option two - all four committees will start working (until then only two had started), and the "sensitive" committee dealing with the border issue will be named "The Committee for Delineating the Line of June 4, 1967", will be established but will not begin its work. The third option - all four committees will start working the next day, and the border committee will keep its original title.

Barak rejected Albright's offer and said he would not go beyond what he has already promised Clinton: that he does not intend to retract the "deposit." He agreed to establish committees and determine their participants, but wanted to ensure the agenda that was agreed upon be retained: that on the following day the normalization and security arrangement committees would convene, and two days later the water committee would convene and only after that would the border committee's turn arrive.

Albright did not hide her dissatisfaction and noted that she was very concerned, and feared that because of this there would not be an agreement. Barak replied that he did not believe this would be the case.

He explained that the issue of the border will be discussed in the most advanced stage, and that the discussion will be in that area, between the border of 1967 and the international border, so the relevant geographic area was more or less known. However the other issues were at a very initial stage of discussion, so they should be discussed first. Barak repeatedly mentioned that in virtually all of these issues, we still did not know the Syrian position and what we would receive to fulfill our needs.

In retrospect, it turned out that on this matter our assessment was wrong. As far as the Syrians were concerned there was no willingness to discuss the other issues significantly, as long as they had not heard that Israel undertakes to withdraw to the 1967 borders.

In this conversation, Amnon Lipkin-Shahak said, in support of Barak's position, that agreements were made and hence it would be wrong to concede to the Syrians and give them other things. Lipkin-Shahak said he was concerned by the fact that the Americans, instead of dealing with the Syrians, immediately ran back to us to propose changes in things on which we had agreed.

I suggested that the Americans demand that the Syrians make a 'counter-deposit,' meaning their consent to our demands – a strip east of the Sea of Galilee under our control, normalization first and Israeli presence on Mount Hermon – and then there would be a Syrian deposit against the Israeli deposit, which would make it easier to continue the process.

The next day I met with Dennis Ross, who reported to me that Clinton and Albright persuaded the Syrians on the matter of the order of the committees, meaning that first the committees would begin their work on the subjects of normalization and security arrangements, then the water and only at the end - the border.

From this conduct you can learn how much time and energy is invested or sometimes wasted, depending on the eye of the beholder, on procedural affairs, and the profound importance attached to these things when everything is so fragile and delicate.

Later that day, which like all of its predecessors and those that followed, racked the tense nerves of all concerned, we received further proof of the extent to which everything depended on one word or another.

On the morning of that day, we were greeted by a report published in the Israeli newspaper *Haaretz*, containing a description of the security package that Israel requested from the United States as part of the peace treaty, and US Secretary of State Madeleine Albright did not even try to pretend that she was not furious.

Barak, as mentioned, urged the Americans to set the talks in a place that would be completely isolated from the media and the possibility of leaks.

The facilities where we were lodged in Shepherdstown were indeed isolated, and the media was lodged in a hotel in the same town but was located far away from ours.

Barak did not initiate any media activity or release 'spins', and it was agreed that members of the Israeli and Syrian delegations would not speak to the press, with the exception of the Americans who released a dry and concise report on the occurrences once a day.

It was clear that the leak published in *Haaretz* was not our doing, but it was highly damaging to the atmosphere that day. However, the more severe damage related to leaks was yet to come, and it was published after we returned from Shepherdstown by the journalist Akiva Eldar in an item on *Haaretz*, elaborating the US draft for the peace agreement - which caused much anger among the Americans, Israelis and Syrians and led to a halt in the negotiations.

Barak noted to the Americans later that day, that in the very same hours when the negotiation teams were having their first discussions, there were incidents in Lebanon which indicated that the Iranians were trying to thwart the process. "I could have been seen by the Israeli public as a hero had I chosen to attack Hezbollah and the Lebanese infrastructure, but I prefer to continue the discussions here," said Barak.

Madeleine Albright updated us that al-Sharaa's response to the idea of adding Lebanon to the talks was, "Suggest it to the Lebanese. If they ask us, we will not prevent it from them, but we will tell them that we do not like the idea of them joining at this time."

At a meeting that day between Barak and Clinton, Barak expressed his disappointment that the Americans enabled the Syrians to "create something out of nothing." Barak's intention was that after the Syrians agreed to the agenda, which dictated that security issues and normalization will be discussed first and afterwards discussions regarding water and the border will commence, they sought to change this agreement, and when their demand was not granted - sought compensation for it.

He added that it was important to be strict with the Syrians in matters of procedure, so as not to create a precedent wherein the Syrians receive the impression that it would be possible to reach a certain arrangement with them, and after a while they could change their mind, and in addition squeeze out a few more things in their favor.

Clinton stressed that what was agreed upon was what would take place, and said that the United States intended to introduce a draft titled: "Peace Agreement between Israel and the Syrian Arab Republic."

Clinton promised to call Assad and talk to him about the need to restrain Hezbollah in Lebanon and for Lebanon to join the peace talks. Yet Clinton also noted that he did not want to call Assad too much, so as not to give al-Sharaa the feeling that he was irrelevant.

In that conversation, Clinton asked Barak how to present the issue of the border in the US draft.

Barak answered that it should present the Syrian position demanding a withdrawal to the 1967 lines, and the Israeli demand that the determination of the border must take into account the vital needs of Israel.

"It must be explained to al-Sharaa," Barak added, "that the determination of the border is not a mere technicality, but a security issue, as well as a national and political one. Furthermore, in determining the border, we must take into account broader interests than each side's claims of the exact location of its military outposts in 1967."

Clinton said to Barak, "I looked at the maps and noticed that since 1967, the Sea of Galilee has receded far enough westward so that the body of land should be enough for your needs."

Barak said to him in reply, "We have to find a way that will allow us to retain sovereignty over several hundred meters east of the waterline on the northeast part of the lake. Only this type of sovereignty will ensure full sovereignty over the waters, because if the border is right on the water - it could create friction between

Israel and Syria later on. Israel needs to be fully secure of its sovereignty over the lake."

Barak believed that water was the most significant point that must not be compromised, since the Sea of Galilee is Israel's largest and most important water reservoir. It was necessary for him to ensure that no disputes and uncertainties would arise later between the Syrians and us regarding Israel's sovereignty over all of the water of the Sea of Galilee, down to the last cubic centimeter, just as the Syrians demanded the very last inch of land in the Golan Heights. Barak thought that if the border would be the waterline, it would leave room for different interpretations in the future, so it was important for him that on the other side of the waterline, Israel would also retain a coastal strip a few hundred meters wide.

Later that day, there was a tripartite meeting between Clinton, Barak and al-Sharaa. The additional Israeli representative on behalf of Barak was me.

Clinton began by saying that he would like to present a draft within forty-eight hours, noted that it would still contain gaps in the form of presenting the Syrian and Israeli positions, and stressed that it is important to hold meetings and to bridge these gaps. Clinton also noted that there were many leaks to the media.

We all knew that the Syrians were leaking incessantly. With our own eyes we saw them briefing a Syrian journalist. They were leaking systematically and constantly emphasizing their positions: a return to the 1967 lines and no Israeli presence in the Golan Heights.

Clinton expressed his dissatisfaction with the leaks, saying, "Every day in which one side is victorious in the media, postpones the agreement for one more day. It is important to make haste so the opponents will not have a chance to kill the process. Hence the importance of rapidly resuming talks with Lebanon, so as not to give leeway to the opponents."

Barak began to answer, saying, "The media reports are harmful. We do not control the Israeli media but I am choosing my words very carefully, so as not to offend the Syrians. However, it is important for you to know: If you say something in the media it requires us to respond. Therefore, you need to lower the media profile for a few weeks. There are leaks on our side as well," Barak admitted and continued, "but on our side, nothing was planned. Most of the damaging leaks came from the Syrians, who feel that they have to justify the fact that they are in Shepherdstown and that there are good reasons for it."

When it was al-Sharaa's turn to answer, he began by saying, "This is a unique historic opportunity that must not be vanquished. It is important for the future generations and for all the people of the Middle East. I feel we can reach an agreement if we are serious and act with integrity. We want an agreement that you can defend in your country and we in our country, an agreement that is balanced, and does not appear as though one side forced itself on the other. It is important for us that the Syrians know that we did not give up even an inch of our land - it is the least they expect of us, and on this basis it would be possible to build good neighborly relations between us. We want a peace treaty and not only an end to the state of war, and only a good and balanced agreement can be the basis for stable peace.

"Syria has invested great efforts to persuade all the political forces in Lebanon to unite on peace with Israel. When we went to Madrid it was difficult for Assad to convince the leadership in Lebanon to come there. There are those who refuse to reach a peace agreement with Israel, such as Iran, which has considerable influence in Lebanon. There is a lot more work that needs to be done in Lebanon to prepare the grounds. A good agreement with Syria will pave the way for full peace in the Middle East.

"We do not ask for even one inch of Israeli land, but want all of our land back. No Jew lived east of the line of 1967 when the war started.

"In your government, Mr. Barak, there is a minister named Ramon, who said that Israel will never return to the 1967 borders as part of a peace agreement with Syria."

At the last comment Barak replied with a smile, "Over that I actually do have control."

Clinton summed up the meeting and said, "If we can bring about a peace treaty, it will make the people of the world see other national and religious conflicts differently."

Later that day, the Syrians once again tried to change the schedule: they sent the Americans to tell us that due to al-Sharaa's fatigue, they could not hold discussions on the normalization and security arrangements on the same day, and wished to postpone them until tomorrow morning. However, since the discussion of the water was planned for tomorrow anyway, then tomorrow we will start everything together.

Barak refused the offer and viewed it as a credibility problem. We were sure that this was a ploy. Barak said, "It is difficult to know the extent to which procedural details can later affect the leadership's ability to make substantive decisions. The Israeli public is constantly watching and testing us."

The arrangement we reached was this: security arrangements and normalization will be discussed the next morning. Only in the evening will the water committee convene, headed by Noah Kinarti, Adviser to the Prime Minister on the issue of water, Prof. Uri Shamir, a water expert, Nahum Mintzker, and legal adviser Roy Sheindorf.

The next morning, January 5, the normalization group convened for its first discussion. This group was led by Brig. Gen. (Ret.) Zvi Stauber, Diplomatic Adviser to the Prime Minister, and its members were the Foreign Ministry Deputy Director General Yoav Biran, Moshe Sinai of the Foreign Office, Ministry of Finance Director General David Brodet, and jurist Daniel Taub.

After the meeting Stauber came to update Barak, and said that the meeting was held in a good atmosphere and a spirit of openness. The Syrians criticized the way in which the Americans managed the proceedings. Walid Muallem, who was head of the Syrian team for the normalization issue, stressed his limitations, and constantly repeated the mantra: al-Sharaa is the one who decides.

It was agreed that in the next meeting there will be a discussion of normal peaceful relations, Americans will present their financial aid package to Syria, and the realization of peace between Israel and Syria over time will be discussed, with us outlining different gestures on the timeline.

Dennis Ross estimated at this stage that the Syrian position is that the coast of the Sea of Galilee, the international border, and the line of 1967 - are one and the same.

Ross also mentioned that Daoudi, Legal Adviser to the Syrian Foreign Ministry, had already rejected the possibility of a territorial swap explaining that Assad would not agree to this.

That morning, the security committee also convened, and included on the Israeli side the Chairman, Head of the Planning Directorate Gen. Shlomo Yanai, Brig. Gen. Dan Harel, jurist Lt. Col. Pnina Baruch of the Military Advocate General Corps, and Col. Udi Dekel of the Planning Directorate.

At the end of this meeting Yanai came to report to Barak, and said that immediately at the start of the meeting the Syrians stated that they are soldiers and cannot deviate in any way from the positions dictated to them. According to the Syrians, in exchange for the return of the Golan Heights, which is Syrian land, Israel does not need to receive anything. According to them, since this was Syrian land in the first place then it is not an Israeli concession at all.

Retired general Ibrahim Omar, the former Head of Syrian Military Intelligence, whom I had already met in the Wye Plantation talks in 1996, repeated the theory that "Peace is security and if there is peace there is no enemy, and therefore there is also no need for security arrangements."

Thus the Syrians repeated their position from 1996.

Omar added that modern warfare is done mostly from the air, and therefore he does not understand the high importance that Israelis attach to the subject of land and the location of Syrian armored forces.

The Syrians stressed that the "relevant" areas on the Syrian side – in which security arrangements will be applied – would only be in the territories Israel would evacuate. This meant only the Golan Heights and not further eastward and deeper in Syrian territory, as we had demanded, and the relevant areas on the Israeli side would be of the same size. They reiterated that they did not accept any foreign presence on Mount Hermon, including non-Israeli; inspection and verification would not be conducted by foreign teams. "You can do this by using aircraft and satellites," said the Syrians.

After we received reports on developments in the committees, a consultation was held in the smaller forum.

Foreign Minister David Levy said he received the impression that the Syrians had no free positions. They came with fixed positions, so as we continued the discussion we would always reach the same disagreements. "In order to avoid crisis," said Levy, "we should not overly extend our stay here."

In the background of this statement was our dilemma whether to stay for the weekend.

Amnon Lipkin-Shahak agreed with Levy's comments, and Barak said, "I will return to the Americans and tell them that the Syrians are not displaying any flexibility. I will remind them that we also have requirements that we view as a 'red line' - if the Syrians will not accept them, we will not reach an agreement."

The border committee was set to convene and the Israeli representatives included the Chairman, attorney Moshe Kochanowsky, Deputy Chief of Special Operations in the Ministry of Defense; Lt. Col. (Ret.) David Shatner, an expert on borders; Prof. Gideon Biger, internationally renowned for his knowledge of borders, and attorney David Kornblit.

Barak briefed Kochanowsky before the committee's convening, and as with all other committee chairmen he had emphasized on the one hand to avoid a display of patronage towards the Syrians, and on the other to display determination regarding our refusal to discuss a border defined as the 1967 border, as long as it is not clear whether our other requirements will be fulfilled.

"The border must be set to reflect, among other things, our vital interests and security concerns, with respect to water and other points of interest for the State of Israel," Barak said.

Meanwhile, General Yanai once more updated Barak of his last meeting with the Syrians and said that he asked the Syrians whether they would agree to withdraw their offensive forces eastward, so that our warning time would be enough to mobilize reservist troops.

General Ibrahim Omar left the room to consult, and came back with a question: how far eastward does Israel want us to move?

Yanai said that he would like to know if the Syrians in general are willing to the principle of moving their troops eastward.

Barak told Yanai that we must stress our demand that security arrangements ensure that a surprise attack cannot occur. It does not have to be only by moving the Syrian forces eastward, it was also possible to distance combat ammunition from the forces, or that some of the forces will be reservists. Yanai mentioned that every time the issue of security arrangements came up in the conversations, the Syrians were quick to say that Barak suffers from paranoia.

Barak said that we had already experienced something of the sort during the Yom Kippur War, so it was not paranoia.

Later that day, Barak met with Albright, who told him the details of a private conversation she held with al-Sharaa. According to her, al-Sharaa said that Israel would have sovereignty over the waters of the Sea of Galilee and up to ten meters to the east of the waters, but added that the five Syrian villages that were on the Sea of Galilee's shore should have access to water. Regarding Mount Hermon, al-Sharaa said that he would not allow an Israeli presence there. Dennis Ross immediately presented him with Lauder's letter, which states that there will be a French-US warning station on Mount Hermon for five years, after which five additional years will be decided on. Al-Sharaa said that what is written in Lauder's document on this matter is correct.

Barak told Albright that for reciprocity's sake he is offering the Syrians to place a warning station in the Galilee.

Albright went on to tell him that al-Sharaa showed understanding for Israel's demand that leaving the settlements in the Golan will be implemented only in the final stage, and that Syria would agree that it would be near the end of the process.

Regarding normalization, al-Sharaa said that it would be very difficult for them to see an Israeli flag flying over the embassy in Damascus, before the completion of the entire withdrawal, but at the time of the withdrawal itself Israeli ministers and elected officials would be able to visit Damascus.

As a gesture of sorts, al-Sharaa said, "We know that the border of 1967 passes in the middle of *Kibbutz Snir*, therefore we are willing to pass the line east of the kibbutz, so that the entire kibbutz remains in Israeli territory."

The Americans left the conversation with al-Sharaa feeling that he has some flexibility.

Barak mentioned to Albright that he suffered substantial damage in Israeli public opinion over the fact that al-Sharaa refused to shake his hand, and the fact that there was no meeting between them except in the presence of the Americans. I told Barak it was important he meet al-Sharaa despite the absence of a handshake. I thought a meeting between them seemed too important to be missed merely due to a lack of courtesy or power struggles.

The extent to which the handshake, or rather lack thereof, was fundamental to the Syrians, could be witnessed again years later, in June 2008, against the backdrop of reports that Israel and Syria resumed indirect talks between them in Turkey, under Turkish mediation.

In the background was the Mediterranean Nations Conference that was to convene a month later, on June 13, 2008, in Paris, and among its participants were Israeli Prime Minister Ehud Olmert and Syrian President Bashar Assad. The two of them were to sit at the same conference table.

In late June 2008, the Syrian Foreign Minister Walid Muallem was interviewed in the newspaper Asharq Al Awsat published in

London, in which he took care to stress that "the arrangements for the conference indicate that there will be no handshake between them."

On January 6, 2000, a meeting took place between Clinton and Barak, during which Clinton and Albright seemed highly encouraged from what they described as the "Syrian flexibility." This referred to Syria's willingness to give Israel sovereignty over the whole east coast of the Sea of Galilee, for an early-warning station on Mount Hermon for the duration of five years with the possibility of Israeli presence there, and that Israeli settlements would only be evacuated at the end of the process.

Barak began to encourage the Americans to put a draft agreement on the table, and added that before everything would be agreed upon - nothing would be agreed upon.

Barak noted that there was an asymmetry regarding the moment Israel would be required to give land in exchange for a paper with promises for the future. "In order for the public to understand that something real is happening," he said, "the public needs to be convinced that it is receiving not only paper but also serious benefits. So we want to know what kind of peace we will receive before we start discussing the border."

Clinton replied to Barak that he believes that in the last twenty-four hours Assad allowed al-Sharaa more flexibility, and I think Clinton would not have said something like that without relying on intelligence information that the Americans had received on the matter.

The next day was ahead of us, and in it the draft agreement prepared by the Americans, which could possibly reveal an additional glimpse of the parties' positions for the first time, and to try and get through the problems of semantics, definitions and fine print that could undermine the entire act of peace.

CHAPTER 20

ALBRIGHT AND CLINTON RUN OUT OF PATIENCE

On Friday, January 7, 2000, the Americans laid down a proposal for the draft peace agreement titled the "American Proposal for a Peace Agreement between Israel and the Syrian Arab Republic."

The proposal reflected the Americans' perception of the agreements and disagreements between Israel and Syria.

Clinton held a tripartite meeting between himself, Barak and al-Sharaa, and presented them with the draft, which stated (brought here in abbreviated form):

> The state of war between Israel and Syria is hereby terminated and peace is established between them. The Parties will maintain normal, peaceful relations… The permanent secure and recognized international boundary between Israel and Syria… has been commonly agreed [and the] Israeli position [is that it takes] into account security and other vital interests of the Parties… Israel will withdraw all its armed forces behind this boundary.

The section that dealt with the implementation schedule was left blank, as it was still in debate.

> [The Parties] recognize and will respect each other's sovereignty… [and] will refrain from the threat or use of

force…and will settle all disputes between them by peaceful means. The Parties will establish full diplomatic and consular relations, including the exchange of resident ambassadors.
…

The Parties will employ the following security arrangements:

1. Areas of limitation of forces and capabilities, including limitations on their readiness and activities, and on armaments, weapon system and military infrastructure… [According to Israel's demand, these areas will include] both the area from which Israeli forces will be relocated and the existing Area of Separation… [According to Syria's demand, these areas will be] of equal scope on both sides of the border.

2. Early warning capabilities shall be in place, including an early-warning ground station on Mt. Hermon, [according to Israel's demand] with an effective Israeli presence, [and according to Syria's demand] operated by the United States and France under their total auspices and responsibilities.

3. A monitoring, inspection and verification mechanism, [according to Israel's demand] composed of the two Parties and a multinational component and including on-site technical means, [according to Syria's demand] through an international presence, to monitor and supervise the implementation of the security arrangements.

4. Each Party undertakes to refrain from cooperation with any third party in a hostile alliance of a military character.

5. Each Party undertakes to refrain from organizing, instigating, inciting, assisting or participating in any acts or threats of violence against the other Party… and will take effective measures to ensure that no such acts occur from, or are supported by individuals on its territory or territory under its control.

6. Both Parties recognize that international terrorism in all its forms threatens the security of all nations, and therefore share a common interest in the enhancement of international cooperative efforts to deal with this problem.

7. Full resolution of all water issues: …[According to the Syrian demand, will be] based on relevant international principles and practices, [and according to the Israeli demand will be via] arrangements that will ensure the continuation of Israel's current use [of water] in quantity and quality…. The arrangements should include all necessary measures to prevent contamination, pollution or depletion of the Kinneret [Sea of Galilee].

Clinton explained to Barak and al-Sharaa that the draft was not an official paper but only a US assessment of the two sides' positions. "We ask," Clinton said, "that you study the paper and pass your comments to us. I am asking wholeheartedly that the contents of this framework document will not reach the media."

At the meeting, which was conducted in a pleasant atmosphere, al-Sharaa said to Barak, "It is very important that when we both go back to our homelands we demonstrate a positive attitude, and we will return a week later to continue working."

Barak replied to him, "There will be no minor victories here. If we reach an agreement, it will be a victory for us all."

Al-Sharaa said, "Now we understand each other better, and we are not ignoring the interests of the other party."

The atmosphere at that meeting was much more relaxed compared to all the forced meetings al-Sharaa had attended. It was evident that when he was alone, without the presence of his delegation, he was much more relaxed and free, and his body language was much more moderate and calm, as was his manner of expression.

On the other hand, you could say that the members of his delegation would also act more freely when he was not around. In my opinion, in the presence of their colleagues, the Syrians were always afraid that something they said would aggravate other members of the delegation, and as a result they would be reprimanded.

In the meeting Barak and I had with Clinton later, without al-Sharaa's presence, the President said that the Americans were under the impression that al-Sharaa responded positively to the draft, and added that he was preparing a letter to Assad which would stress that Barak did not retract and did not intend to retract the "deposit."

Clinton also said that in his conversation with al-Sharaa, the Syrians agreed that for the first five years there will be a US-French warning station on Mount Hermon. Furthermore, they agreed to explore the possibility that it would incorporate Israeli presence provided that this would not be included in the draft. Barak refused that his comment on the "deposit" be given to Assad in writing at that point. "An oral update to the Syrians should suffice," he said.

While we were in Shepherdstown, negotiations were being held between Israeli intelligence officials and members of the CIA.

Clinton said he would guide his people to fully cooperate with the Israelis with respect to the advance warning, in order to find a way to reinforce Israel's warning with the help of the United States, after the withdrawal from the Golan Heights.

At the same time, the various committees continued to convene, with Barak briefing Kochanowsky, chairman of the borders committee, that we could not make progress on the border issue until we saw what happens in the security, normalization and water committees.

Ibrahim Omar, head of the border committee, supplied the Syrian definition for "the border of 1967", and said that it was the line that no Israeli had been eastward of in June 1967. From their standpoint this included the entire Jordan River under Syrian rule, as well as the north-eastern part of the Sea of Galilee. At the same time, Omar noted that he had flexibility and that a gap of a few dozen meters could be bridged.

In order to induce a relaxed and somewhat less buttoned down atmosphere, Barak offered that I meet with Syrian interpreter Bouthaina Shaaban, who everyone knew was much more than an interpreter. The Americans liked the idea but the Syrians rejected it and al-Sharaa did not approve the meeting.

Dr. Bouthaina Shaaban was the woman who was always seen at Hafez Assad's side in his meetings with English-speaking guests. Everyone knew her status at Assad's side was much higher than that of a mere translator and that she was his confidant and woman of trust.

Clinton told us her story as Assad had told it to him in one of their meetings.

Assad met her for the first time during a presidential visit to the high school Bouthaina attended. The girl, who was sixteen at the time, approached him and complained to him that she could not enroll at university because she was a woman, and that there should be equal rights for boys and girls. Following the remark, Assad ordered to change the rules of admission to universities and since then, women could enroll for academic studies in Syria. Bouthaina was admitted to university, and later gained a Master's degree in English Language and Literature, and since her graduation had accompanied Assad as his translator. Over the years she became his confidant and part of his innermost circle.

Since we neared the end of the Shepherdstown talks in those days, it was obvious that another round would be needed, Clinton and Barak tried to reach something that would ensure that the talks would continue and that we could use to successfully reach the final stages.

Clinton told Barak that the United States was devoting much effort to joining other Arab countries to the peace process, and that the Administration is working hard in Congress to prepare the aid package to Israel.

Barak told Clinton that the entry of other Arab countries into the peace circle, especially Lebanon, and the massive US aid to Israel to make up for its strategic loss of the Golan Heights, will be of great assistance for him to reach difficult decisions.

Clinton expressed his concern over what will happen when we return for another round. "You maintained your strategy," said Clinton to Barak, "and you will return to Israel and say you did not agree to the line of 1967, and in fact have not given up on anything so far. However, unlike you, the Syrians have shown flexibilities: They said they would not reach the waters of the Sea of Galilee, which will be under Israeli sovereignty. They agreed to an arrangement of sorts in Mt. Hermon, and agreed to confidence-building measures. You on the other hand have only promised not to destroy settlements in the Golan Heights in return."

It was clear that Clinton was beginning to lose patience.

"Assad cannot even say that he has received some part of what you have agreed to here in writing," said Clinton, and continued, "even the fact that you are not going to retract the 'deposit' you refuse to give him in writing, but only orally.

"I think I can persuade Assad to add Lebanon to the talks, only if I could tell him that you ratify Rabin's 'deposit'," Clinton continued, "Strengthening the relationship between himself and the United States is a secondary matter for Assad - the main thing for him is to get back what he sees as his land. I do not believe there will be progress in the talks as long as the Syrians will feel they have moved forward and met you halfway, while you have not done the same. Only if I can tell Assad that the 'deposit' will be confirmed as soon as the Syrians return to the next round of talks, will I be able to convince him to add Lebanon to the talks."

"The next round must be the last round, in which we go all the way and sign an agreement," answered Barak. "It can be postponed no longer. We must exhaust all degrees of freedom in order to reach an agreement. However, we cannot say this even to our closest aides, because if this were to leak, it would immediately awaken the opponents of peace in Israel and the Arab countries – and they will work to thwart it."

"The negotiations on the border should be postponed until the final days of the final round in order to prevent leaks that might threaten to ruin everything," Barak continued. "I believe my only option to pass the agreement in a referendum would be if the solution would be a borderline which the Syrians could be able to call June 4, 1967 and we will have three things. These are a land strip of a few hundred meters on the north-eastern part of the lake, an effective presence in the Hermon that could serve as a warning station for us and normalization first."

Clinton and Barak agreed that an agreement with Syria and Lebanon should be achieved first, and afterwards all the efforts should be devoted to achieving an agreement with the Palestinians.

In another conversation, Clinton told us that al-Sharaa seemed depressed and in bad shape to him, and raised the possibility of asking Assad to replace him. Clinton said that it seemed to him that al-Sharaa was suffering from bad health, since a short time earlier he had suffered a heart attack from which he was saved at the last minute, and from which he had yet to recover. Clinton hypothesized that al-Sharaa felt that he had failed in his mission, and that he felt that Israel used him to squeeze concessions out of him, while it did not concede anything itself.

"Nevertheless," replied Barak, "and although the Syrians have gone a longer way than Israel this time, still it cannot be expected that Israel will give the Golan Heights before the other elements are discussed. So, the subject of Lebanon can help and I cannot understand why Syria insists not to involve it in the process."

"I cannot convince the Syrians to add Lebanon to the process unless I can say that you will be willing to ratify the 'deposit' during the next round in exchange," said Clinton.

"Even if I could ratify it, it would not be at the beginning of the round," said Barak, and Clinton was quick to respond, "But it is important that it will not be at the end, either."

Barak replied that he agreed to the formulation, whereby if they will successfully add Lebanon to the peace process and if Israel's demands – a land strip east of the lake, a warning station on Mt. Hermon and normalization first – were fulfilled, he would ratify the 'deposit' during the next round of talks.

Later that day, Barak asked me to convey a message to Clinton, through one of his aides. The message was that if the Syrians were to publicize the fact that the next round of talks would be devoted to the matter of the border under the headline of June 4, 1967 - which would mean that there is an understanding that Barak was going to ratify the 'deposit' - Barak would not ratify it. Furthermore, in such an eventuality, the understanding between Clinton and Barak on this matter would be canceled.

Later, on the Secretary of State's initiative, a meeting was held between Madeleine Albright, Barak, Amnon Lipkin-Shahak, and myself.

The meeting was charged, and Albright did not hide her dissatisfaction when she said, "In the entire history of my work with Clinton in the last seven years, there had not been so many phone calls with any head of state as he has had with you. We realized that it was very important for you to make progress in the Syrian track and we took it very seriously. However, you managed to surprise me very much when in the time between my visit to Damascus and obtaining Assad's consent to resuming the talks, and the meeting in the Blair House - you made a decision not to move forward quickly.

"We were able to bring al-Sharaa here and pressured him to show flexibility, but nothing happened on your part. We are pessimistic, al-Sharaa does not know what fate holds for him, yet you – you are pleased."

Albright's words were spoken very angrily and could not be misunderstood. She went on to say, "You have no better friend than Clinton, while you both toyed with his credibility, and made me and my team feel that we were not serving him well, because we did not know what you were planning to do. We may even have lost the chance to reach an agreement due to your error. The Syrians were flexible, while you came with the decision not to give them anything. We cannot proceed unless you show flexibility on the water and the border. I will not conceal this from you I am very concerned."

Barak remained exalted and calm and answered, "Mrs. Secretary, I see things in a different way altogether. The most important goal is to achieve peace. Our goal is not to be pleased. We cannot make mistakes following which we will be pleased in the short term, but will significantly reduce the chances of achieving peace in the long term. I have said before both to the president and to you that for many reasons we cannot speak concretely and in detail on the border, under the headline that the Syrians request (the boundary of 1967), except when we have already reached the last round of talks, and in a state of complete isolation from the outside world (to prevent leaks).

"Only when I know what the Syrians will give us, and only when the other parts of the puzzle are finalized (Lebanon and other Arab countries joining, and US aid) – will I be able to make decisions that are difficult and dangerous to Israel. If Israel concedes the only card that it holds (the Golan Heights) before the start of negotiations, I would be acting against my duty as Prime Minister and would completely lose the trust of the Israeli public."

"I said these things to the President as early as July 1999," continued Barak, speaking in a didactic, monotonous and non-belligerent tone. At times it seemed as though he was a teacher talking to his student: "I emphasized that I will enter a detailed discussion of the border only under the conditions I presented. It would be wrong to say that I made no progress: I told the President that not only do I not retract the 'deposit,' but that I do not intend to retract it, and I see this as progress. Although I said this privately to the President, for me it is as if I have signed a contract. You must understand that I am about to make one of the most difficult decisions ever made by any Israeli prime minister, and that the risks we are going to assume are infinitely larger than those that Assad will assume. Your tone indicates that you do not fully appreciate the risks that we are going to take. We are in dire need of a strip of a few hundred meters from the Sea of Galilee's waterfront, we need a presence on Mt. Hermon - and so far we have received neither one nor the other from Syria. All we have gotten is hints of a beach strip ten meters from the water, hints of a US presence on Mt. Hermon, and a hint of al-Sharaa understanding that normalization will occur before the evacuation of settlements. That's all - just hints. Assad has not taken any risks so far, even if his people come to the next round. I cannot say more or concede more before we enter the stage that would end the negotiations. All I can say at this point I that I mean every word I have said, and promised seriously."

"We understand that you face very difficult decisions," Albright replied to him, "but in the meantime we have spent part of our credit."

She was obviously still not persuaded by Barak's comments, and he proceeded to ask her, "Did you expect me to tell my people to enter discussions headlined 'the borderline of June 4, 1967,' in the current state of the negotiations?"

"I did not expect that, but if you had said three days ago what you said yesterday, that you do not intend to retract the 'deposit' – it would have been very helpful!" Albright replied.

"I do not accept this," Barak answered. "If I had done this, I would have immediately read in the Lebanese newspaper *Al Hayat* that I gave Assad the boundary of June 4, 1967, and right after that I would have found myself wasting days explaining to the Israelis that this was not true. The resumption of negotiations with Lebanon will lead to a fundamental change in the Israeli public's spirits, and will show that Assad intends to move forward and enable me to be more flexible."

From a later conversation I had with Martin Indyk, I learned that the Syrians were pleased, apparently much more so than the Americans. Indyk told me that al-Sharaa agreed that some progress was made on Barak's side, calling it "a hidden promise." He added that if the Syrians would come back for another round they would ask that the border delineation committee be established, and agreed to announce that the talks would resume on January 19, 2000, ten days later.

Clinton entertained Barak and al-Sharaa at his table that evening, while on the Israeli side, Barak took care that Amnon Lipkin-Shahak and Uri Sagi would also be present. Barak used to keep me updated of all the occurrences and the minutiae of their fine details. Since I was the only member of the Israeli delegation who knew all the details, it was evident that other members of our delegation felt frustrated and bitter as a result.

In order to avoid the criticism directed at him on this matter, and in an attempt to restore calm, a meeting was organized between David Levy, Clinton, Shahak, and Albright.

During the dinner with Clinton, al-Sharaa said, "We came unconditionally because we understood that the border of 1967 was agreed upon, and was not open for negotiations. We waited thirty years and if necessary will wait longer, but there will be no peace without this boundary, and there would be great benefits for all if our process is successful. I am in a sensitive spot, it is difficult for me to return to Syria and tell the president that there was no progress on the issue of peace. We were prepared for internal criticism in Syria for holding these talks, because we believed that at the end of this meeting we would discuss the matter of delineating the boundary of June 4, 1967.

"In a telephone conversation I had with President Assad, he told me, 'If the Israelis want everything, tell the Syrian delegation to pack their bags and go home'. I told him that there are two more days and we should wait. I do not understand Barak. In a recent poll in Israel it appeared that there was increased support for the peace process and Barak. We keep track of what is happening in Israel, including polls.

"I am tired, Clinton is tired, Albright is tired, and my entire delegation is tired. We will not go on like this anymore. We came here because we thought we were turning a new page. I will return home and Assad will send someone else in my place. If Barak wants peace, I am willing. There are people in Lebanon, in Saudi Arabia and in Iran, who are trying to sabotage the process. If peace is not dear enough to you, we will wait. I think that peace is important for everyone, and if we want to move forward together under Clinton's leadership, I am ready to do so."

"I believe that at the end of the road we will reach peace," Barak replied to him. "I see this week as a turning point and the seeds of future achievements have been sown here. I respect Assad, and believe that Syria wants true peace, one that will represent the dignity and needs of Syria as well as those of Israel. The paradox is that you surely understand why it is difficult for us to begin negotiations on points that are important to you, before we realize that our demands will be met, in a way that all of our interests will be addressed. I do not intend to jeopardize Clinton's credibility, nor to embarrass Assad. We have not erased all that has been in the past with Rabin, Peres and Netanyahu, but I have said that before the negotiations gain momentum - there are certain things I cannot do."

Here al-Sharaa interrupted him and said, "For us, all that is important is what had been in Rabin's time (when the 'deposit' was given)."

Barak responded, "Not only have I not retracted the 'deposit,' but I have also told the President that I have no intention of retracting it. This does not mean that the negotiations will be easy. I say that you should have already addressed our interests, and this did not happen. I am sure there will be an agreement if we can find the right balance between your needs and ours. I can only show you that I am serious, and ask that you give me some credit, and if not to me - then to Clinton. Let's give the next round a chance."

"In this round of discussions, we put everything on the table: water, normalization and security," answered al-Sharaa. "We opened our minds and our hearts, but you did not act similarly. One of your people, who is probably from Likud, and whom we have known for years, cited today what the Likud said after the Madrid Conference. This means that I was wrong to recommend Assad to renew the talks with you. If we do not demarcate the border on the map now, it will weaken the Syrian position and to that I will not agree. I have been in politics for forty years and have a lot of experience. Tell me that in six months we will begin delineating the border, and that would be fine with me. Give me something, but the ambiguity you are creating and our lack of assurance as to your intentions are very dangerous for negotiations. I will not go on like this. My condition to continue is that next time all the elements of peace will be on the table, including delineating the border of June 1967.

"I want peace and it is a shame we cannot reach it. I am fully invested in the process, and I will not cause the Syrian position to be weakened. I worry not for myself, but for the future of Syria."

"We have no desire to weaken the Syrian position," Barak answered. "The peace of the brave will be between two countries that have mutual respect between them. I think stopping the talks would be a loss for all of us. I suggest an alternative. We will not erase the past - it is there. Nevertheless, I cannot say more than what I have said, but you will not be required to wait for much longer before I have a way to say more."

"What do you mean?" asked al-Sharaa, and Barak replied, "That you should believe that we do not want to embarrass ourselves or Assad or Clinton."

"Assad is not Arafat," said al-Sharaa. "We do not make peace first, and then negotiate for peace. We mock Arafat for the way he made agreements with you. During the next round we will offer nothing more. In Syria there are severe reactions to the peace process. In the last few days we have had many problems in Syria and Lebanon with opponents of the process. I am going to report that we have made no progress and that it is your fault."

"Unlike you, I think we have made progress," answered Barak, "but I cannot tell you what to report. I suggest that the teams will continue their work for two more days, and in the ten days of rest until the next round we will remain in contact through the Americans. If we act responsibly we will reach an agreement and then we will all see that this past week had been important."

Clinton summed up the conversation and said, "It was very interesting to listen to you."

On January 9, we returned from the first round of talks in Shepherdstown, and we started to prepare for the continued discussions ten days later, aware of the fact that we still had a difficult road to cross before signing the coveted agreement.

Chapter 21

"I Swam in the Sea of Galilee"

Immediately upon returning to Israel, we started discussing and reviewing the previous round of talks, and were engaged in feverish preparations for the resumption of the next round, on January 19.

While we were busy with these preparations, details of the US draft, which both parties were asked to study and submit their comments on, were leaked. The publication appeared in the *Haaretz* newspaper by journalist Akiva Eldar, and as stated, caused severe damage. I do not know who the source of the leak was, but it is clear to me beyond any doubt that their aim was to sabotage the talks and the chance to make peace with Syria. It could have been an Israeli who did not find the process to his liking, or an American who thought it would be better to focus on the Palestinian process rather than the Syrian track, or a Syrian attempting to thwart the process.

In my opinion, the chances that it was a Syrian are slim, considering the way the document was leaked and its contents were very inimical to the Syrians. The document stressed that Israel was unmovable on its positions, and that Barak did not give up even a single inch, contrary to the Syrians who had shown flexibility.

At an unbelievable speed, the reprimand call was already on its way to Israel, on January 14, five days prior to the talks' renewal.

On the line was Madeleine Albright, who said to Barak, "We have a real problem with the document's leaking. The Syrians blamed the leak on Clinton, since he sponsored the talks. According to them, the leak has created very serious problems for them. Now they have to deal with the Syrian public's impression that the Syrians have made large concessions and the Israelis received a lot without giving up anything."

Barak replied that there was no evidence that the Israelis had leaked the draft.

To me, he did not rule out the possibility that it was an American leak, nor the possibility of an Israeli leak, coming from the direction of those who wished to thwart the process after deeming the Israeli approach lenient, and overly generous. He also did not rule out the possibility that the leak came from supporters of the process, whose goal was to prove to the Israeli public that Israel had not conceded its principles. If that were the case, the leak was meant to serve as a trial run for the reactions of the public, who in due time would have to approve the agreement with Syria in a referendum.

My estimate was and still is that the leak was made by someone who had an interest in sabotaging the process and gravely harming it.

Barak reminded Albright that since from our standpoint, there would be no agreement unless Lebanon joined the process, and because we believed that the next round should be the last one, in which everything would be finalized - then Lebanon should participate in it.

Albright replied that Lebanon continued to pose an obstacle, and that the Syrians were demanding that Barak publicly ratify Rabin's "deposit" in return for a public announcement that Lebanon would join the talks.

"After the Syrians realized how important and pressing it was for you that Lebanon join the talks, they raised the price for joining it," said Albright.

Barak explained to her again that he was unable to make the "deposit" public, since this was our only leverage against the Syrians, in order to learn what they intend to give in return for the depth of the withdrawal. "If we publicly confirm the 'deposit' to them at this stage," said Barak, "they will have no motivation to give us what we want and need later on. In addition, if the Israeli public hears that we are willing to withdraw to the 1967 borders, and we will not have anything to show for it at the same time - we will not be able to gain its support."

Albright told him that when she asked al-Sharaa, "How do we proceed?" His answer was, "We cannot answer right now."

At this point I was already beginning to grasp that the Syrians were beginning to draw out the process, and that they were not planning to go anywhere on January 19.

Barak told Albright that he would ratify the "deposit" to Clinton only after the Syrians announced that Lebanon would be joining the talks. Thus Barak changed his earlier decision, according to which he told Clinton he authorized him to tell the Syrians that "he had a feeling" that Barak would ratify the "deposit" in the next round of talks.

From the start one could tell that Barak was not running amok towards an agreement with Syria, which stood in stark contrast to the activities of the opposition, who took care to constantly kindle the falsehood that the Syrian story was already over, rigged and staged, and that the whole Shepherdstown affair was nothing but one big sham.

Barak told Clinton that during the talks with the Syrians, he would start talking about the border only if he knew that Lebanon was joining the talks and that all of Israel's requirements would be met.

Barak noted that he was aware that the Syrians may be concerned Israel would agree with the Lebanese on the international border, which would create a precedent by which Israelis would also ask Syria to accept the international boundary rather than that of 1967.

So Barak asked Clinton to promise the Syrians that the border with Lebanon would be agreed only after the agreement with Syria.

At the same time, the Syrians continued to convey messages to the Americans that after the draft's leak, the Syrian leadership's situation was difficult, and that they needed another week before talks resumed.

Al-Sharaa's new demand was that talks between Israel and Lebanon would not be renewed until Israel's border with Syria would be delineated on the map, or alternatively that we would declare that Lebanon would join the talks, but in actuality it would happen only after the border was delineated. The Syrians also offered a third option, that Uri Sagi and Ibrahim Omar would meet and reach an agreement regarding the borderline. This would be based on the line of 1967 and on the security arrangements with Syria, and only then would the resumption of talks and Lebanon's joining them be announced.

On this idea, Albright replied to al-Sharaa that it was not an option, and that this was a "non-starter" - meaning that this was not a starting point for further negotiations.

Al-Sharaa always maintained that the Syrians did not understand what Israel's exact demands were. They took our demands as something very general that included normalization, an Israeli presence on Mount Hermon, and so on.

Barak believed it was time to present Israel's concrete needs to the Syrians.

I had already suggested in Sheperdstown to demand from the Syrians to make their own "deposit" to stand against ours, with details of what the Syrians were willing to give in exchange for the Israeli "deposit."

Clinton told us that Assad was prepared to renew the talks, but without Lebanon, and asked that the US president tell him what Israel's needs were and what he was going to get from Israel.

Clinton raised the possibility of presenting a map to Assad, on which the Israeli demands would be indicated as the Americans understood them.

In one of my face-to-face conversations with Barak, we made a joint assessment of the situation with Syria, and I expressed my opinion that under the current circumstances, Syria would not return to the discussions. I told Barak that our requirements should be made clear to the Syrians, and they should make the chances of these requirements being met clear to us, before we would say anything more precise regarding the line to which we were willing to withdraw.

Up to this point, Barak preferred to define Israel's needs in vague terms: control through sovereignty over the Sea of Galilee, effective Israeli presence on the early-warning station on Mount Hermon, normalization first and the evacuation of settlements later, and was careful not to define the line of withdrawal in exact terms. Barak did so because he wanted to first hear the Syrians' opinion of his demands. The Syrians did not feel that they could state their opinions as long as they did not know all the details from the Israelis. It is possible that this conduct was part of their negotiating tactic and an attempt to elicit more promises from us.

Full Israeli sovereignty over the Sea of Galilee and the warning station on Mt. Hermon necessitated, in my opinion, that we provide a very detailed explanation at that point, in concrete terms, going as far as drawing our requirements on the map. Such an act could reveal whether the lack of information regarding our demands, which the Syrians were talking about, was indeed a true concern, or merely an excuse used on their part to hear from us exactly where the border would be and only then reveal what they were willing to give. I thought that this kind of maneuver would put them to a real test with respect to the Israeli demands, and I thought that this was the right moment to define our basic demands from them in concrete terms: to draw a line on the map and show them our demands, and clearly define the meaning of "an effective presence on Mount Hermon."

The hourglass was running out: the end of Clinton's term was on the horizon, and Barak thought that as soon as the two next presidential candidates would be known, Clinton's scope of action would begin to narrow. At the same time, once we reached an agreement with Syria, we would need about eight weeks to approve such an agreement in referendum.

Based on this calculation, Clinton had until the end of May to present a US initiative. Moreover, since Barak promised to withdraw from Lebanon by July, it was very important for him to know by May if he could get the IDF out of Lebanon as part of an agreement, or would need to do so unilaterally.

On February 7, I met with the US ambassador to Israel, Martin Indyk, to discuss the Israeli demands which the Americans would present to Assad. This time, the group of confidants on the matter was very limited. On the Israeli side there were only Barak and myself, and on the American side were Clinton, Albright, National Security Adviser Sandy Berger, his assistant Bruce Riedel, ambassador Martin Indyk and Dennis Ross, the peace talks' coordinator and the President's special envoy to the Middle East.

From that moment until the Clinton-Assad meeting in March, nothing was leaked, evidence that you can in fact work without leaks.

Barak made sure that all the adjustments, updates and plans went through me, and some of them were made only between the two of us. He preferred it this way, as he saw me as a person of confidence and trusted me. Therefore I was the only one (except Barak himself, of course) who saw the whole picture, and the only one who participated in all the meetings that Barak held in privacy (except for myself).

At that time, Martin Indyk returned to the post of US ambassador to Israel, and Barak said to him, "The only person besides me, who sees the entire picture of all the negotiation channels, is Danny. You will work only with him and me."

These remarks were made against the backdrop of criticism heard from various people in Barak's circle, who claimed I was keeping compartmentalized information from them. In fact, this situation came to be because that was the way Barak wanted it. Naturally this garnered much opposition, and people did not see it favorably. The argument was that I was accumulating too much power and information and preventing access to the Prime Minister, which of course was a fable. It is only natural that it was much less comfortable for all the detractors to deal with the fact that this was the way Barak decided to act.

Security officials, especially Director of the Mossad Efraim Halevy, leaked under the guise of "security sources" that I was blocking their way to the Prime Minister. Such a thing never happened, and I made it clear to Halevy in a conversation between us.

I remember an incident wherein there was a meeting between two Jordanian representatives, led by the Jordanian Foreign Minister, who were sent by King Abdullah to update Barak of the details of a conversation between Abdullah and Assad. The meeting took place at the Mossad visitor's lodge, and Halevy believed that his presence at the meeting was required, since it was held at a facility that was under his responsibility.

However, Barak thought and wanted otherwise. Before the meeting, Gen. Gadi Eizenkot, Military Secretary to the Prime

Minister, informed Halevy that he was merely hosting the meeting and was not meant to participate in it.

Halevy, as expected, was hardly pleased with this notion, and made sure to enter the conference room after Barak and myself and the two Jordanian guests were already seated there. In a demonstration of offense of sorts, he said, "I realize that I am not welcome here." Perhaps he had hoped Barak would change his mind in light of the situation, but Barak did not respond, and Halevy turned around and left the room.

Before the US draft was submitted to the Syrians, there were numerous meetings between Martin Indyk and me, during which we prepared detailed maps on which the villages that the Syrians claimed beside the Sea of Galilee before 1967 were indicated. Under various pretexts I asked the IDF's mapping unit for aerial photos from June 4, 1967, to see the exact whereabouts of the five Syrian villages on the banks of the Sea of Galilee. When we had these photographs, we marked the Syrian villages from north to south: Mishfaa, Musadiyah, Kufar Aqeb, El Kursi and Nuqayb.

We drew a map displaying the minimum needs of Israel, according to which all the Jordan River mountains were under Israeli control, including a corridor of Israeli sovereignty that allows access to the Banias River, which was also under Israeli sovereignty. In addition, we outlined a border passing about 450 to 500 meters east of the Sea of Galilee, and in some places coming within 250 meters of the lake, to keep the locations of Syrian villages around the Sea of Galilee under Syrian sovereignty.

We thought that Assad could call this line the line of June 4, 1967, even though it was not exactly the line of 1967 according to the Syrian point of view. Syria's attitude was that the entire Jordan mountains should be under their sovereignty. Their sovereignty should be on the waterfront of the Sea of Galilee, or at the very least stop ten meters short of the Sea of Galilee's bank, as was decreed by the international border.

We based our work on the document of the US expert Hoff, who researched the border of 1967, and outlined his conception of it.

Hoff was a US military officer who published a research paper on disputed borders, according to his understanding and studies. He used the reports of UN observers and aerial photos from 1967, outlined his understanding of the line of 1967, and published his outline in 1999.

With his outlines as a reference point, we delineated our line east of Hoff's line on the north-eastern part of the lake, and as compensation offered the Syrians the cliffs in the southern area of the Golan Heights, north of al-Hama. This area is located west of the 1967 lines and the international border, and was under Israeli sovereignty on the eve of the war. We also agreed that al-Hama, which according to the international border belongs to Israel, would be Syrian as well. In this way the Syrians would be able to rebuild the villages on the Sea of Galilee's bank, they would be allowed access to the lake under Israeli sovereignty, and the Israelis would be allowed access to al-Hama under Syrian sovereignty.

We thought the offer was very enticing, and could easily be used as the basis for an agreement and a boundary that Assad could call the line of 1967, if only he wished to do so.

Another suggestion we made was to dig a canal or lagoon from the Sea of Galilee to the area in which the Syrian villages were in 1967, so that at least one Syrian village could "sit" on the Sea of Galilee's shore, and the Syrians would have access to the Sea of Galilee in the sense that they could fish and sail in it. We were also willing to allocate a certain amount of water from the Sea of Galilee to the Syrians. This was all under the condition that the entire Sea of Galilee and the strip to its east will be under Israeli sovereignty.

On the issue of an Israeli warning station on Mt. Hermon, we defined the precise number of Israelis who would occupy it and the minimum amount of years for Israeli presence in the station.

Based on these maps, the Americans made their own map which they were supposed to present to Assad during his meeting with Clinton in Geneva.

In the meeting, Clinton was to tell Assad of Israel's needs according to his understanding, present him with Barak's capabilities to fulfill the Syrian needs, and understand from Assad how he would fulfill Israel's demands.

On the basis of the understandings that the Americans would reach at that meeting, talks between Syria and Israel were supposed to resume.

The basis of these understandings was supposed to include Assad's agreements to Israel's vital needs, and in exchange, Barak would ratify Rabin's deposit.

On February 14, a phone call was held between Barak and Clinton, in which Barak said, "We have reached the moment of truth. We need to know if we have a partner for peace in Syria. If there is, we will achieve peace with them. If there is not, we will have to declare a unilateral withdrawal from Lebanon on the basis of UN Resolution 425 at a certain time."

In conversations between Clinton and Barak, the idea began to form that the US president would come to the region. After the draft's leak and Assad's statement that he had to consult his leadership, it was estimated that Assad was trying to buy time and to avoid conducting negotiations as were previously held. The feeling was that the Syrians' degrees of leeway had been exhausted in Shepherdstown. It was clear that decisions regarding Israeli sovereignty over the Sea of Galilee, Israel's presence on Mt. Hermon, a longer timetable than the Syrians agreed to, security arrangements and normalization before the start of the withdrawal – these would all be decided by Assad alone.

At the same time we were all also aware of the hourglass that was running out: not much time was left for Assad's life and Clinton's time in the White House.

The Americans sent a message to Assad through Prince Bandar, the Saudi ambassador to the United States, to the effect that Clinton was prepared to meet with him and assist in formulating a peace agreement with Israel. The message spoke about Clinton bringing all the Israeli requirements to the meeting, and all they were willing to give to the Syrians. Prince Bandar met with Assad, and reported a positive response to Clinton's proposal.

On February 26, there was a meeting between Barak and myself from the Israeli side and Americans Dennis Ross and Martin Indyk. During the meeting, Barak detailed Israel's needs: Israeli control over a 500 meter strip of land in the northeast part of the Sea of Galilee. In the eastern part of the lakeshore, from Nuqayb and southwards, the border would be the international border. In this area, the border would move about 1-1.5 kilometers away from the lake and upwards towards the cliffs of the Golan Heights. According to Hoff's line and the Syrians' claim the boundary passed along the waterfront in the north-east part up to Nuqayb, so we asked only in this part that it be moved a few hundred meters to the east. Elsewhere, the international border was sufficiently far from the waterline.

This expansion was necessary for us to maintain our sovereignty and our control of the Sea of Galilee.

The boundary we delineated took into account the position of the Syrian villages before 1967. Barak asked us to delineate the border so that the vast majority of the land on which the villages resided would be under Syrian sovereignty, and hence in those locations we had to reduce the distance to a mere 250 meters from the Sea of Galilee's waterfront.

According to the boundary we delineated, Israel would also have sovereignty over an eighty meter strip of land along the Jordan mountains, east of the mouth of the lake near Kibbutz Almagor, to the north up to the sources of the Jordan River in the Banias – all to ensure our sovereignty over Israel's water resources.

According to our outline, Kibbutz Snir remained in our territory. We also outlined a strip of ten to twenty meters that would leave the Banias springs under Israeli sovereignty.

(The original map appears in the collection of pictures before Page 289)

Regarding the warning station on Mount Hermon, Barak detailed the minimum number of Israelis that would be at the station. The station itself would be a US station, and the Israeli presence there would be for at least seven years from the date of the agreement's signing.

According to the security arrangements Barak requested, the relevant (demilitarized) zones in the Syrian territory would be from the border that will be set to the area of the "Lega", the Daraa-Damascus highway, east of the line our forces held in the Golan Heights.

Regarding the agreement with Lebanon, Barak said that the agreement should be signed concurrently with an agreement with Syria, and we would have to begin negotiations with Lebanon immediately upon the resumption of talks with Syria.

The next topic was "confidence-building measures", but the Syrians really did not like this term and the Americans "scrapped" it and invented a new term: "signs of good intentions".

Hence, on the issue of "good intentions", we asked for the return of the remains of the late Eli Cohen, the return of the MIAs from Sultan Yacoub, and the return of Ron Arad.

Regarding the timetable for withdrawal from the entire Golan Heights, we asked for a period of three and a half years. The first phase of the withdrawal would take place after three months, in which the Syrians would receive a very narrow strip that includes the Druze villages of Majdal Shams, Masada and Buq'ata.

Against this stage we asked for open borders and the exchange of ambassadors. In the second phase, which would take place nine months later, the withdrawal would include some Israeli communities. The third phase, which would be completed after forty-two months, would end in full evacuation.

In addition, Barak noted that in the framework of relations between Israel and the United States, Israel asks for a "security package" from the Americans that would include Tomahawk cruise missiles. Until then, these missiles had never been given to any country since the Americans claimed it was contrary to their policy of not transferring long-range missile technology.

Indeed, a short time later, Clinton told Barak that the non-proliferation treaty regarding long-range missile technology would make it difficult for him to transfer Tomahawk missiles to Israel, especially considering the US military establishment's concern over the relations between Israel and China, which could lead to technology contained in the Tomahawk missiles finding its way to China.

We also asked for more F-22s – the future aircraft that had not existed yet - and additional warning systems Israel still did not possess.

While we were having these discussions with the Americans, reading drafts and outlining maps and making preparations, we also examined the possibility that Assad would reject all of our proposals. We conducted simulations of Clinton's response in case Assad agreed to our offers, and also in case he refused.

Barak made it clear to the Americans that in his opinion, if Assad wanted to negotiate these requirements - that meant that Assad was not ready for peace. For Barak, the proposal he submitted was the bare minimum that was necessary, our 'red lines' that could not be conceded with respect to the border and water issues. Any Syrian demand to start new negotiations over this would mean that Assad was not interested in a peace agreement.

The day before the scheduled meeting between Clinton and Assad in Geneva, on Sunday, March 26, Barak and I reviewed the US paper which Clinton was to present to Assad for one last time.

The document contained ten dense English pages, in which Clinton explains to Assad that a state of peace will help his transfer of power to his heirs and instilling his heritage, since as a result of peace Syria will be in a state of calm and prosperity. Clinton stressed that his arrival to this meeting indicates he is willing to jeopardize his position and to put his own reputation on the line – in an effort to achieve peace.

Clinton mentioned that his administration's days were numbered and that he had no time to waste. "Either we overcome the differences and achieve an agreement, or it will have to wait for another president and another time," read the document. "This is the moment of truth," stressed Clinton, "You said you were prepared to go into the thick of things and put everything on the table and finish with an agreement, and Barak said the same thing. In order for this to happen, the two of you need to know whether your needs will be met. On the basis of my discussions with Barak, I built my impression of what he is willing to do and what he asks you to do."

Clinton continued to say in the document, that as a result of the pressure he put on Barak, the Israeli Prime Minister had limited his demands to his vital 'red lines,' and went as far as he could toward the Syrian needs.

"I believe that the differences between Syria and Israel are small," the document states on Clinton's behalf. "If we cannot bridge these gaps, future historians will not be able explain why this happened. The only explanation they could give is a lack of courage and a failure of diplomacy. At this stage, it will not be enough to merely resume negotiations, because it would lead to a new breakdown. The two of you, Barak and yourself, bear the task of ensuring that your basic needs can be fulfilled. If this is the case - negotiations could be fruitful. Otherwise, there is no point in continuing."

The document further states that Clinton planned to tell Assad that if he would fulfill Israel's basic needs, Barak would ratify Rabin's deposit, and the next step would be proceeding to discussions between high-level groups to elaborate the understandings that Clinton and Assad would reach during their meeting. Clinton was to point out to Assad that it would be impossible to finish the work on the peace agreement without the latter's presence.

"If you cannot respond positively to Barak's basic demands, I will respect that. However, you must understand that I cannot help you afterwards," said the document.

The document proceeded to list the Israeli willingness to a full withdrawal from the Golan Heights to an agreed boundary, based on the line of June 4, 1967. It also listed all our territorial demands and needs with respect to the Sea of Galilee, the northern part of the Jordan River, the territories on the banks of the Sea of Galilee and the Jordan River, and the Syrian villages.

Barak was willing to make border adjustments to balance his demands, by transferring Israeli land beneath the cliffs near al-Hama to the Syrian side. The document stated that if all these things were to be agreed upon, Barak would agree that al-Hama would be under Syrian sovereignty. This was despite absence of any precedent in international law for a nation giving up an area that belonged to it but was taken from it by force. In the case of al-Hama, it was an Israeli area occupied by the Syrians in 1951.

It is mentioned there that Barak sought a sovereign corridor ten meters wide around the Banias on both sides of the valley. "You can describe the line as the line of 1967, and Barak could say that the line gives Israel complete control and sovereignty over the Sea of Galilee," states the document, whose contents were to be conveyed to Assad.

The document mentioned the possibility that Assad would refuse the notion of five hundred meters of land under Israeli sovereignty on the northeast part of the lake. In this case, Clinton was to tell Assad that he pressured Barak on the matter, and the answer he received was that there is no precedent in the world for a country retreating beyond its international border (this was referring to conceding al-Hama and the border adjustments in the cliffs). However, because Barak wished to satisfy Assad's vital interests, he was willing to do more and withdraw beyond this boundary.

The document noted that Clinton should explain to Assad that the Sea of Galilee was a vital water reservoir for Israel, and hence it was so vital for the Israelis that it will be under their sovereignty, just as the borderline of 1967 was vital for the Syrians. It also stated that the Israelis could prove that except in al-Hama and one of the places near the Banias, all Syrian outposts in 1967 were on the international border or eastwards of it, so a Syrian demand for Israel to withdraw beyond this boundary was not justified. Clinton was supposed to say that Barak was willing to ensure Syrian farmers access to the Sea of Galilee, and that Israel's expectation was that Israeli and Syrian movement all along the border would be unrestricted. Thus, as part of the agreement, the Syrians would be able to fish in the Sea of Galilee and the Israelis would be able to visit al-Hama.

Clinton was also to make it clear that there were limits to Barak's flexibilities.

The document also referred to the Israeli demand for a ground warning station on Mt. Hermon under American control, with the presence of some Israelis, for seven years from the date of Israel's departure from the Hermon. This temporary presence should not undermine Syrian sovereignty on the Hermon.

The document included preparation for the possibility that Assad would refuse to accept this demand. In this case, Clinton was supposed to volunteer to convince Barak to shorten the period of Israeli presence at the warning station, and offer that a "rolling agreement" be signed. Within this agreement, Israel would withdraw all its military forces and civilians from the Golan Heights in about three and a half years, and a small number of Israelis who remained on the Hermon station would be evacuated after seven years. Meaning, this would create a withdrawal in stages, with the final step lasting seven years.

Regarding security arrangements, Clinton was to present to Assad the agreement offered by Barak to define the areas where security arrangements would apply on both sides of the border, in a territorial ratio of ten to four. In other words, for every ten square demilitarized kilometers on the Syrian side, there would be four square kilometers on the Israeli side, the reason for this being that the State of Israel was very narrow in this area, which was not in the same proportion as the Syrian area.

The document further proposed that a monitoring group under American auspices would monitor the implementation of security arrangements on both sides.

The timetable and stages of withdrawal that were listed in the document were to last thirty-nine months after the referendum to approve the peace agreement. This assumed that it would take two and a half months to complete the referendum in Israel, and then in the first phase Israel would withdraw from a strip that would include a few Druze villages, embassies would be opened, and the borders would be opened for people and vehicles. Afterwards, during a period of nine to twelve months several Israeli villages would also be evacuated, and after thirty-six months Israel would begin the final stage of the withdrawal, which would last for three months. It was also noted that Israel would not demolish the settlements in the Golan Heights and would leave them in place.

The document stated that details of the normalization would have to be finalized later. It also stated that an agreement with Lebanon would be signed in tandem with the agreement with Syria. Clinton would indicate that Barak wanted to be sure that the negotiations with Lebanon would resume immediately after negotiations with Syria were resumed, and while it takes place the attacks and terrorism of Hezbollah in southern Lebanon must cease.

It also noted the demand for "signals of peace", to help create an atmosphere of negotiation: to stop attacks on Israel in the Syrian media, allow some Israelis to visit Syria before the peace agreement, and to make humanitarian gestures regarding the fate of Eli Cohen, Ron Arad and MIAs of Sultan Yacoub.

After presenting all these points from the document in his hands, Clinton was supposed to tell Assad that if he agreed to all of the above, then the US president could ratify Rabin's deposit, with Barak's consent and on his behalf. Furthermore, when the border committee would convene it would delineate the border on the basis of the line of June 4, 1967, based on what was presented to him as Barak's requirements and concessions, such as al-Hama.

Clinton was to offer Assad to move on to high-level negotiations in Washington, under American auspices and supervision.

The document also prepared for a possibility that Assad refused everything that was said to him. In this case, the US president was to say, "I respect your position but unfortunately it means that we cannot reach an agreement. I did my best, and I believe that Barak went as far as he could. I cannot help you more in the difficult circumstances we will all face. You will probably not get the Golan Heights, and I will not be able to work with you to build a new future for Syria, a future based on a new relationship with the United States. In this way - you will be left alone."

The document also prepared for the possibility that Assad would ask for time to think about the offer. In that case Clinton was to tell Assad that he does not have much time and that he must receive an answer before he leaves Geneva. Clinton in that case was to express his willingness to stay another night in Geneva, emphasizing that he had to leave for Washington in the morning. He was also to make it clear to Assad that there was no room for negotiation on the conditions themselves. "I worked hard to get Barak to minimize his demands," the document states. "If you cannot respond to these minimum requirements I do not see how a deal can be reached."

All the possibilities, probabilities, preparations, offers and answers accompanied Clinton in the document he took with him on his way to meet Assad.

However, reality, as is its way, was completely different.

At 8:45 PM, on the evening of March 26, a telephone ring pierced the tension and anticipation that hung in Barak's room at the Prime Minister's Office. The two of us were seated there, alert and expectant of Clinton's report, and the news that was to come from his meeting with the Syrian president.

Clinton gave a start and immediately got to the point, "I did my best, but Assad was stiffer than al-Sharaa: He will not concede the water. I did not touch on the remaining issues since as soon as I spoke about water (i.e., the Sea of Galilee) - he stopped me, and would not listen any further."

"If he is unwilling to be flexible on the subject of a strip of land 500 meters around the Sea of Galilee, that means there is no deal," Barak replied, "I will not hide from my people that we have now discovered that Assad refuses to honor our minimum needs! We will proceed to work on an exit from Lebanon based on Security Council Resolutions 425 and 426."

"We will help you with the exit from Lebanon," said Clinton and continued, "Assad is stuck in 1967, he is not in the year 2000. Even in the Arab world his position will not be understood. I told him I know Israel, and that you will not be able to convince the Israeli public to accept a withdrawal from the Golan Heights, unless you will have a ground strip along the lake."

Clinton also said that Assad expressed anger at al-Sharaa after the US president told him that al-Sharaa agreed to Israeli sovereignty over all of the waters and ten additional meters of land east of the Sea of Galilee (according to the international border).

"I told him I will not suggest to you to concede this strip," said Clinton.

The president further told us that during the meeting he quoted to Assad from an article by Amos Oz, published a few days earlier. In the article, he wrote that if an agreement with Syria means that the Syrians dip their feet in the waters of the Sea of Galilee, whereas we receive a signed piece of paper sent by fax, then he has no interest in such a peace.

A day after the Clinton-Assad meeting in Geneva and the President's telephone conversation with Barak, Dennis Ross came to us and gave us the rest of the information on this unsuccessful encounter.

Ross said that the meeting was attended on the Syrian side by President Assad, Foreign Minister Farouk al-Sharaa and Bouthaina Shaaban, Assad's personal interpreter. On the American side were President Clinton, Madeleine Albright, Dennis Ross and Jamal Hilal, an Egyptian-born Christian American who served as the State Department's chief interpreter.

Ross said that in fact, the meeting between Clinton and Assad ended just five minutes after it began.

Although I was not particularly optimistic about the prospects for its success, Ross's description managed to surprise me. I did not think the meeting would go that badly.

Ross said that Clinton opened the meeting by describing the meaning of the rare opportunity before them, and presented the consequences of success and failure.

After Clinton's opening remarks, Assad said he hopes there are no intentions of returning to the initial stage of the negotiations, and immediately asked, "What about my land?"

Clinton responded that Barak was ready for a full withdrawal to a boundary agreed upon by both parties, and that would be based on the lines of June 1967. Assad said, "I do not understand, it has been agreed that this would be the boundary," in reference to what was stated in Rabin's "deposit".

Clinton answered to him, "Israel needs sovereignty over the Sea of Galilee." Upon hearing that Assad immediately said, "Israel does not want peace."

At this point, Ross presented the map on which was outlined the strip of 250 to 500 meters, on the northeast area of the lake, and Assad at once said, "This is impossible."

Afterwards, Dennis recounted, Assad was not interested in anything, and he repeatedly said, "Yet I swam in the Sea of Galilee!" Clinton replied, "And in the future you will also be able to swim in it."

Assad said then, "Except according to what you said, it will be a Sea of Galilee under Israeli sovereignty!"

Clinton reminded Assad that al-Sharaa already expressed consent to this in Shepherdstown. At this point, Assad looked at al-Sharaa with shock and anger and asked, "Farouk, is this true?!" Al-Sharaa, according to Ross's testimony, was very embarrassed and immediately changed colors as well as the subject.

Ross said that Assad would not agree to Israeli sovereignty over the Sea of Galilee and the Jordan River under any circumstances. Clinton tried to explain to Assad that Barak expressed willingness for withdrawals and concessions on his part, that he was going very far in terms of the Israeli public, and that he could not make all these concessions without maintaining Israeli sovereignty over the Sea of Galilee and a strip of land around it.

Assad replied, "If Barak insists on the land strip – then we are stuck."

"True," Clinton said, "We're stuck and for a long time. Now Israel will continue negotiations with the Palestinians, it will leave Lebanon on the basis of UN Resolution 425, and Syria will gain nothing."

Assad did not respond, and seconds later he said, "If that is the case, there is no point in you continuing your presentation."

At this point, as Ross recounted, Farouk al-Sharaa and Bouthaina Shaaban urged Assad to continue listening, but he insisted, "There have never been Jews east of the Sea of Galilee, and the lake is ours."

At this stage of the leaders' meeting, Dennis Ross tried to continue to present the security arrangements, but when he realized that Assad was showing no interest in what he was saying, he ceased to do so. Only later, when he sat separately with al-Sharaa, Ross continued to present them. Al-Sharaa listened to Ross, but did not respond in any way to the timetable and warning arrangements that were presented to him.

Ross told us that Clinton did his best to explain to Assad how much Syria would benefit from a peace agreement with Israel, and how much it would lose without it. However, it was all in vain. His words fell on deaf ears.

Barak responded to Dennis Ross's report, saying, "Now we know that Assad does not want peace. This meeting has saved us negotiations that in any case could not have led to a positive outcome. We cannot continue negotiations with Assad, and we will have to wait for the Syrian regime to change."

The next day, Dennis Ross met with Egyptian President Mubarak, and presented him with the details of the meeting between the two presidents, stating his opinion that Assad's behavior was irrational.

At that meeting, Mubarak talked of his thoughts regarding Assad's obstinacy, explaining that Assad was driven by internal motivations and that his only current goal was to ensure the transfer of power to his son Bashar. Hence he could not afford to make concessions to Israel for fear of the opinion of groups who opposed peace with Israel, fear of the Sunni majority's position and that of everyone who Assad pushed to the side. Within these groups there was severe resentment against Assad and he did not want to intensify it by adding unacceptable concessions in favor of Israel.

On April 5, Dennis Ross gave Barak a message he received from al-Sharaa, to the effect that Assad was sticking to his hardline position, such as an Israeli withdrawal to the borders of 1967, without any adjustments; complete refusal for a ground early-warning station on Mount Hermon, and agreement only to aerial and satellite warning; that the duration of withdrawal would not exceed one year (which was a step back from Assad's consent to a withdrawal time of a year and a half, which was mentioned during Rabin's period); and an exchange of ambassadors that would be made only after the withdrawal and not immediately after signing the peace agreement as we had demanded.

Ross concluded that he believed Assad fears that even the slightest concession on his part would harm the transfer of power to his son.

To conclude this process, I can state with full confidence that the preparations for the discussions and the presentation of our positions were very serious and consistent throughout. All consultations amongst ourselves and between us and the Americans - including the consideration of all the options and possible scenarios for the way negotiations would develop – were done meticulously.

Barak had an organized approach throughout, he defined his areas of flexibility and how far he could go precisely, and made explicitly clear what were the 'red lines' and what we could not concede, even at the cost of not reaching an agreement. Barak did not meander, nor did he change his positions frequently as his detractors claim. He clearly took into account the possibility that Clinton and Assad's meeting would not lead to a breakthrough, although of course we were very much hoping for one.

In those days I completely supported Barak's approach and his insistence on 'red lines.' I saw them as stop lines, things that were impassable and very true to our needs.

Today, in retrospect, I think we could have shown more flexibility in terms of the width of the continental strip around the Sea of Galilee, although I am not sure that Assad would have accepted our demand in this scenario anyway. Moreover, even if we would have agreed to the international border in that area, meaning Israeli control over the waters of the Sea of Galilee and a coastal strip up to 10 meters east of it, and not 500 meters as we requested, I am not convinced that Assad would have agreed. Assad knew his end was near, and at the time was focused on an orderly and peaceful transfer of power in Syria to his son.

However, while the prospect of a breakthrough was small, it was worth a try, because if we would have succeeded, the Middle East could have been entirely different. We would have reached an agreement with Syria, and the price required of us for it – to give up our demand for a 500 meter strip and settle for 10 meters - was worth paying for the sake of peace with Syria.

Regarding other 'red lines' - such as Israeli presence on the early-warning station on Mt. Hermon for a period of several years, and all the other components that we requested - I think it is important we adhere to them in future negotiations as well.

Barak went farther than any other Prime Minister to meet the Syrians' demands. He offered to withdraw to a border based on the line of June 4, 1967, and gave the Americans a concrete proposal on the matter. Yet Israel has certain vital interests that no prime minister can concede, in terms of water, security arrangements, warning, normalization, and the like.

In Shepherdstown, we learned that Syrian Foreign Minister al-Sharaa told the Americans that Syria recognizes Israel's sovereignty over the Sea of Galilee with a land strip the width of between 10 to 30 meters around it. The Americans extended the strip's width to 100 meters, and we demanded 500 meters, because Barak wanted to ensure that there would be no question relating to Israel's sovereignty over the water. A short distance of tens of meters could create, in his opinion, a collision course between Israel and Syria with respect to the access and use of the waters of the Sea of Galilee, and would call into question Israel's sovereignty over all of the waters. Barak argued that we need the continental shell to prevent any future debate over the question of sovereignty over the waters.

To avoid turning the coastal strip into a source of quarrels, and to ensure its existence as an area of peace, there were some suggestions: make it a park, and most importantly – not to raise a fence between Israel and Syria in this area. Thus, along with special arrangements and access through gates and specified passages, the Syrians would be able to reach the Sea of Galilee with Israeli approval without feeling as though they have passed through a fenced border.

These proposals were never submitted to the Syrians but were discussed with the Americans. It was further discussed that a road be paved east of the lake, which would be entirely under Israeli sovereignty, in order to clarify and illustrate the fact that we are sovereign over this location.

Even after the "Geneva disaster" we did not shut the door to negotiations with Syria, but since at the time there remained only a thin opening in that door, it was decided to continue the negotiations on the Palestinian track. In the absence of an agreement with Syria which would enable us to withdraw IDF forces from Lebanon as a part of it, we had to leave Lebanon under UN Security Council Resolution 425 (formed after Operation Litani in 1978). According to the resolution, the IDF forces are to withdraw from all Lebanese territory, Lebanon will be responsible for security in southern Lebanon, and international forces such as the United Nations will help Lebanon to maintain security along the border.

In fact, looking back at the whole process of peace negotiations with Syria in which I participated, from the days of Rabin through Peres and Netanyahu to Barak, one can observe a single stumbling block that accompanied this process throughout, with the waves of peace crashing against it repeatedly. The Syrians would demand their land, that is, the Golan Heights, and would ask to hear the "explicit statement" to that effect in advance. Meanwhile, the Israeli leader would refuse time and again to "part" with this statement and give it to the Syrians, as long as he was unaware of what he would receive from them in regards to all the other issues. He would hold the statement in his "pocket" to be used at the end of the process.

However, that end never came.

***

In a New Year's holiday interview, a few days after his resignation but while still in office, Prime Minister Ehud Olmert said, "Where did Menachem Begin's greatness lie? Begin sent Dayan to meet with Egyptian Vice President Dr. Hassan Tohami in Morocco, and before beginning negotiations, before he even met Sadat, before he knew if Sadat would smile one way or another, if he would say this or that, Dayan told Tohami on Begin's behalf, 'We are willing to withdraw from all of Sinai.' He started from the end. In fact, he said, 'I am prepared to withdraw from Sinai, now let's start to negotiate.'

"If we are not willing to say it, all the talk about negotiations with Syria is worthless. It could be that even if we say it we will find that the Syrians are not willing to pay these prices and there will not be a settlement. Then we can tell ourselves, at least we were close... We are constantly thinking of our fears. Why? Because the only fears we listen to are the fears that we have already experienced. Once, the thought of divisions of Syrian tanks on the Golan Heights, threatening to roll into Israel, rightly frightened us. Today we live in a different reality. We have tools to stop a ground attack without taking over a single meter in Syria, and we have other tools that we can use to win such a battle, no matter where it develops and from how far it comes. The Syrians know this… What I am telling you now, has not been said by any Israeli leader before me: we need to withdraw from almost all of the territories, including the Golan Heights."

Chapter 22

"The Best Friend I Ever Had"

The suspicion, difficulties, sour faces, baffling objections, and icy attitudes that were the staples of each session and attempted dialogue aimed to promote a peace treaty between Israel and Syria gave way to a great deal of cooperation, goodwill, heartwarming gestures and a pleasant feeling, throughout the peace process with Jordan, our eastern neighbor.

The formal peace process with Jordan began as part of the Madrid Conference, but many years before that there was a warm and unique relationship between the two countries that officially were at alternating states of war and ceasefire. All Israeli prime ministers, starting from the days of Golda Meir, met secretly with King Hussein.

This relationship was not official or public, but was known due to leaks that occurred here and there. Israeli prime ministers came and went, but the king remained in place, and the special relations with Jordan were always maintained.

In my opinion, the relations with the Israelis were of great importance in King Hussein's eyes, who assessed that of all the surrounding states, Israel would actually be the one to come to his defense and would help the royal Hashemite regime hold its power in Jordan, in time of need. In September 1970, when Syria mobilized troops with the intention to invade Jordan, Israel prevented it by recruiting reservists, mobilizing troops and declarations that left the Syrians no room for ambiguity.

The king believed that at a time of duress, he could not rely on his neighbors Syria, Iraq and Saudi Arabia, especially considering the first two were incessantly trying to undermine him and Jordanian interests.

The Madrid Conference was convened at the initiative of US President George Walker Bush and under American-Russian auspices in October 1991 in Madrid.

The Jordanian delegation at the conference also included Palestinian representatives, since the State of Israel and its leader, Prime Minister Yitzhak Shamir, sought to avoid separate negotiations with the Palestinians, and in particular Shamir wished to avoid direct negotiations with PLO representatives.

The Jordanian "sponsorship" was a diplomatic solution to this issue, as in actuality the Palestinian representatives in the Jordanian delegation were residents of the West Bank and Gaza Strip.

On April 22, 1993, twenty days after I arrived at the Prime Minister's office as Rabin's Military Secretary, the Prime Minister gathered all the heads of delegations for talks with Arab nations. Elyakim Rubinstein was head of the Israeli delegation for Jordan and the Palestinians, and at his side was Maj. Gen. Danny Rothschild, Coordinator of Government Activities in the Territories.

In Rabin's first briefing there was not one word about Jordan, and hence it was clear that this delegation would focus on the Palestinian issues. Rabin's belief was that the two most important tracks at the time were the Syrian and Palestinian tracks. The assumption was that matters with Jordan would be resolved as soon as the problems with the Palestinians would be solved, which eventually proved to be true.

At a certain point the Israeli delegation for the talks with Jordan even reported that the Jordanians were dedicating the whole of their efforts to handling Palestinian issues and that they had nullified all the Jordanian discussion groups. It was also reported that the Jordanians themselves said the Palestinian issue was the main thing, further evidence for the validity of Rabin's approach.

While negotiations with the Palestinians were taking place under Jordanian auspices, messages were being sent regarding King Hussein's desire to be part of the picture. The king had also contacted Rabin in April 1993, raising concerns about the role of the joint Jordanian-Palestinian delegation. Hussein claimed that there were many foreign elements who were speaking with the Palestinians separately, not as part of the official delegation, but when problems arose in the dialogue with the Palestinians, they were complaining to him as if he were in charge. Hussein also griped that the Americans were not updating him of their talks with the Palestinians, which put him in an impossible situation with the latter. To avoid this situation, the king offered to split the Jordanian-Palestinian delegation into two delegations, each of which would hold discussions separately.

The answer Hussein received from Rabin at the time was that this was what had been agreed in Madrid, and at that point there would be no deviation from it.

The line of thought that guided Rabin at the time was that significant progress on the Jordanian track would only occur after progress on the Syrian and Palestinian tracks, due to the Jordanians seeing Syria as an unfriendly element that could not be relied on if put to the test. Rabin believed that Hussein would fear that progress between Israel and Jordan, if made before progress with Syria, would harm his relations with the latter. As for the Palestinians, the king's approach was different. In many ways, the Jordanians and Palestinians are intertwined, as most residents of Jordan are Palestinians, and it was important for Hussein not to appear as though he were neglecting them to promote Jordan's interests, especially since from his standpoint, the root of the Israeli-Arab conflict was the Palestinian problem. That is also the reason that Hussein agreed to sponsor the Palestinian delegation to the Madrid Conference.

However, the Jordanians had interests of their own: they were concerned by the question of who would control the western side of the Jordan River, with their preference being that it would be Israel; it was important for them to protect their interests in Jerusalem; and they were interested in solving the problem of Palestinian refugees living in Jordan, who were estimated to number around a million and a half people.

In early September 1993, when Oslo "burst" into the world, King Hussein sent a very angry, upset and offended message, in which he resented the fact that he had no idea of the Oslo channel's existence. "I agreed with Arafat on a joint Palestinian-Jordanian effort and have not heard of any change since then. Suddenly, I hear that everything is finished between Israel and the Palestinians, and they are going to the White House to sign an agreement in principle. What kind of cooperation is that?"

As a result, the king decided to fold the Jordanian umbrella over Arafat's head.

The dramatic development in the negotiations with the Palestinians led Rabin to conclude that the time was ripe to move forward in negotiations with Jordan, which at that point were still stuttering against the official Jordanian-Palestinian delegation. It should be noted that even our people in the Israeli delegation to these talks did not know about the meetings with the Palestinians in Oslo. In retrospect, the official talks between these delegations served as a front for the confidential talks.

Towards the end of September a meeting was called at Rabin's office, attended by Director of the Mossad Shabtai Shavit and myself, in preparation for a meeting with King Hussein in Aqaba.

Rabin told us he had known the king for many years, and that in June '75, during his first term as Prime Minister, he suggested to Hussein an interim arrangement whereby the Jordanians would be responsible for the whole of the Palestinian Civil Administration in Judea, Samaria and Gaza. Rabin offered Hussein a free access road from Jordan to Ramallah and Nablus, and Gaza as a free Jordanian port where a Jordanian Army battalion would be deployed. Hussein rejected the offer and said he wanted full peace, including withdrawal from the Territories to the last centimeter, or an interim agreement based on an Israeli withdrawal eight kilometers in depth, all across the Jordan Rift Valley.

Rabin told us that he would devote his conversation with the king to explain the occurrences that led to Oslo; present the prospects and risks that Israel undertakes in this process; and would ask to hear from Hussein what he expects to happen now between Israel and Jordan under these new circumstances, and if and how Jordan could proceed to a full peace treaty with Israel in light of recent developments with the Palestinians.

Rabin's approach was that contrary to the necessity of an interim agreement with the Palestinians, with Jordan it would not be necessary and we could immediately strive for a full peace treaty.

The meeting between Rabin and Hussein was arranged by the Mossad and was top secret - only very few confidants knew of it.

Rabin had other events planned for the day and he had to cancel them. These cancellations worked against us, and stirred the media to pry into our actions. In those days the media kept close track of Rabin's every move, because this was a period abound with processes and events.

We left the Prime Minister's office in a car that did not give away the fact that the person sitting in it was the Prime Minister. We arrived at Ben-Gurion airport, and boarded a small executive jet parked in a remote, hidden location. The pilots knew who they were flying, but did not know for what purpose. From the airport we flew to Eilat airport, where we traveled by car to the yacht harbor, and boarded an Israeli yacht operated by a discreet crew.

The night was very dark, the yacht was sailing without lights and the sea was unquiet. The Mossad ensured coordination with the Israeli Navy in advance, including a cover story about some activity that was allegedly taking place that night, so as to avoid the suspicions of navy ships at the sight of unusual marine activity occurring in the area.

Thus, at the mercy of the sea's motions and heaves, we arrived, late at night and in complete darkness, to the heart of the sea – where we met with the king's royal yacht that was awaiting us, with its lights switched off as well.

With the two yachts sailing alongside each other and rocking over the turbulent waters, we skipped from our yacht to theirs. The Israeli and Jordanian yacht crews helped us, and the move was completed successfully. We entered the ship and immediately the atmosphere was warm, friendly and informal.

To our great satisfaction, although peace with Jordan began on unsteady ground and on turbulent waters, it has proved to be a very stable and calm peace.

After a half-hour journey on the royal yacht, we arrived at the dock of the king's palace in Aqaba.

For me it was the first time I stepped legally on Jordanian soil. Our anticipation was tense and our excitement great.

From the anchorage we walked a distance of some fifty meters in the dark night, and went into one of the palace's rooms, where we were greeted warmly by Prince Hassan, the king's brother. We walked with him for a while and entered another room, where King Hussein awaited us with a smile on his face.

I was very excited to meet the king for the first time in my life. No excitement was evident on Rabin. It seemed as though it was the most natural and routine thing in the world for him.

We came to the meeting dressed according to all rules of protocol, in suits and ties, but the king was dressed informally, wearing a polo shirt and jacket, an appearance that immediately contributed to the warm and friendly atmosphere.

A few minutes after we were seated, a woman fluttered into the room, barefoot and very beautiful – Queen Noor (Elizabeth Najib Halaby). The queen served the guests drinks herself, a gesture that only added to the already pleasant feeling in that room.

Shortly afterwards we were invited to join the dinner table, on which delicious refreshments were served, also by the queen. It was a unique and stirring tribute. It felt as if some relatives had gathered together for a family meal and the landlady was hosting them.

Rabin started with a detailed explanation of the occurrences in Oslo to the king, and then turned to him and said, "This is an opportunity for Israel and Jordan to move forward."

Rabin suggested leaving the meeting with a decision that both sides would begin working as soon as possible to achieve a comprehensive peace agreement between them, and that by the launch of the "Gaza and Jericho First" phase, we would prepare the peace treaty between Israel and Jordan. Immediately after the launch of this stage, the treaty would be made public. Rabin assumed that the launch of the agreement with the Palestinians would help the Jordanians to publicize the final stages of a peace agreement with Israel.

He offered the king to help him rebuild his problematic relationship with the United States, in light of the king's support for Iraq in the first Gulf War. Jordan has a long common border with Iraq and he feared Saddam Hussein, which led to his decision to support the Iraqi ruler during that war.

The Jordanian king responded very enthusiastically to this proposal.

Rabin told the king that he would update the US president that a peace agreement between Israel and Jordan was gradually taking shape, which would help the Americans change their attitude towards Jordan.

In effect, Rabin had built a "peace package", stressing the benefits of this move.

The extent to which Rabin's influence in Washington was important to the Jordanians can be evidenced by the following story:

In March 1995, after the peace agreement between us had already been signed, the king suddenly asked for an urgent meeting between his men and Rabin.

The king's helicopter landed late at night in Jerusalem and from it came Prime Minister Marwan al Qassim, Chief of Staff Gen. Merei, Deputy Commander of the Air Force Gen. Shmasani, Gen. Wahid and Gen. Ali Shukri, the king's Bureau Chief.

At the meeting in the Prime Minister house in Jerusalem, al-Qassim said that the Iranians threaten not only Israel but all countries in the region, and that Jordan must be able to protect the foundations of peace. "Strengthening Jordan will affect the Jordanians psychologically, morally and politically," he explained.

He thanked Rabin for his efforts in the US to secure an aid package for Jordan, and immediately produced a letter from the king with two lists: one containing the means needed to protect the border and the other the means to strengthen the Jordanian army, such as F-16 aircraft and tanks.

Rabin looked at the list and almost fell off his chair.

"The cost of your lists is several billion dollars and the United States will not give it to Jordan now," Rabin said. "You have to make a list with priorities and say what is most important. Also, I do not believe that the United States would give you more than a hundred million dollars a year."

The Jordanians wanted to get everything, and Rabin had to repeat his request time and again that they tell him their priorities, what was more important and what was less important.

The nocturnal meeting at the king's palace in Aqaba was the breakthrough that led to very intensive work on a peace treaty between the two countries. Elyakim Rubinstein, head of the Israeli delegation for talks with Jordan, met often with Prince Hassan and his aides, in order to produce a paper that could be used as a framework and basis for a Statement of Intent.

The secretive nature of the process had been kept and the matter was not leaked, except in a report published in *Yedioth Ahronoth* by Shimon Shiffer one day after the meeting in Aqaba, in which Shiffer speculated that a secret meeting took place, but did not determine it with certainty.

Another interesting meeting that was held as part of the peace process with Jordan took place in London on May 28, 1994.

Along with the public channel there were also confidential meetings, and in fact the official meetings between the delegations were the cover story for the meaningful work that took place behind the scenes.

Along with Elyakim Rubinstein, who headed the official delegation for talks with Jordan, Deputy Director of the Mossad Efraim Halevy was also involved in the talks.

At the confidential meeting in London we were Rabin, Elyakim Rubinstein, Efraim Halevy and myself. From the Jordanian side attended King Hussein, Prince Hassan, former Chief of Staff and member of the royal family Gen. Zaid ibn Shakir, Legal Adviser Hasauna and Bureau Chief Ali Shukri.

This time we learned our lesson, and were even more careful than the last time the two leaders met in Aqaba. We set off late in the evening, after a long workday that was not shortened and no part of which was canceled. For the next day no public events were planned for Rabin, the cancellation of which might have drawn attention.

Once again, a private executive jet was waiting for us at the end of the runway at Ben-Gurion Airport, and once again the pilots knew who they were taking and where, but had no idea why.

We landed in London after a five-hour flight and the British Secret Service men, who were in on the secret, welcomed us and directed the plane into a closed hangar.

Once again it was late at night. We left the plane inside the closed hangar and stepped into cars, and from there, in the cover of darkness, our convoy traveled to the king's residence in London: a castle named Casel Wood. After a half-hour drive we entered the mansion in the dark of night, and the gate shut behind us immediately. We were very tired, it was two in the morning in UK time, and four in the morning in Israel time.

Everyone immediately retired for the night, and I preferred to take advantage of the early morning, as was my habit, for physical activity. Not wishing to go for a run down the street and risk being exposed, I found myself running around the structure and the small yard surrounding it dozens of times.

After breakfast, we met with the king and the meeting between the two leaders began.

Rabin began with an overview of the process with the Palestinians. He openly said to the king, "Part of the Israeli settlements in the Palestinian Territories are a major headache for us, because they impose a heavy security burden on us. I have no problem," Rabin added, "that IDF soldiers will no longer patrol Gaza and elsewhere, and in their place Palestinian police will patrol."

Rabin and the king were in agreement that it was time to move the talks between Israel and Jordan from Washington to our region. Rabin spoke about the problem of terrorism led by Hamas, headquartered in Amman, Jordan, and Islamic Jihad, headquartered in Damascus, but stressed that there are anti-Israeli activities by extremist elements in Jordan as well.

Rabin mentioned the fact that Hamas headquarters, headed by Dr. Mousa Abu Marzouk (later replaced by Khaled Mashal), head of the Hamas Political Bureau and in effect the leader of the terrorist organization, was located in Jordan, and said, "Even the Syrians will not allow Hamas to operate from their territory," and thus hinted to the Jordanians that he expected them to do something about it as well.

Immediately afterwards, Rabin gave a lecture on the state of negotiations with Jordan and his intentions for the future. Rabin had a habit to speak in lengthy lectures. When King Hussein tried to get a word of his own in here and there, he was unsuccessful, and Rabin continued his explanations without stopping for a breath. Hussein listened to his speech intently, and when Rabin was finished he pointedly thanked him for his wonderful portrayal of the affairs. He said that with regard to continuing negotiations between Israel and Jordan, he believed that the public meetings should be held in the presence of a Palestinian representative, in order to have a greater alignment between the Palestine and

Jordanian tracks – which at parts touched on the same issues. Rabin refused this idea and said that he would prefer it to be bilateral, and that the Palestinians would be updated as necessary. Rabin believed that it would be easier to move forward when dealing with each party separately, and King Hussein accepted his position.

Hussein proceeded to state that the two subjects primarily burdening him were borders and water.

Hussein asked that the talks between Israel and Jordan not be moved to Egypt – where the talks with the Palestinians had moved (to Taba and Cairo). Hussein suggested that the talks be held at a certain location along the border between Israel and Jordan. "Jordan is a sovereign state," he said, "and there is no need to conduct talks with it on another country's soil. When the talks take place on the border between the two countries, it means that both sides are equal, and this a symbolic act."

The king's proposal was warmly accepted.

Hussein wanted to start by determining the borderline, but Rabin persuaded him that it was necessary to work simultaneously on all the subjects at hand: borders, water and peaceful relations.

The two leaders agreed to hold a summit meeting in Washington, hosted by President Clinton, the first open meeting between the two of them.

When the two discussed the terrorism issues, Rabin updated Hussein that we told the Americans that Hamas's funding came from Saudi Arabia and from donations collected in the United States by organizations that operated under the guise of innocent humanitarian organizations. Rabin told the king that the Americans did not believe us, and it was only after the truck bomb attack in the parking lot of the World Trade Center that the Americans changed their approach.

Hussein said the same thing had happened to him: "When I told the Americans that the Saudis are funding Hamas, they thought it was a Jordanian ruse meant to drive a wedge between the United States and Saudi Arabia."

The king said that he visited Syria and found "a mood of peace" there, and as if he were overtaken by the spirit of prophecy he said, "I feel that with Arafat, it will not continue in a good way."

I think it was his way of expressing his dissatisfaction with the progress with the Palestinians and that Arafat immediately received a foothold in the Jordan Valley and Jericho, which are near the border with Jordan.

Regarding Jerusalem, Hussein said that a compromise could be found that would form a distinction between the status and political powers of the parties and the religious authorities.

Foreign Minister Shimon Peres received updates on the talks with King Hussein but was not a part of them. On one particular occasion in November he went to a confidential meeting with the king, and later told the media, "Remember the third of November." From there, it did not take long for the media to pounce on the matter and discover that Peres met with the king- and the whole thing erupted.

The Jordanians were greatly annoyed by the leak, which came after a long period in which the talks were confidential and kept secret, and they let us understand that they did not wish to continue the talks through Peres.

Rabin also expressed his dissatisfaction with Peres' statement.

From then and until the public Statement of Intent in Washington, we only updated Peres of the developments in general terms.

There were years of ups and downs between Rabin and Peres, and long periods in which there were mainly downs. However, during Rabin's second term as Prime Minister, it seemed that the two came to peace with each other's existence, and perhaps for the first time were able to set a common goal peace in the Middle East - and they rationally joined forces to achieve this goal.

A contributing factor to their cooperation was that both of them accepted the fact that this was the last chance to change the face of the Middle East in coming years. However, at the same time, the mutual suspicion between the two did not stop for a moment. When Peres acted without Rabin's approval, the latter tended to express his disdain. The competition between the two continued all the time, and one of its highlights was Peres' efforts to be awarded the Nobel Peace Prize as well.

However they managed to conceal their personal feelings, sweep them under the rug and work in unison.

Rabin and Peres took care to have a weekly face-to-face meeting. On rare occasions Rabin would ask me to join a small part of the meeting, to instruct people on different tasks or to issue a summary of the meeting. They would sit for an entire hour, every Sunday, usually before the cabinet meeting.

As the conference in Washington drew near, we were preparing a statement of principles that would be coordinated with the Jordanians. No one knew about it except for Peres and the Americans, who were aware of the meetings between the Jordanians and us but did not know that we had reached an agreed formulation, and discovered it only when we arrived at Washington.

At a meeting on July 1994 between Rabin and Secretary of State Warren Christopher, Rabin said, "There are good prospects for peace with Jordan but the agreement has not been produced yet. The bilateral talks between Israel and Jordan, and moving the talks to the region, created a new opening for success."

Rabin said the components of the peace agreement required more work, including the issues of borders and water.

Christopher told him he met with Hussein and said, "The king has crossed a deep psychological barrier in his willingness to move forward towards peace quickly."

This was uttered a few days before the summit in Washington, where the parties were to sign a declaration in which they commit to peaceful relations and the end of the war era – which goes to show the extent of the Americans' unawareness of the progress made in formulating the understandings between Israel and Jordan.

True to his promise to the king, Rabin took care to speak positively about the Jordanians in all his meetings in the United States, and thus greatly helped to change the American approach towards Jordan and to clear the air between the two countries in the wake of the first Gulf War.

In the discussions between the Jordanians and us, issues such as how to ensure Jordanian rights in Jerusalem were raised. Rabin proposed that when a permanent solution in Jerusalem is discussed with the Palestinians, the historical Jordanian rights in the religious context be taken into account.

After months of secret preparations, and decades of secret meetings between the leaders of Israel and the Jordanian King, everything was ready for the "coming to light" of relations between Israel and Jordan and the Declaration of Principles ceremony on the White House lawn in Washington DC on July 25, 1994, wherein Israel and Jordan would declare the end of the state of war between them and move towards a full peace.

Once we arrived at Washington, and until the last moments before the emotional ceremony on the White House lawn, we continued to refine and improve the wording that would serve as a joint declaration to be signed by Israel and Jordan.

A very short time before the start of the event on the lawn, Clinton called Rabin and Hussein to his meeting room, along with Christopher, Peres, and several members of the entourage.

We sat around an oval table with Rabin, Clinton and Hussein sitting side by side and everyone else around it.

Rabin turned to me and said, "Danny, please produce the paper we are about to sign," and before Peres' astonished eyes I produced the document, which until that moment he had no idea existed, and which revealed that Israel and Jordan had in fact reached an agreed formulation for the Declaration of Principles. Until then Peres thought we were awaiting some kind of general statement to the effect that Israel and Jordan would declare the end of the conflict between them and their commitment to resolve matters peacefully.

Throughout the journey, it was important for both the Jordanians and ourselves that only a small number of confidants would be involved in the process between us, and that nothing would be leaked, so as not to provide all sorts of people with a chance to jubilate over the points of disagreements between us.

Before Peres' astonished gaze I pulled out the document and put it on the table - ready for signing. It should be noted that Peres is very good at controlling his emotions and concealing them. He said nothing, but it was not a pleasant moment for him.

A short time later, all these men came to the White House lawn and on the backdrop of the crowd's applause and palpably great excitement, relations between Israel and Jordan were made public in a declaration of peace.

About two months after the emotional ceremony in Washington, and while work-groups from the two countries were meeting at the border between the two countries in the Aravah, there was another meeting between the king and Rabin in Aqaba.

We arrived at Aqaba by plane, and landed in the king's private airstrip. Hussein was waiting for us there with his vehicle and drove us to the palace. Dealings with King Hussein were always accompanied by human gestures that instilled much ease and indicated the warmth and abundant appreciation he felt for Rabin.

In all the meetings between them, the king made a point to await Rabin outside, and never waited inside the building. He displayed impeccable hospitality and treated all of us, and especially Rabin, with royal manners. For example, he never sat down until Rabin did so before him.

Rabin opened the meeting on the subject of the boundary and said he believed that we should work based on the assumption that an international border between the two nations would be set, from the Gulf of Eilat in the south to the Dead Sea in the north, and from Mehola in the south to the Israel-Jordan-Syria border triangle, west of al-Hama. Rabin asked to leave the matter of the Jordan Valley to a later time, when this region would be discussed in the course of negotiations with the Palestinians.

The boundaries between us and Jordan were never demarcated on the ground but there is a delineation of the armistice line on the maps and a written explanation. For example, there are places mentioning that the border goes through the center of Wadi [*Arabic: valley*] Araba, but over the years the valley changed its shape, and today's maps are also different and more precise than past ones.

"On the matter of security," Rabin said, "Israel wants a strong and independent Jordan under the king's rule. We must ensure that the territories of Jordan and Israel will not be used as a launching pad for terrorist attacks and must develop a mechanism for cooperation and early-warning as part of the war against terrorism."

On the matter of refugees, Rabin said that the final settlement with the Palestinians would discuss it. Regarding the displaced - who had left the West Bank in 1967 and fled to Jordan – we agreed to form a four-way committee that would include Israel, Jordan, the PLO and Egypt, which would try to find a suitable solution to this problem.

Rabin said that when he participated in the talks that led to the ceasefire between Israel and Egypt in 1949, which took place in Rhodes, he asked why they were signing an armistice agreement and not a peace treaty between Israel and Egypt based on the armistice line.

Mahmoud Riad of the Egyptian delegation replied, "We cannot yet fathom your very presence here. Armistice is a temporary thing, so it is possible." Hence, the Egyptians insisted that the determined borderline would not be called a "boundary" but "the armistice line."

"The border between Israel and Jordan is also the armistice line," continued Rabin and said, "It is time that this border becomes permanent. The armistice line is only a line, it does not hold the status of an international border, and hence what we will now decide to be the border – will be the border."

The king praised the good work done by the delegations, but immediately noted, "It is important that we meet often."

The king understood that significant differences could be resolved in direct talks between the two leaders. These types of sessions were much more effective than second-hand reports of exchanges between the delegations.

On the matter of indicating the border the king said, "The British mandate lines were never completely indicated. While we need to follow the channel of a valley that has changed, we do have something to build on."

Ben Shaker, National Security Advisor to the king, suggested the idea that had already come up as an Israeli initiative in the work-groups, whereby the Jordanian lands along the border, which Israeli farmers had been cultivating for years, would be leased.

From this, we learned that the king had given us an optimistic declaration meaning, "we will find a way."

On the issue of water, Hussein said that there is a connection between rights and needs. That is, on the one hand we must rely on the rights granted to us under international law, but the needs must also be considered. Hussein hinted that the solution would be a practical and pragmatic one, in which Israel would also need to receive its share.

Rabin said that we have the ability to provide another one hundred million cubic meters of water to the Jordanians annually, fifty of which are dependent on the construction of two dams: one on the Yarmouk and the second on the Jordan River, and towards this end, we need to raise money in the world.

In the South, in the Aravah region, we would continue to draw between ten and fifteen million cubic meters of water a year and the Jordanians would be compensated by water given to them in the north.

Rabin said that we could give the Jordanians fifty million cubic meters of water immediately, from what flows in the Yarmouk River, where they would take more than they took before, and they would also be able to receive some from the Sea of Galilee. The additional fifty million would be contingent on the dams being constructed as stated, and when Israel would build desalination plants, the Jordanians could also receive water from them.

On the security issue, the declaration in Washington effectively ended the state of war between the two countries. Other issues remained, such as airspace sovereignty. Rabin wanted the peace treaty to include a passage stating that Jordan would not allow hostile forces to pass in its airspace and land, would not make any alliances with countries hostile to Israel and would not allow a hostile foreign army to enter its territory and camp in it, and vice versa.

To that Hussein said, "Anything would be acceptable to us, provided that it will neither undermine our independence nor humiliate us. During the Gulf War, Iraq launched missiles which had indeed passed over our territory, but we could not prevent this. Regarding terrorism, we will continue to fight it and to cooperate in the war to eradicate it. Jordan is moving toward democratization, Israel is a democracy, together let's build an example to others for how democracy and human dignity enable an effective war against terrorism."

On the issue of the refugees Hussein said that it is necessary to instill hope in the refugees. "Refugees living in Jordan will not leave it even if there is a right of return," said the king, a statement meant to reassure us about the possibility of a million and a half refugees from Jordan coming to Israel.

However, said the king, refugees should be compensated financially, and Jordan should be compensated for absorbing them and giving them their full rights.

Rabin said that our perception of the overall solution to the refugee problem was that they must remain in their present locations, and that they should receive generous international aid to improve their residential and living conditions. "We will not accept the PLO's claim to return the refugees to the Territories based on the right of return," concluded Rabin.

Rabin told the king that he spoke highly of the Jordanians in the United States, and promised he would work to convince the United States to help strengthen Jordan.

He also said that while he was acting to improve the Americans' view of Jordan, the Syrians complained to the Americans and expressed their resentment that they were assisting the Palestinians and Jordanians who supported Iraq in the Gulf War. In contrast, Syria, who sent a military force the size of an armed division to participate in the coalition against Iraq, was not receiving any preferential treatment and the United States was not even willing to remove it from the list of state sponsors of terrorism.

In response Ben Shaker, National Security Adviser to the King, said, "We are fighting terrorism and the Syrians are supporting terrorism. So where is the mystery?"

Hussein said that his military needs are still awaiting US approval, and that he expected Israel to help him promote this cause.

Rabin replied, "After we have ended the state of war between us, things will change completely, and we will help you as best we can."

Hussein said the Americans asked him why he needed a large army, now that there is peace.

Rabin at once said that he had no doubt that the Jordanians needed a strong army and that Israel would help him with this.

Rabin understood that one of the internal symbols of power in Arab countries is its ability to impose authority, law and order, and the ability to face internal threats stemmed mainly from the image of a strong nation with military might. In addition, Jordan still had (and has) external threats: the Syrians, Iraqis and Iranians do not cease, in different ways, to undermine the rule of the Hashemite monarchy, and there have been quite a few attempts to attack King Hussein and the foundations of his regime. It should be remembered that Hussein himself inherited the throne following the political assassination of his grandfather, King Abdullah.

"Time is precious and it is crucial that we show some achievements before long," he said.

Hussein's approach showed remarkable courage, because the prevailing public opinion in Jordan did not support peace with Israel. His partners for the idea were few, and they were not to be found in the parliament nor among the public.

We often heard the claim that we were making peace with a very small part of the Jordanians and not with the Jordanian populace itself. So Hussein said he needed to make it clear to the common man that peace would make his life better and was worthwhile for him.

Rabin also believed that it was important to formulate the peace agreement as soon as possible. It was important for him to send a message to the world that the peace process is successful, that the floodgates have opened and that Jordan has become the second Arab country that has a peace treaty with Israel, and that there was a momentum of peace in the region.

Shortly after this meeting, Hussein sent his loyal Head of Bureau, General Ali Shukri, to a night meeting with Prime Minister Rabin in Jerusalem. Ali Shukri was carrying a letter from the king listing all the agreements and topics discussed between the king and Rabin in their previous meetings, as the king understood them.

The letter touched on four main issues: security, water, borders and refugees.

After reading the letter, Rabin said that these issues are important and fundamental, and that he cannot respond to them immediately. "I have to study the matter carefully and only then respond."

Borders and water were the main issues and it was no coincidence that they were left for last.

Over the years, Israel had moved the border fence in the Aravah eastwards, and invaded a bit into Jordan. This was preceded by hydrological tests that indicated that water could be found slightly beyond the indicated border. Therefore, we entered these areas, and drilled for water. Over the years, these plots of land became cultivated green plots of the surrounding Israeli villages. The water resources found there were what made these lands so fertile.

Jordan argued, rightfully, that these are their territories and demanded them back.

Israel's position was that the border there was never demarcated or agreed on, neither during the British rule when Jordan was "Transjordan" and Israel was Palestine-Israel, nor when the Jordanian-Israeli armistice committee delineated the border after the War of Independence. Therefore, Rabin said, now - when both parties were about to draw the line – then they must consider changes in the area over the years, in addition to the political considerations. Lands cultivated by Israelis east of the armistice line are an important source of revenue that could not be abandoned, and moreover Israel has invested heavily in drilling for water and the development of these areas.

My 51st birthday at the Prime Minister's office. Among the congratulators are Prime Minister and Defense Minsiter Shimon Peres, Secretary of State Warren Christopher. Also present: Ambassador Itamar Rabinovich, Media Advisor Aliza Goren, Avi Benayahu and bureau staff (IDF Spokesperson)

With Prime Minister and Defense Minister Peres towards landing at Sharm el-Sheikh, where the International Anti-Terrorism Committee was convening, March 1996 (GPO)

Prime Minister and Defense Minister Shimon Peres appoints me as Director of the Mossad, 1996

With Prime Minister Benjamin Netanyahu at a ceremony for Rosh HaShana at Mossad headquarters

As Director of the Mossad with Director of the CIA, George Tenet

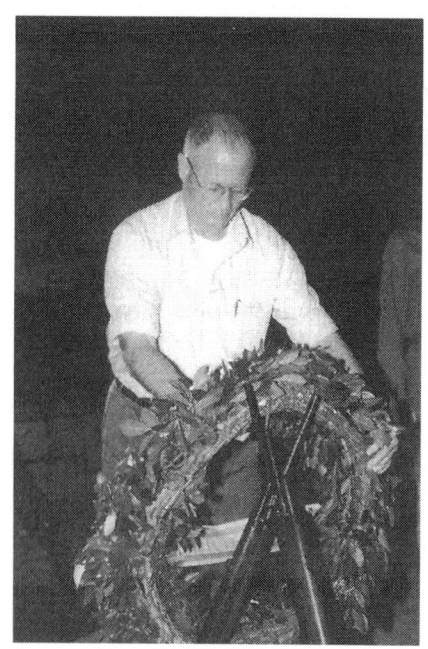

As Director of the Mossad, laying a wreath in memoriam of the intelligence community's fallen (IDF Spokesperson)

As Chief of the Political-Security Staff with Prime Minister and Defense Minister Barak at a meeting with Süleyman Demirel, the President of Turkey (GPO)

With Prime Minister Barak at his meeting with Prince Hassan, King Hussein's brother and heir to the Jordanian throne (GPO)

Shaking hands with Abdullah, the King of Jordan. To my right are Ministers Chaim Oron, Ran Cohen and Fuad ben Eliezer (GPO)

At a meeting between Prime Minister Barak and Nelson Mandela, former President of South Africa (GPO)

At a meeting between Prime Minister Barak and German Chancellor Gerhard Schröder (GPO)

A visit by the President of the United State's wife (and current Secretary of State), Hillary Clinton, at the Prime Minister's office in Jerusalem (GPO)

With President Clinton and Prime Minister Barak on the balcony of the President's cabin at Camp David, during the summit with the Palestinians, July 2000

With Sandy Berger, President Clinton's National Security Advisor, at Camp David, July 2000

Wearing a wig, before meeting the Syrian Chief of Staff General Hikmat Shahibi at the Blair House, Washington

Two weeks before Rabin's murder. The first light of dawn at a visit in the Paratroopers Brigade drill in the south of Hebron Mountain (Image: Robbie Castro)

"The Three Lines Map"
The purple line was offered by President Clinton, in coordination with Prime Minister Barak, to President Assad during their meeting in Geneva in March 2000.

The orange line (Hoff line) – the "June 4, 1967 line" according to a study by Colonel Hoff from the US army.

The dashed yellow line – the international border

I had formed the line that Clinton later suggested together with Martin Indyk, then American Ambassador to Israel. You can clearly see that the area in which the five Syrian fishermen villages had resided near the Sea of Galilee before June 4, 1967, would be under Syrian control.

The line was delineated in a manner which would allow Assad to claim that his demand to return to the border as it was on June 4, 1967, had been fulfilled, while Israel would retain the entire Sea of Galilee under its own sovereignty as well as a strip of land to its east.

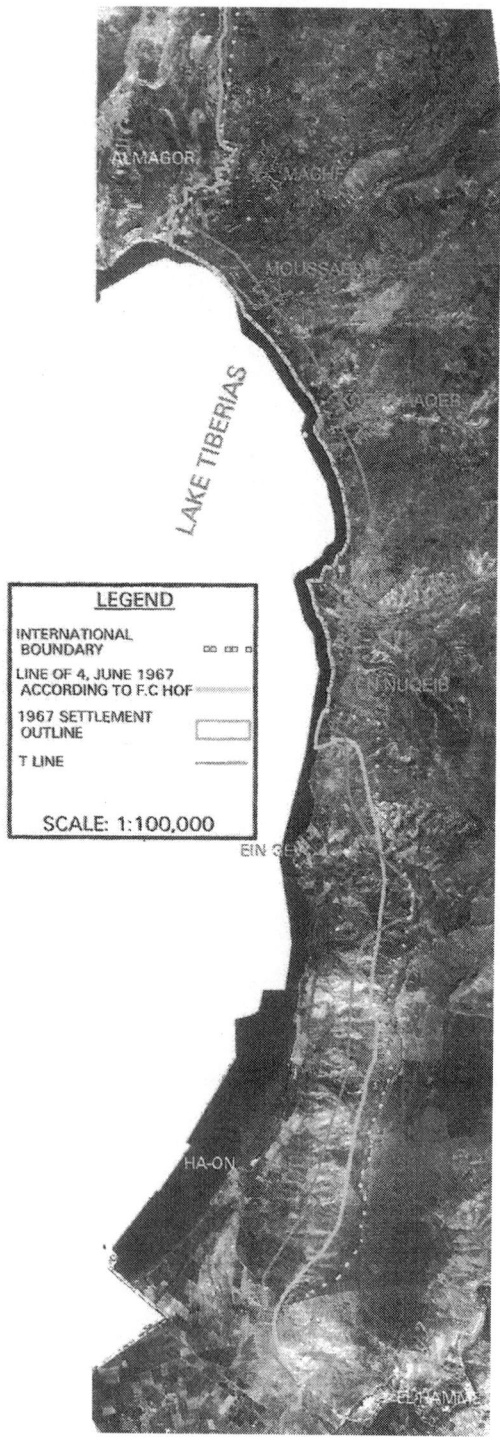

Ali Shukri said the king understood the Israeli government's difficulties to give up cultivated land, which would mean destroying the economic basis for all the communities in the Aravah.

On the matter of water, the Jordanians claimed that under international law, Israel, Jordan and the Palestinians were to share the waters of the Jordan River.

Until then, the Jordanians did not draw water from the river, and they asked for their share of it. Water is a rare and precious commodity in the Middle East, and Jordan requested an additional one hundred and fifty million cubic meters of water a year.

Ali Shukri noted that the king fully understood this issue as well, given the fact that there is also a shortage of water in Israel.

On the refugee issue, the Jordanians began with the formal standpoint that the Palestinians have a right to return to all parts of the land of Israel.

Rabin's position was that the issue of refugees could not be settled between Jordan and Israel, but rather would be discussed in a much broader context that would include the Palestinians.

Rabin said that he would not agree to a right of return to Israel and the Territories. He said he would prevent the flooding of the West Bank and the Gaza Strip with three million Palestinians, since the Territories cannot accommodate so many people. Rabin did not oppose the return of the Palestinians, in limited numbers, from their places of dispersion, but objected that it would be done on the basis of the right of return.

On security issues, there were no particular problems.

In our discussions about progress in the process with Jordan, Rabin said that we had to bind the water and the land in one package, because we could use one to compensate over the other.

In 1923, the British and French divided the countries in the region between them: "Transjordan" and Palestine-Israel were two districts of the British Mandate, and Lebanon and Syria were under French rule. The boundary was determined by two officers: Newcombe of England and Paulet of France.

Newcombe and Paulet measured and demarcated the border between the French and British colonies held in Lebanon, Syria, Palestine and Jordan. In the area between Israel and Lebanon, and between Israel and Syria, the French and the British worked together to mark the border up to the Sea of Galilee, using boundary stones, and in fact this was the border separating the two powers. From there onwards, the land was under sole British control: "Transjordan" and Palestine. The British marked the boundary between the two territories on maps, along the Jordan River, from the Sea of Galilee to the Dead Sea, with the border continuing to cross the Dead Sea to the Gulf of Eilat. The border passed through the center of Wadi Arabah.

This line between the two provinces of the British Mandate was not marked on the ground, except for the first three kilometers from Aqaba northwards.

This line has since been referred to as the international border between Jordan and Israel, as well as the armistice line, part of which was the boundary separating between Judea and Samaria (the West Bank in Jordanian terminology) and the State of Israel until the Six-Day War.

We agreed with the Jordanians in advance that our discussions would ignore the section of the border that passes from south of Tirat Zvi to the north of Ein Gedi and along the Jordan River, since it related to negotiations with the Palestinians. It was clear that this would wait for trilateral Israeli-Jordanian-Palestinian discussions.

With respect to areas where Israel had trespassed across the border into Jordan following the water wells, Rabin asked to prepare ideas for a territorial exchange and a plan that would be lucrative for both parties. Rabin sought a solution in which Israel could continue to cultivate land and make full use of water as we had before, to ensure freedom of movement in regards to farming the land located east of Wadi Arabah, and also to find a way to financially compensate the Jordanians for this.

In the dynamic that developed between Rabin and Hussein and between the two countries, these types of suggestions could be made, because these were two leaders who were looking for ways to bridge the disagreements between them rather than render them unsolvable.

In this case it mainly required courage and vision on the part of Hussein, who had to accept the idea of a territorial exchange or lease in light of the fact that for years Israel had drilled in his territory and cultivated Jordanian lands.

However, there was already a precedent for territorial exchange between the Jordanians and us as part of the armistice agreements between Israel and Jordan in 1949. In order to simplify some of the problems, it was decided at the time to exchange territories between Jordan and Israel. Thus, for example, some of the Arab communities in Wadi Ara were transferred to Israeli control even though the IDF was not there in 1948, and in their place the Jordanians received other territories.

Hussein, like Rabin, was a creative and pragmatic person, responsive to ideas, open to new suggestions, and brought forth an air of optimism.

Rabin and Hussein always gave everyone the sense that problems would eventually be solved. When that is the starting point for problem-solving – then the way to that solution is short and efficient.

"People need to understand that setting the boundary marks a new era in relations between Israel and Jordan," said Hussein, and thus it could be understood that he accepted Rabin's pragmatic approach and saw things in their broader historical context.

Hussein's reference to the border issue as well as the water issue – wherein along with his demand to receive additional water he did not forget that Israel also suffers from a scarceness of this resource – showcases the extent to which Hussein's approach to the process differed from that of Syrian President Assad.

This difference in attitude between Hussein and Assad was not due to a difference in the nature of the conflict between us and them, but from the difference in the two's characters. The Syrians are distant and hard people, and Hussein, who received a Western education, was an open and cordial person.

King Hussein was constantly trying to find the prospects in every matter, and did not devote precious time to "cul-de-sacs." Hussein was a man of "there is a way."

On October 12, there was a meeting between Jordanian and Israeli officials in the Royal Palace in Amman. The meeting began as a private one between the king and Rabin, while Shimon Peres, the king's brother Prince Hassan, and other senior officials from both sides remained outside.

We sat at the palace garden and chatted. It was fascinating to follow the conversation between Peres and Prince Hassan. The two of them spoke a common language - both were visionaries with impressive rhetorical skills. Hassan is a very intelligent person, and it was evident that they both enjoyed sitting there for hours planning for a new Middle East. They ventured into optimistic hyperbole, far-reaching and brimming with vision.

I listened to these two and thought to myself how good it was that there were people like Peres and Prince Hassan, who dare to soar and look into the distance, while at the same time there were also people like Rabin and Hussein alongside them, ones who had both feet planted firmly on the ground, talking "brass tacks" in the next room.

It was a fascinating intellectual experience to listen to their conversation, but cutting to the chase requires a different type of people. The connection between visionaries and realists was good and fruitful. Rabin was a pragmatic realist, who sought to decide on the things done today, tomorrow, the day after, and in one year from now, and exactly how to get there. These features of Rabin completed Peres' high-flying vision.

When the entourage members entered the meeting at the palace in Amman, Hussein opened the conversation with another declaration of Rabin's and his commitment to peace, a commitment which was the most important one in his life. "Rabin and I share a common view that there is no time to lose and the process must be pushed forward," he said.

"We appreciate the king's courage and determination," said Rabin. "Israel's interest is that Jordan will be independent, strong and under your control, and we are opposed to the views that see Jordan as the Palestinian state. We reached the stage where peace is right at hand and all that remains is to finish the issues of borders and water. Israel does not want a single square centimeter of Jordanian land, but as you all know there have been some developments, such as the lands that Israel is cultivating in Jordanian territory and the water wells in these areas. The king and I agreed that the baseline is the armistice line: a line that passes from the Dead Sea along Wadi Arabah, and to the north – from *Nahal Bezek* to al-Hama.

"Israel and Jordan have previously agreed to minor territorial exchanges in 1948, so I believe that this time the solution will also be found in a limited exchange of lands.

"We will need to continue basing our discussions on several wells in the Aravah that will be under Jordanian sovereignty, and we will need to find the arrangements for how to operate these wells in a state of peace. Land will be exchanged on a 1:1 ratio – one square meter per every square meter. We have also agreed on the issue of water, that the Jordanians will receive one hundred million cubic meters of water each year; fifty will be transferred immediately, and fifty more after the construction of the two dams.

"Now we need to keep working on the draft of the peace treaty as we have done so far: without any leaks."

Rabin went on to explain that there would be places where the border would pass close to the main highway, so the Jordanians would have a duty to prevent terrorism that might originate from there.

Peres and Hassan presented ideas for developing the region. After Peres and Hassan finished, Hussein started talking, completely ignoring everything they said, and immediately - continuing from where Rabin had stopped - he said, "We will guide the teams to handle the water, we will examine the possibility of border adjustments and finalize the details. We," said Hussein, "will not go to arbitration."

Four days later, on October 16, Rabin flew back to Amman for a meeting with Hussein. This was after the delegation leaders failed to reach agreements on the controversial issues, and it required the leaders' decision. The scene at the palace seemed as though it had been ripped out of a movie. The team leaders from the Israeli side were sitting across the Jordanian team leaders, by issue: borders, water and security. Heads of delegations, Fayez Tarawneh and Elyakim Rubinstein, also sat along a long table, which was covered in maps and aerial photographs. All the points of disagreement and controversy that remained were raised, and we systematically moved from one to the next. The Israeli representative presented the Israeli position and the Jordanian his position, and Rabin and Hussein finalized the issue.

For example, the Jordanian wanted the agreement to mention that the Palestinians have the right to self-determination. "We'll try to phrase it similarly to the UN's phrasing," he said, and Rubinstein immediately replied, "It would not be good for this to be mentioned, because it would generate unnecessary controversy in Israel. After all, this is an agreement between us and yourselves and not the Palestinians." It was agreed immediately, on the spot, that no specific reference to self-determination would appear, but instead there would be a reference to what appears in the UN's statements.

Regarding the border, Rabin and Hussein sat through the night, reviewed the map one section at a time, and determined where the border would pass at the areas of controversy and which slice the Jordanians would receive as compensation for the cultivated lands that would remain ours. In regards to some areas, it was agreed that there would be no exchange of land, but that the lands would be under Jordanian sovereignty, and an arrangement would be made that would allow farmers from the Israeli side to access the Jordanian side.

Rabin and Hussein instilled a very purposeful and fruitful atmosphere. During that night all matters were finalized, and when morning came – all that was left was to sign the peace treaty.

The first breakthrough in this process was Rabin and Hussein's declaration in the previous meeting that the border would pass in the middle of Wadi Arabah, the second was when they agreed on a territorial exchange, and the third was when they agreed that Israel will have access to, but will not lease the agricultural lands, which will remain under Jordanian control, and that Israel would compensate Jordan for the water we pump in the Aravah.

When the work was done at the dawn of that day, we were tired and bleary-eyed, but we felt the exhilaration that comes with being part of a historical moment. We shook hands with our Jordanian colleagues and phrases such as "we did it", "we made it", and "let's be a role model for other nations in the region", were heard in the room.

We left Jordan with an enormous feeling of satisfaction knowing that a new dawn was rising over the Middle East.

On our way home, the recognition began to seep into us that we were truly on the verge of signing a peace agreement with a second Arab nation, and that millions of people in Jordan and Israel, sound asleep that previous night, did not know that in those very hours, Rabin, Hussein and their associates were working diligently and determinedly on a new peace in the region.

I remember well the first time I drove from Jerusalem to Amman, after many occasions when I had arrived there by air and at night. This was shortly after I left the army, after decades of military service, while I was in the midst of the onboarding process with previous Director of the Mossad. Shabtai Shavit and I crossed the Allenby Bridge on foot, where an armored vehicle was waiting to take us to a meeting with the head of the Jordanian intelligence agency.

Some two years earlier I was still serving as Commander of Central Command, responsible among other things for the defense of the Jordan Valley, the border with Jordan and all operational plans in case the situation with Jordan deteriorated.

I stood countless times on the Israeli side and looked toward the Jordanian side, to study the terrain. And here I found myself, in daylight and openly, riding in an air-conditioned vehicle traveling on an axis that I had been so intimately familiar with from maps, observations, operational plans and aerial photographs.

During the journey, every now and then I thought to myself, at the sight of one location or another: well here, according to the operational plans, a certain squad was to arrive, there another unit would land. During that drive, I recreated everything I had planned for in case of a war with Jordan. When I arrived in Amman, an amazing sight unraveled before my eyes: looking west I could see Jerusalem and the Judean Hills. I was immediately overwhelmed by a sense of satisfaction that we had managed to sign a peace treaty with Jordan, and we could divert all our energy and thoughts from devising offensive and defensive plans to devising ways to develop peace and promote the interests of both countries for the benefit of their citizens.

For Rabin it was very important to instill the sense of peace in the area's residents, turn peace into something that was alive and palpable and a part of everyday life, rather than leaving it as a vague and unrealized idea. Towards this end he tried to recruit the assistance of any foreign leader who met with him.

In a meeting he had at the time with British Prime Minister John Major, Rabin said, "It is important to create economic momentum so that people in the area will feel the results of peace in their living conditions. An Arab leader who signs a peace treaty with Israel assumes much greater risks than I do. He could be murdered, while I could be fired at worst," he said, not knowing that the reality would prove contrary and cruel. Just one year later Rabin would be murdered, and Israeli society would fall into a terrible vortex, from which it has not recovered to this very day.

"On the one hand we see a willingness in some of the Arabs to move towards peace," continued Rabin, "and on the other hand, a huge wave of radical Islamic terrorism is on the rise, whose sole purpose is to harm Israel and Western interests and eliminate the peace process. It is Khomeinism without Khomeini."

A vast majority of the Knesset approved the peace agreement with Jordan and so did the Jordanian parliament. On October 26, 1994, a peace treaty was signed between Israel and Jordan at an impressive and moving ceremony in the Aravah.

Two months later, in early January 1995, Rabin and Hussein held a meeting between them on the question of how to implement the written words into actual real-world projects.

Hussein said that two months had passed and the residents of Jordan were beginning to ask - what are the fruits of peace?

"We tell them not to lose patience and that things will not change overnight," said the king.

Rabin replied, "We have undertaken to withdraw until February 10, 1995, from the existing line to the line we have agreed on. We need to move a fence and evacuate minefields and it takes time. However, we can withdraw from the area between Aqaba and the Dead Sea as early as two weeks from now, and this we shall do.

"We are prepared to immediately begin construction of the pipeline that will allow fifty million cubic meters of water to be transferred to Jordan. We will enable Jordanian citizens to enter Israel with their private cars. In order to develop economic ties immediately, we are ready to start importing and exporting goods to the order of about forty million dollars right now."

The Jordanians asked they be allowed to fly from Aqaba to Europe via Israel, and the Israeli Air Force objected on the grounds that it would interfere with its drills in the Aravah. Rabin suggested that both countries' Air Force commanders would convene, and if they did not solve the problem, then Hussein and Rabin would.

Eventually an aerial corridor was established, along with coordination and control procedures, and it is used to this day by the passenger aircraft of Royal Jordanian Airlines (formerly "Alia") and El Al Airlines in their flights from Amman to Ben-Gurion Airport. Royal Jordanian Airlines also uses this route in its flights to the United States and Europe.

In August, the king asked to meet with Rabin urgently. When we reached Aqaba, we were greeted by an uncharacteristically grave Hussein, who told us he wished to update us of occurrences with Iraq. In those days, Raghad and Rana, Saddam Hussein's two daughters, came to Jordan along with their children and husbands, seeking political asylum from the king.

Hussein Kamel, one of Saddam's sons in-laws, was a very senior officer in the Iraqi army and spearheaded Saddam's weapons of mass destruction program. He claimed to have defected, along with his family and the family of his brother, who was married to Saddam's second daughter, due to his opposition to Saddam's tyrannical rule, and from his place of asylum looked to devise a plan to oust him.

The king began by telling us, "One month before he defected, Hussein Kamel passed through Amman on his way to Moscow. The purpose of his trip was to close a deal to purchase tanks when the embargo on Iraq is lifted.

"We met here, and I told him that Iraq should be part of the peace process, and asked him to convey it to his government. Kamel told me of the internal troubles in Iraq, and I told him about the negotiations between us and the cooperation with Israel which was very beneficial for Jordan. I told him," continued the king, "that we got our lands back and that we are receiving water from you – and that it is all done peacefully and without war. When Kamel returned to Jordan a month later, and requested political asylum from me, he said that what had convinced him to finally make this move was his conversation with me. He told me that Saddam objects to Iraq being part of the peace process, that a month earlier the Iraqis intended to invade Kuwait again, and over the last few days, Iraq had revived operational plans for a possible confrontation with Saudi Arabia and Kuwait. Kamel thought that the way Saddam is taking is incorrect, and that they should not continue to use force and threaten neighboring countries. He tried to influence the Cabinet and the Party, and spoke expressly about mistakes made in recent years by the government in Baghdad, until he gave up."

"When Kamel told me about the situation in Iraq I was stunned," continued the king. "He said that the prisons are full, people are murdered incessantly, and crime is growing rampant. Kamel wants to save the Iraqis from Saddam and to this end he wants to get in touch with Israel."

Rabin understood that Kamel wanted to build a capacity to topple Saddam, and to this end sought the support of Jordan, Israel and others.

"I hope there will be change in Iraq," Rabin said, "but I don't think that Kamel will produce this change. He does not have the charisma and skills to do so. He is an efficient technocrat, who rebuilt Iraq after the war, he built the defense industry in Iraq and was also one of the driving forces behind building the capacities of the Republican Guard – the elite forces of the Iraqi army that encompass several divisions. If he was unable to remove Saddam with all the power he had held, I doubt he could do so from the outside. We have a strategic interest that Jordan will be strong under your leadership. I do not suggest you take risks based on people like Kamel, who are not serious enough. I believe that only pressure and sanctions will bring change in Iraq, and the change should come from within Iraq. No one will intervene to help Kamel overthrow the government in Iraq."

Hussein thanked Rabin for his comments and replied, "Your words were very illuminating."

I think in this instance Rabin saved King Hussein from a crazed adventure that, had he embarked on, could have spelled out big trouble for him.

Rabin's urgent summoning to Amman for this consultation indicated the high degree of respect, cooperation and rapport that existed between the king and Rabin, and how these factors contributed to the peace established between the two countries.

The night meeting in Amman was the last meeting between the two leaders. The next time I met with King Hussein was two months later, when the king - shocked and hurt - came to Jerusalem to attend Rabin's funeral.

At the end of the funeral, the king invited Eitan Haber and me to his room at the King David Hotel in Jerusalem, and said to us, "I know you are hurt and pained, but I want you to know my pain is tremendous. Today I have lost the best friend I ever had!"

Chapter 23

Oslo: "Danny, I Never Thought Anything Would Come of It."

When Rabin arrived at the Prime Minister's office in 1992, the first Palestinian Intifada was already in its fifth year.

Rabin, who was determined to advance the peace process, and mentioned this throughout his campaign, realized that the way to stop the bloodshed with the Palestinians passes through meeting rooms and negotiations.

Throughout the years of the Intifada, the Shin Bet and IDF waged a determined war and an endless pursuit against terrorism. Despite many achievements in this war, terrorism did not stop, and the motivation for young Palestinians to join terrorist organizations had not been eroded.

Rabin knew that it would be impossible to stop terrorism only by military means. He entrenched the perception that the use of military force to relentlessly combat terrorism must be combined with a political channel in which we will strive to reach understandings and reconciliation through negotiations.

Rabin was a very careful and prudent person, and with the Palestinians tenfold so. For the purpose of the negotiations, he had inherited from Shamir a joint Jordanian-Palestinian delegation, established at the Madrid Conference, according to the conception that we did not speak separately with the Palestinians as they were receiving instructions from Yasser Arafat, the leader of a terrorist organization that did not recognize Israel's right to exist; and that in any case the final agreement will be based on the Kingdom of Jordan and an independent Palestinian state would not be established.

However, Rabin thought otherwise.

Even while serving as Minister of Defense in the unity government headed by Shamir, during the Intifada, a process began to mature inside him, in which he realized that contrary to what he had thought before, the Intifada was not a passing episode.

When the Intifada began in 1987, the commonly held view was that this eruption could be suppressed after a certain period of time, and that life will return to its previous state: Israel strong-handedly controlling three and a half million Palestinians in the West Bank and Gaza, who in turn do not display any organized resistance, barring the occasional terrorist attacks.

Rabin's recognition that this was not the case matured over time, and he realized that even at periods of calm, we would still continue to forcefully sit on top of the lid of a boiling pot that threatened to erupt anew at any moment.

I think that at that point in time, in light of attacks and casualties on our side and the Palestinian population's suffering, Rabin began to recognize that if no substantial attempt was made to settle the conflict by way of negotiations and peace, this violent conflict would never end.

Rabin realized it was time to look for a path of dialogue with the Palestinians, in order to reach an agreement that would at least end the mutual bloodshed, if not the conflict itself.

Rabin, "Mr. Security", was a very intelligent man who understood that it is impossible to end the conflict only through the use of military force. Yet for many years, it was convenient for the country's leaders, including Rabin, to maintain the status quo and believe that Israel was strong enough to uphold its control over the Palestinian people for years to come, and that the Palestinian public would humbly accept this.

The Israeli leadership did not internalize the need to think about the day after, and as mentioned, it was easy to proceed as we always had. As the years passed, many diverse military means were put to use: dozens of companies flowed into the Territories, special units such as *Shimshon* and *Duvdevan* were formed, the brigades deployed in Judea, Samaria and the Gaza Strip became divisions and the regimental battalions became brigades. However, that did not lead to a Palestinian surrender, and the Intifada persisted.

It was a flame that could be handled by force of arms, but could not be extinguished.

Rabin was looking for a way to end the bloodshed. He concluded that the 'carrot and stick' method - in which we made gestures to the Palestinians when there was a period of calm, and pummeled them when they rioted – had ceased to work. Rabin was also concerned about the fact that terrorism was increasingly seeping into Israel and that many attacks were committed using cold weapons and firearms.

It had been previously suggested that the change in Rabin's worldview was due to his concerns that Israeli society was not strong enough to deal with terrorism, bloodshed and bereavement, and the Intifada could gravely hurt Israeli society's resilience. However, I can say with certainty that Rabin never expressed such concern. His desire to find another way to resolve the conflict stemmed from his honest wish to end the bloodshed, and to try and lead the State of Israel to a new and better situation.

This had already begun to mature in him during his tenure as Minister of Defense. Hence during his election campaign, when he ran for Prime Minister against Yitzhak Shamir, his platform included the need to negotiate with the Palestinians, Jordanians, Syrians and Lebanese, and a promise to make every effort to try and reach peace agreements between Israel and its neighbors.

When he became Prime Minister, Rabin believed that the way to negotiate with the Palestinians was to do so with an authentic Palestinian leadership in the Territories. His approach was to negotiate with the local Palestinian leadership without any contact with the PLO – which was, as noted, a terrorist organization that did not recognize our right to exist and had sworn itself to Jihadist war against Israel.

Government policy at the time prohibited PLO activity in the Territories, and decreed that it must be suppressed immediately, even if the activity in question was merely the waving of the Palestinian flag.

The Palestinian delegation's representatives to the Madrid peace talks were chosen by the Palestinians themselves. As head of the delegation they appointed Dr. Haidar Abdel Shafi, a Gazan doctor and one of the city's notables, and also asked to include Faisal Husseini, a member of the Husseini family and son of Abdel Kader Husseini, one of the most prominent commanders of the Arab militias during the War of Independence. Faisal Husseini was a political activist, became one of the leaders of the Palestinian population in Judea and Samaria, and was subjected to administrative detention for his activities.

Rabin initially refused to add Husseini to the delegation since he lived in Jerusalem. Rabin did not want to create a situation in which a Palestinian living in East Jerusalem, under Israeli sovereignty, would be a member of the Palestinian delegation. It could create the impression that Rabin no longer viewed East Jerusalem as part of the united Jerusalem, capital of the State of Israel.

However, information slowly began to accumulate, indicating that Husseini was a highly appreciated figure in the Territories, that he was a relatively moderate person. Furthermore, there was pressure from the Palestinians to include him in the talks because they saw him as a prominent leader of the Palestinian population in the West Bank.

Finally, a "creative solution" was found, after it became clear that Husseini had a second residential address at Ein Siniya near Ramallah, and therefore was considered a local resident. Thus, even though in his Israeli identity card Husseini was listed as a resident of Jerusalem, he received the "stamp of approval" to join the Palestinian delegation.

When I arrived at Rabin's bureau in April 1993 he was serving as Prime Minister and Defense Minister, and the Territories had been under curfew for several months due to terrorist activities within the State of Israel. In every situation briefing there was a lingering concern over a major terrorist attack by Hamas, and the number-one task that Rabin set for the IDF was to combat terrorism and provide a sense of security for Israelis within and beyond the Green Line. One of the first things Rabin wanted to do was to reduce the dependence on Palestinian workers inside Israel.

At that period, contact with the Palestinian delegation continued according to what was laid out in Madrid: only through the Jordanian-Palestinian delegation and under Jordanian responsibility. Despite protests expressed by King Hussein, who suggested to separate the delegations, at that stage Rabin opted to continue the previous format in order to create procedural continuity.

At that time, the Palestinian public began to show signs of unrest with the renewal of talks and negotiations between Israel and the Palestinians. We had learned of an incident in which opponents of the process broke into Saeb Erekat's home in Jericho in an attempt to intimidate him. We also received reports through intelligence pipelines that members of the Palestinian delegation, who were to attend talks with Israel in Washington, had been receiving death threats.

In April 1993, the first briefings for negotiators with the Arab delegations to Washington began, and Rabin established the principles for negotiation. According to these principles, the responsibility for overall security in Judea and Samaria and the border with Jordan, with the Gaza Strip and with Egypt - was Israel's. Responsibility for the security of Israelis wherever they may be was also Israel's, and management of civilian aspects would be gradually transferred to the Palestinians.

Here, for the first time, Rabin expressed his willingness to transfer powers of civil administration to the Palestinians. The protocol would refer to this as "the provision of partial administrative powers to the Palestinians in areas of civilian life."

Already at that stage, Rabin said that options should be left open for negotiations of the permanent agreement. That is to say, at that stage the negotiating team would deal with issues relevant to the immediate term, such as specific powers of civil administration, but he was already talking about an interim agreement that would lead to a permanent agreement. "Gestures to the Palestinians are contingent on progress in the peace process," said Rabin, meaning that as negotiations progressed and in order to create a constructive atmosphere, Israel would make gestures to the Palestinians. These gestures would be in the form of removing sieges and curfews, issuing entry passes to Israel for workers, and easing the daily life of the Territories' residents.

In late April 1993, the delegation for negotiations with the Palestinians left for Washington, and reports from there indicated that Faisal Husseini displayed a moderate approach, while Haidar

Abdel-Shafi spoke harshly, saying that it would all stand or fall on the fate of the settlements.

The Israeli delegation members noted the tension between Haidar and Faisal, stating that it was evident that the two were fighting for supremacy.

Even then, early in the talks, we received solid intelligence that Arafat, who resided in Tunis, was actually the final arbiter. Members of the Palestinian delegation to Washington would return to their hotel at the end of the discussions with the Israelis, and immediately contact Arafat in Tunis, to receive his instructions on how to respond to our offers. Hence we realized that while our representatives were physically meeting with the delegation, the final arbiter and true negotiator was the leader of the PLO - Arafat.

In those days, the PLO was still considered anathematic and the formal approach was that we would not hold contacts with it. Israelis who insisted and met with Arafat were sentenced to prison terms, and Rabin, who tried to build an authentic Palestinian leadership in the Territories, began to realize that this would not be successful.

Rabin and Peres agreed that Peres would be responsible for the multilateral meetings that dealt with water, the environment and refugees, and that Rabin would coordinate bilateral contacts and will be the final arbiter. They had weekly meetings where they exchanged views, but it was clear that Rabin was the one who was handling bilateral talks, was deeply engaged and involved in the process, and the final decision was his.

At the same time, the Palestinians began to send us requests for different gestures, one of which was to allow older deportees, who were deported before the Intifada due to subversive political activities, to return to their homes. After the IDF and Shin Bet reviewed the matter, Rabin was persuaded to allow the return of thirty deportees, provided that upon returning to the Territories they would not be allowed to serve as members of official PLO institutions, similarly to the rest of the Territories' residents.

At that stage, in April 1993, Rabin's attitude toward negotiations with the Palestinians was businesslike and devoid of expectations. His approach was that it was impossible to know what the results of the process would be, but he decided to give it a try, and once that decision was made, he handled the matter with all seriousness and responsibility.

Rabin was willing to move forward, and to consider bold proposals. The activity took shape gradually, starting from the first statements and the guidelines he gave the delegation for talks with the Palestinians, and from the way in which he made decisions.

From his conduct at the time, one could not have guessed Rabin's vision for the permanent agreement, since Rabin did not speak of it. In his conversations with us, he did not specify the shape of the final destination, i.e. the permanent agreement, and did not outline the way to reach it. Nevertheless, he always said, "Let's start from here, walk carefully, examine our progress - and then decide what's next." Rabin was always careful to maintain some degrees of freedom and even to backtrack if the need arises.

I have no doubt that Rabin, an analytical and calculated man, had a detailed plan on the way and the goal that he wanted to reach, but he did not share it with us. Only as the process developed we could understand the components of his plan for the permanent agreement. Later I learned that Rabin was willing to establish a Palestinian state whose territory would not exceed fifty percent of the land in the West Bank.

The idea was to move forward gradually and thus bridge the psychological gaps and inherent lack of trust between the parties, in an attempt to build a system of cooperation and coexistence. This gradation, according to Rabin, would allow us to gauge the intentions of the other side and its seriousness and to decide if and how to proceed at every stage.

In late April, there was a discussion between the head of the Israeli delegation to the negotiations, Elyakim Rubinstein, and Rabin, in which they discussed the "issue of Haidar Shafi." Shafi was extreme in his views and we believed he was sabotaging the talks' progress. Rabin and Rubinstein tried to figure out how to get rid of Shafi and remove him from the Palestinian delegation.

Rabin's instructions were to convey a message to the Americans that Shafi's way would lead to nowhere, because we believed he was sabotaging the talks and came to them with a negative and belligerent attitude.

Later, the Americans managed to twist Shafi's arm and tone him down.

In July 1993, Rabin briefed Rubinstein in preparation for another round of talks with the Palestinians, while in the background the first voices were beginning to be heard regarding the idea of 'Gaza first,' according to which the Palestinians would be given civilian responsibility over the Gaza Strip.

"I thought of 'Gaza first', but I do not want the subject to come up in the coming round of talks," Rabin said to Rubinstein and continued, "We must first reach an agreement in principle with the Palestinians, and then we will discuss 'Gaza first' as part of the agreement's implementation."

In those days, Rabin described his intentions in very flexible terms, because the process was still in its infancy. Rabin only provided guidelines, listened to the Palestinian sentiments, and concurrently decided on the next step in the negotiations.

Rabin wanted to try to reach a statement of agreements with the Palestinians, and make the decision to establish various committees that would deal with issues such as human rights, water, land and the transfer of civilian powers to the Palestinians.

The Israeli delegation left for the round of talks, and their reports indicated that discussions with the Palestinians were meaningless. This was because most of the work was being done behind the scenes between the United States and the Palestinians and between the United States and Israel.

As soon as the discussions began, the Palestinians made two demands that enraged Rabin. They asked to discuss the issue of Jerusalem as part of the interim agreement and before the permanent agreement. Furthermore, they asked to discuss the area of jurisdiction, meaning to discuss the land on which Palestinian jurisdiction will apply, or in other words - the basis for a sovereign Palestinian state.

This meant that the Palestinians wanted to receive Palestinian authority over the entire area, except for areas that Israel would wish to discuss as "exceptions", meaning the settlements.

Rabin adamantly refused this request. His approach was that there would be no discussion of Jerusalem at that stage, and that in the interim period Jerusalem would remain one united city under Israeli sovereignty; and that Israel could not accept the notion of giving full civilian and judicial authorities over the entire area to the Palestinians, barring exceptions.

His approach was the opposite of the Palestinian approach: giving authorities on specific matters, not over the land but with regards to the residents, with everything else remaining under Israel's responsibility. As far as Rabin was concerned, authority over territory was not going to be discussed at that stage, and certainly not ownership over territory.

His definition was "providing early powers", meaning the transfer of authority over the residents in all aspects of civilian administration, responsibility for civilian life, public order and civilian police, while physical control of the land is retained by Israel.

Rabin also stressed that Israel was responsible for the security of Israelis wherever they may be, and that responsibility for overall security, borders, control over who comes in and out, and protecting and securing the border – was also in Israeli hands.

These were the guidelines with which Rabin equipped the Israeli delegation.

At that time a sort of "mini-crisis" formed between us and the Americans, who came with a document that, from their perspective, was a proposal for an agreement in principle.

Some of the things in the document did not bode well with Rabin. However, he agreed to accept it, as he understood from Ross and Christopher that this was a US proposal aimed to advance the process, and that the United States would continue to support Israel and protect its interests. So Rabin agreed to accept statements in the document that were not to his liking, such as the term "self-rule authority" for the interim period being replaced by a "Palestinian self-rule authority" for the interim period.

Two months later, in June of that year, the Americans came to Rabin with changes made in the document, which upset him greatly. Rabin railed against the Americans, that they let him understand that the document presented to him in the first place was irreversible, and here they come to him again with changes in the document and demand additional concessions from him.

All this time contacts were also being held between us and the Jordanians, and King Hussein expressed concern over the idea of 'Gaza first,' because he believed that the Palestinians could not ensure security in Gaza. Hussein said that the transfer of security responsibilities in Gaza to the Palestinians might upset the balance in the West Bank, as the Palestinians would expect Israel to evacuate from there as well. The king feared that Israel was about to leave the entire area except for settlements and military bases. Thus, he expressed concern that this could undermine the stability of Jordan, which has a common border with Judea and Samaria, from Tirat Zvi in the north to the Dead Sea in the south.

Rabin assured Hussein and gave him the message that Israel would not leave the entire Gaza Strip, and all that was being discussed was redeployment of Israeli security forces in Gaza, Judea and Samaria. In addition, this would not take place before the framework agreement was reached, of which 'Gaza first' would be the first stage of implementation.

Over the course of the process, we discovered that Arafat was creating difficulties in the negotiations and opposed the idea of granting authorities to manage everyday life. Our impression was that he was trying to delay the progress of negotiations for fear that his presence in Tunis - while Haidar Abdel-Shafi was in Gaza and Faisal Husseini was in Jerusalem – would undermine his authority.

Arafat wanted to be part of the negotiations, and by imposing difficulties on their progress he sent the message that we need to talk with him. Since the beginning of negotiations with the Palestinians, it was clear that Arafat was instructing the members of the Palestinian delegation to present strict and uncompromising positions.

At that stage, the negotiations were still being conducted simultaneously with both the Jordanians and the Syrians, and on this matter Rabin said to the Americans, "I do not remember any occasion in which something good came from simultaneous negotiations with all of the Arabs." Rabin was referring to a situation in which all the delegations meet at the same time and place. In such a situation, one track of negotiations becomes entangled in another, everyone examines the others responses and progress, the extreme position gains traction and everyone aligns themselves according to it... It was better to negotiate separately with each of them.

Rabin gave the example of the negotiations with the Egyptians, which were held separately from the other countries. However, Rabin stressed, "We inherited these concurrent negotiations from the previous administration and we will try to make them work."

In all of his meetings with the Americans, in every step of the way and until his last day, Rabin stressed to them that the United States could be neither a conciliator nor a mediator. The Americans' role, according to Rabin, was to act as an intermediary, to convey the Israeli position to the Palestinians and vice versa, and come up with ideas to overcome obstacles, but to let us know in advance so we are not surprised by them. However, Rabin stressed, the Americans had no authority to mediate or conciliate, and they were not to conduct negotiations in place of direct negotiations; their role was to be a faithful intermediary.

Rabin was very careful to maintain this approach with the Americans, contrary to later periods, such as during Netanyahu's tenure as Prime Minister. Then the Americans assumed a more prominent role in the negotiations in light of the rift between the Israelis and the Palestinians.

Rabin was careful to achieve things through direct negotiations and would involve the Americans only in the event of a deadlock, when they were asked to act as intermediates but definitely not to mediate or conciliate.

During a meeting in April between Rabin and Mubarak in Ismaïlia, Mubarak showed Rabin a map that he received from Arafat. On it, Arafat outlined his vision that he would receive Gaza, Jericho and the Jordan River bridges. Arafat's goal was to make a power-play and convey the message that he was not neglecting the West Bank. However, what lay behind it was essentially an attempt to take control of the entrance and exit crossings already at that early stage.

At the time, as part of the talks with the Palestinian delegation, we offered Faisal Husseini to choose people, whom we would train to apply the civilian authorities in those matters that we wished to transfer to their responsibility. However, the Palestinians refused to do so due to their wariness of Arafat, who opposed the notion that the Palestinians would cooperate in the process of receiving early powers.

As the process progressed, Rabin took one more step toward the Palestinians. He expressed his willingness that immediately after the agreement to redeploy our forces in Gaza, and after our departure from the centers of the Palestinian cities in the West Bank, we would be prepared to transfer almost all the powers of civilian administration to the Palestinians. In this state of affairs, they would have almost complete authority over all Palestinians, except in Jerusalem that would remain united under Israeli sovereignty, while the full responsibility for security and control over the entire area would remain in Israeli hands.

While the Americans were working to formulate a US declaration of principles between Israel and the Palestinians, and the Palestinians were discussing the idea of "Gaza and Jericho First", discussions were held regarding the return of Palestinian deportees to the West Bank. There were two relevant groups of deportees: the older ones, mostly members of the PLO deported even before the outbreak of the Intifada, and the purpose of their return was to send a message to the Palestinians that negotiations were beneficial. The second list was of Hamas deportees who resided in Marj al-Zuhur in Lebanon. This list included three categories: those who would return to prison as they were still involved in terrorist activities; those who would be released immediately; and those who would be investigated by Israel immediately upon their return, and according to the results of the investigation it would be decided if they would be sent to prison for administrative detention, tried in court or released.

At that stage of the negotiations, Rabin had already made statements to the effect that the joint Jordanian-Palestinian delegation was a mirage, and that this situation must be changed. It was also clear that the Palestinian delegation did not act or decide on anything, small or great, without the approval and instructions of PLO headquarters in Tunis.

Against the background of preparations for a turn in the negotiations, which would commence direct talks between Israel and the PLO in Tunis, Rabin received reports from intelligence sources that Faisal Husseini was in a vise. On one hand, Husseini was being pressured by Tunis in an attempt to clip his wings, and on the other hand, he wanted to continue leading the negotiations.

It also became clear that there were differences of opinion between Arafat and the PLO leadership in Tunis, and the Palestinian delegation to the negotiations. The leadership preferred to sign a declaration of principles and begin immediate implementation of "Gaza and Jericho First." This was in order to send a message to the Palestinians that Arafat was not neglecting the West Bank and was not going to be the Mayor of Gaza, but was also establishing a foothold in Jericho. Arafat wanted to receive Jericho as well as the Allenby Bridge in order to maintain the Territories' contact with the external world. Faisal Husseini supported beginning the transfer of authority over civil administration to the Palestinians, in order to start exercising their control over the area. In light of these disagreements and strained relations between Tunis and the Palestinian delegation, the members of the delegation resigned from their posts. However, they retracted their decision later, after Arafat appeased them by reinforcing their status and giving them additional powers.

Meanwhile, in a parallel and secretive track, another process was developing, one that would soon come to light and astonish many people in the region and around the world.

For several weeks, during the summer of 1993, Rabin, me and a few other senior officials received evidence that meetings were taking place between PLO members and Israelis Dr. Yair Hirschfeld and Ron Pundak.

When I and others who were in on the secret asked Rabin about this, Rabin stifled us with a familiar wave of his hand and said, "It's nothing serious."

Later, when I spoke with him about this stage in the informal talks between Israelis and Palestinians, he said, "Danny, believe me, I did not think anything would come of it."

Peres updated Rabin of this activity at an earlier stage, but Rabin did not share it with us, and when he decided to send Director General of the Foreign Ministry Uri Savir to Oslo, he also did not tell us about it.

However, over time there were more and more signs that there is a backdoor communications channel, but its contents were unclear, and it was also unclear how serious or substantive it was.

Some three weeks before Oslo "burst" into the mass media, Rabin called Eitan Haber and me to his office and told us, "Contacts are being held in Oslo under Norwegian auspices, between representatives of the Ministry of Foreign Affairs led by Uri Savir and Yoel Singer, and the Palestinians led by Abu Alaa. This is off the record and keep it to yourselves, even the Americans are not in on the secret. They are trying to reach an agreement in principle there, but I do not think it has much of a chance. There are many problems still remaining but I wanted you to know."

This announcement verified the evidence we had found earlier. To the best of my knowledge, Rabin was truly not overly optimistic about this track, and I think he approved Peres to send Savir to there because he was very doubtful about the results.

From that moment and until the agreement in Oslo was signed I was in on the secret, and from time to time Rabin would inform me of progress that was made in these talks. The agreement signed by Shimon Peres, who was sent to Oslo confidentially, and Abu Alaa, was a "statement of principles" written in general terms, which could be used to move towards bridging the gaps, and all with the aim that this document serve as a basis for further negotiations.

However, much more work was required to turn this document into something that both sides could agree on.

Throughout the development of the Oslo document, Peres was receiving guidelines from Rabin regarding issues he was not willing to concede, such as that Jerusalem would not be a subject for discussion, that responsibility for the security of Israelis and the borders would be Israel's alone, and that there would be no right of return.

In early September 1993, during a "Territories discussion" held in Rabin's office, he introduced for the first time the main tenets of the "Oslo Accords", which were gradually taking shape behind the scenes and in total secrecy in the past months.

"Autonomy is a complicated solution to the problem between us and the Palestinians," said Rabin and continued, "Autonomy requires building a reality of coexistence between the two peoples (at that time Rabin still envisioned the Palestinians and settlers living side by side), and as we know there is no love lost between the settlers and the Palestinians. I would prefer a solution similar to the one we achieved with the Egyptians: that there is a clear line and complete separation between the Israeli and Egyptian sides."

An interim arrangement in which the Palestinian would be given control over their own lives, while living alongside the settlers who would remain in place until the permanent agreement, was a more complicated solution for Rabin. He preferred to proceed immediately to the permanent agreement, in which there would be a line separating the settlers and the Palestinians. This would avoid a situation in which the lives of the two populations would be interwoven with each other and would involve daily friction that could only complicate matters.

"It would have been better to proceed immediately to the permanent agreement," Rabin continued, "but this is not possible because of the problem of Jerusalem. I had high hopes that we would have a local partner, but apparently this is not the case, and at the moment we are attempting to turn the PLO into a partner. I see a big difference between Gaza and Judea and Samaria. In Gaza, we can be more generous towards the Palestinians, and any arrangement we reach need not be a precedent for Judea and Samaria. There is a small amount of settlers in Gaza, living in seventeen small and isolated communities, and so there it will be easier reach a solution of buffering and separation between them and the Gazans. In the West Bank there are close to 200,000 settlers, and the lives of Israelis and Palestinians are more intertwined. I see the plan for the Gaza Strip and a small enclave in the West Bank as a pilot plan for the final agreement and it will also be done incrementally.

"The IDF will remain in the area to provide external protection at the Egyptian border and Rafah terminal, as well as along Gaza's borders with Israel and the sea. The IDF will be responsible for the defense and security of every Israeli wherever he may be. However, Palestinians should progressively be given more areas of responsibilities, and we must see whether they are able to handle them. The Palestinians ask to bring some of their men from the outside and we have agreed to this in principle, but the identity of the people and when it will happen - all of these are subject to negotiations between the Palestinians and us."

Rabin went on to say, "We will have to see whether the Palestinians take it upon themselves to impose order and prevent terrorism. They are able to act forcefully and almost unrestrained against terrorism, since for them there is no Supreme Court and no B'Tselem. 'Gaza and Jericho First' will continue to be implemented during negotiations, the Palestinian Council (which will receive the authorities) will be established only after elections in the Palestinian Authority, and the transfer of civilian powers will not take place before the withdrawal from Gaza is complete.

"I see Gaza and Jericho as a 'test case.' As early as Carter, Sadat and Begin's Camp David, the IDF's redeployment in the Territories was discussed. A timetable was not set then and we will set it according to our own interests. The elections in the Palestinian Authority are contingent on reaching agreements regarding the structure of the autonomy, the Palestinian Council and the nature of the elections - before that there will be no elections and no transfer of powers. I do not object to the establishment of a Palestinian police force - a subject that also appears in Camp David already. I want to make a separation between the negotiations on Gaza and Jericho and the issues of the Palestinian Council and elections. No one has any experience with these matters and they are very complicated.

"I want to emphasize that at this stage there is no talk of evacuating Israeli settlements; the matter of the settlements will be discussed during negotiations for the permanent agreement.

"Apparently the PLO will sign the declaration of principles, but for us to agree to this they need to make several announcements which are very difficult for them: they have to proclaim that twenty-eight out of thirty-three articles in the Palestinian National Charter - that is all the articles that oppose the existence of Israel - are void."

On September 2, 1993, Rabin said to me, "We are working on drafting the papers that will enable us to recognize the PLO. However, I'm starting to feel that Arafat is beginning to flutter when it comes to our demands to cancel most of the clauses in the Charter, his commitment to fight terrorism and resolve the conflict only in peaceful ways, his agreement to holding elections and other matters."

The change in the way the PLO was perceived, from an anathema to a partner to an agreement, was due to Rabin's acknowledgment of the fact that the PLO was the one actually pulling the strings. However, Rabin was unwilling to negotiate with the PLO as long as it did not recognize Israel's right to exist, as long as it did not commit to stopping terrorism and as long as it did not commit to resolving contentious issues through dialogue. Rabin was a realist who chose to accept the facts as they were, because he was very interested in promoting an agreement with the Palestinians. After all, that was the reason the delegation led by Elyakim Rubinstein had been sent to Washington. When Rabin realized that the breakthrough was being made in Oslo rather than Washington, then in his pragmatic way, he immediately changed the plans he had made in advance, accepted the changes and embraced them, rather than adhering to the existing program.

The Oslo process produced substantive results while the process in Washington dragged on and on, since in Oslo dialogue was held with people like Abu Alaa (Ahmed Qurei) and Abu Mazen (Mahmoud Abbas), who were closer to Arafat and managed to persuade him that the Palestinians should adopt the understandings reached there.

In addition, the Israelis who handled the Oslo process were apparently more creative, and were given more freedom to handle the negotiations. The combination of Savir and Singer was good, and doubtless Pundak and Hirschfeld paved the road and prepared the groundwork for this historic move. Perhaps the location of the talks in such a faraway and detached place, which did not attract any media attention or involvement, was also a contributing factor. Another potential factor may have been the fact that in the Washington talks, which were attended by the Americans, the parties were less daring in their proposals and their willingness to make concessions.

In my opinion, the Oslo process shows that eventually agreements are reached through direct negotiations between the parties, who have to make hard decisions that no one can make for them, not even the Americans. It further shows that when media involvement is neutralized and there is isolation from external pressures – the chances to achieve better results improve.

Peres traveled to the United States to report the developments in Oslo to the Americans, who were completely surprised to hear that as they were laboring to promote the talks in Washington – significant things were happening in Oslo.

It was important for Rabin to update the Americans, mostly due to their status as patrons of the process, and as those whose involvement would also be required in the future. However, it was also to allow them to see the agreement, make comments, and to examine our demands of the PLO which were conditions for our recognition of it as the sole representative of the Palestinian people. Rabin wanted the Americans to induce other countries, such as Morocco, Tunisia, Saudi Arabia and the Gulf states, to recognize Israel.

It was clear to Rabin that from that point onwards it would be impossible to move forward without the Americans, to add more countries to the process and pressure the Palestinians to accept our terms for recognizing the PLO, and to create a Palestinian commitment to the United States to fulfill their part in the process.

The Americans were not the only ones surprised by the unveiling of the Oslo process, which until then had been kept in total secrecy. King Hussein was also surprised - and furious.

An envoy on our behalf, returning from a meeting with the king, said that Hussein was angry for not having been updated about the process, despite Jordan officially being part of the Palestinian delegation to the talks in Washington. He also expressed concern over the possibility of Israel and the Palestinians reaching agreements that could compromise Jordan. The king further said, that the day after the agreement is signed he would fold the umbrella he gave the Palestinians in Washington, and the delegations will go their separate ways. This was in accordance with his previous claim that there was no point in a joint Jordanian-Palestinian delegation and that each had to be negotiated with separately.

***

The date for the signing ceremony of the declaration of principles between Israel and the Palestinians on the White House lawn was set for September 13, and on the days leading to it Rabin was debating whether to attend the ceremony.

He believed it was too early for him to meet with Arafat, and in his eyes there was a big difference between a paper signed by Peres and Abu Mazen, and a paper signed by himself and Arafat. Rabin assessed that Arafat would demand to attend the ceremony if he would be there, and was appalled by the possibility of having to shake his hand.

It should be remembered that Rabin had undergone quite a dramatic change, from seeing the world through the eyes of a Defense Minister and Chief of Staff, who for years led the war against PLO terrorism, to a Prime Minister was about to sign an agreement in principle with the PLO. It was not easy for him, although in his characteristic way he did not show any outward signs of this.

His difficulty and great dilemma over participating in the ceremony in Washington indicated the complexity of the matter for him, although he was well aware that at some point he would have to do so. It was a remarkable moment for Rabin, in which his feelings were given a more dominant place than the rational thinking that usually characterized him. The explanation for this was Rabin's extreme dislike for Arafat.

Initially, emotions got the upper hand and Rabin decided not to go, and asked Peres to head the Israeli delegation to the signing ceremony of the declaration of principles instead.

The Americans believed that this decision was wrong, and began to pressure Rabin - including through Clinton - to come to the ceremony in Washington. They argued that this was the first agreement between Israel and the Palestinians, and it was very important to show commitment to the process in the presence of the leaders of both sides.

The weekend before the signing ceremony came, and on Friday the decision was still that Rabin would stay home and Peres would travel. The Foreign Ministry started making arrangements for the excursion while in the Prime Minister's Office, no one was clearing out his luggage or ironing his bow-tie.

However, on Saturday, at seven in the morning, the Point-to-Point (PTP) operational phone at my house rang, and from the other end of the line, Rabin's baritone could be heard: "Danny, wake up and come to my house." Somewhat groggy and still clinging to the last bits of my sleep, I asked anxiously if something had happened, and Rabin answered, "I am also calling Sheves and Haber, we need to talk about Washington."

Half an hour later, I was already at Rabin's house, and I found him dressed in his "day-off" clothes: flip-flops and an untucked shirt. Relaxed and homely, he greeted me, as Leah displayed extraordinarily warm and hearty hospitality.

"I am receiving many phone calls from the Americans, urging me to come to Washington. What do you say?"

Sheves and I were of the opinion that he should go because this is a dramatic turn of events, a breakthrough and the beginning of a new phase in the relations. Although it was still unclear where it would lead, this was the cornerstone of the efforts Rabin led to hold negotiations with the Palestinians.

I told Rabin he needed to participate, even if it meant shaking hands with Arafat. This was because otherwise it would look very strange that on the one hand, he was leading the move for peace with the Palestinians, while on the other, he was careful to be absent from such an important and symbolic ceremony.

Eitan Haber believed that Rabin should not go to Washington because it was not yet time to meet with Arafat.

The discussion was brief and for its duration Rabin said nothing, just listened to us while chain-smoking. After half an hour, he said, "I think that Danny and Sheves are right, I have to go."

The Israeli delegation headed by Peres was planned to leave for Washington on that same evening, leaving us very little time to make arrangements.

Eitan Haber informed Avi Gil, head of the Foreign Minister's bureau, of Rabin's decision to head the Israeli delegation to Washington. In a short while, the Minister's bureau called and told us that Peres was very hurt from this decision as all the preparations were already made. Furthermore, he was hurt because everyone already knew that Peres was to head the Israeli delegation, and this sudden change could be perceived as disregard for his status.

Peres was so offended by the change in Rabin's decision that he decided that if Rabin were to go - he himself would stay. It took a lot of phone calls that day between Eitan Haber and Avi Gil to straighten things out, and it was agreed that the two personages would fly on the same plane, both would be on the stage at the signing ceremony, both would speak and both would sign the document. All this was done in order to dispel Peress concerns that he would not be seen at the ceremony and that the spotlight would be stolen from him.

However, more preparations still needed to be made for the excursion. The Israelis' "change in protocol" needed to be quickly informed to the Americans so they could make sure to "balance" it on the Palestinian side. Thus Arafat would also be on the stage and participate in the signing ceremony alongside his deputy Abu Mazen, and both of them would speak at the ceremony.

The Americans are flexible in these matters, and all ceremonial and procedural matters were properly arranged.

The ceremony on the White House lawn, on September 13, 1993, took place on a particularly hot day. However, the blazing sun that struck mercilessly upon us failed to dispel the great excitement that gripped all those present, and culminated as the leaders emerged from the White House and began to walk towards the main stage.

The sight of Rabin walking alongside Arafat nullified all the clichés at once, and it was impossible not to feel the wings of history beating. I felt I was witnessing an extraordinary and unparalleled moment in the life of the nation which for so many years I had fought for. Even in those solemn moments I was well aware of the many obstacles and hurdles that awaited us, but the spectacle unfolding before my eyes represented a breakthrough that could perhaps lead to a change in our situation in the Middle East and an end to wars and bloodshed.

In the audience sat all the senior diplomatic officials in Washington, including Arab officials such as the Saudi ambassador to Washington, Prince Bandar, a junior representative of the Syrian embassy in Washington and ambassadors of many Arab nations. It was evident that the excitement and sense of solemnity did not skip them as well.

The leaders took their places on the stage with Clinton separating between Rabin and Arafat. Every part of Rabin's body language in those minutes expressed contempt and discomfort. It was clear that he did not know what to do with himself, felt out of place, and his expression was that of one who had unintentionally stumbled into a place where he had no interest in being.

Peres, on the other hand, was shining like a groom on his wedding day, and smiled all the smiles that Rabin spared himself. Those present on stage were speaking of a historic moment and the end of war and bloodshed. However, all these words were dwarfed by the moment of the handshake. When this moment came, it was clear that Rabin was doing so grudgingly, but the deed was done and wrung enthusiastic applause from the audience. Rabin immediately turned to Peres and said to him, with a smile of relief on his face, "It's your turn now."

This was not the final moment of excitement of the day.

Even before leaving for Washington, when it was not yet clear whether Rabin would go, the idea came up, fathered among others by Rafi Edri who was close to government circles in Morocco, that on the way back from Washington Rabin would land in Morocco. While there, he would meet with King Hassan VI, and this would, in effect, be the first public meeting between an Israeli Prime Minister and the Moroccan King.

The plan was shelved at the time when Rabin had decided not to go, and was rekindled when he decided to accept the requests and come to the ceremony. A handful of people in the Israeli entourage were in on this secret, and I handled the final arrangements for it from Washington, where we arrived the day before the ceremony at the White House.

The night before the ceremony, I had a phone call from Washington with Rafi Edri, who was already in Morocco, and brought the captain of the Air Force plane responsible for bringing us safely to Rabat in on the secret. Although I was sure that it was kept in total secrecy, upon our landing in Rabat, I was surprised to see journalist Shimon Shiffer, who decided to skip the trip to Washington and opted to go to Rabat.

After the ceremony in Washington, we left for Morocco feeling excited. For most of us it was naturally our first visit, and this event added an additional layer to the sense of history that accompanied the signing ceremony. There was a feeling that the seeds of peace with the Palestinians were already budding and yielding fruit in the form of an open visit, the first of its kind, to a very important Muslim country.

The visit to Rabat was very moving and picturesque. Parts of it seemed as if they were taken from the Arabian Nights fairy tales. Our delegation was received by an honor guard and Rabin was treated with royal dignity, and the king's attitude towards him was warm and welcoming.

However, all the festivities, euphoria and elation dissipated almost at once upon our return to Israel and the reality that awaited us.

Rabin's utmost concern was always for security matters, and he reiterated time and again that security is the main issue which we would insist upon and for which we would refuse to make concessions. At the same time, we would continue to help the Palestinians and enable them to reach economic achievements, which would grant them the feeling that peace is lucrative and would also have a beneficial effect on the level of security.

While Palestinians were having trouble deciding who would be their representatives to the continued talks in Washington, we started to prepare and decided to establish two main committees: a steering committee chaired by Peres, who would work with Mahmoud Abbas, and a negotiations committee that the Chief of Staff Ehud Barak recommended would be chaired by Head of the Planning Directorate Uzi Dayan. However, I was of the opinion that the issues that would be discussed at the beginning of the process were so sensitive, and the situation so fragile, that the Israeli team should be led by someone with more seniority and experience. Rabin agreed with me and accepted my recommendation to appoint the Deputy Chief of Staff Amnon Lipkin-Shahak for the position.

During the delegation's preparations for the talks, Rabin was invited to visit China. According to the plan, on the way back from China, we were supposed to land for a refueling stopover in Tashkent, the capital of Uzbekistan, where we would be greeted by senior Uzbek government officials led by the president.

Once again, a plan began brewing behind the scenes to change the flight path and to land in Jakarta, the capital of Indonesia, instead of landing in Tashkent. Rabin was supposed to meet there with President Suharto, head of the world's largest Muslim country.

Here as well, the Mossad was involved in organizing the visit and was the one who handled the matter, with complete secrecy. The Indonesians made an uncompromising demand that word of the meeting would not be leaked before it would take place. The Indonesians were so anxious over this that we had been told by the Mossad that if the matter would be leaked, even while the Prime Minister's plane was already circling above the airport in Jakarta, just before landing, the meeting would be canceled. It was supposed to take place on Friday afternoon, and the Indonesians feared that the crowds that would be leaving the mosques after

Friday prayers would hear about the imminent meeting with the Israeli Prime Minister and would begin rioting and sowing chaos in the city streets. The only person from the Prime Minister's staff who was in on the secret was me, and I was in contact with the Mossad. At a certain stage, and after consulting with Rabin, I also updated Eitan Haber and Simon Sheves, and we all maintained full confidentiality, as it was clear that any leak would cancel the historic meeting, whose existence was very important to us.

On the last day of our visit to China we were in Shanghai, and in a free hour we had, Haber and I went for a walk around the local market. As we were walking and staring with astonishment at the local street food stalls, which included mainly frogs and eels, two journalists approached us: Amnon Abramovich and Amir Oren. The two came to us smiling broadly and said, "Say, is it true we're flying to Jakarta?" The blood drained from my face. I was sure that the plan went completely wrong. In an attempt to salvage the situation, I told them this was absolutely incorrect, and that the original plan still stood. To convince them, I produced from my pocket a telegram that had arrived earlier that morning from the Foreign Ministry detailing the landing procedures in Tashkent.

Abramovich and Oren were convinced, and did not run the story, which would have prevented the meeting. After the visit to China, a short while after take-off, Oded Ben-Ami, the Defense Minister's Communications Advisor, took the plane's internal microphone and said, "We wish to inform you about a change in the flight plan. We are not flying to Tashkent but to Indonesia. We could not reveal this until now as it had to be kept secret."

What happened immediately after Ben Ami finished speaking, I could not have imagined: some journalists broke into loud shouts, claiming we had deceived them. There were those who even went so far as to say that it was an actual kidnapping, since we did not ask them if they wanted to go to Jakarta, and some cries of "Liar!"

were also directed at me. Rabin then rose from his chair and said, "Don't shout at Danny. I told him to deny the story, otherwise it would have thwarted a meeting that I think is very important."

In any case, this anecdote did not spoil the satisfaction that accompanied us in those days. We felt that the world was opening up to us: we visited Morocco, and visited Indonesia. There was a sense that Israel was freeing itself of its state of siege, and that Arab and Muslim countries were finally beginning to treat us as a legitimate nation.

Chapter 24

"Dr. Tibi, Please Leave the Room"

When the celebrations had ended and as the initial euphoria faded, we all resumed the difficult, gray, laborious and often even Sisyphean work – of continuing to construct the agreement between the Palestinians and us.

Rabin wanted to begin implementing the Declaration of Principles, but on the Palestinian side nothing was happening. The PLO had never previously been responsible for human life and well-being, and seemed to be finding it difficult to change its "agenda".

Rabin made great efforts towards this end, and among other things, he turned to Mubarak and told him that nothing was moving forward and he wanted his help in shaking up the Palestinians.

In December 1993, some two months after the signing ceremony in Washington, Mubarak summoned Rabin and Arafat to a meeting in Egypt. The meeting started as a private conversation between Rabin and Arafat, and after about forty five minutes they were joined by members of the Israeli and Palestinian delegations.

Rabin began by saying to Arafat, "As I said during our meeting in private, I may have made a mistake by not meeting you immediately after the ceremony at the White House, in order to clarify to you how we understood the declaration we had signed there." Rabin found it necessary to say these things since in the course of negotiations between the two sides, after the signing ceremony, it became clear that each of the parties interpreted the principles agreement in a different way and the gaps were hard to bridge.

Arafat answered Rabin, "The two of us bear full responsibility for what will happen and what will not happen. You are lucky not to be on the Palestinian side." Rabin continued, "During the discussions, we discovered discrepancies with respect to the parties' understanding of the agreement. The agreement deals with the interim period, and subjects that will be part of the permanent agreement (Jerusalem, borders, settlements, refugees, security arrangements for the permanent agreement, the governmental nature of the Palestinian Authority) will be discussed only in accordance with the schedule set by the agreement. This means in the third year out of the five mentioned in the Interim Agreement.

"We are trying to build a very complex thing. When we held peace negotiations with Egypt, we drew a line, which was the border, and each party took its place on the opposing side of the border. Here we are trying to create a life together for Israelis and Palestinians, intertwined with each other.

"I prioritized the negotiations with the Palestinians, and it took me and my colleagues time to realize that the address for conducting these negotiations is the PLO. The negotiations are based on the documents we exchanged regarding mutual recognition, resolving problems by peaceful means, the Declaration of Principles and the accompanying memorandum. These include the following: the permanent status will be discussed separately, settlements will remain in place (during the interim agreement), and Israel is responsible for all matters of security for Israelis and external security (the borders). One of our differences is in the way we interpret the term 'external security.' From our perspective, external security means controlling the borders and crossings, while you claim that according to your understanding the crossings will be under your responsibility or partial responsibility. However, someone who crosses the Jordan River could theoretically be in Tel Aviv tomorrow. It's true that we can close Gaza and the West Bank so that you will not be able to enter Israel - but this is not our intention. I explained it now to Chairman Arafat and found that there are still disagreements on the question of who controls the border crossings."

Arafat listened attentively to Rabin and said, "You have presented an accurate picture of what happened between us. What I said to His Excellency is that I can understand your security needs, but on the other hand – it is written in the signed documents that Palestinian rights will not be infringed (meaning, if every Palestinian who passes through the crossings is inspected by the Israelis, the Palestinians see this as an infringement). Even in the 'Allon Plan,' the border with Jordan was not under your control. I told Rabin that the matter of border security can be solved by joint patrols along with an international element, and so Israel will not be required to have an exclusive military presence along the border with Jordan to protect its security. The crossings are a matter of dignity for us, while it should not bother you, as you already have the upper hand."

Here Arafat used his favorite starting point, that of the underdog, but Rabin was quick to reply, "We are handling negotiations with you as partners."

"And yet you have an advantage. Try to put yourself in our shoes," continued Arafat, in his characteristic way of using emotional manipulation and extortion.

The format of this meeting repeated itself many times in the meetings between the two. At the beginning of the meeting, and to create a common language with Arafat, they negotiated privately or with a recorder on each side, and then the meeting was opened to a wider forum.

At one stage during the meeting in Egypt, Dr. Ahmed Tibi entered the room and took a chair on the side. Dr. Tibi had excellent relations with Arafat and the Palestinians, and acted as their consultant of sorts. Rabin looked at him sharply and said, "Dr. Tibi, you are an Israeli citizen. Who exactly do you represent? I ask you to please leave the room." Tibi heard this, and without skipping a beat – stood up and left.

This format of sessions, starting with face-to-face meetings and then broadening, was designed after we learned that Arafat's behavior contains significant elements of showmanship and hypersensitivity to dignity. Therefore, it was more difficult for him to compromise and change his positions in front of a broader forum and at the presence of his people. In contrast, Arafat felt much more relaxed and at ease in small forums, and was not influenced by the presence of others.

In the meetings between Rabin and Arafat the latter was noticeably tense, and it was clear that he held Rabin in high regard and revered him, perhaps even to the point of apprehension.

In almost every meeting, he repeated the same slogans (in English), such as "look, Your Excellency", "you have the upper hand", "you have superiority over us, so do me a favor, give me this... help me here, add there...". Furthermore, it was always accompanied by a whining tone and an appeal to generosity.

Arafat would sit intent and attentive, listening to every word that came out of Rabin's mouth, and occasionally he would be seen writing notes in a small notebook.

At the stage in which other people would join the meeting, he let them speak, in part because these people were the ones who conducted the negotiations with the Israelis and were more knowledgeable than him on many of the issues. He usually let them argue with us about disputed points, allowing them to "fire all the ammo", and finally he would join and present his opinion.

Over time, you could tell he was becoming more relaxed and loose in the way he sat. Arafat's attitude towards Rabin during the meetings between them was a mixture of respect and awe. It was no coincidence that he was careful to address him as "His Excellency" – he really meant it.

However, even when the atmosphere was more relaxed, Arafat continued to adhere to one rule: he would never get physically closer to Rabin than a handshake's distance. Arafat would kiss everyone he met, but did not dare to imagine kissing Rabin, as he was afraid of him and also noticed the coldness Rabin displayed towards him. With other Israelis, Arafat continued to uphold the "kissing commandment."

The Americans also feared Arafat's hugs and kisses. Prior to the signing ceremony of the Declaration of Principles on the White House lawn, President Clinton was particularly concerned about the possibility of having to participate in Arafat's hugging and kissing exhibition on the stage. The Americans, who are very deliberate and calculated people, much more so than is commonly attributed to them, found a way to prevent this: while the right hand was shaking Arafat's right hand, the left hand was holding Arafat's same right hand near the elbow and by exerting minor force, prevented any chance of uncalled-for proximity.

Rabin did not like Arafat, in my opinion until the end of his days. There was no chemistry between them, but Rabin was a very rationalistic person and with him, reason always prevailed over emotion. For Rabin, if the road to promote the peace process dictated speaking with Arafat, then he would speak with him, but he did not have to hug him. Rabin viewed Arafat as a partner but not as a friend.

Nevertheless, and despite his feelings, Rabin never offended Arafat and took care to keep his dignity as a person, and even behaved very politely towards him. However, he was also not afraid to speak harshly with him when necessary. After Rabin was murdered Arafat said of him, "He was a tough but fair partner."

In the meetings held in the presence of others, Arafat insisted on speaking in English, a language which he did not fully master, to put it mildly. He would often get confused and many times words "disappeared" from his vocabulary. When he would notice that he was having trouble with English, he would switch to Arabic and then required the assistance of Saeb Erekat, who among other things served as his regular interpreter. Rabin did not like Erekat due to his extreme and stubborn positions, and he used to call him "a pain in the…"

Rabin viewed the implementation of the Declaration of Principles as a test for the Palestinians and insisted it be fulfilled.

"Our main problem is security, and without it the Israeli public will not support the agreement," he said. "We need to immediately commence the work of the two important committees: 'Gaza and Jericho First' and the economic committee."

Rabin also addressed the moral aspects of our control over the Palestinian people, and this was another reason he wished to hasten the implementation of the agreement.

Many months later, while Rabin was briefing Amnon Lipkin-Shahak before he departed for another round of talks between the Israeli and Palestinian delegations at Taba, he said to him, "Focus on security matters and only then hear what the Palestinians have to say regarding the early transfer of powers."

It should be emphasized that security issues were Rabin's top priority, and he devoted many hours to these issues in the principles agreement and also in the next agreements, in order to ensure the safety and security of all Israelis within the Green Line and beyond it.

Regarding the economic arrangement between us and the Palestinians, the Ministry of Finance presented two possible economic regimes for the relationship between us. One was a Palestinian free trade zone, which would require a physical border between us and them, with a fence, with inspection stations, with customs and anti-smuggling measures. The second was a regime of a "customs union", which would mean that the rate of customs duty and the import regime of Israel and the Palestinian Authority would be identical: the same laws and the same tariff would apply to both parties. In this case, the border between Israel and the Palestinians would be open economically, but the Palestinians would be subject to the laws that apply to financial relations between Israelis and foreigners.

Rabin wanted that economically, it would be an open border, meaning the unification of customs, and that goods could pass without an import tax being imposed - the same law and the same prices for both sides.

Rabin stressed to Lipkin-Shahak that control over the border crossing between Israel and Jordan at the Allenby Bridge, and between Israel and Egypt at the Rafah terminal, would remain ours.

Since we were discussing a redeployment in Gaza, it was very important for Rabin that border security, including control of the crossings, would be under Israel's responsibility. He asked that the negotiation team ensure that the area remaining in Israel's hands would include blocs of settlements rather than isolated settlements. Thus Gush Katif, which was composed of a cluster of settlements; an additional bloc in northern Gaza that included

Dugit, Nissanit and Elei Sinai; and the two isolated settlements Kfar Darom and Netzarim came to be.

Rabin further stressed that the control and security of the roads would be under Israel's responsibility, and that we must not agree to a situation wherein the Palestinian police would have the power to arrest a settler or any other Israeli.

The Declaration of Principles was an inclusive document that we now had to be break into fine details and breathe everyday life into in practice.

Regarding the Palestinian Charter, the agreement was that the PNC (Palestinian National Council) would void all the clauses that contravene Israel's right to exist and would approve the Declaration of Principles and accompanying memorandum. Arafat had to convene the PNC for it to void twenty-eight of the Charter's thirty-three articles, by a majority of two-thirds.

Rabin dealt with all these details even if they had only symbolic value, such as whether the Palestinian flag would be raised alongside the Israeli flag at the border crossings; if a Palestinian policeman would be on the Allenby Bridge which was under Israeli responsibility; and if Israel would allow the Palestinians to use their own stamps – a characteristic of sovereignty.

Finally, he consented to the flag being raised, the policeman on the bridge and also approved the stamps. Although at that point he had not uttered the words "Palestinian state" – it seemed as though he was gradually nurturing the idea.

At the stage of "Gaza and Jericho First", the Palestinians demanded that the settlers would not be allowed to carry arms when they would enter areas under Palestinian control, but Rabin did not agree to this. Then they demanded that the settlers would only carry handguns and to that Rabin also refused, and he also objected their proposal that a settler would have to produce a license to carry a gun when he entered the Palestinian areas.

Consequently, the Palestinians argued that if Israeli citizens were permitted to bear arms then they demand that a Palestinian citizen would also be allowed to bear arms. Rabin objected, saying that only the Palestinian security forces would carry weapons. He insisted that the army would be allowed to conduct hot pursuit even inside the Palestinian areas, and finally it was agreed by both parties that if a pursuit continued into Palestinian areas – the Israeli forces would conduct it until the Palestinian security forces would arrive and resume the pursuit.

Rabin listed Israel's geographical order of importance, and detailed – in descending order – what we could not compromise on and where we could be flexible. Jerusalem was the most important and no concessions would be made in it; afterwards - parts of the West Bank, which Israel would demand remain under its sovereignty, on account of their importance to national security; next came the Golan Heights; and finally the Gaza Strip, where it would be easier to make concessions than in any other region.

The principle agreement stated that the Palestinians would control Gaza and the West Bank, except for the settlements, specified military areas and in the areas related to the permanent agreement - which Israel would control. The fate of the areas related to the permanent agreement would be discussed during the negotiations for this agreement.

The interpretation of this matter is a subject of dispute between the Palestinians and us to this very day: the Palestinians claim that at the end of the interim agreement Israel should only remain in settlements and military camps, and the rest of the territory is to be transferred to Palestinian control. Israel claims that according to Rabin's approach, the Israeli deployment is not limited to settlements and military camps but also includes security areas.

"One broad security area that I see," said Rabin, "is an area that would ensure we control all the roads leading to Jerusalem.

The second region is the Jordan Valley, because this is a security perimeter bordering with a country with whom we do not have a peace treaty (this was before the peace treaty with Jordan was signed), and that is how I interpret external security. These things relate to the interim agreement – we will discuss the permanent agreement in due time."

"We will not be able to treat Judea and Samaria as we treat Gaza," Rabin continued, "That is to say, that the IDF remains only in the settlement blocs and along the borders and roads. The State will continue to control large parts of Judea and Samaria via the IDF, in part because of Jerusalem, which can be accessed from many directions, and also because of external security."

In late June 1994, Arafat asked to visit Gaza and Jericho. Rabin confirmed only the visit to Gaza, but when Arafat landed in Gaza, an Egyptian and Palestinian request was made that he be allowed to also visit Jericho, and Rabin approved it, on the condition that the transit would be made by flight. In addition, Rabin did not authorize murderers of Israelis to come in the entourage that accompanied Arafat, and for all other escorts, the condition was that whoever entered, would leave immediately after the visit.

Rabin was a very pragmatic man and believed that we should go to an interim agreement, rather than immediately proceed to the permanent agreement. He thought that discussion of the permanent agreement would lead to the talks collapsing immediately, due to serious problems being put on the agenda, such as Jerusalem, settlements, the refugees' right of return, security arrangements, borders and the nature of the Palestinian entity. Rabin understood that discussing these issues while the two parties were not yet ready to make concessions – would lead to a breakdown. Rabin further assumed that an interim agreement would allow the parties to adjust and enable us to examine the Palestinians' seriousness, and if it would be necessary to backtrack, it would be possible to do so during an interim agreement but not under a permanent agreement.

Rabin's approach to the West Bank was affected by the large amount of Israeli settlements, military camps and installations located there. "Without formulating a comprehensive approach to the interim agreement, we will find ourselves giving the Palestinians some parts here and some there," he said. "We will have to determine broad security areas for the interim stage, and additional areas where control over security affairs will be ours and civilian control theirs." In these sayings, Rabin had begun to plant the seeds for the idea that later came to be known as Areas A, B, and C.

"The roads to Jerusalem and the Jordan Valley are first priority," said Rabin, "afterwards the Israeli settlement blocs. The isolated settlements such as Kfar Darom and Netzarim will be harder to protect."

Rabin said that early transfer of powers is very complex. "I do not want the Palestinian populace to be harmed as a result of powers being transferred without an orderly body to receive them existing yet," said Rabin. "It is not clear where the funding for the civilian activities will come from, such as salaries for teachers which are currently paid by the State of Israel through the Civil Administration."

Rabin always said that without an interim agreement there was no chance for a permanent agreement. Without the Palestinians understanding the meaning of being responsible for more than two million citizens - to handle education, garbage disposal, sewage, taxes, electricity and police - and without the Palestinians proving that they were able to fight terrorism, there was no chance of a permanent agreement being reached.

It was important for Rabin to stress, "The agreement in principle we have signed is not a peace treaty, but it is a major step toward peace. We emphasized five points: during the interim period there will be five years that are part of the interim agreement, but in the third year we will begin to discuss the permanent agreement and these discussions will be finished by the end of the five years, and immediately afterwards the implementation of the permanent agreement will begin. During the interim period Jerusalem will stay united in its current state without any division, and it will be discussed in the final agreement. The settlements will remain in place during the interim agreement. Not a single settlement will move," he said.

Rabin insisted until the day he died not to move a single settlement, because he believed that if the fate of the settlements would be discussed before the permanent agreement, it would alter the balance of power. He believed that if we would evacuate settlements, contrary to what we had agreed upon, it would greatly weaken our stand when we begin to discuss their fate as part of the negotiations for the permanent agreement.

The right wing became antagonistic toward Rabin after the IDF departed from parts of the West Bank and Gaza, leaving the Palestinians in control there. Attacks against settlers originating from the areas under Palestinian control led the settlers to accuse Rabin of abandoning them.

Rabin greatly appreciated most of the settlers. He appreciated their willingness to live in dangerous places for ideological reasons, and he highly appreciated the fact that they served in the army, enlisted to combat units and volunteered for command positions.

During the years in which he served as Defense Minister, he had a close relationship with the settlers. For this reason, the hateful statements that came from them after the Oslo Accords were signed, and phrases such as "traitor", and *"Moser ve'Rodef"* (traitor and persecutor), hurt him deeply, and when the community leaders, among them rabbis, wanted to meet with him - he refused.

***

In September 1994, discussions of the interim agreement began, but there were two matters that Rabin insisted on finishing before the start of the agreement's implementation: the Palestinians had to fight radical Islamic terror, which continued to originate from the areas under Palestinian responsibility, and they had to void the relevant articles of the Palestinian Charter.

Palestinian terrorism was not the only thing that concerned Rabin. In every chance he had, especially in meetings with leaders of other countries, he would present his doctrine and concerns regarding negative developments in the Middle East. "In the past, the Middle East was part of a showdown between two super-powers: the United States and the Soviet Union," he would explain, "Today we are witnessing radical Islam's attempts to undermine various regimes, including moderate Arab regimes, and to destroy the peace process. What we are in fact seeing here is Khomeinism without Khomeini. It is a radical Islamic movement, garnering support among extremists in those countries, who believe that by doing so they serve their nation."

In every such meeting, immediately after he began speaking, we would quietly count the minutes until the phrase "Khomeinism without Khomeini" was brought up. Rabin gave the example of Hezbollah, an Islamic-oriented movement influenced by Iran but also by Lebanese interests, and whose purpose was to drive Israel out of southern Lebanon (the IDF was still in southern Lebanon at the time). In this way Islamic and national interests converged.

Rabin believed that this was not a revolution coming from the outside, but an attempt to spread Khomeinism using local citizens who felt that they were serving their own Islamic and nationalist goals. Rabin viewed this as the main reason that these types of movements managed to recruit so many people. It was a radical religious conception of Islam, which decrees the rules of behavior for the people, the individual and the state. It was a global process, starting in the neighborhood mosque with an imam who knew how to excite and incite, and continuing in the construction of kindergartens, schools, clinics and providing services to citizens. Thus the movement manages to take control over areas where ill-fated people lived, people that no other body – including the state – addresses their suffering.

Iran has ambitions to undermine moderate Islamic regimes by means of the Islamic movements, and in addition to build conventional military power in the short term. In the long run it seeks to build unconventional power, including nuclear arms. Rabin believed that this was the main threat to the peace process in the short term, and a threat to the entire world in the long term. When you think about these things today, it is amazing to see just how relevant and true his words on the subject still are to this very day.

Over the course of 1994, Rabin was invited to many ceremonies in which he was given awards for his efforts to promote peace. In all these places Arafat would also be, and the occasion was used for work meetings between the two of them.

In these meetings Rabin tried to be very practical and would immediately present the breadth of his plans and demands to Arafat.

In one of these meetings, at the UNESCO award ceremony in Paris in July 1994, Rabin said to Arafat, "I want to outline the way negotiations will continue. You have problems and I have problems but we will have to overcome them. There are three issues that demand immediate attention. One is the continued implementation of 'Gaza and Jericho,' including things such as the international border crossings in Rafah and Allenby, the area of Jericho and its surroundings, security of the crossings and placing a Palestinian policeman on the bridge. The second thing is continuing negotiations for the early transfer of powers. Lastly, the third issue is convening a quadrilateral committee of Israel, the Palestinians, Jordan and Egypt to discuss the question of displaced persons, the Palestinians from the West Bank and the Gaza Strip who fled during the Six-Day War. We recommend that the committee will be in the presence of the foreign ministers of Israel, Egypt and Jordan, and your representative. Regarding economic issues - as long as there is no mechanism capable of receiving the funds and reporting where they are being sent, the donor countries will not transfer funds. You should make sure your fiscal system is transparent and reports its revenues and expenses."

Arafat seemed totally shocked by Rabin's words. It was clear that this was the first time he encountered a situation wherein he had to handle money according to Western standards, and not as he had been accustomed to. Until then, all the money went directly into his hands and he was the sole decision-maker to whom and what he gave of it, while pocketing some of the money for himself.

Rabin relentlessly continued to say to Arafat, "What's going on with the amendments to the Palestinian charter? You took it upon yourself to do this, so why is it not happening?"

Arafat's reply was, "As soon as I can convene the PNC, I will do it. We already reached a decision in 1988 in the PLO to accept the two-state solution."

Yet Rabin persisted: "I'm talking about the commitment you undertook as part of the Oslo Accords."

Eventually it was agreed in Paris to continue the work of four committees: a committee for early transfer of powers, primarily in the areas of health, education, tourism, social welfare and taxation; completion of the 'Gaza-Jericho' process; a quadrilateral committee for the issue of the displaced persons; and the economic committee.

At a meeting between Rabin and King Hussein in Aqaba, in September of that year, Rabin again addressed the question of the refugees and told the king that Israel would not agree to refugees returning as part of the right of return, neither to Israel nor to the Territories. "The solution," said Rabin, "has to be in the places where the refugees have lived for decades, and there they will receive international aid. Upon its establishment, the State of Israel increased its population by recognizing the Israeli-Arabs as citizens, and the expectation is that the Israeli government will care for them. Why should Egypt, Jordan, Lebanon and Syria, within which these refugees have been living for decades, not do the same?"

King Hussein and Rabin also discussed the Palestinian Authority's powers. The Palestinians suggested establishing a body that would be divided into two parts: legislative and executive – similar to a parliament and government. Rabin, however, did not agree that the Palestinians would have legislative powers, but rather agreed only that an executive branch be established.

Rabin deliberated extensively on the question of whether the IDF would withdraw from the cities first and only then elections would be held in the Palestinian Authority, or the other way around.

Eventually he convinced Arafat that the elections would take place first and then the IDF would exit the cities. The lure for this agreement was a transfer of additional powers to the Palestinians.

Rabin told Arafat that members of the government suggested to him to consider the possibility of opening dialogue with Hamas. "I said I would not do so under any terms," said Rabin. "I explained that you are the leader of the Palestinian people, you are our partner, we have only one address for dialogue - and that is you, and if I want something done with Hamas I will speak with you."

In his meetings with Arafat, Rabin was focused and purposeful, and did all he could to advance the stalled process. At a meeting that took place in one of Israel's Civil Administration's facilities at the Erez crossing, on January 19, 1995, he tried to unclog the bottleneck on issues that the delegations were unable to resolve themselves.

"We can spend all day making mutual complaints, but we need to send a message that we are committed to the process," said Rabin. "Our disagreements strengthen the opponents of peace. We need to continue with security issues, the IDF's redeployment, elections, early transfer of powers and economic issues."

Arafat complained that Israel continued to build new settlements in the Territories, but Rabin immediately interrupted him, "My government has decided to suspend the decisions of the previous government with respect to new settlements in the Territories. Since then, no new settlement has been built. We made this decision even before Oslo and the Declaration of Principles. We further decided that no government funding will be given to existing settlements beyond what is essential for daily life. We cannot prevent private construction in existing settlements, since there is no law in Israel that can prevent privately-funded construction, but we will make sure that the construction takes place solely within the boundaries of existing settlements."

Rabin also referred to Arafat's claims regarding expropriation of land, and said, "Expropriation of land is done according to the IDF's redeployment and for the sake of bypass roads. We have not expropriated land for the construction of houses, and if you have any conflicting information, then I ask to know of it. We need to prepare the settlements for the interim period: paving roads that bypass Arab villages, investing in defensive measures and security arrangements for the settlements. We limited the distance of the security fence from the outlying houses in every town to a range of fifty meters."

Over time, this issue repeatedly served Arafat in his complaints that the settlements continued to develop within their boundaries. However, Rabin told him that beyond the construction of the town's security fence, at a distance of fifty meters from its last house, he did not commit to anything with respect to the town's inner development. Moreover, Rabin realized that the natural growth in the settlements' population must be adequately addressed.

Time and again, he firmly and rigidly repeated his demands to eradicate terrorism within the Gaza Strip and complained about the terrorism that came out of Gaza. At the same time, Rabin was careful to "soften" Arafat with several leniencies: The Allenby Bridge would not operate according to limited working hours, but would remain open as long as Palestinians were on the bridge. Furthermore, one-hundred truckloads of goods could go from Egypt to Gaza through Rafah without the goods having to be unloaded at the crossing and transferred to other trucks in the "back-to-back" system.

However, the problem of terrorism had grown into monstrous proportions following the wave of terrorist attacks that began to wash over the country, one of the first and most tragic of them being the suicide bombing on January 22, 1995, at the Beit Lid junction. As usual, Rabin appeared at the scene of the attack shortly after its occurrence, and witnessed the gruesome sights in what had become a killing field.

Rabin immediately called a situation briefing, decided to commence wide-scale arrests of Hamas and Islamic Jihad members, and ordered to reinforce IDF forces in the Territories and that the area be placed under curfew. He also sent a message to Arafat through Yossi Ginosar, to the effect that the problem of terrorism from Gaza and Jericho endangered the peace process, and that Arafat needed to take care of it immediately and arrest the terrorist Yahya Ayyash, nicknamed "The Engineer", who was behind most of the attacks. Rabin made this a central test for Arafat, who had failed to take action against the architects of terrorist attacks, even though we supplied him with the terrorists' exact names.

Rabin demanded that Arafat confiscate the weapons of all who were not members of his security forces, and that a legal enforcement system be established to try the terrorists and send them to jail. Rabin also demanded that Arafat extradite murderers of Israelis whose names were submitted to him as early as December 1993.

Arafat's answer to this request was both unfounded and outrageous: according to him, the two terrorists who exploded one after the other at the Beit Lid junction were Shin Bet agents, and the attack was a deliberate act of provocation. As evidence, he mentioned the fact that the two of them easily came to Israel from Gaza, and reached as far as Beit Lid completely undisturbed despite carrying such large explosives.

Were they not Shin Bet agents, Arafat said, they could not have done it.

"Enough with his rubbish!" was Rabin's response to this.

As part of the deceitful reality of the Middle East, there were periods in which there was a "golden age" between the intelligence agencies: the Israeli Mossad and Shin Bet, and the Palestinian security services. At the time, cooperation between these services was effective and yielded many results.

Additionally, Arafat negotiated with Hamas and other organizations in an effort to join them to the PA. Arafat claimed that while Hamas's internal leadership (based in Gaza) was inclined to accept his proposals, its external leadership based in Jordan - headed by Mousa Abu Marzouk and Khaled Mashal - was adopting more extremist stances, in part because Syria and Iran supported Hamas and encouraged it to continue its terrorism.

Even today, more than two decades after that period, this description of the internal and external leadership of Hamas and their array of considerations and the pressures they are under - remain the same. You could see the same patterns of behavior and thinking in Hamas during Operation "Protective Edge" against Hamas in Gaza in the summer of 2014.

Multiple attempts were made to reconcile the two sides. In one of them, Rabin initiated a confidential meeting with the heads of the Palestinian security forces in April 1995 in Tel Aviv, in order to create direct dialogue with them without going through Arafat, and to stress to them their role in the war on terror.

The meeting took place in an isolated place, and all participants arrived concealed in vehicles whose windows were shut. The participants at that meeting were Palestinian Chief of Police Nasser Yousef, General Majaida of the Palestinian delegation to the talks, Head of the Preventive Security Force Mohammed Dahlan and Head of General Intelligence Amin al-Hindi.

Rabin began by saying, "I welcome this meeting. The aim of the negotiations is to reach a solution of peace between the two peoples. The Israeli government wants to see a Palestinian entity separate from us alongside the State of Israel, but the main obstacle to this is the terrorism of Hamas and Islamic Jihad. Among us there are also those who oppose the peace process, but barring one exception - the massacre at the Cave of Machpelah - there are almost no cases of Israelis killing Palestinians.

"There were two Israeli groups named *Kach* and *Koach*, whose members made radical statements against Arabs and against peace, and were outlawed by my government. Eight of their activists, who did not commit acts of violence but continued their illegal political activity, were subject to six-month administrative detention and more, and the others we issued restraining orders."

"I am being told everywhere that the Palestinians cannot control terrorism in Gaza," continued Rabin, "and if that is the case, I must answer the question of how exactly I intend to give you control over Tulkarm, Nablus and Qalqilya. The key to the continuation of the process and the development of your economy is the ability to maintain law and order and control the area under your responsibility. For this purpose, I asked Arafat to act decisively against those who use weapons illegally and act against the process; to fight terrorism; prevent incitement; to establish the PA's rule over the areas under its control; and to allow only one armed force to exist, one that is responsible for maintaining law and order. Remember that the great tragedy in Lebanon started with each community holding its own armed force.

"The PLO has never been responsible for the fate of the civilian population. Now you have to worry about food, employment, water, sewage and security, and I know this is difficult. We are in a critical situation in the process and I want to move forward, but I cannot do so unless the leadership of the PLO, together with yourselves, will make serious efforts in your fight against terrorism."

As a display of empathy and to show that he understood them, Rabin said, "We also had problems at the country's outset: the Irgun, led by Menachem Begin, did not obey the provisions of the leadership headed by Ben-Gurion. I was a brigade commander at the time and was sent to command the company that prepared to prevent the arrival of the ship 'Altalena,' which carried weapons that were destined for the Irgun, and intended to anchor at the coast of Tel Aviv. A battle ensued in which the Irgun suffered fifteen casualties and we suffered one, but there was no choice – a resolution had to be reached to ensure that there would only be one armed force and only one government authority. Thus Ben-

Gurion made it clear that there is only one source of authority and only one armed force - the IDF.

"You must bring those responsible for terrorism to justice and make the verdicts public, in order to convey the message that a decision has been made to fight terrorism."

When he had finished speaking, Rabin looked at his watch and said, "I have talked for a long time. I came from the army, but once I became a politician I started making lengthy speeches..."

There was an air of openness, listening and goodwill in the room. The Palestinians listened to Rabin intently and treated him with respect. It was evident they were very pleased that the meeting took place, and that Arafat was absent. It added to their honor, since until that day, they had only met with Rabin as part of an entourage.

At that stage, the Palestinians began to answer him and Nasser Yousef said, "I agree with what you have said, there is no return from the path of peace. Security worries us, too, and our main difficulty is that we are facing armed opposition. The difficult economic situation in Gaza also encourages extremism against the Palestinian government. The diplomatic process is being drawn out, which does not allow us to gain popularity among our public, who is finding it difficult to see the fruits of peace. The Israeli response to the attacks also makes it very difficult for us. Security measures alone will not be able to improve the situation. A Palestinian policeman earns 260 dollars a month and this is a very small sum. Syria, Jordan and Iran are against us. Our circumstances are significantly different from yours."

Amin al-Hindi joined the conversation by saying, "The Palestinian public expects more leniency in the border crossings and permits for students from Gaza to study in the West Bank."

"Providing security for Israelis separately - this method will not succeed in Gaza," said Dahlan. "I suggest that the security presence will be shared - we are willing to put our hands into the fire. Together it will be easier to deal with Hamas. We are working steadily to destroy Hamas and Islamic Jihad, we are pressuring the extremists and negotiating with the moderates. The method is not to fight terrorism, as long as the situation has yet to become unbearable, and to try and recruit Hamas as a partner to the process."

Rabin thought differently than Dahlan and answered, "The more you succeed in the war against terrorism, the more you will succeed in your negotiations with Hamas."

Then as now, the impact of foreign elements on events in the Territories is considerable and it is always what leads to more extreme positions being taken. At that time, Arafat had indeed been making efforts to engage in dialogue and to negotiate with Hamas and Islamic Jihad in Gaza. The members of Islamic Jihad showed willingness that Gaza would cease to be a haven for terrorist activities and tried to convince Fathi Shaqaqi, head of the Islamic Jihad, who was based in Syria. However, the Iranians thwarted the affair, told Shaqaqi that they would view it as an act of treason and warned him that if he would agree to it, Iran would cease all its financial support for the organization. It was the same with Hamas officials in Gaza, who found it difficult to receive authorization from their leadership in Jordan to enter negotiations with the Palestinian Authority.

On the background of the terrorist attacks, handling the lingering and often stuttering process with the Palestinians, and domestic and international pressure, Rabin also had to deal in those days with vicious incitement against him by the Israeli right-wing movements.

Nevertheless, on August 1995, against the background of a turbulent and charged atmosphere, Rabin met with the heads of the settlers' Yesha Council. The meeting was attended by Chairman of the Yesha Council Uri Ariel, Pinchas Wallerstein and Ze'ev Hever ('Zambish').

The atmosphere in the room was tense and gradually became tenser as the minutes passed. Rabin came to the meeting very angry and immediately began by saying, "There is a basic disagreement between us. We will not go to a referendum because I have a mandate. We still have essential disagreements with the Palestinians and therefore the Yesha Council's request to see the maps ahead of the interim agreement, and to be involved in drawing the map, is irrelevant at the moment because even the government has yet to see the map. In general terms, the Palestinian police will require our authorization to enter the 'yellow area' - Area B, which is the area in which the Palestinian Authority has civilian control and Israel has security control. Private lands owned by Jews - even those in the 'brown area,' Area A, which is under civilian and security control of the Palestinian Authority – will remain in Jewish ownership.

"The Palestinian police will have twenty-five police stations in Area B, even though the Palestinians wanted 30, and the movement of Palestinian police will be from one village to another on the basis of Israel's authorization. In Area C, the 'white area,' civilian and security responsibility will be in Israel's hands."

"The discussion of the final agreement will start around 1997," Rabin added, "and by then there will be elections in Israel and the people will decide who they support."

Afterwards, Rabin promised to examine their request to see the map, and later he even enabled one of their representatives - Ze'ev Hever – to meet with the IDF Commander of Central Command Ilan Biran, see the map, comment and make requests.

During the meeting, the settlers' representatives mentioned problems relating to everyday life in the settlements, and Rabin promised them, "We will establish a committee that will be chaired by Noah Kinarti (the Defense Minister's Adviser for Settlements and Development Areas). There will also be a representative of the Ministry of Housing there and a lawyer. The committee will examine the settlers' requests resulting from the natural development of the communities. But remember: my government does not prioritize Judea and Samara, and do not interpret committees' establishment as a renewed impetus for the settlement movement."

In the two months that followed, Rabin was mostly busy promoting the interim stage with the Palestinians and the elections in the PA.

In September, he met with Mubarak in Egypt and said to him, "We hope that Egypt will be more helpful in making connections between the Arab world and Israel. I find it difficult to understand the Syrians, Damascus is a center for extremist groups, and Iran is fanning the flames of terrorism. Even the Arab League has played a negative role and is not encouraging peace."

"We tried to influence the Arab League to create a more positive direction for peace," said Mubarak, "and the problem of terrorism is very difficult for all of us - I also have terrorism in Egypt."

"Egypt has great influence in the Arab world, but I do not feel you use it to promote the peace process," Rabin answered. "You have to help convince that we are on the right track and show more openness. Even informal relationships such as those created with Morocco, Tunisia and Oman can help."

"The Saudis will not agree to direct contact for the time being, but only after you complete the negotiations with the Palestinians," Mubarak said, "But I promise to work with the other Arab nations so that they will support the process."

In late October, we took part in the economic summit in Jordan. It was an impressive and interesting event. Entering the hall in Amman, I could not help but feel excited - the place was full of Arab representatives dressed in Keffiyehs and Djellabas, and there was a lot of openness towards us. Everyone wanted to shake our hands and chat. There was a feeling that a substantial change had occurred in the Arab world's attitude towards us. The Arab representatives expressed interest in doing business with the Israelis, to talk about cooperation, about a new Middle East. There was a sense that we were going in the right direction towards solving the Middle Eastern conflict. For Rabin - who was then at the height of pressures from the right wing, disappointment from the Palestinians' dawdling in the process, and a vicious incitement campaign against him raging in the streets of Israel - these were rare moments of comfort and satisfaction in those days. He looked radiant, very relaxed and smiled often at the representatives of the many countries who approached him, intrigued and excited to meet him.

The peace process with the Palestinians occupied Rabin until his last day. On Friday, November 3, 1995, Rabin met with Chief of Staff Amnon Lipkin-Shahak and instructed him to start preparing for the additional "redeployment." However, he stressed that it should not be done before the elections in the Palestinian Authority, which were set to take place on January 20, 1996.

In these elections, the Chairman of the Palestinian Authority and eighty-two members of the Palestinian National Council were to be elected.

One of the issues surrounding the elections was the matter of 30,000 eligible voters in Jerusalem. The Palestinians wanted to place ballots in Jerusalem and Rabin refused because of the symbolic nature of the matter. It was agreed that these eligible voters would vote at ballots outside of Jerusalem, except for the sick and the elderly who had difficulty traveling, who would be able to vote in the postal agencies of East Jerusalem.

Regarding the candidates, Rabin authorized that Jerusalem residents could only be elected if they had an additional residential address outside of Jerusalem - to prevent a situation in which a resident of Israel would be elected to the Palestinian parliament.

Rabin did not get a chance to witness the elections in the Palestinian Authority – as he was murdered the day after that meeting.

Chapter 25

"Netanyahu Might Win"

Shimon Peres was appointed Prime Minister immediately after Rabin's murder, and upon taking office, he began vigorous negotiations with the Palestinians.

Unlike the Syrian negotiations track, wherein some of the things he was exposed to could be considered a surprising discovery, Peres was very involved in the Palestinian track, and he resumed Rabin's course of action.

One of the first issues that required Peres' attention was the matter of separation. I had already expressed my support of this and thought that we must move to separate the Israeli and Palestinian populations. This meant reducing the number of Palestinians working in Israel to a bare minimum and making an effort to create alternative sources of employment for the Palestinians.

Peres said that the fence's location should be determined according to security and diplomatic concerns. "It will not be long before the fence is seen as the border between the Palestinians and us," said Peres. "For this reason, we need to set up a joint team of army, police and finances – tasked with examining alternatives for protecting the borderline, including in the budgetary aspect. Sometimes you have to take security risks to avoid destroying the economy."

Peres also argued that we were in a period of transition, and should return to the "carrot and stick" policy: Establishing relations between Israeli settlements and Palestinians, meetings between professional associations and constructing industrial parks, while at the same time creating the separation. He stressed. "I am in favor of separation between the two peoples but not between land and land. The intention is to create security separation so that we can better inspect the Palestinians who enter highly populated Israeli areas."

Peres decided to set an earlier date for the redeployment's implementation, i.e. the new deployment of IDF forces resulting from the transfer of Gaza and Jericho to the Palestinians, and planned that by the end of April the redeployment in Hebron would be complete, and the Palestinians would be under Palestinian self-rule there. In May 1996, discussions of the permanent agreement would begin and would last for three years. In August 1996, the additional redeployment was scheduled to start, as according to the plan there were to be three re-deployments, each six months apart from the other.

In meetings with Arafat, Peres repeatedly reassured him that the new government is committed to everything that had been agreed with the previous government.

Peres did not intend to make any further concessions to the Palestinians before the elections in Israel, which at that time were still scheduled to take place in October 1996. People in Peres' circle urged him to hold the elections immediately and thus to bolster his administration for four more years, allowing him to do a lot more than in the year that remained until the elections. Eventually the elections in Israel were scheduled for the end of May due to Peres' conception that "we need a new mandate from the people and not a mandate given because of Rabin's murder."

Elections in the Palestinian Authority took place on January 20, 1996, and Peres was very pleased by that, saying, "No one gave Palestinians authorities, only us. We did it without anyone pressuring us, because we do not want to continue to rule over another people. For years we had said this, and now we are actually fulfilling it."

Arafat won the elections by a majority of 83 percent, and the volume of terrorism was declining, but Peres, who was a realistic man, said something that in retrospect was an accurate prediction of the future - "one terrorist act can devastate the achievement entirely."

Rabin, as Peres, had also realized how fragile and volatile the agreement was. The two leaders understood that it would not be easy to bring it to fruition, as it had not garnered wide public support. No one had forgotten that Rabin passed the agreement in the Knesset by a margin of one MK (Alex Goldfarb). Each time the Israeli public's sense of security was undermined, opposition to the process increased. The Israeli public's support or opposition of the agreement was closely related to their sense of security.

When Rabin was asked what would happen if the PA fails to prevail over the terrorist organizations, he would say that in the worst case scenario, the IDF would reconquer the Territories. I believe that the Palestinians' goal was to reach an agreement with Israel according to their worldview: Arafat wanted to enter the process of negotiations, but without conceding 'red lines' such as the right of return, and he had no problem with the possibility that ultimately an agreement would not be signed.

Some speculated that Arafat entered negotiations with Israel because of his weak and problematic status resulting from his support of Saddam Hussein in the first Gulf War.

Arafat had no problem signing the Oslo Accords, because at that time the discussion of the most difficult issues was postponed to the permanent agreement, and other issues remained vague. During Rabin's term the agreement with the Palestinians had been developing nicely over time, and I am convinced that if Rabin had not been murdered there would have been peace with the Palestinians by now.

Meanwhile, as the elections in Israel drew near, in February-March 1996 the country was swept by a horrendous wave of terrorism, and in its wake Peres decided to intensify the war against Hamas and deport some its members. Peres forbade the deportation of women and children, and ordered to arrest preachers of murder including clerics and politicians. As an almost desperate step in the face of rampant terrorism, Peres decided to establish the Counter-Terrorism Bureau headed by Director of the Shin Bet, Ami Ayalon.

Following these terrorist attacks, for the first and last time, Arafat mobilized his forces and began to fight terrorism, but it was too little too late.

It should be noted that these events did not cause Peres to change his basic approach that the more pressure the United States and Europe put on Arafat, the better the results would be.

On March 13, 1996, the Sharm el-Sheikh summit was convened in the presence of US President Clinton, European leaders, Egyptian President Mubarak, King Hussein, Arafat and other Arab rulers. It was agreed there that the CIA would assist the Palestinians to combat Hamas and Islamic Jihad terrorism, and the US would give Israel $100 million to purchase protective measures and means to combat terrorism.

After a long period of time, Arafat also began, as mentioned, to act against terrorism. He tried to be clever with Hamas and to drive a wedge between the organization's leaders: negotiate with the moderates, and arrest the extremists for investigation. He failed.

The Israeli elections were rapidly approaching, and Peres reiterated, "I have an advantage over my rival Netanyahu, but the terrorist attacks are hurting me. If the attacks continue, we might have to suspend the peace process, and Netanyahu will win."

On April 1996, Peres met with Arafat at the Erez checkpoint. At the meeting, Peres commended the cooperation between the Israelis and Palestinians, which had greatly improved. "Thank Amin al-Hindi and Head of Preventive Security Mohammed Dahlan," said Peres to Arafat, and Arafat was quick to reply, "Do not thank them until they catch Mohammed Deif and Adnan al-Ghoul, the most senior wanted men that Israel asked to arrest." At this, everyone present burst out in great laughter.

On April 30, Clinton entertained Peres for lunch, and noted that Arafat had shown courage in his fight against terrorism, and that support for peace among the Palestinians had grown significantly. Clinton was to meet Arafat later and asked Peres what he thought was important that he say to Arafat.

"We plan to start negotiations for a permanent agreement," said Peres, "and we have committed to redeployment in Hebron on May 3, but it will not happen because Hamas is more active in Hebron than anywhere else in the West Bank. Also, Arafat must void the articles in the Palestinian Charter as he promised, and apprehend the terrorist leaders - only then can we carry out the redeployment in Hebron."

Peres reminded Clinton that Israel imposed a blockade on the Gaza Strip, the removal of which depended on Arafat's ability to fight terrorism. "You should tell Arafat," Peres said, "that he must continue fighting terrorism, and if he does so the US will help him financially. He must also improve his public announcements in which he curses and damns us, and creates an atmosphere of violence and terror."

The date for the beginning of negotiations for the final agreement, which was scheduled for May 4, 1996, at the beginning of the third year since the signing of the Gaza and Jericho First Agreement (of the five years prescribed in the Oslo Accords for the interim agreement), was drawing nearer.

Peres decided that this occasion could not be skipped over without holding some ceremonial event to denote it. It was decided to set up a meeting between Abu Mazen and Uri Savir, in which they would all take pictures, and it would be a sort of declaration of the start of negotiations for the final agreement, when in fact – nothing would be done until after the Israeli elections.

Peres said at the time, that the intelligence material indicated Iran had an explicit strategy to intervene in the Israeli elections and influence their results. This strategy involved operating terrorist organizations that would sabotage his chances of winning the elections and continuing the peace process, all in order to maintain the tension in the Middle East.

Indeed, in the elections held on May 29, Peres was defeated by a tiny margin, and Benjamin Netanyahu replaced him.

On May 31, I was replaced by Maj. Gen. Ze'ev Livne as Military Secretary to the Prime Minister, and on June 2 I began serving as the Director of the Mossad.

***

As Director of the Mossad, I was no longer involved in the negotiations process with the Palestinians, except with respect to intelligence assessments the Mossad gave the Prime Minister, and except once when I was sent to meet with Mubarak regarding the Palestinian track. Netanyahu sought to use my good ties with President Mubarak and Head of Egyptian Intelligence General

Omar Suleiman. These good relations with Egypt and other Arab countries developed during the Rabin and Peres administrations.

Netanyahu found it difficult to maintain a good relationship with Mubarak and I had been sent to him with a message. I came to Alexandria and was greeted warmly at the airport by Gen. Omar Suleiman, the Head of Egyptian General Intelligence.

The message I carried was that four years had already passed during which Arafat made no serious effort to deal with terrorism (except during the months of February-March 1996), to try to appease Hamas and the Islamic Jihad instead of fighting them, and that we were witnessing a rapid change in the positions of the Palestinian Authority. In his public speeches, Arafat spoke against the process and would say that all the roads were open to the Palestinian people - including the renewal of the uprising. Israel would transfer intelligence information to the PA in order for it to arrest wanted persons, and this was not done; or when it was done – those detained were immediately released in the "revolving door" system. In early 1996, Arafat acted against terrorism and proved that he was capable of doing so, but since then he had done nothing against the terrorist infrastructure.

Netanyahu wanted to see if the President of Egypt could help with the matter.

President Mubarak promised to talk to Arafat about his efforts against terrorism, and detailed to me all the arguments Arafat claimed were preventing him from fighting terrorism. These included the continued new construction in the settlements, the need to release Palestinian prisoners jailed in Israel in order to encourage the population, and to avoid imposing blockades.

I also used my meeting with Mubarak to bring up the issue of the Israeli Azzam Azzam, who was jailed in Egypt on espionage charges and the date of his trial drew nearer. I said to Mubarak, "I am looking you in the eye and telling you: Azzam is not a spy. He has never been an agent of the Mossad nor any other security or intelligence agency in Israel, and is not part of any official Israeli body, so it is very important he be released." Mubarak told me that he would try to shorten Azzam's sentence but if Netanyahu continued to speak about this in public, it would create media noise that would prevent him from doing so. With this message I returned to Netanyahu.

Mubarak would later tell Ehud Barak and Clinton that if Netanyahu would have lowered the media profile and noise surrounding the issue of Azzam and would have handled the matter discreetly and behind the scenes - Azzam would have been released. Mubarak claimed that since Netanyahu made the matter public, he put him in a corner, it became a public issue in Egypt, and Mubarak could not act against Egyptian public opinion.

Netanyahu's era was characterized by a severing of relations with the Palestinians, with the exception of the Wye Plantation summit. The summit was convened due to pressure from the Americans and Netanyahu was dragged into it, and after being pressured by Foreign Minister Ariel Sharon, Minister of Defense Yitzhak Mordechai and Minister Sharansky – ended with an Israeli agreement to transfer more territory to the Palestinians.

CHAPTER 26

FULL POWER, ON BOTH TRACKS

My involvement in relations and negotiations with the Palestinians, during Netanyahu's tenure, was very limited as I have mentioned. But when Ehud Barak was elected Prime Minister in May 1999, things changed.

Barak appointed me to the position of the Prime Minister's Chief of Diplomatic-Security Staff. This was a newly formed position in which I acted on behalf of the Prime Minister to coordinate the work being done on security and diplomatic issues, on the peace process and other matters as was required of me. In my role I was in charge of the Political Advisor to the Prime Minister and I coordinated the work of the Military Secretary and the activities of government ministries and official bodies in matters pertaining to security and diplomacy.

In effect, Barak appointed me to be the person in the Prime Minister's Office who organized the PM's activities related to all these matters, with an emphasis on the peace process.

While Barak was busy establishing a coalition, I met with attorney Yitzhak Molcho, who coordinated the Palestinian issue on Netanyahu's behalf. On the Syrian issue, I met with Uzi Arad who informed me that there was almost no activity on this track.

I should mention that Molcho passed me the Palestinian file, which was under his full responsibility, in a highly professional and reliable manner.

In the file I found a memorandum detailing a conversation between Clinton and Netanyahu, prepared by Molcho and Dennis Ross, according to which there would be no third phase of withdrawal, and if there would be – it would not be greater than one percent, when originally it was supposed to include dozens of percent.

According to the Palestinian interpretation of this phase, they were supposed to receive the whole of the territory except for settlements and military bases, while we claimed that Israel alone will determine the extent and location of each phase.

Molcho further told me that there was an agreement with the Americans that the Palestinians were not entitled to an additional withdrawal of IDF forces at that time, because they had not fulfilled the preconditions for such a withdrawal. A timeline with a sequence of actions was drawn, with the last step in each stage being withdrawal. However, before that could happen, there were some things that the Palestinians had to do, and as long as these things were not done – Israel would not withdraw.

"When I conducted the secret negotiations with Abu Alaa before the summit at Wye Plantation," said Molcho, "I kept Dennis Ross updated. When we went to Wye, eighty percent of the agreement had already been drafted. We agreed with Arafat on the principles, and we formulated and finalized the details with Abu Alaa. The Wye Memorandum consists of three subjects: the Palestinians' obligations to us on security matters – fighting terrorism and confiscating illegal arms, Israel's obligations to the Palestinians on transferring land; and the principle that guided the Wye process was reciprocity. If the Palestinians do what they pledged, they will receive a portion of land from us. Or as Netanyahu put it in his famous expression, 'If they give, they will receive; if they do not give, they will not receive'. There will be no advancement to the next stage as long as the previous step's obligations are not fulfilled."

Barak took office as Prime Minister and made the peace process the first priority. He promised to leave no stone unturned on the way to peace. He did not promise to succeed, but he promised to try honestly and without manipulation.

Barak's conception with respect to the peace process was to move forward with full power on both tracks, the Syrian and Palestinian, with no preference for one over the other, and to focus on the track in which a breakthrough would be reached. However, Barak also estimated that the Syrian track was less complex and complicated than the Palestinian track. Despite the dedication he showed to the Wye Memorandum, Barak wanted to examine ways it could be integrated with progress towards the permanent agreement, meaning carrying out the third phase of the withdrawal as part of the permanent agreement.

Barak preferred to reach a framework agreement at first for the permanent settlement (of the Israeli-Palestinian conflict), an agreement that would present the principles for dealing with the basic issues. Afterwards, it would be possible to reach detailed understandings that would eventually form the permanent agreement. Once this agreement was reached, it would include a territorial component, which in practice would be the third phase of withdrawal.

Barak claimed that there were large differences of opinion between Israeli moderates and Palestinian moderates. The package was asymmetrical, because we were giving tangible things such as land and the release of prisoners, and in return they were giving promises about the future: They would ensure order, refrain from terrorism, and would continue the peace – which in itself was a very elusive affair.

In addition, it was important to him that the Palestinians realize that Europe stood with Israel, which was required to make painful compromises and concessions. Barak believed that if Europe would side with the Palestinians, as it had done during Netanyahu's term, Arafat would not feel any obligation or pressure to do what was required of him as part of the agreement: to fight terrorism, confiscate illegal arms and prevent incitement.

Barak believed that during discussions of the Wye Memorandum, Arafat thought that it would stop the process, and that Netanyahu's administration would stop at that point and ask to see it as the basis for the permanent settlement, possibly with the addition of one percent in the third withdrawal phase. According to this perception, Arafat told himself that if this was the case, it was better for him to accept small and disconnected pieces of land – than to get nothing at all. Wye created a long-term interim situation, which Barak believed was very dangerous as it created a mosaic: on the one hand, it disconnected Palestinian areas without contiguity between them, and on the other hand, many small Jewish enclaves were surrounded by Palestinian territories. This mosaic created a volatile and dangerous situation with many points of friction between Jews and Arabs, and with an immediate risk of an uncontrollable outburst - and Barak wished to prevent this whole situation.

Hence, Barak wanted to offer Arafat to carry out a small part of the Wye Memorandum to show that his administration was not afraid to make withdrawals, but postpone the implementation of its main part for several months, until a date that would be set with Arafat's consent. During this time, efforts would be made to try and reach understandings between the parties on the principles for a framework agreement towards a permanent settlement. Thus Israel would give Arafat more contiguous chunks of the land, as part of the implementation of the permanent agreement (in which some of the settlements would have to be evacuated).

"If Arafat will be patient," said Barak, "and assuming we can work out the principles for the permanent agreement in a few months, we will also settle the dimensions of the area that will be under Palestinian control. Then, as part of the final agreement's implementation, I could give the Palestinians a larger amount of land than they received in Wye, and the territory would be more contiguous. If Arafat refuses this idea, even though it serves him well, we'll implement the Wye Memorandum by the letter."

Barak had no intention of touching the settlements until the final agreement was settled, and promised that no new ones would be built in the next fifteen months.

In the Arab world, very positive statements were heard regarding Barak's election as Prime Minister, and especially with respect to the future of the peace process.

Osama al-Baz, Mubarak's political advisory, who we had known since the days of Sadat at Camp David, came to a meeting at the Prime Minister's Office along with the Egyptian Ambassador to Israel at the time, Mohammed Bassiouni, with a message from Mubarak to Barak. "The president is very pleased with you, and believes you are going in the right path and will reach peace with the Palestinians," said al-Baz. "The president is trying to convince Arafat to be patient about the Wye Memorandum's implementation, and he has a feeling that the gap between you can be overcome within a short period of time. President Mubarak believes in you and your judgment, says you are treating the Arabs sensibly, and that you and Netanyahu are completely different."

These statements were made against the backdrop of other expressions in the same spirit that we had heard from many others. There were statements to the effect that leaders considered Barak's election as an opportunity for a new era; you could see the smile on their faces, the feeling of relief, the warm handshakes and open atmosphere which replaced the sense of crisis, suspicion and sourness that marked their attitude towards Netanyahu. Many of them said that they saw Barak as Rabin's successor.

Barak replied to the Egyptian messengers, "Arafat is already seventy years old, I will be Prime Minister for eight years, do the math yourselves… this means that Arafat has to make the deal with me - he has no other choice. There are three options: one is to enter discussions of the framework agreement for the permanent settlement and reach it, and then reach a permanent agreement and a peace treaty with the Palestinians; a second option is that we fail to reach a framework agreement and therefore may have to wait for another generation, until Israeli and Palestinian leaders capable of doing so will arise; or a third option - if we fail, the situation will deteriorate into serious violence, and then it will be much more difficult to return to negotiations."

Arafat was already a seasoned veteran of many types of experiences, and I imagine he smiled to himself when he heard Barak's assertion that he had no choice but to make peace with him. This is because it is impossible to make predictions in the Middle East, here there is no dull moment - and indeed, reality would eventually prove this to be the case.

I do not think that Barak was wrong in his aforementioned assessment, as he truly did intend to serve as Prime Minister for eight years and bring peace. At that time, his statements sounded completely realistic to me as well, and if I were in his place at the time, I probably would have thought the same. Yet then reality set in, and the moral of this story is that in matters related to the Middle East – there is no point in making predictions. Who would have thought that Rabin would be murdered, who could have guessed that Saddam Hussein would be removed from power so easily and quickly. What is clear is that as a leader and as a negotiator, you have only limited influence over the other side's behavior. Barak took into account that there might also be a collapse, but basically he estimated that Arafat was a partner with whom he could work out a deal, just like Rabin and Peres believed before him. At the time, we thought that by shining a spotlight on his lies and insisting on things that were agreed with him, we could bring the Palestinian group to realize that his lies were working against their interests.

It seems as though we failed at that.

Arafat was very suspicious of Barak's proposal to reach a framework agreement. He insisted on the need to implement the next phase of withdrawal, as was agreed during Netanyahu's term at the Wye Plantation. He saw Barak's proposal as an attempt to shirk Israel's obligation to carry out the withdrawal, and he rejected it outright. It took tremendous efforts, many meetings between Barak and Arafat and the intervention of President Clinton, King Abdullah and President Mubarak to persuade Arafat to give the idea of a framework agreement a chance. When he finally agreed to Barak's proposal, Arafat insisted the third phase would be carried out already in 1999, and even before the framework agreement was reached, although discussions over it were to end no later than February 15, 2000.

The compromise eventually found was that if the third phase would be postponed for several weeks, this would not be considered a violation. Additionally, we agreed to release 350 prisoners.

The Palestinians kept complaining about continued construction work in the settlements, and Barak promised to look into the construction activities of Netanyahu's administration, and demolish illegal structures. "I do not need Arafat to pressure me to uphold Israeli law," said Barak. "I will remove illegal construction of my own accord and not because of his complaints."

In the public diplomacy front, we emphasized the United States' return to our side, contrary to the situation during Netanyahu's tenure. The idea was to convey the message that we had regained the confidence of the world's nations, including Arab nations.

Barak sent Clinton messages to the effect that Arafat's statements should not be taken at face value, since he has a tendency to be 'inaccurate.' "Arafat has to decide if we are leaders or horse traders," said Barak, and asked Clinton to pressure Arafat and let him understand that he should compromise and show flexibility.

On November 1999, an international event was held in Oslo in memory of Rabin, attended by Clinton, Arafat and Putin, and it was an opportunity for Arafat and Barak to meet.

The ceremony was very moving. It was said there that a new spirit of Oslo was present, and a new way, for the first time since Rabin's era.

Barak said to Arafat, "After years of talk, now there is action. We opened the Safe Passage (a roadway in Israel that served the Palestinians, connecting the Gaza Strip to the Southern region of the West Bank), we approved the construction of a port in Gaza, and released prisoners (in accordance with the Sharm Memorandum). I am committed to doing all that is possible, along with my commitment to the security of Israel, which I will never neglect. Let us turn a new page in the conduct between us, express ourselves differently, and not attack each other."

Arafat was very excited and still under the impression of the ceremony in Rabin's memory. Unlike his usual manner he was attentive, considerate, relaxed and open. He then turned to Barak and began making a touching speech: "You are my new partner. We will make a peace of the brave and I am sure that our partnership will lead to the success of the process." Barak replied, "Most of the Israeli public elected me because they believe that when I discuss peace, I will not make compromises on Israel's security. The only chance to succeed in the process is if each side understands that there are sensitivities and difficulties on the other side."

In the tripartite meeting held afterwards between Clinton, Barak and Arafat, Clinton said, "If we resolve the conflict through your leadership, it will have a positive effect on the entire world. No one could continue to argue that it is not possible to resolve any dispute through dialogue and peace."

In December 1999, we were invited to a meeting with Arafat at Abu Mazen's home in Ramallah. We were received according to the finest traditions of Arab hospitality: warmly and heartily, with tables laden with refreshments which were solemnly served by the women of the house. Abu Mazen's home was beautiful, spacious and impressive.

The meeting's attendants from the Israeli side, besides Barak and myself, were Yossi Ginosar and Minister David Levy. The Palestinian attendants were Arafat, Abu Mazen, Abu Alaa and Nabil Abu Rudeineh, Arafat's Chief of Bureau.

Abu Alaa spoke first and said, "We understand that you plan to evacuate the entire Golan Heights and at the same time, you are building in the West Bank and not talking about evacuating settlements. Our impression is that you want to please the settlers here to compensate for those you will evacuate from the Golan."

Barak rejected these claims and said, "That is not true. The guidelines of my government state that no new settlements will be built, but I cannot prevent what has already been legally approved."

David Levy noted that illegal Palestinian construction was taking place at a large scale, and that although we were under pressure to demolish these buildings, we rarely ever touched this type of construction.

At that stage, the Palestinian hosts surprised David Levy and entered the room with a birthday cake. It was Levy's sixty-second birthday, and he was greatly moved by the Palestinian gesture. He told those present that his wife asked him to come home to celebrate with his children and family. "However," said Levy, "I told her that I am going to care for the future of our children."

When the meal started, Arafat personally made sure that everyone ate well, as he was prone to do, constantly refilling everyone's plates again and again, while he himself ate nothing.

In a warm and fatherly tone he called towards me from time to time, "General, eat more, eat more!" as he laid food in my plate.

It was no coincidence that Abu Alaa mentioned the matter of negotiations with the Syrians. At that time, the two processes were taking place in parallel. Barak's plan for the Palestinian track was very grandiose, and in practice it turned out to be unrealistic. Barak planned that the Palestinian and Israeli delegations would sit together for ten days, holed up in some isolated place, brainstorm on all matters relating to the framework agreement. This meant laying down guidelines for solving each of the issues pertaining to the permanent agreement: Jerusalem, the refugees' right of return, borders, security arrangements and settlements - and then sit for another ten days and begin to formulate the framework agreement. For ten additional days, the parties would sit with US representatives in order to bridge the sections and issues that the parties could not settle themselves.

That was how Barak saw the way to resolve the conflict at the time.

At one point, Barak wondered whether Israel would be able to process two peace agreements at the same time. Some argued that the answer was negative. Barak believed that if he could bring the Israeli public two agreements, with Syria and with the Palestinians, agreements that would end the conflict once and for all, the public would vote in their favor.

He believed that if in exchange for concessions, painful as they may be, the consideration would be the end of the conflict, it would be very attractive in the eyes of the public. I do not think he was wrong in this assessment of his, because in recent years the Israeli public has grown accustomed to the possibility of concessions, since slowly the people understood that the way to stop the cycle of bloodshed needed to pass through dialogue and mutual compromise. This was evident during the disengagement carried out by Prime Minister Sharon, in August 2005, when the majority of the Israeli public accepted the unilateral withdrawal and did not go out of their way to prevent it. Today, it is clear to any reasonable person that we cannot reach an agreement with the Palestinians without giving up most of Judea and Samaria and part of Jerusalem. Only those who are detached from the reality in the Middle East can still dream of the possibility to significantly improve Israel's situation without making such concessions. Anyone who looks at reality with sober eyes understands that only two basic possibilities stand before us. One is to continue to live by the sword as we do today. The other is to take calculated risks and renew the negotiation, with the understanding that we will be forced to make painful concessions, but also with the knowledge that an agreement with the Palestinians is likely to better our situation and the state of the Middle East.

There is another possibility, which I do not recommend, and it is making relatively small concessions, in exchange for which we will "purchase" temporary quiet. This possibility is entirely disadvantageous, because it will perpetuate the conflict and make it even more difficult to resolve in the future. It is better to strive to resolve the roots of the conflict, with both sides receiving an end to the conflict and bloodshed in exchange. The price tag reads: giving up most of Judea and Samaria and part of Jerusalem. The Palestinians will give up the right of return and the territory of the settlement blocs, and will join the war against terrorism. The agreements will only be achieved if the Palestinians recognize Israel's vital needs, and will also be willing to make painful concessions.

Barak constantly strove to reach a permanent agreement with the Palestinians. In one of his meetings with Arafat, early in the year 2000, Barak said to him, "We are prepared to begin a marathon of discussions. The Middle East cannot be an area in which the sides live normal lives without an agreement between Israel and the Palestinians. In contrast, without agreements with Syria and Lebanon, normal relations in the Middle East can be maintained. The differences between Israel and Syria are not great, but there is no certainty that we will be able to overcome them. This is because the feeling with them is that we are talking to them as if through a sealed glass, we do not have the same intimacy with them that we have with you. Between you and us there are large gaps, but even so, I came to understand that on our side there is willingness to make painful concessions, if this form of willingness will also be seen on yours."

Arafat, as usual, opted to answer in slogans, "It is important to reach a just, full and comprehensive peace. In all honesty, I must say that we are in great pain. We asked that as part of the partial transfer of territory, you would transfer three regions to us, from B to A (to full Palestinian responsibility). You did not agree to this and that has hurt us deeply. You decide unilaterally which area to transfer, contrary to what was agreed in Wye."

Barak told Arafat that we do not need to consult with them about this matter, but as a show of goodwill, he would present to them the areas we intend to transfer in advance. "However, have no illusions - I make no commitment to accept your comments and change my decisions regarding the area that will be transferred to you," Barak stressed.

Despite being the stronger side in our relationship with the Palestinians, we were also suspicious of them. They also needed to fulfill their obligations: to fight terrorism, end incitement and confiscate illegal arms. Therefore, Barak always tried to be considerate, but at the same time firm and determined with regard to obligations.

We were familiar with Arafat's behavior - the bickering and emotional extortion - since as early as Rabin's days: "You are strong, so do me some more favors; shorten the timetable, release more prisoners, give more land."

Although Barak did not show insensitivity towards the Palestinians, he did not manage to build a relationship with Arafat as the one Arafat had with Rabin. Arafat treated Rabin with special dignity due to Rabin being older than him, having the halo of a celebrated military leader, the Chief of Staff of the Six-Day War - things that affected Arafat deeply.

Arafat viewed leaders who were younger than him as rascals. He used to recount how he held the Moroccan king on his lap while he was still an infant. It is quite likely that this tale never actually occurred, but he used it to illustrate how much the others were younger than him.

Arafat appreciated Rabin's maturity and vast experience, while young people like Barak and Netanyahu were toddlers in his eyes.

At that stage, there were still large gaps between us and the Palestinians. While an agreement was in fact signed (an "amended Wye agreement" according to Barak), when the sides sat together, debates over the paper's interpretation began, as always.

Encouraged by Mubarak, Arafat wrote a letter to Clinton in which he raised the argument that there was still no timetable set for the third phase of the withdrawal. This was despite the fact that Barak had told him many times (and was stated in the Sharm Memorandum) that they would not discuss the third phase as long as the sides were trying to reach a framework agreement. Due to this discussion, Israel was supposed to transfer to the Palestinians a portion of six percent of the land, which the Palestinians would deem adequate, but they found it difficult to accept an area that was much smaller than what they believed Israel was supposed to give them.

Barak stressed that Israel had full authority to determine which six percent of the land would be transferred to the Palestinians. Furthermore, we agreed that if the attempt to achieve a framework agreement failed, we would immediately proceed to implement the interim agreement and start discussing the permanent agreement. This agreement would be based on the Oslo Accords and Security Council resolutions 242 and 338, and the principle of "land for peace."

In that period, Barak still hoped to uphold his plan for ten days of brainstorming between Israel and the Palestinians. According to this plan, a framework agreement for the permanent settlement would be formulated within an additional ten days after this, and then there would be a ten-day gathering in which the United States would bridge the differences that still remained between Israel and the Palestinians. Meaning, within thirty days, it would be possible for the two parties to reach a framework agreement, with the help of the Americans.

In this agreement, the parties were supposed to describe in general terms and principles their solution to each of the problems related to the permanent agreement, except for Jerusalem. Barak was not willing to discuss Jerusalem at that stage, and the first time we touched on this issue was only in July 2000, at Camp David.

On the matter of the right of return, Israel objected throughout the way. The Palestinians and the Americans tried to convince us to recognize a Palestinian right to return to all of Israel in principle, when in practice – realization would be sparse and the solution would mostly be based on financial compensation to those who would remain displaced.

On Jerusalem, Barak refused to make any concessions at that stage, and we arrived at Camp David as well with the position that Jerusalem is the eternal capital of Israel and therefore would remain whole and undivided. The idea was that the Palestinian state would build its capital outside of Jerusalem, in the nearby villages.

Barak's first concession on Jerusalem was at Camp David, when he realized that as part of the whole package, the Palestinians would have to make concessions in issues that were vital for Israel, and in order to achieve this, he would have to compromise on Jerusalem. Since he perceived Jerusalem as the most sensitive issue on the Israeli side, he feared that details would leak out of the preparatory meetings, making it difficult for him to reach an agreement. It could have been understood to mean that we were negotiating over Jerusalem even before we received what we demanded from the Palestinians, and this could make it difficult for him to negotiate. Negotiations with the Palestinians were already taking place on the background of terrorist attacks and fierce political resistance from the opposition and parts of the coalition, with the entire right-wing joining forces to thwart the dialogue with the Palestinians.

Barak wanted to reach a framework agreement very much. He knew that such an agreement would serve as a corridor to the permanent agreement, and was well aware that if we failed to reach it, there would be no chance of a permanent settlement.

As mentioned, Arafat agreed, after much persuasion, to try to reach a framework agreement, but insisted that if we did not reach it by a certain date, Israel had to commit to carry out the third phase of withdrawal. Barak agreed to this, and it was determined that if the framework agreement does not materialize, the third phase will be in the middle of the year 2000. In actuality, the first time the two sides discussed the issues pertaining to the permanent agreement, including the territory of the Palestinian state to be established, was at Camp David in July 2000.

We learned from the Americans that the opposition to the idea of the framework agreement was led mainly by Mohammed Dahlan. In discussions on the framework agreement, which were participated by people like Shlomo Ben-Ami and Gilad Sher, Saeb Erekat and Yasser Abed Rabbo, it felt as though the Palestinians were dragging their feet, and in fact Erekat and Abed Rabbo did not have a mandate to make concessions in these areas.

Israel's position was that of a willingness to withdraw from most of the territory, while demanding to keep under its sovereignty the large settlement blocs that constitute some ten percent of the territory. The Palestinians repeatedly demanded the whole of the territory "to the last centimeter" of the 1967 borders. From their standpoint, they had already compromised by not demanding the whole of the land from the river to the sea, but only the West Bank and Gaza. This was based on the great concession made by Arafat, who in the Oslo Accords recognized the State of Israel and its sovereignty over seventy-eight percent of the territory of "historical Palestine," meaning Israel within the 1967 borders. "Arafat's willingness to suffice with the remaining land, only twenty-two percent of historical Palestine, is more than enough, and do not ask us to cede more," said the Palestinians.

Dahlan, who was actually among the supporters of the peace process, believed that the most important thing for the Palestinians at that point in time was to receive as much land as possible. This stemmed from the Palestinian leadership's need to show their public that achievements were reached, such as more land, the release of prisoners, the removal of checkpoints and the easing of blockades.

At the same time, and behind the scenes, a deal with the Syrians was gradually taking shape. After the summit in Shepherdstown, Clinton and Barak tried to formulate a way to reach a breakthrough on the Syrian track. A month later, in March 2000, there was the famous meeting between Clinton and Assad in Geneva, which ended in nothing - a meeting in which Clinton offered Assad, with our consent, far-reaching concessions, but in which we also demanded far-reaching concessions from the Syrians. However, a month before the meeting, we were still secretly working on the Syrian track, which followed the Palestinian one, casting a heavy shadow.

Arafat always believed that Israel was giving higher priority to the Syrian track. He feared that after an agreement between Syria and Israel, he would remain all alone and in a vulnerable position. The reasoning behind this was that Israel after a peace agreement with Syria would be a very tough negotiator with the Palestinians, and would not be willing to agree to concessions that it might have agreed to in that time. Yet contrary to Arafat's belief and despite the preparations being made for Clinton's meeting with Assad, the Palestinian cause was not neglected. It was clear to us that quiet on the Palestinian side would also contribute to the success of the Syrian track.

It was therefore decided to formulate a 'benefits package' for the Palestinians. We discussed a package that would include opening a northern safe passage that would start at the Erez crossing and end in Ramallah through the Beit Horon highway, in addition to the southern safe passage from Gaza to Tarqumiya in the southern Hebron hills. Furthermore, we were willing to transfer tax money from goods that reached Israel and were meant for the Palestinian Authority, money that Israel owed the PA; transfer six percent of the territory; and set a timetable for ending discussions on the framework agreement for the permanent settlement until the end of May. The date for the end of the negotiations for the permanent agreement had long ago been set to September 13, 2000, and we decided to uphold this time-frame. Thus we created a framework of fifteen months from the start of Barak's administration, and into it we crammed a very intensive and ambitious working plan.

In addition, it was decided to open a confidential back-channel that would enable more open and candid discussion than the public channel. The guiding principle set by Barak was that before everything was agreed - nothing was agreed. He believed that this principle would allow the parties to be open, candid and creative. However, this negotiation channel also yielded no results. Barak's proposal for a thirty day marathon of talks between Israelis and Palestinians was accepted by them, but it did not materialize. Although the delegations met many times, no progress had been made. The Palestinians presented rigid positions and did not enable discussions to develop. Then Barak began to realize that it was necessary to hold a summit meeting between the two leaders, Arafat and Barak, with Clinton acting as 'best man.' It had become clear that through their envoys, no progress would be made.

It is obvious that an agreement between Israel and the Palestinians will only be achieved if the leaders are involved, just as it was with the peace treaty with Egypt. Were it not for the direct involvement of Begin and Sadat under Carter's pressure, an agreement would not have been reached, and similarly without the direct meetings between Rabin and Hussein the peace treaty with Jordan would not have been achieved. We understand that each of the leaders keeps the important cards close to his chest, right up to the finish line, the last moments of the endgame. Thus is the nature of negotiations – decisions on the most important issues are left for the last step, in which each party must exhaust its last bits of latitude and compromise in order to reach an agreement.

Thus began the journey to Camp David.

CHAPTER 27

"I'M WILLING TO GO MUCH FURTHER THAN RABIN"

In those days, Barak's everyday life was filled with a myriad of pressures: nothing was moving with the Palestinians, negotiations with Syria stalled, as did the situation in Lebanon, which was intricately connected to Syria. In the background was the constant noise of the opposition parties, who formulated the Jerusalem Law: that Jerusalem will remain the capital of Israel forever and will never be divided. The essence of the law was to prevent any concession in Jerusalem as part of the negotiations with the Palestinians.

Nonetheless, all these factors did not prevent Barak from remaining determined and focused. He knew what he wanted and where he was going. In his frequent meetings with the Americans, he sounded very convincing, and in telephone conversations with Clinton, which took place almost every day, he was able to convince him of almost anything.

Barak restated his willingness to take painful and far-reaching steps, as long as they did not undermine the vital interests of Israel, but to do so in one single instance rather than in stages. "In the 'withdrawal phases' system," Barak said, "I find myself giving another chunk of land every time, which increases the friction between Israelis and Palestinians and erodes Israel's bargaining position. When it comes to painful concessions, it is best to use all the political power I have at once, instead of wasting my political capital incrementally. If I have to give six percent of the territory, it requires almost as much political effort as ceding forty percent. It is better to convince the Israeli public to accept larger concessions in exchange for an enormous payoff in the form of the end of the conflict, rather than sink into struggles for minor concessions without anything to show for them."

On March 26, 2000, the summit between Clinton and Assad in Geneva took place. We attached great importance to this meeting because we knew it will determine the fate of the negotiations with the Syrians for better or worse, and would have a psychological impact on the other side.

We waited for the meeting's results in tense and nervous anticipation, and when Clinton called Barak after it had ended and said, "I did my best but unfortunately I did not succeed." - you could see the great disappointment on Barak's face. However, as usual, he immediately pulled himself together and said, "Now we have to see how to advance the Palestinian track."

At that time, two meetings with the Palestinian took place on the secret track, attended by Israel's Shlomo Ben-Ami whom Barak nicknamed "Shaba" (his initials) and Amnon Lipkin-Shahak who was nicknamed "Alash" (in the same vein). The Palestinian side consisted of Abu Mazen and Abu Alaa, whom Barak dubbed "The Abus."

This channel, which was supposed to be secretive and deniable, was meant to provide a framework for brainstorming, in order to examine how far the Palestinians would go if they got what they wanted, and to present the 'red line' we were willing to reach if our demands were met. The intention was to engage in productive discussions and not turn it into a negotiation, but even there the Palestinians did not show any flexibility.

Barak's strategy was that the official and public negotiation track in Washington, led by Oded Eran, former Israeli ambassador to Jordan, and Yasser Abed Rabbo from the Palestinian side, would address the generic issues. These included issues such as economic relations between Israel and the Palestinians, Palestinians' employment in Israel, water, security coordination, the environment, legal issues and civil issues such as archeology, religion and infrastructure. Meanwhile, the core issues would be discussed only on the secret track. We realized that if there was any chance to make progress on the issues that were bones of contention, it would happen only if they would be discussed far away from the media and public's eye. Our hope was that the brainstorming sessions would give rise to creative ideas and solutions, while the public track was necessary to try and move forward on the remaining issues, and show the Israeli and Palestinian public that the Israeli-Palestinian track lives and breathes.

Despite the seniority of Abu Mazen and Abu Alaa, who represented the Palestinians on the secret track, no progress was being made on it. This led Barak to recognize that in order to make the most the existing prospects, his personal involvement was required, as well as that of Clinton and Arafat, as part of a leaders' summit. Barak came to this conclusion mainly because of the rigid positions the Palestinians were displaying in the secret channel.

They totally rejected the concept of us retaining complete control over the Jordan Valley. They were willing to accept any kind of security arrangement we suggested, as long as it did not include us controlling Palestinian territory. They would not agree to Israel annexing the large settlement blocs to its sovereignty. They even refused that Israeli settlements and residents with Israeli citizenship would remain in place under Palestinian rule.

They agreed to the principle that where security needs required it, an Israeli force will be stationed, but strongly opposed any annexation suggested under the pretext that it would be necessary for security purposes. They repeatedly stressed that they demanded all the territory of the West Bank and Jerusalem up to the last centimeter, according to the 1967 borders, and in exchange for this, they were willing to give Israel any security arrangements it needed.

"We've already made our big concession," said the Palestinians, "by recognizing the 1967 borders. By doing so, we gave up seventy-eight percent of the whole of Palestine, and we did so as early as Oslo - we gave up Jaffa, Haifa, Tel Aviv and Ramla. Twenty-two percent of the territory remains, including the areas of Judea and Samaria and Gaza - and this we will not cede."

We tried to come up with ideas to examine joint control over some of the territory, but they refused. Abu Mazen and Abu Alaa repeatedly stressed that they also could not concede their demand for the right of return for Palestinian refugees into the State of Israel.

Barak decided to go to Camp David, to try to succeed where the envoys had failed, mainly because Arafat did not allow his representatives for the confidential negotiations any leeway for flexibility.

"I'm going because perhaps I will succeed with Arafat," said Barak. "I want to leave no stone unturned on the way to peace, and if that stone is now called 'Arafat,' I want to try with him. Maybe he has not given his people leeway and is keeping the cards to himself."

In my opinion, if Barak would not have gone to Camp David, the question would forever remain open whether we truly gave a full chance to negotiations with the Palestinians, and whether we had not missed the opportunity to reach an agreement with them.

History has shown that consequential matters are eventually determined only by the leaders themselves. In all the efforts and negotiation tracks we had tried until then, no flexibility was shown on the Palestinian side, and they had not backed off on anything: from the right of return to the last centimeter of land. It was clear that Arafat held all the cards in his hands, and only a meeting with him would reveal if there was any chance for Palestinian concessions on the critical issues.

In one of his conversations with Barak, Sandy Berger tried to explain the matter, and said he had learned from the Palestinians that Arafat was not sure that Barak had enough political power to pass a principle agreement in a referendum.

I believe that this claim was an excuse of sorts for the Palestinians, who preferred to avoid discussing the final settlement, because they were required to make concessions for the first time. It is true that Barak came to Camp David with a sparse coalition that relied on a minority - less than sixty MKs - and yet he was sure he could pass the agreement in a referendum, over the Knesset members' heads. I also believe, to this day, that if we had presented to the public in Israel a peace agreement based on Clinton's proposal, one that would have brought an end to the conflict between Israel and the Palestinians – it would have won the support of most of the nation.

On May 5, there was a meeting between Barak, Dennis Ross and Martin Indyk. Barak said we had reached the moment of truth in the Palestinian track.

In May a leak was published, stating that there was a deep crisis in the negotiations between Israelis and Palestinians. The source of the leak was Saeb Erekat, who was part of the negotiating team in the public track, and did not like the idea that material issues were being discussed elsewhere, or rather - where he was not present.

Barak said that if we were unable get the public track to continue and ensure that it dealt only with generic issues, this would seriously harm the entire process, because then it would be impossible to maintain the secret track and discuss the most sensitive issues. At this point, Barak voiced to the Americans the need for the summit between Arafat and himself.

Barak presented his outline for a framework agreement to the Americans, stating that it would include an independent, sovereign, contiguous Palestinian state, with its own gateways to the outside world, a demilitarized state without an army but only a police force. Israel would annex the five major settlement blocs near the Green Line: The Shaked, Hinanit, and Rihan bloc in northern Wadi Ara; the Kedumim, Ariel, Alfei Menashe, Beit Aryeh, Hashmonaim, Giv'at Ze'ev and Mevo Horon bloc north of Jerusalem; the Ofra, Beit El, Mitzpe Yeriho and Ma'ale Adumim bloc east of Jerusalem; Gush Etzion; and the Carmel and Eshkolot bloc in the southern Hebron Hills. This is an area which encompasses some fifteen percent of Judea and Samaria, and some eighty-five percent of the settlers reside in it. The Jordan Valley, which constitutes twenty percent of the territory of Judea and Samaria, would remain under Israeli control, and in the future - when peace and security would stabilize – most of it would be transferred to Palestinian control. The aim was that following the signing of the framework agreement, the PA would control about sixty-five percent of the territory in Judea and Samaria and all of the Gaza Strip.

He added that Jerusalem would remain unified, undivided and untouched by the Palestinians, and there would be no right of return for Palestinian refugees into Israel.

"Time is working against the process," said Barak. "If the chance is vanquished, we will have to face a reality whose price will be horrible. The coming weeks must be devoted to an attempt to bring the positions of the Palestinians and the Israelis closer together, and to hold a summit attended by the leaders Clinton, Arafat and myself in order to reach an agreement."

The Americans undertook to promote the summit, and Dennis Ross took upon himself to lead the efforts to compose a draft that would be used as basis for discussions in the weeks leading to the summit.

However, the Palestinians were in no hurry and wanted to buy time. They may have thought that there was no point reaching agreements with President Clinton, who was at the end of his term, and that it was better to wait for his successor. From the onset, their tactic was not to rush to reach a framework agreement, since, according to a previous understanding - if a framework agreement would not be achieved until the middle of the year 2000, Israel would execute the third phase of withdrawal and would transfer additional territory to the Palestinians. The Palestinians preferred to receive more territory without having to give something in return, before they entered a process in which they would be required to give something of their own for the first time. Dahlan was one of the most prominent people who drove the approach that preferred the third phase to take place before the framework agreement.

On May 7, there was a meeting between Arafat and Barak, again in Abu Mazen's lavish and well-kept mansion in the suburbs of Ramallah. In the heavily guarded convoy that arrived at Abu Mazen's house in the dark of night, came besides Barak also David Levy, Shlomo Ben-Ami, Yossi Ginosar and myself.

Abu Mazen greeted us outside the house with hugs and kisses, and led us inside, where in a side room Arafat, Abu Alaa and Nabil Abu Rudeineh (Arafat's Chief of Bureau) were waiting.

The house was surrounded by Israeli guards, alert and vigilant by the Israeli Prime Minister's very presence inside Palestinian territory.

Barak turned to Arafat and said to him, "We don't have a lot of time. Within two or three months we will no longer have Clinton. At Ben Ami and Abu Alaa's talks in the secret track the atmosphere is positive, but we have to decide what to do with the sensitive issues. I suggest we discuss generic issues in the public track, and the second track will deal with the substantial issues. If we cannot bridge the gaps, we will ask the Americans to help and then reach the 'endgame' (the final stage of negotiations before an agreement is reached)."

After Barak finished speaking there was silence. Then, Arafat replied in a dramatic tone, "Mr. Prime Minister, everything is stuck, there is no progress, and there are words without results. It is the same in the secret track. Nothing is moving."

"For an agreement, each party will need to be flexible," said Barak.

Then Ben Ami intervened, saying, "I feel that progress is being made in the secret track," and Abu Alaa, Ben-Ami's partner in that negotiation track, said, "There are very serious discussions between us, but we need the leaders' help," and thus strayed from Arafat's dramatic message. The latter proceeded to say, "You do not see our problems and we have very serious problems, and the situation is getting worse as long as we cannot present accomplishments to the Palestinian people."

"We are not seeing any flexibility in your positions, so it is impossible to move forward," said Barak.

"The map, which you presented as an illustration to Yasser Abed Rabbo, Dahlan and Saeb Erekat is rejected, and is a surefire recipe for the process' collapse", Arafat said. He was referring to the map which decreed that sixty-five percent of the land would be given to the Palestinians and the rest would remain in Israel's hands, including the Jordan Valley, which only after several years would gradually be transferred to the Palestinians. For Arafat it was out of the question to receive only 65 percent of the territory - he wanted to immediately receive 100 percent of the land in Judea and Samaria. "I get all the territory, you dismantle the settlements - and then there is peace!" concluded Arafat.

Barak said that as long as the Palestinians do not show flexibility, he could not draw a different map for them.

"The only thing you have agreed to is to postpone the schedule, but that is not a precedent, as you had already agreed to it in

Rabin's period," Barak said. "Besides that, you have not shown any flexibility."

"With Rabin everything was different," said Arafat. "When we met him for the first time in Taba, the Israeli side suggested that in the first withdrawal phase we would receive five percent. I talked to Rabin on the phone and he ordered to give us thirty-one percent. That is the difference between the way Rabin treated me and the way you do. Rabin was attentive to me, with him I could talk, he did not give me orders, he listened to me and was willing to change his positions. Rabin even gave the PA money during blockades. In your blockades, everything is shut down and stopped. Rabin never stopped my money and always gave it to me and on time. "

In those days, the atmosphere between Israel and the Palestinians was not one of openness and goodwill, and our relationship was not even slightly reminiscent of Rabin's days. On the Israeli side there was a sense of frustration that things were not moving. Among the Palestinians, there was an air of despair and depression. They believed that Israel was using the discussions regarding the framework agreement as an excuse to avoid carrying out the third phase of the withdrawal, which would entail transferring the entire territory to their control except for settlements and IDF camps.

At the time, Barak believed that implementing the third phase would lead to large-scale and volatile friction between the Israeli population and the Palestinians, and therefore sought to reach a framework agreement that would be the last stop before the permanent settlement – which was the final destination.

For Barak, the positions presented by our representatives in the talks were very close to his 'red lines,' so that in terms of the "endgame" – we had only little leeway for flexibility left.

June 23 was the date scheduled for the third phase's implementation, and Barak very much preferred not to reach this date without a framework agreement, since the third phase would be another instance of the Palestinians receiving land and giving nothing in return. On the other hand, as part of a framework agreement, they would have to make painful concessions and not merely receive.

Clinton agreed with Barak's opinion that a framework agreement would be preferable to carrying out the third phase.

In those days, the Americans visited the region many times in an attempt to promote the process, and Barak and Clinton spoke on the phone often, but the impression was that Arafat was still dragging his feet and buying time.

While we were willing to show flexibility and raise new ideas, the Palestinians had not moved an inch from their basic positions. In effect, this was the tactic Arafat had adopted until the end. The only time he cooperated was in the Oslo Accords, where he was not required to compromise on the core issues, such as the right of return and territory, and gained considerable achievements. For him, he had already made his big concession in Oslo, by agreeing that the Palestinian state will be established in the West Bank and Gaza Strip, and not the entire area of Palestine that also included the State of Israel's territory. Barak asked the Americans to present additional possibilities to Arafat and to tell him that his approach - that the area of the State of Israel within the 1967 borders belongs to the Palestinians, and by not demanding it, they were conceding seventy-eight percent of Palestine - was not acceptable to us. Arafat was not about to compromise on the territory, and repeatedly demanded to receive all of Judea and Samaria. Later, at Camp David, he agreed to territorial exchanges.

The Americans were convinced that a summit meeting was needed in order to move the process forward, and put tremendous pressure on Arafat to come to Camp David. Arafat, who did not like the idea of a summit, came to Camp David begrudgingly. He was not at all convinced of the summit's necessity.

It was agreed that the Americans would prepare a draft agreement that would serve as the basis for discussions. The draft would include the agreed issues, and in any subject where there were disagreements, the Israeli position would be presented and indicated by the letter "I", along with the Palestinian position that would be indicated by the letter "P." The goal was to bridge the gaps between the two sides' positions at the summit.

Barak continued to stress throughout the way that the goal was to reach an end to the bloodshed, end mutual claims and end the conflict, and to achieve this goal, Israel would be willing to go very far to meet the Palestinians halfway.

However, Arafat persistently continued to demand the implementation of the third phase on June 23. "Give me the phase and then I will go to the summit," he said time and again. Yet Barak reiterated that executing the third phase will eliminate any chance for the summit's success, and that if an agreement would be reached, the Palestinians would receive a much larger area than they would receive in the third phase by itself.

Arafat complained that Israel was not upholding its obligations to transfer the three villages near Jerusalem. Abu Dis, al-Eizariya and 'Anata, to the Palestinians. He also complained that Israel was not releasing prisoners, and was not transferring to him the money owed due to taxes collected from Palestinian workers, as well as port and sales taxes - and therefore, he did not trust Barak.

Barak, for his part, said that Arafat had done nothing: he had not disarmed the Tanzim (the armed popular militia of the PLO), had not confiscated illegal weapons, had not ended the incitement and was not fighting terrorism.

"I'm willing to go much further than what Rabin was willing to even consider," Barak said, "And there will not be a better opportunity to reach a settlement with the Palestinians."

Towards the next meeting in the secret track, Barak briefed Ben-Ami and authorized him to discuss all the issues, including Jerusalem which until then he had forbidden to touch upon. "Begin to exchange ideas on how you can solve issues in Jerusalem," said Barak, stressing, "But do not leave the Palestinians any documents or maps."

At the same time, we started to prepare the public relations campaign ahead of the Camp David summit, with the goal being to convince the public in Israel and around the world that the summit was essential, and that the alternative was chaos and deterioration into severe violence.

CHAPTER 28

AFTER 18 YEARS, THE IDF EXITS LEBANON

During the 1999 Israeli election campaign, Barak pledged "to leave no stone unturned" in order to promote the chances of peace with Syria and the Palestinians. He also pledged to withdraw the IDF from Lebanon within a year from the day he would take office as Prime Minister.

Following Operation Peace for Galilee in 1982, which expanded beyond the initial plan, the IDF entered Southern Lebanon. In 1985, the IDF withdrew unilaterally to the area known as the "security zone", where it stayed for about fifteen years, until our exit from Lebanon on May 24, 2000, slightly less than a year after Barak started his term as Prime Minister and Defense Minister. Our presence in Lebanon involved extensive military activity and many clashes with terrorists, which caused heavy casualties to the IDF.

Barak came to the conclusion that we could not accept the conception that it is only possible to protect northern Israel by having the IDF deployed in Southern Lebanon. He was convinced that it was time to withdraw our troops and deploy them on the Israeli side, along our border with Lebanon. Barak assessed that our exit from Lebanon would improve our political situation and lead to more pressure on the Lebanese government and Hezbollah to stop terrorist attacks and the firing of Katyusha rockets. It was clear to all of us that after the withdrawal, IDF soldiers would not be exposed to the same dangers they faced while we were in Lebanon, and the number of casualties will be significantly reduced. This turned out to be accurate.

Barak believed that it would be best to withdraw from Lebanon as part of an agreement. He knew that such an agreement would be possible if we could reach a settlement with Syria. A different, more distant alternative, was to reach an agreement on the withdrawal with the Lebanese government.

As part of the negotiations with Syria, Barak repeatedly demanded from the Syrians and the Americans that peace talks with Lebanon be renewed immediately. The Syrians were decidedly opposed, and announced that talks with Lebanon would begin only after completing the demarcation of the border between Syria and Israel. For them, the situation in Lebanon was a bargaining chip, which could be used to put pressure on Israel.

On January 16, 2000, Dennis Ross informed Barak and me of the contents of US Secretary of State Albright's meeting with Syrian Foreign Minister al-Sharaa. At the meeting, al-Sharaa said, "We will not agree to negotiations with Lebanon being resumed before the border between Israel and Syria is marked." Albright responded, "That is out of the question."

Then al-Sharaa came up with a "creative" idea: Syria would agree to an immediate announcement of the renewal of negotiations between Israel and Lebanon, but they would not actually begin until the demarcation of the border between Israel and Syria was complete.

Albright was utterly opposed to this as well.

In a telephone conversation I had with Dennis Ross, at a later time, I suggested that Dennis would tell the Syrians that the international border between Israel and Lebanon, as marked on maps and on the ground, would not constitute a precedent with respect to determining the border with Syria. I thought that the Syrians were concerned that the determination of our border with Lebanon would force them to agree to the international border between them and Israel, and quash their demands that the border would be the line of June 4, 1967, which is not the same as the international border. Dennis replied that he received the impression that the Syrians would not agree to discussions regarding the border with Lebanon as long as they were not satisfied in regards to their border with Israel.

In early 2000, the Americans continued their attempts to resume negotiations between Israel and Syria. In Southern Lebanon, clashes were occurring between the IDF and Hezbollah, who continued to fire at northern communities, and the IDF responded by firing at Hezbollah targets. Barak sent a message to the Americans that we assessed that the Syrians were encouraging Hezbollah to continue attacking us. The Americans, in response, sent a message to al-Sharaa, stating that the situation was deteriorating, and Hezbollah's attacks could kill the peace process.

Even earlier, in Shepherdstown, Barak made clear to Clinton and al-Sharaa that Syria would also be responsible in case of deterioration on the Lebanese front.

In response to one of the American petitions, al-Sharaa claimed that Damascus was "doing everything in its power" to stop Hezbollah's attacks. At the same time, he asked to convene the Supervisory Committee, which was established to oversee the implementation of the "Grapes of Wrath" understandings, to discuss what he referred to as Israeli violations of the understandings. The basic understanding reached after Operation "Grapes of Wrath" in 1996 was that Hezbollah would not fire from within the villages, but if this did happen, Israel would be able to retaliate against the sources of fire. Both sides, it was agreed, would refrain from firing at civilian targets.

These understandings were violated by Hezbollah day and night, and Israel did in fact respond by attacking, among other targets, sources of fire located in Lebanese villages. These attacks were used to justify the Syrian claims regarding Israeli violations.

On February 14, 2000, at 11:35 PM Israel time, another phone call, one of many, took place between Clinton and Barak. Barak began by saying that he sensed that within the next two weeks, we would know if we had a partner in Damascus for an agreement, which would also facilitate an agreed withdrawal from Lebanon. He added, "We made it clear in the last two weeks that we are willing to take far-reaching measures to protect our citizens and our soldiers, but Hezbollah attacks could lead to the destruction of the peace process. We are at the moment of truth. If we find that we have a partner, we will promptly settle the IDF's withdrawal as part of an agreement. In the absence of a partner, we will be forced to announce a unilateral withdrawal based on UN Security Council Resolution 425. After we are deployed along the border with Lebanon, it would be unwise for anyone to test us. We will respond with great force."

Clinton was in complete agreement with Barak.

At that time, there were many meetings between Dennis Ross and Martin Indyk and Barak. I participated in all of these meetings. The meetings dealt with the Palestinian track and the Syrian track. In the Syrian track, the emphasis was on preparing the summit between Clinton and Assad, which was supposed to bring about a breakthrough in negotiations and pave the possibility of attaining peace with Syria.

In those days, the IDF was making detailed preparations for two scenarios. In one scenario, the withdrawal from Lebanon would be done as part of an agreement, and in the other – it would be done unilaterally, based on Security Council Resolutions 425 and 426.

I took it upon myself to jump start the preparatory work regarding the South Lebanon Army (SLA). At the first discussion I convened, attended by the Head of the Shin Bet's Rehabilitation Administration, the Coordinator of Government Activities in Lebanon Uri Lubrani and representatives of the various ministries, I made it clear that the treatment of the SLA, including evacuation of its troops and their families to Israel and their rehabilitation here, was critical, and had to succeed.

I instructed that the Collaborator's Rehabilitation Administration in the Shin Bet would be responsible for rehabilitating the SLA soldiers and their families, and the IDF would be responsible for their evacuation to Israel.

Later, in another telephone conversation, Clinton told Barak that his meeting with Assad in Geneva would take place on Sunday, March 26, 2000, during a stopover he would make on his way from India to the United States.

In every conversation between Clinton and Barak, the matter of departure from Lebanon was also raised. Barak strove for an agreed withdrawal, and it was his first priority. However, if an agreement with Syria could not be achieved, the withdrawal would be carried out based on Security Council Resolutions 425 and 426. Barak understood that the IDF remaining in Lebanon was the worst alternative. I completely agreed with this notion. In all the discussions, I was of that opinion that our continued presence in Lebanon was much more of a burden than an asset.

After the failed Clinton-Assad summit in Geneva, the president called Barak and said he had done his best, but Assad was much more rigid in his stances than al-Sharaa in Shepherdstown. However, Clinton noted that Assad promised that the Lebanese front would be quiet, adding that the IDF's withdrawal from Lebanon, which

Syria was very concerned about, should be based on the Security Council's resolutions.

From that moment onwards, much effort was devoted to complete the plan to depart from Lebanon. Barak sought to do this as cooperatively as possible. We worked to coordinate the move with the United States, European countries, Russia, China, India, Japan, Arab countries and the United Nations. Our assessment was that Syria would heat up the region via Hezbollah as the withdrawal drew nearer. It was clear to us that we would have to respond. It was a recipe for deterioration. We asked the United States to use its influence over Arab countries such as Egypt to get them to support the IDF's withdrawal from Arab land and appeal to the Syrians to try and prevent an escalation.

Our position was that it would be better if the United Nations would call for Israel to carry out the Security Council's resolutions to withdraw to the international border, and Israel would heed this call, rather than the alternative – that Israel would announce of its own accord that it has finally decided to uphold what was demanded of it many years ago.

In those days, I had many phone conversations with senior aides of various world leaders, including Lord Levy and Jonathan Powell from Britain; Steinmeier and Steiner of Germany; Omar Suleiman and Osama el-Baz from Egypt; the Jordanian Foreign Minister; de Lesamblea and Jean-David Levitte of France; Miguel Moratinos of Spain and others. In these conversations, I updated them of the Geneva summit's failure, the tense situation in Lebanon and the developments regarding the IDF's exit from Lebanon. I asked them to use their influence to restrain Syria and Hezbollah; to support the implementation of Resolution 425; to work to expand the UNIFIL force that would also be deployed in the security zone; and to drive the UN to decide that a UNIFIL force would be deployed there immediately upon the IDF's departure, to prevent Hezbollah from taking over the region.

The Americans asked that we align our positions regarding the international border's delineation, and began to take action. Their plan was that after aligning positions with us, they would present the border's delineation to the United Nations, would finalize it with the United Nations, would present it to Britain, France, Russia and China and also finalize it with them; and then it would be possible to get going and mark the border – first on the map, and then on the ground. Israel pledged to withdraw the army south of the border that would be agreed with the United Nations.

The fate of the SLA fighters was raised in every discussion with the Americans. Our position was that the Lebanese had to take care of the SLA's people as they had done with members of other militias in Lebanon, that is - to find a way to grant them amnesty and integrate them into Lebanese society and the Lebanese security apparatus. However, early on, we already assessed that the members of the SLA would prefer to leave Lebanon. Israel would absorb those who wish to come, and would work to assist those who preferred to settle in other countries.

Barak continued working to coordinate the withdrawal with the powers and the United Nations. He had countless phone calls with Kofi Annan, Chirac, Blair, Putin, Schroeder, Mubarak, King Abdullah and others. In these conversations, he made it clear that Israel would withdraw to the line decreed by the United Nations, would build a new border fence and deploy along it, and UNIFIL forces could be deployed at a much larger scale in the area that Israel would evacuate. He added that Syria saw the withdrawal as a great threat, because it would lead to increased demands for it to withdraw from Lebanon as well.

At that point, Barak had already decided to leave the withdrawal date vague. We knew that as we draw nearer to the date, tensions will increase. We continued to talk about July 2000 as the month in which the withdrawal will be executed, but planned to execute it as surprisingly as possible.

On April 6, 2000, I convened another discussion regarding the plans to rehabilitate the SLA. In the discussion, I was told that we were prepared to absorb only about 600 households. It was not enough. I instructed the participants to continue working round the clock in order to prepare to absorb many thousands and improve the existing program.

We located facilities belonging to the Friends of the IDF charity and military bases in which the SLA fighters and their families would be absorbed when the time came. I asked all the people responsible for the program to be prepared to implement it starting from May 15.

UN Secretary General Kofi Annan appointed Terje Larsen to handle the withdrawal from Lebanon, including the issue of the border between Israel and Lebanon. Barak appointed me to coordinate the efforts being made with all the relevant international and Israeli factors who were involved in the matter. It was agreed that the UN would send a group of expert surveyors that would work with our experts, and they would accurately delineate the border. On the Israeli side, this activity was led by attorney Moshe Kochanowsky, Deputy Director-General for Special Operations in the Ministry of Defense, and Col. Haim Srebro, commander of the IDF's mapping unit.

In my conversations with Barak, we continued developing various alternatives for solving the issue of the SLA. In his meeting with the American team led by Dennis Ross, Barak said, "If the process is done correctly, UNIFIL will immediately enter the area we evacuate. We can then affect General Lahad, commander of the SLA, to split his forces into three ethnic militias - Druze, Christian and Shiite, and the commanders of these militias will be able to discuss their future with the leaders of the various sects in Lebanon."

Barak added, "We will help them as necessary, treat their wounded and provide humanitarian aid and food aid. If Hezbollah shells them with artillery fire, we will help the SLA with artillery fire from our territory. Let no one expect that we disarm the SLA. They need their weapons to protect themselves."

Meanwhile, preparations continued on the Israeli side at an increasing rate. The IDF began to remove excess equipment from its outposts in Southern Lebanon. This was done at night, so as not to encourage Hezbollah to exacerbate its attacks. From early May, the IDF would have to be ready to evacuate Southern Lebanon at short notice.

IDF Chief of Staff Shaul Mofaz did not like the idea of the IDF withdrawing from Southern Lebanon. Contrary to the accepted practice in democratic regimes, he spoke out publicly against the withdrawal and claimed that Barak was taking too big a risk in his decision. I thought Mofaz went too far. A military official must not publicly criticize the decisions of the Prime Minister and the government, especially when that criticism goes so far as to imply that the Prime Minister and Defense Minister is actually endangering the safety and security of the residents of northern Israel. I told my opinion to Barak, but he decided not to take action to stop these damaging remarks.

In my opinion, Barak made a mistake when he allowed the Chief of Staff to continue his public criticism against the Prime Minister's decision. At the time, statements made by "anonymous military sources" appeared in the media, claiming that Israel was taking hair-raising risks in its withdrawal from Lebanon.

On April 11, Barak met with Clinton in the White House. The meeting lasted four hours and covered a wide range of topics. Of Lebanon, Barak said that we were preparing the withdrawal in accordance with UN Security Council Resolution 425. "We will return to the line where we were deployed in 1978, on the eve of Operation Litani," he said. The UN had already confirmed that this course of action would uphold Resolution 425, which calls for Israel to withdraw from all Lebanese territory. He added that it was important to expand UNIFIL, so that it could effectively control the area evacuated by Israel. Barak also updated the president that he recently rejected recommendations by the IDF to attack Syrian targets in Lebanon, despite Hezbollah's attacks and even though Syria was behind these attacks. He acted thusly to avoid an escalation in the Southern Lebanon front.

The IDF continued to dilute its order of forces and the abundant equipment it stored in Southern Lebanon. According to the Chief of Staff's recommendation, Barak authorized to transfer the "Taiba" outpost and later the "Rotem" outpost from the IDF to the SLA, and to further reduce the number of our soldiers in Lebanon. The outposts that were transferred to the SLA, as well as IDF outposts, were attacked by Hezbollah, and the SLA soldiers began to flee them.

On May 21, 2000, Hezbollah took over the "Taiba" outpost without a fight, and the collapse of the security zone accelerated. That was the moment when Barak decided that the withdrawal had to be carried out immediately, otherwise the SLA would collapse and the IDF would remain in Lebanon, holding outposts that no longer constituted a complete defensive array. The threat to IDF soldiers in this situation would be immense. In view of this, Barak ordered to carry out the withdrawal in one night, between the 23rd and 24th of May 2000.

The IDF withdrew its forces at night under very difficult conditions, and while Hezbollah was firing at our forces. The withdrawal was carried out very successfully, and the IDF completed it on the morning of May 24, with no casualties among our troops.

The hasty withdrawal led to IDF equipment and vehicles being left in the field and photographed by Hezbollah. These images, along with pictures of SLA soldiers and their families fleeing to the Israeli border, and pictures of Hezbollah fighters taking over the security zone, created the false impression that the IDF ran away from Lebanon.

I state that the IDF did not run away from Lebanon. The hasty withdrawal was necessary due to the collapse of the SLA. As a military operation, it was done flawlessly, in extremely difficult circumstances.

The SLA soldiers were granted entrance to the State of Israel, housed in a transit camp and then transferred to various locations in the country. Their treatment was very lacking at first but steadily improved over time. However, to this day, claims are occasionally heard that they "were abandoned" and that their treatment is still lacking.

About two weeks before the IDF's withdrawal from Lebanon, Barak met with General Lahad, the Commander of the South Lebanon Army, in his office in Tel Aviv. Lahad wanted to know how the SLA issue will be handled in the event of withdrawal. Barak made it clear to him that the best scenario would be for the SLA to remain in the form of three militias - Shiite, Christian and Druze, each of which would protect a strip containing the villages where its people live. Israel will not take the SLA's weapons, and will help the SLA deal with Hezbollah without our soldiers being in Southern Lebanon. Barak argued that in this format the SLA commanders will be able to receive the support of Lebanon's sectarian leaders, to negotiate with the Lebanese government about their future, and eventually integrate into Lebanese society and the Lebanese army.

Lahad informed Barak that he intends to travel for a few weeks to Paris, where his family lived. About two weeks later, as noted, the SLA began to collapse and the IDF made an early withdrawal.

At the time, Lahad was in Paris and not with his forces in the field. This did not deter him from sharply criticizing Barak for the way the withdrawal was carried out, and claiming that Barak hid his intentions from him and did not tell him that the withdrawal was set to take place within a very short time.

Lahad's claims are false. At the time of his meeting with the General, Barak did not know that he would be forced to order an immediate withdrawal. It was imposed on us by the situation that developed in the field, the same field from which Lahad was absent.

Thus, 18 years after IDF forces entered Lebanon in Operation Peace for Galilee, they withdrew and were deployed along the international border. UN surveyors, who had begun mapping the border, did not have time to finish the job before the IDF withdrew, and continued after the IDF was already deployed along the line set by us. Yet as we had pledged, the IDF withdrew its forces and changed their deployment according to the UN experts' measurements. The latter often changed their decisions in relation to the exact location of the border due to Lebanese pressure and allegations that the delineation was biased in Israel's favor, prompting the IDF to deploy, build a fence and move it time and again.

At one point we got tired of this, and demanded Kofi Annan to declare the final line. Israel deployed along this line, but Lebanon continued to complain that it was not the border in some places. Eventually, Kofi Annan declared that Israel had fully completed its withdrawal, and that the UN rejects Lebanon's claims to make additional changes to the borderline.

One of the bones of contention was the area of the Shebaa Farms, which remained under Israeli control. This area was under Syrian control until the Six-Day War, but the Lebanese claim that it belongs to them, and that Syria had given it to Lebanon. The UN, however, claims that the area is Syrian and connected to the Golan Heights, and therefore its fate should be determined in the negotiations between Syria and Israel. The Shebaa Farms issue has become bloody over the years, and for a long time Hezbollah continued to attack IDF soldiers in this area.

The village of Ghajar also caused quite a headache. This village was conquered from the Syrians by *Sayeret Matkal* during the Six-Day War. Its residents are Alawites and thus are part of the sect that is a minority in Syria, but which the ruling Assad family belongs to.

The border delineated by the UN surveyors divides the village into two parts: its southern part is controlled by Israel and its northern part is controlled by Lebanon. Since we did not want to disrupt the lives of the locals, we did not build a fence separating the two parts of the village. The place remained a weak point, and Hezbollah took advantage of it several times to infiltrate into the village in order to attack IDF soldiers. When Israel began building a fence north of the village to plug the gap, a protest arose from Lebanon, to the effect that Israel was taking over the northern half of the village. The solution was to build a security fence south of the village and monitor the passage of local villagers into Israel.

I supported the withdrawal from Lebanon before the decision was made, and to this day I am certain that it was a most correct move. After years of nonstop incidents between the IDF and Hezbollah in Southern Lebanon, and Katyusha rockets being fired at communities in the Galilee, the sector cooled down and there was a dramatic drop in the level of conflict. Most of the time the border remains relatively calm, and the northern communities returned to flourish economically.

In July 2006, the Second Lebanon War broke out, but since the end of the war and until the time of this book's publication, our northern border with Lebanon has usually been quiet.

CHAPTER 29

"DEAR FRIENDS, WE ARE NOT MAKING PROGRESS"

In the midst of preparations for Camp David, we learned from the Americans that people around Arafat were running an intimidation campaign, according to which this whole summit was nothing but an Israeli-US trap, designed to elicit concessions from him. We assessed that the ones disseminating this approach were Abu Mazen and Abu Alaa.

Barak continued to detail his viewpoint to the Americans, listing everything he was willing to give the Palestinians, and constantly reiterating, "I am taking a political risk, endangering the integrity of my coalition and government and I run the risk of creating a rift within the Israeli public. The risks I am taking are much larger than Arafat is taking with respect to his people. If he will reject all my generous offers at the summit, we will find ourselves – he and I, the Palestinian people and the Israeli people – on the brink of disaster. After the Israeli public will learn how far we went in the proposals we submitted to Arafat and were rejected by him, they will be united in the opinion there is no partner for dialogue on the other side. All this will lead to accelerated separation between the Palestinians and us. The United States must make it clear to Arafat that while he has not shown any flexibility, I go further than any prime minister has gone before me. He must understand that both of us have to take risks and come to the summit, and that it is much less dangerous than to avoid going, because then we will crash and burn. The summit could prevent grave deterioration between the sides."

Madeleine Albright returned from a meeting with Arafat and informed us that the Palestinians threatened that if they saw that nothing was happening, they would unilaterally declare an independent state in the forty percent of the West Bank's territory under their control, and would continue their efforts to obtain the rest of the territory.

At the mention of this scenario, Barak said that if such a thing were to happen, on the very same night, Israel would declare the annexation of the large settlement blocs that encompass fifteen percent of the territory, and the entire Jordan Valley, which is another twenty percent. "Then," said Barak, "we'll see what they will do."

Albright told Arafat that if he did so, it would be a pyrrhic victory: a victory that comes at such an exorbitant price that it is tantamount to defeat.

She explained to Arafat that his views were vague and his areas of flexibility unclear, so the process could not move forward, because until Barak saw flexibility on Arafat's part, he would be unable to keep showing flexibility on his part.

In the meantime, we made sure to pass messages to many countries, that this summit could be a historic event in which Israel was willing to make greater concessions than any prior or future government. Arafat would make a critical mistake if he unilaterally declared a Palestinian state. We were making generous and far-reaching offers to Arafat, and if, God forbid, the summit failed – we would show the entire world just how generous and far-reaching we were. Arafat would then be revealed as a refuser of peace and the entire world would turn its back to him.

During the preparations for the summit, Barak had a marathon of night conversations with Clinton. I was amazed every time to discover how much patience and time Clinton devoted to the conversations with Barak.

In one conversation, Clinton mentioned the possibility of the worst-case scenario, and said, "I'm concerned. We cannot predict the outcome of the summit and must take into account the possibility that it will fail. The Palestinians are talking about territorial exchanges and I do not know your position on the matter, they want part of East Jerusalem and you oppose it. How will we solve these problems? I suggest you make gestures to Arafat so he reaches the summit in a constructive mood. The summit will have to take place somewhere completely isolated from the media, to avoid leaks that may harm our efforts. This is why I have chosen Camp David, which is an easy place to isolate, and due to its small dimensions, each side can only bring twelve people."

"I am on the same page with you on these issues," Barak replied. "Arafat is taking advantage of the fact that I have not given him the three villages near Jerusalem (Abu Dis, 'Anata and al-Eizariya) even though the Knesset approved it, following violent and severe riots which broke out that day, and after Palestinian policemen opened fire on our security forces. Since then, Arafat has assumed a sullen pretense, but every time we make gestures to him he asks for more – so it was recently when after we transferred 200 million NIS to him. He swallowed the money in seconds and within twenty-four hours sent additional requests. I cannot give him the villages as long as I will not be convinced that he has taken all steps to ensure that the Palestinian security forces will not fire at us again. These 'favors' are not the main thing - the important thing is to reach an agreement, because time is working against the process.

In Israel, there is increasing criticism against concessions. I am taking enormous risks, politically and also on a personal level. I might become a target, as I have gone far beyond Rabin and Peres, against the political beliefs of the majority of the members of my government and a large part of the public. We have not forgotten what happened to Rabin when he took similar steps. In contrast, Arafat is being rude and undermining our confidence. He has to be convinced to talk constructively, to describe the summit as a win-win situation rather than one of winners and losers."

"Our approach," Barak continued, "is that if we leave the summit with an agreement, we will see it neither as our victory over the Palestinians nor their victory over us. An announcement by one of the parties regarding their 'victory' would only arouse the opposition forces on the other side, and therefore we need to talk about an agreement from which both sides emerge victorious."

"I'm not afraid to take risks," said Clinton, "provided I am convinced that success is possible." It was very important for Clinton that the summit would succeed, as its failure would also be his failure as 'best man,' host and mediator.

Barak believed Arafat would only show flexibility in a summit, which would have a dynamic that was difficult to reproduce in other types of meetings, and when he would see the whole package, he could realize what he stood to lose if he did not reach an agreement. Barak also asked to test once and for all if Arafat intended to tone down his positions and finally make some compromises, and to meet the Israeli demands halfway.

As the summit's date drew nearer, the phone calls between Barak and Clinton became more and more frequent, and took place almost every night and sometimes several times in the same day. In the final conversations before the summit, Clinton pressured Barak to make gestures towards the Palestinians, and talked about releasing prisoners and transferring the three villages, so that

Arafat would arrive in a good mood and would be able to present achievements to his public.

"As soon as I announce the transfer of the three villages, the National Religious Party will resign from the government," Barak said, "and *Shas* and *Yisrael BaAliyah* also threaten to do the same. It is important for me to start the summit while I still have a coalition. I cannot ignore internal Israeli considerations. There is a difference between a situation wherein I come to the summit while there is still a majority coalition that supports me, even if during the summit some parties will leave the coalition, compared to a situation wherein I come to the summit already without a majority in the Knesset."

Barak knew his coalition was very flimsy and believed he would not have another opportunity to discuss the final agreement, as the political system would not afford him even the partial support he received when he left for the summit.

The Americans allocated each delegation twelve places in Camp David, where they were to hold discussions on the core issues, and twenty additional places in the nearby town of Emmitsburg, where the generic issues were to be discussed.

It was determined that the summit would be closed and isolated, and the agreement was that no one would have contact with the media except for American Press Secretary Joe Lockhart, who would deliver reports to journalists on behalf of both sides.

On July 9, two days before the summit's opening, Barak updated Clinton that the National Religious Party and *Yisrael BaAliyah* had left the coalition, and that *Shas* was still considering its next steps. "The State of Israel, and I personally, are taking great risks, and I expect you to help us reduce the risks we are taking upon ourselves to a minimum," said Barak, hinting at a large security package, including advanced weapons, financial aid, intelligence and defensive measures that the Americans would give to Israel as compensation for the territory it was going to lose.

Late in the morning of July 11, we arrived at Camp David, a beautiful place, green and peaceful, located in the midst of a thick forest. Small golf carts were waiting for us and we each loaded our luggage on one of them and rode towards our cabin.

These were charming log cabins, each named after a different tree. Each cabin had two bedrooms and a sitting room. I shared a room with Gilead Sher, and together with us in the cabin were Shlomo Ben-Ami and Dan Meridor. The only ones who had their own cabin were Barak, who received a large cabin with a bedroom, living room and a study that became a headquarters, and secretary Einat Gluska – who was awarded one by virtue of being the only woman in the delegation.

The first formal meeting between the Americans and us took place as early as midnight. In it, our hosts informed us that we had only one week at our disposal before Clinton would have to leave us for the G8 summit – the meeting of the leaders of the eight major industrialized countries in the world (the United States, Russia, Canada, France, Germany, the United Kingdom, Italy and Japan) held in Okinawa, Japan.

We also learned that Oded Eran, who was at the nearby town in order to continue the public negotiation track, found himself without a partner after Arafat decided to bring Saeb Erekat to Camp David. We asked the Americans to solve the problem because this had been agreed on in advance and from our side a delegation of experts and auxiliary staff was waiting for the Palestinians. Arafat sent a representative only a few days later, but nothing developed from these conversations because of the reluctance displayed by the Palestinians.

Upon our arrival, the first conversation between Barak and Clinton took place, in the presence of Bruce Riedel, who was in charge of the Middle East in the National Security Council, his deputy Rob Malley and myself.

Barak presented the delicate political situation in Israel: "I have formed a coalition that will last at least until the start of the last stage," said Barak. "When I became Prime Minister, I decided that my most important goal is to achieve peace. I assumed that parts of this coalition would leave even sooner. I supported the 'Tal Law' (the first law that legally anchored the ultra-orthodox Jews' 'exemption' from military service) so that the ultra-orthodox would abstain in a no-confidence vote two days ago, and I could come to Camp David with a sitting government.

"Even if the government had fallen, I would come to Camp David, but for the public it is very significant that the government is still serving during my time here. I could have formed a unity government with the *Likud*, stabilized a broad coalition and avoided risking my political position, but then we could not advance the peace process."

Clinton told us that he had already met with Arafat who came before us, and that he found him relaxed. Everyone was concerned about Arafat's mood as he believed from the onset that this summit was an Israeli-American conspiracy designed to drag him into making concessions. Clinton also said that Arafat was aware of the political price Barak had to pay on his way to the summit (the National Religious *Party*, *Yisrael BaAliyah* and *Shas* leaving the coalition) and he believed that Barak was serious in his intentions.

It was agreed that the parties would not surprise each other, and Clinton said he told Arafat that if the Camp David summit failed, he would blame neither party (that is not what eventually happened), but the consequences of failure would be dire.

Clinton said that if an agreement would be reached, the United States could appeal to the G8 nations and Congress, and ask for extensive financial aid meant to enable the implementation of the agreement, to rehabilitate the refugees and provide them with adequate compensation.

In an attempt to explain his complex situation to Clinton, Barak said, "For us Israelis, survival is a very tangible and daily matter. I am obligated to remember that in two generations, Israel will be the only expression of the continuity of the Jewish people, since due to assimilation and intermarriage, the Jewish identity of our communities in the Diaspora could be significantly eroded. I always remember that I must ensure the future of the State of Israel without endangering its existence. So I am willing to make concessions, but not at any price. Only twice in the long history of the Jewish people, we had independence: once, it lasted for about four hundred years, and the next time we were independent for about a hundred additional years. Now we have the third kingdom of Israel, the third time we are independent in the thousands of years of this people's history. Therefore, I will not in any way agree to demands that will endanger the State of Israel and its continued existence as a Jewish and democratic state."

Barak referred to the US proposal that we start working according to pairs of topics, and in each topic, we would put our demands against the Palestinians' claims: "It cannot work that way," Barak said. "We have to see the whole thing as a complete package. Only thus will the parties be able to show flexibility on some of the issues in exchange for achievements in other areas."

Clinton agreed with Barak, and it was not the first or last time that Barak managed, in his logical way, to cause things to happen exactly the way he wanted them. Clinton once said, "I know only two people who can think many moves ahead, and their names are Ehud Barak and Bill Clinton…"

Immediately afterwards all the teams gathered, led by Clinton, who said, "Time is short and it is important to move forward as quickly as possible. We must stay isolated from the media and nothing is agreed until everything is agreed."

This notion of "nothing is agreed until everything is agreed" was a concept that Barak instilled.

This was due to the fact that during the negotiations with the Palestinians, we learned that every time we presented an idea that seemed to include an Israeli concession, the Palestinians had decided that this was already theirs, and started the next stage from that point. Clinton's remarks made it clear that nothing was 'yours' or 'ours,' until everything was finalized. Otherwise, the parties would be afraid to make offers during the negotiations.

Another thing that Clinton's remarks made clear was that the United States was the one that would manage the summit, the schedule and order of events.

To encourage and compliment Arafat, Clinton said that the Americans and Israelis were very happy about his decision to bring representatives of other political factions to Camp David, such as the communist Hassan Asfour and Yasser Abed Rabbo, who headed a small party that had made a coalition with Arafat.

Barak said, "We have come with a sense of heavy burden and great hope. Seven years after Oslo, nine years after Madrid, fifteen years since the eruption of the Intifada and thirty-five years since the PLO was founded, the time has come for a peace of the brave, to find a way to live side by side in peace and mutual respect, and to ensure a better future for our children. There will be no similar opportunity again, and if God forbid we fail, we both could face very serious problems."

"Barak said important things," Arafat said, "and we hope that what happened here between Sadat and Begin will repeat itself."

Clinton went on to meet with the parties, and in the next meetings he presented a plan, which would later serve as the basis for the

American's later proposal, known as the "Clinton Plan", for resolving the conflict.

The key elements of these initial ideas were: there would be no right of return to Israel for Palestinian refugees; the Jordan Valley would remain under Israeli control for a few years and would serve as a security zone; we would redefine "the Jerusalem region" and increase its territory beyond the current municipal borders; the nearby villages would be defined as part of Jerusalem, and would serve as the basis for the establishment of Al-Quds, the Palestinian capital. In this way, it would be possible to say that the Palestinians had established their capital in Jerusalem.

Barak said he was worried about the fact that Arafat had yet to make any concrete proposal regarding the negotiations. "We come with maps and present positions, in an attempt to bridge the gaps, and the Palestinians bring nothing!" he complained.

Regarding refugees, Barak said that in the early 1950s, just after the War of Independence and soon after its establishment, Israel had absorbed 650,000 Jewish refugees who fled or were expelled from Arab and Muslim countries. These people left behind vast wealth, and when discussing a solution to the refugee problem, they would need to be taken into account as well as the way to compensate them. If that could be achieved, then the State of Israel could make a humanitarian gesture, and allow the entry of one thousand refugees per year for ten years on the basis of family reunification, up to a total of ten thousand refugees. Barak repeatedly stated that this would be done on humanitarian grounds of family reunification and not on the basis of the right of return, which Israel utterly opposed.

Clinton proposed to examine a solution for the issue of Jerusalem in three levels: the practical level – how the day-to-day lives of all the city's residents would be conducted; the religious level – how the holy places would be administered; and the political level - where would the border between Jerusalem and Al-Quds pass, where sovereignty would be Israeli and where it would be Palestinian.

At that stage, the Americans also supported the notion that Jerusalem would not be divided but members of all religions would have free access to it. Clinton proposed the idea that the city's administration would be based on districts that would all be under Israeli sovereignty, with each district enjoying self-governance, and above them would be the city's elected council and in it representatives from all districts.

Barak suggested that in the Greater Jerusalem area (Jerusalem and the surrounding villages), some regions would be defined as Israeli, some as Palestinian regions, and in others there would be special arrangements (such as in the Old City).

Barak said he was concerned that Israel's concessions would be perceived as problematic by parts of the Israeli public. Hence he requested two additional components to help package the agreement and make it easier for the Israeli public to digest. He asked that during the summit, Clinton would already start petitioning additional Arab and Muslim nations to join the peace process with Israel, and also asked for generous US aid to Israel.

"Uprooting 40,000 settlers from their homes is not only practically difficult, it is also very expensive, and will cost the state $10 billion," said Barak.

One of the ideas Barak suggested was that the Americans would purchase from us the residential and industrial areas in the settlements, and transfer them to the Palestinians for free. "Do not give us money to evacuate settlements, but in exchange for the property instead," said Barak, when the Americans told him that Congress would not approve financial aid to fund the settlers' evacuation.

"I am worried that someone will try to harm you physically," said Clinton to Barak. "I remember Rabin's terrible murder, and I am worried about the opposition of a considerable part of the public to your actions."

"I am willing to take personal and political risks," said Barak. "We have brought the Israeli public to a state of internal rift as a result of the process. There are opponents and proponents. So if, God forbid, we do not reach an agreement, despite our generous offers, and Arafat feels he has the support and sympathy of the United States, it will be a recipe for disaster as it will encourage him to take destructive measures."

It was settled that the issue of Jerusalem would be discussed one day after the discussions regarding the other issues, because of its sensitivity, and Shlomo Ben-Ami was appointed head of the Jerusalem group. Amnon Lipkin-Shahak was appointed head of the settlements group, and the head of the IDF Planning Directorate Gen. Shlomo Yanai was appointed to be in charge of security arrangements. Elyakim Rubinstein headed the discussion group for the refugees and I was appointed to deal with bilateral issues between us and the Americans. Gilead Sher was initially part of Ben Ami's group and later the two of them also handled the borders issue.

Clinton said he wanted to talk to President Mubarak and persuade him that Egypt would give additional territory to expand the Gaza Strip, rather than the territorial exchange that the Palestinians demanded in return for the territory that would remain in our hands. It was clear that the chances of such an idea to succeed were slim, since no one was in a hurry to give away land. You could see the extent to which Egypt would fight to receive its last grain of sand in the way they handled the Taba affair.

I worked opposite of Bruce Riedel, a CIA veteran who was loaned to the National Security Council and served as Clinton's advisory on the Middle East. I presented to Bruce the request for aid: two and a half billion US dollars to redeploy the IDF; one billion US dollars in compensation for the loss of capabilities and territory in the form of intelligence and long-range weapons; one billion US dollars towards roads and bridges that would allow contiguous movement for the Palestinians; one billion US dollars for safe passage between Gaza and the West; one billion US dollars for the borderline between Israel and the Palestinians; 10 billion US dollars for construction of desalination plants and the separation of infrastructure (water, electricity) between us and the Palestinians; three billion US dollars towards strengthening the IDF; and two billion US dollars for infrastructure in Jerusalem. All this did not include the financial solution for the Palestinian refugee issue nor the US acquisition of the settlements we would evacuate.

I read the list from the page, and Riedel wrote down every word and did not respond. My impression was that the Americans in general were not frightened by numbers. I think the request was not excessive. In US terms, this was pocket change compared to the US annual budget, which comes to trillions of dollars. Indeed, the next day Clinton told us, "We are working on the numbers you presented to Riedel and they seem reasonable to me."

At the time, the atmosphere with the Palestinians was comfortable. This was in no small part due to the stunningly beautiful location that created a tranquil, relaxed and serene atmosphere.

Along the camp's paths we had friendly meetings with the Palestinians and we dined at mixed tables in the dining room, where we were served excellent meals.

We had a joint basketball game where the Israelis and Palestinians played against one another, and one night we watched an American war film together, in which the Americans take command, successfully of course, of a German submarine. The Americans supplied the popcorn.

The main people with whom we had dealings were Mohammed Dahlan, Hassan Asfour, Muhammad Rashid, Saeb Erekat, Yasser Abed Rabbo and Nabil Shaath.

We hardly even saw Abu Alaa and Abu Mazen, and we remembered that they - along with Arafat himself – were the main opponents to the summit.

On the night of the summit's second day, Barak called a meeting, and told us there was a chance that during the next day the Americans would introduce their own initial suggestion for resolving the conflict. Barak told us that for now, the Palestinians were still unwilling to enter a real discussion and show flexibility, and that they were not presenting any idea of their own.

Barak said that we had to make it clear to the Americans that we were very close to our utmost far-reaching positions. "We did not come here to take part in a Mediterranean bazaar," said Barak, "the positions we have presented are almost our final positions. From our perspective, this would demonstrate how serious we are. The Palestinians, in contrast, have immediately declared: we want all the territory, and that's it. We wanted to give dialogue a chance, and are presenting them with a line that is nearly final and very advanced, a line that includes many concessions, while they are not making any concessions, only demands. It is important to achieve the end of the conflict, and we will not accept any formulation that implies Israeli responsibility for the refugee problem. Tomorrow, you will concentrate on the dialogue with the Americans so that they will soften the Palestinians."

The next day I had another meeting with the Americans, in which I emphasized the matter of upgrading strategic relations between Israel and the United States in the sense of creating a defensive alliance of sorts, mainly meaning that a threat to use non-conventional weapons against Israel would be considered a threat against the United States itself.

In addition, I asked for two defensive measures as part of the aid package: the F-22 future combat aircraft, and Tomahawk cruise missiles.

On the third day of the summit, on July 13, Barak told Madeleine Albright and Martin Indyk that Arafat had to understand that the United States and Israel have 'red lines,' and if he decided to 'blow up' the negotiations – it would not be a picnic for him. Barak believed that Arafat would be willing to make difficult decisions only when he understood that the alternative would be disastrous for him.

"If everything collapses here, I will have no alternative but to form a unity government with the Likud," said Barak, "and such a government would not be able to accept the positions we present today. All this will only lead to the collapse of the process and of relations between the Palestinians and us."

In the afternoon, the Americans gave us a paper with their own proposal, which was not acceptable to us. It talked of territorial exchanges, and of the borderline between us and the Palestinian state being based on the 1967 lines.

We said the wording should be that this line must be affected by the strategic needs of Israel, and the situation that has developed in the area since 1967 (settlements and security needs). In addition, we wanted to add the issue of Jewish refugees expelled from Arab and Muslim countries. These refugees left their belongings behind and would also need to be compensated for the great suffering they had undergone and the property they had lost.

Naturally, Jerusalem, with all the sensitivity surrounding it, was put on the center stage.

With regard to Jerusalem, Barak briefed us that it would remain united under Israeli control, with free access for all to the holy places. Its municipal area would be expanded and within it a Palestinian capital could be established. Sovereignty would remain Israeli, including in the places where the Palestinians would have municipal powers.

Barak changed the structure of the teams and assigned me and Meridor to handle Jerusalem issues, Gilead Sher and Ben-Ami to borders, Lipkin-Shahak and Yanai to security issues, and Rubinstein and Gidi Grinstein to the refugees issue. The Palestinian teams opposite of us were Abu Mazen and Nabil Shaath on the issue of refugees, Asfour and Abu Alaa on the issue of borders, Dahlan and Rashid on security issues, and Yasser Abed Rabbo and Saeb Erekat on the issue of Jerusalem.

Meanwhile, behind our backs, the Americans pulled a trick on us. On July 14, we received from them a draft of the US proposal that was not presented to us earlier, and that there was no way we could accept, as it mentioned transferring sovereignty in the Arab neighborhoods of Jerusalem, which are far away from the Old City, to the Palestinians. According to the draft, the Palestinians would be given control over almost the entire border with Jordan, contrary to our view that for security reasons, we needed to be responsible for the Jordan Valley, and to withdraw gradually over ten years.

The Americans submitted the draft to us and the Palestinians at the same time, without coordinating it with us and contrary to our earlier understanding that neither side would surprise the other.

Barak flew into a rage, said that this was unacceptable and that if this paper would continue being passed around it will cause great harm, as it would become a starting point for negotiations on Jerusalem. To make things worse, it contained big concessions on our part, without any Palestinian concession.

He demanded an urgent meeting with Clinton, who immediately agreed.

Barak came to the meeting with the signs of anger on his face easily discernible even at first glance.

As soon as he entered "Aspen," Clinton's cabin, Barak did not hide his exasperation and stated he was very disappointed by this draft paper. He stressed that it contained sections he would not accept, and said that he was also disappointed by the process between him and Clinton on a personal level, and as a friend and a leader.

"I am willing to sacrifice my entire political career for peace, but I will not be subject to American manipulation," said Barak. "I presented my viewpoint to you extensively many times, I said I was willing to take risks, but stressed that I must not be surprised by the United States - and here I am surprised. After seeing the first proposal for the paper, I met Albright and gave her a document with our requests for amendments. Despite this, in the draft you have prepared there are positions associated with Israel which were not coordinated with us, and worst of all – you have already presented it to the Palestinians! Now they have a new basis for negotiations without them actually having given anything in return. Our most crucial positions on Jerusalem and the Jordan Valley have been compromised!"

While Clinton was quick to say, "Delivering the paper without coordination with Israel is my mistake," we believed that this "mistake" was not made innocently.

The Americans thought that the document contained concessions from both sides and its purpose was to force the Palestinians and us to begin to confront bridging the gaps between our positions.

"If so, it would be better for us if the document will be returned to the Americans as if it had never been," said Barak, "and we will refrain from referring to it for the rest of process."

Clinton immediately accepted the suggestion to shelve the document and said, "In fact, the Palestinians don't have a plan. They just react to what you and I say to them."

The Palestinians had only one plan and it was called the 1967 borders, and in Jerusalem they demanded that every part that was occupied during the Six-Day War would return to Palestinian ownership, including the Old City and the Temple Mount.

They were only willing to discuss the principle of settlement blocs, but stressed that the blocs' size must not exceed two percent of the territory, while we were talking about ten percent and agreed to territorial exchanges to compensate for the area that would remain under Israeli sovereignty.

Gradually, the atmosphere at that conversation on the porch of Clinton's cabin softened. The atmosphere at this conversation and others was always tranquil and at eye level, in no small part thanks to Clinton's phenomenal ability to give his companions the pleasant feeling that he was entirely attentive and concentrated on them.

"The Jerusalem issue is more complex than what you feel and appreciate," Barak said to Clinton. "In the past, I have spoken with Mubarak, with King Abdullah and previously with his father King Hussein, and presented to them my outlook on Jerusalem, which is that the city will remain under Israeli sovereignty. Outside of Jerusalem's municipal borders, in the villages of Abu Dis and 'Anata, a city called Al-Quds will be established, and this will be the Palestinian capital. Muslim neighborhoods in Jerusalem will remain under Israeli sovereignty and will enjoy a high degree of municipal self-administration, in the sense that some of the municipal authorities will be delegated to committees that will manage the Muslim quarters. This means responsibility over issues such as education, garbage collection, and so on. In the Old City and the Temple Mount, sovereignty will remain Israeli, but we will establish a special regime there, which we will discuss later on. When I presented this to the Arab leaders, they didn't seem to fall off their chairs. Hence I assume that if Arafat will accept these ideas or something similar to them, he will receive the support of the Arab world."

Barak said these things in response to Arafat's repeated claim that if he were to make concessions in Jerusalem – he would be murdered.

On that same day, close to midnight, Clinton called Barak and Arafat to a tripartite meeting with him. Each one of them brought along one of his aides: Clinton brought Bruce Riedel, Arafat brought Nabil Abu Rudeineh and Barak brought – as always – me.

Clinton opened the meeting by saying, "Dear friends, we are not making progress and must start moving faster."

Immediately afterwards, he began to summarize his impression of how the matters at hand had developed up to that point. "On the issue of refugees, we need to find a framework for a solution, with the US approach being that there will not be a right of return to within the borders of Israel but to Palestine, and after the solution is settled, we need to find a way to implement it. On Jerusalem there has been no progress, and each side demands sovereignty. I asked you to conduct a simulation in which each side assumes that its demand has been accepted and now has to solve the other side's problems."

Arafat intervened at this point to slip in a phrase he would use whenever he wanted to impress someone, "If there is a will, there is a way."

Clinton proceeded, "On borders and territory, there was little progress, but the two main obstacles are the Palestinians' demand that Israel withdraw to the June 1967 borders, with very slight amendments, while Israel is talking about annexing around ten percent of the territory that includes the major settlement blocs, where approximately eighty percent of the settlers live. The second obstacle is Israel's demand for security control in the Jordan Valley for about ten to fifteen years, while the Palestinians demand sovereignty over the entire Jordan Valley and could accept a phased Israeli withdrawal that would last no longer than two years."

"Our mission is to reach an agreement and we must ensure that everything possible was done to achieve it," Clinton proceeded, and turned to Arafat. "Mr. Chairman, we cannot move forward if you do not begin to treat these meetings as a summit, meaning that all discussions are meant for exchanging ideas so that we can show creativity, openness and flexibility, and nothing is agreed until everything is agreed. Since time is short, we will continue working on Saturday, but because this is a sacred day for the Jews, representatives of both sides – Israelis and Palestinians – will not record the talks in any way."

The idea was to cause the Palestinian side to be more open, since if nothing was recorded, it became more of an exchange of opinions, which could dispel their fear of saying things that would later be used against them.

Arafat was very nervous due to the occasion, and said, "We must do everything to speed things up. We have to make great strides forward. I suggest that the people work non-stop, day and night, until we achieve the coveted agreement."

"I agree with the Chairman," said Barak. "Time is of the utmost importance. I feel that either we reach an understanding now or never will. If we will not achieve an agreement, many people in our region will suffer on account of it."

"Israel will have to give territory back to you and it will shrink geographically," said Clinton to Arafat, "This is not a trivial matter, because no country has done so to date. For seven years, I tried to persuade Russia to give back to Japan a few islands it occupied during World War II, but I did not succeed. Both of you are wise and courageous and I will do my best and will be at your disposable all the time."

Clinton's remarks poured like honey on Arafat's tongue, and he was quick to say, "Your words are very encouraging, and I promise you on my behalf and on behalf of my partner Barak that we will fulfill your bidding."

During the summit Barak and Arafat rarely met, and I think this was a mistake on Barak's part. He should have initiated more meetings and shown more empathy towards Arafat. However every time I directed Barak's attention to the matter, he would answer, "As if all the problems could have been solved if only I had handed him pastries."

In meetings between him and Arafat in the presence of Clinton and others, Barak tried to be affable towards him and build a relationship with him, among other things by making statements such as "I completely agree with the Chairman's comments." Barak made a serious effort to give Arafat the feeling that he was listening to him, was attentive to him, appreciated his opinion and relies on it. Yet no real warmth formed between the two of them, who both made "equal" efforts.

On the next day, Barak met with Dennis Ross, and Ross voiced his disappointment from Barak's demand to shelve the draft on Jerusalem that the Americans had prepared.

Barak told Ross that things could have been different if the Americans would have included in the draft his comments on the first paper as they were conveyed to Albright, or had they prepared a new document with the updated Israeli and Palestinian positions.

This is the method for building an agreement: writing what was agreed, specifying the positions of the two sides on disputed issues, then trying to bridge the differences through negotiations.

"By the way you responded, we understand that you rejected this document completely," said Ross. "I ask you to present to me your final 'red lines.' We want to know how far you are willing to go on each one of the core issues (Jerusalem, refugees and the right of return, borders, settlements, security arrangements and the nature of the Palestinian entity to be established)."

Barak, who held tough negotiations and fought fiercely for his positions there, said to Ross, "In the last few months, the Palestinians have not strayed from their basic positions. Now you ask me for my 'red lines,' which means I will make more concessions, I will present what else I am willing to concede. However it will not work that way. If the Palestinians refuse to budge, there will be no agreement. I feel that you have not managed to get Arafat to understand that if he will not move forward, his losses will be significant. If any Israeli prime minister signs a paper that cedes part of Jerusalem, we condemn ourselves to the start of the disintegration of the Israeli nation."

Reports that continued to come to Barak's cabin that day revealed that the Palestinians had expressed willingness for Israel to withdraw from the Jordan Valley gradually and over a period of two years. They demanded sovereignty over the Old City including the Temple Mount. They insisted on the refugees' right of return, saying, "Let's agree in principle that we have the right to return and then we can discuss the numbers." The Palestinians were convinced that the majority of the refugees do not want to return to Israel, and the main issue was the matter of the 300,000 Palestinian refugees in Lebanon. The Palestinians also asked that the final borders would be the 1967 borders, with minor amendments on the basis of reciprocity.

Israeli's counter-proposal talked about expanding Jerusalem's municipal area to include Givat Ze'ev in the north, Gush Etzion in the south and Ma'aleh Adumim in the east. Two municipalities would be established – Israeli and Palestinian, with the second being based on Abu Dis, 'Anata and al-Eizariya. Sovereignty over the Temple Mount would remain Israeli and the Palestinians would continue to manage day-to-day life at the site through the Waqf, just as they do today. A network of roads and bridges would be built to allow the Palestinians to reach the Temple Mount directly from their neighborhoods without having to pass through Israeli neighborhoods.

At the same time, Barak began hearing rumors about a new document being prepared by the Americans. The source of the rumor was one of the American participants to the negotiations, who seemed to imply such a document was being drafted in a conversation he engaged in during one of the meetings.

Barak was extremely dissatisfied with this and asked to meet urgently with Clinton. Barak came to the meeting wearing a frown, turned angrily to Clinton and said, "I've heard rumors that you are preparing a new document that transfers the neighborhoods of Beit Hanina and Shuafat (which are in the outskirts of the far side of the municipal area of Jerusalem) to Palestinian sovereignty, and gives the Palestinians full autonomy in East Jerusalem, so that apart from the issue of security – everything is in Palestinian hands."

"We have not completed any such document and I promised you that nothing will surprise you," Clinton replied.

"A US document suggesting that Israel give up its sovereignty over East Jerusalem will force me to pack my bags and go back home," said Barak. "I did everything possible to make this summit happen, but there is no way we can agree to Palestinian sovereignty in Jerusalem. What's more, I expect you not to bring up the subject of territorial exchanges at the beginning of the negotiations. There is a huge difference between such an idea appearing at the end of the negotiations, as a means to achieve an agreement and as an American suggestion, compared to it popping up right now at the beginning of the negotiations. "

"If so, it would be better if there will be no American paper," said Clinton, "but a document formulated by the parties instead."

"I feel that Arafat wishes to hold both ends of the stick," said Barak. "If Israel will receive ninety-nine percent of Arafat's claims, there will be an agreement, and if we do not accept them – he will take what has already been offered and see it as the starting point for the next negotiations, while he has conceded nothing."

During that day Gilead Sher and Ben-Ami reported their findings after a night of discussions with the Palestinians. The two had introduced Israel's willingness to cede most of the control along the Jordan River and for the presence of an international force to oversee our security deployment, as long as we would be there. The withdrawal would be gradual, and Israel would continue to control the valley, but in contrast to the starting position that Israel would remain there for many years, now Israel was willing to compromise on a shorter timetable.

At least ten percent of the land in the West Bank would be annexed to Israel, including the area that is home to about eighty percent of the settlers in the large settlement blocs. The Palestinians wanted territorial exchanges in return for this, and we offered something that resembled a territorial exchange: a passage between Gaza and the West Bank, which would be within Israeli territory but would only be used by the Palestinians. They would receive service in our naval ports, would not have to build a port, and could use our airports. The idea was to suggest creative solutions that would not require us to give territory out of the sovereign territories of Israel.

"On the issue of Jerusalem," said Ben-Ami to Barak, "I went further in my proposal than you had authorized me to, and suggested that the outskirts - neighborhoods like Beit Hanina, Sur Baher and Shuafat - will be partially transferred to Palestinian sovereignty, and these neighborhoods will be part of Al-Quds, the capital of Palestine.

"I explained to the Palestinians," continued Ben-Ami, "that we would connect Ma'ale Adumim, Gush Etzion and Givat Ze'ev to

Jerusalem, and this will be a form of exchange of territories and populations. Within the heart of the Old City and the neighborhoods bordering it, Israeli sovereignty would be kept, and in the neighborhoods near the Old City – such as Sheikh Jarrah and Wadi al-Joz – there will be an autonomy with municipal functions that the Jerusalem Municipality will delegate to the neighborhoods' administrators (a similar model exists in London). In the Old City, a specific regime will be in place, which we have not yet defined, and we will allow Arafat to establish his office there."

Barak was not frightened by these sayings. The recognition had already begun to brew, that if we would not offer a very revolutionary solution for Jerusalem – nothing will move.

The Palestinian position on the matter was that the Jewish neighborhoods in Jerusalem would be under Israeli sovereignty and the Arab ones under Palestinian sovereignty, including the neighborhoods close to the Old City, as well as the Old City itself except for the Jewish Quarter. Regarding our demand for ten percent of the West Bank, they said they would only accept two percent.

"It was a theoretical exercise designed to test if it would provoke them to participate in the negotiations," said Ben-Ami. "We proposed a bold deal. Now we need to go to Clinton and say, 'we have come up with something new and daring, we have wildly exceeded the authority Barak granted us, and even so we received nothing from the Palestinians in return.'"

"Tell the Americans that Barak is not sure we can live with Ben Ami and Sher's proposal," Barak said. "Say that Ben-Ami told the Palestinians that we are presenting a puzzle whose parts are interdependent. If I concede something on the eastern border, and you do not concede some other issue – the concession I offered ceases to exist."

At the very start of the summit it was stated that until everything was agreed, nothing was agreed. However, the Palestinians used a different tactic: they would write down our offers, and in the next session regarded our proposal as if it was already in their pockets, and formed a new starting point, while taking care – as usual – to concede nothing.

"Stress to the Americans that you have presented these positions as part of a theoretical discussion, and that we do not agree that they will appear as part of the US paper," Barak said.

On July 16, at 9:00 PM, Clinton came to Barak's cabin on his own initiative, and said he was returning from the most difficult meeting he ever had with Arafat. "I told him I did not think that the Israelis would present such a compromising stance on Jerusalem," Clinton told us. "I said that I expect him to accept the Israeli proposal for the borders (the territory containing eighty percent of the settlers and the border with Jordan under Israeli sovereignty, and Israeli security deployment in the Jordan Valley for several years, with gradual withdrawal), and I expect him to finally introduce his own proposal. Until now, you are only listening and making no counter proposal. Israel cannot cede the territory which is home to about percent of the settlers. Any agreement has to bring an end to the conflict. I told him, 'You keep telling stories, but you cannot expect any more concessions from Israel!'"

Clinton said that at his words, Arafat started to tremble all over. He apologized and said, "I have no one to talk to in my team, and you are actually a sort of psychiatrist for me."

Clinton went on to say that he told Arafat that the Israelis had been very reasonable in their offer, and he (Arafat) was not being so.

"Do not be afraid to show flexibility," said Clinton, "I will protect you with all my strength. I expect you to make some suggestions to me. Until now, you have not been negotiating in good faith."

Clinton turned to Barak, "I believe that you have an excellent team and your people talk to you honestly, openly and without fear. On the other hand, I feel that Arafat's people are so afraid that they avoid telling him the truth. I said to Arafat: Do not treat the Israelis as if their demands are illegitimate and only what you demand is legitimate. You have to take their demands into account."

"This morning was perhaps the hardest day of my life," Barak replied. "Ben-Ami and Sher went, during the last night of discussions, much further than I had authorized them to, and if this did not cause Arafat to stray from his initial positions – it means we should probably prepare for war. They went beyond what I can live with. We built our country as a shield for the Jewish people and the State of Israel cannot exist without Jerusalem. Arafat can get almost everything he dreams and wishes for. I believe that the only way to move Arafat forward is to say to him, either we achieve an agreement here and now or such an agreement will never be achieved. I have burned a lot of political bridges behind me with the intention to give negotiations a chance. If we leave here without an agreement, within a few days, we will establish a national unity government or we will go to elections. Perhaps Arafat will declare independence and on that same night, we will annex the large settlement blocs and establish a security zone in the Jordan Valley. I estimate that these developments will lead to confrontation between us and the Palestinians. Then there would be no way to hide from the world who is responsible for the deterioration. After we show how far we went in Camp David, it will be clear to the entire world that Arafat carries all of the blame for the summit's failure. You have to make it clear to Arafat that if this happens, he will stand before the United States and the entire world as a culprit."

CHAPTER 30

THE SUITCASE PACKERS

As the days continued to pass, you could feel how disappointed Clinton and his people were from the Palestinians and how much they appreciated us.

At one meeting, Clinton could not help but erupting in shouts at Abu Alaa, "You are not negotiating in good faith and you are dragging your feet!"

In contrast, in personal meetings and the statements he made, you could see how much he appreciated Barak.

That same evening, after another meeting he had with Arafat, Clinton again came to Barak's cabin, a gesture which clearly exemplified the extent to which he appreciated him. He said, "Arafat said he will come very close to your territorial needs, so that you will annex between eight and ten percent of the territory, and in return he wants a territorial exchange, if only a symbolic one. He is leaving it to my judgment to determine which areas these will be. Arafat recognizes that Israel has security needs on its eastern border, but he refuses that Israel will annex land on the pretense of security. Additionally, he refuses that a twenty-five kilometer-wide portion of the eastern border will remain under Israeli sovereignty forever because he wants this line for himself. For him, this is annexation of territory under the guise of security needs."

"As for the end of the conflict," continued Clinton, "Arafat says he understands the need for this, but it can only be declared after there is an agreement and it is implemented in full. I told him that I could not give money to the Palestinians except in return for the end of the conflict, and I told him that Barak could also not pass an agreement in the Knesset except in return for the end of conflict."

"I have lost faith in Arafat," Barak replied, "and I understand that this summit will not be able to survive another crisis like the one we had in the past twelve hours. You have to use the momentum while Arafat is on the defensive, and talk to him about the Temple Mount. Israel cannot give up sovereignty at the Mount, and the fact should be stressed to him, that along with Israeli sovereignty, the Palestinians will manage the day-to-day religious and administration issues, just as they do today. The neighborhoods near the Old City will be under full Israeli sovereignty."

This conversation was taking place on the background of a severe sense of crisis, while informal contacts between all the teams continued to take place in order to conceive new ideas.

On July 17, there was another two-on-two meeting between Clinton, Barak, Bruce Riedel and myself. Clinton said that his impression was that Arafat thought we could reach an agreement. He told us that the Palestinians would be willing to recognize Israeli sovereignty over parts of eastern Jerusalem, because in case of an agreement - the whole world would recognize Jerusalem as the capital of Israel anyway.

Clinton asked Barak to describe to him how he saw the division of functions in the various neighborhoods in Jerusalem and how it would work, and what special arrangements would exist in the Old City and the Temple Mount. "I must nudge Arafat from his position on Jerusalem," said Clinton.

Barak continued to insist on full Israeli sovereignty over the Temple Mount, and said, "If this is not resolved, it means we have done nothing."

Clinton answered that he understood Israel's claim to sovereignty on the Temple Mount, but explained that he was trying to find something to give Arafat in return, to convince him that this deal would be beneficial for him.

Barak explained that according to his conception, the ongoing management of religious affairs and daily life on the Temple Mount would be given to the Palestinians. Yet in addition to the existing situation, wherein Jews could enter the Temple Mount but not pray on it, he demanded that Jews would be allowed to pray there. In the Old City, there would be a special regime under Israeli sovereignty, which would be managed by a local council with representatives from all the holy places, and would take into account all religious, archaeological and tourism aspects of the place.

Clinton asked, "What can you give the Palestinians in the Old City symbolically?" Barak replied, "For me, sovereignty means the supremacy of Israeli law, the overall security and planning and building authorities (all of which would remain ours). Everything else can be discussed."

Clinton suggested that perhaps we could enable the Palestinians to establish their own office in the Old City. Then they might feel more comfortable and be more responsive to our demands.

Barak was tense during meetings with the US President, and whenever he talked about concessions, his tone of voice became resolute and decisive: "I cannot make any more offers," he said to Clinton, "before I know that sovereignty in the Temple Mount and the Old City is ours."

At noon that day, there was a big discussion of the Israeli team on the back porch of Barak's cabin. The discussion was attended by all members of the Israeli delegation, as well as Oded Eran and Col. Daniel Reisner, Head of the International Branch in the IDF Military Advocate General.

"We have gathered to discuss the issue of Jerusalem with the aim of moving the summit forward," Barak said. "We have reached the edge of the concessions we could possibly make in other subjects. The Jerusalem issue seems to be the most charged. Our opening position is clear: there will be two municipalities in the greater Jerusalem area, with the whole of the current municipality of Jerusalem under Israeli sovereignty. The Palestinians will build Al-Quds in Abu Dis and the villages around Jerusalem, which will lead to the formation of Palestinian territory, Israeli territory and the area of the Temple Mount and the Old City, in which there will be a special regime. All this is without compromising the principle that the entire municipal area of Jerusalem is under Israeli sovereignty. "

The feeling was that if the problem of Jerusalem could be solved, it would be easier to solve the other problems, since Israel's position on the refugee issue was categorical, and there was only one starting and final position: there was nothing to discuss, and salvation would not come from there. This was also the Americans' opinion. However, our thinking, which was mistaken in retrospect, was that if Arafat would get almost everything he wanted with respect to Jerusalem, territory, borders and security arrangements – he would be able to bite the bullet regarding the right of the return for Palestinian refugees into Israel, which would not materialize.

In practice, this was not the case. While our intelligence assessments indicated that the Palestinians would not agree to give up the right of return, we nevertheless had to try.

Barak assessed that our position on Jerusalem would not be accepted by the Palestinians, and realized some creative thinking was required with regards to the question – what else could be done in Jerusalem?

Is functional autonomy (which refers to some parts of municipal authorities) in the neighborhoods a solution or a problem? Or perhaps it would actually be better to make a more painful cut? Perhaps things should be left vague? Or postpone some of the issues to a later time?

Barak asked to hear the opinions of the delegation's members and this time, more than in the past, he was very attentive to what the others said.

My opinion was that we needed a solution that would last for many years, and there must not be a source of clashes in Jerusalem, which could be hazardous to the peace agreement. Therefore, the solution had to be clear and sharp, so as not to leave room for different interpretations that would lead to conflicts. Jerusalem's current borders were not written in stone, and other borders could be set, for example – transferring the distant Arab neighborhoods, such as Shuafat and Beit Hanina, to Palestinian sovereignty; establishing a form of functional autonomy in the neighborhoods near the Old City; and in the Old City – which would be under Israeli sovereignty – municipal powers should be given according to districts. Arafat wanted a foothold in the Old City, so when a Palestinian Embassy in Israel would be established – it would be in the Old City. Among all the possibilities for municipalities I suggested two separate municipalities, rather than one over-arching municipality with two secretariats under it: for Jewish and Arab Jerusalem. I thought it would be right to establish a boundary line between the two cities, and that it was crucial that it be delineated on the maps and demarcated on the ground. In short – I thought that we needed to ensure complete separation between the Palestinian and Israeli territories.

This was also the attitude of most of the speakers. The gist was that we were willing to transfer the distant neighborhoods even if it meant that the Israeli right-wing would see Barak as dividing Jerusalem. Ceding the Arab neighborhoods did not seem so terrible to me, especially considering that in any case, only Arab-Palestinians live in these neighborhoods and Israelis stay away from there. Perhaps the time had come to say things outright and plainly: there are neighborhoods where we are sovereign "de jure" but not "de facto" – and there is no reason not to transfer them to the sovereignty of those who already manage them "de facto." Everyone knew that at that time it was Jibril Rajoub's security forces who controlled these Arab neighborhoods, and our security forces failed to prevent their activities there.

For Barak, this was a historic moment. He emphasized the moment's significance and noted that this was a unique moment that tore each one of us apart from the inside. The weight of a moment, in which a decision had to be made on very crucial issues with historic significance, landed on Barak's shoulders. There are moments in the life of a nation and the life of a leader in which difficult and overwhelming decisions must be made: so it was when the Partition Plan for Palestine had to be accepted or to announce the establishment of the State; so it was on some days during the Yom Kippur War, when all seemed to be lost and doomed, and the decision had to be made on how to continue conducting the war; such were the decisions that Begin had to make at Camp David, twenty-two years before we came there; and such was Rabin's decision regarding the Oslo Accords.

"I do not see myself, or any other prime minister, signing over our sovereignty in the Temple Mount," Barak said, "but on the other hand, we cannot ignore what is going to happen if we do not reach an agreement."

Barak believed that if the summit collapsed, it would have far-reaching and devastating consequences on the region. He therefore asked to make an effort and find the furthest point we could reach without crossing our 'red lines,' in order to indicate for ourselves our utmost degrees of freedom for the continued negotiations and to fully exhaust the chances for peace.

As usual, Barak was purposeful and practical, and began assigning tasks to the team.

The most far-reaching offer would be presented, based on the following components: two different municipalities; a mechanism for coordination between municipalities; special arrangements (especially transportation) that will allow the Palestinians to visit the Temple Mount; the establishment of a regime of functional-religious autonomy in the Temple Mount and of a municipal functional autonomy in the Old City, all under Israeli sovereignty.

From the jurists, Barak asked to suggest a range of formulations, according to which the Israelis had sovereignty over the Temple Mount and the Palestinians managed it.

Barak asked us to present to him the minimum requirements of the Palestinians, so as to be able to examine the differences between the maximum that we were willing to reach and the minimum that the Palestinians would be willing to accept – and then to see if we could bridge the gap between the two.

Immediately afterwards, there was an update meeting between Barak and Clinton, and the president said that he met Arafat and told him that the Israelis were working very hard to find solutions, and that he should do the same.

Clinton told us that Arafat decided to remove Abu Alaa and Abu Mazen from the talks, both of whom had demonstrated a negative attitude and had not supported anything, and now was relying on Muhammad Rashid and Mohammed Dahlan.

Barak asked the Americans to pressure Abu Alaa and Abu Mazen, so that they would adopt a positive attitude and also help Arafat take responsibility.

Barak told Clinton about the tasks he gave us, and Clinton replied, "What you have done is very important and I'm glad you listened to me. If we succeed, you will have the privilege to achieve what Rabin and Ben-Gurion did not manage to achieve: to end the historic conflict between the Israelis and Palestinians, and make Jerusalem the internationally-recognized capital of Israel."

"I feel a heavy burden on my shoulders," said Barak. "The responsibility is all mine, but I was surprised by the sense of burden expressed by the people in the discussion. In practical terms, any solution will have to be approved by the Knesset, and the entire agreement will have be passed in a referendum. Every slight change in Jerusalem's sovereignty, and any exchange of territory, require a majority of 61 MKs even before the referendum. We have to include in the complete package generous US military aid, steps toward a defense pact between Israel and the United States and diplomatic relations with as many Arab countries as possible following the agreement. Moving the US Embassy to Jerusalem could also help."

Barak was worried that the Palestinians, who showed no flexibility up to that point, would find it difficult to do so during the short hours remaining until Clinton's departure for the G8 summit at Okinawa, Japan, and he asked the president to cancel or postpone his departure. "The summit is entering a very sensitive state. If we cannot reach understandings on the fundamental issues within a day, I think there will not be an agreement," he said.

Barak assumed that if the Palestinians made no progress in the next day, then the chances that something might change on their end would be extremely slim to non-existent.

Clinton promised to postpone his trip for 18 hours, and Barak said to him, "I cannot go beyond a certain point and at this stage,

I cannot reach the final step that will connect between all the components of the deal, if I am not convinced that an agreement will be signed. Furthermore, I need to know what the United States undertakes to us regarding aid in weapons and money. I cannot show you the bottom lines before your trip, because at this point I am not convinced that an agreement will be achieved. And if something leaks, everything will 'blow up' even before your return, and then certainly an agreement would not be reached."

Clinton suggested he shuttle between Arafat and Barak, and examine a possible basis for an agreement during this. He asked us to prepare questions for him, through which it would be possible to discover Arafat's leeway, and whether he could accept an agreement in which he would only receive sovereignty over the outer neighborhoods of Jerusalem – without offering him autonomy in the inner neighborhoods for the time being. "We'll start at a distance from him and see where his minimum requirements can be met," said Clinton.

At the same time, Stauber and I met with the Americans and presented them with the updated list of Israeli demands for aid in case an agreement is signed. We asked for a description of the future relationship between the United States and the Palestinian state, including in security and intelligence issues.

We asked that the Americans would be responsible for the Palestinian state remaining demilitarized, that they give us securities for the event of a breach of the agreement by the Palestinians, and make sure that there would be no Palestinian claim against us on account of the occupation.

As part of the bilateral relationship between the United States and us, we discussed upgrading relations with the United States to the level of a defense pact. We asked for access to advanced technologies that were withheld from us until then, compensation for our losses from canceling the Falcon deal with China due to US demand, authorization for arms deals with India, and signing an economic memorandum of understanding that would guarantee Israel the same level of financial aid for the next seven years. In addition, we asked the United States to persuade as many Arab and Muslim nations as possible to join the peace process with Israel, that the intelligence cooperation be deepened between Israel and the United States, and asked to be given very generous financial aid including three billion dollars to purchase the settlements that Israel would leave.

At one in the morning, on July 18, there was a meeting in Clinton's cabin, its participants being the president, Shlomo Ben Ami, Barak and myself, Sandy Berger, Madeleine Albright and Dennis Ross.

"The foundation of our positions is a united Jerusalem under Israeli sovereignty, annexation of the large settlement blocs where approximately eighty percent of the settlers live, a declaration of the end of the conflict and that there will not be a right of return," said Barak, and gave Clinton a document that still did not include his last and final positions.

Clinton looked at the document, and his face turned red with anger. "I'm not going to the Palestinians with this kind of proposal!" he said furiously. "On Jerusalem there is a lot here less than what I already discussed with them."

According to the document submitted to Clinton, Barak took a big step backwards. This was because he did not want to start the negotiations from the point where he had already conceded and crossed his 'red lines.' This greatly angered Clinton: "We and the Palestinians waited for 13 hours to see the document," he said to Barak. "I will not go with anything less than what you already offered. This is a retreat from what you offered during the night, this is an unrealistic and unserious attitude." In his rage, Clinton let loose all the frustrations, angers and disappointments he had accumulated from Barak, and snapped at him, "I went with you to

Shepherdstown and wasted four days there, then I made a fool of myself, I went to Geneva to meet with Assad and felt like a puppet!"

Barak, with his unwavering ability to exhaust, persisted, "We do not expect Arafat to accept what we have offered, but we expect him to present a different position than the one he has presented so far."

"That's not true!" Clinton interrupted him. "The Palestinians have moved on the subject of territory by agreeing that Israel annexes between eight and ten percent of the land. Arafat waited all day for me to come, now you want me to go to him with a bunch of backwards steps? I will not go to him with this paper!" he concluded angrily.

Barak tried to calm him and said, "Jerusalem is the most sensitive part of our national identity."

"I know that!" Clinton interrupted Barack in a firm tone of voice.

Yet Barak continued, "I sent Ben Ami and Sher to negotiate with the Palestinians, and it was a depressing affair. They went beyond my 'red lines' - I understood our agreement was that the whole idea is to test whether Arafat would even be willing to budge from his positions, and he didn't budge. I do not know anything about a change in Arafat's approach. If it is assumed that this is the way to elicit a new position from me as a starting point for further negotiations – then you are mistaken. What Arafat said is that he intends to meet us halfway on the matter of territory, but he left his position vague. Maybe we also need to do the same. What I learned from the last six months and the last few days here, is that we are expected to speak clearly and concretely, while completely general statements by Arafat are deemed acceptable..."

"I think that Arafat was specific," Clinton shushed him. "Can you quote a number you heard from Arafat?" Barak asked.

"Yes, he is willing that you annex an area of eight to nine percent, which includes the settlement blocs," said Clinton. "As for territorial exchanges, I understood from him that he would agree that

I determine the size of the area that Israel will transfer to the Palestinians."

"Arafat has accustomed us to an attitude that we wouldn't accept even in a kindergarten," Barak continued. "I'm afraid we've become accustomed to him throwing tantrums and not moving on. We are asked to divide Jerusalem at the beginning of negotiations, and all to satisfy Arafat's childlike behavior? I can take many risks, but I have no intention of being seen as a 'sucker' by the Israelis. Eventually I will have to ask myself, how is it that I am asked to cross a line (regarding Jerusalem) which I intended to consider crossing only at the end, and only when there is a 'done deal.' If I budge before we know if Arafat is indeed a partner to an agreement, he will consider what he hears as a starting point for the next negotiation. When I see that there is movement on his part with respect to Jerusalem, we will also move. You can tell Arafat that it is not Israel's final offer, but Barak wants to know how he plans to proceed. The public did not give me a mandate to divide Jerusalem, and I can do it only if I know that I am near the end of the process, and that there is going to be an agreement."

It was a difficult meeting at one in the morning, and an hour later Barak was called to a private meeting in Clinton's cabin. He returned from the meeting at four-thirty in the morning, and told me that in it, Clinton once again said that he would not go to Arafat with our offer. Barak told him that he should not expect any more concessions from him until we understood what the Palestinian position was, and we knew that we were about to reach an agreement.

"So how do we proceed?" asked Clinton, and Barak offered to do what Kissinger did when he shuttled between Syria and Israel after the Yom Kippur War. Kissinger assessed what each party could do, what Party A would give Party B in return, he spoke with both sides and understood the limitations of the negotiation field and the limitations of both parties' flexibilities.

"There are things I cannot do since I have not received a mandate from the public," said Barak to Clinton. "There is a difference between me saying something, compared to that same thing being part of the parties' leeway of flexibility that is presented as your assessment."

"I understand the need for Israeli sovereignty in the holy places, but I am trying to find something to give to the Palestinians, so they could see it as an achievement."

Clinton proposed the idea of "Palestinian custody" in the Temple Mount, with sovereignty belonging to Israel. He repeated his request to have some kind of "quasi-sovereign" Palestinian hold in the Temple Mount's vicinity, such as a visitors center or something similar, of which the Palestinians could say, "This is ours."

"Until I know that we have a deal I cannot go any further," Barak insisted.

Clinton also talked about our requests for economic and security aid and said that he would give Israel eighteen billion dollars out of the thirty-two billion we asked for, and the rest he would try to recruit from the rest of the world. He expressed his consent that we begin formulating a defense pact treaty between Israel and the United States, under the in-principle understanding that the pact would include US intervention in favor of Israel in the event of a missile attack on Israel, in the event of an attack with unconventional weapons and in the case of a full-scale war.

"Regarding Geneva," Barak told me, "I said to Clinton that he has no reason to feel that I sent him there like an idiot. I told him he was wrong, and in due course we will all see that this was an important landmark in the process of peace negotiations with Syria. When a new negotiation starts, the proposal submitted in

Geneva will define the boundaries of the solution to achieving a peace agreement between Syria and us. "

At the same time meetings between the Americans and us continued, and between Ben-Ami and Sher and Dahlan and Saeb Erekat. In these meetings, Ben-Ami and Sher hinted that in Jerusalem a fair settlement could be reached from an Israeli standpoint, and Erekat and Dahlan went to report this to Arafat.

On the evening of July 18, Sandy Berger, Dennis Ross and Rob Malley suggested to try to reach an agreement that would not include Jerusalem, in which the current status quo would remain, and over the next two years, the matter would be discussed in the presence of the two nations: Israel and Palestine. The current agreement, which we would currently sign, would declare the end of the conflict, and as for Jerusalem – it would be written that the status quo would be preserved and that both sides pledged to solve problems through peaceful means and negotiations.

"Where will their capital be?" asked Barak, and Ross answered, "They will have to declare a temporary capital."

We knew that Arafat would not accept such a proposal, and we also had a problem with it. The chances of such an agreement surviving would be slim, since as long as the issue of Jerusalem was not resolved, it would stand like a bleeding abscess between the two sides, and could even lead to the agreement being violated. In the practical level, such an agreement would give the Palestinians great gains in the form of their own state and territory that they would receive from Israel. We, on the other hand, would only receive the "end of conflict" if the Palestinians agreed to it, and the revocation of the right of return, which was unlikely to happen. In exchange for these achievements, we would exhaust all of our leeway and would have no assets lefts when the time came to discuss the matter of Jerusalem again.

"This suggestion is very problematic," said Barak.

During a meeting between Barak and Clinton that took place about an hour later, Barak said that he did not believe that the Palestinians would accept the American proposal. He stated that this was since they would not agree to declare the end of the conflict while the whole of Jerusalem remained under Israeli sovereignty, and while it is unclear how the issue would be resolved in a few years' time.

Barak explained to the president that this proposal was also problematic for Israel, because it created ambiguity on the matter of control and sovereignty over Jerusalem, leaving the charged issue to later negotiations without leaving any assets in our hands to be used as bargaining chips with the Palestinians.

"The Israeli public may think there is a hidden agenda behind this, one that leads to large-scale concessions in Jerusalem," Barak said to Clinton. "We cannot accept Arafat's office being in the Old City at this early stage, because we said that the status quo in Jerusalem must be preserved."

During their meeting, Barak gave Clinton a document with comments on the Americans' proposals. After studying it, Clinton suggested that if Arafat did not agree to end the conflict, the parties might suffice with the declaration that "all conflicts will be resolved by peaceful means and negotiations."

It should be noted that years earlier, as a condition for Rabin's agreement to negotiate with him, Arafat sent a letter that included a similar commitment. There was a similar assertion in the Oslo Accords. Yet as is well known, over the years Arafat did not uphold his commitment.

Clinton expressed his impression that Arafat wants a deal, and would like the affair to end successfully. "However," said Clinton, "Arafat is terrified of the possibility that the Palestinians would agree to Israeli sovereignty over the holy places. I'm trying to find a way in which Barak would not have to make concessions in Jerusalem, and Arafat could also say he has not conceded – by preserving the status quo, and by eliminating the possibility of discussions over Jerusalem leading to conflicts and war."

"I am convinced that if I agree to Arafat's office being in the Old City as part of the status quo, and to Palestinian custody over the mosques, I will not be able to enlist support for this in Israel," Barak said, "because people will see this as a sign of further concessions in the future."

"Look at the positive sides. Assuming an agreement is reached, it will contain solutions to the problems of refugees, settlements, borders, security arrangements and the nature of the Palestinian entity to be established, and will declare the end of the conflict," Clinton said, and turned to compliment Barak. "You are Israel's great hope, there is an opportunity do something historic here."

In the course of their conversation, Barak made another significant step in an attempt to reach a peace agreement, and said to Clinton, "I am willing for you to initiate a proposal of your own that will be presented as an American idea. If Arafat accepts the idea, tell him you estimate that you can convince me too. The proposal would be that the Temple Mount would be under Israeli sovereignty, with some form of Palestinian custody and permission for Jews to pray on the Mount. In the Old City, Arafat will receive sovereignty over the Muslim Quarter and the Church of the Holy Sepulcher. If during your contacts with the Palestinians you find that everything stand or falls on this, you can also offer him sovereignty over the Christian Quarter, with Israeli sovereignty over the Jewish and Armenian Quarters. The outer Muslim neighborhoods will be transferred to Palestinian sovereignty, inner Muslim ones will remain under Israeli sovereignty and a special regime will be in effect there, with neighborhood administrations receiving municipal authorities from the Israeli sovereign power. We will construct transportation solutions that will allow Muslims from the outer neighborhoods to attend prayers on the Temple Mount, without passing through Israeli sovereign territory.

"An area of no less than 11 percent, where eighty percent of the settlers live, will be annexed to Israel. In addition to this, we will not transfer Israeli sovereign territory (territorial exchanges) to the Palestinians, and there will not be a right of return for Palestinian refugees to Israel. Security arrangements will be established according to the concept of a demilitarized Palestinian state. For a few years, Israel will control approximately one quarter of the Jordan Valley, to ensure control over the crossings between Jordan and Palestine."

"I will not be able to confirm my conversation with you," Barak stressed. "Present it as a US suggestion, but do not come to ask me for more ideas and concessions. I have reached the farthest end of what I can agree to."

It was clear that Clinton was very excited to hear these things and was surprised by them: he never imagined that Barak would go so far, and said, "Ehud, you're the bravest person I've ever known, and if Arafat won't accept this offer, he needs psychiatric help!"

Clinton returned from his meeting with Arafat and told us that he presented the momentous proposal to him, and that Arafat's face crumpled at this. However, Clinton stressed that his impression was that the Palestinians intend to consider the proposal seriously.

At that stage, Yossi Ginosar informed us that the Palestinians were preparing a letter, in which they thanked Clinton for his efforts and the summit, and stated that they wish to take the offer home, consult, and come back in two weeks to continue the summit.

"This is exactly the scenario I feared in advance," said Barak, "that the Palestinians will take what was offered to them by the Americans as a sure thing that has already been achieved, and this will be the starting point for negotiations in two weeks. They would like to have a series of summits, each of which begins where the last one ended, and in this way, they will gain more and more concessions. I will not agree to that under any terms. The decision has to be made here, this time, at Camp David.

"I am also concerned about the possibility that the Palestinians will present the US proposal and say that the Israelis have already conceded, while they have not conceded anything," Barak continued. "That will put us on the defensive. Therefore we have to go home now. I am giving the order to prepare the aircraft that will take us home. We'll tell the media that US officials are accusing Arafat and the Palestinians of causing the summit's failure, that Barak and the Israeli delegation are preparing to return home after extremely difficult discussions, in which it was revealed that the Palestinian side is not a partner. We will stress that Israeli sources state that every effort was made to reach a permanent peace, while maintaining Israel's national interests, and warn against one-sided violence."

While we were making these moves, with our luggage already packed and piled on the lawn outside the cabins on its way to the plane, on the morning of July 19, Sandy Berger came running to Barak and said to him, "I think you have displayed extraordinary courage! Clinton had his most difficult meeting with Arafat yesterday, and afterwards Dahlan, Hassan Asfour and Erekat came to us with twelve questions about the proposal that was given to them, with some of the questions opening parts of the proposal for negotiation. We replied to them that we will not consider any of their questions before they state that they accept the president's proposal as the basis for an agreement. We told them, 'If you say so, the president will speak to Barak and will convince him to also accept your proposal as the basis for an agreement.'

"At two in the morning," continued Berger, "We received a message from Arafat that his impression is that serious steps were taken during the summit, but he is of the opinion that he has to leave for consultations, and return in two weeks. Clinton said this was unacceptable, and that he was willing to continue the talks and negotiations only if Arafat accepts the principles presented by the president as the basis for an agreement. Then, at three-thirty in the morning," Berger went on to say, "I received a message from Arafat that he cannot accept the president's principles as a basis for an agreement. This morning, I reported this to Clinton, who received it with great disappointment, and intends to tell Arafat that there is nothing more he can do for him. The president will also stress that the Israeli side was very serious and very flexible, but Arafat has to decide whether he wants an agreement or not."

"Arafat's tactic is to find out most of our ideas and proposals, so they can be used as a starting point in the next phase of negotiations," said Barak. He gave Clinton a letter in which he thanked him for his efforts, and explained that in light of the developments and the fact that the Israelis came a long way for the sake of achieving an agreement, while the Palestinians on the other hand did nothing, he no longer saw any point in staying at Camp David.

That day at noon Barak met with Clinton, who thanked him for the letter and said, "I will protect you, support you and attest that you were very brave. It is very depressing! It seems that the Palestinians are afraid to take bold steps. I told Arafat that I am very disappointed that he did not accept my proposal. I told him my disappointment is both on a principle level and on a personal level, because it is the end of my involvement in the process after eight years. I'm disappointed because I think that the Palestinians are missing another historic opportunity, that they will not find a better Israeli government in the future. You, the Palestinians, have not introduced any initiative of your own, and I hope you are not returning to a conflict with the Israelis. Arafat told me that he likes me very much and thanks me, but what the Israelis actually want is to turn occupied land into land under Israeli sovereignty, and if he would agree to this – he would be killed."

"The Palestinians very much want to stay and continue," the president went on to say. "Look at the difference between Arafat and the two of us: you and I see the proposal as a basis for negotiations, but Arafat cannot see it that way. He has to argue with you about it, and when they say 'no,' they really mean 'yes,' but with reservations and questions. Arafat said that before he concedes anything in Jerusalem, he has to speak with other Muslim leaders face-to-face, which is why he wanted the intermission. I told him, 'You cannot leave - Barak has needs too, he also needs to talk to his people, and once the two of you leave here, and things will leak - there is no chance that the negotiations will resume!'

"I believe that before we decide to finish," Clinton suggested, "You and Arafat should meet face-to-face. I understand that you don't want to complicate matters for yourself by enabling him to make use of what you say to him, but otherwise he could claim that you did not even meet him during the summit. I have to leave for Okinawa, so we will have to agree on a work plan during my absence. I will shorten my stay there and will return on Sunday."

"I went far beyond what I thought..." said Barak, but Clinton continued, "When we came here, your strategy was to put your final offer on the table – at the end. Arafat came without intending to reach an agreement. What he had in mind was a rolling summit: a meeting, intermission, and so on. In fact, until today, they have not really listened, but now they are frightened because I am about to leave, and perhaps you as well, and there will be no more meetings. I suggest you consider a meeting between you and him, and it is important we call Mubarak and Abdullah so they support Arafat. I told Arafat he did not read you and the situation in Israel correctly."

Clinton meant that Arafat did not understand the enormous difficulties Barak was facing in the context of domestic politics. He did not understand how fragile Barak's political situation was when he went to Camp David with his coalition beginning to crumble. Arafat did not understand how the Israeli democracy works, and his perception was that if Barak was the Prime Minister, he could do anything that came to his mind.

"Until now, it was not a negotiation, and I discovered that I do not, in fact, have a partner," said Barak. "I made a lot of compromises even before the summit, and gradually prepared the Israeli public for even more painful compromises. In every step in our conversations here, we moved towards the Palestinians, and they in turn stayed stuck in the same place. There was only one part where they showed some flexibility, and then they changed their mind. I do not think I will meet Arafat. We were careful enough, and did well not to leave him with any Israeli or US document that would enable him to leave the summit with a baseline for the next summit. Already on the first day of the summit, I said that I am worried about the possibility that Arafat will try to buy time, and leave here with a more compromising Israeli position that he will use as a baseline for the next stage. In fact, he needs the meeting with me to nail this line down and to be able to say, 'Barak offered me this and that,' and I will not have this. I will not have Arafat saying that he has Israeli suggestions that are contrary to my commitments to the public, without an agreement. The compromises I have made, I can only explain in the context of an agreement and the end of the conflict."

"I cannot meet with Arafat," Barak reiterated, "I cannot accept his nature and his character. If Arafat does not respond positively to the US proposal in the next two hours, I will return to Israel. The proposed line is not a prologue for a new deal; if he wants changes,

I will also ask for changes. You think Arafat can be led to respond positively to the proposal, because he is afraid of your pressures, but he is even more afraid of having to make difficult decisions.

"I understand Arafat's need to receive the support of Mubarak, Abdullah and other Arab leaders, when it comes to decisions on Jerusalem. I am convinced that the other leaders will support Arafat and back any decision he makes on the matter. Mubarak and Abdullah told me they would do so, and Abdullah also said that the King of Morocco, who is the Chairman of the Jerusalem Committee in the Arab League, would do the same. Arafat will be backed by the Arab world, as long as he has some sovereignty in Jerusalem and the custody over the Temple Mount."

"So how do we proceed?" Clinton asked.

"The best way is to keep the pressure on Arafat," said Barak. "If Arafat comes up with a counter proposal, a completely different one – then I'm packing my bags and leaving. I cannot afford beating around the bush on this matter. If Arafat agrees to the proposal with reservations, we can use the previous US proposal that referred to solving all of the problems except for Jerusalem as a fallback. Jerusalem will remain in its current state, and we will discuss it in two years from now. In the meantime, we will make peace and declare the end of the conflict."

Clinton expressed doubts about the possibility that Arafat would accept this alternative, and Barak replied that Arafat faced two options: to accept a recognized Palestinian state as part of an agreement, or to unilaterally declare independence in the absence of agreement.

"If Arafat will make a unilateral decision, it will greatly strengthen the political right-wing in Israel, and within days I will either form a unity government or go to new elections," Barak said.

"After the elections, which I believe I will win, I will form a unity government, meet with world leaders and show them what I was willing to do to end the conflict. I am certain I will receive their support and understanding after they will see how far I was willing to go, and how stubborn and uncompromising Arafat was. He will be left without any achievements if he unilaterally declares an independent state. His nation would consist of non-contiguous blocs in Judea and Samaria, and of Gaza that would be isolated from the West Bank, without any land connection between all the parts of this puzzle. In this state of conflict, we can operate more freely against terrorism, liberated from the need to take considerations regarding the negotiations into account."

Eventually, and in retrospect, Barak failed to achieve the empathy he was so certain he would receive from a large part of the Israeli public. The notion that has taken root was that he did not do enough to protect Israel and went too far in his concessions to Arafat. His insistence in Camp David was of no avail to him, and he was labeled as one who was willing to make sweeping concessions.

On the evening of July 19, Clinton came to a meeting with Barak after he had met with Arafat.

It was clear to us all that the moment of truth had arrived – the moment when Arafat finally said something, rather than merely asking questions and expressing grievances.

Earlier, Barak tried to ask Arafat via Clinton, if he was willing to discuss a permanent agreement that included the end of the conflict on the basis of the US proposal.

"It's time he says his opinion, instead of wasting time and gnawing at the points he finds problematic," Barak told us.

In our conversations with the younger representatives in the Palestinian delegation, we received the impression that Dahlan, Hassan Asfour and Mohammad Rashid recognized the breakthrough in the US proposal, and if it was their decision to make – they would have adopted it as the basis for further negotiations.

Clinton returned from a meeting with Arafat and said that the Palestinians seemed scared to him. Arafat claimed once again that not enough preparations were in fact made for the summit, and complained that Barak did not meet him. Clinton reminded Arafat that Barak had already agreed to give him a lot before the US proposal was even put on the table.

"The Palestinians are begging to go home," said Clinton, "because Arafat wants to consult with Arab leaders."

We thought that Arafat could just as well conduct all these consultations from Camp David. In fact, his great desire to leave the camp was mainly due to his wish to evade the US pressure and the need to make difficult decisions, as well as his wish to display the concessions which he believed he had already gotten from Barak.

Clinton told Arafat that his request to convene again in two weeks' time was out of the question. At that stage the Palestinians expressed their willingness to stay in Camp David for a few more days, to discuss the issue of Jerusalem and keep the momentum.

"The only thing that happened on the Palestinian side – is bullshit," said Barak. "We are adults, not children, and we also understand that essentially, until this moment, the Palestinians have not held any negotiations. They have manipulated both of us. They knew in advance that the issue of Jerusalem would be discussed at the summit, and should have said honestly, at least to you, that they have no flexibility on this issue. This would have raised some very serious questions about their true attitude towards the negotiations in the seven years that have passed since 1993. All the negotiations, dialogue and talks since Oslo were based on the assumption that one day, we will discuss a permanent agreement, in which we will have to find solutions to the fundamental issues – one of which is Jerusalem. If the Palestinians have no intention of making any concessions on this matter, they should have said so in advance, just as we have announced that we would never agree to the Palestinians' right of return to Israel. I cannot order my people to continue any kind of dialogue before I hear something from the Palestinians. We will not leave and return in two weeks, it is out of the question!" Barak concluded angrily, not attempting to conceal his disappointment. However, he did not lose his famous composure, and continued, "As a result of the process between us and the Palestinians, I face a difficult political challenge within the Israeli public. Whether an agreement is reached or not, they will say I went too far. Therefore, I will not talk with the Palestinians on Jerusalem individually, because this is an extremely sensitive issue and their only purpose is to gain concessions and flaunt them.

"If Arafat does not respond positively to the US proposal, this means that in the past few months he has been wrapping us around his little finger," said Barak. He pledged, "If we are forced to fight, at least we understand what we will fight for. After Arafat rejected our proposals, I can unite the public in the war against him. No one can blame me that I was unwilling to make concessions or did not do everything to avoid conflict. Everyone will understand that Arafat could not rise to the moment, and was unwilling to make difficult decisions."

Barak went on to talk about how Ben-Gurion established the State of Israel without Jerusalem, and that we won the war that was imposed on us, and after it – we had Jerusalem. If the Palestinians were unable to make a decision to establish their state with a little less than what Arafat dreamed of (i.e., without Jerusalem), then maybe Arafat was unworthy of this role, and the Palestinians did not deserve a state.

Clinton said that Saeb Erekat, Abu Alaa and Abu Mazen were willing to accept his offer to postpone Jerusalem for a later discussion, while concluding all the other issues.

"What if we leave now, and next week the Palestinians come back and say they are willing to negotiate with you on the basis of this proposal?" Clinton asked Barak.

"I will not come to another summit!" Barak snapped. "I will not enter the same room with a villain who has proved himself as such. I went further towards him than any other prime minister in the past, and further than any will in the future, I tell you. I can also make an oath right now to keep Jerusalem united, which would shut down any possibility of compromise in the future."

"Are you sure this is what you want - that either Arafat answers the US proposal or you will go back home?" Asked Clinton and Barak immediately replied, "Yes."

Clinton complained that Barak had not actually held any direct negotiations with Arafat throughout the entire summit. Barak replied again that the Palestinian side had not even entered the negotiations, and had not shown that they were ready to negotiate.

Clinton persisted in his attempts to set up a meeting between Arafat and Barak, and once again tried to prod Barak: "Do you think it is right to do what you said, even without trying to look Arafat in the eye?"

"I am willing to negotiate only with those who are willing to negotiate with me," answered Barak. "I am going to announce that we have not found a partner here, but a manipulator who betrayed your trust and mine."

Clinton tried to urge Barak to leave an opening for dialogue and recalled that in Oslo, Israel undertook to recognize some of the Palestinians' claims.

"I cannot lie to the Israeli public and I do not intend to do so," said Barak. "I see here that Arafat and the Palestinian national movement are unable to take advantage of an historic opportunity and make decisions."

Barak went on to explain that the Oslo Accords did not seem to him to be the best and most desirable solution. It should be remembered that when Rabin presented the agreement for the government's approval, Barak – then Israel's Interior Minister – abstained, but despite his opposition, he was in favor of the process as it meant creating a time corridor toward a permanent agreement. During this period, the two sides were supposed to live side by side without violence (Intifada and terrorism), to cooperate and find a way to solve the problems. "In a few months, we will probably stand before a unilateral Palestinian decision to declare independence and we will have to fight," said Barak. "I was ready to go all the way to break this terrible cycle of bloodshed, but I am not afraid of confrontation. With the same determination with which I was willing to strive for peace – we will fight in a violent confrontation, if there will be no other way."

This conversation between Clinton and Barak took place under the abrupt time frame of the president's departure for Japan. Clinton was very keen to ensure that the dynamic of the talks would continue during his absence from Camp David, and after Barak's last statements he said to him once again, "Don't you think you should say these things to Arafat directly, rather than pass them through me?"

However, Barak refused once again, "I cannot begin negotiations, except with someone who agrees that your suggestion can serve as a rough outline for the end result of such negotiations."

CHAPTER 31

"I Do Not Want To See Anyone"

All throughout the summit, I tried time and again to convince Barak to meet with Arafat. I told him that as I see it, the main idea of the gathering at Camp David is that negotiations would be conducted under the auspices of the leaders, but also with their direct involvement.

From the outset, we came to Camp David after the negotiators from both parties – and mainly from the Palestinian side – completely exhausted what little leeway they had. We were well aware of the Palestinian positions and had heard the intelligence officials' assessments that the Palestinians would display rigid positions. We came to Camp David nonetheless, based on the assumption that only Arafat could show flexibility if he wished to, and that only in a summit, where the leaders would discuss all of the package's components, could we exhaust the possibility of reaching an agreement. Now came the moment for the leaders to make decisions. I thought that a meeting between him and Arafat could encourage Arafat to enter negotiations and present more flexible positions. Since we are already here, I said, you have to exhaust all chances, and even if we fail, we will know that we have done everything we could.

Barak, as was his way, was firm and quite uncompromising in his position.

I further told Barak that as long as Clinton told Arafat that it was a US proposal that would be the basis for further negotiations, and that Clinton would try to convince us only after Arafat would accept it – the concern that the Palestinians would claim this was an Israeli concession would lessen. I think he could have spoken with Arafat in a way that would not have played into his hands by allowing him to claim later that he had in his hands a compromising Israeli position, which would be used as a baseline for the next meeting.

As expected, I failed to convince Barak.

Clinton wanted to know what Barak intended to do when he returned to Israel after the summit. Barak told him that he would make it clear to the Knesset and the Israeli public that he was not willing to risk Israel's vital interests, "and then the fact that I did not meet Arafat will be of great help to me," he said. Barak continued, "I will have to face a very problematic Knesset (at that stage, only 33 MKs supported him), and I expect you to make a public statement at the right moment, and say to the Israeli public that the Israeli side showed extraordinary courage and a real desire to bring the conflict to an end. However, this did not happen because of the Palestinian positions and Arafat's fear of making courageous decisions. "

"I will say that you displayed historical wisdom, courage and responsibility, and make it explicitly clear who is to blame for the crisis," said Clinton.

"What was Arafat's position regarding the proposal to finalize all the issues and keep the current status quo in Jerusalem, and to re-discuss it over the next two years?" asked Barak, and Clinton replied, "Arafat considers this to be a very bad proposal, because he's afraid that in this situation, eventually he will not get anything in Jerusalem."

Immediately after this conversation, Barak gathered the Israeli delegation and said, "The Americans have raised three suggestions: the first – that I speak with Arafat; the second – that we will continue the discussions here between the teams; and the third – that we erase all the proposals made so far on Jerusalem, and start discussing it again from the beginning."

In that meeting, and this time in the presence of all the delegation's members, I once again told Barak that it was very important that he meet with Arafat. However, Barak once again rejected the idea, and once again dismissed me with his regular carbohydrate-related saying, "And if we would have eaten pastries together, would it have changed anything?"

In negotiations, there is great significance to every detail, including human warmth and direct contact between the participants. Over time, it has been argued that Barak's insistence not to meet with Arafat at Camp David was one of the main reasons for the talks' failure. I am of the opinion that given the way things developed at the summit, and despite my recommendation that the two of them meet, it would be highly presumptuous to think that a meeting between them could have turned the picture on its head.

It was apparent that Arafat had not developed a connection to occurrences at the summit based on commitment, interest, understanding and internalization. The mindset he came to Camp David with was that it was a conspiracy meant to drag him into a US-Israeli trap. In retrospect, it is clear to me that he did not come to the summit with the required level of maturity to make far-reaching concessions on charged issues. His inability to reach a level of remarkable and courageous leadership - is at the heart of Camp David's failure.

At that stage, Arafat preferred to maintain the situation in which he did not reveal his 'red lines' with respect to the material issues of the permanent agreement: the refugees and the right of return, the fate of Jerusalem, the Temple Mount, settlements, security arrangements, the issue of borders and the nature of the Palestinian state to be established.

Camp David was in fact the first time since the Oslo Accords, in which Arafat found himself in new territory, where he was required to make concessions, and it simply did not suit him.

In this state of affairs, the question arises if it was not a mistake to bring him to the summit. My opinion is that the summit was necessary, even though it did not end with an agreement. It should be remembered that the summit came in relation to what preceded it: the assessment that all contacts between the negotiating teams have exhausted themselves. Additionally, elections in the United States drew nearer, and Clinton was close to the transition period between the end of his term and a new president taking his place. During this period, the incumbent president's power decreases significantly. The combination of these circumstances created concern regarding the stagnate state of negotiations with the Palestinians, which could deteriorate the regional situation and result in another bloody conflict.

The need for a summit was based on the assessment that significant concessions and fateful decisions would only be made by the leaders themselves, and that this possibility should be fully exhausted.

Yet in practice, there were no substantive meetings between Arafat and Barak. I think we should have insisted on this and convinced Barak, even though I have already mentioned that you cannot hang the failure of the summit on the fact that such a meeting did not occur.

Arafat was aware of the fact that Barak had the authority to go beyond the range of flexibilities he gave the negotiators on his behalf. Hence the fear was that if Barak would present a compromising position during the meeting, it would immediately be engraved in Arafat's mind as the starting point for the next meeting, without him showing any flexibility.

I kept telling Barak that he was wrong in his approach, and that he should try and meet with Arafat. "After all, this is the reason we came here," I said to Barak. "Until now, the negotiations were done by proxy. We came here to fully explore the possibility that those who wield executive power, you and Arafat, will exhaust direct negotiations." Nevertheless, Barak continued to insist, and continued to refuse.

It was important that a meeting between Barak and Arafat take place; a meeting of this kind is something that creates opportunities, prevents crises and allows intimate dialogue. However, it is certainly not the essence of the whole thing, and certainly it would not have supplied Arafat with the concessions he so desperately wanted to gain.

Today, more than ever, it is clear that Arafat was not willing to make concessions that would allow for an agreement between the Palestinians and us. Arafat did not want to go down in the annals of history as the one who conceded the things that he saw as the most crucial for the Palestinians. He recognized our right to a secure existence here, but he did not accept the State of Israel being the national home of the entire Jewish people. If he would have accepted that, he would have understood that there was no possibility for him to receive the right of return. I believe Arafat had trouble even recognizing the existence of a Jewish people. He recognized that there are Israelis, and that there are Jews who live in various countries around the world. However, he refused to accept the definition of Israel as the national home of the Jewish people.

The concern, which also came from intelligence sources, was that the Palestinians would begin to develop the concept of the binational state: a single state from the Mediterranean to the Jordan, where both Jews and Arabs would live. This would be a democratic state based on the determination of the majority, which in any demographic estimate would be Palestinian within a few years, and thus the end of Israel as a Jewish and democratic state would come about. Hence I believe we had to insist on a solution that would clearly separate between the two peoples.

Later in the night of July 19, Clinton recounted to Barak a conversation he had had with Arafat: "Arafat promised that he would make every effort to prevent the failure of the negotiations. You have taken a big step by agreeing to our proposal on Jerusalem, which talked about dividing the city and shared sovereignty over the Temple Mount. Yet the Palestinians cannot enter negotiations that are not based on their sovereignty over the Mount. However, I am under the impression that they accept the fact that you will never relinquish sovereignty over the Temple Mount."

"I think the only formula that will enable us to move forward in the negotiations will be if we do not talk about sovereignty," Barak offered. "If we leave aside the issue of Jerusalem, and discuss the other matters." Barak's suggestion was a continuation of the US proposal, according to which we would finalize all the other issues, and declare that there were no more changes and mutual claims with respect to refugees, borders, settlements and security arrangements, and that the Israeli-Palestinian conflict has ended. Then it will be possible to begin implementing the agreement, and continue to discuss the remaining issues later. A similar model was used in the peace agreement between Egypt and Israel with respect to Taba.

I thought it was not a good proposal. Jerusalem is a fundamental and important issue, and I thought it was wrong to enter a situation where such an important matter remains pending. This has explosive potential that could devastate all the agreements reached on other issues, and turn the picture on its head.

Clinton believed that Arafat would agree to negotiate on the basis of the American proposal, which talks about a two-state solution, rejects the right of return, leaves only five percent of the territory, where approximately eighty percent of the settlers reside, under Israeli sovereignty, divides Jerusalem, gives sovereignty over the Temple Mount to Israelis at the first stage, and then shares it with the Palestinians or a third party. "However," Clinton stressed, "Arafat did not accept the notion that already at the beginning of the negotiations you will get sovereignty over the Temple Mount."

Barak's consent to the possibility that at some point sovereignty over the Mount will become shared sovereignty – was already a major concession. His initial position was that sovereignty on the Mount had to be ours and that the ongoing management of the Mount would be Palestinian – as is the current situation. This carries great weight in terms of the Israeli public, as it means that Israeli law applies in the Temple Mount. For example, in case disturbances break out on the Mount, the Israeli police is the one that goes in and is responsible for returning order. As we know, this is not an imaginary scenario and has happened many times. The Temple Mount is a very volatile place, as reality has proven time and again.

Upon hearing Clinton's last statement, Barak said that if this was the case, it was better not to leave the issue of Jerusalem for a later discussion.

"Arafat will not give up sovereignty over the Mount, and neither will I. So there is no point in leaving the subject for another time," said Barak, and immediately proposed to appoint a small group of Americans, Israelis and Palestinians, who would try to find a formula that both parties could accept regarding the Temple Mount.

"This should be a formula that will give us sovereignty, and Palestinians custody," said Barak. "What matters to us is the symbolic aspect of sovereignty. I cannot continue the negotiations with the Palestinians before they respond positively to your proposal. We have accepted the proposal, they have not. As long as they do not accept it, there is no point in continuing negotiations. If the problem of the Mount is resolved, it will allow us to continue negotiations on other subjects. "

This was an example of the process of Barak "feeding ideas" to Clinton. To illustrate his determination and seriousness, Barak said, "If that does not work, I will have to leave tomorrow night. I am going to be exposed to immense risks, because Arafat will certainly blame us for the failure of the talks. So I need your word and the support you will give me for doing my best. I was willing to go very far to meet the Palestinians halfway, and they bear all the blame for the failure."

Clinton later returned from his meeting with Arafat, in which he introduced him to the idea of establishing a small team for negotiations regarding the Temple Mount. Barak asked him, "Did Arafat seem to accept the notion that if we reach an acceptable formula regarding the Temple Mount, he would be willing to accept all the other components (Jerusalem, right of return, borders, settlements, security arrangements) as a basis for further negotiations?"

"That is what I understood from him," said Clinton, "and I told him, that he should not take this to understand that you have changed your position on the Temple Mount. The message is that you are willing to look for a solution that will satisfy both sides. The position will change only if you reach an agreement in the discussion."

The next day, on July 20, Clinton departed and went to Okinawa, while Barak learned from Albright that there was in fact no Palestinian consent to the rest of the components in the American proposal. This was in contrast to what had been implied by Clinton, that the greatest difficulty was the Temple Mount, and when it would be resolved - the Palestinians would accept the rest of the US proposal as a basis for further negotiations.

We tried to understand what caused Clinton to mislead Barak. Perhaps it was a misunderstanding, perhaps Clinton sought to prevent the summit's collapse in his absence, or maybe this was truly the way Clinton understood Arafat's words.

This drama developed during the afternoon of that day, when a US delegation that included Madeleine Albright, Martin Indyk and Dennis Ross arrived at Barak's cabin. From the Israeli side Barak, Gilead Sher and I were present.

Albright looked entirely smug and said that she felt the difficult atmosphere has dissolved. She said that at her meeting with Arafat in the morning, she found him and the rest of the Palestinians willing to put new ideas on the table and talk.

Albright went on to say that the Palestinians wanted to form a group that would continue discussing the subjects that make up the US proposal, and her statements implied that the Palestinians accepted the proposal as a basis for negotiations that would lead to an agreement.

Albright proceeded to say that we needed to talk about work procedures for the next day, and before that, Dennis Ross would ask us several questions raised by the Palestinians.

Upon hearing the questions Ross presented, Barak realized that they implied something completely different than what was told to him by Clinton.

Barak understood from Clinton that the Palestinians accepted the US proposal, and all that remained was to solve the issue of the Temple Mount. However, from their questions, Barak realized this was not the case.

The Palestinians wanted to know what would be the status of the Christian holy sites in Jerusalem; what would be the status of the underground water reservoir ("the aquifer") in territories under our sovereignty in the West Bank; who would be responsible for the Palestinians' construction planning during the period in which we would continue to control the Jordan Valley (for twelve years); and which powers they would have there?

Barak listened to the questions presented by Ross on behalf of the Palestinians, and was filled with rage: "I will not answer any questions, and I will not allow my people to answer any questions! What the Palestinians are doing is not negotiation. I expect them to stop asking questions and start giving answers, such as whether they accept the notion that they will have less than sovereignty in the eastern neighborhoods of Jerusalem (where they were offered only civil sovereignty with the exception of planning and construction authorities)? How will they respond to our demand to annex 650 square kilometers in the large settlement blocs? Do they agree to joint custody over the Temple Mount? Also, I would like to hear them affirm that there will be no territorial exchanges. I will not have any more farces. I need a clear answer from the Palestinians that they do in fact adopt Clinton's proposal as a basis for negotiations."

Barak's tone of voice left no doubt regarding his fury, whereupon Albright shrunk in her chair and her face turned red. Indyk and Ross began to comprehend that there was a problem which they were not aware of, and the atmosphere in the room became tense and unpleasant.

"I'm not here to wait for Clinton to return without doing anything," said Barak, and offered to start talking about the generic issues, such as the economic regime in the free trade zone and the regime along the border. Barak also expressed his willingness to an informal meeting on the refugees.

"If Arafat cannot say 'yes' to the US proposal, I'll know what to do. If he says say 'yes,' I am prepared to enter any discussion. If he does not say 'yes', it means that he wants more," said Barak. "If we fail in our attempt to set the Clinton proposal as a basis, it would strengthen extremists on the Palestinian side. We need to get a definite and immediate answer from Arafat, otherwise I will not meet him."

At this stage, Albright managed to pull herself together and said to Barak, "You are brave and very creative in your suggestions, but your behavior is the opposite. On the one hand, you went a long way towards Palestinians, but on the other hand, you demand to receive a definite and immediate answer from Arafat without leaving any room for flexibility."

From this it could be understood that Clinton did not share with her Barak's position that he could not continue without a clear answer from Arafat. It could also be understood that he did not update her that he told Barak that Arafat had responded positively to the proposal, so that if the issue of the Temple Mount would be resolved between the parties, the Palestinians would agree to see the US proposal as a basis for further negotiations on the other issues.

"The proposal raised by the president is beyond what I can give. However, I agreed to see it as a basis for further negotiations. If Arafat does not see it this way, then there is no point in wasting time and it is clear that this is the end of the summit," said Barak.

Ross started to say, "But the Palestinians' questions..." and Barak interrupted him and said, "I do not accept that asking questions is negotiating. We are already on the eighth day of the summit and Arafat still has not begun to negotiate!"

At this point, Albright began to show signs of irritation and said, "Yet you're the one who wanted the summit, how exactly did you expect it to work?"

"If we want an agreement, Arafat had better start negotiating," Barak replied. "I think we did more than we needed to give this summit a chance to succeed. When I said I wanted a summit, I did not agree to sell Israel out in the process."

Ross went on to say that Arafat sent a letter to Clinton in which he wrote that if the solution on Jerusalem seemed adequate to him, then he would agree that Clinton would decide what should be the solution to the territorial issue.

Clinton answered Arafat that in that case, he would suggest a territorial exchange, wherein Israel would receive nine percent of the territory and give the Palestinians only one percent in return.

Barak spoke about the proposal that came up between him and Clinton, to establish a small discussion group that would deal with the Temple Mount. Barak said he knew that Arafat could not accept a situation in which he would lose sovereignty over the Temple Mount already at the beginning of the negotiations, and therefore it was necessary to negotiate to find a solution. "I expect the Palestinian concession of their claim to sovereignty over the Mount to be given to Clinton as a deposit," said Barak. "Eventually, we will find a formula that will be less than sovereignty (such as custody), and against it I will deposit my agreement to concede two of the Old City's quarters with Clinton.

"I want to draw your attention to the fact that Arafat is trying to paint a picture that will serve him if the talks fail. He is asking questions, and eventually will say that he did not receive adequate answers and therefore Israel is to blame for the summit's failure.

"You must tell Arafat that you do not see a way forward, as long as he does not answer the president's proposal. Make it clear to him that you do not want him to commit to every detail of the future discussions, but what is expected of him now is to answer the question of whether he accepts the president's proposal as a framework and basis for further negotiations," Barak said.

"This is the first time that the Palestinians are beginning to negotiate at the summit, but you're not ready to do so," said Ross, and gave the impression that Barak and the Americans were not speaking the same language.

"They are not negotiating, and it's time for them to start answering our questions," Barak said again - and thus, in an air of crisis, the meeting ended.

The entire Israeli team assembled at Barak's quarters and he informed us: "We have reached a crisis whose essence is this: the president introduced very far-reaching ideas, and Arafat does not want to answer them. I do not want to be seen as one who is unwilling to negotiate, and I want you to continue discussing with the Palestinians on generic issues such as water, borders governance, economics and work in Israel. I am prepared to start informal, one-on-one (Israeli and Palestinian) talks on other issues, such as refugees, security arrangements, territory, settlement blocs and the border. I would like to warn all of us of a dangerous development, that our willingness to stay here is seen as a Palestinian achievement – since they are not providing answers and yet we stay and talk. Regarding territory, keep in mind that our demand is to annex 650 square kilometers, which is eleven to twelve percent of the land in the West Bank, and we will not agree to territorial exchanges, and additionally oppose the demand for the right of return."

Later that day, Barak told Gilead Sher and me that an awkward situation has formed in which the Americans at Camp David were unaware that the president was waiting for Arafat's answer regarding his proposal.

At another meeting that day between Barak and Albright, the Secretary of State tried to straighten things out after what happened in the morning. Barak did not feel comfortable with the explanations he received, but wished to avoid creating a crisis and offending the Americans, and therefore authorized our people to continue informal meetings on matters pertaining to the core of the conflict.

"This is very generous of you and I thank you for it very much," said Albright.

"Informal negotiations will not begin before we know Arafat's answer to the president's ideas," Barak clarified. "I am very disappointed. I expected that the rules of the game would change. I do not see that the crisis is gone, only that it has been postponed."

On the evening of that same turbulent and overwhelming day, Barak called me to his cabin and told me that he needed to gather himself, to think and plan his next steps in light of the complex situation that has formed and the disappointing developments.

Barak felt that Clinton deceived him in order to ensure that he stayed at Camp David, and he was very hurt by this. He saw this as an acute crisis of confidence with the Americans and decided to act accordingly. He secluded himself, displaying his disapproval of the situation in which he found himself.

"A dour development is taking place here, contrary to what I understood from the president. There is a big difference between what I understood from him and the instructions he left for his people. I see this as a serious crisis, and I have to consider my response to it when he returns. Until then, I do not want to see anyone," Barak said to me.

He turned to his cabin and locked himself inside it for the coming days, with me being the only connection between him and the outside world.

After two days of voluntary confinement, which Barak imposed on himself, Albright decided to break the cycle of seclusion. This came after all her attempts to contact Barak in the past few days had failed.

I received a call from her personal assistant, who told me that Albright was striding vigorously to Barak's cabin. I immediately informed him about the unplanned development, and when

Barak realized that he could not refuse to see her, he quickly put on a tracksuit and running shoes. To me he assigned the role of gatekeeper, wherein I was supposed to wait for Albright at the entrance to the cabin, and tell her that Barak went out for his morning jog.

When the Secretary of State approached me, I was waiting for her at the door and felt like a complete idiot. I told her that Barak went out for some exercise, but Albright persisted, and asked me emphatically, "What is happening to him?"

I explained to her that Barak took the situation hard, he was hurt and offended by the lack of coordination and understanding on the American side, and that he was accompanied by a great sense of discomfort because he was certain that things could have been different. I explained to her that he felt in need of self-examination due to the developments, and for this reason he asked to be alone and undisturbed.

It was clear that the answer did not satisfy the Secretary of State. She looked nervous and asked, "Is he not feeling well?"

Contrary to what was said by certain people afterwards, Barak was not depressed. After realizing that the summit had in fact – and contrary to all of his hopes – failed, he tried to think how to proceed from that point. Barak came to Camp David with great expectations and realized that he was going to come back empty-handed.

Barak maintained strict isolation. We brought him his meals directly to the cabin so he could avoid having to go to the communal dining room, and he refused any possibility of socializing with other people. He requested that we tell anyone who asked to see him that he did not want to be disturbed.

Throughout that entire weekend, I was the only person who saw him in his cabin. I found him writing and mostly reading. He read newspapers, and two books: Churchill's book on the decision-making process during World War II and a book about Ben-Gurion. Apparently, Barak sought to draw strength and ideas from other leaders, who found themselves at critical decision-making crossroads.

It was clear that a heavy weight rested on his shoulders, and he was going through difficult turmoil on the way to deciding on his next steps.

CHAPTER 32

"ARAFAT CANNOT MAKE A DECISION"

On Saturday evening, the end of the "confinement" was announced, and all the Israeli team members gathered on the back porch of "Dodge Wood", Barak's Cabin.

Barak asked each person to report on the progress made in their meetings with the Palestinians.

Maj. Gen. Shlomo Yanai, Head of the IDF's Planning Directorate, reported that on the issue of security arrangements - the Palestinians accepted our demands, except for Israel's demand for security control over the Jordan Valley for twelve years, and Israeli supervision at the border between Jordan and the Palestinians to prevent the smuggling of prohibited weapons.

Yossi Ginosar reported that the Palestinians misunderstood Clinton's proposal. They did not understand, for example, the meaning of the custody Clinton offered them over the Temple Mount, the difference between this custody and the division of sovereignty over Jerusalem according to quarters, and consequently they found it difficult to understand the basis that they were being asked to adopt for further negotiations. Ginosar reported that the Palestinians were seeking to make progress on the security and territorial issues, but they were not trying to provide an answer to the president's proposals.

Amnon Lipkin-Shahak, who dealt with the Temple Mount, said that among most of the Palestinians he discovered complete ignorance of the subject matter, in the context of what is sacred and why the site is important for Jews. Regarding the refugees, the Palestinians insisted that the right of return be recognized.

On the other hand, Oded Eran, who was in the refugees committee, found a possibility for Palestinian flexibility with regard to the right of return. They expressed their willingness to omit the term "right" and leave the term "return." Eran also noted that he believed that progress could be made with them on other issues.

Dan Meridor was less optimistic than Eran on the refugee issue, saying that the Palestinians insisted on the right of return and were unwilling to accept our figures. Our offer stated that no Palestinian would return on the basis of the right of return, but on humanitarian grounds of family reunification. We offered that 1,000 people would enter Israel every year on this basis, for ten years, up to a total of ten thousand refugees.

Shlomo Ben-Ami said that as long as the president's ideas had not been accepted by the Palestinians, he believed this was a Palestinian tactic aimed at wearing down these ideas.

"Progress in the negotiations will depend on what we will achieve regarding Jerusalem," Ben-Ami said to Barak, "and the critical issue is the Temple Mount. Maybe you should speak with Arafat about this."

I also told Barak again that Arafat is the man who we should focus on, because his people would not do anything without him.

Israel Hasson, who was Deputy Director of the Shin Bet, said his impression was that there were numerous Palestinians ready to move forward on security, territory and refugees.

Elyakim Rubinstein from the refugee team said that in all levels pertaining to the refugee issue there were differences of opinion between them and us. Rubinstein identified that the biggest problem with the refugee issue related to those who are in Lebanon and amount to approximately three hundred thousand people.

Two hundred thousand additional refugees are in Syria, a million in refugee camps in the West Bank, a million to a million and a half in refugee camps in Jordan, and another million in camps in Gaza.

It was amazing to follow everyone's reports, and see how some of us came back with different reports from different meetings with the Palestinians. This suggests that the Palestinians did not speak in one voice, they expressed different positions, and all these positions together did not essentially change anything. The final decision-maker, in any case, was Arafat.

Barak began to sum up and was noticeably still very angry: "The basic situation has not changed since the president left. So far, we have used all of our 'ammunition' and have not hidden it, even if it was presented as the president's far-fetched ideas. The Palestinians' refusal to address the American ideas actually reveals their true faces. I will stay here and try to make the most of this summit until the end, since in a short time, Clinton will enter a transition period prior to a new president taking office, and he will be substantially weakened. Clinton is very involved in the details, he spent seven years of his reign to try to achieve an agreement between the Palestinians and us. It is very doubtful whether the next US president will invest even ten percent of the energy Clinton invested in the matter, and even more so if the negotiations come to a deadlock.

"It would be a most grievous error to come to confrontation with the Palestinians, without having tried to solve the conflict. We have reached the moment of truth in which we must find out for certain if the other side is willing to accept a state on about ninety percent of the territory, concede the right of return and accept a radical solution in Jerusalem, with the end of the conflict being the anchor and main lever to influence the public.

"This should be followed by bringing an end to the conflict with other Arab nations, and ending incitement against us. This entire package will be achieved in part in the agreement, in part in understandings with the Americans, and in part in oral understandings with the Palestinians. From our perspective, the agreement has to be such that the area that is home to about eighty percent of the settlers belongs to us, and without territorial exchanges. We still have to discuss the border regime and the question of the meaning of separation, and consider the amount of time required to move the settlements that we will have to evacuate. This whole process should last for at least five years. It is also necessary to discuss the legal matters, such as the status of refugees who return to Israel – residents or citizens, and the issue of dual citizenship for Palestinians remaining in Israeli sovereign territories."

Barak decided that once Clinton returns, and in accordance with Arafat's answer, he would decide whether to choose the possibility that meant signing an agreement that would contain everything that had been agreed up to that point, including the end of the conflict, and leave the unresolved matters to further negotiations under a binding time frame.

On Sunday, July 23, Barak invited Albright and Ross to a meeting, and told them that in view of the developments, he wanted to make some changes in Clinton's proposal. Since Arafat made no significant step forward, and had not expressed a willingness to make any concessions in exchange for the generous offers he had received – Barak asked to withdraw from some of the more consequential proposals.

According to the US proposal, sovereignty in Jerusalem would be divided according to the principle of "what is Muslim – is Palestinian, and what is Jewish – is Israeli", including the neighborhoods near the Old City. The Old City would be divided into five districts: the Temple Mount, the Jewish Quarter, the Muslim Quarter, the Armenian Quarter and the Christian Quarter. The Jewish and Armenian Quarters would be under Israeli sovereignty, and Jewish access to the Temple Mount would be through the Wailing Wall. The Muslim and Christian Quarters would be under Palestinian sovereignty. Initially it was said that the Temple Mount would be under Israeli sovereignty and Palestinian administration, as custody. Clinton estimated that Arafat would accept this offer, but not at first, because he could not give up sovereignty over the Temple Mount without negotiating. It was estimated that after receiving concessions on other issues, Arafat would cede sovereignty over the Mount.

Later, it turned out that Clinton's assessment was wrong: Arafat was not about to give up the Temple Mount at any stage.

Additional neighborhoods that would be under Palestinian sovereignty, according to the US proposal, are the outlying neighborhoods adjacent to Jerusalem's municipal border: Wadi al-Joz, Shuafat, Sheikh Jarrah, Sur Baher and others. The Israeli neighborhoods that would be annexed to Israeli Jerusalem would include all eleven neighborhoods built on land that was Jordanian until 1967: Gilo, French Hill, Tzameret HaBira, Givat HaMivtar, Ramat Eshkol, Ramot, Neve Yaakov, Pisgat Ze'ev, East Talpiot, Ramot Alon and Har Homa.

Now Barak announced that he was unwilling to accept this proposal as it was, and that he was changing it. Palestinian sovereignty would only encompass the outer neighborhoods far from the Old City. There would be no division of sovereignty by quarters in the Old

City. Sovereignty – over all quarters – would be Israeli, and a special regime will be in place to enable the Palestinians to manage their lives under Israeli sovereignty, Israeli law and Israeli police.

Barak expressed willingness that near the Temple Mount Arafat would have a small complex under his sovereignty, in which he would establish an office and would entertain visitors from abroad. In the holy sites in the Old City, there would be joint custody: inside the structures – custody would be Muslim-Palestinian, and outside of them, custody would be Israeli.

"This is the limit of what I can possibly agree to," Barak said, "and I think that in Arafat's terms, it's still the deal of a lifetime because he is receiving a state on at least ninety percent of the territory; economic cooperation with Israel; large-scale financial aid to solve the problem of refugees and their rehabilitation; international recognition of his state; membership in the UN, a transportation corridor through which he can reach his complex near the Temple Mount; and special arrangements that will enable the Palestinians to easily reach the Al-Aqsa Mosque from their neighborhoods. I will need to agree to divide Jerusalem, but this is contingent on a majority vote of at least 61 MKs in the Knesset," Barak continued. "If we cannot finalize this difficult matter now, I have no doubt that the alternative is a national unity government in Israel."

According to the arrangement Barak proposed, Israel would receive the end of the conflict, and annex the large settlement blocs. All the infrastructure the settlers will leave could remain in place: houses, roads and industrial areas - where the refugees will be able to settle. Israel's borders will be recognized, and Jerusalem will indeed be "divided." However, it will retain its Jewish majority and cover an area that is the largest in the history of the Jewish people, because the region of Jerusalem will encompass Givat Ze'ev in the north, Ma'aleh Adumim in the east and Gush Etzion in the south.

"If we do not reach such an agreement, what would Arafat's alternative be?" Barak continued. "In the absence of an agreement, Arafat will declare a state that will not be recognized by the world, and no one will help rehabilitate the refugees. Israel will separate from the Palestinians and they will not be able to work in Israel. We will immediately announce the annexation of the large settlement blocs and all of the Jordan Valley."

Then Barak stopped talking for a moment, and spread a map of Jerusalem on the table before Albright and Ross and said, "Friends, after much long thought in the last two days, I wish to inform you that Israel will not be able to do more!"

Madeleine Albright shrank in her chair, expressionless. It was clear that these were not the things she expected to hear, and she began by saying, "You know that Clinton will be back in half an hour. Until now, I understood that you wanted us to prod Arafat to accept the president's proposal, and I still think there is a possibility that he will indeed accept it. Now you propose changes to these ideas, and this puts us in a very embarrassing position."

Barak, who was well aware that the president was supposed to be back in half an hour, orchestrated this "incident" on purpose, in order for Albright and Ross to hurry and update Clinton of the changes.

"Maybe it's embarrassing," Barak replied, "and I am in favor of the president putting pressure on Arafat. However, as I understand, the president's previous proposal was rejected by Arafat, and therefore is off the table, and we have realigned our positions."

Dennis Ross was unnerved by the sudden change Barak imposed on them and said, "Do you really want us to present your new ideas to the Palestinians?"

"Yes," Barak replied, "Why is it that only Arafat has the right not to accept certain ideas, and try to pull us toward his ideas?"

Ross, who could not hide his embarrassment in view of the developments, said, "Yet for several days we tried to nudge Arafat to accept the president's ideas after all, so what will we do now?"

"Arafat did not respond to the president's ideas, and was not even asked to do so. What I proposed now is more advanced than what was raised in last night's discussions between the Palestinians and us, and it is the most that we can do. Perhaps if Arafat had accepted the president's ideas last week, I would agree. However, today, after being exposed to the public's response to the leaks that came out of these talks, I know I cannot pass the president's original ideas in the Israeli public. If Arafat had agreed a week ago, I could have been able to sway Israeli public opinion to accept this offer, under the understanding that Arafat accepts it too. However, because Arafat does not agree, and conditions have changed, I have to bring these things into account. "

It was clear that the Secretary of State was still under the effect of Barak's harsh words, and she said, "Mr. Prime Minister, you have every right to do as you see fit - but what is the president supposed to do now?"

"I clarified the limits of my ability to move forward," replied Barak. "I made it clear to the president that there are things that the State of Israel cannot accept under any circumstances, such as the right of return or territorial exchanges. I suggest that Clinton find out Arafat's answer to the presidential proposal, and then we'll decide what to do."

Two hours later, there was a meeting in "Aspen," President Clinton's cabin. The meeting was attended by, besides the president, Bruce Riedel, Barak and myself. Clinton began by telling us that during his stay on the Okinawa Island, he visited the memorial site for the casualties of World War II. A third of the island's residents were killed in that war, and the names of the dead from both the Japanese and the American sides are inscribed on the monument.

"Each of us must think of the terrible price of war and draw encouragement to try and achieve reconciliation and peace," said Clinton. "The monument is a symbol of the end of the war and the heavy price it entailed. Okinawa Island is a large volcanic rock with many natural caves formed by the volcanic processes. The caves were used as shelter for residents of the island fleeing the Japanese who threatened to kill all of them. I spoke with seven other leaders who participated in the G8 summit, and I explained that a lot of money would be needed to pay for the peace agreement between Israel and the Palestinians, including for the refugees' rehabilitation. I said that the United States is prepared to contribute half of the required sum, and asked them to contribute the second half. My impression is that they understood this."

Barak, who was in a particularly practical mood, returned the conversation from the Japanese Islands to the Camp David summit in the United States, and with a stern expression said, "After you left, I found myself in a very awkward situation. Immediately after you presented your proposal, I told you that this was a lot more than the Israeli side could bear. As for Arafat, he never even bothered to respond to your proposal, and after you left, I discovered to my amazement that he was not even asked to do so.

"The Secretary of State told me that in order to continue the talks, despite all this, we should take your ideas off the table. During this period, there was a series of leaks from the Palestinian delegation, including an interview given by Abu Mazen. As a result, the Palestinian responses have become more extreme, and the rug that enabled any movement for the parties to make progress was pulled from under out feet. The Palestinians have not swayed from their positions, and on the core issues, they even went backwards.

"As a result of all these developments, we found ourselves negotiating indirectly with the Palestinians through Jonathan Schwartz (the Legal Advisor to the US delegation), who was trying to find a formulation that would allow the continuation of direct talks between us.

"The Palestinians are demanding, as a precondition, sovereignty with full powers over the Temple Mount and the neighborhoods near the Old City. On the matter of Jerusalem, I went to the farthest edge to which any Israeli Prime Minister can conceivably go.

"Over the last twelve months, twelve weeks and twelve days - Arafat has tried to get as many concessions as possible from us, so that he can use them without committing to an agreement. We have disclosed our positions, but they have not disclosed theirs.

"I do not see any sign of flexibility on the Palestinian side, and am concerned about the process that is leading to the opposite of what I had in mind. I came to Camp David in good faith, I thought that in the pressure cooker of intensive meetings in a confined location, we could move forward – but I will not do so at any cost. In view of Arafat's refusal to your proposal, I must realign our ideas as I have said to Albright. "

"For two days I was alone, and I devoted all of this time to deep and serious contemplation," continued Barak. "I believe that Arafat did not take the opportunity and did not answer your proposal. In his insistence on the Temple Mount, and the leaks from Camp David, he has created a situation in which I cannot accept your ideas.

"My farthest line is that most of the outer neighborhoods in Jerusalem will be under Palestinian sovereignty, and the inner neighborhoods will be under Israeli sovereignty (including all the Muslim neighborhoods). These neighborhoods will be managed by neighborhood secretariats, who will receive their authority from Israel and have a certain connection to the Palestinian city of Al-Quds. I am willing to accept that only one of the inner neighborhoods will be under Palestinian sovereignty. In the Old City, there will be Israeli sovereignty with a special regime that enables freedom of religion for members of all religions. Arafat will have a small complex under his sovereignty near the Temple Mount in the Muslim Quarter, which will be under Israeli sovereignty, and the holy places there will be in joint custody. The Temple Mount will be under Israeli sovereignty, mainly to prevent underground excavations in the area of the mosques. In places holy to Muslims on the Temple Mount, there will be Palestinian tutelage. Free access will be given to members of all religions, and Israelis will have a right to pray on the Temple Mount."

At this point, Barak produced a map and on it demonstrated to Clinton that the distance between Abu Dis – where the Palestinian parliament would be built – and the Temple Mount was smaller than the distance between the Knesset and the Temple Mount. This meant that despite Arafat's close proximity to the Temple Mount from Abu Dis, Israel was willing to get him even closer to the Mount by setting up an office nearby, and by providing easy and close access to the Temple Mount.

"This is the farthest line of concessions I can pass in the Israeli public under the current circumstances, wherein Arafat does not concede the right of return. If he would have conceded, I too could have made concessions. This is not a tactic but the plain truth. For the Palestinians it is a fair and very advanced deal," Barak said to Clinton. "When you meet with Arafat, I suggest you present to him the alternatives to not reaching an agreement, in the most blatant manner, which means the outbreak of violence. Arafat should understand that it is either now or never. In exchange for his agreement, he will gain much over the next few weeks and months. This includes a sovereign and contiguous state on about ninety percent of the territory, entry to neighboring countries, and cooperation with Israel, including a free trade zone. He will also gain permits for Palestinians to work in Israel, the right of return for Palestinians to a Palestinian state, a large monetary fund that will subsidize Palestinian refugees' rehabilitation, and part of what is now Israeli Jerusalem. Israel will gain the end of the conflict and eighty percent of the settlers will continue to live in their communities in the settlement blocs that will be annexed to Israel. Israel would be willing to participate in the refugees' rehabilitation in symbolic and humanitarian aid; there will not be a right of return for Palestinian refugees to Israel, and Jerusalem will be recognized worldwide as the Israeli capital.

"This is a great opportunity that is being submitted to Arafat, and he must decide whether he wants to be a historic leader, the first to establish a Palestinian state, or to remain a gang leader."

Clinton met with Arafat once more in a final attempt to explain to him the magnitude of the proposal he received, how important and fateful his willingness to accept it would be, and how all those involved are at a crucial decision-making crossroads.

His impression from the conversation, as recounted to Barak, was that Arafat had started to show understanding and willingness to delve deeper into negotiations.

"I told Arafat that I do not want him to come to me again with the demand for the 1967 borders, and with the UN resolutions he keeps analyzing for me every time. I do not want to waste time," Clinton said. "I told him not to tell me he was ready, unless he was ready to discuss the refugees, security arrangements, and finally borders and Jerusalem."

"Did he give you an answer to your question as to whether he is willing to negotiate on the basis of your offer?" asked Barak, and the president replied, "Yes."

The president stressed that George Tenet, Director of the CIA, whom Arafat held in high esteem, received the impression that Arafat was ripe for peace. Given Arafat's conduct and the results of negotiations with him, one can learn how the Americans tend again and again to receive the wrong impressions from Middle Eastern statements and gestures.

Indeed, in meetings held immediately afterwards between the Americans and Palestinians, it became apparent that Arafat's positive response to Clinton was entirely opposed to the Palestinians' behavior, and their positions remained rigid and uncompromising.

At midnight on July 25, there was a telephone conversation between Clinton and Barak, and the president began by saying, "Usually I'm optimistic, but during the meetings we held, Saeb Erekat admitted to me that Arafat is unable to make difficult decisions. I asked them to suggest a counter-proposal against my proposal, but have not received one. I told them, Barak is serious, he made serious offers, he commented on my proposals while you are not commenting and only say what you cannot do, and never what you can.

"I mentioned to them the possibility that perhaps we could confine ourselves to a partial agreement at this stage, and continue the negotiations later. Erekat replied honestly that the Palestinians would not agree to this.

"We now face three possibilities: we reach an agreement after all, we reach an agreement without dealing with the issue of Jerusalem which will be postponed for the time being, or the summit will fail. Erekat tried to argue with me and said that the Palestinians have also made suggestions. I told him that he is not taking into account Barak's condition and the harsh criticism by the Israeli political right, since according to leaks coming out of Camp David, a picture is portrayed that the Palestinians were tough, while the Israelis were lenient - which hurts the Israeli peace camp.

"Erekat almost burst into tears and said, 'Arafat will turn seventy-two years old next month, he cannot make a decision, even though I think it is possible to reach an agreement'.

"I am very disappointed right now," said Clinton, and it was evident in his voice that he was beginning to understand that on the other side there was a stone wall that could not and perhaps never had the intention of opening a window to allow the peace process to develop.

Barak, who had heard the sounds of the summit's crash even earlier, at once said, "We have to think how we announce this, since obviously we cannot detail the ideas that came up here, so that Arafat will not use them as the baseline for the next meetings."

As a contingency plan, preparations were made in case the summit failed, and it would be necessary to issue a formal announcement about it.

Clinton promised to Barak, "If things do not change, I will tell the media that you have done all you could, and that Arafat did not respond as he should have."

"I would suggest that you use the following wording: 'Israel made courageous steps, but we found that there is no partner. All that was said at Camp David will not be used as a starting point for any future negotiations'," Barak began, in his characteristic way, to issue orders – even though this was the president of the United States.

"I will say you acted with courage, that the Palestinians did not respond properly, and that if there is no deal – then all that has been said here is null and void, and it will not be a basis for the future," said Clinton.

"If the summit does indeed fail, we will need your assistance in a few other matters, such as transferring your embassy to Jerusalem. I took many risks here, things leaked, people know how far I was willing to go, and I do not want the Israeli public to feel that we have lost something as a result of these negotiations, but rather that we have actually benefited. Recognizing Jerusalem as Israel's capital could be appropriate compensation," said Barak.

Clinton and Barak decided that they would let Arafat consider until the next morning, and then decide on his answer to Clinton's proposal. "If Arafat gives a final negative answer to your proposal, tell him that there is no point in making additional proposals," said Barak.

"If Arafat will ring me back, do you think the two of you should meet?" asked Clinton, and Barak replied, "Perhaps I should meet him, but you are more effective when it comes to putting pressure on Arafat. If anything positive can come out of a meeting, there is a greater chance that it will happen at a meeting between the two of you, without my presence."

A few hours later, Dennis Ross came to us, and reported that the Palestinians have declared that they cannot concede their sovereignty over the Temple Mount, and that they cannot accept the president's proposal as a basis for further negotiations.

It became apparent that it would still be possible to bridge the issue of the Temple Mount, but on the right of return, Arafat could not present to his people a situation in which he had even considered the matter.

For Arafat, it was convenient to describe the failure of the Camp David talks as occurring in light of the issue of the Temple Mount rather than the right of return. Otherwise, he would have to explain to the Americans why his answer was not given earlier. After all, if the issue of the right of return is an absolute deal-breaker as far as he is concerned, and he was aware of this in advance – what was even left for him to mull over?

The Temple Mount was Arafat's guise to excuse his "days of contemplation", although in fact it was clear to him from the outset that he could not give up the right of return.

On the other hand, in order not to be seen as responsible for the summit's failure, Arafat chose to buy time, and hence did not immediately refuse Clinton's proposal, which included the abolition of the right of return.

On the morning of July 25, the day the summit ended, all of the Israeli team gathered at Barak's cabin. There was a feeling of great disappointment in the air stemming from the fact that all of Israel's sincere and far-reaching efforts were unsuccessful, and from the clear recognition that Arafat was not capable of making difficult decisions.

It was there, for the first time, that I concluded that he was not a real partner, and that it was apparently impossible to reach a peace agreement as long as Arafat ruled and led the Palestinians.

At the closing session in his cabin, Barak said, "I bear the ultimate responsibility for any result, and every stage and step of the way in which negotiations here were conducted. The end of this round of talks is not the end of the efforts to make peace. The battle for peace will continue in the days and months ahead, but keep in mind that there is also a struggle between us and the other side. The developments in the last 24-48 hours only go to show how much we do not have a partner, even when we go very far, even to the edge of every Israeli and every Jew's position.

"The diplomatic process has stopped here on account of the other party's demand to cede full sovereignty over the Temple Mount to them. The Temple Mount is a place that touches the roots of the State of Israel's existence, a place that is the foundation of the independence that has enabled four generations of Zionism to overcome the obstacles, through much blood and sweat, and form a sovereign state in the land of Israel.

"If there is an almost singular point on which the entire people of Israel can be united and base their willingness to fight for the country, it will be this: the recognition that the Palestinians refuse to concede the Temple Mount. The proposals Clinton submitted to Arafat are far-reaching, and they speak mainly of the division of sovereignty over the Temple Mount. Arafat's very explicit and negative answer requires us to see what has happened here as the end of one chapter and the beginning of another."

Barak went on to talk about how the true struggle that will await us when we return from Camp David, will be over the outstanding issues raised at the summit, for the first time in many years.

At a certain point Clinton, Albright and Riedel joined the discussion in Barak's cabin. Clinton asked Barak whether he would like to meet Arafat and Barak answered, "My people think I should, and I am willing."

The president showed Barak a draft of the statement that he was about to issue from the summit, which said that Barak displayed courage and determination, while Arafat disappeared and was dumbstruck. It would further state that an effort was made to prevent the outbreak of violence and allow the continuation of dialogue.

"Saeb Erekat said that Arafat cannot make a decision, and he was as if paralyzed," Clinton said, adding, "The Palestinians came with a wrong strategy to the negotiations, namely: not to show flexibility. Arafat is already seventy-two years old, and has never been anything but the head of a resistance movement. He is surrounded by old people, who are just as fixated as him. However, there is also a group of young people who are willing to listen, and they must be nurtured. Arafat lives in a virtual world, not in the real world. In the world that we live in, we must constantly make decisions and consider different alternatives, and for the Palestinians it doesn't work that way. This is because they have lived for so many years with a very strong sense of victim-hood. Erekat said to me, 'The Arabs never treated the Palestinians properly. But something happened here, because we had real discussions on fundamental issues that we never dealt with before, and we even changed our positions (the "change" in their positions was manifested in their agreement that Israel would retain seven percent of the territory, and two quarters in the Old City will be under Israeli sovereignty)'.

"For the Palestinians, it was a historic summit," Clinton continued, "because it forced them to deal with the most sensitive issues and have internal debates about them."

"The Palestinians should have accepted your proposal. Even Arab leaders were willing to accept it and support Arafat. Even the intelligence I have tells me that they were willing to live with it," said Barak.

"How will you act now?" Clinton asked. "On one hand, you have to be strong enough to survive politically, but on the other hand, you should not kill the process that has now begun between the Palestinians and themselves. You Israelis are used to making decisions, but the Palestinians have gone through very difficult internal debates here."

"I fear that the lesson the Palestinians will learn is that whoever does not decide, is rewarded," said Barak, "and this must not happen!"

"I agree with you," said the president, and Barak continued, "It should be clear that all the ideas raised here have ceased to exist, so as not to be used as the baseline for the next session.

"Now Arafat will make use of what he meant to achieve in the first place: he revealed the limits of our flexibility, while he himself, not only did not show flexibility, but also strengthened his standing by not compromising in Jerusalem. I took big risks. After all, I could have been sitting in a national unity government, waiting for the clash between the Palestinians and us, which is drawing nearer. Now I have to act quickly or my government will fall. I can do so only if it is clear that your judgment as the leader of the free world will prevent the things we said from being used against us, and the things we were willing to undertake here."

Barak once again asked Clinton to consider the possibility of transferring the US embassy in Israel to Jerusalem. "This will send a message to the Palestinians," Barak said, "that as long as they are stuck in their positions, they lose more and more. And on the other hand, it is a message to Israelis and Jews around the world, that the United States supports, in practice, Israel's willingness to achieve peace at the price of very large concessions."

"In my closing remarks, I will say that the process is not over and we will continue it. I will also say that if the Palestinians unilaterally declare a state, the United States will not recognize it and will move its embassy in Israel to Jerusalem," the president said.

A heavy sense of missed opportunity accompanied that day. We felt that at last we had touched upon the five most painful and bleeding aspects of the conflict: Jerusalem, refugees, settlements, borders and security arrangements. We arrived at Camp David with a lot of goodwill and a great willingness to discuss these issues, and promote understandings between the parties regarding them. It was very disappointing to discover that the Palestinians were not willing to enter an in-depth discussion of these issues.

Based on many sources, including intelligence ones, we were aware of the possibility that within the next few months we might be in the midst of a difficult and bloody Intifada.

I thought that the negotiations should continue with the intent of reaching stabilization. We were not expecting anything more than that after Arafat's reaction to all that was offered to him, and following our realization that he was not a partner.

Expectations for a breakthrough and for closing the gaps in these core issues were a distant dream back then, and unfortunately still are today.

Nevertheless, I still think that peace with the Palestinians can be achieved already in our generation, but only after the Palestinians will overcome their internal problems, overcome Hamas, regain control of Gaza, fight terrorism determinedly, end incitement and disarm all the armed organizations. I believe that at some point, the Palestinians will realize that they have only two possibilities: deterioration of the situation between us and them to severe violence, or making significant concessions and moving on to times of peace.

The Israeli side will have to accept that alongside the State of Israel, there will be an independent, contiguous and demilitarized Palestinian state in most of the territories of Judea and Samaria and the Gaza Strip. The future border between the two countries will be based on the line of June 4, 1967 – with the required territorial and security adjustments. The border would be such that Israel will contain the major settlement blocs adjacent to the Green Line, and the Israelis will have to agree to territorial exchanges.

Both sides will have to accept a solution in Jerusalem according to the principle that the Arab neighborhoods will be under Palestinian sovereignty, the Jewish ones under Israeli sovereignty, and a special regime will be in place in the Temple Mount and the Old City.

The Palestinians will have to accept the fact that Israel is the national home of the Jewish people, and there will not be a right of return for Palestinian refugees into it.

I thought in the past that if this type of negotiation is unsuccessful, Israel will have to take unilateral action that would lead to complete separation from the Palestinians. Towards this end, it will be necessary to move isolated settlements to the large settlement blocs under Israeli sovereignty, outside or inside the Green Line. Israel will continue to control about thirty-five percent of the West Bank, including the Jordan Valley, which constitutes twenty percent of the territory, and which would be declared a security zone primarily used for military activity. Existing settlements will remain in place, but no new ones will be built. Another fifteen percent of the territory, which contain the large settlement blocs, will be annexed by Israel. A robust and smart fence and compound barrier will separate between the Israelis (including settlers) and the Palestinians, and Israel will have full control over people entering and exiting its territory.

At the present day, after we have tried to unilaterally separate from the Gaza Strip, I came to the conclusion that such a step could not be implemented in the West Bank. Israel will not be able to evacuate some sixty thousand settlers living in isolated settlements, except as part of a permanent agreement that will also declare the end of the conflict between the Palestinians and us.

Every leader who sets forth on the thorny, laborious and total path that leads to peace must be courageous and possess a sober outlook and the ability to look to the future, beyond the limited boundaries of the present moment.

Barack possessed these qualities, and this was also how he acted at Camp David. Contrary to popular belief, Barak had not retracted his far-reaching proposals because of polls indicating that the public was not ready to make concessions in the Temple Mount. Barak changed his mind because he realized that Arafat could not be a partner to a permanent agreement.

When he came to Camp David, Barak truly intended to reach an agreement with the Palestinians. Going to the summit was not meant to position him as "the first one to take the fall" or to expose Arafat's true nature. Barak reached the summit to confront the problems in full, and to solve them. Arafat's true nature was revealed during the summit.

It was clear to Barak that the core issues would be put on the table and discussed at the summit for the first time, and he was ready for it. In retrospect, we know that the summit is a major milestone in shaping Israeli public opinion on some very sensitive issues. The Israeli public understood then for first time, that a day will come in which we will have to give up most of the territory of the West Bank and Gaza, and sovereignty over part of Jerusalem. Evidence of this can be found in the behavior of the Israeli public, which endured, understood and accepted the disengagement from Gaza carried out by Prime Minister Ariel Sharon. Except for local settlers, and their usual right-wing supporters, there were no riots or a national resistance to the move.

Barak displayed a sober outlook and realized that without concessions there was no chance to advance the process. In doing so, Barak presented a historical perspective, political courage and leadership.

Barak went to Camp David on the background of his assessment that we can see the large glacier approaching us, and it bears news of the deterioration of the situation – unless there is a positive breakthrough in our relations with the Palestinians.

In view of this situation, he faced three choices: One was to avoid doing anything dramatic and prepare for deterioration. Another was go to the leaders' summit in order to fully exhaust the chances of reaching a permanent agreement. The third option was to carry out the third withdrawal phase (according to Oslo) and cede additional territory, which according to the Palestinians should include the remainder of the territory of Judea, Samaria and Gaza except for settlements and military bases. All this – while still within the framework of the interim agreement and before the permanent settlement. The Israeli interpretation was that if there will in fact be a third phase – Israel would decide on the size and whereabouts of the territory to be given to the Palestinians, rather than all the remaining territory as the Palestinians claimed.

Despite the known results of the summit, I thought then, and still think now, that Barak made the right choice when he decided to go to Camp David.

At the end of the summit, we returned to Israel with a feeling that sluggish negotiations would continue for the time being, thus delaying the outbreak of violence. It was estimated that in the absence of the third phase's implementation, or alternatively a peace agreement being signed – this outbreak would come.

However, despite these less than exhilarating forecasts, and although we were long prepared for this possibility – the Al-Aqsa Intifada managed to catch us by surprise. Perhaps this was due to our great hope and genuine wish that it will not happen, which at times managed to eclipse the writing on the wall.

The surprise was less on account of the events themselves, but more from their spreading into the State of Israel, the participation of Arab-Israelis in them, and that it went on for such a long time.

One of the main things that changed after returning from Camp David was the process towards unilateral actions, meaning physical separation between us and the Palestinians.

The separation fence was launched.

The first stage was the construction of artificial cliffs meant to make it difficult for Palestinian vehicles to enter Israeli territory. At the same time, instructions and funding were given for the construction of rigid barriers against vehicles in places prone to penetration. Plans for the implications of our separation from the Palestinians commenced: planning the route of the barrier that will separate between us and them, which includes the separation fence, plowed roads, an array of barriers and warning measures. Work began on the civilian aspects of the fence, such as the construction of water, electricity and transportation infrastructure for the settlements that will remain beyond the barrier line.

To this day, we have almost completed building the seven hundred kilometer separation fence alongside the pre-1967 border with the West Bank. The fence dramatically reduced the terror attacks initiated in the West Bank and directed towards Israel.

The idea was that one day – when there is peace and the border is determined – the separation fence will be torn down.

The Berlin Wall has already demonstrated to the world that many years of separation, enmity and war can be dismissed by a few bulldozers.

Let us pray that the same will happen here.

Chapter 33

To Practice What You Preach

After Ehud Barak was defeated by Ariel Sharon in the 2001 elections, I spoke to him at length and tried to persuade him to take on the role of Defense Minister in Sharon's government. I was happy to see Ehud heeding my advice and accepting the position. Yet how great was my surprise when a few days later, he announced that he had changed his decision, turned down the Ministry of Defense and retired from the political life to enter the business world.

I thought then, and still think so today, that Barak made a mistake. At the time, in 2001, Israel still faced enormous challenges. The Second Intifada was already claiming many victims among us, the threat of a nuclear Iran continued to develop, terrorism had not ceased for a moment, and Barak was the most suitable person to fill the post of Defense Minister. I further thought that his decision to take a time-out would impair the Labor Party's ability to recover, and would make it much harder for him to return to politics if he would decide to do so in the future. I think that the developments after the 2001 elections proved me right.

While the Al-Aqsa Intifada raged on, the IDF had neglected its reserves and many reserve units were untrained. Under our noses, Hezbollah's power grew to dangerous proportions, and Iran continued its efforts to obtain a nuclear bomb.

Years later, during the Second Lebanon War that erupted in 2006, we learned a painful lesson about the results of complacency and neglect of the reserve units' training and preparation for combat.

Barak found it difficult to return to politics, and failed in his first attempt to be reelected as Chairman of the Labor Party. Amir Peretz won that campaign, defeating Binyamin Ben-Eliezer and Shimon Peres.

With Barak's resignation, I finished my term as Chief of the Political-Security Bureau, and wished to have a short rest after an interesting, intensive and exhausting period. Less than two weeks later, I was offered the position of Chairman of the Board of Koor Metals Ltd., one of the leading companies in its field in the country. The position in the company, which is owned by Pini Oslerne, a wonderful friend blessed with many talents, opened a wide window into the industrial and business world for me, and I was fascinated by it.

One day, in 2002, Professor Tzvi Arad, president of Netanya Academic College, called me and asked that we meet. I was happy to agree. At the meeting, Arad and Dr. David Altman raised the idea that I would establish a center for strategic studies at the college, and among others would recruit Ehud Barak to it.

I accepted the challenge, and along with my work as Chairman of the Board at Koor Metals, I enlisted myself to the matter, on a completely voluntary basis. As CEO, I recruited my good friend, Dr. Moshe Amirav, while I served as the center's chairman. Later Trevor Spiro, a Jewish philanthropist from London who contributed much, joined me as co-chairman. We decided that it would not be a regular academic center, but a practical one: we would not make do with research and reports, but would try to work in the field to assist in managing and solving conflicts throughout the world. We chose the name "Center for Strategic Dialogue", and soon afterwards, the center was already on its feet. We received assistance from the Netanya Academic College, were allocated some professors and researchers, Dr. Reuven Pedatzur was appointed Academic Director of the center and we were on our way.

In March 2003, about one week after the outbreak of the Second Gulf War, we held our first symposium at the Waldorf Astoria hotel in New York, which dealt with the war on terror. It was attended by Abdul Rahman Wahid, former President of Indonesia; Carl Bildt, former Prime Minister of Sweden; Louis Freeh, former Director of the FBI; James Woolsey, former Director of the CIA; Ehud Barak and myself. The symposium garnered much attention, and the Netanya College, which no one had heard of before, was put on the map.

In June 2003, we held a large conference at Netanya College, entitled "After the Iraq War, Towards the Road-Map - Prospects and Risks." Among other attendants at the conference were Mikhail Gorbachev, former President of the Soviet Union; Abdul Rahman Wahid, former President of Indonesia; Frederik de Klerk, former President of South Africa, Ehud Barak; Mr. Motegi, Japanese Deputy Foreign Minister; Berend Shmidtbauar, former Intelligence Minister of Germany; and James Woolsey, former Director of the CIA.

We held additional symposiums; we sent a delegation headed by Dr. Alon Liel, former Director General of the Ministry of Foreign Affairs and our ambassador in Turkey, to Cyprus. The delegation engaged in dialogue with Turkish-Cypriots and Greek-Cypriots to help resolve the years-long conflict there.

To the center's executive committee I recruited such personages as Mikhail Gorbachev, Frederik de Klerk, the last white President of South Africa, Abdul Rahman Wahid, Berend Shmidtbauar, Ehud Barak, Prince Hassan of Jordan, Louis Freeh, James Woolsey, Sandy Berger and others.

On the tenth anniversary of Rabin's murder, we held a major symposium at Netanya, wherein speeches were made by, among others, Dr. Abdul Salam Al Majali, former Jordanian Prime Minister; Osama el-Baz, President Mubarak's political advisory; Lionel Jospin, former Prime Minister of France; foreign ministers from seven countries and many others.

Over time, Prof. Yossi Ginat replaced Dr. Amirav, while I finished my volunteer role after five years of chairing the center.

For about two years, I served as Chairman of Koor Metals. I enjoyed my job very much and found it to be highly interesting. Material conditions were improved and life was comfortable and relaxed, but I found no rest in light of the problems that Israeli society was facing. I felt that I needed to re-enlist myself so I can contribute from my experience, and I decided to return to public activity.

At the end of 2002, it was decided to hold early elections for the sixteenth Knesset. It was a difficult and turbulent period: near-daily terrorist attacks caused many casualties among Israelis, and the al-Qaeda terrorist attacks that were carried out on US soil on September 11, 2001, led to the collapse of the World Trade Center, damaged the Pentagon, crashed four passenger planes and took the lives of thousands – Americans, Israelis and other nationals.

One hour before the candidate list for the Labor Party primaries was closed, I arrived at the party's head office in Hatikva Quarter, and registered as a candidate. I had no political experience. In the consultations that I held before the decision, I spoke to many people with extensive experience in politics who told me that I was making a mistake. I had no foothold among party members, I was not a guest at their celebrations and did not participate in their moments of pain and sorrow, had not developed personal relationships with activists, enumerators and voters. Hence, I was told that even though I served as Major General, Rabin's Military Secretary, Barak's Chief of Staff and Director of the Mossad – my chances were minimal. However, there were others, including Ehud Barak and Ophir Pines, then the party secretary, who encouraged me to make the move.

The primaries were set to take place in nine days, by all accounts a short time to run an effective campaign, and I debated what I should do, since as mentioned, I had neither any political experience nor political connections. Luckily, a group of talented and efficient young people enlisted to help me. They had read in the newspaper about my decision to run, contacted me on their initiative and showed up to work. For nine days, I covered the length and breadth of the country, appeared countless times before activists and voters, and I was elected at the eighth place in the Labor Party primaries. After the reserved seats were added, I was positioned at the thirteenth place.

I was elected to the sixteenth Knesset, then the seventeenth Knesset, and I served as a Knesset member for five and a half years. I was a member of the Foreign Affairs and Defense Committee, the Finance Committee, the House Committee, Chairman of the Committee on Foreign Workers and other committees. I came full of energy, saw my role as an MK as a mission rather than a career, and tried to promote many issues, some of which I even succeeded. I headed the Lobby for the Separation Fence, the Lobby for the IDF Soldiers, the Lobby for the IDF Disabled, and the Lobby for the Protection of Sderot and the Gaza Envelope Towns. I dealt with accelerating the construction of the separation fence, hastening the addition of protective measures in the Gaza envelope towns, the rights of disabled IDF soldiers, the rights of IDF widows and many other issues.

Along with MK Avshalom Vilan ("Meretz") I enacted the Reserve Service Law. This law regulated the designation of the reserves army, its management, responsibility and authority of senior officials in the defense establishment with respect to the reserves, as well as remuneration and compensation for the reserve soldiers on account of their service, for the first time in the country's history. I was involved in raising the electoral threshold to two percent, though I failed in my efforts to raise it to 2.5 percent. I was similarly unable to pass the Civil Service Law - alternative service for those who do not serve in the IDF, mainly intended for minorities, the ultra-Orthodox and those who were rejected for military service due to medical or other problems.

The Second Lebanon War broke out in response to Hezbollah's murderous attack against an IDF patrol. Three of the patrol soldiers were killed and the late Ehud Goldwasser and Eldad Regev, may they rest in peace, were kidnapped.

I justified the government's decision to respond forcefully and strike Hezbollah. However I said at the beginning of the war, in closed forums and in public appearances, that the goal should be to exact a very high price from Hezbollah, and the method should be based on the use of massive firepower while avoiding a large-scale ground attack. I know Lebanon well, have gained much experience in fighting terrorism, and it was clear to me that the conquest of Southern Lebanon will exact many victims from us, but will not achieve its goal - to end the rocket fire.

The government erred by not accepting Lebanese Prime Minister Fouad Siniora's request for a cease-fire after the first week of combat.

The many flaws revealed during the Second Lebanon War were due to overly ambitious goals set by the government, and the fact that the government debated for three weeks without reaching a decision - whether to use only firepower, or to conquer Southern Lebanon by the force of a few divisions. When the government decided to commence a ground operation, it was after the details of the ceasefire were already finalized at the UN Security Council, and the IDF was allotted only sixty hours to reach the Litani River, while in the previous three weeks of combat, the IDF advanced a mere eight kilometers.

It was clear that the decision was wrong: the cease-fire was set to go into effect within days, the ground attack was unlikely to achieve any significant achievement, and within sixty hours, there was no way to reach the Litani River with a significant order of forces.

I tried to prevent the operation in discussions at the Foreign Affairs and Defense Committee, which were attended by the Chief of Staff, the Defense Minister and the Prime Minister, and having failed to do so – I appeared in all the television and radio channels, trying to convince that this was a terrible mistake. As mentioned, the IDF launched the ground operation. About a third of the fighters killed in the entire war fell in its final hours, and the IDF did not manage to accomplish its mission.

There were other reasons for the failures: the reserve forces, who had not trained for years, were not prepared for their missions, much equipment was missing, and frequent changes to the missions they were given did not allow for efficient and focused use of the forces.

At the end of June 2008, I resigned from the Knesset, after five and a half years, for three main reasons. The first was that I called for Prime Minister Olmert's resignation immediately after the release of the Winograd Commission's full report, due to his responsibility for the failures of the Second Lebanon War. I argued that he should be held responsible for the government's flawed actions and for the consequences of his decision to go to war, and that he should lead by example rather than making do with the dismissal of the Defense Minister, the Chief of Staff, Commander of Northern Command, and two division commanders. As is known, Olmert refused to resign.

The second was that I was of the opinion that the Labor Party had to resign from the coalition after the release of the Winograd Report, and that it must not be used as a safety net and lifeline for Olmert, who continued to serve as Prime Minister. I had many conversations with Barak on this matter, and I expressed my opinion publicly many times. Barak chose to stay in the government, despite his commitment during the campaign for the party's leadership that he would resign from the government immediately upon the release of the full Winograd Report. As someone who worked to cause Olmert to resign, or alternatively – for my party to resign from the coalition, and whose efforts were unsuccessful - I thought that in this state of affairs, I had to "practice what I preached."

The third reason was that I found that ethical standards among quite a few of the politicians were eroding away, personal example was gradually disappearing, personal and political considerations were playing an increasingly dominant role, and many considered their seat in the Knesset to be more desirable and worthy than their ideology. I did not want to continue to be there.

Around the time of my resignation, a temporary cease-fire ("*tahadiyeh*") was reached with the Hamas regime in Gaza. The Israeli government made a mistake when it did not use the ceasefire in order to protect as many homes as possible in Sderot and in the Gaza envelope towns.

On December 27, 2008, the IDF launched Operation "Cast Lead" in order to strike a severe blow against Hamas, after eight years of Katyusha rockets and mortar fire on Sderot and the Gaza envelope towns. The operation was justified. The mission that was set was an achievable one: not to topple Hamas and its regime, but to cause as much damage and casualties to Hamas as possible. This time the IDF acted well, recovered and regained its confidence, which had partially been lost in the Second Lebanon War.

The calm period that was reached following Operation "Cast Lead" was temporary, and the security situation in the Gaza envelope settlements began to worsen. On November 14, 2012, the IDF launched an additional operation against Hamas. Operation "Pillar of Defense" started with the targeted killing of Ahmed Jabari, commander of the military wing of Hamas, and its purpose was the strengthening of our deterrence, striking a severe blow to the rocket apparatus, causing grave damage to Hamas and other terrorist organizations, and minimizing the attacks against our civilian home front.

The operation was based on firing at terrorist targets and it did not include a ground incursion. The "Iron Dome" missile defense system was highly effective and intercepted hundreds of rockets fired at Israel.

On November 21, 2012, the operation ended with the declaration of a ceasefire.

Once again, the quiet did not last for long and on July 8, 2014, the IDF launched Operation "Protective Edge." This operation lasted fifty days and ended on August 26 in a ceasefire.

In this operation, the IDF operated intensively from the air and its aircraft destroyed many targets. The operation also included a limited ground offensive including several brigade-level combat teams.

The ground incursion was only decided upon after the threat of attack tunnels dug by Hamas became clear, and that some of them reached into Israeli soil. This was perceived as a severe and imminent threat and it was necessary to destroy these tunnels.

Operation "Protective Edge" lasted too long, and faults were found in the transmission of intelligence to combat units. However, the biggest fault in terms of intelligence was that the military and political echelons had not properly assessed Hamas's willingness to fight and its readiness for a long-term battle.

Another fault was that the upper echelons had failed to fully understand the dangerous nature of the attack tunnels. It was only after thirteen terrorists managed to infiltrate into Israel through an attack tunnel that the military and political leadership realized that a ground offensive must be launched in order to destroy the dozens of underground attack tunnels.

The "Iron Dome" system intercepted 735 rockets and mortar shells, but despite the IDF's forceful attacks, Hamas continued firing rockets until the operation's last day.

Since then, there has been a tense quiet in the region, occasionally violated by the activities of "rogue" organizations while Hamas attempts to prevent attacks against Israel due to its fear of the IDF's response.

Since the outbreak of the series of revolutions in the Muslim world, the world has become less stable and less safe. The Arab nation-state that formed the basis for the regional order has been undermined, and some countries are experiencing a process of disintegration based on the ethnic identity of their inhabitants.

The uprisings were an expression of social and economic discontent and brought three elements to the front of the stage: the Muslim public that took to the streets en masse and toppled the old regimes; the social networks used to develop and realize the revolution; and terrorist groups growing noticeably stronger against the backdrop of the collapse of the nation-state.

These terrorist organizations are of an extremist Islamic orientation and have a common goal with Iran: to build, on the ruins of the existing world, an Islamic religious caliphate which will be based on the laws of the Quran (Sharia) and will dominate the world.

The nature of the threat to Israel has changed: instead of large-scale armies, we are threatened by the terrorist organizations that surround us. Hezbollah in Lebanon and Syria; ISIS, Jabhat al-Nusra, Al Qaeda and others in Syria; Terror cells in the West Bank; and Jihadist organizations including ISIS in Sinai and Hamas in the Gaza Strip.

The current threat requires us to prepare in a different way in order to handle it. It is very difficult to gather accurate intelligence on terrorism since it is an elusive threat that is difficult to identify and to fight.

Hence the need to combat terrorism all year round, every day, every hour and in every place and create a continuous struggle in which we must constantly take the initiative and pursue the enemy.

It is very grave that Muslims who are citizens of European countries, the United States and other Western countries, in addition to many citizens of Islamic countries, volunteer to join the ranks of terrorist organizations, particularly ISIS.

Thousands of Jihadists from Western countries and tens of thousands from Muslim countries are fighting in Syria and Iraq.

Europe is now facing a great danger. These terrorists will return to their homelands with combat experience and very high motivation to carry out terrorist attacks in order to kill infidels and promote the ideal of the Islamic caliphate.

Such attacks have already been carried out in France and Belgium, and the security forces in several European countries have managed to prevent additional terrorist attacks orchestrated by the veterans of Syria and Iraq.

The war against terrorism is based on accurate intelligence in real time, on special forces on constant standby and on precise and deadly weapons.

It is a long and difficult battle that requires much patience and determination. No person involved in terrorism is immune and we must hit the entire chain of command, from leaders to perpetrators.

Israel has developed the "targeted thwarting" method, which combines precise intelligence in real-time with available operational capabilities of the highest level.

Cyber intelligence has become a very significant component. There is a huge space with infinite information, websites and networks from which we need to mine relevant information and supply it within a short time-frame. The defensive dimension has also become critical as a result of the capabilities and attempts of hostile elements to infiltrate our cyber systems, draw information and paralyze computer-based systems and the communications between them.

Terrorism cannot operate without financial resources. Money is sent from Iran and Muslim communities around the world, which collect money for charity, but it eventually finds its way to terrorist organizations. It is very important to block the money path and prevent it from reaching hostile hands.

If Iran achieves nuclear capabilities, it will constitute an existential threat to Israel.

On April 2015, in Lausanne, Switzerland, a "framework agreement" was reached between the six world powers and Iran regarding Iran's nuclear program. Until June 30, 2015, the parties will formulate a nuclear agreement, and only afterwards will they carry out their obligations. This agreement has its shortcomings - it will only be in effect for ten to fifteen years and it is unclear what will happen afterwards. Iran's breakthrough time to develop a bomb will be one year, a very short period by all accounts. It is essential that once Iran decides to produce enough fissile material to build a bomb, it will require a much longer period until achieving its target.

The agreement allows Iran to enrich uranium using 5,060 centrifuges, which will continue spinning in Natanz. Although the framework agreement defines a mechanism of close inspection over the nuclear program, its test will be in the implementation. Without an agreement that enables unannounced and intrusive inspections in each and every facility, it will be impossible to ensure that Iran is upholding its commitments.

The agreement does not require Iran to refrain from terrorist attacks and involvement, aid, training and guidance of terrorist organizations. In addition, the agreement does not require Iran to destroy its fleet of long-range surface-to-surface missiles and to stop their production. These missiles are designed to carry non-conventional warheads, including nuclear ones, in the future.

Removing the sanctions on Iran will annul the main factor that has brought Iran to the negotiating table. Furthermore, reinstating the sanctions in case Iran breaches the agreement will be a long and very problematic process. Hence, it is important that the sanctions be removed gradually and only after the West will ensure that Iran has complied with all the demands.

Chapter 34

A Look to the Future

I have dedicated 42 years of my life to public service. This has mostly focused on protecting the people and the nation in the course of my service in the IDF and the Mossad; promoting national interests in my roles in the Ministry of Defense and the offices of prime ministers who also served as defense ministers; and parliamentary and public activities as part of my membership of the sixteenth and seventeenth Knessets.

The State of Israel is very dear to me and I pray that the people of Israel will indeed reach a state of rest and quiet and will achieve the peace we deserve more than any nation in the world.

The State of Israel faces difficult and complex challenges, some of them existential.

The major issues any Israeli government has to promote are education, welfare, nurturing the outlying areas, fighting political corruption, striving for peace with our enemies, fighting terrorism and preventing Iran's acquisition of nuclear capabilities.

Israeli society is remarkably diverse. It has long-standing residents and immigrants, religious and secular, urban people and members of agricultural settlements, rich and poor, Jews and minorities, and various descendants of the Diaspora who have immigrated to Israel from all over the world, have gone through the Israeli melting pot and became a single society here. The key to our capacity for survival, for the growth and strengthening of our economy, culture and security is our social cohesion, the citizens' sense of belonging to the country, the willingness to work for the common good and the connections between the various layers of the population. We must ensure that the social cohesion is not lost and will come to our aid when we need it most, when the entire people will have to be enlisted to protect our homeland.

In current Israeli society, cracks have begun to form, and social cohesion is beginning to weaken. The huge gaps between the uppermost decile and the lower deciles are unbearable. The State of Israel is still struggling to properly absorb one million immigrants who arrived in large waves of immigration from the former Soviet Union and the Ethiopian immigrants.

To our great shame, Israel is home to approximately 1.8 million people below the poverty line, half of whom are children. The gaps between Jewish citizens and minorities have hardly been closed. Children from poor families are expelled from educational institutions to the street, and this leads them to crime and violence. Our society has become extremely violent, the elderly are beaten and robbed, and people are murdered in intolerable and inconceivable lightness. All these signs indicate that Israeli society is ill.

The government's main challenge is to treat these problems and fix them.

We must expressly place education at the top of our national priorities. Prioritizing education means increasing budgets, promoting the status of teachers, building additional classrooms so that the number of students per class will not exceed 28 students, and education towards values, rather than focusing on achievements and the pursuit of grades.

The values by which we should educate are love of the people and country; respect for the cultural and historical heritage of the Jewish people throughout history; love of others; patience and tolerance towards those who are other and different; behavior according to proper moral standards; providing tools for distinguishing between right and wrong, between permitted and forbidden; the essential nature of contributing to the society that we are all part of; the need to help the weak and underprivileged; education towards telling the truth; providing independent learning tools; encouraging creative thinking, and more.

Education must be available for everyone, regardless of financial situation. Through an improved and modern educational system, we can fix most of the flaws in our society and take more and more people out of the cycle of poverty and into the cycles of productivity and contribution. When Yitzhak Rabin decided to put education on the top of the national agenda, he allotted education the biggest budget, even bigger than the defense budget. Rabin realized there was no choice but to take calculated risks regarding security in order to ensure our future by means of an excellent education. Since then, the education budget has withered, and in 2014, the government allocated to education a budget which was only about two thirds the size of the defense budget.

The economic plan must serve educational and social goals. We must close the gaps between rich and poor, and provide adequate pensions to the underprivileged, the Holocaust survivors, the disabled, the sick, the elderly and to impoverished families.

We must create many jobs and fight unemployment, raise the minimum wage and encourage local and foreign investors to build their factories here rather than in countries where there is cheap labor available.

Israel should be a world center of higher education, science and technology, and this can be achieved. We must turn to the Nobel Prize laureates among the Jewish people, and convince them to dedicate one or two years to Israel. Their contribution in the fields of education, research, science and technology could be huge and could significantly advance these areas in Israel.

The burden on the eighteen-year-olds is divided unequally and unfairly. Only seventy percent of eligible candidates are recruited to the IDF. Minorities, barring the Druze, Circassians and Bedouins, the vast majority of the ultra-orthodox and people with medical impairments are not recruited. When David Ben-Gurion decided on the exemption of *yeshiva* students from service, they were but a few. Over the years, the number of those not drafted on the basis of "their Torah is their profession" has soared and in 2014 amounts to approximately eleven percent of the total number of those eligible to be drafted. There is no justifiable reason for having the burden of serving the country be so distorted and so unequal.

In recent years, the ultra-Orthodox have begun to enlist in the IDF. This is a welcome process, but their numbers are very small. We are also witnessing Muslim and Christian Arabs volunteering for military service; this is also a very important step, but it too is a drop in the ocean.

It is essential to build a framework for national service for those who do not serve in the IDF: A civilian national service, in which young men, and perhaps in the future young women too, will serve – mainly within their communities. Hence, we could assign young people to positions in education, community centers, auxiliary staff at hospitals, traffic police and more.

National service will grant similar rights as military service, and its greatest advantage is giving people who did not serve in the army the sense that they serve the country in a different way, and thus have also contributed to its strength and to its public's well-being.

Our political system needs to change.

The governmental system is unstable, and a new government is established almost every two years. There is no long-term national vision, and no strategic and multi-year work plan. I am in favor of changing the system.

Firstly, the electoral threshold must be raised to five percent. Thus, the small parties will vanish, there will be fewer parties in the Knesset, and the governmental coalition can be based on a small number of parties – which would stabilize it and reduce the smaller parties' power to extort the ruling party.

Another change is to elect half of the Knesset members in regional elections. The country will be divided into sixty districts, and each electoral district will send a representative to the Knesset. This change will result in a much stronger link between voters and elected officials, and will encourage talented young people, who have no chance of being elected in the current system, to go into politics. The remaining sixty Knesset members will be elected as they are today, through the political parties and in national elections.

We must not give up on peace. We may not manage to reach peace with the Palestinians and other countries, but we must try time and again and must not despair. It is our duty to prevent the next war, and if it is forced on us – to win it as quickly as possible and in an unequivocal and resolute way.

If Israel does not initiate a renewal of peace talks with the Palestinians, we are likely to find ourselves entrenched in another round of armed conflict with Hamas and facing a possible eruption of another Intifada in the West Bank.

Such a situation could ignite the northern border, which would cause Israel to be forced to fight on three fronts. We must do everything in our power to prevent the next war.

The "sitting and doing nothing" policy of Prime Minister Benjamin Netanyahu, who was elected to serve as Prime Minister for the fourth time now, could deteriorate the situation in the Middle East and even further deteriorate our international standing.

The absence of a diplomatic process could lead to a situation of 'one state for two peoples,' and for all matters and purposes, it would be an Arab state, between the Jordan River and the sea. It would be the end of the Jewish state.

The Arab Peace Initiative has been adopted, first by the twenty-two nations of the Arab League, and then by all fifty-seven Muslim nations. According to the initiative, these countries declare that peace is their choice and they recognize that there is no military solution to the Israeli-Arab conflict.

These are statements of the utmost importance, suggesting a deep strategic change in the Arab world's approach to Israel.

Israel is asked to withdraw in all fronts back to the lines of June 4, 1967. However, there is room for border adjustments agreed by the parties. A Palestinian state will be established in the West Bank and Gaza Strip. The issue of the refugees will be solved by means of an agreement between the parties. The term "right of return" is not mentioned in the Arab Initiative. East Jerusalem will be the capital of the Palestinian state, and in return, the Arab nations see the conflict as having reached its end and similarly the mutual claims.

The Muslim countries will enter peace agreements with Israel, and security will be ensured for all countries in the region.

I believe this is an opportunity that must not be missed!

A new situation has formed in the Middle East. Egypt, under the leadership of Abdel el-Sisi, sees the Muslim Brotherhood and Hamas as enemies that must be eliminated.

The moderate countries - Egypt, Saudi Arabia, Jordan, the Palestinian Authority and the Gulf States - see Iran as an existential threat and terrorism as a most dangerous threat that must be eliminated.

The struggle for hegemony in the Muslim world between the Sunni axis led by Saudi Arabia and the Shiite axis led by Iran is intensifying and is reaching new heights.

The struggle is expressed via proxies in Syria and in Yemen, where Iran supports the Houthis and Saudi Arabia supports the elected president.

This situation is the basis for a common strategic vision for Israel and the moderate Arab countries. In my opinion, Israel should adopt the Arab Initiative as a basis for negotiation and add the following: no Palestinian refugees will return to Israel on the basis of the right of return. Refugees who wish to return to Israel will return to the Palestinian state.

An international compensation fund will be established to compensate the Palestinian refugees and Jewish refugees who were driven out of Arab countries.

The border will be based on the one of June 4, 1967, with the necessary adjustments. Israel will annex approximately seven percent of the West Bank territories, an area where the major settlement blocs adjacent to the separation fence are located. There will be territorial exchanges in a ratio of 1:1. In Jerusalem, the Jewish neighborhoods will be under Israeli sovereignty and the Arab ones under Palestinian sovereignty. Special arrangements will apply in the Old City, with the Jewish and Armenian Quarters under Israeli sovereignty and the other two quarters under Palestinian sovereignty.

The Temple Mount would be under the sovereignty of God, or shared Israeli-Palestinian sovereignty, or sovereignty over it will remain undefined. The Islamic holy sites will be managed by the Waqf, and the Jewish ones will be under Israel's responsibly. The agreement is a regional agreement, and its main component will be the agreement with the Palestinians. Negotiations based on the Arab Initiative will allow the immediate commencement of reconstruction efforts in the Gaza Strip.

Israel does not have the luxury to give up on peace and therefore we must try time and again, on the basis of the Arab Initiative along with the Israeli initiative.

We must separate from the Palestinians on the basis of a two-state solution in regional negotiations and this type of process must be given a chance.

A nuclear Iran is an existential threat to Israel, and this must not happen. Iran possesses missiles with a range of 2,500 km that can reach Vienna and Warsaw, is developing missiles with a range of 4,000 kilometers that can reach London, and is heading towards a nuclear bomb.

We have successfully convinced the world that a nuclear Iran is not merely a problem for Israel, but a problem for the entire world. If Iran breaches the agreement, military action may be required, mainly through the air, using aircraft and long-range cruise missiles in order to seriously damage the nuclear program's main sites. This may not destroy all the facilities, but it will send Iran many years back in its efforts to obtain a nuclear bomb. It is very important that such an operation will be carried out by the international community, led by the United States.

If Iran continues with its nuclear program, despite the agreement, and the world decided not to take military action, Israel cannot sit back idly and watch Iran acquire nuclear capabilities. We will have to act to stop the Iranian efforts.

We will have to continue fighting terrorism. We have gained tremendous experience in this war. We cannot eradicate terrorism by military means alone, but we must fight it with all our might, to thwart its intentions and impair its abilities. We should continue conducting targeted killings and attacking the entire chain of terrorist activity, from the leaders of the organizations through the preachers, recruiters, the masterminds and to the perpetrators of the attacks themselves. The Shin Bet, the Mossad, the IDF, with an emphasis on the special forces, and the police, with an emphasis on its own special forces, will have a crucial role to play in this war.

The State of Israel is not a "nation unto itself." We are part of the family of nations, and in the reality of the global village, events occurring in the Middle East can affect distant states and peoples. The United States will continue to lead the world and the relationship between us and the Americans are the cornerstone of our security strategy, and are a very significant contributing factor to our capacity for survival. We will have to continue to nurture and develop these special relations. There can be arguments between friends. There have already been arguments between the United States and us, but we must remember that in addition to being independent and masters of our own destiny, we will have to make great efforts to maintain our alliance with the United States and keep it strong.

Europe is becoming an increasingly influential force. The EU, NATO and the open European market are powerful forces in today's global village. Developing our relations with Europe, joining the European market and strengthening ties with the EU and NATO will empower the State of Israel and serve our vital interests.

Russia, China and India are large economies with high potential for growth and development. Our foreign relations will have to devote special efforts to build more and more bridges of cooperation between these countries and Israel.

Peace with Egypt and Jordan is a highly important component of our national security strategy. Even if peace is not as warm as we want it to be, it is essential that it be protected from all harm. We must cultivate our relations with Jordan and Egypt, consult with them regarding negotiations with the Palestinians, and keep them in the picture regarding our contacts with additional Arab and Islamic nations, if and when such contacts occur.

We must continue to encourage immigration to Israel. Our citizens are the most important resource we have. Jews from around the world should already see Israel as their home, not just a place of refuge when trouble befalls them. I see the existence of the State of Israel and the immigration to Israel as the essence of today's Zionist vision.

When conditions are better, when there will be peace or at least a calm that lasts for many years, we can direct more and more resources from security to education, industry, welfare and the outlying areas. Yet we must not deceive ourselves - even if we reach the coveted peace, we will need a strong IDF and excellent security services. These will always guarantee our security and our independence, and guarantee that peace agreements will not be breached and will remain stable.

There is enormous potential in the Jewish people. Israel can become a blossoming garden and a world-leader in many areas. I am sure that in a state of peace or a long calm, and with a stable political system, we can develop the economy and lead it to greater achievements than those we have reached so far. We can become one of the most developed and leading economies in the world. Additionally we can develop all areas of life and soar to huge achievement, bigger than anything we have experienced before.

We are commanded to hand to our children and grandchildren a better nation, free of political corruption, without violence, with a stable system of government; a nation that continues to do everything to prevent the next war, but to win it decidedly if it is forced on us; a nation that strives for peace, and that places its citizens, their rights, standard of living and education at the center of national considerations.

The State of Israel was established from the smoking embers that remained of the Jewish communities that were destroyed during the Holocaust by the Nazis and their collaborators. We won the War of Independence against all odds. Alongside our struggle for independence and our development, we were able to build an advanced society and reach unprecedented achievements in many areas.

We have returned here after two thousand years of exile, and we will stay here forever.

EPILOGUE

During my military service I lost the best of my friends, commanders and soldiers. The routes of battles and military cemeteries across the country are saturated with the blood of the fallen. There are long rows, too long, of graves, where those who gave their lives for the people and the country are buried.

Our independence and our ability to continue living here we owe first and foremost to the fallen soldiers who stormed into the fires of hell, and sacrificed their most precious belonging so that Israel could continue to live in security, and in the future perhaps in full peace. We also owe it to the wounded and disabled who continue to bear the scars of war and its horrors throughout their lives.

What I have achieved in my life I could not have achieved without the vast support and infinite love that I have received from my family, and especially from Tova, my beloved wife, who gave me boundless support, raised our five sons by herself and was able to fill the roles of both mother and father, since I was a 'present-absentee' for almost all of these years.

We have five sons – Omer, Nir, Tal, Roey and Itay. They are wonderful boys, talented and smart. Our family is closer than most, and this is also thanks to Tova. We have wonderful and devoted daughters-in-law, four grandchildren, Lior, Adi, Tamir and Dolev, and two granddaughters, Tamar and Maya. Our grandchildren are the sweetest and smartest in the entire world. Today, as I follow their development, I understand what I have missed by not closely accompanying my own childrens' development and growth.

To my family I owe everything, and for them I would do anything, I love them dearly and am very proud of them and their achievements. Like me, they believe that the foremost duty is to act like a human being: honestly, fairly and generously; to act with courage and without being afraid to express their views and defend them determinedly. They understand the need to contribute to society and to promote it, do so and set a personal example in their behavior.

I admit, my happiest hours are the hours I spend with Tova, with the children and the grandchildren.

The journey of this book's writing begins in the assassination attempt by Mossad operatives, under my leadership, of one of the leaders of contemporary Arab terrorism. The end of the book looks to the future, noting the major challenges that the State of Israel faces and expressing a wish that we will soon reach a state of full and comprehensive peace.

Our life in this country moves constantly between these extremes.

I was born in this country, raised in it and more than once was ready to sacrifice my life for it. For most of my adult life, I accompanied it through its bloodied foothills and glorious peaks. I did this as a young soldier in Sayeret Matkal, as a commander leading his troops into battle, and as a partner to the most important, moving and nerve-racking crossroads of our national biography.

I have experienced the warrior's determination in war and combat and the hope for peace. Of the two, I have always preferred the latter. I willingly devoted the best of my abilities to reviving the vision of peace. I never abandoned the dream to give my children and grandchildren the opportunity to live in the country that I was born and raised in, albeit a slightly different one – one which would be a nation of peace and well-being. A nation where childrens' laughter will replace missile fuses, and family vacations will replace reserve duty; a nation in which loving mothers will be free of the destructive, threatening and debilitating fear of the Casualty Officer knocking on the door; a nation living in peace and prosperity with its neighbors in the region, and where struggles against terrorism and violence, and bereavement over soldiers lost in battle, are no longer part of daily reality, but a distant historical memory.

I will end my book, which blends into the story of this land, with a verse taken from the *"Kaddish Yatom"* (the orphan's mourning prayer). It was with this verse that Yitzhak Rabin would end many of his speeches on the matter of peace, and which represents the longing within the prayers of every Jewish person:

He who makes peace above, in his mercy he will make peace upon us
And upon all his people of Israel, and say Amen.

APPENDIX I

Non-Paper regarding main goals as agreed upon by Prime Minister Rabin and the President of Syria, Assad in 1995. The process of preparing the document appears on page 275.

AIMS AND PRINCIPLES OF THE SECURITY ARRANGEMENTS

AIMS

1) The most important priority is to reduce, if not, eliminate the danger of surprise attack.

2) Prevent or minimize friction on a daily basis along the boundary.

3) Reduce the danger for large scale attack, invasion or major war.

PRINCIPLES

1) Security is a legitimate need for both sides. No claim of security, or a guarantee for it, should be achieved at the expense of the security of the other side.

2) Security arrangements should be equal, mutual, and reciprocal on both sides, with equal [in cases of geographic difficulties being approached or addressed as follows] particularly insofar as geography and difficulties with geography are concerned, being as follows:

The purpose of the security arrangements is to ensure equality in overall security in the context of a state of peace between Syria and Israel. If, during the negotiations on security arrangements, it appears that the implementation of equality in principle insofar as geography is concerned with regard to a particular arrangement is impossible or too difficult, the experts of the two sides will discuss the difficulty of this particular arrangement and resolve it either by modifying it (which includes supplementing or subtracting from) or by mutually agreeing to a satisfactory solution.

3) The two sides acknowledge that security arrangements should be arrived at through mutual agreement and, as such, should be consistent with the sovereignty and territorial integrity of each side.

4) Security arrangements should be confined to the relevant areas on both sides of the boundary between the two countries.

APPENDIX II

A letter from Ronald Lauder to the President of the United States, Bill Clinton from November 12, 1999 which delinieates the agreement arrived upon between Israel and Syria and appears on page 318.

RONALD S. LAUDER
SUITE 4200
767 FIFTH AVENUE
NEW YORK 10153

The Honorable William J. Clinton
President of the United States
The White House
1600 Pennsylvania Avenue
Washington D.C. 20500

November 12, 1999

Dear Mr. President,

It appears that some misunderstandings have arisen regarding some of the issues we discussed in our last meeting. In order to be of assistance in clarifying these matters, I have meticulously reviewed all the records of the hours we spent in those intensive five weeks of meetings about relations between Syria and Israel during the summer and fall of 1998. I would like to share with you the last positions of both sides which reflect where our efforts ended.

While great progress was made, the talks were left at a crucial juncture and were not completed because the security zones between Syria and Israel could not be finalized until a map of the June 4, 1967 line was provided by Israel.

During the process, there was much discussion and exchanges of views and, as you can well imagine, the two parties were very far apart on some issues. However, as the talks proceeded, most of those differences were narrowed and real progress on many previously unresolved issues were made.

As I mentioned to you, some of the points dated August 29, 1998, that I shared with you in our previous meeting, were never accepted by Syria. In subsequent visits, we reached agreement on the points attached in the letter. I believe these points still need to be finalized by defining the security zones on both sides of the border.

I am also sending you the points that were agreed to by both sides on September 12, 1998, in the hope that they will assist you and your Administration in your pursuit of a lasting peace between Israel and Syria. I am ready to further clarify any remaining questions in regard to my efforts and to do all that I can to assist you in obtaining the goal we share of peace between Israel and her neighbors.

Sincerely,

Ronald S. Lauder

Treaty of Peace Between Israel & Syria

Israel and Syria have decided to establish peace between them. The peace will be based on the principles of security, equality, respect for sovereignty, territorial integrity, and the political independence of both. The Parties agree to the following provisions:

1. Israel will withdraw from the Syrian land taken in 1967, in accordance with Security Council Resolutions 242 and 338, which established the right of all states to secure and recognized borders in the "land for peace" formula, to a commonly agreed border based on the line of June 4, 1967. The withdrawal will be effected in three stages and completed over a period of 18 months with normalization implemented during the third stage and declaring an end to the state of war during the first phase of withdrawal.

2. Due to the existing agreements between Syria and Lebanon, the two tracks should go simultaneously both in solution and in signing peace agreements between Syria and Israel and Lebanon and Israel.

3. In the framework of the peace process, Syria and Lebanon with other parties will discuss paramilitary activities across the borders with Israel with the aim of finding an appropriate solution.

4. The adoption of the paper reached between the parties during previous negotiations on [Aims and Principles of Security Arrangements] including the establishment of demilitarized zones of limited forces on both sides.

5. In the case of a pressing need for ground early warning station it is agreed that:

   a. EWS can remain on Mt. Hermon for a duration of 10 years after total withdrawal: five years followed by a yearly extension for another five years upon agreement by both sides for a total of 10 years.

   b. It will be an American-French facility under their total auspices and responsibilities.

6. Peace to comprise of diplomatic and normalized relations including the opening of embassies and various agreements about peaceful relations provided that it is done according to laws and regulations.

7. The issue of water is to be addressed by Syria and Israel according to international laws and norms including the development of new water resources.

8. Syria believes that the achievement of a just and comprehensive peace will solve a lot of problems in the region in the forefront of which is the achievement of real and lasting peace between Syria and Israel.

12 Sept. 1998

INDEX

Abbas, Mahmoud. See Abu Mazen

Abd al-Shafi, Haidar — 488, 490, 491, 493, 496

Abdullah bin Hussein (King) — 12, 23, 24, 26, 27, 32, 34, 35, 36, 46, 98, 105, 177, 212, 227, 254, 439, 441, 442, 443, 445, 446, 448, 449, 450-454, 457, 460, 465, 473-477, 480, 481, 483, 488-490, 495, 496, 506, 530, 546, 556, 568, 612

Abed Rabbo, Yasser — 566, 571, 576, 603, 608, 610

Abramovich, Amnon — 513

Abu Alaa, (Ahmed Qureia) — 500, 501, 504, 552, 559, 560, 570-572, 575, 576, 595, 608, 610, 623, 629, 630, 647

Abu Marzouk, Musa — 13, 16, 17, 54, 449, 533

Abu Mazen (Mahmoud Abbas) — 504, 506, 509, 512, 548, 559, 570, 571, 572, 574, 595, 608, 610, 629, 630, 647, 675

Abu Rudeineh, Nabil — 559, 575, 613

Abu-Sief Mohammed — 20-22, 38, 39

Admoni, Nahum — 42

Al Baz, Osama — 555

Al-Ghoul, Adnan — 547

Al Hindi, Amin — 534, 536, 547

Al Majali, Abdel Salam — 694

Al Qasim, Marwan — 446

Al Qawuqji, Fawzi — 115

Albright, Madeleine — 332, 342, 348, 356, 357, 361, 362, 380-383, 391-393, 395, 403, 405-407, 412-414, 416, 431, 582, 596, 609, 611, 615, 632, 658-661, 663-665, 670, 673, 676, 683

Alon, Hanan — 131

Al-Sharaa, Farouk — 302, 304, 314, 315, 345, 346, 348, 349, 351-353, 355-363, 367, 370, 376, 383-388, 391-393, 395, 397-399, 402, 403, 405-409, 413, 414, 430-435, 582, 583, 585

Altman, David — 692

Amidror, Ya'akov — 277

Amir, Yigal — 187

Amirav, Moshe — 692, 694

Amit, Meir — 101

Annan, Kofi — 587, 588, 592

Arad, Ron — 99, 162, 163, 220, 422, 428

Arad, Tzvi — 692

Arad, Uzi — 313, 340, 551

Arafat, Yasser — 181, 182, 217, 319, 322, 329, 346, 409, 442, 451, 486, 491, 496-499, 504, 506-510, 515-520, 522, 524, 528-537, 544-547, 549, 552, 554-560, 562, 563, 565-568, 571-579, 595-601, 603, 604, 606-609, 612-616, 618-621, 623-627, 629-631, 633, 634, 636-649, 651-664, 667-685, 687

Arbel, Edna — 68, 90

Arens, Moshe (Misha) — 9, 130, 157, 159, 205

Ariel, Uri — 538

Arnan, Abraham — 120, 124

Asfour, Hassan — 603, 608, 610, 640, 645

Ashkenazi, Gabi — 277

Aslan, Ali — 256

Assad, Bashar — 242, 392, 433

Assad, Family — 593

Assad, Hafez — 16, 65-66, 191, 217, 218-223, 226-231, 233-236, 238, 240-241, 248-250, 253-256, 258, 263, 272-275, 277, 279-280, 287-290, 292, 296-298, 300-303, 307, 314-316, 318-325, 329-334, 336-347, 351-2, 355, 357-9, 362-5, 367, 369, 371, 373, 376, 379-380, 384, 386, 388, 393, 398-409, 415-421, 423-435, 470, 474, 566-7, 570, 584-5, 633

Ayalon, Ami — 12, 14, 18, 19, 40, 53, 79

Ayyash, Yahya — 533

Azzam, Azzam — 549-50

Bachar, Reuven (Ruby) — 44

Baker, James — 321-2

Barabash, Gabi — 176

Barak, Ehud — , 52, 122-4, 127, 130-1, 142, 158, 165, 178, 183, 185, 190, 196, 202, 206, 210, 232, 235, 239, 242, 244-7, 249-257, 259-274, 277, 280-1, 298, 302, 313-4, 316, 320-339, 341-8, 351-7, 359-371, 373-388, 390-3, 395, 397-409, 411-8, 420-437, 465-8, 470, 512, 550-1, 553-560, 562-592, 595-606, 608-621, 623-649, 651-685, 687-8, 691-5, 698

Barak, Esther — 245

Barkai, Razi — 325

Barkan (Berkowitz), Yehuda — 116

Bar-Lev, Rafi — 201

Bar-Natan, Zvika — 44

Bassiouni, Mohamed — 555

Batikhi, [General] Samih — — 94

Baumel, Zacharia — 99, 162

Begin, Benny — 52

Begin, Menachem — 60, 345, 437, 503, 535, 568, 603, 628

Beilin, Yossi — 224

Beinish, Dorit — 149-150

Ben Aharon, Yossi — 188

Ben Ami, Shlomo — 575-6, 606, 619, 632-3

Ben Artzi, Abraham — 156-7

Ben Shaker, Zaid — 456, 459

Ben-Ami, Oded — 513

Ben David, Mishka — 17-8, 40

Ben-Eliezer, Binyamin (Fouad) — 168, 170, 466, 692

Ben-Gurion, David — 115, 170, 535, 630, 647, 666, 708

Berger, Sandy — 573, 632, 636, 640-1, 693

Berri, Nabih — 163, 306

Biger, Gideon — 390

Bildt, Carl — 693

Biran, Ilan — 183, 538

Biran, Yoav — 388

Blair, Tony — 587

Bouchiki, Ahmed — 28

Brochiel, Amnon (Bruchi) — 120-1

Brodet, David — 388

Bush, George H.W. — 321

Bush, George W. — 440

Carter, Jimmy — 503, 568

Ceausescu syndrome — 219

Çiller, Tansu — 172

Chirac, Jacques — 587

Christopher, Warren — 181, 215, 220, 223, 225, 227-232, 236-7, 240-2, 264, 273, 281, 293, 301, 304-5, 307, 315, 452-3, 462, 495

Churchill, Winston — 665

Ciechanover Commission, Joseph Ciechanover — 43, 48-50, 52, 77-8, 80-1, 83-5, 93, 100

Clinton, Bill — 35, 168-170, 172, 212, 227, 234, 272, 287-8, 291-2, 315-6, 318, 322-4, 326-334, 336-8, 344-6, 352-6, 358, 361, 370, 375-380, 382-5, 387, 393, 395, 397-403, 406-9, 412-6, 420-1, 423-434, 450, 453, 468, 470, 507, 510, 519, 546-7, 550, 552, 557-9, 563, 566-571, 573-5, 578, 583-5, 589, 597-607, 610-5, 617, 619-620, 623-5, 629-635, 637-649, 652, 654, 656-662, 664, 667, 669-671, 673-5, 677-685

Cohen, Eli — 220, 422, 428

Cohen, Reuven — 126

Deif, Mohammed — 547

Dagan (Huberman), Meir — 101, 121

Dahlan, Mohammed — 534, 536-7, 547, 565-6, 575-6, 608, 610, 629, 636, 640, 645

Daoudi, Riad — 338, 342-4, 357, 388

Dayan, Asi — 121

Dayan, Moshe — 138, 437

Dayan, Uzi — 297, 512

De Charette, Areva — 305

De Klerk, Frederick — 693

de Lesamblea — 586

Dekel, Udi — 389

Demirel, Suleiman — 369, 465

Dichter, Avi — 127

Dirani, Mustafa — 163

Djerejian, Ed — 321

Dole, Robert — 173

Dulles, Allen — 93

Edri, Rafi — 510-1

Eichmann, Adolf — 82

Eizenkot, Gadi — 417

Eldar, Akiva — 383, 411

El-Sana, Taleb — 181

Enan, Menachem — 367

Eran, Oded — 571, 600, 626, 668

Even Baruch (Yussim), Sarah — 111, 112

Erekat, Saeb — 489, 520, 566, 573, 576, 600, 608, 610, 636, 640, 647, 679, 683

Ezra, Gideon — 52, 148, 182

Feldman, Tzvi — 99, 162

Freeh, Louis — 693

Friedman, Henya — 107-8

Gelber, Shlomo — 126, 201

Gosha, Ibrahim — 16

Gil (Jankh), Yehuda — 57-76, 102

Gil, Avi — 305, 508-9

Gilutz, Hanan — 126, 201

Ginat, Yossi — 694

Ginosar, Yoseph — 532, 559, 575, 639, 667

Gluska, Einat — 600

Goldberg, Eliezer — 140

Goldenberg, Dudu. See Topaz, Dudu

Goldfarb, Alex — 545

Goldstein, Baruch — 134-9, 144, 152

Goldwasser, Ehud — 696

Gonen, Yitzik — 126, 201

Gorbachev, Mikhail — 693

Gore, Al — 272, 332

Goren, Aliza — 175-7, 305, 462

Greenstein, Gidi — 610

Haber, Eitan — 94, 164, 176, 178, 212, 483, 500, 507-9, 513

Halaby, Najib Elizabeth. See Noor (Queen)

Halevy, Efraim — 32-3, 36, 106, 417-8, 448

Hamudout, Yitzchak — 137

Haniyeh, Ismail — 34

Hrawi, Elias — 306

Harel, Dan — 277, 388

Hariri, Rafik — 215, 306

Hasauna, Awan Shaukat — 448

Hassan VI (King of Morocco) — 510

Hasson, Israel — 668

Hayke, Giora — 121

Hever, Guy — 99

Hever, Zeev (Zambish) — 538

Hilal, Jamal — 431

Hirschfeld, Yair — 224, 500, 503

Hoff, Fred — 419, 421, 470

Hoffi, Yitzchak (Echo) — 101

Hollander, Shmuel — 176

Huberman, Meir. See Dagan (Huberman)

Hussein Bin Talal (King) — 12, 23-4, 26-7, 32, 34-6, 46, 105, 177, 212, 227, 254, 439, 441-3, 445, 448-454, 457-460, 465, 473-8, 480, 489, 495, 506, 530, 546, 568, 612

Hussein, Raghad — 481

Hussein, Rana — 481

Hussein, Saddam — 98, 446, 481-3, 545, 556

Husseini, Abdel Kader — 488

Husseini, Faisal — 488-490, 496, 498-9

Indyk, Martin — 247, 289, 298, 304, 308, 312, 318-9, 325, 357, 373, 405, 416-8, 421, 470, 573, 584, 609, 659-660

Israeli, Chaim — 209

Jadallah, Salah (Khaled) — 180

Jibril, Ahmed — 190

Jospin, Lionel — 694

Kahane, Meir — 135-6

Kamel, Hussein — 481-3

Katz, Yehuda — 99, 162

Kennedy, John Fitzgerald — 93

Khalil, Hassan — 280, 297

Khomeini, Ruhollah — 480, 527-8

Kinarti, Noah — 387, 539

Kissinger, Henry — 226, 634

Kochanowsky, Moshe — 390, 399, 588

Kohl, Helmut — 91, 131

Kornblit, David — 390

Lahad, Antoine — 588, 591, 592

Landau, Uzi — 52

Langer, Rani — 124

Lanir, Niva — 164

Larsen, Terje — 378-9, 588

Lau, Israel — 180

Lauder, Ron — 313-6, 318-320, 323, 326, 333, 336-342, 344, 391

Lerner (Yussim), Dina — 111, 112

Levi, Moshe — 140

Levinger, Moshe — 151

Levitte, Jean-David — 586

Levtzur, Uzi — 127, 129, 157

Levy, David — 351, 357, 375-6, 389-390, 406, 559-560, 575

Levy, Michael — 345, 586

Levy, Shaul — 119-120

Liel, Alon — 693

Lipkin-Shahak, Amnon — 12, 176, 185, 273, 277-281, 283-8, 293, 298, 301, 305, 375-6, 381, 390, 403, 406, 512, 521, 540, 570, 606, 610, 668

Lipschitz, Zohar — 162

Livne, Ze'ev — 14, 53, 548

Lockhart, Joe — 599

Lubrani, Uri — 585

Madenlater, Ahuva — 116

Magen, Aliza — 81, 86

Major, John — 479

Malhin, Zvi — 82

Malley, Rob — 318, 325, 354, 601, 636

Marzel, Baruch — 135

Mashal, Khaled — 11, 13-22, 24-8, 34-7, 39, 45, 52, 54, 56, 73, 79, 81-3, 86, 89-90, 94, 100, 102, 133, 449, 533

Mazen, Abu — 504, 506, 509, 548, 559, 570-2, 575, 595, 608, 610, 629-630, 647, 675

Meir, Golda — 226, 339

Meir, Yitzhak — 90

Majaida, Abdel Razek — 534

Melnick (Corporal) — 137

Merei, Mohammed — 446

Meridor (Rubin), Liora — 124

Meridor, Dan — 600, 610, 668

Miller, Aaron — 298, 318, 325

Mintzker, Nahum — 387

Mitzna, Amram — 132

Mofaz, Shaul — 137, 182-3, 185, 589

Molcho, Yitzhak — 551-2

Moratinos, Miguel — 313, 319, 586

Mordechai, Yitzchak (IItzik) — 12, 14, 18-9, 35, 39-40, 53, 79-80, 132, 319-320, 340-1, 550

Muallem, Walid — 246-250, 252-266, 272-3, 280-1, 297-300, 308, 312, 315, 319, 352, 357, 388, 392

Mubarak, Hosni — 227, 322, 433, 497, 515, 539, 546, 548-550, 555, 557, 563, 587, 606, 612, 643-4, 694

Muchtar, Abraham — 120-1

Nader, George — 339-342

Navon, Yitzhak — 170

Nazal, Mohammed — 16

Netanyahu, Benjamin (Bibi) — 12, 14, 18, 23-4, 26, 28, 35-6, 39, 41-3, 46, 53-6, 66, 78, 83, 85, 91, 93-4, 102-3, 127, 173, 185, 285, 309, 311-6, 318-

321, 323, 326, 329, 336, 339-342, 361, 407, 437, 463, 497, 543, 547-552, 554-7, 563, 709

Newcombe — 472

Noor (Queen) — 445

Obeid, Abdul Karim — 162

Olmert, Ehud — 338, 378, 392, 437, 697-8

Omar, Ibrahim — 280, 297, 299, 327, 352, 357, 389-390, 399, 414

Or, Ori — 52

Oren, Amir — 513

Oslerne, Pini — 692

Oz, Amos — 377, 430

Paikov, Abraham — 107-110

Paikov, Nehama — 108

Paikov, Rachel — 108, 111

Paikov, Shoshana — 108

Paikov, Yehudit — 107, 110

Paris, Mark — 298, 312

Patton, George Smith — 129

Pedatzur, Reuven — 693

Peled, Musa — 129

Peled, Rafi — 43-4, 47-50, 80, 147

Peled, Yossi — 130

Peres, Shimon — 9, 15, 55, 102, 132, 176, 223-4, 227, 244, 291-7, 302-9, 311-2, 315, 325, 339, 352, 361, 407, 437, 451-4, 462-3, 474-6, 491, 500-1, 505-510, 512, 543-9, 557, 598, 692

Peretz, Amir — 692

Perry, Ya'akov — 147

Pines, Ophir — 695

Paulet — 472

Poraz, Maoz — 183

Poraz, Nir — 183

Powell, Jonathan — 586

Primakov, Yevgeny — 305-6

Prince Bandar — 421, 510

Prince Hassan — 36, 445, 447, 448, 465, 475, 693

Pundak, Ron — 224, 500, 504

Putin, Vladimir — 558, 587

Qureia, Ahmed. See Abu Ala

Rabin, Dalia — 156

Rabin, Leah — 176

Rabin, Yitzhak — 7-8, 15-6, 34, 54-5, 85, 102-3, 130, 132, 140-2, 144, 150-1, 155-185, 187-191, 197-8, 204-7, 211-8, 220-7, 229, 231-245, 254, 256, 259, 266, 273, 275, 277-9, 285-6, 288-294, 296-7, 302, 315, 318, 323, 328, 331, 336-7, 339, 345, 348, 359-362, 370, 379-380, 401, 407, 412, 420, 425, 428, 431, 434, 437, 440-461, 469, 471-483, 485-541, 543-6, 549, 556-8, 563, 563, 577, 598, 606, 628, 630, 637, 649, 694, 707, 719

Rabin, Yuval — 157

Rabinovich, Itamar — 219, 224-5, 234, 236, 244, 246-7, 263-4, 280, 293, 297, 462

Rahamim, Mordechai — 126

Rajoub, Jibril — 628

Rashid, Mohammed — 608, 610, 629, 645

Regev, Eldad — 696

Reisner, Daniel — 626

Reshef, Amnon — 128, 196

Revivi, Rotem — 137

Riad, Mahmoud — 456

Riedel, Bruce — 354, 416, 600, 607, 613, 624, 683

Rigley (General) — 87, 90

Ross, Dennis — 190-1, 225-8, 234, 236, 247, 261, 263, 269, 273, 275, 277, 279, 281, 288-290, 293, 295-8, 306, 312, 314, 318-9, 325, 339, 342-4, 346-7, 357, 369-370, 373, 375, 382, 388, 391, 416, 421, 431-4, 495, 552, 573-4, 582, 584, 588, 615-6, 632, 636, 659-662, 670, 673-4, 681

Rothschild, Danny — 440

Rubinstein, Elyakim — 49, 68, 90, 357, 367, 375, 440, 447-8, 477, 493, 504, 606, 610, 669

Sadat, Anwar — 98, 221-2, 234, 296, 300, 345, 373, 437, 503, 555, 568, 603

Sadeh, Tehila — 100

Sagi, Uri — 263, 314, 334-6, 338, 341-3, 357, 367, 374-5, 406, 414

Salameh, Ali Hassan — 28

Saramago, José — 26

Sarid, Yossi — 52, 80

Savir, Uri — 293, 297, 308, 500-1, 504, 548

Schmidbauer, Bernd — 91

Schroeder, Gerhard — 587

Schwartz, Jonathan — 676

Seale, Patrick — 314-6, 332-3

Segal, Avraham — 110

Segal, Miriam — 110

Segal, Rivka — 110

Segal, Sarah — 110

Segal, Shimon — 107, 110

Segal, Ya'akov — 110

Segal, Yoseph — 110

Shaaban, Bouthaina — 249, 262, 357, 399, 431, 433

Shaath, Nabil — 608, 610

Shai, Hezi — 162

Shalev, Meir — 83

Shalit, Gilad — 34

Shamgar, Meir — 140, 152

Shamir, Uri — 387

Shamir, Yitzhak — 440, 485-6, 488

Shapiro, Isaac — 176

Shapiro, Shimon — 174-5

Shaqaqi, Fathi — 537

Sharansky, Natan — 550

Sharon, Ariel (Arik) — 35-7, 130, 185, 341, 379, 550, 561, 688, 691

Sharvit-Baruch, Pnina — 388

Shatner, David — 390

Shavit, Shabtai — 59, 63, 81, 10-2, 127, 443, 478

Sheindorf, Roy — 387

Sher, Gilead — 566, 600, 606, 610, 618, 619, 621, 633, 636, 659, 663

Sheves, Simon — 164, 176, 207, 213, 507-8, 513

Shiffer, Shimon — 447, 511

Shihabi, Hikmat — 235, 244-6, 248, 256, 262-274, 277, 278-284, 286-8, 298, 301, 352

Shmasani — 446

Shomron, Dan — 128, 131, 156, 158, 197

Shukri, Ali — 24, 26, 36, 95, 446, 448, 460, 471

Siboni, Moshe — 126, 201

Sinai, Moshe — 388

Singer, Yoel — 297, 500, 504

Siniora, Fouad — 696

Snir (Shukragi), Danny — 126, 201

Sofrin, Amnon — 133

Spiro, Trevor — 692

Srebro, Haim — 588

Stauber, Zvi — 388, 631

Steiner — 586

Steinmeier, Frank Walter — 586

Suharto — 172, 211, 512

Suleiman, Omar — 357, 549, 586

Tamari, Dubik — 142, 200

Tamari, Nehemya — 141-2

Tamari, Shay — 142

Tarawneh, Fayez — 477

Taub, Daniel — 388

Tenet, George — 464, 678

Teomim, Moshik — 117

Tibi, Ahmed — 181, 518

Tohami, Hassan — 437

Tolkowsky, Dan — 80

Topaz, Dudu — 117

Verstandig, Tony — 298

Vilan, Avshalom — 695

Wa'ava, Mihail — 298, 353, 357

Wachsman, Esther — 181

Wachsman, Nachshon — 180-4

Wahid, (General) — 446

Wahid, Abdul Rahman — 693

Walker, Ned — 321

Wallerstein, Pinchas — 538

Weizman, Ezer — 90, 176

Werner, David Yechiel, Rabbi Werner — 113

Woolsey, James (Jim) — 693

Ya'alon, Moshe (Bogie) — 18-9, 40, 53, 79-80, 127, 185, 206, 209-210

Ya'ari, Menachem — 140

Yanai, Shlomo — 388, 390-1, 606, 610, 667

Yassin, Ahmed — 33-4, 36-7, 180

Yatom (Yussim), Dov — 111-2

Yatom (Yussim), Moshe — 111-3

Yatom (Yussim), Pesia — 111-3

Yatom, Adi — 124, 717

Yatom, Dolev — 124, 717

Yatom, Ehud — 8, 192-3

Yatom, Eti — 8, 113, 116, 192

Yatom, Itay — 124, 193

Yatom, Lior — 124, 717

Yatom, Maya — 127, 717

Yatom, Moshe (Moshik) — 8

Yatom, Nir — 124, 193

Yatom, Omer — 124, 193

Yatom, Pnina — 8, 110-1, 113, 192

Yatom, Roey — 124, 193

Yatom, Simcha — 8, 111-3, 116, 192

Yatom (Yussim), Shlomo — 111-2

Yatom, Tal — 124, 193

Yatom, Tamar — 124, 717

Yatom, Tamir — 124, 717

Yatom, Tova — 9, 12, 92, 124, 193-7, 717

Yavin, Haim — 27

Yeltsin, Boris — 324

Yousef, Nasser — 534, 536

Zamir, Tzvi — 101

Ze'evi, Rehavam (Gandhi) — 66

Zemin, Jiang — 171

Zloczower, Ralph — 90

Zoabi, Abdul Rahman — 140

Zuckerman (Zur), Baruch — 126

Printed in Great Britain
by Amazon